UNIQUE PUBLISHERS

S. T. COLERIDGE

SELECTED POEMS

A Critical Study with Complete Text, Paraphrase, Annotations, Explanations with Critical Comments, Important Passages for Reference to the Context, Discussion of Important Textual Aspects and Selected University Questions with Answers

A Critical Evaluation

Dr. S. Sen, *M.A., Ph.D.*

Thoroughly revised by
Dr. G. S. MANSUKHANI
M.A., Ph.D.

Ex-Head of the Department of English
S.G.T.B. Khalsa College
University of Delhi
and
Retd. Deputy Secretary
University Grants Commission

For any query/suggestions,
please write us at **info@uniquepublishers.in**
9583-978-978

Price : ₹350
ISBN 13 : 978-93-95259-70-5
ISBN 10 : 93-95259-70-1
Code : 1.21.3

Edition: 2023

Published by: Amarjeet Singh Chopra, Unique Publishers (I) Pvt. Ltd.

Email: info@uniquepublishers.in, ***Website:*** www.uniquepublishers.in

Corporate Office: J-2/1, Block B-1, Mohan Cooperative Industrial Estate, Mathura Road, New Delhi-110044. **Tel.:** +91-11-41076666

Printed at: Aapte Udhyog, Noida

PREFACE TO THE LATEST EDITION

We take a pleasure in bringing out the 15th edition of S.T. Coleridge : Selected Poems. We have been encouraged by the appreciation shown by the academic community, and hope this edition will also benefit students, like its previous editions. We invite and look forward to suggestions for improving the book further in its subsequent editions. Every care has been taken to make this book user friendly and helpful. Few more chapters on S.T. Coleridge has been added with University Questions and Answers. University Questions with Answers have been included with all the important poems of S.T. Coleridge to help students prepare themselves for the examination.

New Delhi
2007 **Dr. S. Sen**

PREFACE TO THE 1st EDITION

Literary history classifies Coleridge as one of the great Romantic poets- the others being Blake, Wordsworth, Byron, Shelley and Keats. Many readers see him as primarily a great poet, whose poetic output was sadly diminished, even stifled, by an unfortunate taste for philosophy. To others he was essentially a philosopher, who happened to have brilliant poetic gifts; others see him as a man of immense and varied talents who frittered away his life in a series of brilliant gestures - in poetry, journalism, political and religious writings - and left no substantial work in any of these fields. Yet even the work completed and published in his lifetime was impressive in its scope. He published a substantial body of poetry, including a number of the finest poems in the language.

In the present edition, we have given a wide selection of Coleridge's poems - besides the famous trio of *The Ancient Mariner, Christabel* and *Kubla Khan,* there are the lovely conversation, pieces, some political poems and some other short items. Each poem is extensively annotated and critically discussed. The chapter, Select University Quesitons with Answers, classifies textural topics under suitable headings and discusses them critically and in detail. Modern critical thought and views on Coleridge and his poetry have been incorporated in the discussion to enlighten the reader on the various aspects of the poems.

We take this opportunity to express our gratitude to the enlightened critics and commentators on Coleridge and his poetry without whose views our work would have been incomplete.

We welcome suggestions for improving the book.

New Delhi **Dr. S. Sen**
1986

CONTENTS

(XII) STYLE AND ARTISTRY OF METRICAL COMPOSITION

1

INTRODUCTION TO SAMUEL TAYLOR COLERIDGE

(A) LIFE AND WORKS OF S.T. COLERIDGE

(1) 1772-1794. Coleridge has been born at Ottery St. Mary, Devonshire, on Oct. 21, 1772. His father, a man of great learning but eccentric tastes, has been the vicar and headmaster of the King's School there. He has initiated his son into the mysteries of astronomy, and has taken him through a course of desultory reading. He has died in 1781, leaving Coleridge to go as a sizar to Christ Hospital. He forms there a friendship with Elia (Charles Lamb), and early has distinguished himself for his attractive disposition, versatility, and youthful enthusiasm. In 1791, he has gone to Jesus College, Cambridge, and becomes an ardent republican. In conjunction with Southey, he becomes engrossed in a communistic scheme for the amelioration of his fellow men. In 1794, he leaves the University finally without taking a degree.

(2) 1795-1800. Soon after leaving Cambridge, he marries Sarah Frickers, a sister of Southey's wife. His republican ardour has by this time considerably cools down. The Coleridge's have settled down first at Clevedon, and thereafter at Nether Stowey, Somerset, where he forms an intimate friendship with Wordsworth, and comes under the wholesome influence of the great poet and his sister. The few months spend there are the best of his life; his domestic troubles has not yet commenced; his poetic imagination, though ethereal and airy from his very boyhood, has not yet lost its creative power. All the best work which is peculiarly his own belongs to this period. In 1798, appears the famous *Lyrical Ballads* to which he has contributed *The Ancient Mariner*.

About this time, he is rendered financially independent through the kindness of some friends, and starts for a tour through Germany with the Wordsworths. German philosophy and literature particularly fascinates him; he is perhaps, the first English man of letters completely to imbibe the spirit of German thought of the day, and subject the mind of his contemporaries to its influence.

(3) 1800-1816. On his return to England in 1800, Coleridge aimlessly moves from place to place. During an illness sometime before, he has started taking opium. The habit gradually grows upon him till its shadow darkens the remainder of his life. The days of his literary achievement are now over; he is simply planning, never executing.

Coleridge has a wonderful gift of speech. Partly through the persuasion of friends, partly to eke out his living, he starts a series of lectures on Shakespeare and Milton. With his wonderful imagination and insight and felicitous use of language he always keeps his audience enthralled.

His health is gradually failing, and he resolves to try the effect of warmer climates. He reach Malta in April 1804, and is well received by the English colony there. Later, he is appointed Public Secretary of Malta and its dependencies. It is another proof of his remarkable versatility that he proves a thorough man of affairs and makes his mark as a secretary. The climate also suits him. But, cut off from friends and congenial intellectual environment, he finds his life unbearable.

(4) 1816-1834. All this time, he has been living in virtual separation from his wife and children. His friends are anxious that he shall regain those exceptional powers which he has frittered away in dreams and fragments. He is , therefore, placed in the house of a surgeon, Mr. Gillman, under whose kind protection and treatment he passes the rest of his life.

During several lucid intervals, he still give proofs of his great poetic power, subtle knowledge of psychology, and fine critical grasp of thought. Youth and Age, the charming songs in *Zapolya,* and *Law Sermons* belong to this period. He retains his wonderful hold on the minds of his contemporaries till the very last. His reputation and his fascinating gift of talk still brings young and old devotees of learning to his surgeon's residence in Highgate. Till his death in 1834, he never loses the poetic frenzy of his eye or the dreamy grace of his melodious speech.

THE WORKS OF COLERIDGE

Coleridge's works may be discussed under three heads : (i) his poetry, (ii) his dramas (iii) his literary criticism. His poetic output that really matters is very limited. According to Stopford Brooke, "all that he did excellently might be bound up in twenty pages, but it should be bound in pure gold."

(i) His Poetical Works. The early poems of Coleridge have been published in the spring of 1796 in the volume entitled *Poems on Various Subjects.* The manner is artificial and stiff, under the strong influence of 18th century poetic diction, modified by sentimentalism and melancholy. His political sonnets betrays the influence of Godwin but are pompous in style. More promising, however, are the poems dominated by the young poet's love and minute observation of natural scenery – *The Song of the Pixies* (1793); *The Lines on Autumnal Evening; Lewti* (1794) and *Religious Musings* (1794-96).

Then comes his golden period of intimacy with Wordsworth and Dorothy, which leads to the planning of *The Lyrical Ballads* and the flowering of Coleridge's best poetry-the true Wordsworthian pieces like *The Lime Tree Bower, Frost at Midnight, Fears in Solitude* (1797-98), followed by the master-pieces stamped with his own original sensibility – *The Ancient Mariner, Christabel* and *Kubla Khan*. Then the poetic fount begin to dwindle in energy and after a few spurts in *Dejection : An Ode* and *Love and Hope* it becomes exhausted and the vacuum thus created has to be filled by critical and philosophical activities which yields richer and more voluminous works, though quite fragmentary and discursive. The creative life of Coleridge is at once a miracle and a melancholy spectacle of waste and sudden collapse of divine imagination.

(ii) His Dramas. His first drama, written in collaboration with Southey is *The Fall of Robespierre* (1794). It shows influence of Shakespeare but is married by rhetorical declamation and poor characterisation. His other dramas are *Remorse* (1798), which is a tragedy in blank verse and *Zapolya* (1817), a romantic tragedy in imitation of Shakespeare's *Winter's Tale.*

(iii) His Literary Criticism. Coleridge's chief critical work is *Biographia Literaria* (1817). It is a sort of loose autobiography, embracing a variety of subjects like religion, politics, literature and criticism. It contains a valuable criticism of Wordsworth's theory of poetic diction.

(B) MAIN CHARACTERISTICS OF S.T. COLERIDGE'S POETRY

1. INTRODUCTION

Coleridge, for many years is a neighbour, friend and collaborator of Wordsworth, and their partnership is not only mutually beneficial but also extremely fruitful for the English poetry which they have liberated from the eighteenth century shackles and put along the road to new freedom and achievement. But temperamentally they are contrasted figures, though they both react enthusiastically to the bright prospects which is opened by the French Revolution and then recant their faith with equal bitterness, as the high hopes has fallen to earth with broken wings. Of the two, Coleridge is more subtle and comprehensive, more gifted with the poetic vein and faculty divine, but his will power is weak and many of his mighty schemes either remains in the limbo of 'might have beens' or are partially fulfilled. He is indolent and dreamy and likes to lie on the floating lotus like Vishnu and wake up a while only to sleep again for ages. He himself is the best anatomist of his chronic ailment :

To me hath Heaven with bounteous hand assigned
Energetic Reason and shaping mind :
The daring ken of Truth, the Patriot's part
And Pity's sigh that breathes the gentle heart
Sloth-jaundiced all.

His imagination is fed on the romances, travel-books, voyages and *The Arabian Nights,* entertainments and the lure of the remote and the weird is stronger on his mind than the claims of the practical duties. He is a young proselyte of the revolutionary doctrines, plans the scheme of Pantisocracy, the settlement of a group of kindred souls in the solitude of America which come to nothing but procurs him the friendship of Southey. Later on, he marries romantically and suffers all his life for his hasty love. Then comes his habit of opium taking, first as a palliative for his rheumatic pain but thereafter as a matter of course, natural to every addict. These are his fatal enemies and the wonder is not that he did not produce more but that he is able to do so much in philosophy, criticism, poetry, public talks and lectures as well as in his animated conversations.

Wordsworth is a lonely but tough man and his energy is equal to any crisis and wrung out a meditative optimism from the intractable materials of personal suffering and 'the still sad music of humanity.' All his great characters are solitary, calm, patient and victorious, though charred by their suffering. But Coleridge, mighty philosopher and subtle-souled psychologist as he remains passive and helpless in the grip of sorrow and hardship and his characters also, the Mariner and Christabel, are passive, helpless sufferers like himself.

2. HIS ROMANTICISM AND ITS INFLUENCE

Coleridge is a typical representative of the true romantic spirit which is marked by a fondness for that beauty which has strangeness added to it and naturally flies away from the familiar daylight realities of our common existence into the regions remote, exotic and mysteriously unfamiliar. Thus, medievalism, the supernatural and their combined effect in the primitive ballad poetry became the favourites of Coleridge and are transmitted by him to Keats, then to Tennyson and the Pre-Raphaelites, especially Rossetti. His opium dream and curiosities about the psychic states and even the hidden working of the sub-conscious come as a legacy, again, to Rossetti, Poe and thence to Baudelaire. His practice, equally romantic, of colouring the external nature with the moods of the observer is an anticipation of the employment of that psychological landscape which becomes prominent in Tennyson and in the modern poets like Pound, Eliot and Edith Sitwell. Many of his lyrics are full of that subjectivity, self-pity and self-analysis which are regarded as the keynote of true romanticism, which together with melancholy, characterise the romantics. His suggestive style and the aura of dim but alluring association which clings to words and images represents a development of the romantic manner which eventually is culminated in the symbolist poetry and prose. As a pure poet, also he represents a phase of romanticism, while his love of freedom, his successful experiment in versification and his sense of the brotherhood of all creatures, including even the ass, are the traits which connect him with the romanticism and the speculations of the day.

To sum up, Coleridge's whole career is romantic in the sense that his life is full of brilliant promises and broken aims. He finds expression for many unheard of his mind in poems like *Dejection: An Ode.* He is a melancholy man given to brooding over the failure of his life infact, he has the 'romantic melancholy' to the full.

Coleridge's poetry represents the culmination of romanticism in its purest form. *The Ancient Mariner* and *Christabel* mark the triumph of romanticism as fully as Wordsworth's narrative poems mark the triumph of naturalism. It is by virtue of these poems that he has been called by Saintsbury "the high-priest of romanticism."

There is a certain romantic note present in the best works of Coleridge. "In pictorial power" writes Buchan, "felicity of phrase and word music he is one of the greatest masters. In his subtly suggestive treatment of the supernatural, he stands almost alone. It is not only that he eliminates from his supernaturalism the crude material horror, then popular with the writers of the romantic school; he also gives it a psychological foundation. This is particularly apparent in *The Ancient Mariner,* the backbone of which is provided, not by the marvels of the narrative, but by the spiritual history of the hero. Wordsworth sought to save naturalism from the hard liberalism of Crabbe by touching reality with imagination, Coleridge redeemed romance from coarse sensationalism by linking it with psychological truth."

3. THE TREATMENT OF NATURE

The early nature poetry of Coleridge betrays the clear influence of Wordsworth and echoes the favourite ideas of the latter, such as the sentience and holy plan of Nature, the harmony between the life of Man and the Spirit rolling in the natural universe outside and the beneficial, educative influence of Nature on young minds :

> And what if all of animated nature,
> Be but organic Harps divers'ly framed,
> That tremble into thought, as o'er them sweeps
> Plastic and vast one intellectual breeze,
> At once the Soul of each, and God of all.

O ! the one life within us arid abroad,
Which meets all motion and becomes its soul
A light in sound, a sound-like power in light
Rhythm in all thought and joyance everywhere.

But the spell of Wordsworth did not last long and Coleridge eventually adopts the idealistic attitude, sanctions by the contemporary German philosophers, which rests on the reality of the human mind, which imparts whatever reality one may perceive in the external nature. Coleridge will have us believe that in looking at external objects he is seeking only the symbols of his subjective thoughts and feelings rather than trying to find out any new fact through observation.

The point has been elaborated in his *Dejection : An Ode* where he clearly states :

O Lady! we receive but what we give
And in our life alone does nature live
Ours is her wedding garment and ours her shroud...

so that he cannot hope to win from external forms that joy whose fountain lies within. Using the favourite symbol of Wordsworth, namely, the wedding of Man and Nature, he asserts that joy is the main bond of union, which gives in dower a fairer charm and brightness to nature-joy, which is a notion born of the perfect harmony of heart and mind in the observer. If this joy is defunct, the observer may see the external objects without feeling any magic power in them and his own grief, meanwhile, may colour the goings on in the external world of Nature. The contrast with Wordsworthian faith is quite obvious and it is also quite evident that for Coleridge there was no external agency but human love and friendship for providing support and consolation in misery :

Flowers are lovely : Love is flower-like;
Friendship is a sheltering tree;
O ! the joys that come down shower-like;
Of Friendship, Love and Liberty,
Ere I was old.

In his treatment of nature, there is no Wordsworthian tendency to spiritualize the objects and moods perceived in observation, but there is a marked tendency in Coleridge to spread a touch of eeriness, a sort of weird haze over the whole landscape to create the appropriate setting or atmosphere. The natural objects shimmer in an elusive light which does not belong to them. Moreover, his observation is more sensitive and delicate than Wordsworth's and comes, at times very close to Shelley or Tennyson's minute perception of the fleeting and atmospheric lights and shades. While describing the practice of Wordsworth to spread the strange colouring of imagination over the familiar scene, he observes in his

Biographia Literaria: "The sudden charm, with accidents of light and shade, which moonlight or sunset diffused over a known and familiar landscape, appeares to represent the practicability of combining both."

Coleridge himself loves twilight or the magic of moon light and notes with great fidelity the subtle effects of light and colour. One may take the description of Geraldine in Christabel as a fit case in a point :

A damsel bright
Drest in a silken robe of white
That shadowy in moon light shone.

Other details are her neck that 'make the white robe wan; her blue-veined feet and gems entangled in her hair that wildly glittered here and there.' What is true of the depiction of this lovely phantom is equally good in respect of his description of aerial and sky phenomena of changing light and colour. Rossetti, the painter poet, has compared him to Turner in the skill to capture and reproduce the aerial glitter: 'With him colour is always melted in atmosphere which it shines through like fire within a vein in crystal. It is liquid colour, the dew on flowers or a mist of rain in bright sun shine. His images, are, for the most part, derived from water, sky, the changes of weather, shadows of things rather than the things themselves, and usually the mental reflections of them.' He has noted the peculiar tint of yellow—green in the sky; the rich and amber light of sunset cloud, the last red leaf of autumn; the rich attire of water-snakes—blue, glossy green and velvet—black and their tracks on moon-lit water : 'every track was a flash of golden fire', and when they rear, the elfish light fell off in flakes. In the same poem, we have other touches also;

(i) About, about, in reel and rout
The death-fire danced at night;
The water, like a witch's oils,
Burnt green, and blue and white.

(ii) The upper air burst into life !
And a hundred fire-flags sheen,
To and fro they hurried about !
And to and fro, and in and out,
The wan stars danced between.

The early poems are full of vivid descriptions of mountainous scenery and of the glorious splendour of the sun lying on it, while everywhere one can find brief and well-defined pictures of the different seasons, sounds and moods of nature. Yet there is no indication of spiritual communion in solitude which filled him with horror, even though he has a hunger for 'the vast and the sublime' and looks upon the universe of Nature, 'the infinite I am', as an echo of the might and glory of God, so that its contemplation amounts to the silent worship of the Creator and His too human Son.

4. THE TREATMENT OF SUPERNATURAL

Coleridge makes the supernatural as the region and haunt of his genius and shows the way to its most artistic use. There are two ways of treating the supernatural, one external and decorative and the other suggestive and psychological. In the beginning, the supernatural horrors multiplies through a number of direct and vivid descriptions, in the second, they subtly suggests and intensifies through the depiction of their effect on the human victim. The greater effectiveness of the second is evident enough and could be gauged by comparing the terrible effect produced by the Weird Sisters in Shakespeare's *Macbeth* as they appear as forces of darkness in the first scene, with their motto-'fair is foul and foul is fair', with the greater familiarity of their appearance in the later scene, which gives an elaborate picture of their literal cauldron and its conventional trappings. Vague fear is always intenser than the fear defined as an objective reality, as Coleridge himself has described :

> Like one, that on a lonesome road
> Doth walk in fear and dread.
> And having once turned round walks on,
> And turns no more his head;
> Because he knows, a frightful fiend
> Doth close behind him tread.

Coleridge is well acquainted with the Gothic novels of horror where the supernatural is simply an external machinery, part of the medieval setting. It is thrilling but not artistic. Coleridge himself has not been able to avoid it completely in his first characteristic poem, The *Ancient Mariner,* where we have such a sensational touches as the hundred companions of the Ancient Mariner falling down suddenly like lifeless lumps, each with a fixed stare on the sinner, who see this curse for seven days and nights but can not die or the picture of the spectre bark with Death and Death-in-life, gambling intently for the possession of the Mariner.

But in *Christabel,* the element of the sinister is infused in the atmosphere and the nature of the daemonic force is unfolded gradually through a number of suggestive details which builds up the suspense till the full force of its potency is reached in the transformation of the poor victim into the likeness of the Evil one.

Similar is the method in *Kubla Khan* where the touch of the weird mystery is added 'to the deep romantic chasm' which becomes a place as 'holy and enchanted.'

As e'er beneath the waning moon was haunted
By woman wailing for her demon-lover.

A single comparison here is charged with all the mystery and shuddering thrill of the contemporary German ballad. This artistic treatment of the supernatural opens a wide vista of possibility before the poets and novelists who follows this track.

Coleridge knows how to handle that type of the supernatural whose essence is entirely psychological. Coleridge's supernaturalism is at once refined and suggestive. It is very unlike the coarse sensationalism of his predecessors-the Eighteenth century writers of the "tale of terror." Coleridge refrains from being crude, elaborate, conventional or unrefined; and to every word he says he leaves ten unsaid. He creates an atmosphere of mystery and horror in *Christabel* by means of suggestive and meaningful details like:

Sixteen short howls, not over loud
Some say, she sees my lady's shroud...

Bus when the lady passed, there came
A tongue of fire, a flit of flame

Coleridge only suggests horror and leaves the rest to the responsive imagination of the reader.

5. COLERIDGE'S NARRATIVE POWER

Coleridge is a Born Story-teller. He knows the art of telling a story in verse. As a narrator he is superior to Wordsworth. He possesses considerable narrative skill and power.

His Narrative Poems have a Quick Movement. His narrative poems, like *Christabel,* have a swift movement. Contrasted with *Christabel,* Wordsworth's *Michael* moves very slowly and leisurely. In *Christabel* one event follows another with breathless rapidity.

He Avoids Unnecessary Details. Coleridge avoids carefully all unnecessary details in *Christabel.* Every detail in this poem either carries the story forward or helps in creating the atmosphere of mystery and horror. There are neither unnecessary characters nor events in *Christabel.*

He Creates Suspense. Coleridge is a master of suspense. He always kept the reader guessing as to what will happen next. In *Christabel,* he creates suspense at every step. The reader continues guessing whether Geraldine would succeed or fail in her evil mission. The story grips our imagination from the beginning to the end.

He Possesses a Dramatic Sense. Like all good narrators, Coleridge possesses a dramatic sense. The dramatic touches in *Christabel* heighten the effect of narrative. In this respect, he is again superior to Wordsworth who has little or no dramatic sense.

The Interest is Continuous Throughout his Poems. The story never grows dull. The interest is continuous throughout his poems. He employs many tricks to engage the attention of the reader. Sometimes he repeats the idea; at other times he introduces a new situation or character.

His Narratives Appear to be Convincing. Lastly, Coleridge possesses the art of making his supernatural stories appear natural and convincing. Though he refers to strange and supernatural events, yet they never strike the reader as incredible. The spell (magic) is not allowed to break at any point. Truly, Coleridge is a great spell-binder—a gifted story teller and a successful narrator.

As a Lyricist. Coleridge is a capable lyricist. In most of his personal poems, he interweaves skilfully the landscape with lyrical utterance. *In Dejection: An Ode* and *Frost at Midnight* Nature and personal effusions are inseparably linked. For instance :

I see the old moon in her lap foretelling
The coming on of rain and squally blast,
And Oh! that even now the gust were swelling.

Occasionally he, like Shelley, provides us with instance of a lyric—cry—the piercing note of sadness. For example :

A grief without a pang—void, dark and drear,
A stifled, drowsy, unimpassioned, grief,
Which finds no natural outlet, no relief
In words, or sigh, or tear. *(Dejection: An Ode)*

6. THE DREAM-ELEMENT IN COLERIDGE'S POETRY

The admirable poem written to Wordsworth after reading *The Prelude*, it is clear that Wordsworth has wrote the poetry which Coleridge most admires. He himself would have liked to have been such a poet, gathering the meaning of life as he see it. But a poet cannot write the poetry he wants to write but only the poetry that is within him. "Within Coleridge, there was a strange territory of memory and dream, of strange birds, phantom ships, Arctic seas, caverns, the sounds of unearthly instruments and of haunted figures, flitting across a scene where magic reigned in a world beyond the control of reason. Some have sought for a moral in *The Ancient Mariner*, but the poem itself is like some Arabian tale, where all moves in a wind and unexpected sequence. *Kubla Khan,* though sometimes judged as a fragment, is best considered as a complete poem, and almost as a definition of Coleridge's poetry, the song of an Abyssinian maid created at the call of magician. These poems are far removed from the gravity and 'high seriousness' of Spenser, Milton, Wordsworth. The poet in them is no longer the arbitrator of life, but the controller of a dream-territory, called out of the sub-conscious."

Imagination and its Surrealistic Character. Coleridge's imagination is sometimes surrealistic in character. In *Kubla Khan*, there was 'a dream' within a dream. Much modern poetry has followed Coleridge in this manner, removing verse from its older and more normal purposes. The strange thing is that Coleridge should have given this lead, for it is one of which Coleridge as critic would have little approved.

The most remarkable thing about Coleridge is his imaginative sensitiveness. He is a visualist and his mind has made all sorts of pictures. "He was of imagination all compact" as a great poet must be. In his imaginative flights, he has seen a 'soul in things' at the heart of all the manifestations of life and nature of which he is a very keen observer. He has always impassioned by ideas and his imagination is only at its height when he run away from human reality. The mystic realm of imagination is more vivid to him than the world of reality from which he easily escapes into it. His fancies from afar are, though a little reckless, extremely fine and lofty.

7. THE MUSIC OF HIS POETRY

Vision and feeling together will never make a poet great unless he possesser the gift of poetic expression also. Coleridge is richly endowed with this quality also. Coleridge alone knows the spell of that unique music of verse in which his imagination finds expression. He is a singer always. Music and imagination are so perfectly blended that it seems impossible to improve the harmony. The fine harmony of his diction, the perfect form of utterance that human words can reach, clearness and simplicity- these have won for Coleridge a unique place among the English poets.

8. HIS ATTITUDE TOWARDS MAN

The Romantic Poets have Intensely Felt for Man: His hopes, sorrows and joys from the substance of their poetry. Coleridge's feeling is not passionate either for Man or Nature when he has worked in actual, he has passion in his work. But in the world where Man and Nature are of the stuff which dreams are made of, his imagination is at once kindled to an amazing degree. The French Revolution, no doubt, has stirred his feelings but there is no endurance in it. The love of liberty as well as other human affections do not arise his emotion. Love is treated with little fire. From love he wanders into fantasies of thought. He does not love passionately and so cannot be expected to sing of that sacred passion.

9. SYMPATHY WITH ANIMAL LIFE

Coleridge is a man of wide sympathies. He hates the type of men who have no natural pity or love for the animal world. He feels the law of love pervading the whole creation. The spiritual world of nature would be angry with a man who will feel no pity or love for living beings. Such men will be punished by hardness of heart. The moral of his great poem, *The Ancient Mariner*, is beautifully worded and is conceived in a truly spiritual mood:

> He prayeth best, who loveth best
> All things both great and small;
> For the dear God who loveth us,
> He made and loveth all.

10. COLERIDGE : THE POET OF THE INNER LIFE

Lastly, Coleridge, the subtle psychologist, shows in his poetry a remarkable knowledge of the inner side of human life. As a writer has remarked, Coleridge is as familiar with the avenues of the soul as Wordsworth is with the dales of his much loved country. He can translate soul hieroglyphics as accurately as his fellow-poet can portray the landscape and the flower. To illustrate this aspect of the poetry of Coleridge we take, for instance, his view of the close relationship of the spirit of love for God's creatures and the capacity to pray is so beautifully portrayed in his *Ancient Mariner* :

> A spring of love gusht from my heart
> . . . .
> The self-same moment I could pray.

In the same poem the poet forcibly brings home the reader the lesson of the necessity of love and human fellowship which is realised by the *Ancient Mariner* through an experience of the horrors of utter solitude:

> O Wedding-Guest ! this soul hath been
> Alone on a wide wide sea !
>
> So lonely "twas, that God himself
> Scarce there seemed to be :
>
> O sweeter than the marriage feast
> 'Tis sweeter far to me.
> To walk together to the kirk,
> With a goodly company !

Take again the following as descriptive of the two-fold effect of remorse:

> Remorse is as the heart in which it grows:
> If that be gentle, is drops balmy dews

Of true repentance but proud and gloomy
It is a poison-tree, that pierced to the inmost
Weeps only tears of poison.

In the following famous lines again the poet gives us another eternal truths about human life with which he is so familiar:

Life is but thought: So think I will
That youth and age are playmates still.

Here is yet another of the same kind:

Work without hope draws nectar in a sieve
And hope without an object cannot live.

In this way the poetry of Coleridge will be found interspersed with similar observations on human life, showing an insight into the inner man, which is supposed to be next only to that of Shakespeare.

11. AS A POETIC ART

As a poet art Coleridge is more pure, subtler and more skilful than Wordsworth who is given to didacticism and whose poetry has 'a palpable design upon us' which a true artist, such as John Keats, naturally abhors. Coleridge, of course, has recorded that nobody can be a great poet unless he is, at the same time, a great philosopher, yet in his poetry philosophical and moral wisdom is always held in solution and is seldom allowed to obtrude itself on our attention so as to mar the poetic effect.

He quite naturally and spontaneously has achieved that simplicity of style and pellucid purity of diction which Wordsworth can attain but seldom after a good deal of pain and deliberate striving. Then there is the 'elfin music', 'the witchery of sound' which he has managed to produce by a subtle handling of the alliterative effects and internal rhymes, a music which does not depend upon a faithful adherence to a fixed patterns, because Coleridge has paved the way for the later metrical experiments in the direction of freedom and flexibility where accent syllables may be fixed in a number but the unaccented ones may vary from one verse to another.

His lyrical note is more genuine and narrative skill that shows itself to great advantage by its rapidity and cumulative effect of growing tension and suspense, is combined with great dramatic intensity of a brief but significant snatches of dialogues. He knows the art of charging his plain words with a wealth of suggestion and making the familiar objects of common observation pregnant with profound symbolical significance.

Development of His Poetic Career. ***Coleridge's Beginnings.*** Wordsworth and Coleridge are most intimate friends. Their development until the time of their meetings, offers great analogies. Coleridge, like

Wordsworth, goes through a phase of revolutionary ardour; his first poems are imitative in character. He begins by imitating the artificial style of the 18th Century, and the themes of his early poems are those of pre-Romanticism.

Coleridge's Part in 'Romantic Revival'; His Handling of the Supernatural. If Wordsworth represents that side of the Romantic Revival which is best described as the return to Nature; Coleridge has justification for the phrase 'Renaissance (or Renascence) of wonder'. He revives the supernatural as a literary force, emancipates it from the crude mechanism which has been applied to it by fashionable (dilettante) writers of the Terror School like Horace Walpole and Mrs. Radcliffe; and invests it instead with that air of suggestion and indefiniteness which gives the highest potency to it in its effect on the imagination. He goes directly to the supernatural and makes artistic use of it to create the spirit of romance which is a strange wed to beauty. With Wordsworth, he has a programme, a literary manifesto in "Preface to the Lyrical Ballads", in which he expresses his intention of Naturalising the Supernatural i.e., he is intended to present the supernatural in such a manner that it will appear to be natural. Indeed, the very centre of his art lies in his faculty of evoking the mystery of things. Gifts with a powerful imagination, he knows how to handle that species of the supernatural whose essence is entirely psychological. It is this which constitutes a great measure of the deep romanticism of his work.

Coleridge's Defects *(i) The Fragmentary Character of his Work.* Coleridge is more noteworthy for what, he has suggested to others than for what he did in himself. His poetry is, even more than Wordsworth's unequal; he is capable of large tracts of dreariness and flatness; he seldom finishes what he begins. *The Ancient Mariner* indeed which is the fruit of his close companionship with Wordsworth, is the only completed thing of the highest quality in the whole of his work. *Christabel* is a splendid fragment; for years the first part lays incomplete and when the odd in accident of an evening's intoxication has led him to begin the second, the inspiration has fled. For the second part, by giving to the fairy atmosphere of the first a local habitation and name, has robbed it of its more precious quality; what it has given in exchange is something the public can get better from Scott. *Kubla Khan* goes unfinished because the call of a friend breaks the thread of the reverie in which it is composed. In the end Coleridge becomes addicted to opium and this has fouled the springs of poetry. Coleridge never fulfills the promise of his early days with Wordsworth. 'He never spoke out'. But it is on the lines laid down by his share in the pioneer work rather than on the lines of Wordsworth's that the second generation of Romantic poets—that of Shelley and Keats—has developed.

(ii) Lack of Human Interest. When we try Coleridge's poetry in its relations to the world of human action, passion, sensation and thought, we are forced to admit that, despite all its power and beauty, it at no moment succeeds in convincing us. The poetry of Coleridge is deficient in human interest. "His poetry leaves too much of the feeling of a walk through a fine country on a misty day." We may have many peep at beautiful scenery and occasional glimpses of the sublime but the medium of vision has been of variable quality and somehow we come home with an uneasy suspicion that we have not seen as much as we might.

(iii) His Fleeting Poetic Impulses. Coleridge's political or politico-religious odes are the offspring of youthful democratic enthusiasm, the supernatural poems, so to call them for want of a better name, has their origin in an almost equally youthful and more than equally transitory passions for the wild and wondrous. Political disillusion is fatal to the one impulse, and mere advance in years extinguishes the other vision of *Ancient Mariner* and *Christabel* which does not revisit the mature man, and the Toryism of middle life will hardly inspire odes to anything.

(iv) Wonderful Music of Coleridge's Poetry. Coleridge with all his defects is a singer always, as Wordsworth is not always, and Byron never. He is endowed with a glorious gift of song. If a critic like Swinburne seems to speak in exaggerated praise of Coleridge's lyrics, we can well understand their enchantment for a master of music like himself. Probably it is the same feeling which makes Shelley describe France as "the finest ode in the English language".

12. WORDSWORTH'S INFLUENCE ON COLERIDGE'S POETRY

The meeting of Coleridge and Wordsworth in 1797 has been an event of outstanding importance in the history of English poetry. Coleridge has been residing at Nether Stowey, which is three miles from Alfoxden, where Wordsworth has settled with his sister. The Wordsworths come to meet Coleridge, and soon there sprang up a friendship between Coleridge and the Wordsworths.

Some change in Coleridge is attributable to Wordsworth's influence upon him. Coleridge by nature is unsteady, and also rambling in his speculation; it is Wordsworth who has checked his rambling tendency, helps and encourages him to concentrate his poetic energy along a definite channel. Again Wordsworth's philosophy of nature influences him and colours to some extent his nature-poetry, which reveal deeper insight and perception. His earlier nature-poems are descriptions of the sights and sounds of nature, and though the details have a beauty of their own, they are not harmonised into lyrical unity by the stress of emotion. The later group of nature-poems shows a deeper sense of calm, a more contemplative mood and, above all, a consciousness of unity pervading the universe, of a spirit operating everywhere "at once the Soul of each and God of all".

But Coleridge do not fully and unreservedly accept Wordsworth's philosophy of nature. According to Wordsworth, nature lives her own life and heals and soothes man in his sorrows and suffering. But Coleridge opposes this view where he says in *Dejection an Ode* :

> O Lady we receive but what we give
> And in our life alone does nature live.

Nature to him is cold and inanimate, and if any glory or joy is to be found in her, it is due to the reflective mind of man and not any quality present in her :

> Ah, from the soul itself must issue forth
> A light, a glory, a fair luminous cloud
> Enveloping the Earth

Both Coleridge and Wordsworth has revolted against the artificial poetic diction of the eighteenth century. But Coleridge do not wholly subscribe to Wordsworth's theory. He will not give any importance to rustic speech, nor will he accept the dictum that, "there is no essential difference between the language of prose and metrical composition." To Coleridge, the language of poetry is distinct from that of prose.

The best poetry of Coleridge is ultimately his own; it is not influenced by Wordsworth at all. Coleridge's genius finds its own way, and attains its fullest and most poetic expression in *The Ancient Mariner, Christabel* and *Kubla Khan*.

Prof. Quiller Couch suggests that Coleridge gives more to Wordsworth than he receives, because his (Coleridge's) presence and talks are more inspiring. In 1797-98, Coleridge write such lines as these:

> 'No sound is dissonant which tells of Life'
>
> (*This Lime-Tree Bower*)
>
> That crowds, and hurries and precipitates
> With fast thick warble his delicious notes. (*Nightingale*)

These lines may be said to be Wordsworthian. But Wordsworth do not attain the intensity of such lines in 1798; he may then write *We are Seven, Simon Lee* etc. Coleridge may teach a thing or two to Wordsworth, and Wordsworth may improve on them and make them his own. "But that other note-the lyrical note of the *The Ancient Mariner*-is incommunicable. He has bequeathed it to none, and before him no poet has approached it; hardly even Shakespeare on the harp of Ariel."

Conclusion. Coleridge has possessed the most vigorous mind among the elder English Romantics (i.e., the English Romanticists of the first generation). In some of his pieces, he is their most exquisite poet. But his work, his life, and even his thoughts are marked by an unhappy fate, which prevents him from reaching complete self-fulfilment. His nervous energy is unable to cope with an intellectual and artistic ambition which has demanded the most exacting efforts for its fulfilment. He becomes a slave to opium, and to a deep-set disease of his own personality, from which he has never recovered.

Coleridge, the Metaphysician as he is called has produced more work in Criticism and Philosophy than in poetry, poetry beings but one of the many pursuits of his life and engaging him only in the earlier part of it. As Mr. Hales has said: "he did not take the Muse for better or worse and cleave only to her. It is in his young manhood that he is devoted himself to her; in the later period political and critical questions mainly occupies him." Most of his work in poetry again is of a fragmentary nature. As we know, 'he was a born procrastinator... .a living Hamlet, for ever plotting and designing but seldom acting.' His last pieces—*Christabel, Kubla Khan,* etc. are brilliant fragments. This small and fragmentary amount of Coleridge's poetry is, however, of exquisite quality. Mr. Stopford Brooke says: "All that he did excellently might be bound in twenty pages but it should be bound in pure gold." This remark, however, is properly true only of the poetry of the 'Nether Stowey' period—the *annus mirablis*—the flowering-time of his poetic genius. His earlier poetry, as the poet being turgid, rhetorical, diffuse and harsh in diction and rhythm. Later, however, he outgrows all his deficiencies and produces a few selected pieces like *The Ancient Mariner, Christabel, Kubla Khan, Love etc.,* which have taken their place among those masterpieces in English poetry which the world will not willingly 'let it die'.

2

COLERIDGE AND THE ROMANTIC MOVEMENT

(A) CHARACTERISTICS OF THE ROMANTIC SCHOOL OF POETRY

Q. 1. What do you understand by romantic poetry? Write a note on the Romantic Movement in English poetry, referring to the characteristics of this school of poetry as manifested in the various Romantic poets.

Ans. The Romantic Movement in English poetry has started as a conscious reaction against the Neo-classical poetry of the eighteenth century. Towards the close of the eighteenth century the great intellectual, moral and religious changes which marks the end of the Age of Reason gains momentum and results in the Romantic Movement. Like all great movements, the Romantic Movement is resulted from the preparations of a preceding age. Its greatness lay in the way in which it draws together the formerly scattered elements of thought and feeling, into a new and significant pattern. Thoughts and feelings can lie inertly side by side, like chemicals; they can be so combined that active forces are released. The French revolution, Methodism, Idealist philosophy, which insist on the supreme importance of mind, and the work of Blake, Wordsworth and Coleridge are all expressions of creative forces working at different levels within society. Broadly, what the Romantic Movement attempts to re-assert is an organic, as opposed to a mechanical, view, of life; it has set out to bring God back into a living universe, and it has placed a higher value on private vision than upon general theories which has degenerated into dogma. At its best the Romantic Movement adds a new dimension to man's vision of himself and the world about him, and is, as Coleridge is aware, a magnificent attempt 'to reconcile the heart and the head'.

The publication of *Lyrical Ballads* in 1798 by Wordsworth and Coleridge may be regarded as the founding event of the Romantic Movement. The chief Romantic poets besides Wordsworth and Coleridge are Scott, Byron, Shelley and Keats. We discuss now the salient features of Romantic poetry and its manifestation in the works of the poets is termed as Romantic poets.

Emotion and Imagination. The essential qualities of romantic poetry are emotion and imagination. Neo-classical poetry appeals chiefly to reason. Romantic poetry has a predominantly emotional appeal. Besides, neo-classical poetry shows very little exercise of the imagination of the writer. Such purely imaginative poems of Keats' *La Belle Dame Sans Merci* and Coleridge's *Kubla Khan* can not have been written by an eighteenth century poet. As for emotion, there is hardly any romantic poem which does not appeal chiefly to the heart as is distinguished from the head. Even Wordsworth's *Ode To Duty* which aims at teaching us a lesson, has an emotional appeal. Poets like Keats or Shelley, indeed, are intense and passionate. Even when the romantic poet wishes to teach a lesson, he does not do so like the 18th century poets; he teaches by appealing to us through our emotions. Shelley's *Ozymandias,* for instance, aims at teaching us a lesson but the lesson is not directly preached. The poet succeeds in impressing the moral upon us by raising in us a certain feeling or emotion. Of pure didacticism there is little in the work of romantic poets, except in the later poems of Wordsworth.

Nature. The 18th century poets are little interested in nature. Even when they do refer to her in their poems, they do so casually and without having any genuine appreciation of her beauty or significance. The romantic poets, on the contrary, has a deep and sincere love for Nature. Wordsworth is the greatest Nature poet in English literature. He gives Nature a high status as an independent subject for poetry and developes a full-fledged philosophy regarding her.' This is his chief contribution to romantic poetry. Coleridge, Scott, Byron, Shelley and Keats are also ardent lovers of Nature though they can be distinguished from one another in their attitude to Nature. Nature is a very important subject in their poetry. *Nutting, Frost at Midnight, Lake Leman, Ode to the West Wind, Ode to Autumn* are all Nature poems as they contain nature description as well as the poet's love for nature. They also reveal what significance Nature holds for the poets.

Humanitarianism (Love for Liberty etc). The romantic poets has sincere love for man, or rather the spirit of man. Wordsworth, Coleridge and Shelley has a superabundant enthusiasm for humanity. Wordsworth is deeply interested in the simple village folk who lives in contact with Nature. Coleridge shows his love of humanity in *Reflections on Having Left a Place of Retirement* when he says that he would like to serve mankind. Both Wordsworth and Coleridge shows admiration for the ideals that inspires the French Revolution. Shelley's whole poetry is an evidence of his humanitarian ardour. Shelley visualises the golden age of men, when there will be no slavery of any kind and love will reign. He expresses these ideas in his *Hymn to Intellectual Beauty* and *Ode to the West Wind.*

Byron too has a great love for liberty. He denounces tyranny in his *Ode to Napoleon*.

Lyricism. The Romantic poets are deeply subjective. They write deeply personal poems, revealing their own nature, feelings and thoughts. This subjectivity leads them to write lyrics. All the Romantic poets have fine lyrics to their credit but Shelley surpasses them all in this respect. Shelley's lyricism is exquisite, incomparable. The *Ode to the West Wind* is a supreme example of his lyric gift. Wordsworth too wrote excellent lyrics, such as, *The Solitary Reaper*.

Supernaturalism. Besides the above more or less common features, there are certain qualities of romantic poetry which are possessed by particulars poets. Supernaturalism is an outstanding romantic quality. It gives to certain poems an atmosphere by virtue of which the romantic poetry is often called the 'renascence of wonder'. Coleridge is a great master of supernaturalism in *The Ancient Mariner*. He is psychological, refined and suggestive. Scott too writes supernatural poetry, e.g. *William and Helen* though his supernaturalism is rather crude. Keats gives supernatural touches to some of his poems such as, *La Belle Dame Sans Merci and Eve of St. Agnes*.

References to Distant Lands and Past Ages. Romantic poets often draws upon the Middle Ages. Keats loves the Middle Ages for their passion and chivalry and art; Scott for their action and adventure as also chivalry. Keats' *The Eve of St. Agnes*, Coleridge's *Love* and Scott's *William and Helen*—all have been inspired by medieval times.

Melancholy Note. There is a note of melancholy in Romantic poetry. It may be a nostalgia for past glory, or experience of sheer sadness. Byron shows this melancholy in *Lake Leman*. Byron's melancholy comes to have a special appeal over the continent. Keats wrote an *Ode to Melancholy* and Coleridge an *Ode to Dejection*.

Other Characteristics of Romantic Poetry. Romantic poets are lovers of Beauty—beauty of nature as well as of man. Keats wrote "Beauty is Truth, Truth is Beauty" and "A Thing of Beauty is a joy for ever". Indeed Keats' sensuous love of beauty is his chief quality as a romantic poet. Shelley writes A *Hymn to Beauty* (Intellectual Beauty, of course). Greek mythology has a fascinating effect on Keats and Shelley and to some extent also on Byron. Keats loves Greek mythology for the sensuous charm of its stories and writes several poems pertaining to it. His fancy contains references to Proserpine, Pluto, Jove, etc. Shelley's poems, too contain abundant reference to it. *The World's Great Age Begins Anew* contains references to Ulysses Battle of Troy, Sphinx etc.

Style of the Romantic Poets. The style of the romantic poets deserves special mention. In the 18th century, conventional and artificial diction has been employed and a particular metre (the heroic couplet) is thought to be the best metre for writing poetry. The romantic poets introduces several new metres and stanza forms with remarkable success. Their poems, especially those of Coleridge and Shelley, are marked by delightful melody and cadence. *The Ancient Mariner* and the *Ode to the West Wind* are musical. The romantic poets also coins special phrases and uses fresh and beautiful words (as against conventional and artificial words of the 18th century poetry). Wordsworth and Keats are especially known for their phrases. We come across such phrases as "unchartered freedom", "trailing clouds of glory" and "virgin sense" in Wordsworth and "azure-lidded sleep", "purple riot" and "warmed jewels" in Keats.

(B) COLERIDGE AS A ROMANTIC POET

Q. 2. In Coleridge romanticism attains a fullness of complexity. Discuss with illustrations.

Or

Discuss the salient features of Coleridge as a Romantic poet.

Ans. Along with Wordsworth, Coleridge is the co-founder of the Romantic Movement by virtue of his contribution to the writing of the *Lyrical Ballads* published in 1798, the official date of the commencement of Romantic Movement. Coleridge's poems are few in number but show Romantic features at their best.

Humanitarianism and Love of Liberty. Like Wordsworth, Coleridge too has dreams of the political regeneration of mankind and has a great enthusiasm for the French Revolution though its cruelty later on repelled him. His love for humanity is expressed in *Reflection on Having Left a Place of Retirement* where he bids farewell to his cottage in order to go to the city and work for relieving people of their distress. He condemns those theoretical lovers of mankind who do nothing practical for humanity. In the *Ode to France,* he regrets the failure of the French to live up to their revolutionary ideals. *Fears in Solitude* expresses his love for mankind and his abhorrence of injustice and inhumanity.

Importance of Imagination. The quality which distinguishes the poetry of the beginning of the 19th century, the poetry which we can roughly group together as the Romantic poetry, is the quality of its imagination and this quality is seen as a kind of atmosphere, which adds strangeness to beauty. Watts-Dunton uses a phrase which has become famous, "Renaissance of Wonder" for "that great revived movement of the soul of man, after a long period of prosaic acceptance in all things, including literature and art." It means a reawakening to a sense of beauty and strangeness in natural things, and in all the impulses of the mind and the senses. Poetry is realised as a personal confession, or as an evocation, or as "an instant made eternity." At countless points the universe of sense and thought acquires a new potency of response and appeals to man, a new power of ministering to and mingling with, his richest and intensest life. Glory of lake and mountain, graces of childhood, dignity of the untaught peasant, mystery of the Gothic castle, radiance of Attic marble all these springs of the poet's inspiration and the artist's joy begins to flow. Wordsworth is the poet of a peculiar mystic idealism who discloses, in the rapt communion with nature, an undreamed of access to the "life of things." Coleridge is allured to rare and remoter tracks of humanity, lurking places of strange dreams and fantastic anomalies of belief. Shelley and Keats find the world controlled not by laws of nature, but of beauty. In Byron the artist's self-assertion takes a more defiant and lawless form, even to the abnegation of art. What all these poets aimes at is the emancipation of the world and of the mind and of the vehicle of poetry from the bondage of fact, opinion, formality and tradition and the right to look through :

> Charmed magic casements opening on the foam
> Of perilous seas, in faery lands forlorn.

Two great movements of European thought stands in an intimate but complex intellectual relation to Romanticism the revolutionary naturalism of Rousseau and the transcendental movement in Germany from Kant to Hegel. Rousseau the apostle of the French Revolution, preaches the worth and dignity of man as man, and the power of natural scenery to respond to his needs. Kant and his successors is exalted the mind as mind. The ideal is more and more explicitly identified with the real; to will goodness, or to imagine beauty, is alone to live truly. Art is thus not merely a heightening of the actual, but an escape from it. It insists on the power and autocracy of the imagination which alone gives a varied, subtle, intimate interpretation of the world of "external nature" and of that other world of wonder and romance which the familiar comradeship of Nature generates in the mind of man.

Supernatural Rendered Real through Imagination. Coleridge is always peculiarly engaged with the inquiry into the quality by which poetic imagination gives an air of reality to the marvellous. It is his critical ingenuity which conceives the design of "a series of poems.......of two sorts; the one, of common subjects such as will be found in every village" is poetically treated, the other, of subjects mainly "supernatural, but is made real by the dramatic truth of such emotions, supposing them real." He is peculiarly fascinated by the "interception" of the spiritual world, the straggling branches of marvel which startle and waylay the observer. He looks into the void and found it peopled with presences. His is the uncommon eye that beheld the unseen. With rare felicity of phrase and imagery he makes the supernatural natural, giving to the unreal, weird and mysterious phenomena of this world a sense of actuality and substance.

In *Christabel* the element of the marvellous is not obtruded, but slowly distills into the air. The first part is a masterpiece in the art of suggesting enchantment by purely natural means. The castle, the wood, the mastiff, the tree with its jagged shadows are drawn with a quivering intensity of touch which conveys the very atmosphere of foreboding and suspense:

> Sir Leoline, the Baron rich,
> Hath a toothless mastiff bitch;
> From her kennel beneath the rock
> She maketh answer to the clock
> Four for the quarters, twelve for the hour,
> Ever and aye, by shine and shower,
> Sixteen short howls, not over loud
> Some say she sees my lady's shroud.

The marvellous, too, when we come to it—the serpent-nature of Geraldine—is of a subtle weirdness, for no prodigies of the external world touch the imagination so nearly as distortions of human personality.

The Ancient Mariner abinds in this supernatural element. All nature is pillaged to supply the mysterious atmosphere he creates. The sun is flecked with bars :

> Heaven's mother send us grace!
> As if through a dungeon-grate he peered
> With broad and burning face

Nothing can exceed the terror and horror, is suggested by the appearance of the phantom ship and its inmates :

> And is that woman all her crew?
> Is that a Death? and are there two?
> Is Death that woman's mate?

And we have the weird ship moving zig-zag across the water when there is absolute calm and no wind to push it along.

Dreamy Quality. The mystery, the strangeness, the weirdness of the supernatural cast a peculiar spell on the dreamy imagination of Coleridge. In *Kubla Khan* we have an instance of dream-poetry at its finest. According to Saintsbury, the nineteen lines "But oh!.......war" (L. 12-30) reach the highest point of English verse-music. And the three lines—

A savage place, as holy and enchanted
As e'ver beneath a waning moon was haunted
By a woman wailing for her demon-lover!

represent the very summit of romantic poetry, condensing within themselves the whole world of romantic imagination in the same manner as the famous lines of Keats :

Charmed magic-casement, opening on the foam
Of perilous seas, in faery lands forlorn.

There is in *The Ancient Mariner* the abrupt movement of stages, exactly like what happens in a dream. Its visual impressions are brilliant and its emotional impacts change rapidly. The poem clings to the memory with the peculiar tenacity of a dream.

Medievalism. Coleridge thus took upon himself the treat of the supernatural in such a manner as to give it "a semblance of truth" and "to procure for it a willing suspension of disbelief for the moment." To accomplish this, Coleridge often goes back to Middle Ages to create the necessary background for his supernatural characters and incidents. The romanticism in Coleridge consists among other things, in his introduction of medieval elements in his poetry, which enables him to call up all the magic and enchantment of the distant past. In the *Ancient Mariner* several references give a medieval touch-such as mention of the cross-bow, vesper-bell, the shriving hermit, the prayer to Mary Queen. The very idea of penance for a wrong done has a Catholic overtone and is medieval in spirit. *Christabel* of course, has a palpably medieval atmosphere—moated castle, feudal lords, bards, pages and chivalry. The ballad form used in *The Ancient Mariner* and in *Love* is also an influence of the Medieval literary tradition.

Nature : Minute Description and Pantheism. Closely connects with this quality is the power of observing and depicting the subtle aspects of nature, richly and faithfully. In *The Song of the Pixies,* he paints the russet suites landscape of the eighteenth century idyllists from the rich and varied palette which we are accustomed to call Celtic. The beauties of nature, the clouds, the furze, the dew, are drawn with delicate feeling, full of half-lights and elusive suggestion. Stopford Brook praised "the perfect pictorial skill and truth of his descriptions." Takes the description of the ice in *The Ancient Mariner* :

And now there came both mist and snow,
And it grew wondrous cold,
And ice, mast high, came floating by
As green as emerald.

and of the night in *Christabel* :

> The night is chilly, but not dark.
> The thin grey cloud is spread on high.
> It covers but not hides the sky.
> The moon is behind and at the full;
> And yet she looks both small and dull.
> The night is chill, the cloud is grey:
> Tis the month before the month of May,
> And the spring comes slowly up this way.

or this, which has a touch of "romantic" weirdness :

> Nought was green upon the oak
> But moss and rarest mistletoe:

The Ancient Mariner is full of word pictures. When there is no breeze and the ship is motionless, it is "as idle as a painted ship upon a painted ocean". We have several natural pictures like the moving moon going up the sky and a star or two beside, the slimy things crawling upon the slimy sea, the ice crackling and growling and roaring and howling. The distinctive note of Coleridge's nature pictures is that, he dwells upon the uncommon and rare phenomena of nature. In *The Ancient Mariner*, for instance, he refers to "a copper sky" "the bloody sun" and the death-fires dancing at night and the water burning green and blue and white like a witch's oils. Coleridge is a great lover of colour : the ice is as green as emerald, the water-snakes moves in tracks shining white and they are blue, glossy green and velvet black.

The lines reveals a minute realism, an imaginative apprehension of the silent and unseen processes of nature and the vivid aspects of external nature which is characteristic of a singular watchfulness for the minute fact and expression of natural scenery and a closeness to her exact physiognomy. As he himself says :

> That outward forms, the loftiest, still receive
> Their finer influence front the world within;
> Fair ciphers of vague import, where the eye
> Traces no spot, in which the heart may read
> History and prophecy...

In *Frost at Midnight* we see evidence of Wordsworth's influence in the lines is addressed by Coleridge to his baby. Coleridge refers to a Divine Spirit behind nature and to the moral and shaping influence which she exercises over those who seek her company. Later on he modifies his attitude to Nature and believes that we interpret the moods of Nature according to our own moods. In other words, if we are happy, Nature looks to us happy too and if we are dejected, Nature also looks dejected. Nature therefore, has no moods and feelings of her own. We receive from

Nature only that which we give to her. This belief finds expression in his *Dejection: An Ode*. His love for Nature makes him give us beautiful pictures of it. He has a preference for the uncommon and rare phenomena of nature and this preference is illustrated in *The Ancient Mariner*.

Insight into Human Mind and Psyche. No poet, except Shakespeare, has shown such a profound insight into the working of the human soul or has expressed it with finer accuracy as Coleridge in his poems. Subtle-souled psychologist Shelley called him. He is as familiar with the avenues of the soul as Wordsworth with the dales of his much loved country. He can translate soul hieroglyphics as accurately as his fellow pot can portray the landscape and the flower. He can descend to the depths of our consciousness and discover the secret springs of action; it is only in questioning ourselves that we can unravel the universe; the true, the only events are those of the soul and the special domain of Coleridge's poetry is this inner theatre. He can describe vividly the feeling of fear :

> We listened and looked sideways up!
> Fear at my heart, as at a cup,
> My life-blood seemed to sip!

or the distraction of an agonize soul :

> I looked to Heaven, and tried to pray,
> But ere ever a prayer had gusht
> A wicked whisper came, and made
> My heart as dry as dust.
> I closed my lids, and kept them close,
> And the balls like pulses beat;

or in *Christabel* :

> Her limbs relax, her countenance
> Grows sad and soft; the smooth thin lids
> Close o'ver her eyes; and tears she sheds-
> Large tears that leave the lashes bright!
> And oft the while she seems to smile
> As infants at a sudden light!

Lyricism : The Music of His Poetry. Coleridge is a great musician. His best poems are marked by a delightful melody. He has been called an epicure in sounds (i.e., a lover of melody). *The Ancient Mariner* illustrates the witchery of his music :

> The fair breeze blew, the white foam flew
> The furrow followed free;
> We were the first that ever burst
> Into that silent sea.

The alliteration and the simplicity of the words is used to add the melody of the lines, and suggests the very swift movement of the ship :

> Down dropt the breeze, the sails dropt down
> "Twas as sad as sad could be.

Here the artistic repetition of words is noteworthy. It immediately suggests the stillness of the atmosphere. Indeed, in this poem Coleridge has attained the highest level of verbal music ever reached by an English poet. And this he did by the use of the simplest words possible. The poem is perfect in rhythm, sound and cadence and magical in its metrical felicities. He is really a "master of harmony". Love also illustrates this.

Conclusion. Coleridge may be called the most romantic of the poets of the Romantic revival. His poetry, more than even that of Wordsworth, shows the unfolding of the process of the Romantic revival. His early poems are more or less experimental, but they show his ardent delight in natural beauty and his self-consciousness as an artist. His feeling for the beauties of the physical world and his spiritual interpretation of the universe may be traced in some of his early verse, like—*The Song of the Pixies* (1793), *Lines on an Autumnal Evening* (1794), *The Eolian Harp* (1795) and *Religious Musings* (1796). His revolutionary ardour and his subsequent feeling of despair and indignation break out in the *Odes to the Departing Year* (1796) and *To France* (1797); these poems are full of fire and passion, and displays a poetic eloquence hitherto lacking in his work. His emotional response to the beauties and glories of nature is poetically expressed in practically all his poems. Coleridge has planted his supernaturalism on the truth of human emotions and so made the supernatural appear to be natural. The three great poems of Coleridge—*The Ancient Mariner, Christabel* and *Kubla Khan*—all contain supernatural elements (the last one having just a touch of it)—and they are his most romantic poems.

Thus, all the features of the Romantic revival are fully manifested in the poetry of Coleridge. In his poetry, there is bold adventure, joy of discovery, romance of action. There is the glamour of untravelled regions, elements of mystery and marvel. There is Nature in a variety of moods : familiar, weird, tender, tumultuous, gay, desolate, soothing or horrifying. All these features are linked into a vital unity with a psychological insight. Truly, in Coleridge's poetry, romanticism—attained a fullness of complexity.

(C) COLERIDGE AND THE LATER ROMANTICS

Q. 3. "Coleridge bridges the gulf between Wordsworth and the younger romantics. He sings of the beneficent effect of nature". Discuss Coleridge's contribution to the nineteenth century romanticism in the light of the above statement.

Ans. Coleridge and Nineteenth Century Romanticism. Coleridge bridges the gulf between Wordsworth and the younger romantics. He sings of the beneficent effects of nature on the human mind in the manner of Wordsworth, glorifies childhood as the period of peace and innocence and of communion with God and in his earlier phase, he welcomes the French Revolution as the new dawn for humanity. But more than Wordsworth, he lets in a new aestheticism in English poetry through his worship of the beauty of women, he revives interest in Gothic art and medieval legends, he starts the cult of Spenser, the great favourite of Keats, he dreams of faery lands which have no location in time and place, he treats the supernatural with unsurpassed mastery. He gives new imagery to Shelley, a new medievalism to Keats, Laudanum and the Gothic to the Pre-Raphaelites, religious fervour to the Oxford Movement and "patriotism" and worship of all things English to Lord Tennyson. Across the whole length of the nineteenth century falls the shadow of Coleridge. With him we enter the world of Romanticism proper.

The Cult of the Middle Ages. The romantic movement draws the attention of the poet to the Middle Ages. The name *Lyrical Ballads* suggests the blending of new lyricism with the ballad poetry of the past. Dr. Johnson has ridiculed the ode and sonnet school but these becomes the favourite metrical forms for the new poetry. The new poets has turned to ballads not only for the variety of the stanza as being opposed to the heroic couplet but also for the flavour of old romantic tales and their dramatic appeal. They are resuscitated the superstitious beliefs of the people which has found less sympathy in a more sophisticated age. They, of course, has ignored the barbarism and cruelty of feudal society, the hypocrisy and corruption of the church, the denial of all those human values in life which has made the Renaissance a great period of creative literature quite different from the soulless scholasticism of the Middle Ages. This aspect is partly stressed by Morris and Swinburne in their earlier work. To Coleridge and Keats, the medieval world is one of pure romance where even witches put on such lovely forms that the doom of their victim has become a pleasurable experience to the poet.

Christabel is the first expression of the medieval spirit in the new poetry. The hall, the moat, the bard, the friar, the rushes, the carving, the brands all together by subtle suggestion create the indefinable thing, the atmosphere. Keats is more lavish in his detail; he makes things too palpable to have that ethereal suggestive quality which is characteristic of Coleridge. He is also less correct in his details as in the too many inconsistent pictures in Bertha's manuscript in the *Eve of St. Mark* and notorious carpets in the *Eve of St. Agnes* Coleridge is more careful and is a master in achieving utmost-poetic effect through minimum of detail. Yet the medievalism of

Christabel is not the chief feature in that poem. The primary thing is the hypnotic effect of the superior will power of Geraldine on Christabel.

Anticipates Keats and Shelley in His Nature-poetry. Much of Coleridge's nature poetry bears the obvious imprint of Wordsworth's thought. No doubt, Wordsworth himself is indebted to Coleridge for much of his idealism. While in the *'Christmas Eve'* Coleridge echoes his friend's pantheism :

> Tis the sublime of man,
> Our noontide majesty, La know ourselves
> Parts and proportions of one wondrous whole

In *Dejection : And Ode* : he says that Beauty is within us and not outside in nature. This conforms more to his Platonism and is opposed to the attitude of Wordsworth :

> O lady we receive but what we give
> And in our life alone does nature live.

Coleridge is a poet of moods and nature generally accords with his own dominating feeling. He can give truthful pictures of natural scenes when he chooses and there is often that love of detail, and what is more, a stress on individual details, which later characterised the Pre-Raphaelites. Wordsworth is seldom interested in details for their own sake as Coleridge is, for example, in the picture :

> How solemnly the pendent ivy-mass
> Swings in its window; all the air is calm.
> The smoke from cottage chimneys, tinged with light.
> Rises in columns.

Coleridge has often picked such sense not in the mountains but in the plains. For mountain scenery, he generally prefers Switzerland and the Alps or the bleak and dismal mountains of the English of north. Like Shelley, he rejoices in the torrents and the avalanches of the snow-covered mountains. He also associates with them the emotional upsurge in the human heart and as in *Prometheus Unbound*, he makes nature rejoice in the happy millennium of humanity. It is new kind of poetry he has given to his generation when he has written in the *Chamouni Hymn* :

> God ! let the torrents, like a shout of nations,
> Answer! and let the ice-plains echo, God!
> God! sing ye meadow-streams with gladsome voice!
> Ye pine-groves, with your soft and soul-like sounds!

Like Shelley, he has a tendency to etherialise nature; beneath the external form, he seems to penetrate to its changing non-material substance. Thus he asks to the solid Mont Blanc to :

> Rise like a cloud of incense, from the Earth !

This will naturally draw his attention rather to the more dynamic aspects of nature, to movement and to change, than to objects that are static and in repose. It is not given to Wordsworth to sing of the constant shiftings of huge masses of snow on the high mountains, where :

> ....the avalanche, unheard,
> Shoots downward, glittering through the pure serene
> Into the depth of clouds.

Shelley alone probed into these mysteries of nature. But Coleridge will not be himself if this were the sole or even dominating characteristic of his nature poetry. He is more like a newly emancipated spirit that is interested in tasting as many forbidden fruits as possible. He also describes objects in repose and in sharp relief in the manner of Keats and Rossetti. The solitary leaf in *Christabel*—to which his attention is drawn by Dorothy—is an example of his stress on solitary detail.

Eye for Colour and Exotic Details. Keats glories in colours; he luxuriates in the deep golden colour of autumnal sunsets but Coleridge observes the subtler shades and nuances has been brought about by shifting light like an impressionist. Even the pre-Raphaelites are not so concerned with these fleeting effects in nature. In the *Lime-Tree Bower My Prison,* Coleridge watches the pale colour of the transparent foliage, observes a broad and sunny leaf and its shadow, the richly tinge walnut tree and the deep radiance on the ancient ivy, and because of the black mass of ivy, the dark branches of the elm trees

> ....gleam a lighter hue
> Through the late twilight.

His love of exotic scenes and dream-nature distinguishes him from Wordsworth. The imagery of *Kubla Khan* is as exotic and suggestive as the palm trees beneath which the Indian maiden is discovered in *Endymion.* His exoticism is best seen in *The Rime of the Ancient Mariner.* The sense of guilt and pursuit through distant lands forms the subject of *The Ancient Mariner.* He relates his story to a Wedding-Guest and curiously enough holds him with "his glittering eye". It is, however, not the guest who falls a victim to hypnotic and superior will-power; the Mariner holds him only to tell him how he has been guilty of shooting the Albatross for apparent reason. The Mariner and his friends are punished for this sin with a terrible nightmare. They see strange colours on the water at night-time :

> About, about, in reel and rout
> The death-fires danced at night;
> The waters, like a witch's oils'
> Burnt green, and blue, and white.

The fascinating character of this horror cannot be missed. The sea is rotting and the crew are going to die, yet the Mariner can hardly take his eyes off these colours. To know what lay behind the story of the Mariner, compare with the above stanza the following :

But yesternight I prayed aloud
In anguish and in agony,
Up-starting from the fiendish crowd
Of shapes and thoughts that tortured me:
A lurid light, a trampling throng,
And whom I scorned, those only strong... (*Pains of Sleep*)

Coleridge is describing the pains of sleep as he has endured them in his real life. Like the Mariner and Christabel, he has a strange and inexplicable sense of shame and horror :

Deeds to be hid which were not hid.

In his prose passage on the *Wanderings of Cain* he describes the same agonizing experience again. "He pursueth my soul like the wind", says Cain, "like sand-blast he passeth through me; he is around me even as the air; that I might be utterly no more; I desire to die.. For the torrent that roareth far off hath a voice; and the clouds in heaven look terribly on me; the mighty one who is against me speaketh in the wind of the cedar grove; and in silence am I dried up." This can describe very well the feelings of the Mariner; he has the same sense of unutterable guilt of fear. The reason of this paralysis of the will-power, this sense of guilt and shame and the nightmare of being ever pursued through space is, as in the case of De Quincey, opium.

Opium and the Supernatural. The supernatural is intimately connected with opium in the poetry of Coleridge. This may appear to be fantastic at first sight and example of poets can readily be given who write of the supernatural without in the least being addicted to that fatal drug. But Coleridge's treatment of the supernatural is not the same as that of other poets. Without going into a detail comparison of their different treatments, one can readily see that in Coleridge, the supernatural means the pursuit of the victim, the complete collapse of his will power and the intense pain resulting from a fascination, not horror exercised by the supernatural being. Coleridge's Geraldine is the prototype of Keats' *Lamia*, the serpent-woman who can assume a fascinating form and works the ruin of her lover. The serpent-eye of Geraldine are noticed by Christabel only when she is completely within her power. Sir Leoline does not see any sign of the witch in her. She is exceedingly beautiful like a lady of a far off country and to make her alluring, Coleridge lets his look linger on her for a little while as she is undressing. Keats may be say to have enlarged on the following lines in his description of the undressing of Madeline :

> She unbound
> The cincture from beneath her breast;
> Her silken robe, and inner vest,
> Dropt to her feet, and full in view,
> Behold her bosom and half her side-
> A sight to dream of, not to tell !
> O shield her! shield sweet Christabel !

The Fatal Woman and Her Victims. The fatal woman usually has a male lover and she is not interested in tormenting female victims. But Coleridge's purpose is not to write a poem of love and beauty like the later nineteenth century poets. The theme is haunting his mind is the paralysis of human will and this he could depict very well with the aid of a female character. She is in a dizzy trance when she goes to meet her father and her fearful dreams have given her a sense of guilt. The Ancient Mariner has killed the Albatross; the dreams of Christabel have wrought such a change in her that the poet asks, "Can this be she? The lady who knelt at the old oak tree?" and "Sure, have I sinned", says Christabel to herself. Coleridge did not complete the poem and we do not know if Christabel have been shriven by a priest like the Ancient Mariner. There is also a faint suggestion in the prolonged embrace of Geraldine that she wants to catch not only the daughter but also the father in her snare.

The last line, suggests the fatal character of her beauty but is not meant to evoke a feeling of horror. He has already told the reader that she is a sight to dream of. She is the first of that long line of fatal women who enchant their lovers in proportion to their power of evil. They become an obsession with Swinburne, Pater, the Pre-Raphaelites and the Decadents.

Love of Liberty and Abhorrence of Tyranny. Coleridge is a firm believer in human dignity and liberty. He fiercely denounces

> Statesman blood-stained and priests idolatrous.

The blood of Christ, he says, has been bartered away for war; and state and religion make widows groan and orphans weep for bread. In his sonnet on Burke, he laments the fact that a wise statesman like him shall make "Oppression's hireling crew rejoice". Lafayette, whom Burke calls an "unspeakable ruffian", is lauded in another sonnet as heralding a new dawn in the long night of winter. It is not, however, in the expression of bright hopes for future that Coleridge is at his best, he is most effective in his denunciation of tyrants and in such passages, he is the direct predecessor of Shelley.

Conclusion. Coleridge has started his career as a poet of love and nature; he has brought it to a climax by his treatment of the supernatural; and then it comes to an abrupt end with the complete deadening of his imagination. He has touched lightly on all those keys which are to give new melodies to the next generation, though he can not create symphonies of his own. His early intellectual death matches the early physical death of Keats and Shelley who, however, has lived a fuller life than Coleridge.

(D) FRENCH REVOLUTION AND COLERIDGE

Q. 4. How far is Coleridge's poetry influenced by the ideals and trends of the French Revolution which in many ways has inspired the Romantic Movement?

Ans. Coleridge, like Wordsworth, is filled with revolutionary ardour, when the French Revolution burst upon France with its cry of Liberty, Equality and Fraternity. He greets the fall of the Bastille as a promise of the time when

> Liberty, the soul of life, Shall reign,
> Shall throb in every pulse, shall flow thro'every vein.

All his youthful enthusiasm is roused (Coleridge was then 17) and he feels deeply in his blood the passion of the moment—a revolutionary passion which challenged established beliefs, and even conceived wild projects to serve the cause of Freedom. His mind is filled with Utopian dreams; with Southey and some others he has planned the scheme of Pantisocracy—a sort of communistic society on the banks of the Susquehenna in America, where he hoped to realise his dreams of equality.

Soon after, his enthusiasm cooled. The aggressive designs of France in her attack on Switzerland totally destroyed his belief that she was the champion of liberty. His feelings about the Revolution—his earlier enthusiasm and his later disillusionment are expressed in two odes—*Ode to the Departing Year* (1796) and *France: An Ode* (1797); "they form the transition between his first hopes and his later conservative despair."

The *Ode to the Departing Year* is an emphatic denunciation of the brood of hell-the kings who had combined against France. It calls on the Spirit of the Earth to avenge the wrongs of the poor and to speak in thunder to England, who has leagued herself against liberty, and joined "the wild yelling of Famine and Blood." The revolutionary character of the poem is noticed in the sentiment of the poet who, like Wordsworth, was on the side of France against his own country.

When France attacked Switzerland, the disillusionment of Coleridge was complete. In the *Ode to France*, he recollects what he had first felt about the Revolution some years earlier; he has wished that England has been fighting against liberty, might have been defeated by France :

> Yet still my voice unaltered sang defeat
> To all that braved the tyrant-quelling lance.
> And shame too long delayed and vain retreat...

The Reign of Terror in Paris does not extinguish his hopes; he has thought that the evils are are brought by the reign of blood and terror, are unavoidable, in view of the vast change for the better in human life: the sun of liberty has been rising behind the storms of the Terror :

> "And soon," I said, "shall wisdom teach her lore
> In the low huts of them that toil and groan
> And conquering, by her happiness alone
> Shall France compel the nations to be free,
> Till love and joy look round, and call the earth their own"

But the attack on Switzerland by France shook his faith in the has Revolution; he is disappointed and has fell back upon the sense of liberty in his own soul. The world has failed him and he takes refuge in the solitudes of nature. The conclusion of the ode on France is in a lofty strain. He asks the forgiveness of Freedom for having identified her with France, and asserts her to be unquenchable even if she must be driven for her resort to the elements themselves :

> Thou speedest thy subtle pinions,
> The Guide of homeless winds, and playmates of waves.

The poet sends out his being to the sea and air and possesses all things "with intensest love".

This magnificent poem has been pronounced by Shelley as 'the finest ode in the English language. It is the last and the greatest poem produced by Coleridge under the influence of revolutionary enthusiasm.

The last vestige of his faith in the revolution is destroyed when England was threatened with invasion. "France was no longer the apostle of freedom but the apostle of despotism". Coleridge has once dissolved the tie of patriotism in the interest of the wider love of man; but now he has laid aside his wild hopes of love for mankind and has fell back on his old patriotism:

> O my mother isle
> How shouldst thou prove aught also but dear holy
> To me, who from thy lakes and mountain rills
> Thy clouds, thy quiet dales, thy rocks and seas
> Have drunk in all my intellectual life
> All sweet sensations, all ennobling thought

Coleridge has lapsed into conservatism (as did Wordsworth) when the Revolution has failed him; but the change, in the case of Coleridge is much more rapid than in Wordsworth, for Coleridge is less firm and less temperate than Wordsworth. His enthusiasm has been warmer and it has died more quickly. With the passing of his enthusiasm his will and poetic energy has also passed away. "Almost all his best poetic energy also passed with the Revolution: afterwards everything is incomplete. The weakness of will was doubled by disease, and trebled by opium, and his poetic life, even his philosophic work, was a splendid failure", says S.A. Brooke.

Coleridge, however, never lost his admiration and love for the ideals that the French Revolution stood for. He always holds dear the liberty of man, love for one another, and egalitarian society in which there would have been no exploitation of the poor.

3

COLERIDGE'S TREATMENT OF THE SUPERNATURAL

Q. 1. What are the features that render Coleridge's treatment of the supernatural unique?

Or

"The very centre of Coleridge's art lies in his beauty of evoking the mystery of things, and making it actual, widespread and obsessing" Discuss.

Or

Discuss Coleridge's treatment of the supernatural in the light of the statement that he endeavoured to "procure for the shadows of imagination that willing suspension of disbelief for the moment that constitutes poetic faith."

Ans. Introduction. Though Coleridge's poetic achievement is small and sometimes fragmentary, yet he remains unequalled in one sphere of poetry—that of the supernatural. While planning a new volume of poems to be jointly written by Wordsworth and Coleridge, Coleridge undertakes to deal with the supernatural. He has written in, *Biographia Literaria* : "It was agreed that my endeavours should be directed to persons and characters supernatural or at least romantic, yet so as to transfer from our inward nature a human interest and a semblance of truth sufficient to procure for these shadows of imagination that willing suspension of disbelief for the moment which constitutes poetic faith." It is with this idea in his mind that he has composed *The Rime of the Ancient Mariner*. The two other poems dealing with the supernatural element are both left incomplete—*Christabel* and *Kubla Khan*.

Break with Existing Cult of Supernaturalism. Before Coleridge, the supernatural element has entered into English Literature (apart from drama) in a rather gross and crude form. It has appeared in the works of Horace Walpole. Mrs. Radcliffe and Monk Lewis has introduced the supernatural element in a crude form in their romances. They have tried to produce an atmosphere of mystery and horror by artificial devices like sudden transformation; noise and thunder, mysterious whisperings and awful appearances. Coleridge totally has discarded such grotesque and ludicrous grossness. He has given an inward quality to his conception of the supernatural; he brings supernaturalism into intimate relation with individual experience and gives a new psychological interest to it. The difference between Coleridge on one side and Walpole and Mrs. Radcliffe on the other is the difference between the maker of horror and the maker of horrors. Coleridge creates the atmosphere of mystery by indefiniteness and by subtle suggestion while the other two employ crude description and pile horrors in order to send a cold shiver down the reader's spine and to curdle the reader's blood.

The treatment of supernatural by the earlier writers is of the objective kind. Coleridge's treatment is of a fine kind; the supernatural is brought in line with subjective experience. Coleridge himself wrote in reference to the supernatural class of poems in the *Lyrical Ballads*.. ."the incidents and agents are to be in part at least supernatural; and the excellence aims at, is to consist in the interesting of the affections by the dramatic truth of such emotions, as will naturally accompany such emotions, supposing them real" Thus Coleridge, even before he writes *The Ancient Mariner* lays stress upon three essential features of the poems of the supernatural class; (i) psychological interest, (ii) dramatic truth, and (iii) "reality" of the supernatural.

Exploration of Human Psyche through Supernaturalism. Supernaturalism in Coleridge is neither a presentation of sorrow by external devices, nor as mere exhibition of the effects of the supernatural on human conduct and behaviour, but it is an exploration of what Pater calls, 'soul-love'; the deepest emotions of the soul are explored by the experience of the supernatural. Secondly, the incidents and emotions arising from them are so full of human interest that they acquire a dramatic truth and produces a 'suspension of disbelief' which constitutes poetic faith. It is the dramatic truth of the Mariner's emotions in *The Ancient Mariner* that gives an air of reality to his weird experiences. Thirdly the supernatural in Coleridge appears to be real-not objectively but psychologically real. 'Reality does not consist merely in the external appearances of things perceptible to the senses, but also in the deeper passions and experiences of the soul. The supernatural experiences of the Ancient Mariner are in this sense as real as his sailing in the ship or his meeting with the Wedding—Guest.

The three poems, *The Ancient Mariner, Christabel* and *Kubla Khan*, are the best examples of Coleridge's use of the supernatural. The poet does not employ any crude device to produce the sense of the supernatural. "It is delicacy," says Pater, "the dreamy grace in the presentation of the marvellous which makes Coleridge's work so remarkable. The palpable intruders from a spiritual world in almost all ghost literature, in Scott and Shakespeare even, have a kind of coarseness or crudeness. Coleridge's power is in the very fineness with which as with some really ghostly finger, he brings home to our inmost sense; his inventions, daring as they are." The secret of Coleridge's unique success works on the mind and not merely on the external objects. He knows with his psychological insight that the mysterious world of the supernatural must remain a mystery, and that subtle suggestion only can produce this sense of mystery, not crude description. It is with delicate touches of suggestions, combines with psychological insight, he brings out all the shadowy mysteries of the unseen world. The art with which Coleridge excites supernatural wonder and curiosity produces an atmosphere of what Aristotle calls "the higher illusion of reality". It is the human note in his poems dealing with the supernatural that helps to create this sense of reality. When the Mariner recovers from his spell and returns to his normal self, a natural human interest emerges in his weary words.

O wedding guest ! this soul hath been
Alone on a wide, wide sea
So lonely it was, that God himself
Scarce there seemed to be

O sweeter than the marriage-feast
'Tis sweeter far to one
To walk together to the kirk
With a goodly company

And in this chastened and humanised mood, he derives the simple moral :

He prayeth well who loveth well
Both man and bird and beast.

Towards the end of *Kubla Khan*, the poet is presented as a supernatural being :

His flashing eyes, his floating hair !
Weave a circle round him thrice,
And close your eyes with holy dread,
For he on honey-dew bath fed,
And drunk the milk of paradise.

The description is psychologically accurate, for a poet in the frenzy of creative inspiration may achieve the level of a supernatural reality.

Imaginative Use Inducing a Sense of Reality. Coleridge has aroused the sense of supernatural mystery by taking the imagination to some distant unknown place as in *The Ancient Mariner* or to some distant past, as in *Christabel*. A known place, or the living present has no wonder or mystery; it is distance that is romantic and produces a sense of mystery and wonder. In Christabel, the poet takes us back to the old medieval days, which bring to our mind the associations of magic, superstition, and witchery. In *The Ancient Mariner*, he takes us away from the busy haunts of men to the distant seas, where the Mariner is left alone,

> Alone, alone, all, all alone
> Alone on a wide wide sea !

At such a place and in such a situation, the Mariner with a consciousness of guilt, may very well have a supernatural experience. The poet thus creates what is called 'dramatic probability' and produces 'that willing suspension of disbelief which constitutes poetic faith.'

Coleridge produces the sense of horror, not by describing the spectre-woman and her death–mate or other external phenomena at length, but by portraying the effect of these external things on the Mariner's mind. Coleridge's method is psychological. For instance, at one point in the poem, the poet wishes to tell us how horrifying the Mariner's face appeared. He does not describe the face itself, he simply describes the effect of the face upon the pilot.

> I moved my lips-the pilot shrieked
> And fell down in a fit.

In *Kubla Khan*, the mighty fountain being forced out of the earth is definitely vested with a supernatural energy, but describing it Coleridge employs familiar and natural similes.

Feeling of Wonder Evoked in the Use of Supernatural : The Romantic Feature. The Romantic Revival has been otherwise called the Renaissance of Wonder. Apart from the fact that the romanticism of the early nineteenth century is a revolt against the classical tradition of eighteenth century, it is marked by certain positive trends, the most important of which is the awakening of the feeling of wonder. Wordsworth takes upon himself to give the charm of novelty to things of everyday and to excite a feeling of wonder by directing the mind to the glory and loveliness of the world before us. Coleridge, on the other hand, undertakes to awaken the feeling of wonder by depicting the supernatural and the mysterious. The pervading sense of mystery is the key to Coleridge's supernaturalism; it is that species of supernaturalism whose essence is psychological. If Wordsworth has given the charm of novelty to common things of life and nature, Coleridge has made the supernatural appear to be natural by a hundred delicate touches and subtle suggestion. "It is this finer, more delicately marvellous supernaturalism, fruit of his own more delicate psychology," says Pater, "that Coleridge infuses into romantic adventure, which itself was then a new or revived thing in English language."

Conclusion. The supernaturalism of Coleridge's poems is no matter of "stage-lighting as with Monk Lewis; of hysterical declaration as with Mrs. Radcliffe; of stage accessories as with Scott; it is an atmosphere that suffuses the entire tale; the outcome of a hundred delicate touches and subtle hints makes convincing to the reader by the profound psychological insight of the poet." Coleridge lays the scenery of such poems as *The Ancient Mariner* and *Christabel* in the midst of untravelled seas and the deep forests of romance. It is supernatural, but of the ancient, common, simple kind which belongs to all mankind. We find nothing unnatural in the supernatural dread conveyed in the lines-

> Like one, that on a lonesome road
> Doth walk in fear and dread

Q.2. How does Coleridge make the supernatural look natural ?

Or

What devices are employed by Coleridge to make the supernatural appear natural?

Or

Coleridge superbly surmounts the difficulty of making the supernatural credible. How does he achieve this artistic triumph?

Ans. While giving us the history of the composition of the *Lyrical Ballads* and his own share in it, Coleridge writes in his *Biographia Literaria.*

"My endeavours were directed to persons and characters supernatural, or at least romantic; yet so as to transfer from our inward nature a human interest and semblance of truth sufficient to procure for these shadows of imagination that willing suspension of disbelief for the moment which constitute of poetic faith". Coleridge with an artistic mastery achieves a blend of the supernatural and the natural to fulfil his role in the contribution to the *Lyrical Ballads.* His technique is successful in rendering the supernatural real enough to the reader, not only while reading the poem, but even afterwards; for he conveys a sense of a whole reality in which the supernatural exists without difficulty.

Truthful Nature Pictures. With a view to giving his stories an air of plausibility, Coleridge gives accurate descriptions of his nature pictures. Scenery is generally kept true to nature. In *The Ancient Mariner* every phase of landscape, seascape and cloudscape is touched upon, from the quiet scenery of an English woodland to the vibrant scenery of the tropics, The poet touches with equal power and beauty every phase of life at sea.

And yet there is no false note struck anywhere. Even the best geographer cannot spot any defect in the poet's geography. What better and lovelier description can there be of the coming night in the Tropics :

> The sun's rim dips: the stars rush out:
> At one stride comes the dark.

Things are seen at a distances look very small and vague. As they come nearer, they look bigger and clearer. What more scientifically accurate description of the phantom ship (as it appears to the Mariner) can there be then in the lines quoted below- :

> At first it seemed a little speck
> And then it seemed a mist,
> It moved and moved, and took at last
> A certain shape, I wist.

For the purpose of creating an atmosphere of realism the poet sometimes personifies the Forces of Nature and invests them with human qualities: the Sun, the Moon, the Storm blast have all been personified.

Blend of the Natural and Supernatural Element. Coleridge has blended the natural and supernatural phenomena so skilfully and successfully that no reader can draw a line of demarcation between the two, saying that here the natural ends and the supernatural begins. His way of describing natural scenes is such that they appear to be supernatural. At the same time the poet presents his supernatural phenomena so that the supernatural world becomes a reality. The poet invests his tales with 'a human interest' and 'a semblance of truth' and, consequently, produces 'willing suspension of disbelief' for the moment, in the reader's mind. The fantastic and the real, the human and the supernatural, the probable and the improbable, are so well dove—tailed that the effect is one of realism. The transition from the natural to the supernatural and vice versa is so well and so dextrously managed that the reader is hardly conscious of it. *The Ancient Mariner* is a masterpiece of vivid description. However, it is most remarkable for the way in which the transition from the detailed, matter-of-fact and accurate description of the voyage towards and from the South Pole to the equally matter-of-fact description of the avowedly supernatural manifestation of the phantom ship is managed with so little change of tone that in a rapid reading, we fail to realise that the transition has been made. There is no question of an incursion, a border raid, of the supernatural on the natural; both are parts of a whole. *Christabel* abounds in supernatural touches-the dying fire leaps in a fit of flame; Geraldine sees the spirit of the dead mother of Christabel and speaks to her with altered voice; the serpent women casts an evil spell upon the innocent Christabel so that she cannot disclose the real nature of the sorceress to anyone, not even to her dear father. But the total effect is one united impression of realism. In *Kubla Khan* we have the description of the sacred river being "flung up momently". The lines certainly have a supernatural aura but the similes employed are familiar and natural :

> Amid whose swift half intermitted burst,
> Huge fragments vaulted like rebounding hail
> Or chaffy grain beneath the thresher's flail
> And mid these dancing rocks at once and ever
> It flung up momently the sacred river.

Touches of Human Interest. Coleridge's poems have a psychological background. They are invested with human interest. The poet never loses touch with nature and human life and with man's spiritual possibilities. He is a master of human psychology and knows well how man will react under given conditions. He imagines the dramatic situation in which he places his characters. But the emotional reactions of these characters are convincing and true. In *The Ancient Mariner*, the poet portrays the Mariner's state of mind and makes us share the feelings and thoughts that arise in his mind as a result of the various happenings in the story. When he catches sight of the skeleton-ship :

> Fear at my heart, as at a cup,
> My life-blood seems to sip !

Again, the Mariner's reaction to the experience he has at the time when the two hundred crew has died and has cursed him, is described in the following lines :

> I could not draw my eyes from theirs,
> Nor turn them up to pray.

Now any man under similar circumstances will have reacted exactly in the same manner in which the Mariner did.

Suggestiveness. One of the most effective methods used by the poet to make his stories look real is that of infinite suggestiveness. He deliberately leaves many things in his supernatural tales vague and indefinite. He gives the picture in broad outlines so that the details may be filled in by the reader himself according to his own temperament. The path he pursues so as to create horror in his readers is indirect. While describing the first vision of Christabel, the poet says :

> With open eyes-ah woe is me!
> Asleep, and dreaming, fearfully
> Fearfully, dreaming, yet I wis,
> Dreaming that alone, which is.

Now every reader has to conjure up before his mind's eye the exact picture of the horror Christabel see in her vision, and this picture will differ with different readers according to their temperament. He writes first :

> Behold ! her bosom and half her side
> Are lean and old and foul of hue

Surprising, no doubt, and repellent, but direct. This is the technique of *The Ancient Mariner* and this, Coleridge feel will not do. So he rewrite it with a suggestive quality :

> Behold I her bosom and half her side
> A sight to dream of, not to tell.

And we "eithei shiver deliciously or turn away the too patent garden path according to temperament," as one critic puts it.

Gradual Introduction of Supernatural. In none of Coleridge's poem is the supernatural element brought in abruptly. Coleridge first takes his readers around familiar places and wins their confidence through vivid portrayal of minute details. Then minor hints of the supernatural are introduced, finally the entire scene takes on a supernatural look. Thus the reader readily accepts it. The atmosphere is built up in this way in *The Ancient Mariner* as well as *Christabel.*

Supernatural Just a Different Level of Reality. Unfortunately, the oft-quoted passage about Coleridge's role in the collaboration with Wordsworth in the composition of the *Lyrical Ballads* has encouraged critics to over-simplify Coleridge's contribution. Up to a limit it is true that Coleridge directs himself to purpose and characters supernatural, that he deals with those poems in which "the incidents and agents are to be, in part at least, supernatural; and the excellence aimed at is to consist in the interesting of the affections by the dramatic truth of such emotions, as would naturally accompany such situations, supposing them real. And real in this sense they have been to every human being who from whatever source of delusion, has at any time believe himself under supernatural agency. However, Coleridge, in his modesty, is a little less than just to the *raison d'etre* of his supernaturalism.

There is not merely the willing suspension of disbelief in reading his supernatural poems; they deal equally with reality—only, it is a different level of reality from Wordsworth's. Coleridge, as Professor Otto and Aldous Huxley point out, is not so much a poet of the supernatural as the super sensible. His poetry is a record of the numinous' experiences which are common to both savage and mystic. In Coleridge's world the so-

1. Pertaining to divinity

called supernatural events are not disconnected from the natural world; they are parts of one complete system is governed by a principle which is neither subject nor object exclusively, but which is the identity of both, which can be conceived neither as infinite nor as finite exclusively, but as the most original union of the two. After all, if only we could see far enough, we shall see that the distinction between natural and supernatural is one created by man in his ignorance. What he thinks he can understand, he is pleased to call natural; what wholly baffles him, he calls supernatural. *The Ancient Mariner* is not an elaborate fairy tale or a piece of literary patchwork, its trance is not that of sleep but of intense vision. "My outward sense is gone, my inward essence feels". The highest powers of the mind work in harmony with energies normally 'unconscious'. The distinction between poetic reality and human reality is very often merely conventional. All beauty draws itself from the existence of the ideal within the real; even in the bodily stateman can converse with the ideal beauty.

4

COLERIDGE AS A POET OF NATURE

Q. 1. Consider how Coleridge treats Nature in his poetry. How far does his attitude seem to show an evolution in his poetry?

Ans. Love of Nature: a Romantic trait. One of the main characteristics of the Romantic movement is the awakening of a sense of mystery in nature. The poets of the Romantic school not only loves Nature for her external beauty and grandeur, but sight deeper truths underlying her physical manifestations. They describe their emotional reactions to nature rather than her external aspects. Hence it iss that each Romantic poet has his own conception of nature.

Minute Observation of Nature. Though the nature poetry of Coleridge has an individual note, he is undoubtedly influenced by Wordsworth, it is after his acquaintance with Wordsworth that his descriptions of his natural scenes shows an intensity of affection and accuracy of perception, which has been absent in his early works. But his nature-poetry has a subtlety and delicacy rarely found in Wordsworth, and "he reaps a richer harvest through the senses than Wordsworth". "His senses", says Cazamian, "invest his impressions of nature with an extraordinary freshness and splendour, and at the same time with a shrewd and minute precision which reveals the analytical mind." Wordsworth's idealisation of the commonplace no doubt impresses Coleridge; "Wordsworth had shown the wonder of ordinary sights and sounds; it remained for Coleridge to exhibit their mystery."

> The upper air burst into life
> And a hundred fire-flags shone
> To and fro they were hurried about
> And to and fro and in and out
> The wan stars danced between.

The landscape of *Kubla Khan* is visualised with clarity:

> And there were gardens bright with sinuous rills
> Where blossomed many an incense bearing tree;
> And here were forests ancient as the hills,
> Enfolding sunny spots of greenery.

The deep romantic chasm slanting down a green hill across a cedarn cover and the mighty fountain being momently forced from it had been described vividly.

Sense of Colour. Coleridge has the eye of the artist, and his sensuous perception is hardly less keen than that of Keats. But his poetry, shows evidence of his keenness of perception, is not sensuous, for nature is always seen by him through the human atmosphere. "The shaping spirit of imagination" works upon the outward forms, and everything is seen in a "fair luminous mist"; it is then that we have the highest poetry of Coleridge. But when the shaping power of imagination declines, he cries in despair :

> I see them all so excellently fair,
> I see, not feel, how beautiful they are
> ... ...
> It were a vain endeavour
> Though I should gaze for ever
> On that green light that lingers in the west:
> I may not hope from outward forms to win
> The passion and the life, whose fountains are within...

Coleridge possesses the faculty of minute and subtle observation, and paints the outward forms of nature with a degree of delicacy to which neither Wordsworth himself nor perhaps any other worshipper of nature, Keats excepts, ever quite attains. It is in a highly sensitive apprehension of the external aspects of nature, says Pater, "that Coleridge identifies himself most closely with one of the Lake school, a tendency, instinctive, and no more matter of theory in him as in Wordsworth. That record of the

> green light
> Which lingers in the west

and again of

> the western sky
> And its peculiar tint of yellow green....

is a characteristic example of a singular watchfulness of the minute effect and expression of natural scenery prevailing over all he writes." *The Ancient Mariner* too is full of images of light and luminous colour in sky and sea. Ice as green as emerald sends a dismal sheen. Life-in-Death has red lips and yellow locks and her skin is as white as leprosy. The water-snakes are beautiful because of their colours and the play of light.

> And when they reared, the elfish light.
> Fell off in hoary flakes.

Coleridge has a sense of colour comparable to that of Keats in poetry and of Turner in painting. But with his extraordinary sense of colour and form he never lavishes it at every turn; he merely suggests with a rare sense of poetic finesse :

> The thin grey cloud is spread on high...
> The one red leaf, the last of its clan......
> The level sunshine glimmers with green light...

"With him colour is melted in atmosphere which shines through like fire through a crystal. It is liquid colour, the dew on flowers or a mist of rain in bright sunshine", as Symons point out.

Nature Invested with Mystery. Coleridge envelops Nature with a sense of awe and mystery to suit the supernatural element in his poems. In *Kubla Khan* we have a naturally beautiful place invests with a mysterious and awe-inspiring aspect :

> A savage place as holy and enchanted
> As e'er beneath a waning moon was haunted
> By woman wailing for her demon-lover.

In *Christabel* we have the natural events, scenes and sounds of night being used to create a sense of mystery and a haunting atmosphere. *The Ancient Mariner* too abounds in the phenomena of nature has being invested with a supernatural aura. As Cazamian points out, "the very centre of Coleridge's art lies in his faculty of evoking the mystery of things, and making it actual, widespread, and obsessing." Nor is Vaughan wrong when he says: "Nothing, in short, that he found in the outer world attained its rightful value from him until, 'by sublimation strange' it had passed into the realm of shadows which Schiller conceived to be the true region both of poetry and of action."

Nature and Human Beings : A Harmonious Relationship. Nature to Coleridge is a background to highlight the moods of his characters. If the Mariner describes the sun as peeping through the ribs of the phantom-ship :

> As if through a dungeon gate...
> With broad and burning face..,

it is because the Mariner himself is experiencing a kind of imprisonment. In *Christabel* the single red leaf hanging on the oak tree exemplifies Christabel's isolation and her precarious situation. The description of Nature in *Dejection*: *An Ode* also draws a colouring from the poet's own moods.

God's Spirit in Nature : Pantheism. Coleridge is not a nature poet as Wordsworth is, but with Wordsworth he has a part in bringing to English poetry a genuine love of nature and spiritual insight into her processes. He loves nature for her own sake, and his love took almost the form of a reverent worship, for he sees behind all the phenomena of nature the veil presence of God :

> Father of Earth and Heaven
> All-conscious presence of Universe
> Nature's vast ever-acting energy
> In Will, in Deed, impulse of All in All

Coleridge's deep delight in the common aspects of nature finds a beautiful expression in the poem *This Lime Tree Bower My Prison*. Once Lamb and other friends of Coleridge goes out for a walk in the countryside but Coleridge can not accompany them owing to an unfortunate accident. Sitting alone in his garden, he imagins the delights which his friends will enjoy but which he can not share. The poem describs the details of the scene through which his friends would pass, is a charming specimen of natural description combines with human interest. The truth of the description is the beauty of the poem, and the influence that passes from nature to the soul of the poet is very much like that which Wordsworth describes in his poetry :

> Henceforth I shall know
> That Nature ne'er deserts the wise and pure:
> No plot so narrow, be but nature there
> No waste so vacant, but may well employ -
> Each faculty of sense, and keep the heart
> Awake to Love and Beauty!

Coleridge's nature poetry rises to grandeur when he describes the sunrise over Mont Blanc in his *Hymn before Sunrise in the Vale of Chamouni*. Wordsworth is confined his nature poetry to the manifestations of nature in the Lake District; it is left to Coleridge and Shelley to depict the more violent and magnificent aspects of nature. The poetic energy of Coleridge fully rises to the occasion in the presence of that magnificent spectacle of sunrise over the snow peak of the Alps. He surveys the glorious scene and feels his own soul expanding under its mighty influence.

Coleridge's fundamental conception of nature is that every object oft nature—from a simple flower to the mighty mountain—is pervaded by the presence of God. His attitude towards nature passes through two phases. In his younger days he conceives that there are multitudes of spirits, by whose operation nature grew, and who informs all the organic and inorganic forms of nature. They are all in the service of God, and it is God, the all-conscious spirit, who informs all forms of nature. The whole universe thus resides in God. Nature is alive in God, and each of her forms is informed by a distinct spirit, has a distinct life of its own. This idea forms the basis of *The Ancient Mariner*, where the guilty man is first punished by the avenging spirits, and then is redeemed by the seraph band."

The Mind Creating Nature : German Influence. The poet passes to the second phase of his conception of nature when he conceives that it is our own thought that makes nature appear as it is to us. This view is partly the result of his study of the transcendental philosophy of Germany. The existence of the external world is not actual, but phenomenal. It is in our thought that we give forms to external objects, and thinking of these we build up the world of nature ourselves. Nature thus lives in us, and when we receive impression from nature, we do not receive something distinct from us but our own thoughts, is reflected from the external world. This idea is expressed both in *The Eolian Harp* and in the *Dejection and Ode*. In *The Eolian Harp,* Coleridge's imagination is aroused by the music of a harp when it is touched by the wind. Similary when the thought of man touches the external world of nature, it breaks into harmony :

> And what if all of animated nature
> Be but organic harps diversely framed,
> That tremble into thought, as o'ver them sweeps
> Plastic and vast, one intellectual breeze
> At once the soul of each, and God of all.

"We each in our thinking", explains Brooke, "make the outward world for ourselves; but our thinking in this sphere is in its source the one Thought of God in which, infinitely varied through a myriad secondary forms of thought, the universe consists."

This idea again is beautifully expressed in 'the *Dejection* and Ode when the poet says :

> O Lady! we receive but what we give
> And in our life does Nature live.

When one feels in one's soul the 'one intellectual breeze', which makes the harmony of the universe, one is spiritually conscious of the Divine Presence; "whosoever knows this as the truth, rejoices in it, and from him goes forth over the whole appearance which the world takes to him, a light, a glory, a fair luminous cloud that makes glorious all things,—a sweet and potent voice, the echo of God in his own soul that turns the universe into music."

Conclusion. Coleridge shows a delicate touch in the painting of nature, specially the fleeting charms of Narture. He can produce broad and general effects of Nature as skilfully as subtle and precise delineations. He is capable of investing a sense of mystery on the common and ordinary aspects of Nature. While in the earlier poems, Coleridge describes Nature as separate from human beings, under the influence of Wordsworth he develops a pantheistic attitude. Later his attitude towards Nature undergoes further change. He comes under the influence of German thinkers to believe that Nature takes on its form from our own thoughts.

5

COLERIDGE'S NARRATIVE SKILL

Q.1. Coleridge's narrative skill and art of story-telling are commendable. Discuss.

Or

Write a critical note on the narrative style of Coleridge with illustrations from the text.

Ans. The form that has appealed to the Romantic poets, besides the lyric, is the ballad. Coleridge uses the ballad form with artistic skill. He tells a tale so well that we become rapt listeners willing to believe even supernatural incidents as if they are the most natural things to happen in the given situation.

Dramatic Beginning. Perhaps, the best known and more appreciated of his narrative poems is *The Ancient Mariner*. The very beginning of the poem draws and keeps the attention of the reader. With the Wedding Guest the reader too is hypnotised into attending to the Mariner's tale. Coleridge's artistic skill is noteworthy-he knows what will grip the attention. The wrinkled hand and the glittering eye of the Mariner are enough to awe the Wedding—Guest and rivet the reader's attention. Curiosity is at once aroused and one wants to read on. The opening of *Christabel*, similarly, is striking. Once again Coleridge shows his narrative skill in evoking and holding one's attention. The bleak and cold night with its silence broken by the owl, the unexpected crowing of the cock, the howling of the mastiff, the shrunken full moon-the natural setting is perfect for the tale to follow.

Building up Dramatic Action. Suspense is another quality that Coleridge uses with, artistic finesse. This is a part of his narrative skill. In *The Ancient Mariner* we have a deceptively calm beginning to the Mariner's tale. Familiar details of the journey are given. The Wedding-Guest appropriately beats his breast at having to listen to such a pedestrian account. But now the dramatic turn comes. The storm blast comes and with it the ship is driven toward the South Pole. The descriptive skill is used to enhance the narrative art in the poem. The mysterious atmosphere is built up; there is an interplay of human emotions with the Albatross being fed and played with by the sailors. Then comes the single line that the Mariner has shot the Albatross with his cross-bow. The dramatic quality is enhanced and the reader's imagination is gripped. The complete calm of the ocean and the motionless ship, the hanging of the dead Albatross round the Mariner's neck, the appearance of the skeleton ship zig-zagging its way along a calm ocean with no wind to help it move-these episodes build up the tension and prove the power of Coleridge's art. The story by itself is simple, but is made interesting because of Coleridge's narrative art.

In *Christabel*, similarly, the dramatic quality is built up with the help of suspense. When Geraldine appears, suspense is intensified. An ominous atmosphere is further created by the reaction of the mastiff and the dying brand leaping into light as Geraldine passes by. The climactic moment is prepared for by Coleridge in a remarkable manner. How subtly, yet with remarkable horrific effect, Coleridge conveys to us the sense of evil embodied in Geraldine. The effect of the evil on Christabel is again portrayed dramatically.

Nature Description Enhances Dramatic Sense. The nature descriptions are used by Coleridge to enhance dramatic effect, just as music is used in drama and movies. The natural scenes harmonise with the events. In Christabel the full moon, covered but not fully hidden by a cloud, looks dull and small-a clear sign that all is not well. In *The Ancient Mariner*, nature, violent and furious, calm and soothing, or still and stagnant serves to increase the dramatic effect of the incidents.

***Love* : A Ballad within a Ballad.** In *Love* we have a ballad within a ballad. The lover wins the love of Genevieve by narrating to her the sad tale of a knight who goes crazy because of unrequite love. The medieval atmosphere is used to enhance dramatic effect. The two stories are interwoven. The element of action, adventure and medieval chivalry in the knight's story works toward the climax when Genevieve, overwhelmed by the pathos of the story, rushes into her lover's arms.

Human Interest and Psychological Insight. Psychological insight enhances the dramatic quality of Coleridge's narrative poems. The change that has come over the old Mariner would not have been so well conveyed through description as it is through giving the reaction of the pilot and his boy. The effect of guilt on the Mariner's mind too is vividly conveyed. Christabel is transformed by the contact with evil, but Coleridge does not say so directly. He hints at the change, but the hints have more dramatic effect than direct description would have had.

Even *Kubla Khan*, though not basically a narrative poem, has some dramatic qualities. The description of the scene has dramatic effect—the place is "savage, holy, enchanted", and is associated with a waning moon and a "woman wailing for her demon lover". The image of the poet in an ecstasy of creation is not without dramatic touches.

Conclusion. Coleridge has possessed a powerful narrative skill. He can invest a tale with drama even while giving to it a symbolic significance. More than Wordsworth, Coleridge has possessed the skill of telling a story effectively. Pictures alternate with incidents and images with episodes. There is action, excitement, thrill and subtle psycho–analysis. All these features combines to hold the reader's interest-the most important aspect of narrative poetry. The form of the ballad and the ballad metre are used with facility and felicity by Coleridge. This again is part of his narrative art.

6

COLERIDGE : A GENERAL ESTIMATE

Q.1. Write a critical note on Coleridge's extraordinary contribution to the development of English literature.

Or

"Coleridge as a literary figure will remain ever-inspiring". Discuss.

Ans. As a poet. Coleridge is a strange and baffling figure both in life and poetry. By sheer force of genius he has ushered in the great age of English romantic Poetry along with his friend Wordsworth. His fame rests now on a surprisingly small output, hardly half a dozen pieces and some of them mere fragments. His early poetry when he is brooding a good deal on the complex questions of philosophy and politics and reform of mankind, is usually formless, wordy and diffuse. But a very distinct change comes over the spirit of his poetry after his meeting with Wordsworth in 1797. There is a growing sense of wonder and delight and fresh rapture in his handling of the themes of nature. Such poems as *This Lime Tree Bower,' Frost at Midnight, Fears in Solitude*, belong to this period. But the full flowering of his genius has come (in 1797-98) with the *Ancient Mariner, Christabel* (1797-1800) and *Kubla Khan* (1797-98) and Coleridge at his highest has no rival even among his great contemporaries. To have written one of these poems alone have brought him within the small' circle of the the supreme makers of verse. Each of its kind is unique.

Coleridge's reform in English poetry has mainly concerned with the technical side of the art. Before his time the rhythms employed by English poets has been almost exclusively iambic or trochaic and the tradition tendency is to confine them more and more within the heroic couplet. The heroic couplet from its narrow limits gives little scope for liberty or variety of movement, and howsoever effective for the purposes of the epigram, is an inadequate vehicle for the expression of powerful emotion. Coleridge, advancing along the line of invention is opened by Chatterton, converts the ancient rhythms and metres of the language into vehicles for his own imagination, thought. His ear is haunted by the possibilities of the metrical tunes suggests to him by his study of ballad poetry; and he is associated these with the strange, and as it seems to him, supernatural experiences of his own imagination, with genius akin to that of a musician. In *The Rime of the Ancient Mariner* he shows that it is possible, through the ballad form, to give expression to a marvellous series of supernatural incidents. *Christabel* is an illustration of the beautiful and picturesque effects that may be created in the fancy by the combination. Coleridge has consciously formulated the return of English verse to the principle of accentuation which is most suitable to its spontaneous rhythm. *Christabel* is written in lines of four accents, where the number of syllables varies on a very large scale, the pattern of the melody swelling or subsiding with the needs of the musical suggestion; while the light, ample cadence of the anapaest is introduced with delicate facility among the shorter measures. This example of judicious freedom is at the source of the vast development in prosody which accompanies the expansion of modern English lyricism.

There are two main elements in Coleridge's poetry (i) psychical and (ii) intellectual. The former lends to the poet's work a pervading sense of mystery and the latter accounts for the power of limpid expression and masterly execution of rhythmic effects which are so evident in the best of his poetry. In his handling of mystery or the supernatural Coleridge takes a line of his own.

He has very little to do with crude horrors, gibbering ghosts, witches' cauldrons, creaking gallows, dark corridors and trap doors. He does not deliberately set out to make the flesh creep but brings home to the readers the dramatic truth of the emotions which he deals with. He forces on the readers, to use his own vivid phrase "a willing suspension of disbelief.' He gets his marvellous magical effects by a hundred little subtleties-hints and nuances and suggestions. As Compton Rickett observes regarding *The Ancient Mariner* "The Mariner himself gathers up into his own person the elements of romance-with the glittering eye, his skinny hand, his arresting voice, and the spiritual misery that drives him into speech to ease his tortured soul. The Supernaturalism of the poem... is an atmosphere that suffuses the entire tale; the outcome of a hundred delicate touches and subtle hints, makes convincing to the reader by the profound psychological insight of the poet". The same writer observes on *Christabel*: "Whether it be taken as an allegory or merely as another excursion into the dream-world of fantasy its beauty and magic are indisputable". Summing up Coleridge's achievement the critic finally comments; ' 'His supreme strength lay in his marvellous dream faculty; one might add that the dream faculty lay at the root of his greatness as a poet and his weakness as a man. But there is no finer dreamer in English verse; this quality is that gives distinction to *The Ancient Mariner* and *Christabel* and makes of *Kubla Khan* so superb a triumph."

"After *Christabel* the poet never reached the height again, though a few minor pieces survive of his later writings, dealings with *Dejection, Love* and *Hope*, that show some measure of his ancient cunning. It was not a decline of poetic power as in Wordsworth's case, but an arrest of poetic power, of creative imagination. His imagination was as rich as ever, his intellect as restless and keen, but they sought expression in channels other than those of verse". (Compton Rickett). Various explanations have been offered to account for this sudden disappearance of creative power, such as defects of character especially infirmity of will. But Rickett points out, "The peculiar character of his poetic inspiration, its sudden outbursts, its dream like character, the mysterious way in which it would come and go, leaving him unable to complete what he had begun; these things suggest something that might well visit a youthful imagination, and then, when the flush of youth and youth's sensibility had passed, itself melt away. The wind bloweth where it listeth."

As a Philosopher. As a philosopher, Coleridge has been a sower of germinal ideas. His indebtedness to German philosophy has probably been overrated. He becomes acquainted with it at a time when his normal personality has already been formed, and he is never thoroughly acquainted with it. The doctrine of Kant, interprets in as much as it is founded a new metaphysics, encourages his own tendencies. He takes up the distinction between understanding and reason, only to push it to conclusions very far removed from those of Kant. He borrows from Schelling what in his intellectual absent-mindedness he fails to acknowledge. Taken as a whole his work reveals a general parallelism with the intuitive, idealistic, and historical movement of ideas which gives German Romanticism its essential character. But, he himself declares that he is just as much the disciple of national tradition, and of Burke. He is not the master, but the immediate predecessor of Carlyle. John Stuart Mill sees in him the principal source of the reaction which an age animated with the will to believe, and basing his inner life upon the feeling of spiritual mystery, shows against the rationalism of mechanical explanations, and the extension of a scientific ideal to the things of the soul. Through the intermediary action of thinkers who are also believers as F.D. Maurice, Coleridge's influence has helped to nurture the decisive revival of idealism in the time of Carlyle, and in adjoining circles of thought.

As a Literary Critic. In literary criticism his achievement is lasting. No one before him in England has brought such mental breadth to the discussion of aesthetic values. His judgements are all permeated by a trend of thought that is strongly under the influence of doctrinal preconceptions; even in this domain he is the metaphysician. The well-known differentiation between imagination and fancy, which Wordsworth has interprets after his own fashion, is a way of laying stressive association of the mind as opposes to the passive association of mental pictures; but for Coleridge it has a mystical significance. This feeling for the secret link existing between problems, together with his habit of intermingling, even perhaps of confounding them, by no means deprives him of a penetrating sharpness of vision of precise points. In *Biographia Literaria* certain intentions as well as certain successes or failings, of Wordsworth are caught and illuminates to their depths, so searching is the light, that it is even cruel. His remarks on Shakespeare show a sound intuition of the profound unity of dramatic art. Accustomed as he is to reach to the heart of things, to find there the same vital impulse which animates his own thought, and to see this secret life produces what becomes the apparent world of the senses, Coleridge is thus able to discern with an unerring insight the paths along which a central impulse has radiated so to speak, towards all the fundamental ideas, aspects, and characteristics of a work. Modern English is indebted to Coleridge for some of its soundest principles as well as much of its terminology and many of its famous dicta.

Q.2. "Critics have spoken of the fragmentary nature and imperfection of Coleridge's work". Elaborate this dictum with reference to Coleridge's decline as a poet.

Ans. Coleridge's period of poetic creation is incredibly brief. His is not a case of decline in poetic faculties as is the case with Wordsworth, but a case of arrest of poetic power, of creative imagination. His imagination is as rich as ever; his intellect as restless and keen, but they has sought expression in channels other than those of verse. *Dejection: An Ode* has been described as the poet's dirge to his own imagination. To the magic heights of *The Rime* and *Christabel*, Coleridge never rose again. Some have sought the causes in external circumstances and others have offered a more psychological approach.

Among the external causes the failure of his health from 1801 onwards is an important one. He has inherited a tendency to gout which is accentuated by carelessness and indifference. Ill-health brings depression and lowering of animal spirits. Recourse to opium results not only in a deadening of natural sensibilities, but also in the prevention of resurrection of poetic powers.

A contributory cause is Coleridge's natural indolence. He has described himself as a great "tomorrower." Says Margoliouth, "one thing was not given to Coleridge, self control without submission to outside authority." C.H. Herford puts it thus: "phenomenal wealth of ideas and equally phenomenal weakness of will embarrassed and distracted his subtle and delicate poetry."

Domestic unhappiness and estrangement from friends, adds to indolence and irresolution, proves harmful to what is most characteristic of Coleridge's poetry-its spirit of peace and gentleness. Under their stress as Courthope points out, creative faculty gradually withers.

The second group of causes concerns the inner life of Coleridge. The first of his sources of inspiration to fail him was the revolutionary enthusiasm, though it does not prove fatal to poetry. It is interesting to note that Coleridge's stay in Germany coincides with his death as a poet. In other words "Metaphysics destroyed the poet in Coleridge."

In his characteristically pungent way Quiller-Couch describes these explanations of Coleridge's arrest of poetic power as "foolish". "Let us ask ourselves", he writes "if it is conceivable within one man's measure to produce a succession of poems on the plane of *The Rime of the Ancient Mariner*". The question is indisputably answered by *Christabel* and *Kubla Khan*, both fragments. "The quality of Coleridge's poetic genius", in the words of Compton-Rickett, "does not suggest long life". Coleridge's poetry is dream poetry. Such poetry as *Kubla Khan* and *The Rime* "comes not with observation. It draws its sustenance from mysterious half-lights of dreams." "The dream faculty and the power to word its message", observes O. Elton, "to a perfectly felicitous tune, is too finely strung and too liable to be jarred by outer vexations and inner disharmonies for a long lease to be expected of it." C.E. Vaughan asks: "Is it reasonable to suppose that any poet could have gone on living forever in an air so rarefied as that *The Rime of the Ancient Mariner, Kubla Khan*, and *Christabel* ?" The wonderful dream palaces Coleridge built for himself in the clouds, the colours and forms of which are charged with a thousand suggestions from the unearthly and enchanted world of dreams cannot have endure

7

COLERIDGE AND WORDSWORTH : A COMPARATIVE STUDY

Q.1. Compare and contrast Wordsworth and Coleridge discussing their mutual influence.

Ans. From 1795 up till 1802, Coleridge and Wordsworth have enjoyed a friendship. During this time they have collaborated in producing the *Lyrical Ballads,* a volume of verse to which Coleridge has contributed his *Ancient Mariner*. This volume, produces in 1798, is said to have ushered in the English Romantic Movement.

Different Approach. But in planning the poems for this volume, the differences between these two poets at once come out. Wordsworth is to write poems on common subjects "such as will be found in every village" and make them appear significant with his "original gift of spreading the atmosphere of the ideal world over (familiar) forms and incidents". Coleridge, on the other hand, is to write on "supernatural" subjects, "made real by the dramatic truth of such emotions, supposing them real." In other words, while Wordsworth makes the "natural" appear as "supernatural", Coleridge makes the "supernatural" appear as "natural." Thus, "Coleridge represented perfectly that side of the romantic imagination which seeks to lose itself in dream and marvel". Coleridge revive the elements of wonder and mystery, whereas, Wordsworth revive interest in nature. Coleridge by writing *The Ancient Mariner* make the supernatural appear like the natural (credible and convincing); Wordsworth by writing *The Solitary Reaper, Immortality Ode* and *Tintern Abbey* make the natural look like the supernatural, sublime and marvellous.

Attitude to Nature. Wordsworth spiritualises nature. He regards nature as a living presence, a sacred entity which can influence the mind of man:

> A motion and a spirit impels
> All thinking things, all objects of all thought
> And rolls through all things.
> * * * * * * *
> Well pleased to recognise

In nature and the language of the sense
.......the nurse,
The guide, the guardian of my heart, and soul
of all my moral being. *Tintern Abbey*

Coleridge feel that it is we ourselves who endow nature with a spirit:

O! Lady, we receive but what we give
And in our life alone does nature live. *Dejection : An Ode*

Coleridge again is attracted by the mysterious aspects of nature, whereas Wordsworth by everyday homely scenes and objects. Thus, in *The Ancient Mariner* we have descriptions of such queer natural phenomena as:

All in a hot and copper sky
The bloody sun, at noon....

Or

The water, like a witch's oil
Burnt green and blue and white.

Or

And straight the sun was flecked with bars
... ...
As if through a dungeon grate he peered
With broad and burning face.

On the other hand, Wordsworth delights in "meadow, grove and stream" or the "tall rock, the mountain, and the deep and gloomy wood".

Wordsworth, again, is not only a poet of nature but also a prophet of nature. He reads a deeper meaning into nature and believes that if we surrender ourselves to nature we will gain in holiness, beauty and strength.

Dream *versus* Reality. Coleridge's imagination is stirred more by dream than by reality. Coleridge is at his best when he abandons himself to vision and dreams. Wordsworth is at his greatest when he touches facts with imagination. Coleridge provides us an escape from the world of reality by transporting us to a land of mystery and wonder.

Word Painting. Wordsworth attaches great importance to sensations but in this case they are not important for their own sake. They have an impact on his feelings and thought. In the case of Coleridge sensations come to assume a significance such as we find only in the poetry of Keats and the later nineteenth century poets like Rossetti, Morris and Swinburne. Coleridge's sensibility is of an aesthete who is delighted by refined sensuousness for its own sake. He takes pleasure in describing things, often criticises himself for being bad at description (quite unjustifiably of course) and longs for the art of the painter to do justice to his subject.

Poetic Output. Wordsworth's poetic output is greater than that of Coleridge. Excepting a few masterpieces like *The Ancient Mariner, Kubla Khan,* and *Christabel,* Wordsworth's poetic achievement is much more considerable. He write a large number of lyrics, sonnets, odes and narrative poems that will die only with the English language.

Lyricism and Mastery of Words. As a lyric poet Wordsworth again surpasses Coleridge who as Grierson says, "was not essentially a lyric poet, because he lacks the passion and intensity of lyrical utterance." Coleridge is a narrator rather than a lyrical poet. He is a gifted story teller. Wordsworth is an inspired singer who write such immortal and imperishable lyrics as *Tintern Abbey, Immortality Ode,* and *The Solitary Reaper.* Coleridge's lyricism in *Dejection and Ode* is reflective rather than inspired. It lacks the quality of rapture.

Coleridge, however, is a master of words. His poetry is rich in musical quality. In *The Ancient Mariner* he gives us rare musical effects with the help of most familiar words :

> The fair breeze blew, the white foam flew
> The furrow followed free

He can likewise paint a scene with a few bold strokes :

> The sun's tins dips, the stars rush out
> At one stride comes the dark.

Wordsworth's command over words is not as astonishing as that of Coleridge. At his best Wordsworth cannot be easily surpassed. For instance:

> The sounding cataract
> Haunted me like a passion: the tall rock
> The mountain, and the deep and gloomy wood,
> Their colours and their forms were then to me
> An appetite

Resemblance Despite Differences. Coleridge's criticism of Wordsworth makes us forget the close resemblance between—even identity of—the views of the two poets. Both have begun their careers as ardent supporters of the French Revolution and the cause of human progress. They give up their open support to the French Revolution but remains—in the period of their best creative activity—confirms believers in human progress and democrats. Both are opposed to the rule of the aristocracy and monarchy and hates the commercial civilization of the upper classes. Both are under the influence of the materialist radical tradition of Locke, Hartley and Godwin. The views of these three philosophers are not identical, but they belong to a common tradition to which the poets are loyal. They have no liking for the clergy and instead of a personal God worships nature (Wordsworth in particular) and treats all living things as sacred (particularly Coleridge). Their political opposition to land-owning aristocracy make them critical of the culture of the ruling class. Their criticism of old poetic diction is a part of their general struggle against the culture of a class that has ceased to be progressive historically. Perhaps not many people realize that Coleridge have been as much a critic of neo-classical poetic diction as Wordsworth. But it is a fact that the views of the two friends has been identical in one phase of their intellectual development.

Conclusion. Speaking of Wordsworth and Coleridge, Cazamian observes: "Their development, until the time of their meeting, offers great analogies. Coleridge, like Wordsworth, went through a phase of revolutionary ardour. The daring of a personal inspiration, and that of a fresh-created language, come to him at the same time; and this is the hour when his social zeal, his hopes for mankind, freed from the hope of any immediate realization, are transformed into a spiritual idealism. Wordsworth's influence contributes to this result; but Coleridge is indebted to none but himself for the more philosophic and mystical character with which he invests their common doctrine."

8

SYMPOSIUM OF CRITICS ON S.T. COLERIDGE

GENERAL ESTIMATE OF COLERIDGE

Swinburne : As a poet, his place is indisputable: it is high among the highest of all time. Other and stronger men, with fuller control and concentration, genius, may do more service, may bear more fruit; but such as his they will not have in them to give. The highest lyric work is either passionate or imaginative. Of passion Coleridge has nothing but for height and perfection of imaginative quality, he is the greatest of lyric poets. This is his special power and this is his special praise.

Hazlitt : He is the only person from whom I ever learn anything. There is only one thing he can learn from me in return, but that he has not. He is the first poet, I ever know. His genius at that time had angelic wings, and feed think on manna. He talkes on for ever, and you wish him to talk on for ever. His does not seem to come with labour or effort, but as if borne on the gusts of genius and as if the wings of his imagination lifts him from off his feet. His voice rolls on the ear like the pealing organ, and its sound alone is the music of thought. His mind is clothed with wings; and raises on them, he has lifted philosophy to heaven....

Courthope: Coleridge's reform in English poetry is mainly concerned with the technical side of the art. Before his time the rhythms employs by English poets has been almost exclusively iambic or trochaic, and the traditional tendency has to confine them more and more within the heroic couplet which, from its narrow limits, give little scope for liberty or variety of movement, and however effective for the purposes of the epigram, is an inadequate vehicle for the expression of powerful emotions. Coleridge, advancing along with the line of invention openes by Chatterton, converts the ancient rhythms and metres of the language into vehicles for his own imaginative thoughts. His ear has haunted by the possibilities of the metrical turns suggest him by his study of ballad poetry; and he associates these with the strange, and as it has seemed to him supernatural experiences of his own imagination with genius akin to that of a musician. In *The Rime of the Ancient Mariner* he shows that it is possible, through the Ballad form, to give expression to a marvellous series of supernatural incidents; *Christabel* is an illustration of the beautiful and picturesque effects that may be created in the fancy by the combination of dactylic with iambic and trochaic rhythms in the line of four accents.

Dawson : What of the works of Coleridge ? It may be said briefly that it is upon his poetry that the fame of Coleridge is built. His *Friend* is full of the ripest wisdom; his *Biographia Literaria* of isolated passages of great beauty; his *Lectures on Shakespeare* have long held their place as masterpieces of critical insight, but it is after all, by his poetry that future generations will know him. *The Ancient Mariner* and *Christabel* stand alone in English literature. Coleridge has an extraordinary power of interpreting the supernatural, the night side of Nature, that weird, subtle, spiritual undercurrent of life which invests with mysterious significance this hard outer world. In doing this he has done superbly what no other has attempted with more than partial success. He possesses force of imagination and felicity of epithet, and each in an extraordinary degree. His words are music and his power of producing on the ear the effect of fine music merely by the assonance of the words is unrivalled. No great poet has written less, but the best of what he has written is so perfect of its kind that here can be no mistaking the superscription of immortality with which it is stamped.

The faults of Coleridge's style are its occasional confusion and difuseness. This, however, is most apparent in his political poems, and is probably attributable to the fact that Coleridge find the themes uncongenial. It is in the world of pure imagination he is most at home, and it is there he attains his highest literary excellence. In delicate and airy fancy, not less than in imaginative intensity, he has few rivals. Such a poem as *Kubla Khan,* a mere dream within a dream, may illustrate the one, and *The Ancient Mariner* the other. His force as a thinker and metaphysician is a waning force, but his poetic fame has never stood so high as now. This result is accurately perceived immediately on his death by the review that had persistently ridiculed him for many years when it wrote "Coleridge of all men who ever lived, is always a poet, in all his moods, and they were many, inspired". It is so the best poems of Coleridge still impress us, and when the logician and the metaphysician weary us, we turn with ever fresh delight, to the bard. The pity of it is that Coleridge is so seldom the bard, and so often the metaphysician; for who will not give all the prose writings of Coleridge for another twenty pages of poetry like the *Ancient Mariner.*

Woodberry : His sensitiveness to Nature is two-fold; in the first place he notices in the objects and movement of nature evanescent and minute details, and as his sense of beauty is keen, he sees and records truly the less obvious and less common loveliness in the phenomena of the elements and the seasons, and this give distinction to his mere description and record of fact; in the second place he often feels in himself a mood induced by nature, but yet subjective-states of his own spirit, which sometimes deepens the charms of night for example, by his enjoyment of its placid aspects, and sometimes imparts to the external world a despair has been reflected from his personal melancholy. In his direct treatment of Nature, however, as Stopford Brooke points out, he seldom achieves more than a catalogue of his sensations which, though touched with imaginative detail, are never lifted and harmonised into lyrical unity, though he can moralise Nature in Wordsworth's fashion and when he does so the result remains Wordsworth's and is stamped with that poet's originality and in his own original work Coleridge never has been equalled either the genius of Shelley, who can identify nature with himself, or the charm of Tennyson, who can at least parallel of nature's phenomena with his own human moods. Coleridge will not be thought of as a poet of nature except in so far as he describes what he observes in the way of record or gives a metaphysical interpretation to phenomena. But in those poems in which he describes nature directly and without metaphysical thought, there is no trace of anything more than a sensuous order of his own perceptions. Beautiful and often unique as his Nature poems are, they are not creative.

Hales : Poetry is with Coleridge but one of many pursuits; he does not take the Muse to him for better and worse and cleave only to her. It is only in his young manhood that he is devoted himself to her; in the later periods of his life political and critical and religious questions mainly occupies him. What of poetry, almost all his writtings are a collection of fragments rather than complete achievements. He is for ever designing and plotting, not acting. He is conscious of his weakness in the respect, but has not strength to overcome it. He is a living Hamlet full of the most splendid thoughts and the noblest purposes, but a most incompetent doer. "Carmen relguum" he notes at the end of *The Three Graves*, a fragment of a Sexton's Tale, "In future tempus relegatum" (Tomorrow and Tomorrow and Tomorrow). At the end of his introduction in 1817 to *Kubla Khan* or *A Vision in a Dream*—a fragment, he adds, "yet from the still surviving recollection in his mind, the Author has frequently purposed to finish for himself what had been originally as it were, given to him but the to-morrow is yet to come". And it never came. The incompletion of *Christabel* is a severe loss to our literature. The two parts, we happily possess, are of wonderful beauty and power. They were the immediate inspiration of the *Lay of the Last Ministrel* ("It is to Mr. Coleridge" writes Scott. "That I am found to make the acknowledgement due from the pupil to his master"); and certainly Scott himself never succeeds in surrounding any one of his works with so fine an atmosphere of glamour and romance. Moreover, Coleridge's spiritual insight is incomparably profounder than that of Scott; he sounds depths of feeling and thought beyond the reach of the northern Minstrel's plummet. In the scanty amount of what he has produced Coleridge reminds one of Gray; but the causes of sterility are different. Gray has suffered from fastidiousness, Coleridge rather from an overwhelming abundance of interests and ideas. "His Mind", writes Southey, "is in a perpetual St. Vitus', dance: eternal activity without action". If no man can serve two masters, still less can he serve half-dozen. "*Expede Herculem*": in such a way we must be content to infer how splendid an artist was there in Coleridge.

K.E. Royds : A correspondent of H. Crabb Robinson has once written to him "of all men, there seems most need to say, 'God bless poor Coleridge.' One can almost believe that an enchanter's spell is upon him forcing him to be what he is, and yet leaving him the power of showing what he may be". It is this tantalizing feeling of unfulfilled possibilities that, in spite of Lamb's objection to the use of the adjective "poor" in connection with such a man remains our feelings about him. The tragedy of his wasted manhood is real enough and not to be minimized. It is one of those who know him best who write, while aware of his achievements. "It vexes and grieves me to the heart that when he is gone nobody will believe what a mind goes with him—how infinitely and then ten thousand fold the mightiest of his generation". Yet this sense of what he may have done must not be allowed to overshade on the realisation of what he do. In the course of the story we have seen something of the great work that he and Wordsworth together accomplishes for English poetry, freeing it from the chains of eighteenth century convention and bringing to it once more genuine love of Nature and spiritual insight into her processes. Coleridge especially breathed into it fresh the spirit of high romance, wedded to modern knowledge of the "phenomena of mind". As a critic among much else that is valuable, he give Shakespeare back to the English people.

As a theologian, champion of orthodoxy as he grow conservative, he has influenced greatly such rising men of the younger generation as F.O. Maurice, Kingsley and Newman. He has been claimed as the teacher of greatest influence behind the Tractarian movement.

And the last note shall be personal. As a man he has won and has kept the love, admiration, and friendship of some of the noblest men of his generation. Nor let it be forgotten that against the 'body that did him grievous wrong' after years of slavery and misery he has rose up and conquered. This is not the least worthy of remembrance among his achievements.

Critics have compared his last years of quiet life on Highgate Hill to the pale shining out of the sun before its setting. Rather will we say, wears from the fight of the night of darkness that has engulfed him, Coleridge claims to heights where, aloof from the struggle, with the violent ardours of youth left behind, yet with forward looking thoughts, he spends what strength is left in brave endeavour to point others towards the sunrise.

T.F. Huntington : It only remains to say a word about his place in literature. As a journalist he moves on a high plane of thought and morality, and, by scorning the tactics of the mere politician and bringing his intellect to bear upon the momentous events of his time, because at least in the broad view he take of all political problems, he is the legitimate successor of the great Burke. As a theologian his influence is even more far-reaching. He is the mentor at whose feet sits such men as Thomas Arnold, Julius Hare and Frederick Maurice. He sights to moralise and spiritualize the religion of England, and to find on the shadowy border between psychology and theology some relation between the human and the divine. As a philosopher his special praise is again to be found in his influence. He left no system of philosophy and his exposition of the transcendentalism of Kant and his followers is not thorough or systematic enough to be final. He is the means, however, of introducing England to German thought, and thus of inaugurating, against the materialism of Locke and Paley the revolution out of which arose the transcendental movement, headed by Carlyle in England and by Emerson in America, the result, in a way of Coleridge's influence upon the intellect of his time. But great as is his influence in theology and metaphysics, his position as a critic is even more commanding. He is easily at the head of English philosophical criticism. Modern English criticism is indebted to Coleridge for some of its soundest principles, as well as much of its terminology and, many of its famous dicta. He also revolutionises the accepted view of Shakespeare and says that his work is not the product of the wild, irregular genius of a pure child of nature, but of a poetic wisdom, which is as remarkable for its disclosure of judgements as for its manifestation of genius.

As a poet Coleridge's work is very much a matter of definitions. If we say, with Matthew Arnold, "that poetry is at bottom a criticism of life; that the greatness of a poet lies in his powerful and beautiful application of ideas to life, to the question how to live" Coleridge must give precedence to many others and to none of his contemporaries more than to Wordsworth; but if we say, with Matthew Arnold again that "poetry is simply the most delightful and perfect form of utterance that human words can reach", and add with Coleridge himself, that the immediate object of poetry is "pleasure, not truth" then the rank has been assigned to the creator of the *Ancient Mariner*, of *Kubla Khan* and of *Christabel* must be high among the highest. In the fine harmony of his diction and the pure power of his imagination, in the ability to do by means of words what the musician do by means of notes, what a painter does by means of colours, he has, among lyrics poets, few equals—he has no superior.

Extract from *Blackwood's Magazine*, 1819. The longest poem in the collection of the *Sibyline Leaves* is the *Rime of the Ancient Mariner*—and to our feeling, it is by far the most wonderful also the most original, and the most touching of all the productions of its author. From it alone, we are inclined to think, an idea of the whole poetic genius of Mr. Coleridge may be gathered, such as he could scarcely receive an important addition either of extent or of distinctness, from a perusal of the whole of his other works. To speak of it at all is extremely difficult: above all the poems with which we are acquainted in any language—it is a poem to be felt—cherished—mused upon—not to be talked about-not capable of being described—analysed—or criticised. It is the wildest of all the creations of genius—it is not like a thing of the living, listening, moving world-the very music of its words is like the melancholy mysterious breath of something sung to the slipping ear—its images have the beauty-the grandeur—the incoherence of some mighty vision. The loveliness and the terror glide before us in turns—with, at one moment, the awful shadowy dimness- at another, the yet more awful distinctness of a majestic dream.

Charles Lamb : (Abstract from A Letter To Southey Rejoinder to Southey on his criticism of The Ancient Mariner). If you write that review in Crit. Rev., I am sorry you are so sparing of praise to *The Ancient Mariner*—so far from calling it as you do, with some wit, but more severity, 'A Dutch Attempt', etc. I call it a right English attempt, and a successful one, to dethrone German sublimity. You have selected a passage fertile in unmeaning miracles, but have passed by fifty passages as miraculous as the miracles they celebrate. I have never felt so deeply the pathetic as in that part,

> A spring of love gush'd from my heart,
> And I bless'd them unaware.

It stung me into high pleasure through suffering. Loyd do not like it; his head is too metaphysical, and your taste too correct; at least I must allege something against you both, to excuse my own dotage.

William Wordsworth : (From Preface to 2nd edition of Lyrical Ballads, 1800). The poem of my Friend has indeed great defects; first, that the principal person has no distinct character, either in his profession of Mariner, or as a human being who having been long under the control of supernatural impressions might be supposed himself to partake of something supernatural; secondly, that he does not act, but is continually acted upon; thirdly, that the events having no necessary connection do not produce each other; and lastly, that the imagery is somewhat too laboriously accumulated. Yet the poem contains many delicate touches of passion, and indeed the passion is everywhere true to nature: a great number of the stanzas present beautiful images, and are expressed with unusual felicity of language and the versification, tho' the metre is itself unfit for long poems, is harmonious and artfully varied, exhibiting the utmost powers of that metre, and every variety of which it is capable. It, therefore, appeared to me that these several merits (the first of which, namely, that of the passion, is of the highest kind) gave to the poem a value which is not often possessed by better poems.

THE ANCIENT MARINER

William Wordsworth : ***On the Origin of The Ancient Mariner Circumstances Leading to the Development of the Poem.*** In the autumn of 1797 he (Coleridge), my sister, and myself has started from Alfoxenden pretty late in the afternoon, with a view to visit Linton and the Valley of Stones near to it: and as our united funds are very small, we have agreed to defray the expense of the tour by writing a poem to be sent to the *New Monthly Magazine* set up by Phillips, the book seller, and edited by Dr. Aikin. Accordingly we set off, and proceeded along the Quantock Hills towards Watchet; and in the course of this walk has planned the poem of the Ancient Mariner, have been found on a dream, as Mr. Coleridge said, of his friend Mr. Cruikshank. Much the greatest part of the story was Mr. Coleridge's invention, but certain parts I have suggested; for example some crime is to be committed which should bring the old Navigator, as Coleridge afterwards has delighted to call him, the spectral persecution, as a consequence of that crime, and his own wanderings. I have been reading in *Shelrock's Voyages* a day or two before, that while doubling Cape Horn they frequently see albatrosses in that latitude, the large sort of sea-fowl, some extending their wings twelve or thirteen feet. 'Suppose said I, 'you represent him as having killed one of these birds on entering the South Sea, and that the lutelary spirits of these regions take upon them to avenge the crime'. The incident is thought fit for the purpose, and adopts accordingly. I also suggests the navigation of the ship by the dead men but do not recollect and I have anything more to do with the scheme of the poem. The Gloss with which it is subsequently accompanied is not thought of by either of us at the time, at least not a hint of it is given to me, and I have no doubt, it is a gratuitous after thought. We began the composition together on that to be a memorable evening: I furnished two or three lines at the beginning of the poem, in particular—

> And listen'd like a three years' child:
> The Mariner had his will.

These trifling contributions, all but one (which Mr. C; has with unnecessary scrupulously recorded) sliped out of his mind, as well they might. As we have endeavoured to proceed conjointly (I speak of, the same evening), our respective manners have proved so widely different that it would have been quite presumptuous to me to do anything but separate from an undertaking upon which I can only have been a clog... We have returned by Dulverton to Alfoxenden. *The Ancient Mariner* grows and grows, till it become too important for our first object, which is limited to our expectation of five pounds; and we begin to think of a volume which is to consist, as Mr. Coleridge has told the world, of poems chiefly on supernatural subjects, has taken from common life, but looks at, as much as may be, through an imaginative medium.

William Hazlitt : (*Extract from The Spirit of the Age, 1825*). Of all Mr. Coleridge's productions, *The Ancient Mariner* is only one that we can with confidence put into any person's hands, on whom we wish to impress a favourable idea of his extraordinary power. Let whatever other objections be made to it, it is unquestionably a work of genius of wild, irregular, overwhelming imagination, and has that rich, varied movement in the verse, which gives a distant idea of the lofty or changeful tones of Mr. Coleridge's voice.

Humphry House : *An Interpretation of Ancient Mariner.* The poem up to.... Part IV and the opening stanzas of Part V, has taken together with the ending, Part VII, is relatively easy to interpret as a tale of crime, punishment and reconciliation, with the recovery of love in the blessing of the water-snakes at its climax. But the reminder of Part V and the whole of Part VI do not seem at first sight to have quite the same coherence and point. It is here that readers may still find "unmeaning marvels" and an elaborate supernatural machinery which dissipates concentration. There are wonderful details in the verse, some of the finest descriptions of all; but they may seem to fall apart and to have too little bearing on each other and on the whole. Many publishes accounts of the poem do not adequately face the implication of the detail in these Parts. It is, therefore, best to summarise shortly what happens.

The Mariner hears a roaring wind and sees the fires and lightning in the sky. But the ship moves on untouch by the wind, and the reanimate dead men work it : a troop of blessed spirits has entered into them. These spirits makes various music. The ship goes on, move from beneath by the spirit of the South Pole. Through the two voices the Mariner learns that it is this Polar Spirit that requires vengeance for the Albatross's death, and that he will have more penance to do.

In Part VI, the Voices says that the ocean is under the power of the moon.

The ship is now moved northward by the angelic power while the Mariner is in his trance. He wakes to see the final curse in the eyes of the dead men. Then that spell is snapped, and he feels at last a sweet breeze on himself alone. He arrives at his home port, steep in cool night. Then, as the Gloss says: "The angelic spirits leave the dead bodies. And appear in their own forms of light". This acts as the signal which brings out the boat from land.

In Part VII a dreadful rumbling sound comes under the water and the ship sinks.

A quite normally accepted and simple interpretation of Parts V and VI treats them as a further necessary extension of the expiation theme. In the blessing of the water-snakes the Mariner has reconciled himself to the creatures, but it remains for him to reconcile himself also with the Creator: therefore he has to suffer once more (this time from the curse of the dead men's eyes) and to win the power of recognising the beauty of the angelic music.

This is broadly acceptable; but it takes us very little distance in understanding the complicated machinery. Is there any serious import in the answers to such questions as these : What is the function of the Polar Spirit? In one aspect he appears as the friend and avenger of the "pious bird of good Omen", and yet he is made to work under obedience to the angelic troop, who are thus plainly, in the spiritual hierarchy, superior to him; and he is bought off by the promise that the Mariner's penance shall continue. It may have seemed better to have make the angelic troop themselves the protectors of the Albatross and make them require the further penance. Why shall the ship move first by the Polar Spirit and then by the angelic power? Again, what is the significance of the two winds in parts V and VI? Put the problem in another way : are the avenging by the tutelary spirits of the South Sea and the reanimation of the dead bodies to work the ship here just out of politeness, because Wordsworth have suggested them? The first main problem here is to decide whether there is any meaning in the two different kinds of supernatural being.

Walter Pater : *The Ancient Mariner : A Romantic Poem (An abstract from Appreciations 1889*). *The Ancient Mariner*... .is a 'romantic' poem, impressing us by bold invention and appealing to that taste for the supernatural, that longing for *le frisson*, a shudder, to which the 'romantic' school in Germany, and its derivations in England and France, directly ministers. In Coleridge, personally, this taste have been encouraged by his odd and out-of-the-way reading in the old fashioned literature of the marvellous-books like *Purchas' Pilgrims,* early voyages like Hakluyt's, old naturalists and visionary moralists, like Thomas Burent.... Fancies of the strange things which may very well happen, even in broad daylight, to men shut up alone in ship for off on the sea, seems to have occurred to the human mind in all ages with a peculiar readiness, and often have about them, from the story of the stealing of Dionysius downwards the fascination of a certain dreamy grace, which distinguishes them from other kinds of marvellous inventions. This sort of fascination *The Ancient Mariner* brings to its highest degree : it is the delicacy, the dreamy grace, in his presentation of the marvellous, which makes Coleridge's work so remarkable. The too palpable intruders from a spiritual world in almost all ghost literature, in Scott and Shakespeare even, have a kind of crudity and coarseness. Coleridge's power is in the very fineness with which, as by some really ghostly finger, he brings home to our inmost sense his inventions, daring as they are the skeleton ship, the polar spirit, the inspiriting of the dead corpses of the ship's crew. *The Rime of the Ancient Mariner* has the perfect adaptation to reason and the general aspect of life, which belongs to the marvellous, when actually present as part of a credible experience in our dreams.... The modern mind, so minutely self-scrutinizing, if it is to be affected at all by a sense of the supernatural, needs the more; finely touche than is possible in the older, romantic presentment of it. The spectral object, so crude, so impossible, has become plausible, as :

> The bolt upon the brain
> That will show itself without;

and is understood to be but a condition of one's own mind, for according to the scepticism, latent at least, in so much of our modern philosophy, the so-called real things are but spectral after all.

It is this finer, more delicately marvellous supernaturalism, fruit of his own more delicate psychology, that Coleridge infuses into romantic adventure, itself also then a new or revived thing in English literature; and with a fineness of weird effect in the *Ancient Mariner* unknown in those older, more simple, romantic legends and ballads. It is a flower of medieval or later German romance, growing up in a peculiarly compounded atmosphere of modern psychological speculation, and putting forth in it wholly new qualities. The quaint prose commentary, which runs side by side with the verse of *The Ancient Mariner,* illustrates this a composition of quite different shade of beauty and merit from that of the verse which it accompanies, connecting this, the chief poem 'of Coleridge, with his philosophy, and emphasizing therein that psychological interest of which I have spoken, its curious soul-love.

Completeness, the perfectly rounded wholeness and unity of the impression which it leaves on the mind of a reader who fairly gives himself to it-that, too, is one of the characteristics of a really excellent work, in the poetic as in every other kind of art, and by this completeness, *The Ancient Mariner* certainly gains upon *Christabel*.... It is Coleridge's one great complete work, the one really finished thing in a life of many beginnings.

Harold Bloom : *The Ancient Mariner and the wandering Jew tradition.* Poetry and potentially its criticism alone of all human talk need not be reductive. Coleridge in *The Ancient Mariner* tells a story that relates itself clearly to a major Romantic archetype, the Wanderer, the man with the mark of Cain, or the mocker of Christ, who must expiate in the perpetual cycle of guilt and suffering, and whose torment is in excess of its usually obscure object and source ... In Coleridge, Shelley and Byron it becomes something more, a personal myth so consuming that we hardly know whether to seek it first in the life or in the work.

The Ancient Mariner is in tradition of the stories of Cain and of the Wandering Jew, but it does not reduce to them. It is a late manifestation of the Gothic Revival, and its first version is clearly to be related to the ballad of The Wandering Jew in Percy's *Reliques* but its historical sources also tend to mislead us when we attempt to describe it in its own terms, which is the business of criticism. The Ancient Mariner, bright-eyed and compulsive, is a haunter of wedding feasts, and in a grim way he is the chanter of prothalamium. Yet he does not address himself to bride or groom but to a gallant who is bridegrooms next of kin. His story means most, he implies, when it is juxtaposed with the special joy of the wedding celebration, but it is not relevant to these being joined by a sacrament. Its proper audience is an unwilling one; its function is monitory. The message can only be relayed from a lurker at the threshold to a prospective sharer of the feast.

The world of the Mariner's voyage is purely visionary..., without apparent premeditation or conscious motive, the narrator murders the Albatross.

The murder is a gratuitous act, but then so is the initial appearance of the bird. There is a tradition of seemingly motiveless malevolence that goes from Shakespeare's Iago, Milton's Satan to the protagonist of Poe, Melville and Dostoevsky........ the tradition climaxes (in our times) in violence that yet confirms individual existence and so averts an absolute despair of self. Coleridge's Mariner belongs to this tradition whose dark ancestors include Cain, the Wandering Jew and Judas whose act of betrayal is portrayed as a desperate assertion of freedom by Wilde, Yeats, and D.H. Lawrence.

This tradition's common denominator is that of a desperate assertion of the self and a craving for a heightened sense of identity. This is what the Mariner brings about for himself, in a death-in-life purgatorial fashion; for his companions he brings only a terrible death and a mechanical life-in-death following his own partial redemption.

Several influential modern readings of *The Ancient Mariner* have attempted to baptize the poem by importing into it the notion of Original Sin and the myth of the Fall. But the Mariner is neither disobedient in his dire action nor altered in nature by its first effects. There is nothing in him to suffer the depravity of the natural heart, nor is the slaying of an Albatross at all an adequate symbol of a lapse that demands expression in the language of theology. Coleridge felt the poem has been already too overtly moral.

J.L. Lowes : ***The design of The Ancient Mariner.*** Behind *The Ancient Mariner* lie crowding masses of impressions, incredible in their richness and variety. That admits no doubt. But the poem is not the sum of the impressions, as a heap of diamond dust is the sum of its shining particles: nor is the poet merely a sensitized medium for their reception and transmission. Beneath the poem lies also innumerable blendings and fusings of impressions, brought about below the level, of conscious mental processes. That too is no longer open to question. But the poem is not the confluence of unconsciously merging images, as a pool of water forms from the coalescence of scattered drops: nor is the poet a somnambulist in a subliminal world. Neither the conscious impressions nor their unconscious interpenetrations constitute the poem. They are inseparable from it, but it is an entity which they do not create. On the contrary, every impression, every new creature rising from the potent waters of the Well, is what it now is through its participation in a whole, foreseen as a whole in each integral part a whole which is the working out of a controlling imaginative design. The incommunicable, unique essence of the poem is its form.

And that form is the handiwork of choice, and a directing intelligence, and the sweat of a gorging brain. The design of *The Ancient Mariner* did not lie, like a landscape in a crystal, Pellucid and complete in Coleridge's mind from the beginning. It has been there potentially, together with a hundred hovering alternatives, in a melange of disparate and fortuitous suggestions. To drive through that farrago, 'straight forward as a Roman' balanced opposition of daemonic and angelic agencies, and the unfolding consequences of tie initial act that involves more than the spontaneous welling up of images from secret depths. Beyond a doubt, that ceaseless play of swift associations which has been flashed is like flying shuffles through Coleridge's shaping brain, present and cooperating from the first.

For the action has a beginning, and a middle and end. It is the first half of the poem the agency of an avenging daemon is in the ascendent; in the second, the prevailing power of an angel band. It is an overt act of the mariner which precipitates the daemonic vengeance; it is an inner impulse counter to the act which brings to pass the angelic intervention; and in the end it is 'the penance of life' which falls upon the rescued wanderer, a fated wanderer still. Exciting force, rising action, climax falling action, catastrophe-all are there. And through the transfer to the Mariner of legendary associations of the Wandering Jew, undying among the dead, Cruikshank's dream its figures metamorphosed into Death and Life-in-Death is built into the basic structure of the plot. And under the influence of another ship, is sailed by an angelic crew, the suggestion of the navigation of the Mariner's vessel by bodies of the dead is so transformed as to provide that cardinal antithesis of angelic and daemonic agencies on which the action of the poem turns. And finally, by a stroke of consummate art, ship and poem alike are brought back in the end to the secure, familiar, happy world from which they have set out. The supernatural machinery is a masterpiece of constructive skill. But only, I think, in the light of the genesis of its component parts can the triumph of the faculty which has shaped them into unity be fully understood.

R.P. Warren : *Two basic themes (Summarised by Humphry House).* The whole discussion of this problem has been clarified and ennobled by Mr. Warren's long essay, which may be summarised. He maintains that the poet has "two basic themes both' of them very rich and provocative." The primary theme, which is "the outcome of the fable taken at its face value as a story of crime and punishment and reconciliation," is the theme of sacramental vision, or the theme of 'One Life.' The secondary theme is "concerned with the context of values in which the fable is presented" and is "the theme of the imagination." The two themes are finally fused in the poem. He aims to establish the existence of this secondary theme by two lines of argument : first, that there are parts of the poem not otherwise easily intelligible, such as parts V and VI; and second, that the symbolism of the poem is richer and more coherent than the redemption, visionary, theme alone requires. Mr. Warren elaborates the contrast of the "Two lights" in great detail.

He points out quite rightly and fully the "pervasive presence of the moon and moonlight in Coleridge's work", especially in association with creativeness. In *Sonnet to the Autumnal Moon,* 1788, she is called the "Mother of widely-working visions,", and in *Songs of the Pixies 1796,* "Mother of wildly-working dreams". *Christabel* and *The Ancient Mariner* are bathed in moonlight; the moon is over the deep romantic chasm of *Kubla Khan;* it is prominent in *The Nightingale, Cain* and *Dejection.*

Mr. Warren maintains that the association is so recurrent and persistent in Coleridge's writing, between creation or the activity of the secondary imagination and the moon light, half-lights, dim lights, gloom, luminescent clouds and so on, that the association between them can justifiably be regarded as habitual: and that as it goes back even into his very early poems, it can without injustice be taken as established (even if not consciously) at the time of writing the Mariner. He quotes from the *Biographia* passage in which Coleridge recalled the origin of the *Lyrical Ballads* themselves: "The sudden charm, which accidents of light and shade, which moon-light or sun-set, diffused over a known and familiar landscape. These are the poetry of nature."

The Albatross, besides being associated with human nature on the level of the primary theme, is also associated with the moon, mist, cloud and fog-smoke on the level of the secondary theme of the imagination:

> In mist or cloud, on mast or shroud,
> It perched for vespers nine;
> While all the night, through fog-smoke white,
> Glimmered the white Moon-shine. (L. 75-78)

Furthermore the bird is associated with the breeze, which Mr. Warren takes to be the "creative" wind, for which there are countless parallels in other poets.

J. Colmer : *The Theme of One Life in Ballad Form.* In *The Rime of the Ancient Mariner* Coleridge explores the theme of the one life in ballad form through 'incidents and agents......in part at least, supernatural.' The colour, solidity, and movement of the descriptions and the hypnotic power of the narrative makes it possible for young readers to find complete satisfaction in the story alone. But within the narrative framework a complex vision of life is developed. At a deeper level then the purely narrative, at which it has all the appeal of an old minstrel's song that 'holdeth children from play and old men from the chimney corner' it may be seen as a spiritual adventure, and the specific references to Christian doctrine invite us to some relationship between the Mariner's crime of killing the Albatross, his punishment and subsequent expiation and the fall of man. Nevertheless a search for deeper moral significance is not at the expense of the rich complexity of the poem, and the idea that it embodies a dramatic tension, between Coleridge's Christian belief and his fears that the universe is ruled by arbitrary laws might explain why many of the elements like the death of the crew cannot easily be brought within any simple moral interpretation. Whatever else it is, it is a poem centrally concerned with the one life and the redeeming power of imaginative love.

S. A. Brook : *Supernaturalism in The Ancient Mariner.* In *The Ancient Mariner* the events are natural, but behind them lies a supernatural world. The thoughts which Nature's powers awake in a sensitive soul are believed by Coleridge to have corresponding existence which derive their being from nature. These bodiless beings may be felt by us as enemies or friends and in circumstances 'made emotional by loneliness, they may themselves be felt as actual presences by man. But this could only be in primeval, solitude where dwell things to dream of, not to tell, or in the midst of untravelled seas, or in the deep forests of romance. In these remote mysterious seas and woods Coleridge lays the scenery of *The Ancient Mariner* and of *Christabel*. It is supernatural, but of the ancient, common simple kind which belongs to all mankind. We feel the same thrill he desires to convey in *Christabel* if at night we are lost in forest:

> Like one, that on a lonesome road
> Doth walk in fear and dread

The same expression of the possibility of marvel and, horror, of mysterious sins and their forgiveness, and of the chance of meeting some forgotten spiritual life which have been before man came on earth, which creeps over us as we read *The Ancient Mariner*, belongs to sea men who have been lost in unvisited spaces of ocean, vext with everlasting calm. I have never met a sailor whose ship has been among the lonely places of the sea, who do not know of their haunting, in the air that has sighed in the rigging, the voices of the creatures that are half of the water and half of the air above them. With wonderful but unconscious skill scenery is kept extraordinarily true to Nature. The single motive—"He prayeth well who loveth well, both man and bird and beast"—is so slight that it does not take the whole out of the world of the dreaming phantasy, out of the mystery of the great and solitary sea; and yet, when it comes in at the end, it throws back its single impression on the whole and gives it lyric unity.

S. Dutt : *Dramatic Probability of Supernatural Elements.* For the appreciation of the novel and original character of *The Ancient Mariner* as well as the intimate connection of 'suspension of disbelief' with 'dramatic probability,' it is necessary to explicate what are but implicit suggestions in Coleridge. Considers as a tale, Coleridge's poem is radically different from all previous tales of the supernatural, not on account of its richer or finer artistic qualities, but because of its inner dramatic stress. And its supernatural incidents acquire from this very dramatic stress a different quality corresponding to what Leigh Hunt calls 'conditional truth to nature.

It is obvious that by presuming 'dramatic probability' or 'dramatic truth' in a supernatural tale, which is a tale of one's intimate experience, Coleridge implies the presence of an inner mental drama underlying and informing it. On the consistent character of this drama depends the whole power of illusion of suspension of disbelief, for it is not difficult to see how the presence of it affects the supernatural elements of the tale. Involved in this inner drama, the supernatural incident necessarily appears shadowy and uncertain: its reality becomes largely relative and it scarcely lends itself to judgement on its own merits and apart from the situation imagined. The supernatural, shedding largely its supernatural marvel, raises only the kind of speculative wonder implied in Prof. Beers' intriguing queries about the Ancient Mariner's experiences, viz., "Did the mariner really see the spectral bark, hear spirits talking, or is it all but the phantasmagoria of the calenture which attacks the sailor on the tropic main, so that he seems to see green meadows and water-brooks on the level brine?"

H.D. Traill : ***Realism in The Ancient Mariner.*** *The Ancient Mariner*, however is as real to the reader as the hero *Beau de Chagrin*. We are convinced of the curse upon one of the doomed wretches as upon the other; and the strange phantasmagoric haze which is thrown around the ship and the lonely voyager leaves their outline as clear as if we see them through the sunshine of the streets of Paris. Coleridge triumphs over his difficulties by sheer vividness of imagery and terse vigour of descriptive phrase : two qualities over which his previous poems did not prove him to possess by any means so complete a mastery. For among all the beauties of his earlier landscape we can hardly reckon that of intense and convincing truth. He seems seldom before to have written as Wordsworth nearly always seems to write, "with his eye on the object"; and certainly he never before has displayed any remarkable power of completing his word-picture with a few touches. In *The Ancient Mariner* his eye seems never to wander from his object, and again the scene starts out upon the canvas in two or three strokes of the brush. The skeleton ship, with the dicing demons on its deck; the setting sun peering "through its ribs, as if through a dungeon-grate"; the water-snakes under the moonbeams, with the "elfish light" falling off them "in hoary flakes" when they reared; the dead crew, who work the ship and "raise their limbs like lifeless tools"—everything seems to have been actually seen and we believe it all as the story of a truthful eye-witness. The details of the voyage, too, are all chronicle with such order and regularity, there is such a diary-like air about the whole things that we accept it almost as if it were a series of extract from the ship's "log". Then again the execution : a great thing to be said of so long a poem ; is marvellously equal throughout; the story never drags or flags for a moment, its felicities of diction are perpetual, and it is scarcely marred by a single weak line.

A. Douglas : ***The Ancient Mariner A Symbolic Poem.*** The Mariner is ultimately saved from his fate worse than death by the gentle spirit who decrees that he shall win his way back to partial release through loving all things. And so through a role of gentleness and sentimentality does Coleridge pursue his way through life. He plays the role and preaches the gospel of benign love ....

It (shooting the Albratross) is, significantly, an utterly unjustified act and..... it is followed by a remorse out of all proportion to the deed. It is clearly a fantasy symbolising guilt. The Mariner has killed the source of kindness, safety and guidance... The odd omission of any justification, provocation or motivation is best explained as a symbolic device suggesting their sub-rational, neurotic source. In view of the bird's mission and the pattern of emotional disturbance in Coleridge's childhood, it will seem that this fantasy of killing the Albatross is associated with some deeply burned guilt, either incestuous or Oedipal.

With Coleridge a weak or waning moon is pretty clearly a powerful symbol for loss of mother love. The figure appears in *Christabel* :

> The moon, is behind, and at the full;
> And yes she looks both small and dull.

But the most astonishing moon symbolism occurs in *The Ancient Mariner*. At the most awful moment in that poem, when the nightmare Life-in-Death has won the Mariner's soul, and the night is thick and dark then comes the Moon. The passage describing her coming has forever astonished and puzzled with its mystifying error in astronomy

> Till clomb above the eastern bar
> The horned Moon, with one bright Star
> Within the nether tip.

The figures come at the end of a long stanza that reaches a climax of feeling in these lines. Can this impossible bit of astronomy be a Freudian slip? It seems inexplicable, yet if the moon holds reference here to motherhood, how wonderful that Coleridge shall put the star within the nether tip, "enfolded", so to speak. Is it possible that we have here the unconscious yearning of the narcissist in a magnificent bit of pure expressionism altering the very face of the heavens? Like a mother, the moon holds the little star within her arm. It is not so strange an idea in the mind of a poet dominated by the need of a universe essentially benevolent, essentially loving. Soft, gentle and benevolent presence in the sky, serenely she floats among the stars quietly shedding her light on all below : the lovely complement and partner of the strong male Sun.

C.M. Bowra : *The Ancient Mariner : A Myth of Guilt and Redemption.* *The Ancient Mariner...,* is a myth of guilt and redemption, but of course it is also much more. Its symbolical purpose is but one element in a complex design. Though Coleridge has his own poetry of a guilty soul, it is not comparable in depth or in insight with the poetry of some other men who have given the full powers of their genius to writing about crime and the misery which it engenders. Nonetheless Coleridge's introduction of this theme into *The Ancient Mariner* gives to it a new dimension. What might otherwise be no more than an irresponsible fairy-tale is brought closer to life and to its fundamental issues. The myth of crime and punishment provides a structure for the supernatural events which rise from it but often make their appeal irrespective of it. Much of the magic of *The Ancient Mariner* comes from its blend of dark and serious issues with the delighted play of creative energy. Coleridge has good reasons for fashioning his poem in this way. In the first place, the combination of different themes is responded to his own complex vision of existence. For him life has both its dark and bright sides; its haunting responsibilities and ravishing moments of unsullied delight. He has seen that the two are closely interwoven and that, if he speak with the full force of his genius, he must introduce both into his poem. In the second place, he see life not analytically but creatively, and he knows that any work of creation must itself be an extension and an enchantment of life. He must preserve the mystery and the enchantment which he know in his finest poems, and for him these come alike from the beauty of the visible world and the uncharted corners of the human soul. The shadow cast by the Mariner's crime adds by contrast to the brilliance of the unearthly world in which it is committed, and the degree of his guilt and his remorse serve to stress the power of the angelic beings which watch over humankind. The result is a poem shot with irridiscent light. It appears to us now in this way, now in that, and there is no final or single approach to it.

In creating *The Ancient Mariner* in this way Coleridge has obeyed the peculiar and paradoxical nature of his genius. In him, the poet and the metaphysician are uneasily blended, and the creative spirit, which is capable of such rapturous flights, has worked most freely when it is free from metaphysical speculations.

Graham Hough : *The Ancient Mariner, A Rebirth Myth.* The poem is more than an allegory of guilt and regeneration. In any ordinary sense the Mariner is very little guilty. But he has broken the bond between himself and the life of Nature and in consequence becomes spiritually dead. What happens to him when he blesses the water-snakes in the tropical calm is a psychic rebirth : a rebirth that must at times happen to all men and all cultures unless they are to dry up in living death. The whole poem is indeed a vivid presentation of the rebirth myth as it is conceived by Jung : the psychologist who has done most to explain these recurrent forms of imaginative literature. But such explanations of poetry are not convincing to everyone and are not easily demonstrable, so I will not labour the point. What we must explain is that it is not the final 'Moral', it is the living symbolization of this universal psychic experience that gives the poem its lasting power. It is as though Coleridge has tapped a deeper level of consciousness here than he is ever to reach again.

Allan Grant : ***The Ancient Mariner, the Story of a Voyage into the Interior.*** At the same time the Mariner's tale is a story of a voyage into the interior. Not only the unfathomable depths of the sources of human action is to be discerned in the unpremediated shooting of the Albatross that causes him his suffering and the spontaneous blessing of the water-snakes that begins his restoration: the story also takes us beyond the human world altogether. Again it is a voyage of extreme contrasts, of suffering and of expiation, of the human and social world and an altogether alien cosmos with its own terrible, yet beautiful order. It is exactly right that the listener shall be a wedding guest and that the Mariner denies him his expectations of the nature enjoyment of the music, the celebration and the happiness of the feast. It is also right that the guest shall be afraid of the Mariner and feel that he is a being from another world; he is exactly that.

George Whaley : ***The Ancient Mariner, A Personal Allegory.*** *The Ancient Mariner* in addition to its other unique qualities is both an unconscious projection of Coleridge's early sufferings and a vivid prophecy of his sufferings that were to follow. The poem is probably not originally intended to be a personal allegory: but that is what, in Coleridge's eyes, it became latter as the prophecy is slowly, inexorably, and lingeringly fulfilled.

As far as I know *The Ancient Mariner* has never been interpreted as a personal allegory. To do so (and the evidence for it is weighty) not only gives a clue to the sources of the poem's intensity but also explains beyond cavil its moral implications. *The Ancient Mariner* is, however, of primary importance as a poem; and no specialised interest : moral, biographical or allegorical—can be allowed to assail the integrity to which, as a poem, it is entitled. But the interpretation I have suggested does bring the reader into intimate contact with Coleridge the man. Even to attempt to understand him will induce sympathy, and from sympathy some understanding can grow.

D.W. Harding : ***Depression and the Sense or Isolation.*** The human experience round which Coleridge centres the poem is surely the depression and the sense of isolation and unworthiness which the Mariner describes in part IV. The suffering he describes is of a kind which is perhaps not found except in slightly pathological conditions, but which, pathological or not has been felt by a great many people. He feels isolated to a degree that baffles expression and reduces him to the impotent, repetitive emphasis which becomes doggerel in school room reading :

> Alone, alone, all, all alone,
> Alone on a wide wide sea!

At the same time, he is not just physically isolated, but is socially abandoned, even by those with the greatest obligations :

> And never a saint took pity on
> My soul in agony.

With this desertion the beauty of the ordinary world has been taken away :

> The many men, so beautiful !
> And they all dead did lie.

All that is left, and especially, centrally, oneself, is disgustingly worthless :

> And a thousand thousand slimy things
> Lived on; and so did I.

With the sense of worthlessness there is also guilt. When he tried to pray :

> A wicked whisper came and made
> My heart as dry as dust.

And enveloping whole experience is the sense of sapped energy, oppressive weariness :

> For the sky and the sea, and the sea and the sky
> Lay like a load on my weary eye,
> And the dead were at my feet.

This, the central experience, comes almost at the middle of the poem. It is the nadir of depression to which the earlier stanzas sink, the rest of the poem describes what is in part recovery and in part aftermath. You need not have been a Mariner in a supernatural Pacific in order to have felt this mood. Coleridge knew it well, and *Dejection* and *The Pains of Sleep* deal with closely related experiences.

E.B. Gosse : ***The Ancient Mariner is the Romantic Urge to Explore the Eternal Soul.*** But in truth the Mariner tells us little of our relation to Wordsworthian nature, to wino, sun and moon. Our premise has been that his tale deals with no literal geographical voyage. Rather it is emblematic of the romantic urge to explore the eternal soul and the temporal emotions. The voyage was Coleridge's as it becomes the readers': plunged like, all men in the mist and gloom of life on this planet, he sought to comprehend the life-giving source which calls up that mist, to appreciate the luminosity that informed that gloom. *The Ancient Mariner* is the finest fruit of that labour.

F. Marsh : ***Journey of Psychic Exploration.*** It is just as essential (as in *The Waste Land*) in reading *The Ancient Mariner* to wrestle with images to interpret the symbols.

The Ancient Mariner, in addition to being the story of crime and expiation, takes us on a journey of psychic exploration where natural and symbolic coexist.

The reception of the bird and the splitting of the ice are not coincidental. The connection, I suggest, is causal. The ice like the later lack of wind and rain is an image of the absence of creative vitality and spontaneous feeling. The bird images just such life and feeling. But as yet there is no real insight, no conscious understanding (the light is mist, cloud, fog-smoke), and the Mariner kills the bird.

Critics have given this action every significance from symbolic, murder and fall of man to the "violation of a great sanctity at the animal, human and spiritual levels" and "the act of pride, the unbridled assertion of the self." Mr. George Whaley who... suggests that the Albatross "is the symbol of Coleridge's creative imagination, his eagle" is perhaps the most helpful. Since the bird images life stirring in the frozen depths, is in fact the life that broke the frost, the crime is as much a crime against the Mariner's own soul as against nature and the external order of the universe.

To my mind the unmoving ship, beating sun, the rotting water create a more powerful image of the sick soul than even Eliot's rock with 'no water. Since all life once emerged from the sea, the sea should by nature abound with life; when the very sea rots, consciousness is indeed paralysed and ill.

Humphry House : ***The Mariner is not a Spiritual Adventure.*** The poem's very richness at once tempts and defeats definiteness of interpretation. As we commit overselves to the development of one strand of meaning, we find that in the very act of doing so we are excluding something else of importance.

An example of this difficulty occurs on the threshold of interpretation, in the opinion we form about the Mariner's relation to ordinary human beings and the relation of the voyage to ordinary human life. Dr. Tillyard, struck (as everybody must be struck) by the similarities in spirit between the poem and the seventeenth century voyages :

> We were the first that ever burst
> Into that silent sea—

as voyages of adventure and discovery, and using, to support his argument, the later Coleridge passage in the *Biographia* about the range of hills which must be crossed by an inquiring spirit, maintains that the Mariner himself is a mental and spiritual adventurer, 'an unusually enquiring spirit', that he together with the rest of the crew are, from the accepted social point of view, self-appointed outcasts and criminals; and that the sea-voyage indicates spiritual adventure, which they go out of their way to seek.

How is this present in the poem? The beginning of the Mariner's own account of the voyage contains no hint that he think of the voyage as a high spiritual enterprise at variance with the current is limited social ideas, a conscious seeking of adventure. The ship starts off in an atmosphere of communal agreement and pleasure:

> The ship was cheered, the harbour cleared,
> merrily did we drop
> Below the kirk, below the hill,
> Below the light house top. (21-24)

The voyage it seems, begin normally, commonly, happily, the crew at one both with the society and with each other. In the literature of sea-going the antecedents are rather to be found in such voyages as that described by Herodotus certainly is used by Coleridge when he write :

> The sun now rose upon the right-

the voyage in which the Phoenician seamen doubles the Cape without knowing that there is a Cape. Adventure come upon them unaware.

The Mariner, says Wordsworth in rude complaint, 'does not act, but is continually acted upon'. There is surely an important element of truth in this though it does not in the least derogate from the poem's merit.

There are only three points in the poem at which the Mariner may be said to 'act'; these are the shooting of the Albatross; the blessing the water-snakes; and the bitting of his arm. Each of these actions has a very different character. The shooting of the Albatross comes quite suddenly and unexplained; superficially it is unmotivated and wanton. The Mariner himself never makes any explicit attempt to explain it; nor does the poem contain, from his point of view, any defence of it. We shall return to this. In the first phase of his recovery, in the crisis at the centre of the poem, when he blesses the water-snakes, he does so unaware, and this word 'unaware' is deliberately repeated and occurs each time significantly emphatically, at the end of the line. That is to say, he do not really know what he is doing; he could find no adequate spring of action in himself, and retrospectively attributes his undeliberate blessing to a supernatural influence on him :

> Sure my kind saint took pity on me

He himself think he is more acted upon than acting. Against this must be set the one clear occasion in the poem on which the Mariner does deliberately act. In Part III, when all the crew, including himself, have been stricken dumb by the drought, it is he who sees the sail; it is he who, by prodigious effort, bites his arm, sucks the blood and finds voice to cry out. This is his one 'tremendous effort; it is a moment of terrible hope for him and for the whole crew. But the hope is blasted , not just negatively, but positively, appallingly blasted. The crew all die cursing him with their eyes and he alone survives.

This is crucial to the whole poem's dramatic effect and by inference, also to its moral effect. On the one occasion when the Mariner does consciously, deliberately and with all his effort act, his action leads ironically to the climax of the disaster. The irony is enforced by the two lines that end this part :

> And every soul, it passed me by,
> Like the whizz of my cross-bow!

The disastrous anticlimax of this action and this hope is made to throw back to the earlier, unexplained act of the shooting. One main element in the poem's theme is that the Mariner's experience involves a tangle of terror, incomprehensibility and frustration. He is certainly not a great courageous spiritual adventurer, though he has a great spiritual experience.

E. E. Stoll : ***No Allegory or Symbolism in The Ancient Mariner.*** If..... allegory or symbolism had been intended, why does some hint of that not appear in the marginal glosses? Why, indeed, were these added? They are not at all necessary for the understanding of the poem, are not like Mr. T.S. Eliot's notes appended to *The Waste Land*. In prose, they speak still, though more explicitly and philosophically, the language of superstition; they only amplify and in explaining by no means explain away. Their purpose is but to heighten the illusion; they credibilize the marvels, providing an approach to them, a middle distance, which makes them appropriately more remote. In the poem itself, this principle of perspective is happily observed. The marvels occur on unknown, distant seas with the meridian of marvels and when the Mariner and his ship, equally bewitched, arrive, the effect of the mere sight of them, on the normal, everyday Hermit, Pilot, and pilot's Boy is startling, shocking. The effect of that in turn upon the Wedding-Guest and also the reader is convincing. And as important to the transition and the illusion is the effect upon the Mariner himself before that :

> Oh! dream of joy ! is this indeed
> The light house top I see ?
> Is this the hill ? is this the kirk ?
> Is this mine own countree ?

It is like the ending of *The Midsummer Night's Dream*, as day breaks and the lovers wonder whether the adventures of the night are a dream or not. Dreaming without awaking is not dreaming. In the figurative sense of the word "perspective", to be sure, the Wedding-Guest, in his momentary, palpitating interruptions of the narrative "Why look'st thou so?" "I fear thee *Ancient Mariner*"—represents the middle distance; and the marginal comment is the nearer distance, though still from us remote.

And none of literary figures concerned with The Ancient Mariner, in its composition or in its appearance, seems to have detected allegory or symbolism in it.... The retribution is greater, simpler, less regardful of distinctions, than in life we should have it, but yet has something of a natural movement; punishment, repentance, a gush of love for other living things, prayer and relief, yet further penance for, as in ancient legend and somewhat as in life, "the train of cause and consequence knows no end." And, "given that world" as Lowes says, "one of tutelary spirits and a retribution that is endless, and of a leading figure who, like the wandering Jew and the flying Dutchman, is immortal"—has given that world, its inviolate keeping with itself becomes the sole condition of our acceptance for the movement, of its validity.

For *The Ancient Mariner* is a structure, a perfectly ordered, a finely "complex design wrought out through the exquisite adjustment of innumerable details." It is not an opium dream like *Kubla Khan*; and that is the answer to the symbolists of psycho-analytic and biographic bent.

M. Ware : *Moral Purpose.* The moral tag near the end of the poem has been variously dealt with, or more frequently dismissed as superfluous and intrusive........Professor E.E. Stoll... Pronounces Coleridge's final remarks as an unimportant part of his poem : "they are in keeping with the medieval spirit, which is given to simple, open moralising". And Humphry House feels that the tag, when it is detached from the rest of the poem, constitutes simple 'almanac art'. When, however, the tag is considered in the context, House finds, "after the richness and terror of the poem, it is no more a banal moral apothegm, but a moral which has its meaning because it has been lived." The moral at the end of the poem is, as Professor Stoll contends, "open moralising," but moralising which has been systematically developed throughout. In *The Rime of the Ancient Mariner,* the central figure's ability to pray obviously indicates that a workable reconciliation to the 'Holy of Holies' has been effected. The poem is most frequently considered a comment upon man's obligation to love his fellow creatures and to observe the natural bonds which unite all creation. Such ideas are unquestionably inherent in it. But in Coleridge's sweeping moral conclusion, the word love is only of secondary importance Coleridge tells us quite plainly that the ability to pray follows love.

E. Dowden : *The Moral of The Ancient Mariner.* The Mariner is punished for shooting an Albatross; the curse passes away when he blesses the water-snakes. Coleridge might have called his critic's (Mrs. Barbauld's) attention to the fact that the professed moral is serviceable at least as an artistic device. The beautiful stanza beginning :

> He prayeth best who loveth best
> All things both great and small;

sets forth his professed moral. Its real effect is admirably described by Mrs. Oliphant, when she says that the soothing words "bring our feet back to the common soil with a bewildered sweetness of relief and soft quiet" after the imaginative strain with which we follow the tale of the voyage through strange seas. If any reader requires a moral he can find it elsewhere; he can find it in that passage which tells how a sense of the incomparable beauty and the rapturous life of the world quickens and redeems the withered soul of the Mariner. "How do you know", asks Blake, "but every bird that cuts the airy way is an immense world of delight closed by your senses five?" It is the opening of our senses and our hearts to the miracle of beauty and of life everywhere surrounding us that (if we must have a moral) is the highest spiritual fact wrought by the poem.

B.R. McElderry : *The Moral Sentiment is Obtrusive.* Keeping in mind professor Lowes' impressive defence of the moral as a structural element it is hard to see how Coleridge could have made an *Arabian Nights* tale of his poem without producing a new work. However, he may in this context have fallen into a natural exaggeration (one would expect Mrs. Barbauld to produce a violent reaction!) or he might have meant here by "moral" the quotable formula at the end. Certainly the repetition of :

> He prayeth well, who loveth well
> Both mass and bird and beast

at most the end of the poem does make the moral sentiment obtrusive...

It will be agreeable to believe that Coleridge did mean "some day" to revise this passage, for it is the one part in the poem that is definitely unsatisfactory to most readers. Professor Lowes argues eloquently, and I think, convincingly against Coleridge himself the validity of the moral as a structural element; he adds much to our understanding of how it is used. But has it ever been seriously contended that the idea of crime and punishment interfered with the poem's proper function? It is the obtrusiveness that disturbs, and this at only one point, the very end of the poem. Professor Lowes does not discuss this.... The formula is repeated for emphasis and the last lines of the poem impress it upon us that the Wedding-Guest has been a good pupil and has learned his lesson well. "A sadder and wise man/He rose the morrow morn." The return to the world of everyday, is bare and unrelieved. The finely dramatic effect of the sermon in the mouth of the Mariner himself, reading into his terrible experience a significance vital to him, is largely blotted out in the grey of the "morrow morn." The absence of poetic quality at so emphatic and strategic a point at the very end of the poem is, I believe many readers feel, a genuine flaw in the artistic unity of the work.

KUBLA KHAN

Graham Hough : ***Meaning of the Dream-Poem.*** *Kubla Khan* has the same quality of enchantment (as that of *The Ancient Mariner*), but it is more puzzling, partly because it is a fragment but for another reason, too : it is a fragment of a private experience, not of a universal one. Its origin is well known. It is composed in an opium dream; and before it can all be written out "a person on business from Porlock" interrupts the poet at his task, and when he returns to it, as commonly happens with dreams, all is gone. An immediate inspiration is again in *A Book of Voyages* that Coleridge was reading just before he fell asleep; and Livingstone Lowes has shown that echoes from many other travels are found in short fifty lines. But here it will be harder to look for the controlling purpose: if there is one, it is in Coleridge's private biography, in a region that is not accessible to his own inspection, and is still less to ours. Only a poet with a mind like Coleridge's as sensitive as his town Aeolian harp, can catch the dream-images in all their strangeness and authenticity, and the abiding fascination of the poem is that it is a fragment of psychic life of a kind which in the nature of things is rarely communicable to the outside world. Writing of this kind, without the usual logical and conceptual frame-work is sometimes 'pure-poetry'; it is not readily susceptible to analysis perhaps of a psychological kind.

However, this is not wholly impossible. The poem as it stands does present a meaning, consistent both with itself and with what we know of Coleridge's mind. The fact that a poem is not wholly or certainly explicable shall not discourage us from explaining it as well as we can. The opening lines suggest by a passage in *Purchas's Pilgrimage* that Coleridge is reading as he has entered his dream or reverie, describes an ideal landscape watered by a sacred river, of paradisal happiness, in which Kubla is such an all-powerful lord that he can create his pleasure-dome by mere decree. But in the succeeding lines (12-30) comes images of fear, enchantment, violent and uncontrollable energy, oblivion and death and foreboding of strife. The paradisal landscape is cleft by a chasm which is savage and fearsome, and from it a mighty fountain is forced, throwing up huge rocks: and the fountain turns out to be the sacred river itself bursting out after an underground sojourn like classical Alpheus from which its name Alph seems to be derived. It flows for a little in the open then disappears for good. And Kubla hears prophecies of war. The idyllic calm of the opening lines is threatened, and the movement of Alph seems to echo or symbolize this. Lines 31-6 add little, but bring us back to the pleasure-dome, shows it is reflected in the river, and bring it closely into contact both with the fountain (uncontrolled bounding energy) and—the caves (final annihilation).

Then we come to the last eighteen lines, of which Lowes said "the pageant is as aimless as it is magnificent." And here is the most characteristic dream-feature of the poem : the sudden switch from Kubla and Xanadu landscape. The poet now speaks in his own person and has a vision of an Abyssinian maid singing of Mount Abora. Mount Abora is Milton's Mount Amara (so written in an earlier manuscript), and Mount Amara is a fabled paradise, as we can see by consulting *Paradise Lost,* (IV, 268-84). So the Abyssinian maid is singing of a paradisal landscape very like that of the opening lines; singing in fact of the same cluster of ideas under different name and guise. And if he, the poet could re-live in his imagination her song, he himself can build the magic pleasure-dome as Kubla has done, he himself can become what Kubla is, a figure of power, of mystery and enchantment.

Explanation can be pushed much farther. This is enough to suggest that the poem, for all its dream-like air, is not unintelligible as Lowes suggests, and that what underlies it is the recurrent Coleridgean theme of poetic inspiration. Alph, the sacred river of the Muses, the poetic imagination itself, which is terrible as well as seductive, and threatened ultimately with conflict and extinction, as Coleridge later is too bitterly to know. Could he only recapture at will the vision of it, and the paradise through which it flows, all his dream-of poetry will get written and he will become the inspired magical prophet-bard which the quintessential romantic poet asks to be.

J. B. Beer : *Rich Complexity*. Coleridge's own assertion is that the poem is unfinished is probably sincere, for his notebook contains various notes on *Kubla Khan* and the *Tartars* which are no doubt collected with a continuation in mind. One can contain a poem in the middle, however, as well as at the end; and it is likely that this is his plan. Certainly it is difficult to see how the poem can be carried on after the last stanza: the argument is there brought to an end with overwhelming finality.

The argument of the poem as a whole might conceivably provide the basis of expansion at other points in the poem: its general drift is not very far removed from that of *Religious Musings* for example, a much longer poem. Nevertheless, it is clear that such an attempt on Coleridge's part would have been mistaken and probably impossible. The images of the poem are so tightly drawn together and so closely interlocked that any addition will upset its balance.

The chief characteristic of the poem, indeed, is its extraordinary compression: and if one is to make any objection to the poem it must be on these lines. As with the 'moral' of *The Ancient Mariner*, the trouble is not that the poem has no meaning, but that it has too much. The reader can hardly be expected to bring to mind all the complicated involutions of sense which it contains in the time that it takes him to read fifty lines of poetry. On the contrary, his attention is far likely to be caught throughout by the fascination of the sensuous imagery in its own right.

Nevertheless if *Kubla Khan* is a petrified forest, it is also an enchanted forest. At every point it glows directly and at every point also, it reflects the intense subterranean energy of a mind which can not rest in its endeavour to apprehend all experience and reduce it to one harmony. It will always remain possible to enjoy it as a simple stream of images, and to ignore the opportunity which it affords of exploring the intricacies of Coleridge's visionary world. To fascinate by these intricacies, one has first to share something of Coleridge's excitement at the potentialities of the basic images involved. Once we begin to sense this excitement however, and its climax is modelled itself into a single pattern, a paradigm that is also a focus of his major speculations in art and life, we may see that in this context more than any other poem is what Coleridge himself is the first to call it : "a vision in a dream".

Elizabeth Schneider : *Oscillating Images*. The central statement, through the first half of the poem, is one of the bright affirmation. The talk and activity are of building, the pleasure-dome and a delightful Paradise materialize. But even as the words give they take away with half-Miltonic negatives. Pleasure itself is rhymed with one of them—measureless; deprivation haunts the language. The negations recur in sunless, ceaseless, lifeless, a second measureless. The demon-lover is not a Paradise; he is as-if brought in to cast his shadow. Images of awe and mystery underlie Paradise in the subterranean river and ocean, and the ancestral threat of war is heard far off. The whole poem oscillates between giving and taking away, bright affirmation and sunless negation, light flowing music that nevertheless stands still and rings the portentuous sound of dome time after time.

The spirit of the poem, moreover, is cool and rather non-human. One feels no real warmth even in the sunny garden. And though the verse is nominally well-peopled, Kubla, the wailing woman, and the Abyssinian maid are not really there, and their half-presence leaves the place less human than if the theme are a poetic scene of nature alone. Even the poet, who is half-present in the end, is dehumanized behind his mask of hair and eyes and magic circle and is only present as mirrored in the exclamations of nebulous beholders, or rather, he will be mirrored if he has built his dome and if there has been beholders. Nor is there any human or personal feeling in the poem; the poet's "deep delight," impersonal enough even if it is there, exists only to be denied.

"Here in these interwoven oscillations dwells the magic, the "dream", and the air of mysterious meaning of *Kubla Khan*. I question whether this effect is all deliberately thought out by Coleridge, though it may have been. It is possibly half-inherent in his subject. Paradise is usually lost and always threatened, in Genesis and Milton, in the Paradise garden of Irem of Aloadin of Abyssinian princes. The historical Kubla did not apparently lose his in the end, but it too has threatened with war and dissension and portents. The Paradise of Coleridge's poem was not exactly lost either. What has lost, the closing lines tell us, is the vision of an unbuilt Paradise, an unwritten poem. His Paradise in that sense is truly enough a dream. What remains is the spirit of "oscillation", perfectly poeticized, and possibly ironically commemorative of the author.

CHRISTABEL

Charles Tomlinson : ***Meaning of Christabel.*** As far as the poem goes (it is a 'fragment') it is complete. The climax of :

> And turning from his own sweet maid
> The aged knight, Sir Leoline,
> Led forth the Lady Geraldine.

leaves Christabel in that condition of pathological isolation which the Mariner also feels and which Coleridge must himself have known. It follows upon the carefully ordered series of psychological knocks to which

Christabel has been subjected and beneath which her innocence is crushed. Mr. Humphry House says of the poem in his excellent book on Coleridge that it is 'fragmentary and finally unsatisfying' and that its mystery remains both incomplete and clueless. If one feels a certain incompleteness about the poem, it is because we are left with *Christabel's* pathological isolation which is never, unlike that of the *Ancient Mariner*, to be resolved (Indeed, of the Mariner's it will perhaps be more true to say that it is only partially resolved). The 'story' of course, is never completed and the element concerning the broken friendship between Sir Leoline and the father of Geraldine, relevant as they are to the poem's theme of the division of the inmost being end of the most intimate relationship, are never knit up into a more organic significance. *Christabel* offers, however, despite its abrupt conclusion in psychological status, a completeness concerning what does happen, if only we pay attention to the premonitory nature of the symbols at the opening and see the poetic interest as centring on the uncertain balance which is represented here between health and disease, good and evil, and the end as a tragedy in which neurosis, not death, strikes the final blow. One has in *Christabel*, in allegorical form, that same concern which is tormented the self-analyst of the notebooks and the reader of John Webster's Folio on *The Displaying of Supposed Witchcraft* : 'the mind's failure to guide the will'. For Christabel, bewitched, suffers simultaneously with the disintegration of personality the disintegration of the will.

Raymond Wilson : *The Striking Metre of Christabel.* Perhaps the most striking feature of the poem is its metre, which is manipulated by Coleridge with extraordinary sensitiveness. In claiming that the metrical principle of *Christabel* is new, Coleridge is doing less than justice to pre-Augustan lyric forms, but there can be no doubt that a free rhythmical movement, is based on counting are stressed syllables to the line, with a variable number of unstressed syllables, must have seemed revolutionary to readers still conditioned to the restricted measures of the heroic couplet:

> The night is chill; the forest bare;
> Is it the wind that moaneth bleak?
> To move away the ringlet curl
> From the lovely lady's cheek–
> There is no wind enough to twirl
> The one red leaf, the last of its clan,
> That dances as often as dance it can,
> Hanging so light, and hanging so high
> On the topmost twig that looks up at the sky...

In passages like this, the rhythms are as exquisitely modulated as the language is direct and pure, and in its description of glimmering wood and shadowy castle the first part of *Christabel* has moments of great beauty.

Even in part one, however, the poetry inclines towards stiltedness when it deals with action and characters. The passages just quoted continues :

> Hush, beating heart of Christable !
> Jesu, Maria, shield her well !
> She folded her arms beneath her cloak
> And stole to the other side of the oak.
> What sees she there?

Apart from the formal address to the heart and the archaic religious formula, the picture of Christabel, arms is folded beneath her cloak, has a theatrical 'period' which is heightened by the melodramatic use of the historic-present in 'What sees she there ?'

DEJECTION : AN ODE

Raymond Wilson : *Dejection* has all the vividness of the earlier Conversation Poems, and in the self-analysis that Coleridge gives of his failure—a postmortem by a merely alive medically, Coleridge on the poet that has died inside him thought and feeling are integrated more surely and powerfully than in any other of his poems. On a miniature scale, the poem resembles a tragedy. From a calm but menacing beginning it works to a tragic climax and subsides into something not unlike 'calm of mind, all passion spent'. A true tragic climax cannot, however, exist at the level of hysteria, and *Dejection,* superbly successful as it is in creating both the despair of loss and (paradoxically) the wonder of what is lost, breaks down at the very point where it ought to reach its greatest strength. Its pathos is more convincing than its tragic power, for at the moment when Coleridge becomes conscious of his restored power to feel, the poetry turns self-conscious and bardic in its declamation, not embodiment, of tragic emotion :

> Thou mighty poet, even to frenzy bold!
> What tell'st thou now about?

The tone is forced; not surprisingly, since the motion it expresses is not a natural, but an agonise is release.

FROST AT MIDNIGHT

Raymond Wilson : In *Frost at Midnight,* one of his finest poems, Coleridge harmonizes the physical world about him with his own mood. The inmates of the cottage have retired for the night and only his 'cradled infant', Hartley, sleeps at his side. He is contained in the 'hush of nature', which mutes 'the goings on of life' and makes them inaudible as dreams'. From the very first lines of the poems the silent operation of the frost is indistinguishable from the stealth of his own mind working in contemplation.

The Frost performs its secret ministry........and as it does so his mind ministers to its own 'abstruser musings'. As his eyes come to rest on the fragile life of a soot-flake on the grate, he recognises, even explicitly, that it is intimately associated with his mind's activity:

Only that film, which fluttered on the grate,
Still flutters there, the sole unquiet thing,
Methinks, its motion in this hush of nature
Gives it dim sympathies with me who live,
Making it a companionable form,
Whose puny flaps and freaks the idling spirit
By its own moods interprets, everywhere
Echo or mirror seeking of itself..........

As the flame plays with a furtive life of its own, so the poem develops in an interplay of memory and thought emerging from the shifting back into a psychically external environment, until the mind comes full circle to rest in the almost traced contemplation of :

Silent icicles
Quietly shining to the quiet moon.

It is interesting to relate Coleridge's practice here to what Keats in his letters call 'negative capability'. A poet having 'negative capability' surrenders himself completely to the objects of nature which he portrays and by taking part in their existence, gives them a sensuous reality in poetry.

Richard Gravil : In *Reflections* Coleridge is reflecting on the scene he presents, summarising his experience in somewhat general terms. The presence of Sara is stated in the presentation of the past, but is not active in the poem. The detail of the cottage is not particularly sharp, and the setting is rather abstractly presented as 'the Valley of seclusion'. Bristol is poetically called 'Bristowa'; the merchant is 'a son of commerce', an allegorical figure whose 'thirst for gold' (which may be a totally unfair judgement on the stranger) needs to be calmed by nature. The skylark is made the subject of a formal, moralising simile (19-28). The mount is also allegorically used, and is unrealistically described. Remnants of poetic cliche and rhetoric appears in the third paragraph on rose-leaf beds, pampering the coward heart', 'the sluggared Pity's vision waving tribe', 'the bloodless fight Of Science, Freedom and the truth in Christ'.

There is at the end of the poem the 'return' to the opening subject, which is common to the structure of all the conversation poems. But the reiteration of five words from the opening lines (Cot, Jasmin, Rose, Myrtle and sea) is purely formal. Only the sea has figured at all in the meditation. We are unlikely to feel that the repetition expresses more than nostalgia.

Frost at Midnight begins with an image of present activity and proceeds to specify very precisely the atmosphere in which the meditation is taking place and by which it is heightened. The co-presence of the sleeping baby and the 'ministry' of the frost is felt throughout the poem. The thoughts in the poem—whether about frost, or the moon, or the sooty film—are not ready-made and merely 'hung' on the peg of an appropriate image. The frosty calm is vexing the poet's meditation. The sooty film mirrors the poet's unquiet soul, and provides a direction for its thoughts. Paragraph two is caused by the imagery of paragraph one. The 'eternal language, which thy God/Utters' (60-61) has already been demonstrated by such communicative images. Finally, radiance of the moon—the timeless element in that night landscape.

The poem is marked by its subtlety in following the course of the poet's thought, which is at once intimate and yet concerned with vastness of time and space : past, present and future; earth and heaven. From the soot on the grate to the quiet moon, we are kept conscious of the moulding, shaping elements of nature and their 'sympathies' with each other and with man. The images are invested with clarity and separateness, but they are also unified in a felt harmony.

MISCELLANEOUS

Richard Gravil on *Christabel*. Quite literally, Coleridge transfers to this poem much of his own domestic experience; the relationship between Sir Leoline and Christabel partly reflects his own relationship with his children at this time. Like Hartley, Christabel is child of nature, and like Coleridge's children she experiences partial rejection in consequence of her father's state of mind. Presumably the complete poem would have been largely about the trial of innocence. As it stands, the fragment shows an innocent Christabel is caught between Geraldine's veiled wickedness and Sir Leoline's lack of insight. The child's only ally in the fragment is the poet, whose dream has the ring of truth. We do not know to what extent love, in the person of Christabel's betrothed knight, would have proved triumphant in the completed poem.

Beneath the fantastic surface, then, the poem deals with human universals. On the surface, too, Coleridge displays a skilful blend of symbolism and psychology. The veiled moon (of line 19) looks 'both small and dull'—an indication of troubled and obscured vision which is taken up later in the poem when Christabel's eyes ('so innocent and blue') imitate Geraldine's serpent-like glance ('a snake's small eye blinks dull and shy'). In her enchantment, Christabel becomes what she fears—her 'hiss' of indrawn breath, also, is both naturalistic and symbolic of the spell she is under.

The poem exhibits a conflict between some kind of embodied evil, and the girl's natural and religious grace. Geraldine is perhaps possessed by evil, rather than evil in herself. The portrait is ambiguous. We do not know whether she is to be pitied or feared, whether she will be redeemed or defeated by the forces of good. All that we have is a fascinating depiction of evil, mysterious and erotic, insinuating itself beneath Christabel's spiritual guard.

Richard Gravil on *Conversation Poems.* *This Lime-Tree Bower, Frost at Midnight* and *The Nightingale* are the finest examples of a form Coleridge invented: the 'conversation poem', or 'poems of friendship'. *The Eolian Harp* also belongs to this group, and *Reflections, To William Wordsworth, Fears in Solitude,* the verse *Letter to Sarah Hutchinson* and ever. *The Pains of Sleep* share some of the characteristics of the form. The critic G.M. Harper is first to apply the term 'conversation poem', which Coleridge uses only in *The Nightingale,* in this wider sense. Other critics prefer to include these poems in a broader group which M.H. Abrams calls 'the greater Romantic lyrics'.

The *Conversation Poem* is a development of lyric poetry, which terms we must define. Originally a lyric poem is intended to be sung, and is usually written in stanzas (groups of lines with a fixed pattern of rhyme and metre). Formally it may resemble ballad poetry, except that ballads tend to be longer. Moreover, the ballad is essentially a narrative poem-telling a story, usually objectively and in the third person—whereas the lyric is a personal utterance, expressing mood, feeling or reflection...

The development of a freer conversational cadence is not the only characteristic of the conversation poems. They are written in the style of intimate talk to an understanding auditor and in most cases we know who the imagined addressee is. The poems are addressed to his wife (early in their marriage), to William and Dorothy Wordsworth, to Charles Lamb, to his son Hartley, and to Sarah Hutchinson. This is far from being a formal gesture. Coleridge has a great gift for friendship and a great need for it. He wrote in a letter, 'Man is truly altered by the coexistence of other men: his faculties cannot be developed in himself alone, and only by himself'. His friends inspires powerful emotions in him, and grateful meditation on such emotions is part of his strategy for deepening his own self-awareness. That is not to say that the poems are self-centred, for one of their most striking characteristics is the generous, loving spirit we feel in them all.

In discussing lyric poetry, we sometimes speak of a 'lyric persona, when it seems improper to identify the speaker with the poet. In these poems, however, the speaker is undoubtedly Coleridge himself : this unambivalent indentity is one of the distinguishing features of the *Conversation Poems*. Furthermore, we know the precise biographical context of the poems, sometimes because we are explicitly told what the context is, and sometimes because it is easily inferred. The poems are usually about Coleridge in a particular state of mind, at a particular time. So speaker, auditor, and biographical context are made unusually explicit.

Furthermore, we have in each poem a precise specification of space and time. Sometimes the place and date of composition are stated: this habit is shared by all the Romantic poets, as in Shelley's stanzas written a few miles in *Dejection*, near Naples, Wordsworth's *Lines written a few miles above Tintern Abbey*: on revisiting the banks of the Wye during a tour, July 13, 1798. More characteristic of Coleridge is the care with which he specifies the time of day, the atmosphere, his exact surroundings, so that each poem has an easily visualised setting. It is not that he wants a picturesque frame for his meditation. Rather, the peculiar quality of these poems is that the landscape, or fireside, or nocturnal sounds, or garden sights, stimulate the meditation that takes place and helps to influence the direction his thoughts take. When a dramatic change occurs in the course of the poem it may be caused by some train of association in the poet's mind, or by a freak of memory, or by something outside him altogether; inner and outer are partners in the process. Remember that Coleridge thought of art as 'the reconciler of nature and man'. In these poems, he comes closest to fulfilling his poetic aim of 'infusing the thoughts and passions of man into everything which is the object of his contemplation' and reconciling 'what is nature with that which is exclusively human'.

S.T. COLERIDGE : SELECTED POEMS

9

THE RIME OF THE ANCIENT MARINER

(A) TEXT, PARAPHRASE AND ANNOTATIONS IN SEVEN PARTS

Facile credo, plures esse Naturas invisibles quam visibiles in rerum universitate. Sed horum omnium familiam quis nobis enarrabit? et gradus et cognationes et discrimina et singulorum munera? Quid agunt? quae loca habitant? Harum rerum notitiam semper ambivit ingenium humanum, nunquam attigit. Juvat, interea, non diffiteor, quandoque in animo, tanquam in tabula, majoris et melioris mundi imaginem contemplari: ne mens assuefaeta hodiernae vitae minutiis se contrahat nimis, et tota subsidat in pusikllas cogitationes. Sed veritati interea invigilandum et, modusque servandus, ut certa ab incertis, diem a incertis, diem a nocte, distinguamus. -T.BURNET, Archaeol. Phil. P-68

ARGUMENT

How a Ship, having passed the Line, was driven by storms to the cold Country towards the South Pole; and how from thence she made her course to the tropical Latitude of the Great Pacific Ocean; and of the strange things that befell; and in what manner the Ancient Mariner came back to his own Country (1798).

PART I

IT is an ancient Mariner,
    And he stoppeth one of three.
'By thy long grey beard and glittering eye,
    Now wherefore stopp'st thou me ?
The Bridegroom's doors are opened wide,
    And I am next of kin;
The guests are met, the feast is set :
    May'st hear the merry din.'

An ancient Mariner meeteth three Gallants bidden to a wedding-feast, and detaineth one.

He holds him with his skinny hand,
    'There was a ship', quoth he.
'Hold off ! unhand me, grey-beard loon !'
    Eftsoons his hand dropt he.

L. 1-4. Ancient Mariner—Coleridge uses the word 'ancient' not merely to signify extreme old age but also to lend some supernatural charm. Anything which is very old and very distant has got some unearthliness about it. Note the abrupt beginning. **One of three**—one of the three wedding guests, whom he chooses particularly to listen to his tale. Note that "three" has a mystical significance. **By**

COMPLETE PARAPHRASE

PART I

L. 1-8. An ancient Mariner has stopped one of the three guests who are going to a wedding party. The guest has resented it and asks why he has been stopped. He is anxious to go soon because he is a near relative of the bridegroom. He says that the reception has started, the guests have assembled and the feast has been arranged. The guest has enquired the Mariner with 'grey beard' and 'glittering eye' to tell him why he is being stopped.

L. 9-12. The Mariner has caught him by the hand and began to tell his story. The Guest did not like this. He has asked him in anger to leave him and keep away. The Mariner immediately left his hand.

---

thy long grey beard ...eye—In the name of your long grey beard and bright eyes. 'Long grey beard' and 'glittering eye' are touches of mystery. At the same time these terms give a vividness to the description of the old man. 'Glittering eye' is a mark of sharp intelligence or of great will power which the ancient Mariner exercises over the wedding guest. These striking features are referred to again and again in the poem. **wherefore**—why. **Wherefore....me**-why do you detain me? It is not a mere inquiry but an expression of annoyance, impatience, nervousness and also a consciousness of some coming mystery yet to be revealed.

L. 5-8. The Bridegroom's ... wide—i.e., the marriage party is eagerly waiting for the wedding guests. The statement also reflects the impatience of the wedding guest. **I am next of kin**—I am very closely related to the bridegroom, and hence, it is all the more necessary for me to join the marriage party as early as possible. **the feast is set**—the marriage dinner is laid on the table. **May'st hear the merry din**—you can hear the noise made by the marriage party who are enjoying the happy function. **din**-confused noise. **The guests are met...merry din**—This is an other dramatic touch of the poet to express the impatience of the wedding guest.

L. 9-12. Holds him-detain him, skinny hand-bony and thin hand. **He holds him....hand**-It is not the skinny hand but the will power of the ancient Mariner that detains the wedding guest. **quoth**-said. Note how the old man begins his story without heeding the guest's words. This is another weird touch. **Hold off**-Take off your hands, **unhand me**—leave me or take your hand off me. loon-a mean or worthless fellow or a rascal. **Eftsoons**-soon afterwards or immediately. The archaiç phraseology suggests the atmosphere of by-gone days. However, in the very next line we will be told that he has got a great will-power by which he can detain the wedding guest as he actually-holds him with his glittering eye.

He holds him with his glittering eye-
The Wedding-Guest stood still,
And listens like a three-years' child :
The Mariner hath his will.

The Wedding-Guest is spell-bound by the eye of the old seafaring man, and constrained to hear his tale.

The Wedding Guest sat on a stone :
He cannot choose but hear;
And thus spoke on that ancient man,
The bright-eyed Mariner.

'The ship was cheered, the harbour cleared,
Merrily did we drop
Below the kirk, below the hill,
Below the light-house top.

The Mariner tells how the ship sailed southward with good wind and fair weather, till it reached the line.

The Sun came up upon the left,
Out of the sea came he !
And he shone bright, and on the right
Went down into the sea.

Higher and higher every day
Till over the mast at noon—
The Wedding-Guest here beat his breast,
For he heard the loud bassoon.

L. 13-16. He holds him... eye.—The ancient Mariner like a hypnotist detains the wedding guest by merely looking at him fixedly and by exercising his will-power. The guest is fascinated into listening to the old Mariner. **Listens like a three years' child**—listens most helplessly or with the greatest possible attention, with the docility of a three-year old child. The change in the wedding guest's attitude is complete. (These two lines were Wordsworth's contribution). **The Mariner hath his will**—The Mariner has got his way in detaining as well as in compelling the wedding guest to listen to his story.

L. 17-20. Sat on a stone—This is a natural touch. Besides, sitting signifies complete surrender on the part of the wedding guest to the will of the Mariner. **He cannot choose but hear**—the wedding guest is compelled to listen to the ancient Mariner though in the beginning he was in a hurry to attend the marriage party. **Spoke on**-continued relating the story. **bright-eyed**—this is a synonym for 'glittering eye' signifying the uncanny look and the will power of the Mariner.

L. 21-24. The Ship was cheered-The friends and relatives who came to see off the sailors and passengers on the ship bade them farewell and wished them a prosperous voyage. **The harbour cleared**—the ship got out of the harbour. **Merrily did we drop**—With a joyous heart-or with a favourable wind we put

L. 13-16. After releasing the hand the Mariner holds the Guest with his glittering eye. The Wedding-Guest is spellbound. He become helpless like a child and the Mariner has complete hold over him.

L. 17-20. The Wedding-Guest is spellbound and is compelled to hear the story. He, therefore, sit on a stone and the old man begins his story.

L. 21-24. As the ship set sail, people has cheered it and ha give in good wishes. The port is left behind and the ship begin to move with the tide. As it advance the church, the hill and the lighthouse disappeare one after another.

L. 25-28. The ship moves southwards. The sun rises on the left side from the horizon. It shine brightly and goes down on the right.

L. 29-32. As they moves on, the sun rose higher and higher. At last when they reach the Equator, it appeares at noon right at the top. As the Mariner is telling this, the sound of musical instruments make the Wedding-Guest remember his relatives and the party. He feel very restless and beat his breast.

L. 33-36. The guest remember the marriage ceremony that is been going on. The bride is as beautiful as a red rose. She has entered the hall. Before she has walked the musicians nodds their heads as they play on their instruments and sings.

---

out to sea with the ebbing tide. **kirk**—church. Again an archaic word. Note the abrupt and dramatic way of beginning the story. The realism and vividness of the description here will help us to believe the fantastic happenings that are to follow. In truth it is a voyage from the world of reality into the world of imagination.

L. 25-28. upon the left—i.e. in the east which was on the left side of the ship as she left the harbour and got out into the open sea. **Out of the sea came he**—This is a realistic touch. Those who have gone on a voyage must have seen how the sun seems to rise exactly Out of the sea where the sky and the sea seem to meet. **On the right...the sea**—i.e., set in the west, which was on the right side of the ship. The whole stanza is beautiful for the simplicity of language. The ship is apparently travelling southwards.

L. 29-32. Higher and higher...at noon—the sun rose higher and higher in the sky till he shone exactly over the head i.e., reached the meridian. It also indicates the ship nearing the equator where the sun gets more and more overhead, **beat his breast**—expressed his impatience and helplessness. It is a realistic touch. **he heard the loud bassoon**—he heard the music of the marriage party. A bassoon is a wind instrument producing a deep sound.

The bride hath paced into the hall,
Red as a rose is she;
Nodding their heads before her goes
The merry minstrelsy.

The Wedding Guest heareth the bridal music, but the Mariner continueth his tale.

The Wedding-Guest he beat his breast,
Yet he cannot choose but hear;
And thus spake on that ancient man,
The bright-eyed Mariner.

'And now the STORM-BLAST came, and he
Was tyrannous and strong :
He struck with his o'ertaking wings,
And chased up south along.

The ship driven by a storm toward the south pole.

With sloping masts and dipping prow,
As who pursuel with yell and blow
Still treads the shadow of his foe,
And forward bends his head,
The ship drove fast, loud roared the blast,
And southward aye we fled.

And now there came both mist and snow,
And it grew wondrous cold:
And ice, mast-high, came floating by.
As green as emerald.

And through the drifts the snowy clifts
Did send a dismal sheen
Nor shapes of men nor beasts we ken—
The ice was all between.

The land of ice, and of fearful sounds where no living thing was to be seen.

L. 33-36. paced into the hall—stepped into the hail. **Red as a rose is she**—she is beautiful as a rose i.e., exceedingly beautiful. **Nodding their...goes**—tossing their heads to music as they pass through the half before the bride. The **merry minstrelsy**—the joyous band of musicians.

L. 37-40. This stanza is a repetition of the lines in the preceding stanza as is the case with all ballad poetry.

L. 41-44. Storm Blast—sudden gust of violent wind or stormy weather. **he was tyrannous and strong**—The storm is personified. The storm was exceedingly powerful and violent or destructive. **He struck....wings**—The storm swept at a higher speed than that of the ship and hence, it overtook the ship very easily. The storm is described as a bird of prey. **chased us south along**—i.e., drove our ship southwards.

L. 37-40. The Wedding-Guest is impatient to leave but is helpless. Under the magic influence of the Mariner he has to listen to the tale that the old man continues to tell.

L. 41-44. Soon after a furious and violent storm comes. It is very strong and has drove the ship up to the South Pole.

L. 45-50. The blast is blowing fast and loud. Under its force the ship is driven southward very fast. The masts of the ship are bent forward so that it appears to be something fleeing before a cruel pursuer.

L. 51-54. They have reached a region where there is a lot of mist. It abounds with icebergs. It is very cold. The icebergs are emerald green in colour and are as tall as the mast of the ship.

L. 55-58. The snow-covered cliffs shine in a gloomy light; neither a human figure nor a beast is visible. Everywhere there is nothing but snow.

L. 45-50. With sloping masts and dipping prow—Some of the annotators have wrongly taken "sloping masts" in the sense of "bent masts" and have explained that due to the heavy wind the masts are bent. However, if the masts are bent by the force of the wind they will positively break because they are made of such wood which cannot be bent without being broken. The masts look sloping because the ship itself bends forward with the rolling waves of the sea in a stormy weather. Prow is the fore part of a ship or boat. When the wind is heavy and strong and the waves rise high, the ship is rocked continually on the rolling waves, and naturally the fore part is actually dipped into the water every time the ship descends from the crest of a rolling wave, **with yell and blow**—with shouts and threats of violence and blows because in the case of the ship it is being actually struck by the wind. **Still treads.....foe**—i.e., is so closely followed by the enemy that the enemy's shadow falls on the victim and the victim treads the shadow. **drove fast**—moved with speed pushed by the storm. **aye**—all the time. The lines draw a vivid picture of the progress of the ship in a heavy storm.

L. 51-54. wondrous cold—exceedingly cold. **Ice mast-high**—huge blocks of ice (better known as icebergs) as tall as the ship's mast. **emerald**—a precious stone, bright green in colour. The ship has now entered the polar region, the land of mist and snow.

L. 55-58. drifts—currents. It may be used in the case of water, snow or rain. Here it stands for the heavy currents or gusts of wind and rain mixed with snow. **snowy clifts**—'Clifts' has been variously interpreted as cliff. i.e., rocks or as clefts or openings, in the icebergs or in the storm, or as icebergs themselves, **dismal sheen**—gloomy and fearful brightness, shapes of men- forms of human beings. **ken**—discern; make out. **The ice was all between**—The ice was lying everywhere.

The ice was here, the ice was there,
The ice was all around:
It cracked and growled, and roared and howled,
Like noises in a swound!

Till a great sea bird, called the Albatross, came through the snow-fog and was received with great joy and hospitality.

At length did cross an Albatross,
Thorough the fog it came;
As if it had been a Christian soul,
We hailed it in God's name.

It ate the food it ne'er had eat,
And round and round it flew.
The ice did split with a thunder-fit;
The helmsman steered us through!

And lo I the Albatross proveth a bird of good omen, and followeth the ship as it returned northward, through fog and floating ice.

And a good south wind sprung up behind;
The Albatross did follow,
And every day, for food or play,
Came to the mariner's hollo!

In mist or cloud, on mast or shroud,
It perched for vespers nine;
Whiles all the night, through fog-smoke white.
Glimmered the white Moon-shine.'

L. 59-62. It cracked...howled—An example of onomatopoea in which the sound signifies the sense. The sound of cracking and growling, roaring and howling gives us an exact picture of the icebergs crashing against one another. **Like noises in a swound**—Swound is archaic for swoon, or fainting fit. Whether it is a fact or not, people believe that when one is in a fainting fit or in a state of unconsciousness, one hears confused voices or sounds. The line adds to the supernatural atmosphere of the scene. Besides, "just as the intense cold forms so marked a contrast with the fiery heat of the coming scene to which all this is but leading, so do these fearful noises prepare, by contrast, for the fearful silence to follow". (P.T. Creswell)

L. 63-66. At length—after a long time. **did cross**—i.e., appeared. **Albatross**—a very large seabird found mostly in the tropics particularly in the south of Cape of Good Hope. The Albatross looks much like a goose though it is much bigger than a goose. **Thorough**—through. **As if it had been...in God's name**—We heartily welcomed the Albatross as if it was a human being with divine associations. Of course, on a long voyage even birds are welcome because there is no other life visible except the passengers and the crew. The coming of the Albatross is mysterious and sudden, **hailed**—greeted. It should be noted that every word in the line will be contradicted afterwards by the Mariner's conduct.

L. 59-62. There is ice on all sides. The icebergs are cracking and a fierce sound is produced. These noises seems to be like the noises heard in a fainting fit or dream.

L. 63-66. At last, an Albatross come through the mist. The Mariners welcomes it in the name of God as if it is a human being belonging to the Christian faith.

L. 67-70. The Albatross has got food from the sailors. Such food it has never eaten before. It fly around the ship. As it do so the icebergs splits up and the way become clear for the ship. The steersman has guided the ship through the split ice.

L. 71-74. A favourable south-wind begin to blow and drive the ship from behind. The bird is still following it. It become friendly with the mariners. Everyday it eat and play with them.

L. 75-78. The bird come to the ship and sit on the mast or ropes at the time of evening prayers. It continues to do so for nine days. At night the moonlight has shone through the mist.

L. 67-70. It ate the food.......eat—The Albatross took human food as it was offered by the sailors, and hence, the food it took from the hands of the sailors was something which it had never formerly eaten. **split**—break to pieces. **thunder-fit**—loud sound resembling the peals of thunder. The Mariner's belief is that it was because of the appearance of the Albatross that the ice began to split. This is of course a superstitious belief which is perfectly in keeping with the supernatural atmosphere of the scene. **The helmsman...through**—as the ice broke up the ship sailed on easily.

L. 71-74. sprung up behind—began to blow from behind to move the ship forward hollo-cry or call. **For food.....hollo**—whenever the sailors called the Albatross either to take food from their hands or to play, it at once responded to their call.

L. 75-78. shroud—ropes from the mast head fastened to ship's side. This word is significant here. 'Shroud' generally means the winding sheet or cloth for the dead body. The poet uses it probably to strike the keynote of the coming death of the sailors and the sails serving as a shroud for them. The word add just a touch of horror anticipating the scene which is yet to be unrolled. **vespers nine**—nine evenings. Nine is a mystic number like 3, 7, 13 etc., which also helps to add to the supernatural atmosphere of the scene. Usually 'vesper' is used for 'evening prayer.' Again the association of divinity with the bird. **fog-smoke white**—fog which looks like thick white smoke. **Glimmered**—glittered or sparkled or shone brightly.

'God save thee, ancient Mariner !
From the fiends, that plague thee thus !
Why look'st thou so?' With my cross-bow
I shot the ALBATROSS.

The ancient Mariner inhospitably killeth the pious bird of good omen.

PART II

The Sun now rose upon the right:
Out of the sea came he,
Still hid in mist, and on the left
Went down into the sea.

And the good south wind still blew behind,
But no sweet bird did follow,
Nor any day for food or play
Came to the mariners' hollo !

And I had done a hellish thing,
And it would work 'em woe:
For all averred, I had killed the bird
That made the breeze to blow.
Ah wretch ! said they, the bird to slay,
That made the breeze to blow !

His shipmates cry out against the ancient Mariner, for killing the bird of good luck.

Nor dim nor red, like God's own head,
The glorious Sun uprist :
Then all averred. I had killed the bird
That brought the fog and mist.
'Twas right, said, they, such birds to slay,
That brings the fog and mist.

But when the fog cleared off, they justify the same, and thus make themselves accomplices in the crime.

L. 79-82. fiends--devils or evil spirits. The word suggests that something evil prompted the Mariner to shoot the bird. **plague thee thus**—torture you so much. **Why look'st thou so?**—Why do you look so pale and horrified? **God save thee,....thou so**?' The wedding guest notices in the face of the ancient Mariner marks of extreme pain fear and horror-ball of which are due to the Mariners s consciousness of sin for having killed the Albatross, which he confess in the next line, **With my cross-bow...Albatross**—How dramatically and how briefly the Mariner describes the climax of the story, namely, the killing of the Albatross, which in itself may be a trifling incident but is full of significance in the context of the story. The first part of the poem ends with a direct reference to the wanton act of killing the Albatross.

L. 83-86. Practically a repetition of L. 25-28 in Part I except the reversal in the direction of the sun and the ship. Having doubled Cape Horn, the ship is sailing northward.

L. 79-82. The Wedding—Guest sees sign of pain on the face of the Mariner and ask him the reason for it. The Mariner can not say much. In an abrupt manner, he state that he has killed the Albatross with his cross-bow.

PART II

L. 83-86. As the ship has moved northward, the sun rises on the right and set in the sea on left. But all along it is hidden in the mist.

L. 87-90. The beneficial south wind continues to blow from behind, but the bird is no longer there. It no longer responds to the mariners' call for it to have food or play.

L. 91-96. The sailors accuses the Ancient Mariner of having committed a wicked crime which will bring trouble for all. They condemn his action for they have thought that the bird has brought the good breeze.

L. 97-102. The fog clears and brilliant sunshine appears. As the sailors see this, they changes their attitude towards the killing of the Albatross. Now they have opined that the Albatross has brought the mist and fog and that killing such birds is right.

L. 87-90. We notice how earlier events are repeated with significant changes-the Albatross is not there nor does it come for food or to play to the Mariner's call.

L. 91-96. a hellish thing—a mean and cruel act, namely, the killing of innocent Albatross. **it would work 'em woe**—The killing of the Albatross would bring some kind of misfortune to the sailors, **'em**—them, **averred**—asserted, declared. **I had killed...breeze to blow**—Mark the superstition of the sailors; they unanimously believed that the wind ceased to blow simply because the Albatross had been killed by the ancient Mariner. **Ah wretch**—the sailors curse the ancient Mariner and call him a miserable creature.

L. 97-102. Nor dim nor red—neither very faint nor extremely bright. **Like God's own head**—as bright and glorious as God itself. Every God or saint is painted with a halo round his head probably because brightness is considered as a mark of purity or holiness, **glorious sun**—bright sun. **uprist**—rose up. **Then all averred......mist**—Mark how the sailors are fickleminded. A moment ago they declared that the Albatross was a bird of good omen and hence it was a sin to have killed such a bird. But now that the mist and fog have cleared they declare exactly the opposite thing. This shows that they do not judge things by any moral standard but by the standard of utility or selfishness. As often as the omens change, so often do the sailors change their mind. Thus, the sailors make themselves accomplices in the crime along with the ancient Mariner and suffer no less than he. What is more, do they not have the redeeming feature of consistency.

The fair breeze blew, the white foam flew,
The furrow followed free;
We were the first that ever burst
Into that silent sea.

The fair breeze continues; the ship enters the Pacific Ocean and sails north-ward, even till it reaches the Line.

Down dropt the breeze, the sails dropt down,
'Twas sad as sad could be;
And we did speak only to break
The silence of the sea !

The ship hath been suddenly becalmed.

All in a hot and copper sky,
The bloody Sun, at noon,
Right up above the mast did stand,
No bigger than the Moon.

Day after day, day after day,
We stuck, nor breath nor motion;
As idle as a painted ship
Upon a painted ocean.

Water, water, every where,
And all the boards did shrink;
Water, water, every where.
Nor any drop to drink.

And the Albatross begins to be avenged.

The very deep did rot ! O Christ :
That ever this should be !
Yea, slimy things did crawl with legs
Upon the slimy sea.

L. 103-106. These lines are often quoted to illustrate the use of alliteration-a figure of speech in which the first letter of each of the words in the same line has the same sound, and it has a musical effect upon the ear. Mark breeze and blew; foam and flew; furrow, followed and free; first and burst, silent and sea. The lines reflect the swift movement of the ship. **furrow**—a track cut out by the ship in the water as it moves forward. **The furrow followed free**—the water was easily cut by the ship because there was no ice to block the passage and a fair wind pushed at the sails. **that ever burst**—who ever appeared or sailed. The ship has entered the Pacific Ocean. A new phase has begun but it has been introduced without fanfare, smoothly, as if the listener too knows all about 'that silent sea'.

L. 107-110. Down dropt...dropt down-the wind ceased to blow and consequently the sails hung still. **'T was sad...could be**—The whole situation was miserable because the ship was stranded in mid-ocean without wind or wave. **We did speak.. .of the sea**—We spoke only to forget the monotony or wretchedness of the situation. Besides, there being no sound of wind or wave it was a relief for words to break that silence. Note how the quality of stillness is conveyed by the

L. 103-106. The wind is favourable and the white foam fly from the surface of the water, and as the ship advances, leaves behind a clear track. They are the first people to have suddenly entered the great Pacific Ocean.

L. 107-111. Suddenly the wind has stopped blowing and the sails of the ship has hung loosely. An atmosphere of utmost sadness has prevailed. There is complete silence all around. The only sound audible is made by the sailors speaking to one another.

L. 111-114. It is extremely hot. The sky has changed colour to dull copper. At noon the sun is of blood red colour and it shines right on top of the ship. It appears to be no bigger than the moon.

L. 115-118. For days together they can not move and remain stuck at one place. The wind do not blow and the ship do not move. It looks like the picture of a ship in the painting of an ocean.

L. 119-122. Although there is water on all sides, it does not help the sailors. The wooden planks are contracting because of extreme heat. On the ship the supply of drinking water is exhausted and more is not available even though there is water all around them.

L. 123-126. Even the sea begins to rot. Repulsive creatures can be seen crawling about with ugly legs on the sticky and muddy-looking water.

---

slow, rhythmic movement of the verse. A sense of helplessness is created by the halting lines.

L. 111-114. All—used for emphasis **a hot and copper sky**—When the sun shines brightly at noon, the whole sky looks like a sheet of heated copper. (The Mariner's guilt and the fate of the ship are closely linked to nature's mood) **The bloody sun**—the red-coloured sun. Of course, the sun never looks bloody at noon. Mark the contrast with the 'glorious sun' in Line 98. **Right up...did stand**—the sun always reaches the meridian at noon and noon is also the hottest period in the tropical countries. **No bigger than the moon**—i.e., as small as the moon.

L. 115-118. Day after day...day—The repetition of the words signifies monotony of the situation. **We stuck**—our ship stood motionless. **nor breath nor motion**—neither wind nor tide. **As idle as...painted ocean**—As motionless as a ship in a painting. These are famous lines perfectly picturising a becalmed ship on a completely still ocean.

L. 119-122. All the boards did shrink—the wooden planks of the ship contracted or got warped due to extreme heat. **Water, water..to drink**—the idea is that there was plenty of water in the sea but it was not drinkable.

L. 123-126. The very deep did rot—The sea was so still that it began to rot. A stagnant pond, for instance, rots. The poetic exaggeration conveys the horror of the situation. **O Christ...should be**—O God, that such a dreadful thing should happen! This is an appeal to God for mercy and help. **Yea**—Yes: used for emphasis. **slimy things**—slippery and hateful creatures covered in mud. **Crawl with legs**—Move slowly in the mud that is the sea. The lines convey hideousness of the spectacle. It is an expression of hatred and loathing for creatures of the sea or for the lower creations of God. The idea is that it is only the sinner who hates God's creations while the pious soul loves all creatures, great and small.

About, about, in reel and rout
    The death-fires danced at night;
The water, like a witch's oils,
    Burnt green, and blue and white.

And some in dreams assured were
    Of the Spirit that plagued us so:
Nine fathom deep he had followed us
    From the land of mist and snow.

And every tongue, through utter drought,
    Was withered at the root;
We could not speak, no more than if
    We had been choked with soot.

A Spirit had followed them; one of the invisible inhabitants of this planet, neither departed souls nor angels; concerning whom the learned Jew, Josephus, and the Platonic constantinopolitan, Michael Psellus, may be consulted. They are very numerous, and there is no climate or element without one or more.

    Ah ! well a-day ! what evil looks
    Had I from old and young!
    Instead of the cross, the Albatross
    About my neck was hung.

The shipmates, in their sore distress, would fain throw the whole guilt on the ancient Manner; in sign whereof they hang the dead sea-bird round his neck.

PART III

There passed a weary time. Each throat
    Was parched, and glazed each eye.
A weary time! a weary time!
    How glazed each weary eye,
When looking westward, I beheld
    A something in the sky.

The Ancient Mariner beholdeth a sign in the element afar off.

L. 127-130. **reel and rout**—a whirling and confused motion, as of a dance. **death-fires**—The phosphorescent light which is common at night in the sea, as they are generated by a kind of sea-fish. **Witch's oils**—ingredients which the witches use for magic preparations. The reader must be reminded of the witches and their boiling cauldrons in Shakespeare's Macbeth.

L. 131-134. Some in dreams assured were—Some of the sailors in a state of half-wakefulness were convinced. **The spirit**—the Polar Spirit who felt offended at the killing of the Albatross and who wanted to avenge the bird. **plagued**—tortured. **Nine fathom deep**—much below the water. Note again the use of 'nine' a mystical number.

L. 135- 138. through utter drought—through extreme dryness. **withered at the root**—was absolutely dry. **choked with soot**—suffocated or filled with smoke particles i.e., unable to speak.

L. 139-142. Ah! well-a-day!—Alas! an expression of distress and despair. **What evil looks...young!**—The Mariner means to say that though the sailors kept quiet and could not speak at all, their very looks cursed him bitterly. **Instead**

L. 127-130. Round about the ship death-fires shines. The fires are of different colours and looks like the fire produces when the witches burnt oils for their evil incantations.

L. 131-134. Some of the sailors has dreamt that they are victims of a revenge of the Polar Spirit which has been following them nine fathom deep in the sea since the Albatross has been killed in the land of mist and snow.

L. 135-138. There is no water to drink. The sailors' tongues has dried at the very root. It is not possible to speak. They feel as if they are suffocated by smoke.

L. 139-142. What a sad day it is! young and old, all the sailors looks at the Ancient Mariner with anger. They have hung the dead Albatross round his neck in the place of the cross.

PART III

L. 143-148. They have passed a very tiresome time. Their throats are dry and the eyes of the sailors has looked glassy. When the Ancient Mariner has looked westward, he see some object, 'but he can not properly make out its shape.

---

of the cross,... was hung—the Cross is holy to the Christians because it is an emblem of Christ who died on the Cross for man's salvation. Christians wear the Cross round their neck as a protection against evil influences. Here the Mariner says that instead of the Cross he was made to wear the dead body of the Albatross round his neck. The dead body of the Albatross here represents the curse of the Mariners and the punishment for the crime of having killed the bird. The sailors by this act fix the sole responsibility of the sin on the old Mariner. Like Part I, this part too ends with a significant reference.

L. 143-148. Weary time—a tedious and miserable time. **glazed**—glassy. When the eyes are fixed and motionless due to fear or horror they look glassy or glazed. **A weary time! a weary time!**—The words are repeated here for the sake of emphasis. It adds to the intensity of suffering. **I beheld...in the sky**—I saw some strange sign at a distance. This sign on a nearer view was found to be a skeleton ship. This indefinite term· a something' is used only to mystify the situation.

At first it seemed a little speck,
And then it seemed a mist;
It moved and moved, and took at last
A certain shape, I wist.

A speck, a mist, a shape, I wist !
And still it neared and neared:
As if it dodged a water-sprite,
It plunged and tacked and veered.

With throats unslaked, with black lips baked,
We could nor laugh nor wail;
Through utter drought all dumb we stood !
I bit my arm, I sucked the blood,
And cried, A sail ! a sail !

At its nearer approach, it seemeth him to be a ship; and at a dear ransom he freeth his speech from the bonds of thirst.

With throats unslaked, with black lips baked,
Agape they heard me call :
Gramercy ! they for joy did grin,
And all at once their breath drew in,
As they were drinking all.

A flash of joy;

See!see! (I cried) she tacks no more !
Hither to work us weal;
Without a breeze, without a tide,
She steadies with upright keel!

And horror follows. For can it be a ship that comes onward without wind or tide?

L. 149-152. **Speck,**—a small point or dot. **a mist**—a larger shadow as compared with a speck, but the outlines of the shape not yet clear. **A certain shape**—some form or other or a definite form. **wist**—knew. The lines describe the slow approach of a ship from the distance. Things at a great distance appear like a speck or a small point but as they draw nearer and nearer they appear bigger and bigger to the view and also more well marked and definite in their form.

L. 153-156. **dodged**—tried to avoid or escape. **Water-sprite**—water spirit. The superstitious mind believes that all the elements of nature-earth, air, water, fire, ether-are presided over by deities or spirits. The elements of supernatural is reinforced. **Plunged**—went deep into the water. **tacked and veered**—changed course by turning against or with the wind. The object moved in a zig-zag manner. How unusual in a becalmed ocean.

L. 157-161. **unslaked**—unmoistened. **black lips baked**—lips parched by heat and thirst **wail**—cry out with pain. **I bit my arm...blood**—The ancient

L. 149-152. The thing at first seems merely a small spot. Then it looks like a patch of mist. Gradually as it is moved nearer, it takes on a definite shape.

L. 153-156. Certainly the thing is developed from a spot and a mist to a definite shape, as the Ancient Mariner lookes at it. It is coming nearer still. The way it moves in a zig-zag manner suggests that it is trying to escape some spirit of the water.

L. 157-161. The throats and lips of the sailors are dried up because of heat and thirst. As such they can neither laugh nor weep. Finding no other way the Mariner has bit his arm and moisten his throat with his own blood. He then cries out that a ship is approaching them.

L. 162-166. With dry throats and lips they have looked with surprise at the Ancient Mariner when he has announced the approach of the ship. They have thanked God for mercy. They can not speak but have showed their teeth in joy. They draw in their breath as if they have already drank water.

L. 167-170. The Mariner has pointed out to his companions that the ship is no longer changing her course. It is coming to do good to them. The surprising thing is that it is moving steadily without the help of wind or tide.

Mariner moistened his throat with his blood in order to speak. **a sail**—a ship was visible.

L. 162-166, With throats...baked—A repetition of the first line in the preceding stanza for the sake of emphasis. **Agape**—with mouth wide open i.e., with wonder and curiosity. **Gramercy**—great mercy; many thanks to God. **They for joy did grin**—The sailors when they heard of the ship tried to laugh with joy but because they had lost their power of speech due to extreme thirst, they simply opened their lips a little and showed their teeth partly so that their expression of joy mixed with a feeling of pain was more like a grin than like a smile. **all at once their breath...drinking all**—The sailors thought that the ship visible at a distance was bringing water for them, and hence they mechanically drew a long breath fancying that they were actually drinking water. A remarkable psychological and pathetic touch to indicate the feelings of the suffering sailors.

L. 167-171). she tacks no more—the ship is not changing her course any more i.e., she is coming straight forward. **Hither to work us weal**—The ship is coming here in order to give us relief. **Weal** means comfort, happiness, **without a breeze...upright keel**—The ship is mosing without any wind or wave. This enhances the unnatural atmosphere. **Steadies with upright keel**—balances herself upon the water without leaning sideways. 'Keel' is the backbone of a ship i.e., the main plank from stem to stern to which all other side planks are joined to make the complete body.

The western wave was all a-flame.
  The day was well nigh done !
Almost upon the western wave
  Rested the broad bright Sun;
When that strange shape drove suddenly
  Betwixt us and the Sun.

And straight the Sun was flecked with bars,
  (Heaven's Mother send us grace!)
As if through a dungeon-grate he peered
  With broad and burning face.

It seemeth him but the skeleton of a ship.

Alas ! (thought I, and my heart beat loud)
  How fast she nears and nears !
Are those her sails that glance in the Sun,
  Like restless gossameres?

Are those her ribs through which the Sun
Did peer, as through a grate?
And is that Woman all her crew?
Is that a Death? and are there two?
Is Death that Woman's mate?

And its ribs are seen as bars on the face of the setting Sun. The Spectre-Woman and her Death-mate, and no other on board the skeleton ship.

Her lips were red, her looks were free,
  Her locks were yellow as gold:
Her skin was as white as leprosy.
The Night-mare Life-in-Death was she,
  Who thicks man's blood with cold.

Like vessel, like crew I

L. 171-176. **The western wave...a-flame**—The western horizon was coloured red due to the setting of the sun. **The day was well nigh done**—The day was nearly at an end. **Almost upon...bright sun**—i.e., the sun was on the point of setting in the western horizon. The sun always looks at its biggest when it just rises or sets. The moment it is realised that there is something unnatural about the ship, it is no longer described as a ship; it is described as a shape. **drove suddenly**—Note that all supernatural phenomena in the poem appear or occur with a suddenness.

L. 177-180. Straight—immediately, **flecked with bars**—marked with long narrow lines. **Heaven's mother**—Virgin Mary, mother of Jesus Christ. send us grace-protect us against any evil, **dungeon-grate**—prison bars, **he peered**—the sun peeped. **With broad and burning face**—with a large and glowing appearance. The picture conveys the spectral nature of the ship.

L. 181-184. My heart beat loud—indication of fright, **nears and nears**—draws nearer and nearer. **glance in the sun**—shine in the sunlight.

L. 171-176. The day has almost come to an end. The western horizon is filled with the colour of the twilight. The broad sun stood on the western horizon. At that moment the strange thing has come in between the sun and their ship.

L. 177-180. Immediately, the sun seems to be streak with bars. It looks like a prisoner peeping from behind the prison gate with a broad and red face. The Mariners prays to Virgin Mary for mercy.

L. 181-184. The skeleton-ship is advancing fast. The Ancient Mariner's heart beat fast. He is surprised to see its sails which looks like moving cobwebs shining in the sunlight.

L. 185-189. The Mariner has noticed with horror the thin masts and boards of the skeleton ship. The sun has peeped through them like a prisoner. He has noticed only one person - a woman on the ship. He has wondered whether that is the only crew. Then he has noticed another like Death and wonders whether it is the mate of the woman.

L. 190-194. The women has red lips, a bold, immodest look and hair as yellow as gold. Her skin has a whiteness similar to that of the disease leprosy. She is the horrible spirit Life-in-Death who, like a dreadful dream, freezes any man's blood.

---

restless gossameres—cobwebs which are fluttering in the breeze. **Are those her sails...gossameres?** The phantom ship had for her sails nothing but something light and filmy which looked more like cobwebs. The whole description of the ship and her surroundings strikes horror in the heart of the Mariners as well as in that of the reader.

L. 185-189. her ribs—the main planks which make the skeleton ship. **Peer**—peep. **grate**—interwoven frame work. **all her crew**—all the inmates of the ship. Students should note that the whole stanza is put in the form of questions which help only, to mystify the scene and intensify the horror and terror of the whole situation. **Death**—a skeleton.

L. 190-194. Her lips were red...were free—There is nothing unnatural about the lips or the looks of the woman and yet red lips and free looks in a woman make her conspicuous. **yellow as gold**—extremely bright or unnaturally yellowish. **leprosy**—Coleridge is here thinking of white leprosy in which case the whole body turns abnormally white. The red lips and free looks suggest life while leprosy suggests death, so the description befits Life-in-Death. **Night-mare**—an evil spirit that was supposed to haunt and originally suffocate people to death in sleep. **Life-in-Death**—The name is significant. Death is an end of life but Life-in-Death is, lingering death, and hence, it is far more painful than death. **Who thicks...cold**—who thickens man's blood with horror, i.e., a reference to blood congealing in horror.

The naked hulk alongside came,
And the twain were casting dice;
'The game is done ! I've won ! I've won !'
Quoth she, and whistles thrice.

Death and Life-in-Death have diced for the ship's crew and she (the latter) winneth the ancient Mariner.

The Sun's rim dips; the stars rush out:
At one stride comes the dark;
With far-heard whisper. o'er the sea,
Off shot the spectre-bark.

No twilight within the courts of the Sun.

We listened and looked sideways up!
Fear at my heart, as at a cup,
My life-blood seemed to sip!
The stars were dim, and thick the night,
The steersman's face by his lamp gleamed white;
From the sails the dew did drip-
Till clomb above the eastern bar
The hornd Moon, with one bright star
Within the nether tip.

At the rising of the Moon,

One after one, by the star-dogged Moon,
Too quick for groan or sigh,
Each turned his face with a ghastly pang,
And cursed me with his eye.

One after another,

Four times fifty living men,
(And I heard nor sigh nor groan)
With heavy thump, a lifeless lump,
They dropped down one by one.

His shipmates drop down dead.

L. 195- 198. The naked hulk—the skeleton ship. Hulk means the main body or frame work of a ship. **the twain**—i.e., the two inmates of the phantom ship, namely, Death and Life-in-Death, **were casting dice**—were gambling. **The game is done**—The gambling is over. **I've won... won**—Life-in-Death cries out triumphantly that she has won the soul of the ancient Mariner.
quoth—said. **whistles thrice**—whisper joyously thrice. Note again the number thrice which lends a mystic horror to the situation. The very cry of joy and the whistling of Life-in-Death sends a chill through our bones.

L. 199-202. The sun's rim dips-the circle of the sun sinks into the sea. **The stars rush out**-with the setting of the sun the stars become visible in the sky. **At one stride...dark**—immediately after setting of the sun. This is true of the tropics where there is no twilight. **With far-heard whisper**—with a faint sound at a distance. **Off shot**—went away. **The spectre-bark**—the phantom ship.

L. 203-211. Fear at my heart...seemed to sip—A fine simile. Fear is personified and represented as a monster who takes the Mariner's life blood in a cup and

L. 195-198. When the skeleton-ship come alongside their ship, the Mariner see that the two in the ship are playing at dice. The winner is to get the Ancient Mariner and the loser, the rest of the crew. Life-in-Death exclaim that she has won the Mariner and has whistled thrice in the joy of victory.

L. 199-202. The Sun goes down into the waters of the sea. The stars appears in the sky and the darkness has covered the world with a suddenness. The skeleton ship has disappeared quickly with a whispering sound heard from a distance.

L. 203-211. They have heard the sound from a distance and looks sideways out of fear. The Ancient Mariner feel as if fear are drinking his lifeblood from his heart as a man drinks from a cup; i.e. he is overwhelmed by fear. The darkness become more dense. In the light of the lamp the face of the steersman is shining white. The dew drops from the sails. The crescent moon rises above the eastern horizon with one bright star within its lower end.

L. 212-215. In the light of the moon it is closely followed by a star, each sailor has turned towards the mariner with pain. They cast cursing glances at him. It all happens with such quickness that they can neither groan nor sigh.

L. 216-219. Two hundred of his companions is falling down dead. They are dropping one by one without sighing or groaning.

---

drinks it. In other words, fear seemed to dry up or freeze the blood in his veins, **thick the night**—the night was very dark. **steerman's**—helmsman who plies the ship or holds the steering wheel. **gleamed white**—looked absolutely pale because of extreme fear and agony. **clomb**—old form of 'climbed', **the eastern bar**—the eastern horizon. **The hornd moon**—i.e., the crescent moon which is pointed at both ends and resembles a horn, **nether tip**—lower end. **The hornd Moon.....nether tip**—The popular superstition is that if the moon is followed by one single star at its lower end it portends some calamity. The details of description are intended to mystify the supernatural elements and intensify horror. It is to be noted that throughout the poem the moon is associated with benevolence. The evil here arises from the star.

L. 212-215. star-dogged Moon—the moon followed by a star. 'Dogged' when used as verb means 'closely followed'. **Too quick for groan or sigh**—i.e., unusually quick or in the twinkling of an eye. **ghastly pang**—horrible pain. 'Ghastly' means unearthly. **cursed me with his eye**—looked with the bitterest feelings at the ancient Mariner.

L. 216-219. Four times fifty—i.e., two hundred. **And I heard...groan**—The sailors fell dead on the deck so mysteriously that no expression of their dying moment was visible. Generally when people die they gasp or cry, as a mark of their last sign of life but in the case of the sailors the death was not natural but brought about by some supernatural agency, and hence no sigh or groan was heard. **With heavy thump**—with a sound resembling the falling of a heavy body. **A lifeless lump**—heap of dead bodies lying together upon the deck. Death claims what he has won in the grim game of dice.

The souls did from their bodies fly,-
They fled to bliss or woe
And every soul, it passed me by,
Like the whizz of my cross-bow !

But Life-in-Death hegins her work on the ancient Mariner.

PART IV

'I fear thee, ancient Mariner !
I fear thy skinny hand !
And thou art long, and lank, and brown,
As is the ribbed sea-sand.

The wedding-Guest feareth that a Spirit is talking to him;

I fear thee and thy glittering eye,
And thy skinny hand, so brown'.—
Fear not, fear not, thou Wedding-Guest !
This body dropt not down.

But the ancient : Mariner assureth him of his bodily life, and proceedeth to relate his horrible penance.

Alone, alone, all, all alone,
Alone on a wide wide sea !
And never a saint took pity on
My soul in agony.

The many men, so beautiful !
And they all dead did lie :
And a thousand thousand slimy things
Lived on; and so did I.

He despiseth the creatures of the calm.

I looked upon the rotting sean,
And drew my eyes away;
I looked upon the rotting deck,
And there the dead men lay.

And envieth that they should live, and so many lie dead.

L. 220-223. **The souls...fly**—The common idea all over the world is that when the body dies the soul leaves the body and flies somewhere. **They fled to bliss or woe**—The souls fled to heaven (the place of eternal bliss) or to hell (the place of eternal pain). **whizz**—the sound made by the string of the bow. This line is significant in the sense that it reflects the consciousness of guilt on the part of the ancient Mariner who regrets that he killed the innocent Albatross. The reminder of the end of Part I is clear.

L. 224-227. lank—lean and thin. **The ribbed sea-sand**—the sands on the sea-beach looked like ribs because the ripples of the sea arrange the sands in that manner when they roll over the beach and withdraw. **I fear thee...sea-sand**—These occasional addresses to the ancient Mariner by the wedding guest help to intensify the dramatic effect upon the reader and also serve as a change to the monotonous narrative. The wedding guest fears ghost. that he is talking to a ghost.

L. 220-223. They all are dead and their souls fly either to heaven or to hell. As they have died the Mariner is reminded of his crime-their souls are passed by him with the same sound of the cross-bow like that makes when he has killed the Albatross.

PART IV

L. 224-227. The Wedding—Guest after hearing about the death of sailors, is afraid. He tell the Ancient Mariner that he fears his thin and brown and wrinkled body. He fears that the Mariner is a ghost.

L. 228-231. The Guest has repeated that he has feared the Mariner's shining eyes and wrinkled hand. The Ancient Mariner allay his fear and tell him that he himself is not one of the dead.

L. 232-235. The Mariner is absolutely alone on that vast ocean. His soul is in bitter pain and no saint has took pity on him.

L. 236-239. All the sailors, beautiful human beings, are lying dead. In contrast, the ugly creatures of the sea are living; just like them the Mariner too live on.

L. 240-243. The Mariner sees the sea. It is rotting. He can not bear the sight and turns away his eyes. Nothing beautiful can be seen because the deck also looks horrible, being covered with dead bodies.

L. 231. This body dropt not down—The ancient Mariner assures the wedding guest that he did not die like the other sailors on board the ship, so he is no ghost.

L. 232-235. Alone, alone...wide sea! That the ancient Mariner was all alone in the midst of his dead comrades is a fact but his feeling of loneliness is more due to the horror of the scene and also the consciousness of his guilt than his actual surroundings. **Never a saint...agony**—No God or angel ever tried to relieve his pain-the pain due to the consciousness of guilt. These are powerful lines bringing Out the terror of the lonely situation.

L. 236-239. The many men...so did I—The psychological significance of the Mariner's confession should be noted. The Mariner distinguishes between human beings and creatures of the sea and declares the former as beautiful and the latter as ugly and hateful. The poet believes that when one makes such a distinction of God's creations, one offends God and has to pay the penalty as the Mariner did. Coleridge's idea is that one should love all creatures, great and small, and therein lies the best form of worship of God. The Mariner has not shown any repentance so far. The note of despair in 'so did I' is noteworthy.

L. 240-243. I looked upon...dead men lay—The same hatred and disgust for the creatures of the sea and the same love and sympathy for human beings are reflected in this stanza as in the preceding one. the rotting sea-the sea in which the water was foul and the creatures were no less ugly and hateful, **drew my eyes away**—This reflects the loathing and disgust of the Mariner for the lower creations of God. **the rotting deck**—the deck of the ship which was made ugly by the dead bodies of the sailors.

I looked to heaven, and tried to pray;
But or ever a prayer had gusht,
A wicked whisper came, and made
My heart as dry as dust.

I closed my lids, and kept them close,
And the balls like pulses beat;
For the sky and the sea, and the sea and the sky
Lay like a load on my weary eye,
And the dead were at my feet.

But the curse liveth for him in the eye of the dead men.

The cold sweat melted from their limbs,
Nor rot nor reek did they :
The look with which they looked on me
Had never passed away.

An orphan's curse would drag to hell
A spirit from on high;
But oh! more horrible than that
Is the curse in a dead man's eye !
Seven days, seven nights, I saw that curse,
And yet I could not die.

L. 244-247. looked to heaven—turned my eyes to the sky to think of God. or ever-before. **a prayer had gusht**—a feeling of regret had come to my heart. **A wicked whisper**—a sinful impulse not to pray or think of God at all. **made my heart.......dust**—made me absolutely incapable of praying to God. The stanza paints exactly the feeling of the sinner's heart-how an impenitent heart fails in the very attempt to pray to God and suffers agony.

L. 248-252. I closed my lids.....close—By closing one's eyes one tries to pray because the closing of the eyes helps one to concentrate attention on God. **The balls like pulses beat**—i.e., the eye balls were very restless or in other words, the mind could not concentrate for prayer. **Lay like a load**—lay heavily, **the sky and the sea.., weary eye**—The idea is that even by closing the eyes the ancient Mariner could not forget the external world or his physical surroundings, which continually disturbed his mind and did not permit him to pray to God or forget his crime of killing the Albatross. It reminds one of "Hell flies with Satan." Note the sense of weariness conveyed by the dragging rhythm. **The dead were at my feet**—The ancient Mariner means to say that he was conscious of the sea and the sky as painfully as the dead bodies of the sailors-both of which did not allow him to think of God.

L. 242-247. The Mariner looks towards the sky and tries to pray. But he can not pray. Evil thoughts has hardened his heart and has made him incapable of praying.

L. 248-252. The Mariner has closed his eyes and has kept them closed. His eyeballs are throbbing with weariness. Everything around seems to lie like a heavy burden on his eyelids. All around him on the deck are lying the dead bodies of the sailors.

L. 253-256. Cold perspiration is coming out of the dead bodies. They are neither decaying nor giving out a foul smell. There is a cold curse in their open eyes which he can not forget.

L. 257-262. The curse of an orphan can pull down an angel from heaven to hell. But the curse in the eyes of a dead man is more horrible than that. The Mariner see that curse for seven days continuously, yet can not have the relief of death.

L. 253-256. The Cold sweat ...limbs—The cold sweat is a mark of the fear and agony of the sailors who died mysteriously. **Nor rot nor reek did they**—Generally dead bodies decompose but in the case of the sailors their dead bodies did riot decompose or give out any foul smell. It was all due to their unnatural death. **reek**—give out a foul odour. **The look...passed away**—The look of extreme anger and pain with which the sailors died haunted the Mariner always.

L. 257-262. An orphan's curse...on high—An orphan is one who has no parents, no home, no shelter, and hence everybody should have sympathy for him. Even an angel who wrongs such a helpless creature would not be pardoned but severely punished **from on high**—from heaven. **Seven days, seven nights**—here the definite is used for the indefinite for the sake of emphasis. Note again the use of a mystical number, **yet I could not die**—The words reflect the agony and despair of the Mariner. He could not die because he had been won by Life-in-Death in the game.

The moving Moon went up the sky,
And no where did abide:
Softly shẹ was going up,
And a star or two beside-

Her beams bemocked the sultry main,
Like April hoar-frost spread;
But where the ship's huge shadow lay,
The charmed water burnt away
A still and awful red.

In his loneliness and fixedness he yearneth towards the journeying Moon, and the stars that still sojourn, yet still move onward; and every where the blue sky belongs to them, and is their appointed rest, and their native country and their own natural homes, which they enter unannounced as lords that are certainly expected and yet there is a silent joy at the it arrival.

Beyond the shadow of the ship,
I watched the water-snakes:
They moved in tracks of shining white,
And when they reared, the elfish light
Fell off in hoary flakes.

By the light of the Moon he beboldeth God's creatures of the great calm.

Within the shadow of the ship
I watched their rich attire :
Blue, glossy green, and velvet black,
They coiled and swam ; and every track
Was a flash of golden fire.

O happy living things ! no tongue
Their beauty might declare:
A spring of love gushed from my heart,
And I blessed them unaware:
Sure my kind saint took pity on me,
And I blessed them unaware.

Their beauty and their happiness.

He blesseth them in his heart.

L. 263-271. These lines serve as a relief to the tragic tension of horror and terror and also as a turning point in the Mariner's expiation. The description of the moon and the natural surroundings is a happy digression from the subjective world to the objective world. **a bide**—stop or stay. **bemocked**—caused to be mocked, formed a striking contrast. **the sultry main**—the hot water of the sea. **hoar-frost**—white frozen dew-drops. **Her beams bemocked...spread**—The cool moonbeams formed a striking contrast with the hot water of the sea. The moonlit sea looked as if overspread by hoar-frost. **The charmed water...awful red**—The

L. 263-266. The moon continues its journey in the sky. It does not stop anywhere, nor is it disturbed. There are one or two stars by its side.

L. 267-271. The cool white rays of the moon has spread over the red hot sea like frozen dew covering the land in April. But in the shadow of the ships where the moonlight do not reach, the sea water is under a charm and looks fearfully red.

L. 272-276. Beyond the shadow of the ship, the Mariner see the water snakes playing. In the moonlight the lines has formed on water by their movement looks brilliantly white. When they raise their heads shining white beads of water falls off into the sea like white flakes of light.

L. 277-281. Within the shadow of the ship the Mariner see the rich colours of the snakes. They are brilliant green and black in colour. As they move and swim, they produce tracks in the water. Moonlight lit up these tracks and make them look like flashes of golden light.

L. 282-287. The Mariner has appreciated the beauty and joy of those creatures which is beyond description. He is filled with love for them and has blessed them spontaneously. It seems that some kind saint has at last taken pity on him and has enabled him to bless those creatures.

---

water of the Red sea which was under a supernatural spell for the time being was sparkling and giving out continuously a red glare.

L. 272-276. They moved...white—When the snakes swam in the sea the water sparkled and formed streams of light. **When they reared**—when the snakes put up their heads above the sea water. **elfish**—supernatural like an elf; suggestive of supernatural beauty as well as joy. **hoary flakes**—white particles.

L. 277-281. their rich attire—the beautifully coloured skin of the snakes. **glossy green**—shining green. **velvet black**—smooth and glossy black. **coiled**—twisted or curled. **every track Was a flash of golden fire**—every movement of the snakes was followed by a stream of light. (L. 272 to 281 give a memorable description. The Mariner's interest in the snakes indicates the renewal of his interest in life around him. This marks the beginning of his redemption.)

L. 282-287 happy living...declare—The ancient Mariner envies the lot of the snakes in the sea and says that they are so beautiful that they cannot be described by anybody properly. This admiration on the part of the ancient Mariner for slimy creatures for which he had a deep loathing and hatred earlier in part IV is a sign of his sympathy and love for the lower creations of God. **might**—could. **A spring...unaware**—suddenly the Mariner felt some attraction for the snakes or slimy creatures; he prayed for their happiness perhaps unconsciously. Now the ancient Mariner makes no distinction between human beings and the lower creations of God. He feels that they deserve to live. This is a change of mind. **Sure my kind saint...me**—The ancient Mariner believes firmly that his guardian angel had been kind to him so he could admire or love the snakes and pray for them because formerly when he was a sinner he had shown a deep hatred and loathing for them.

The spell begins to break.

The self-same moment I could pray;
And from my neck so free

The Albatross fell off, and sank
Like lead into the sea.

PART V

Oh sleep! it is a gentle thing,
Beloved from pole to pole!
To Mary Queen the praise be given!
She sent the gentle sleep from Heaven,
That slid into my soul.

By grace of the holy Mother, the ancient Mariner is refreshed with rain.

The silly buckets on the deck,
That had so long remained,
I dreamt that they were filled with dew;
And when I awoke, it rained.

My lips were wet, my throat was cold,
My garments all were dank;
Sure I had drunken in my dreams,
And still my body drank.

I moved, and could not feel my limbs :
I was so light, – almost
I thought that I had died in sleep,
And was a blessed ghost.

He heareth sounds and seeth strange sights and commotions in the sky and the element.

And soon I heard a roaring wind :
It did not come anear;
But with its sound it shook the sails,
That were so thin and sere.

L. 288-291. The self-same moment—The very same moment. **And from my neck...the sea**—The dead body of the Albatross is only the visible mark of the sin committed by the ancient Mariner, it is a kind of token of memory or consciousness of his guilt. Hence, the moment he begins to pray for others, he enjoyed God's grace. The visible sign of his sin thus falls off. It is a wonderful artistic device to represent a psychological phenomenon.

L. 292-296. Beloved from pole to pole—loved by all the people of the world, pole to pole-from one end of the world to the other. **Mary Queen**—Virgin Mary, mother of Jesus Christ. **the praise be given**—Mother Mary should be given the

L. 288-291. As soon as the Mariner has blessed the snakes, the chain of the curse begain to break. He is able to pray. The Albatross, that is hanging like a heavy curse, fall from his neck and sink into the sea.

PART V

L. 292-296. Sleep is a blessing. It soothes and refreshes man. That is why people all over the world love it. The Mariner has praised Virgin Mary, the Queen of Heaven, who has sent sleep to him. At last he can sleep without effort.

L. 297-300. The Mariner has dreamt that the buckets which has remained empty so far, are filled with rain drops. When he awake from sleep, rain fell.

L. 301-304. The dryness of his throat has gone and his lips are wet. All his clothes are wet with rain. He feel as if he has been drinking in his sleep and his body is still enjoying the bath.

L. 305-308. Now as he has moved he feel very light. It makes him feel that has he is a new man. He almost think that he has died in sleep and is only a happy spirit in heaven.

L. 309-312. The Mariner hear shortly afterwards the loud noise of the wind. It do not come near the ship. The sails however begin to move under its effect because they are thin and dry.

---

credit of sending such a sweet thing as sleep which the whole world loves, slid-gently descended.

L. 297-300. silly—empty, **it rained**—another sign of divine grace.

L. 301-304. garments—clothes. **dank**—wet or damp. **sure**—surely. **drunken in my dreams**—drank the raindrops while asleep. **still my body drank**—still all my limbs were drenched or wet.

L. 305-308. could not feel my limbs—felt my body to be so light that I seemed no more a creature of flesh and blood but a spirit of the other world. **a blessed ghost**—a strange and happy spirit of the other world.

L. 309-312. Mark how in this stanza the ancient Mariner sees strange sights and hears strange sounds. These are all hallucinations from which the heated brain of a sinner must suffer until he is completely absolved. Mark how the wind roars and yet does not touch the sails but only fills them with sound. These create a supernatural atmosphere. **sere**—dry or worn out.

The upper air burst into life !
    And a hundred fire-flags sheen,
To and fro they were hurried about
    And to and fro, and in and out,
The wan stars danced between.

And the coming wind did roar more loud,
    And the sails did sigh like sedge;
And the rain poured down from one black cloud;
    The moon was at its edge.

The thick black cloud was cleft, and still
    The Moon was at its side :
Like waters shot from some high crag,
    The lightning fell with never a jag,
A river steep and wide.

The loud wind never reached the ship,

    Yet now the ship moved on !
Beneath the lightning and the Moon
    The dead men gave a groan.

The bodies of the ship's crew are inspired, [inspirited, S.L.] and the ship moves on;

They groaned, they stirred, they all uprose,
    Nor spake, nor moved their eyes;
It had been strange, even in a dream,
    To have seen those dead men rise.

The helmsman steered, the ship moved on;
    Yet never a breeze up-blew;
The mariners all 'gan work the ropes,
    Where they were wont to do;
They raised their limbs like lifeless tools—
    We were a ghastly crew.

L. 313-317. burst into life—suddenly exhibited signs of life, i.e. began to blow, **fire-flags**—something like flashes of lightning or may be comets. **sheen**—bright, **to and fro**—here and there. in and out-faintly visible stars. wan-dull, pale.

L. 318-321. sigh like sedge—whistle like reeds; grass found on river banks. Mark the suggestive touches-**sigh like sedge; one black cloud; the 'noon was at its edge.**

L. 322-326. cleft—broken up. **Like waters...crag**—like a mountain stream. crag—rock. with never a **jag**—without a break. **A river steep and wide**—

L. 313-317. There is commotion and movement in the upper air. Flashes of lightning are seen moving back and forth. In between these flashes are to be seen the dim stars appearing and disappearing.

L. 318-321. The wind nears and roars louder. The sails moves and produces a sighing sound like the sound produced by the reed-like grasses. Heavy rain fell from a dense dark cloud on the border of which has shone the bright moon.

L. 322-326. The dark cloud is broken up in two, but at its side is the moon. The lightning flashes as if it is a broad river of water falling unbroken from the top of a high cliff.

L. 327-330. The howling wind do not reach the ship, but the ship is moving forward. The lightning flashes and the moon shine. The dead men suddenly begains to groan.

L. 331-334. The dead men has groan and move. Then all of them stand up. It is a most amazing sight. One will not believe it even in a dream.

L. 335-340. Although no wind has blown, the ship is moving. The steersman has guided the ship and the other sailors has also started to work at their posts. They are moving their limbs as if they are lifeless machines. All of them has formed a dreadful group of sailors.

---

the lightning flashes are compared here with a large river pouring down from a precipitious rock, i.e. lightning fell like an unbroken water-fall.

L. 327-328. **The loud wind...moved on!**—another device to lend a supernatural touch. **The dead men gave a groan**—This is a suggestion of grave terror and grim horror, and the same suggestion is drawn out further in the next stanza. groan-an expression of great pain.

L. 331-334. The whole stanza is intended to intensify the horror and terror of the scene. **stirred**-moved, **uprose**—got up. **It had been...dead men rise**—The event would have been strange even in a dream.

L. 335-340). The helmsman steered—the man incharge of the steering wheel worked at the helm. **All'gan work the ropes**—all began to use the ropes for fixing and adjusting the sails. **wont to do**—used to work. **like lifeless tools**—without any sign of real life, i.e. mechanically. **a ghastly crew**—a strange and horrible body of mariners; a spectral crew. The lines show intense and horrific realism.

The body of my brother's son
Stood by me, knee to knee
The body and I pulled at one rope,
But he said nought to me.

'I fear thee, ancient Mariner !'
Be calm, thou Wedding-Guest!
'Twas not those souls that fled in pain,
Which to their corses came again,
But a troop of spirits blest:

But not by the souls of the men, nor by daemons of earth or middle air, but by a blessed troop of angelic spirits, sent down by the invocation of the guardian saint.

For when it dawned—they dropped their arms,
And clustered round the mast;
Sweet sounds rose slowly through their mouths,
And from their bodies passed.

Around, around, flew each sweet sound,
Then darted to the Sun;
Slowly the sounds came back again,
Now mixed, now one by one.

Sometimes a-dropping from the sky
I heard the sky-lark sing;
Sometimes all little birds that are,
How they seemed to fill the sea and air
With their sweet jargoning!

And now 'twas like all instruments,
Now like a lonely flute;
And now it is an angel's song,
That makes the heavens be mute.

L. 341-344. Stood by me knee to knee—stood very close to me. **The body of my brother's son...knee**—There is some particular significance about the mention of a close relation. The poet wants to intensify the feeling of horror and terror by bringing together the dead nephew and alive uncle making them work at once at the same rope. **The body and I**—the lifeless body of my brother's son which was for the time being revived by some supernatural agency. **nought**—nothing.

L. 345-349. Be calm—do not be frightened. **'T was not those souls...blest**—The ancient Mariner assures the wedding guest that it was not the departed souls of the sailors but a band of angels which inspired their dead bodies, and

L. 341-344. The Mariner's nephew is one of the crew. His has reanimated body stand beside the Mariner, and works at the same rope but without speaking a word.

L. 345-349. On hearing the account of the reanimation of the bodies, the Wedding-Guest again get frightened. The Ancient Mariner has stayed his fear and tells him that the souls of those men do not return to the bodies. What inspire them, are some heavenly spirits.

L. 350-353. When it is early morning, the arms of the bodies fall and all of them has gathered around the mast. They are being worked by spirits. As the spirits has passed out of the bodies sweet sounds has come out of the mouths of the dead sailors.

L. 354.-357. Each sweet sound hovers about the ship for some— time and then rushes upwards straight. Then these sounds come back slowly. Sometimes they come in groups and sometimes, one by one.

L. 358-361. Sometimes the sweet song of the skylark came to the Mariner's ears. Sometimes he feels that all the birds of the world has come together and are filling all the atmosphere with their sweet song.

L. 363-366. The music is of a varying nature. Sometimes, it is like that of an orchestra and sometimes, like that of a single flute. At times it sounds like an angelic choir so compelling in power that has made even the heavens silent.

---

hence, they were not ghosts and there was no reason to be afraid. **souls that fled in pain**—The souls which left the bodies of the sailors because they suffered from so much of heat and thirst. **corses**—corpses or dead bodies. **a troop of spirits blest**-a band of good spirits or angels.

L. 350.353. When it dawned—when the day broke. **clustered**—gathered together. **Sweet sounds......passed**—the blessed spirits that got into the sailors' dead bodies began to sing ethereal songs which rose to the sky.

L. 354-357. darted to the sun—shot up to the sky or to the heavenly bodies. **Slowly the sounds came back again**—probably the sky echoed the sweet sounds. **Now mixed, now one by one**—the sweet sounds sometimes mingled together and sometimes resounded in single notes.

L. 358-362. a-dropping—while dropping. **that are**—that exist. **fill the sea and air**—ring or resound in the surroundings. **sweet jargoning**—sweet notes of confused music, i.e. the notes of in music, ,not properly arranged and yet they are sweet. Note the praise for the lower creations-the birds.

L. 363-366. 'twas like all instruments—the sweet sounds were mingled together like the music of several instruments in an orchestra, **like a lonely flute**—as a single note of music proceeding from a flute. **it is an angel's song**—it is an exquisitely sweet music, **makes the heavens be mute**—makes the Heaven silent. It seems as if the heavenly bodies stop their movement in their orbits and listen to the music with close attention. Note the sense of universal peace and harmony projected in these lines and their contrast to the earlier images of dryness and stagnation.

It ceased; yet still the sails made on
A pleasant noise till noon,
A noise like of a hidden brook
In the leafy month of June,
That to the sleeping woods all night
Singeth a quiet tune.

Till noon we quietly sailed on,
Yet never a breeze did breathe:
Slowly and smoothly went the ship,
Moved onward from beneath.

Under the keel nine fathom deep,
From the land of mist and snow,
The spirit slid: and it was he
That made the ship to go.
The sails at noon left off their tune,
And the ship stood still also.

The lonesome Spirit from the south pole carries on the ship as far as the Line, in obedience to the angelic troop, but still requireth vangeance.

The Sun, right up above the mast,
Had fixed her to the ocean:
But in a minute she 'gan stir,
With a short uneasy motion—
Backwards and forwards half her length
With a short uneasy motion.

Then like a pawing horse let go,
She made a sudden bound :
It flung the blood into my head,
And I fell down in a swound.

L. 367-372. The sails made...noise—The sails of the ship which caught the sweet notes of the blessed spirits went on trembling for some time and produced a faint harmony, even when the singing ceased. **A hidden brook**—a stream covered by trees or rocks and concealed from view. **Leafy month of June**—In the month of June the trees have got a fresh set of leaves after spring. **sleeping woods**—quiet woods. **Singeth a quiet tune**—The gentle murmur of the small stream hidden by dense leaves of trees in month of June is like a lullaby to the quiet woods through which it Rows.

L. 373-376. Never a breeze did breathe—There was not a single breath of wind, i.e. the air did not move at all. **Moved onward from beneath**—driven forward by the Polar spirit which has been following the ship from the land of mists and snow.

L. 367-372. The sweet sounds of the angels stops but still the sails of the ship continues a sort of music till noon. It is like the quiet music of a wood-stream producing a sweet murmur in the quiet of the night.

L. 373-376. Till noon they moves on quietly although there is still no wind. The ship moves on, being propelled from below.

L. 377-382. Nine fathom deep under the main mast of the ship is moving the Polar Spirit. That is making the ship move forward. At noon the sails of the ship has stopped their music. The ship also come to a standstill.

L. 383-388. The sun stand exactly above the mast and the ship stand motionless on the ocean. Very soon it begin to move unsteadily. It moves awkwardly back and forth half its length.

L. 389-392. Then it take a sudden jerk like an impatient horse that has been let loose. Because of this the blood has rushed to the Mariner's head and he fell down unconscious.

L. 393-397. The Mariner can not tell how long he lay in that state of unconsciousness. But before he regains consciousness he clearly hear two voices in his mind.

L. 377-382. Under the keel-Just below the centre of the ship. The keel is the backbone of the ship that runs from the stem to stern, **nine fathom deep**—i.e. quite deep under water. **From the land...slid**—The spirit came from the South Pole where there is perpetual snow and mist, **left off their tune**—ceased vibrating or flapping.

L. 383-388. fixed her to the ocean—made the ship motionless. **The sun...ocean**—This gives a supernatural touch. she'gan stir-the ship began to move. **With a short uneasy motion**—i.e. with a jerk; not smoothly.

L.389-392. pawing horse—a restless horse which scratches the ground with its paws in impatience. **It flung the blood into my head**—the sudden leap of the ship made my blood rush to the head. **fell down in a swound**—fell into a fainting fit. **Like a pawing horse... bound**—The simile is most appropriate here. A restless horse, when it is suddenly released, jumps forward with a jerk; so the ship which was held fast to the ocean by the sun was suddenly moved by the polar spirit from below the water and so she made a forward leap. Coleridge deliberately uses dreaming or fainting in order to confuse reality and vision. Thus, he makes the supernatural acceptable to the reader.

How long in that same fit I lay,
I have not to declare;
But ere my living life returned,
I heard and in my soul discerned
Two voices in the air.

The Polar Spirit's fellow—daemons, the invisible in-habitants of the element, take part its his wrong; and two of them relate, one to the other, that penance long and heavy for the ancient Mariner hath been accorded to the Polar Spirit, who returneth southward.

'Is it he ?' quoth one, 'Is this the man ?
By him who died on cross,
With his cruel bow he laid full low
The harmless Albatross.

The spirit who bideth by himself
In the land of mist and snow,
He loved the bird that loved the man
Who shot him with his bow.'

The other was a softer voice,
As soft as honey-dew :
Quoth he, 'The man hath penance done,
And penance more will do.'

PART VI

FIRST VOICE

'But tell me, tell me! speak again,
Thy soft response renewing—
What makes that ship drive on so fast?
What is the ocean doing ?'

L. 393-397. same fit—same state of unconsciousness. **I have not to declare**—I cannot say or I do not have the power to say. **ere my living life returned**—before I came back to my senses. All this time the Mariner had been in the power of Life-in-Death, so Coleridge uses the term 'living life' as deliberate antithesis. **In my soul discerned**—I distinguished two voices whether there were actually any voice in the air or not. The voices are supposed to be voices of justice and mercy.

L. 398-401. The first voice is referred to the Ancient Mariner and ask in the name of Christ whether he is the man who has killed the innocent Albatross.

L. 402-405. The Polar Spirit live alone in the land of mist and snow. That Spirit love the Albatross. The bird love the Mariner who, instead of returning the love, has killed him.

L. 406-409. The other is the voice of Mercy. It is gentler. It says that the man has suffered for the crime and will undergo more suffering.

PART VI

FIRST VOICE

L. 410-413. The First Voice (Justice) request Mercy to gently reply to two questions: (1) How the ship is moving fast ? and (2) What the ocean is doing?

L. 398-401. **quoth**—said. **By him who dies on cross**—in the name of Jesus Christ who died on the cross. **With his cruel bow**—it is not the bow but it is the man that uses the bow who is cruel. **laid full low**—killed completely. This is the voice of the spirit of Justice.

L. 402-405. **who bideth by himself**—who lives all alone. **He loved the bird ....bow**—The Polar Spirit loved the bird, Albatross; the Albatross loved the ancient Mariner but the ancient Mariner killed the Albatross. The effect of the repetition of the world 'loved' is striking.

L. 406-409. **The other was a softer voice**—this voice was of Mercy whose heart is always soft unlike that of Justice whose heart is stern. **As soft as honey-dew**—extremely soft and sweet; 'honey-dew' has a supernatural touch. It is the drink of Gods. **hath penance done**—has made amends or paid the penalty for the crime of killing the Albatross.

L. 4 11-413. Thy soft...renewing—repeating your gentle voice. **What is the ocean doing**?-How can the ocean move the ship without any wave or wind?

SECOND Voice

'Still as a slave before his lord.
The ocean hath no blast;
His great bright eye most silently
Up to the Moon is cast–

If he may know which way to go;
For she guides him smooth or grim.
See, brother, see! how graciously
She looketh down on him.'

The Mariner hash been cast into a trance; for the angelic power causeth the vessel to drive northward faster than human life could endure.

FIRST VOICE

'But why drives on that ship so fast,
Without or wave or wind?'

SECOND VOICE

'The air is cut away before,
And closes from behind.

Fly, brother, fly ! more high, more high !
Or we shall be belated :
For slow and slow that ship will go,
When the Mariner's trance is abated.'

The Supernatural motion is retarded; the Mariner awakes, and his penance begins anew.

I woke, and we were sailing on
As in a gentle weather :
'Twas night, calm night, the moon was high;
The dead men stood together.

All stood together on the deck,
For a charnel-dungeon fitter:
All fixed on me their stony eyes,
That in the Moon did glitter.

L. 414-422. Still as a slave before his lord—always as obedient as a servant to his master. **The ocean hath no blast**—No wind is blowing over the ocean. **His great bright eye**—is it the reflection of the moon in the ocean or is it all the water of the sea lit up by the moon beams which stand here for the eye of the ocean'? The latter is more likely. **If he may know...go**—In order to know which way the

L. 414-417. The Second Voice replies that there is no wind on the ocean. It is as calm and quiet as a slave before his master. At that moment the ocean is busy absorbing the light of the moon.

L. 418-421. The ocean seem to be looking to the moon as if to receive orders as it is the moon who directs the sea in calm as well as in storm. Mercy points out to Justice the kindness with which the moon is looking at the ocean.

L. 422-425. Justice ask why the ship is moving so fast when there is neither wave nor wind to help it? Mercy replies that it is because the air pressure has been decreased in front and increased behind the ship.

L. 426-429. Mercy further says that they must fly away otherwise they will be late, because on the Mariner's waking up the speed of the ship will slow down.

L. 430-433. The Mariner wakes and found the ship moving as smoothly as in calm weather. It is a peaceful night and the moon is shining. The dead men are standing in a group.

L. 434-437. All the dead bodies are on the deck although they are really fit for a cell for keeping dead bodies. The eyes of the dead are still fixed on the Mariner and they are shining in the bright moonlight.

---

water of ocean should move, **she guides....grim**—It is the moon that rules the ocean in calm or in rough weather. It is not a mere poetic fancy but a natural truth that it is due to the attraction of the moon that there are tides, **graciously**—kindly.

L. 424-425. The air is cut away...behind—The second voice offers an explanation, which is scientific. When the air is cut away from before the ship a vacuum is created and consequently, the ship is drawn. forward by the vacuum as the air behind it simultaneously presses the ship. That is exactly how the ship is made to move, but how is it done when there is no wind or wave? Coleridge leaves this vague. Probably, it is the Polar Spirit who moves it.

L. 426-429. We shall be belated—We shall be late in reaching our place, i.e. we shall be detained, trance-fainting fit or a state of unconsciousness. **abated**—subsided.

L. 430-433. In these lines we note the contrast between the natural and supernatural and also find that the supernatural motion of the ship is retarded when the Mariner becomes conscious and the Mariner's penance begins anew. There is a touch of cold terror and horror about the last line.

L. 434-437. For a charnel-dungeon fitter—An underground room, in which the bones of the dead are generally treasured up, was the most suitable place for the dead men who stood on the deck. **charnel-dungeon**—an underground room in which the bones of the dead are kept. **stony eyes**—fixed looks or glassy eyes, having no speculation or intelligence in them. Note the horrible image of the lifeless glittering in the moonlight.

The pang, the curse, with which they died,
Had never passed away:
I could not draw my eyes from theirs,
Not turn them up to pray.

And now this spell was snapt: once more
I viewed the ocean green,
And looked far forth, yet little saw
Of what had else been seen—

The curse is finally expiated.

Like one, that on a lonesome road
Doth walk in fear and dread,
And having once turned round walks on,
And turns no more his head;
Because he knows, a frightful fiend
Doth close behind him tread.

But soon there breathed a wind on me,
Nor sound nor motion made :
Its path was not upon the sea,
In ripple or in shade.

It raised my hair, it fanned my cheek
Like a meadow-gale of spring—
It mingled strangely with my fears,
Yet it felt like a welcoming.
Swiftly, swiftly flew the ship,
Yet she sailed softly too :
Sweetly, sweetly blew the breeze—
On me alone it blew.

L. 438-441. The pang, the curse...passed away—The dying look of the dead men which reflected the utmost anger, hatred and revenge was always haunting the Mariner. **I could not draw...pray**—this shows how much the ancient Mariner was affected by his sense of guilt. He could neither forget the dying looks of sailors nor could he think of God in order to repent for his sin.

L. 442-445. this spell—the charm; the fainting fit was due to supernatural influence, was snapt-was broken, **yet little saw...seen**—He was so much overmastered by his sense of fear that for some time, though he was free from the fainting fit, he could not see properly any natural thing around him-the moonlight, the ship or the shadow of it, the waves or any other thing.

L. 438-441. The dead bodies has still retained the signs of pain and the curse with which the men has died. The Mariner can not look away. It is impossible for him to look up for prayers.

L. 442-445. Now, at last, the spell broke and once again the Mariner has the ocean in its natural colour. He see far into the distance but does not find what he has seen at another time.

L. 446-451. The Mariner feel like a man journeying on some lonely path in fear-like one who has turned his head once to look back but is afraid to do so again, because he suspects that he is being followed by some evil spirit.

L. 452-455. Very soon the Mariner feel a wind blowing. It is so subtle that it produces neither sound nor motion. It leave no track on the sea or ripples in the water. Even the shades in the water do not change.

L. 456-459. The wind has lifted his hair and has gently stroked his cheeks. It is as fresh as the wind blowing over the meadows. The gentleness of the wind is accompanied by his fears. It has a pleasing effect.

L. 460-463. The ship has moved fast but gently. The gentle breeze has blown only on the Mariner and on nothing else.

L. 446-451. **lonesome**—lonely. **having once turned round**—having once turned his head backward and seen some strange and frightful thing which may be altogether imaginary due to the feeling of fear, **fiend**—some devilish, ghostly figure. Doth close...tread-follows him very closely. The passage offers a striking description of the Mariner's mind.

L. 452-455. **There breathed a wind on me**—I felt a puff of wind blowing on me. **Its path was not...in shade**—The wind did not blow upon the sea, and hence, the water was not in the least disturbed to form ripples or waves. This is another supernatural touch to create a sense of mystery.

L. 456-459. **It raised......cheek**—The wind was sufficiently strong to make the Mariner feel its gentle touch, **meadow-gale of spring**—the south wind which gently blows over the green fields in the spring season. It is a refreshing image. **like a welcoming**—The breeze seemed good.

L. 460-463. This stanza is also an instance of alliteration: swiftly, swiftly; she sailed softly, sweetly: blew the breeze.

Oh ! dream of joy ! is this indeed
The light-house top I see ?
Is this the hill ? Is this the kirk ?
Is this mine own countree ?

And the ancient Mariner beholdeth his native country.

The angelic spirits

We drifted o'er the harbour-bar,
And I with sobs did pray—
O, let me be awake, my God !
Or let me sleep alway.

The harbour-bay was clear as glass,
So smoothly it was strewn !
And on the bay the moonlight lay,
And the shadow of the Moon.

The rock shone bright, the kirk no less,
That stands above the rock:
The moonlight steeped in silentness
The steady weathercock.

And the bay was white with silent light,
Till rising from the same,
Full many shapes, that shadows were,
In crimson colours came.

The angelic spirits leave the dead bodies.

A little distance from the prow
Those crimson shadows were:
I turned my eyes upon the deck--
Oh, Christ ! what saw I there ?

And appear in Their own forms of light.

Each corse lay flat, lifeless and flat,
And, by the holy rood !
A man all light, a seraph-man,
On every corse there stood.

L. 464-467. Oh ! dream of joy—The Mariner cannot trust his eyes: he cannot believe that he is nearing his native shore. The recollection of the familiar places and things is slowly reviving after the super-natural state of unconsciousness. **kirk**—church. **countree**—country. **Is this mine...countree?** these questions are significant. On the one hand, they help the progress of the description while, on the other, they bring out the feelings of doubt mingled with the sense of joy of the Mariner, who feels a great relief not merely on seeing his native soil and other familiar things but also on feeling that he is no longer tortured by the supernatural hallucinations. Note the reverse order in which the familiar landmarks appear (cf. Ll.23-24).

L. 464-467. The Mariner see before him the light house, the hill and the church of his own land. It is too good to be believed. He considers it a joyful dream and has wondered whether he has really reached his native land.

L. 468-471. The ship sails over the harbour bay. The Mariner weep convulsively and prays to God. He wishes that either what is viewed by him shall be real or he may go on dreaming forever.

L. 472-475. The water in the bay is so calm and clear that it looks like a sheet of glass. On the coast is spread the moonlight and the water has reflected the moon.

L. 476-479. The hill and the church is standing on its top are shining in the light of the Moon. There is deep silence prevailing and the weather-cock stands unmoving.

L. 480-483. Calm and peaceful white moon light spreads all over the bay. From it appears some reflections of crimson colour.

L. 484-487. Those shadows are at a little distance in front of the ship. Then the Mariner looks towards the deck of the ship. He is surprised to see strange things there.

L. 488-491. He see that all the dead bodies are lying flat on the deck. He is awe-struck to see that near each dead body there stand a bright angel.

L. 468-471. drifted......harbour-bar—sailed on smoothly over the bar of sand that lies across the mouth of the harbour. **O, let me be awake...al way**—The Mariner prays that either if his sufferings have been real his escape too may prove real; or if they have been a dream, his dream may last for ever.

L. 472-475. was clear as glass—i.e. was transparent. **So smoothly it was strewn**—The water of the bay was so clear and unruffled, **shadow**—reflection; another touch to lend a supernatural charm. The calm sea-scape offers a pleasant respite after the Mariner's unrest.

L. 476-479. steeped in silentness—bathed in perfect stillness. **The steady weathercock**—the weather-cock was steady because there was no wind at all.

L. 480-483. rising from the same—rising from the bay. **Full many shapes**—great many forms or figures. **that shadows were**—those forms which rose from the dead bodies were not creatures of flesh and blood but spirits of another world. **In crimson colours**—reddish coloured. This is a fine colour effect offering a striking contrast to the white moonlight.

L. 484-487. prow—the fore part of a ship. **Those crimson shadows**—those bright angelic forms which were nothing but the spirits moving the dead sailors. **Oh, Christ!...there?**-This is an expression of extreme wonder and horror.

L. 488-491. corse—corpse or dead body. **the holy rood**—The holy cross on which Jesus Christ died. **A man all light**—an angelic form or a luminous human form, **seraph-man**—an angel.

This seraph-band, each waved his hand !
    It was a heavenly sight !
They stood as signals to the land,
    Each one a lovely light ;

This seraph-band, each waved his hand,
    No voice did they impart—
No voice; but oh ! the silence sank
    Like music on my heart.

But soon I heard the dash of oars,
    I heard the Pilot's cheer;
My hand was turned perforce away,
    And I saw a boat appear.

The Pilot and the Pilot's boy,
    I heard them coming fast :
Dear Lord in Heaven ! it was a joy
    The dead men could not blast.

I saw a third—I heard his voice:
    It is the Hermit good !
He singeth loud his godly hymns
    That he makes in the wood.
He'll shrieve my soul, hell wash away
    The Albatross's blood.

PART VII

This Hermit good lives in that wood
    Which slopes down to the sea.
How loudly his sweet voice he rears !
He loves to talk with marineres
    That come from a far countree.

The Hermit of the wood,

L. 492-495. seraph-band—a body of spirits or angelic forms. **Each waved his hand**—Each of the spirits moved its hand as a signal to the shore. (This stanza and a few other foregoing and following stanzas are full of supernatural touches which students should note while discussing the treatment of the supernatural in the poem).

L. 496-499. No voice did they impart—Not a word did they speak. **impart**—utter; give forth. **Oh! the silence...on my heart**—though the angelic forms did not speak a single word yet their very silence was as sweet as music.

L. 492-495. The angels are waving their hands. It is a heavenly sight. Standing there they are like signals for people on land.

L. 496-499. The angels only moves their hands. They do not produce any sound. But this silence is soothing. It has impressed the Mariner like sweet music.

L. 500-503. Very soon he has heard the sound of oars being worked and also encouraging words of the Pilot which has given him hopes of rescue. But by some force his head has turned in another direction where he see a boat.

L. 504-507. The boat carrying the Pilot and the Pilot's boy is coming fast towards the Mariner's ship. He is over-joyed to see them. The joy is too great to be interfered with even by the sight of the dead bodies on the deck.

L. 508-513. In the boat, there is a Hermit too who has composed and has sang hymns in his solitary abode. His voice has given the Mariner further hope that he will hear his confession and absolve him of the crime of killing the Albatross.

PART VII

L. 514-518. This pious Hermit has lived in the forest which come up to the sea. While praying he raises his sweet voice. He is very fond of talking to the sailors who has came from far off lands.

L. 500-503. **the dash of oars**—the sound of the playing of the oars i.e., the movement of some boat. **the Pilot's cheer**—It is call of the pilot. The pilot brings the bigger ships into harbour. **perforce**—by force; of necessity. Note that even the Pilot appears suddenly.

L. 504-507. Dear Lord in Heaven—It is a kind of oath, expressing joy. **it was a joy......blast**—Even the dead men could not possibly destroy the joy of the Mariner when he heard the voice of the Pilot and the Pilot's boy. **blast**—blight; destroy.

L. 508-513. 1 saw a third—the third person, the Mariner saw was the Hermit. **Godly hymns**—pious songs or prayers to God. **shrieve**—absolve: to hear the sinner's confession and then pronounce absolution for the sins confessed. **wash away the Albatross's blood**—purge the Ancient Mariner's soul of the sin of having killed the Albatross.

L. 514-518. Which slopes down to the sea—which stretches to the seashore, he rears—he raises. **Marineres**—archaic spelling for Mariners.

He kneels at morn, and noon, and eve—
He hath a cushion plump :
It is the moss that wholly hides
The rotted old oak-stump.

The skiff-boat neared: I heard them talk,
'Why, this is strange, I trow !
Where are those lights so many and fair,
That signal made but now ?'

Approacheth the ship with wonder.

'Strange, by my faith !' the Hermit said-
'And they answered not our cheer!
The planks looked warped ! and see those sails,
How thin they are and sere !
I never saw aught like to them
Unless perchance it were

Brown skeletons of leaves that lag
My forest-brook along:

When the ivy-tod is heavy with snow,
And the owlet whoops to the wolf below,
That eats the she-wolf's young.'

'Dear Lord ! it hath a fiendish look—
(The Pilot made reply)
I am a-feared.'—'Push on, push on !'
Said the Hermit cheerily.

The boat came closer to the ship,
But I nor spake nor stirred;
The boat came close beneath the ship,
And straight a sound was heard.

L. 519-522. He kneels......eve—He prays to God regularly every day. **plump**—thick. **oak stump**—a part of oak tree trunk. **It is the moss..... oak-stump**—It is the green vegetation growing on the old stump of an oak tree which makes the Hermit's hassock or seat to kneel on for offering prayers.

L. 523-526. The skiff-boat neared—the small light boat drew near. The 'skiff' itself is a light boat; the term 'boat' is redundant. **trow**—think. **Where are those lights...but now?**—The lights refer to the angelic forms which had waved as a signal to the shore.

L. 527-532. by my faith—a kind of oath expressing firmness of conviction on the part of the man who takes the oath, **answered not our cheer**—did not

L. 519-522. The Hermit has offered prayers thrice a day-morning noon and evening. An oak-stump has covered by moss served as his cushion.

L. 523-526. As the boat has come near the Mariner hear their talk. They have come on the signals given by the fair luminious angels. They are surprised not to find them.

L. 527-537. The Hermit, too, has astonished by the disappearance of the angels. They have not even responded to their shout of joy. Moreover the boards of the ship has seemed to have shrunk and the sails are too thin and dry. The Hermit says that he has never seen anything like them except the brown dry leaves that floats along the stream in the forest in the autumn season when the ivy bush is covered with snow and the young owls has hooted to reproach the wolf which eats its cubs.

L. 538-541. The Pilot replies that the whole thing has the look of an evil spirit and that he is afraid. The Hermit has encouraged him and asks him to move ahead.

L. 542-545. The boat comes near the ship but the Mariner neither speak nor moves. As the boat has came just near the ship a loud sound has heard.

---

respond to our greetings. **warped**—contracted or shrunk and distorted. sere-worn out; withered. **aught**—anything. **perchance**—by chance.

L. 533-537. Brown skeletons on leaves—discoloured, dry leaves, **lag**—float idly or lie scattered. **ivy-tod**—ivy bushy. **heavy with snow**—thickly covered with snow, **owlet**—a young owl. **whoops**—cries mockingly. **the wolf below**—the wolf lying underneath the tree on which the owlet is sitting. **That eats...young**—It is a fact that the wolf has a tendency to eat its young. This blend of natural and unnatural things lend a peculiar charm of horror and terror.

L. 538-541. Dear Lord-an expression of fear and wonder. **it hath a fiendish look**—the ship has a devilish or ghostly look, a-feared-afraid or frightened. **Push on**—ply the boat to reach the ship. **cheerily**—cheerfully.

L. 542-545. Stirred-.........beneath the ship—not under but alongside the ship. As the ship was quite tall and the boat comparatively small, it stood lower than the ship. **straight**—immediately.

Under the water it rumbled on,
Still louder and more dread;
It reached the ship, it split the bay;
The ship went down like lead.

The ship suddenly sinketh.

Stunned by that loud and dreadful sound,
Which sky and ocean smote.
Like one that hath been seven days drowned
My body lay afloat;
But swift as dreams, myself I found
Within the Pilot's boat.

The ancient Mariner is saved in the Pilot's boat.

Upon the whirl, where sank the ship,
The boat spun round and round:

And all was still, save that the hill
Was telling of the sound.

I moved my lips—the Pilot shrieked
And fell down in a fit;
The holy Hermit raised his eyes,
And prayed where he did sit.

I took the oars : the Pilot's boy,
Who now doth crazy go,
Laughed loud and long, and all the while
His eyes went to and fro.
'Ha, ha !' quoth he, 'full plain I see,
The Devil knows how to row.

L. 546-549. rumbled on—produced a heavy, rolling sound as of thunder **and more dread**—and more fearful. **it split the bay**—the loud sound broke up the water of the bay. It is a fact that when a very loud sound is produced the water nearby is seriously disturbed because of the sound waves, **went down like lead**—sank as if it were made of lead, a heavy metal. The ship and its ghastly burden had to be got rid of, as Creswell says. Coleridge adopts the device of sinking it along with its dead crew.

L. 550-555. Stunned—greatly surprised. **Which sky...smote**—the loud sound disturbed greatly the water of the sea and also resounded to the sky. **Like one...drowned**—like a body which has drowned and after some time comes to

L. 546-549. The sound became louder and more dreadful under the water. It reaches the ship and cause an opening in the water under it. As it has happened, the ship sink like a heavy burden.

L. 550-555. The Mariner become almost unconscious at the occurrence of the loud sound which has shook the sky and the ocean. After the ship has sank, he do not draw but floats on the water like a decomposed dead body. He is, however, quickly taken into the Pilot's boat.

L. 556-559. A whirlpool has formed where the ship has sank. The boat is moving over it in a circular motion. All round there is complete silence except for an echo in the hills.

L. 560-563. The Mariner has moved his lips to speak to them. The Pilot gets frightened, shrieks and falls down unconscious. The Hermit too has raised his eyes towards the sky and begin to pray immediately from the place where he is sitting.

L. 564-569. The Ancient Mariner begin to row the boat. The servant of the Pilot has gone mad because of the fear that he is in the presence of the Devil. He goes on laughing and rolling his eyes. Then he says that he clearly see the Devil rowing the boat.

---

float on the water surface because it has swollen up. **lay afloat**—lay floating. **swift as dreams**-very quickly and also quite unconsciously. Dreams are imperceptible and rise and melt quickly.

L. 556-559. **the whirl**—the rapid circular motion of water which is produced by the sinking of the heavy ship. **spun round and round**—moved round and round very quickly with the circular motion of the water. **telling of the sound**—echoing the sound.

L. 560-563. **moved my lips**—tried to speak. **shrieked**—cried out in fear. **fell down in a fit**—fell into a state of unconsciousness. The Mariner appears so horrific. Note the consummate skill with which Coleridge conveys to the reader the change brought about by the horrible experiences in the Mariner's appearance. No direct description could be as striking as the description of the effect his appearance has on the others.

L. 564-569. I took the oars—I began to ply the boat. **doth crazy go**—goes mad. **Laughed loud and long**—laughed in fear and not in joy; the Pilot's boy has gone mad at the very sight of the ancient Mariner taking the oars. **His eyes...fro**—His eyes moved restlessly as those of a mad man or of one extremely frightened, **'full plain I see**—I know well enough. **The Devil...to row**—This is said about the ancient Mariner whom the Pilot's boy takes to be an evil spirit suddenly taking possession of the dead body and trying to ply the boat. Mark how natural the touches are here and yet how easily they help to create a supernatural horror.

And now, all in my own countree,
I stood on the firm land !
The Hermit stepped forth from the boat,
And scarcely he could stand.

'O, shrieve me, shrieve me, holy man!'
The Hermit crossed his brow.

'Say quick' quoth, he, 'I bid thee say-
What manner of man art thou ?'

The Ancient Mariner earnestly entreateth the Hermit to shrieve him; and the penance of life falls on him.

Forthwith this frame of mine was wrenched
With a woful agony,
Which forced me to begin my tale;
And then it left me free.

Since then, at an uncertain hour,
That agony returns :
And till my ghastly tale is told,
This heart within me burns.

And ever and anon throughout his future life an agony constraineth him to travel from land to land;

I pass like night, from land to land;
I have strange power of speech;
That moment that his face I see,
I know the man that must hear me :
To him my tale I teach.

What loud uproar bursts from that door!
The wedding-guests are there:

But in the garden-bower the bride
And bride-maids singing are:
And hark the little vesper bell,
Which biddeth me to prayer!

L. 570-573. 1 stood on the firm land—the Mariner felt sure that he stood on solid land and not on the rocking ship in the sea which had been the scene of his ugly dreams and hallucinations and also actual suffering, **stepped forth**—came forward. **scarcely he could stand**—the hermit also was so frightened by the unnatural sight and events that he could hardly stand erect.

L. 574-577. crossed his brow—made the sign of a cross on his forehead as all Christians do when they are in fear and want to avert some evil influence. Even the Hermit is not quite sure that the Mariner is human. **What manner...thou?**—Are you a human being or some supernatural spirit?

L. 578-581.forthwith.....frame—body. **wrenched**-twisted or convulsed with great pain. **woful agony**—extreme pain, **begin my tale**—this is the penance of

L. 570-573. Now the Mariner has reached his own country and is standing on its firm land. The Hermit comes out of the boat but even he is so frightened that he can not stand properly.

L. 574-577. The Mariner has appealed to the holy man to save him. He, at first, crosses his brow and then has asked the Mariner to say what kind of man he is.

L. 578-581. As soon as the Hermit has asked him the Mariner feels an extreme pain inside him. It compells him to relate his story only after which he has felt relieved.

L. 582-585. From that time onwards at some moments suddenly he feel the agony. The burning sensation and pain has continued till he has related his story.

L. 586-590. Just like the night, the Mariner has travelled from country to country. He has developed an uncommon power of story-telling. He can recognise the person who will listen to him as soon as he see his face. Then he tell him the tale and has also taught him the moral.

L. 591-596. Loud sound of music is heard. They are coming from the wedding-hall where the ceremonies are going on. The bride is in the garden where her maids are singing. Just then comes the sound of the church bell and the Mariner feels as if he is being called for evening prayer.

---

his life, **it left me free**—He felt relieved after speaking out his story. This sense of relief is based on a psychological fact that when one commits a sin or a crime or even a mild offence one feels restless at heart until one talks about it to somebody else.

L. 582-585. an uncertain hour—at any time. **That agony**—the consciousness of guilt and the consequent feeling of pain and horror. **ghastly tale**—a tale dealing with fearful incidents and scenes. **This heart...burns**—The Mariner feels the dreadful horror of his guilt.

L. 586-590. **I pass...land**—Just as darkness travels swiftly from one corner of the world to the other with the setting of the sun so alsp the ancient Mariner travels from one country to another to relate his tale. **strange power of speech** —a great power of attracting and detaining people by speech. **That moment...hear me**—by the very form of the face of a man the Mariner can judge that he is a potential listener and that he will have no power to resist the tale, **teach**—relate.

L. 591-596. What loud uproar...that door—What a great noise of merry-making is coming from the wedding house: This is an artistic touch to produce a change of atmosphere and a touch of realism. **Bride-maids**—the attendant maids of the bride, **hark**—listen, **vesper bell**—the evening church bell. **Which biddeth prayer**—Which invites one to attend the prayer in the church. Note the contrast of the noise of the wedding feast and the light sound of the little vesper bell. The wedding no longer interests the wedding guest.

O, Wedding-Guest! this soul hath been
Alone on a wide, wide sea:
So lonely 'twas, that God himself
Scarce seemed there to be.

O, sweeter than the marriage-feast,
'Tis sweeter far to me,
To walk together to the kirk
With a goodly company !

To walk together to the kirk,
And all together pray,
While each to his great Father bends,
Old men, and babes, and loving friends,
And youths and maidens gay !

Farewell, farewell ! but this I tell
To thee, thou Wedding-Guest !

And to teach by his own example love and reverence to all things that God made and loveth.

He prayeth well, who loveth well
Both man and bird and beast.

He prayeth best, who loveth best
All things both great and small;
For the dear God who loveth us,
He made and loveth all.

The Mariner, whose eye is bright,
Whose beard with age is hoar,
Is gone; and now the Wedding-Guest
Turned from the bridegroom's door.

He went like one that hath been stunned,
And is of sense forlorn
A sadder and a wiser man,
He rose the morrow morn.

L. 597-600. This soul hath...there to be—In the utter loneliness felt by the Mariner, even God scarcely seemed to be there. The stark loneliness of a person haunted by guilt is well brought out.

L. 601 -609. Note the tone of repentance and complete conversion from a hater of birds and beasts to a pious worshipper of God and his creations. Even the marriage feast is not as sweet as the prayer and goodly company in a church. After the horrific loneliness at sea, the Mariner longs for the peaceful company

L. 597-600. The Mariner tells the Wedding-Guest that he has been alone in the midst of a vast ocean. It is so lonely that even God has not seemed to be present there.

L. 601-604. The Ancient Mariner tells the Wedding-Guest that he like going to the church with good people much more than attending a marriage.

L. 605-609. The Mariner continues that it is a great pleasure to walk to the church with other people and to pray with them. It is nice that old and young men and women, all shall together bend in prayer before God.

L. 610-613. The Mariner has bade farewell to the Wedding-Guest. Before going he has told him that real prayer lay in loving all men and birds and beasts.

L. 614-617. The best prayer is to love all the creatures of God. God has made them as He has made men and He loves all equally.

L. 618-621. The Mariner who has a bright eye and a grey beard has gone away. After that the Wedding-Guest do not go to the marriage but has gone away from the house of marriage.

L. 622-625. The Wedding-Guest leaves the place like a person is deprived of his thought and sense. Next morning when he gets up he is a wiser and a sadder man.

---

in church. **all together pray**—pray not alone but in a body i.e., in a congregation. **each to his...bends**—each person kneels down iii- order to pray to God who is regarded as the Father or Creator of all. **babes**—little children. Note that the diversity of the congregation is stressed. The Mariner has learnt from experience that all of them are to be loved without distinction.

L. 610-617. **He prayeth well...beast**—This is the moral of the poem. The Ancient Mariner has learnt it at a dear cost. He means to say that the best form of worship is to love all the creations of God whether they are human beings or birds or beasts without any distinction. **All things both great and small**—all creatures alike, i.e. men, birds, and beasts and even plants and trees. He **prayeth best...love the all**—The argument is that the best form of worship is to love all creatures or rather all creations of God without making any kind of distinction as we generally do. God has created this universe in which all great and small things exist and he loves them all. Those who do not love God's creatures cannot love their creator.

L. 618.621. **with age is hoar**—grown white due to old age. **Turned from...door**—gave up the idea of visiting the bridegroom.

L. 622-624. **stunned**—extremely surprised or shocked. **of sense forlorn**—deprived of his senses or feelings, **sadder**—more sober. **morrow morn**—next morning. The wedding guest has undergone a serious change as the result of hearing the Mariner's story.

(B) EXPLANATIONS WITH CRITICAL COMMENTS

1. L. 21-24. The ship.....Lighthouse top. The passage is taken from Coleridge's poem *The Ancient Mariner*. It occurs in the first section where the Mariner describes how the ship has started. He says that they have started very happily. The greetings and good wishes of friends are with them. He mentions the church, the hill and the lighthouse top.

The stanza with its picturesqueness, conjures up before our imagination an image of the little village harbour as the ship puts out on its voyage and also the cheers of onlookers asembled on the quay. But those who witnessed its departure would little dream of the fate awaiting it.

2. L. 28-32. Higher and higher.....bassoon. In this passage from the first section of Coleridge's *The Ancient Mariner*, the Mariner is continuing his narration. As the ship has moved towards the Equator the sun stood higher and higher at noon, till on the Equator it has stood over the mast at noon. At this point the guest has heard the loud sound of bassoon coming from the feast hall and as he has felt that he is being prevented from attending the feast, he beat his breast in utter helplessness.

The story so far has been a plain, matter-of-fact narrative. In spite of the fascination exercised over him, the guest cannot conceal his irritation when the sounds from the feast break in. These sounds remind him of his strange circumstances, but they do not have the power to break the spell. After this, however, the listener is all attention. He is reminded of the marriage feast only when the Mariner has finished his tale. Traill says: "The details of the voyage are all chronicled with such order and regularity, there is such a diary-like air about the whole thing, that we accept it almost as if it were a series of extracts from a ship's log.

3. L. 45-50. With sloping.....we fled. These lines give a picture of The Ancient Mariner's ship as it is driven southward by a violent storm. The storm blows from behind. By the force of the storm the tall, erect masts of the ship are bent forward. The front part of the ship sank under the water by the drive from behind. Thus the ship has moved fast before the storm, but still it can not outspeed the storm. The ship here is compared to a man who, being pursued by an enemy, runs fast for fear of life. The enemy is pursuing from behind, shouting and striking the man. His shadow is cast before the man who is being pursued. The man dare not look behind to see the enemy. He runs at top speed, bending his head forward. But however fast he runs, he cannot outdistance his enemy. So also the ship was driven fast by the roaring and striking storm from behind but it cannot get rid of the storm.

The stanza is remarkable for its picturesqueness and the aptness of the simile. The speed and the situation is suggested by the fast moving metre.

4. L. 59-62. The ice.....a swound. In these lines The Ancient Mariner gives details of the polar region. The place is not only dark but also full of confused noises, due to the constant breaking of the icebergs. As the icebergs are driven by the storm they crash against one another and crack up. A loud and confused noise is thus produced. These noises are like those heard by a man who falls into a fainting fit. This is a reference to the belief that an unconscious man hears confused sounds.

An impression of utter desolation is produced by the simple description.

5. L. 79-82. God save thee....the Albatross. This stanza marks the end of the first section of *The Ancient Mariner*. The Mariner has been narrating his story to the Wedding-Guest. At this stage the Guest notices signs of great mental agony on the face of the Mariner. He has felt that the old man is troubled by evil spirits and has prayed to God to protect him from them. He also asks the Mariner the cause of his trouble. In reply he can not give an elaborate explanation. He only said that he has killed the Albatross. It reminds us of the previous stanzas where the Mariner has been lingering on the description and not proceeding with the story. The reason for this reluctance is that this is to be the most painful confession of the crime.

This dramatic way of saying it has helped us to concentrate attention on the confession and the crime. The stanza also brings out the poet's skill both in keeping up the reality of the story as a story told to a listener and in suggesting, without direct narration, some point of appearance or description which he wants to convey to the reader. The first part of the the poem closes with the mention of the word, Albatross, is suggesting to the reader the idea that the killing of the bird is the crisis of poem. This fact is kept in our mind by the conclusion of almost each part of the poem.

6. L. 99-102. Then all ....fog and mist. The Albatross, the bird of good omen, which has followed the ship for nine days is cruelly slain by The Ancient Mariner. At first his companions has rebuked him for that wanton act of cruelty. They have said that it is a dastardly crime to kill the bird that has brought the breeze. A little later, however, when the sun rise in all its glory and the fog and mist has cleared away, they have changed their attitude and said that *The Ancient Mariner* has done right in killing the bird which is responsible for the mist and fog.

This attitude of the sailors makes them really contemptible creatures who have not even the virtue of consistency. In his marginal commentary to the poem, Coleridge points out that by justifying the action of The Ancient Mariner, the other sailors make themselves accomplices in the crime.

With the change of weather there came a change in the outlook of the sailors regarding the killing of the bird. The Albatross has brought fog and mist and is therefore a bird of ill omen. The Ancient Mariner has therefore done the right thing by killing the bird. Their attitude towards the crime is merely selfish and is not based on moral principles. They judged the deed not on merit but by the result it has on them; they are therefore not merely accomplices in the crime, but also utterly inconsistent in their assertion.

7. L. 103-106. The fair breeze.....silent sea. This beautiful stanza is the description of how the ship in Coleridge's *The Ancient Mariner* enters the Pacific Ocean. The Mariner is telling, the Guest in Section II that the wind is favourable. The white foam is being thrown up as the ship advanced and left behind a clear track because of the calmness of the sea. According to him, he and his companions are the first to have entered that silent sea.

The sea has been mentioned in such a way as if both the Mariner and the Guest knows it well. The stanza is remarkable for vividness of description and fineness of versification. The alliteration makes it smooth and sweet to hear. The rhythm suggests the wonder of a great discovery.

8. L. 115-118. Day after day......painted ocean. For some days after the Albatross is killed by The Ancient Mariner. The ship driven by the favourable south wind entered the calm Pacific Ocean. It still sails northward and reached the equator. The sun now have stood directly overhead. It is intensely hot and the sky is assumed a copper colour by the heat of the sun. All of a sudden the wind has stopped and the ship stood motionless. There is also no current in the sea water. This continues for some days. The ship is as motionless as a ship painted in a picture remains all the time in the position in which it has been drawn by the painter; so the ship of the Mariner remained still and in the same position for some days, for want of wind and current.

The simile used for the motionless state of the ship is striking and powerful. The stanza, as a whole, is a specimen of Coleridge's power of word-painting.

9. L. 119-122. Water, water......to drink. As the ship of The Ancient Mariner is suddenly becalmed, their sufferings begains. The sun is pouring fire. So great is the heat of the sun that the planks of the ship are getting twisted or shrunken. Besides, their supply of fresh drinking water is soon exhausted. They are almost dying of thirst. Thus it is their tragedy that with the limitless water of the ocean around them they have no water to drink, as the sea water is not suitable for drinking. The punishment of The Ancient Mariner and his fellow-sailors' begins here.

10. L. 123-126. The very deep.....slimy sea. This is the description of the prevailing rottenness around the motionless ship has given by the Mariner in *The Ancient Mariner*. The situation is so terrible that even the sea seems to have become rotten. There is dirt all around. In the mud of the sea, dirty creatures are crawling about.

The stanza, particularly the last two lines, illustrates Coleridge's power to describe the horrible. The full effect is best seen and appreciated when these lines are read slowly. The repetition of the word 'slimy' and the addition 'with legs' create the extreme sense of hideousness of the spectacle.

11. L. 127-130. About, about.....blue and white. These lines describes the punishment that has came upon the old Mariner and his companions for killing the Albatross. Their ship lay becalmed at the equator. There is no stock of drinking water in the ship. The sea is looking unnatural. It seems to be rotting in the intense heat of the sun. At night various phosphorescent lights coming out of the decaying animal matter in the ocean begains to dance in a confused manner around the ship. To the superstitious mariners these lights seems to foretell death. The sea water which is rotten begins to burn with strange colours of green, blue and white. It seems to be not water but witch's oils, prepares from various loathsome ingredients which is described by Shakespeare in his *Macbeth*. The sea-water too seems to be charm and spread horror into the minds of the mariners.

12. L. 153-156. A speck.....veered. In these lines, The Ancient Mariner describes the gradual approach of the skeleton ship. He and his companions has passed a long and weary time, in thirst and loneliness. One day, looking towards the western sky, when the sun is setting, The Ancient Mariner sees a strange sight. At first, the thing has appeared like a dot in the horizon. As it come nearer, it has looks like a moving piece of mist; it is still too indistinct to be clearly distinguished. Then as it come still nearer, the Mariner find it has a definite shape-it is a ship. It is moving so fast that it has appeared to be escaping from the pursuit of a water spirit. Besides, its course is very unsteady. This strange behaviour of the ship makes. The Ancient Mariner thinks that the ship is trying to escape from a water spirit that is pursuing it to take revenge.

The poet skilfully suggests the supernatural nature of the ship. The ship of The Ancient Mariner is becalmed, for there is no wind and tide. But in the same sea there is another ship which iss moving fast and very irregularly. How can this second ship move thus, without wind or tide, unless there is something supernatural about it.

13. L. 190-194. Her lips.....cold. In these lines, The Ancient Mariner describes one of the crew of the phantom ship, namely Life-in-Death. On a nearer view of the ship The Ancient Mariner has found that there are two figures on the deck of the ship. One is Death and the other is Life-in-Death, the companion of Death. Life-in-Death has the beauty of a woman. Her lips are red, the look of her eyes are bold and open. Her hair is golden. But her skin is of an unnatural colour. It is as white as the skin of a woman who is suffering from leprosy. Now a normal, healthy woman cannot have such a white skin as that of Life-in-Death. Life-in-Death is like a nightmare that congeals men's blood.

The horrible description corresponds to the strangeness of her character as is evident from the name. The appearance of the skeleton ship is a mere device to demonstrate the respective awards by higher supernatural agency to the two categories of human sinners. Death will indicate lighter punishment; and Life-in-Death, a more severe punishment, though leading to the laborious pleasure of a godly life. The strangeness of her character is indicated by contrasts: red lips and yellow locks stand for life; leprous-white skin stands for Death.

14. L. 199-202. The Sun's run.....spectre bark. This stanza is describing the night-fall in tropics from *The Ancient Mariner* by Coleridge is striking. The ship of the Mariner is driven by some spirit from the south to the tropical region where they have suffered from thirst and scorching heat of the sun.

The Mariner has seen with fear the skeleton-ship and its inmates. At that time darkness overtook them suddenly and the skeleton-ship has disappeared. Describing it he says that the edge of the sun has gone down into the sea and the stars has appeared. The darkness covered the entire scene swiftly. The skeleton ship has disappeared in the darkness. Only a faint sound is made by it is heard from a distance. The stanza shows Coleridge's great power of word-painting. The absence of twilight in the tropics has been described remarkably through the simplest words.

The fearful climax of human destiny is followed by the description of nature; man, nature and God are forming the eternal themes of poetry. The darkness suddenly appeares because there is no twilight in tropical regions (the ship is near the Equator). 'The dark' is personified. The phantom-ship suddenly disappeares with a hissing sound which is heard from a distance.

15. L. 203-207. We listened.....gleamed white. These lines describes the horror felt by time Mariner at the strange disappearance of the spectre ship. Night comes rapidly in the tropical sea. It is a very dark night but the stars are dim pale. As the ship dartes off, it produces a hissing sound which cannot be heard from a distance. The mariners listenes to the sound. They have not the courage to look directly at the disappearing ship and looks only sideways. The Ancient Mariner's fear is so great that all his life-blood seems to be suck dry. Fear seems to sip all his blood, in the same manner as a man sips tea out of a cup. In other words, The Ancient Mariner becomes pale with fear. He also find in the lamp light that the face of the helmsman is white with fear.

16. L. 232-235. Alone, alone......in agony. The stanza is taken from Coleridge's *The Ancient Mariner* Part IV. The horrors is described and the Mariner tells the Guest that all his companions is dead. The Guest fears that he also may be talking to a ghost. His fear is intensified by the strange appearance of the Mariner. The Mariner, however, assures the guest that he is not a ghost. He tells him that the signs of pain and ghastliness on his face have resulted from the utter loneliness that he has had to suffer. This stanza describes the oppressive solitude. It is all the more terrible because he is alone in the midst of a vast ocean with dead companions. He feels that he is forsaken even by God and no holy saint has pity on his tortured soul.

By repeating the words 'all', 'alone' and 'wide' the poet marvellously depicts the terror of loneliness.

17. L. 236-239. The many men......so did I. The Ancient Mariner here describes his condition after the death of his two hundred companions. He is left alone on the wide sea. Even a saint of heaven whom he has invoked do not come to his help. His companions are all strong, beautiful men. They are dead. The only living creatures are the ugly aquatic animals living in the mud. They are moving about the ship. Like them, The Ancient Mariner, too is living. He seems to be one of them, because he too is living. His mind is, therefore, filled with a hatred for his own self. He look upon himself not as a man, the beautiful creation of God, but as an ugly, slimy thing.

This shows that there is in him even now a hatred for lower creatures and his heart is not chaste. It is this disdain for lower creatures which has led the Mariner to kill the Albatross. His sense of loneliness is the punishment for his want of sympathy with his humbler fellow-creatures.

18. L. 244-247. I looked......as dust. In these lines The Ancient Mariner describes his utterly helpless condition in the far-off sea. The sea is rotting. He can not look at it, because he see there only ugly aquatic animals. He tries to look up to the sky and pray to God for relief from his suffering. But no prayer has came out of his mouth because his heart is not yet softened with pity and love. It is only a wicked thought that has found expression in the shape of a whisper that has came out of his heart. The result is that his heart is left dry as ever-utterly devoid of noble feelings. Thus his condition is so miserable that he can not even say a Christian prayer.

The distant sea, the nearer deck and upward heaven are the possible objects on which the Mariner can look or concentrate his mind. But in each case there is some positive obstacle—disdain for the sea-creatures, the reminder of his crime and the impurity of his heart. As a result the Mariner can not find peace or rest anywhere. His heart is still filled with antipathy and aversion for the ugly sea-creatures and can not find peace in prayer. Pride and disdain constitute sin and so long as sinful thought will persist, the mind will be bereft of gentler feelings and all good aspirations will wither.

19. L. 257-262. An orphan's.....not die. In these lines, The Ancient Mariner describes his suffering after the death of his companions. He does not find any consolation from the sea or the sky. When he looks at the deck of the ship he see horrible sights there. The dead bodies do not show any sign of decomposition that is caused by death. The sweat falling from their bodies has evaporated. There is still the same dreadful look of curse in the eyes of the dead men. It seems as if they are still cursing him, though they are dead. The curse of an orphan is powerful enough to bring an angel from heaven to hell. Even an angel has to suffer torment in hell if it is cursed by an orphan, so great is the power of an orphan's curse. The curse in the eyes of a dead man is even more powerful. And this curse now fell upon The Ancient Mariner. For seven days and nights he remains in that state, being exposed to the cursing looks of the two hundred dead men. Every moment he has prayed for death, which will be a welcome relief from his torment. But he can not die and has to suffer more.

Curses are believed to have great power over men's spiritual welfare. Cruelty to a helpless orphan will, under the moral order of God, drag down even an angel from heaven to hell. The reason is that in the heart of every being it is God who dwells; that is why even the most powerful man cannot be exempted from divine punishment for moral violation.

20. L. 263-266. The moving Moon.....two beside. The stanza occurs in part IV of *The Ancient Mariner* written by Coleridge. The Mariner is saying that in that loneliness he is utterly bewildered. He does not know what to do and where to go. He is surrounded by dirty things—dead bodies and slimy creatures. As he looks up he see the Moon whose journey is described here. It goes on moving up the sky without stopping anywhere. She is going up gently with a star or two by her side. They seemes to him to enjoy a free, happy life in their native home. The Mariner desires to share their happy condition. It is made clear by the comment in the margin: "In his loneliness and fixedness he yearneth towards the journeying Moon and the star...."

The picture is a symbolic fulfilment of the Mariner's desire to have a welcoming home and to be able to move into it with freedom, a thing which he can not hope for in that situation. The contrast between the tortured life of the Mariner is surrounded by the dead bodies of the crew and the peaceful loveliness of nature above him is to be noted. When the Mariner is haunted by the looks of the dead sailors the moon continues her quiet unchanging course. The permanence of Nature and the mutable and painful character of human life is a fundamental note of poetry.

21. L. 288-298. The self-same moment....into the sea. The stanza marks the end of Part IV of *The Ancient Mariner* is written by Coleridge. As soon as the Mariner is able to appreciate the beauty of the creatures of God and feels love for them, he gets pity from god. It is possible for him to pray. The curse begains to lose its effect. The very moment he is able to pray, the Albatross fell off quite freely from his neck. It sinks into the sea like lead or a heavy burden. As he has regained the power to pray, the power of the curse breaks.

As in the other parts, here also in the very last lines appears the incident to which the whole section has been leading. It comes suddenly and is mentioned briefly. This point is, indeed, the dramatic centre of the whole poem and on it, is based the moral of it.

This incident is obviously modelled on the falling off of Christian's burden in *Pilgrim's Progress* when he sees the Cross.

22. L. 292-296. O sleep....soul. After The Ancient Mariner has atone for his sin by loving and blessing the water snakes, his redemption becomes complete. The dead body of the Albatross, which is so long hanging around his neck like a dead weight of sin, fell off. The Mariner fell into a refreshing sleep, of which he has been deprived so long. In these lines The Ancient Mariner sings his song in praise of sleep. Sleep is a soft and soothing thing, that is dear to all people of the world. It is the balm of hurt minds. It is the great nourisher of life. The man who is denied the blessing of sleep is a miserable wretch, indeed. Sleep is a divine blessing. It is a gift of God to toil-worn men and animals. May Virgin Mary, the mother of Jesus Christ, be thanked for giving sweet sleep to men, says the Mariner. It is the divine sleep which descends from heaven into the body and soul of the Mariner. The Ancient Mariner now fell asleep not only in body but also in tortured soul and feels the sweet effect of sleep and was restores to calm and serenity.

The soothing nature of sleep is well-known in life and literature. In sleep the mind does not function and cares and anxieties of wakeful life come to an end.

23. L. 313-317. The upper air......between. As The Ancient Mariner awoke from a refreshing sleep he has heard the roaring sound of the wind blowing violently at a distance from his ship. The whole sky has became vocal with the noises of busy activity. The sky which seems to be dead is so long animated. Bright flashes of lightning has occurred in different directions and looks like white banners. The stars looks pale in contrast with the brilliance of the lightning flashes. These pale stars seems to be moving quickly between the clouds driven by the storm. Thus the spell of silence in the sky is broken by thunder and lightning.

Coleridge here sketches a storm with delight in the wild effects of sky and cloud. Every detail comes from the known world, which is the firm background of the supernatural events which accompany it in this poem.

24. L. 324-326. Like waters....and wide. When he has become conscious of the beauty of created things and has been able to pray, sweet sleep descends on The Ancient Mariner and brings peace to his soul. He dreams that it has been rainy and awakes to find heavy showers pouring down from one black cloud. The cloud soon is cleft into two and from the broken cloud flashes of lightning darted forth continuously. The lightning seems to fall like a deep and wide river flowing down from some high mountains. The beautiful image has been employed to convey the idea that the lightning is continuous.

Coleridge is here speaking of what is called sheet lightning (and not forked lightning). Sheet lightning comes down from the sky to the earth like a long sheet without a break. A fork lightning is one which flashes from one end of the sky to the other like a set of forks. This is a remarkable simile. The sheet lightning is compared to a waterfall. As a cataract flows down from a high hill, so the lightning, like a continuous flood of light, pours from the sky above. These are "lines noteworthy for their minute and sensitive appreciation of natural scenery, and the realistic description in the interest and simplest of language," as Creswell says.

25. L. 358-362. Sometimes a dropping.....sweet jargoning. The Ancient Mariner realises that the bodies of the dead companions were animated by a troop of blessed spirits. There is proof for this when he hears the sweet sounds coming from their mouths and filling the atmosphere. These musical sounds seems to dart forth everywhere. Sometimes, they sounds like individual melodies, and at other times combine to make a magnificent concert. One moment it is like the song of a lonely skylark when dropping from the great height to which it has soared. Another moment it will be like the music of all the little song-birds in the world combining in one magnificent harmony.

26. L. 367-372. It ceased....quiet tune. This delicate stanza occurs in Coleridge's The Ancient Mariner. The Mariner tells how beautiful and soothing are the sound that the sails produces as the ship sails on after that torturous has fixed state in the tropical region.

The sweet sounds of the angels, says he has stopped. Still, the sail has continued producing a sweet sound till noon. This sound is as sweet as the sound produces by a small stream is hidden among trees in a wood during the month of June. The calm song lulls the woods to sleep and rest for the night. The sounds that he has heard are as sweet and as soothing.

The simile here, as elsewhere in this poem, is dramatically appropriate. The pleasant noise of the wind in the sails suggests to the Mariner the woodland sounds of his home. Choice of words like the 'hidden brook', 'the leafy month of June' and the 'sleeping woods' is very skilful. It gives not only a musical form and melody, but are also sensuous and picturesque in suggestion. The lines gives an unsurpassed impression of gentle continuity and peace.

The contrast of these lines with the dryness and stagnation describes earlier is noteworthy.

27. L. 406-409. The other was......will do. These are the words of the Second Voice, which represents the spirit of Mercy, that The Ancient Mariner has heard in his trance. The First Voice representing Justice, emphasised the sin of The Ancient Mariner who has killed the loving Albatross that is the beloved of the Polar Spirit. Clearly Justice is in favour of giving more punishment to The Ancient Mariner for his sin. But the voice of Mercy has pleaded on behalf of The Ancient Mariner. The voice of Mercy is soft and tender like honey-dew. It is pointed out that The Ancient Mariner is already paying the penalty for his sin by a process of terrible suffering. He will be performing more penance when he goes back to his native land. Hence he shall be spared further punishment at that moment.

The Mariner is thus assured in his dream of divine mercy and final salvation.

28. L. 446-451. Like one......him freed. In these lines, taken from Part VI of Coleridge's *The Ancient Mariner,* the Mariner expresses his haunted state even after the curse has abated. When a man goes on a solitary journey he walks in fear. Having once looks back and seen an evil spirit pursuing him hotly, he does not look behind again. In fear he walks on though the spirit may not be pursuing him. The situation of the Mariner is similar. Having been once under the spell of horror he can not easily believe that it is over.

The passage shows how tormented he was and exhibits remarkably Coleridge's understanding of mental states.

29. L. 534-537. Brown skeletons.....she wolf's young. In these lines the Hermit describes the sails of the ship of The Ancient Mariner towards which they are drawing in a small boat. The sails seem to be unnatural, being completely dried up and of a brown colour, by exposure to sun and rain. He had never seen the like of them. These sails, according to him, can be compared only to the dried leaves which fall from trees and become thin and sere. They decay and only the veins of the leaves remain. The leaves become mere skeletons of a brown colour. The Hermit has seen them float on the stream in winter. In this season the ivy-bushes are covered with snow-fakes. The song of all birds becomes silence in the dead of winter. It is only the owl that screeches at night. Its screech are mixed with the hungry howls of the he-wolf which eats away its young ones, if the mother-wolf did not guard them carefully. The gruesomeness of the imagery is quite appropriate in a supernatural story.

30. L. 578-581. Forthwith....free. In this stanza of Coleridge's *The Ancient Mariner,* the Mariner describe what has happened to him when the Hermit has asked him to tell him about himself. The painfulness of the confessionary process is clearly brought out. His body at once felt a severe pain which compells him to tell the whole story. After having done this he felt relieved. This, as we learn from the lines following it, is the penance of his life. This alone brings him comfort. He washes his sin by confessing it and by describing the punishment. He urges his audience to learn a lesson from his tale and to love and pray as he has once so disastrously failed to do. In this he finds relief and comfort.

31. L. 597-600. O Wedding-Guest......to be. The Mariner has experienced worldliness marked by human pride and has hatred for other creatures, and the resultant sorrows and sufferings; he has also known purity of heart following upon godliness and consequent inner peace and repose. Hence he contrasts the two paths of life; and ends following the true pleasure of life in seeking God in the world. He has known intense suffering and loneliness. He is so lonely on the wide sea that he has felt as if God has left him. Though God is present everywhere, yet not being god-minded due to his arrogance, he has to suffer all alone on a silent sea and can not find any solace. When through the dawn of love in his chasten heart he can turn inwards to feel the divine reality pervading all objects he can feel happy, and his mind now has turned away from the empty pleasures of worldly life.

32. L. 614-617. He prayeth.....loveth all. In these lines *The Ancient Mariner* sums up the grand moral of his tale. It is a truth that has been driven home to him by his crime and punishment. Prayer, to *The Ancient Mariner*, does not mean uttering some set of words in the Church. The essence of prayer is universal love-love for all the creations of God, great and small. To pray to God means to love all His creations. God is Love, says the Bible. He loves all His creations, without making any distinction of them. The Ancient Mariner has learnt this grand moral lesson from his own experience. He now inculcates this grand moral lesson in the Wedding-Guest.

The moral arises easily and naturally out of the very constitution of the poem and does not at all appear to be an imposition from outside as the result of after-thought. A crime born in hate must, in the nature of things, find its expiation through love; and thus the large love for "all things great and small" is the cosmic need of the poem itself and an aural reflex from its central life principle. The poem is a revelation, says Stopford Brooke; makes by Coleridge of what he has believed to be always the case in the spiritual world.

(C) INTRODUCTION TO *THE RIME OF THE ANCIENT MARINER*

Sources of *'The Ancient Mariner'*. The incident of the Albatross has been taken by Coleridge from a book entitled *A Voyage around the World by the way of the Great South Sea* by Shelrocke. In this book the second captain of the ship shoots at an albatross which continually hovers near the ship. The interpretation of the incident is to be attributed entirely to Coleridge. The poem is published in 1798 in *Lyrical Ballads* but is afterwards revised. It is one of the poems written in 1797 when Wordsworth and Coleridge are on tour together and some details are suggested by Wordsworth.

The Origin of the Poem. Coleridge's great contribution to the Lyrical Ballads is *The Ancient Mariner,* his one perfect and complete achievement. The way in which this marvellous poem comes to be written is common place enough. On the afternoon of November 13, 1797 Coleridge,

Wordsworth and his sister set off together from Alfoxden on a walking expedition 'with a view' Wordsworth tells us, 'to visit Linton and the Valley of Stones near it and as our united funds is very small, we have have agreed to defray the expenses of the tour by writing a poem to be send to the *New Monthly Magazine*. Accordingly we set off, and have proceeded along the Quantock Hills towards Watchet, and in the course of this walk it his planned the poem of the *The Ancient Mariner*, has founded on a dream, as Mr. Coleridge says, of his friend, Mr. Cruikshank—'a dream of a skeleton ship manned by skeleton sailors.' With this dream as the starting point, other hints and suggestions are taken from various sources. Wordsworth, who has been reading in Shelrocke's Voyages about the Albatrosses of the South Seas, suggests that the mariner should have been represented 'as having killed one of these birds on entering the South Sea, and that the tutelar spirits of these regions take upon themselves to avenge the crime.' He also contributs a few lines, but soon the manners of the two 'proved so widely different' that he withdraws, and Coleridge has completed the work himself.

With consummate skill he welds the story into an artistic whole. For vividness of imagery and descriptive power the poem is unsurpassed. We move in a world of unearthly weirdness whose mystery and charm is unbroken by an inconsistency. He sees the invisible and almost touches the intangible in this realm, where the things that are too seldom dreamt of in our philosophy loom within our ken. Absolutely simple in both metre and language, the poem is indeed, as Coleridge himself pronounces it, 'inimitable'.

It is futile to try to discover from where all the materials and ideas for such a great work of art have been derived. Coleridge is a voracious reader and the books he read and the men he meets left a profound influence on him. Like the bee, he roams in a garden of flowers, gathering the materials for his honey in strange and little known places. For the reader it is enough to know that what is presented to him is an exquisite work of art and he need not bother about the sources from which the poet might have drawn his material.

Purpose for Writing *The Ancient Mariner*. Coleridge wrote *The Ancient Mariner* to fulfil his plan of writing a series of supernatural poems, in which the incidents and characters are to be at least in a part of supernatural and yet to present them as would impress the readers with a sense of their reality. This is a part of the literary programme he has made along with his friend Wordsworth. There is another purpose behind the composition of the poem, and this is purely mercenary. It is to defray the expenses of a journey to Linton and neighbourhood that he has undertaken in the autumn of 1797 along with Wordsworth and his sister Dorothy.

(D) CRITICAL SUMMARY OF THE POEM

Part I. An Ancient Mariner, with a long grey beard and glittering eyes, stops one of the three guests on their way to a wedding feast, and wants him to hear his story. The Wedding-Guest stands hypnotised and "cannot choose but hear." The Mariner goes on with his tale. He tells how his ship leaves the harbour and under a favourable wind sails southwards to the tropics. Then comes a furious and thundering storm-blast which drives it to the land of mist and snow. The mariners see no beast, or bird there. At last an Albatross comes flying to the ship and follows it. Along with its coming, the weather clears up and a favourable wind begins to blow. The sailors hail it as a bird of good omen and feed it with affection. But, alas, The Ancient Mariner, in a moment of wanton impulsiveness, shoots the bird with his cross-bow and this marks the beginning of their sorrows.

Part II. All goes well for a while. The fog thins away. The sun rises "like God's own head." The ship sails merrily along. The sailors approve of the Mariner's crime by saying that it is right to kill such birds as it brings the fog and mist. But suddenly the wind falls so that the ship cannot move. The ship is becalmed. The sun burns fiercely. The silent sea rots; the slimy creatures crawl about; the sailors suffer from unbearable thirst. At night unearthly fires flit across the waters. The Spirit of the sea pursues the ship nine fathoms deep from under the sea, and take its vengeance upon the sailors for the slaughter of the harmless Albatross by persecuting them with horrible sights and unbearable thirst. All the sailors hate The Ancient Mariner hangs the dead Albatross round his neck as a punishment for his brutal act.

Part III. The sailors have an awful time, and are almost dead with thirst when The Ancient Mariner sees a tiny speck in the horizon. The Mariner thinks that a ship is coming towards them. He bites his own arm and sucks the blood to moisten his lips to proclaim to the other sailors the approach of a ship that will put an end to their agonising thirst. But, alas, it proves to be a skeleton ship, sailing steadily without breeze or tide. The next moment the Mariner sees in the ship Death and Life-in-Death playing at dice, their stake being The Ancient Mariner. The latter wins, signifying that all the sailors are to die immediately and thus to be relieved of their suffering except The Ancient Mariner who is to suffer life-long agony, i.e., doomed to live a life in death. The phantom ship then disappears. One after another all the two hundred sailors drops down dead. The Ancient Mariner alone is left behind to expiate by life-long suffering and penance.

Part IV. The Ancient Mariner lives all alone on a wide, wide sea. Not a saint takes pity on his soul in agony. The men, all so beautiful, lie dead on the deck; while a thousand slimy creatures live merrily on. The sight of the dead sailors meets him on all sides. He tries to pray, but a wicked whisper comes, and makes his heart 'as dry as dust.' The sea and the sky lie like lead on his weary eye, and the dead men lie at his feet. He is persecuted by his guilty conscience and the cursing looks of the dead sailors. Soon the moon rises and covers the whole sea with white light. The Ancient Mariner watches the water snakes moving in 'tracks of shining white.' He admires their beauty. A spring of love gushes out of his heart and he blesses them unconsciously. At the same moment, he is able to pray; the dead Albatross falls off his neck and sinks like lead into the sea.

Part V. The Mariner then falls into a deep sleep. When he wakes up, he finds that rain has moistened his 'baked' lips and quenches his thirst. He is so light that he cannot feel his limbs. He feels as if he has died in sleep and is a blessed ghost. He hears strange sounds and sees strange movements in the sky. The rain pours down from one black cloud, with the moon at its edge. The dead men gives a groan and suddenly rise, as if from sleep. The Mariners work at the ropes and the ship moves on. The Ancient Mariner and his nephew pull the same rope, without speaking to each other. The dead bodies come to life, animated by a troop of heavenly angels. But the next morning the angels leave the bodies. Still the ship moves on. The vengeful Spirit of the South Pole 'makes the ship go.' At noon the ship comes to a standstill. But in a moment it begins to stir and then makes a sudden bound. The Ancient Mariner falls down into a swoon. In that condition he hears two spirits' voices talking about his crime. One of the voices says that The Ancient Mariner does a great crime in killing the Albatross that has loved the Mariner. The other voice says, "The man has done enough penance and will do more of it."

Part VI. When The Ancient Mariner wakes up, he finds the moon calmly shining in the sky and sees the dead bodies standing with their stony eyes fixed on him still. But soon the spell is broken altogether. A light breeze begins to blow and the ship enters the harbour which the Mariner at once recognizes to be that of his own country. To his great astonishment, he finds the corpses lying flat, with a seraph standing on each and silently waving his luminous hand like a bright signal. The silence sinks like music into his heart. But soon he hears the flash of oars and sees a boat coming fast, bringing the Pilot, the Pilot's boy and the good Hermit. The Ancient Mariner rejoices, for he thinks that the pious Hermit will wash his soul clean of all guilt.

Part VII. But as the boat approaches, there is heard a loud thundering noise below it and the ship goes down like lead into the sea. But *The*

Ancient Mariner is at once saved in the Pilot's boat. His strange aspect frightens the Pilot and sends the Pilot's boy crazy. The Mariner finds himself on the solid land of his own country. He prays to the Hermit to wash his soul clean of all guilt. The Hermit asks him who he is; and forthwith his body is 'wrenched with a woeful agony' which forces him to tell his ghastly tale. Since then at uncertain intervals this woeful agony returns and he is relieved only when he has told his tale of woe to some sympathetic listener. The Mariner tells the Wedding-Guest that he passes, like night, from land to land; he possesses a strange power of speech and of knowing the right man who will hear his tale. To him his tale relates. The Ancient Mariner, before parting, tells the Wedding-Guest that "he prayeth well, who loveth well all things both great and small," and then he suddenly vanishes.

(E) CRITICAL APPRECIATION, INTERPRETATION AND DEVELOPMENT OF THOUGHT

Cold Reception of the Poem on Its First Appearance, but now Regarded a Masterpiece and Best of the Author's Poems. This famous poem of Coleridge, now justly is regarded as a masterpiece in English poetry, is curiously enough, on its first appearance, very coldly received. Even the poet's own friends, Southey, Lamb and Wordsworth, does not show any appreciation of it. Southey speaks of it as 'a very Dutch attempt at sublimity.' Lamb has said that 'he dislikes all the miraculous part in it.' Wordsworth thinks that the poem has 'great defects.' Time has, however, abundantly vindicated the excellence of *The Ancient Mariner* and it has now come to be regarded as one of the world's great poems, and the greatest written by its author. 'For,' as Mr. Traill says, ' this weird ballad abounds in those very qualities in which Coleridge's poetry with all its merits is conspicuously deficient, while on the other hand it is wholly free from the faults with which he is most frequently and justly chargeable'.

The 'Rime of *The Ancient Mariner* ' is the High Water Mark of Coleridge's Excellence as a Poet. In the thin volume of his poetical work, this poem ranks the best. Not only this, it holds a lofty position in the entire romantic poetry for its dexterous treatment of the supernatural, vivid and sensuous nature-imagery, smooth flow of its musical metre, simplicity and dramatic appropriateness of language and above all its truth to human sentiment and its profound ethical and spiritual implications.

The Simple Realistic Force of its Narrative. Perhaps the greatest achievement of the poem is the simple force of its narrative. To achieve this is of course Coleridge's main object; he has undertaken to "transfer from our inward nature a human interest and sentence of truth sufficient to procure for those shadows of imagination that willing suspension of disbelief for the moment which constitutes poetic faith." It is a difficult task. But Coleridge has triumphed over his difficulties by sheer vividness of imagery and tense vigour of descriptive phrase—two qualities over which his previous poems does not prove him to possess by any means so complete a mastery. Among all the beauties of his earlier landscapes we can hardly reckon that of intense and convincing truth. He seems to seldom write as Wordsworth nearly always seems to write, "with his eye on the object;" and certainly he never before has displayed any such remarkable power of completing a word-picture with a few touches.

In *The Ancient Mariner* his eye seems never to wander from his subject, and again and again the scene starts out upon the canvas in two or three strokes of the brush. The skeleton ship with dicing demons on its deck; the setting sun "peering through its ribs, as if through a dungeon grate," the water-snakes under the moonbeams, with 'elfish light' falling off them, 'in hoary flakes' when they rear; the dead crew who work the ship and "raise their limbs like lifeless tools" every thing seems to have been actually seen; and we believe it all as the story of a truthful witness.

The Execution of the Poem. Then again the execution is marvellously equal throughout: the story never drags or flags for a moment, its felicities of diction are perpetual, and it is scarcely marred by a single weak line.

What could have been better said of the instantaneous descent of the tropical night than-

> The sun's rim dips the stars rush out,
> At one stride comes the dark

What more vividly imagines of the "cracks and growls" of the receding ice-bergs than that they sounds "like noises in a swound?" With what consummate art are we left to imagine the physical traces which the Mariner's long agony has left behind it by a method far more terrible than any direct description-the effect, namely, which the sight of him produces upon others—as he is a Devil in human form? Perfect consistency of plan, in short, and complete equality of execution, brevity, self-restraint, and an unerring sense of artistic propriety-these are the chief notes of *The Ancient Mariner*, a masterpiece of ballad minstrels (Traill).

The Skilful Blending of the Natural with the Supernatural. The great charm and power of the poem lie in the skill with which the unreal is made to look like the real. Descriptions of the natural phenomena are given with such minuteness and detail, and dove-tailed into the imaginative and supernatural parts with such nicety, as to make the whole story look quite probable. The dreadful silence of the far seas; with hot stagnant waters, with the intolerable blazing sun overhead, and the vast unknown furnish a background of reality on which the emotion of a sensitive human soul is portrayed with absolute freedom and yet carry conviction with them. "I never met", writes Stopford Brooke, "a sailor whose ship has been among the lonely places of the sea, who did not know of their hauntings, who will be surprised to see the phantom ship, who does not hear in the air that has sighed in the rigging the voices of the creatures that are half of the water and half of the air above them."

The poem is a magnificent plea for universal love and sympathy Stopford Brooke says, "The poem is a revelation made by Coleridge of what he believed to be always the case in the spiritual world. That world is on the side of pity and love, and men who violate these are punished by hardness of heart. They cannot pray, they cannot be wise, they cannot bless the living of the land and sea and sky. Nature for them is dead; and if there be powers bound up with Nature, those are their enemies till they change their hearts. And Coleridge imagines the lonesome spirit of the South Pole who loved the Albatross, and his fellow demons, the invisible inhabitants of the elements and great Ocean that always looks at the Moon, and the Sun and the Moon, who act with the Polar Spirit. Death and Life-in-Death-the spiritual powers which execute the sanctions of the Law of Pity." The poem is a magnificent plea for universal love and sympathy. The Mariner is relieved of his soul's agony only when he blesses the slimy creatures. Then only a prayer gushed from his heart. Well does the poet say-

He prayeth best, who loveth best
All things both great and small.
For the dear God who loveth us,
He made and loveth all.

The Ballad Element in the Poem. "Coleridge drank deep of the spirit of the folk-ballad, and at no point has he more completely caught the primitive spirit of the ballads than in their childlikeness. It is a difficult feat for the poet to keep his own thought within the circle of the Mariner's mind and the Mariner's thought within the circle of a child's mind. Like the old ballads, the poet deals with elementary feeling and primal affections of humanity (as the Mariner's) and this simplicity of sentiment is equally matched with a simplicity of language and style. Then there are the elements of moral as in the old ballad. He has used, for the sake of effect, the traditional tricks of ballad style viz., the ballad metre, medieval rhyme and alliteration, repetition of phrases and lines, archaisms and a noble simplicity of language, vigour and energy of narration. Yet he touches the ballad to a finer issue."

Development of Thought. One of the chief problems of the story-teller is the right choice of a dramatic narrator. Coleridge makes the Mariner himself tell his own story a perfectly natural thing, considering the abnormal and sensational quality of many of the happenings. In the first part the Mariner sets upon the voyage in a cheerful mood, overcomes the usual calamities of seafaring; and commits the crime which 'presses a supernatural trigger.'

In Part II, even after the killing of the Albatross of the fair breeze continues for some time that is a test of the sensitivity of the shipmates consciences. They do not feel that the killing of the bird is wrong in itself; they only judge it by its immediate consequences on their material welfare, which for the moment has appeared to be favourable. And then begins the train of disasters starting with the complete stifling of the breeze and the parching heat of the tropical sea.

In Part III, the supernatural appears concretely on the scene in the shape of the ghostly skeleton-ship and its two shipmates, Death and Life-in-Death. It is an irony of fate that the appearance of the ship on the horizon fills the mariners with a frenzied joy for a time; but soon they realise their mistake. The game of dice between the Spectre-Woman and her Death-mate is a symbolic weighing of the guilt of the Mariner and his mates. The winning of the game by the Spectral-Woman leads to the death of all the two hundred shipmates of the Mariner and to his being singled out for further persecution and penance. The horror of the situation reaches a peak in this part.

In Part IV, the psychological strain from which the Mariner is suffering reaches its point of highest tension. The blackness of his sin fills him with horror and makes him disgusted with the whole world, including himself. Thoughts of repentance come to him but are scotched by the 'wicked whisper' which dries up his heart. But the unremitting sight of the dead men at his feet for a whole week, the suffocating loneliness, the physical and emotional stings of calamity, the disgusting feel of slimy shapes created by a fevered brain-these have a softening and humanising effect on the hardened heart of the Mariner. He recovers a feeling of love for living things and that is the beginning of his spiritual regeneration. After having plumbed the depths of degradation, he begins to scramble up towards human dignity. That is the theme of this part, the most central in the poem.

In Part V, miraculous events follow each other and show the curse upon the Mariner dissolving away. The supernatural element is no longer maleficient, it is now beneficent. While the gentle sleep and the refreshing rain may be regarded as aspects of the 'natural supernatural', the mysterious movement of the ship and the inspiring of the dead bodies of the crew by the troop of angelic spirits, the snatch of a conversation between two spirits which the Mariner hears in a dream, all show the kindly interest which the supernatural beings are now taking in the physical and spiritual well-being of the Mariner. The kindly forms of the supernatural in this part may be instructively contrasted with the terrifying forms of it in Part III.

In Part VI, the miraculous and the natural again join hands and bring the Mariner home, both physically and spiritually. The fit of unconsciousness or trance in which he overhears the dialogue between spirit of Justice and Mercy is due, as the gloss say, to the dizzy speed at which the ship is driven forward by the power of the seraph-band. The work of the seraph-band is done when they have made the Mariner feel repentance for his sin and gratitude for the mercy of God, and have brought him back to his own country: they make their exit in a supernaturally telling way and leave the Mariner in the world of every day reality, the world from which he has set out so adventurously in Part I.

In Part VII, the last part of the poem, the Mariner re-establishes contact with the normal life from which he has dashed off adventurously in Part I. But his appearance is so unusual that men stand in awe of him : a most startling instance of his weird appearance is found in the unhappily crazing effect it had on the Pilot's boy. Now the Mariner has learnt his lesson in blood and sweat of body and soul, the ship with its dead crew is no longer wanted : it is made to scuttle itself miraculously. In the closing stanzas of the poem there is a conscious attempt at the summing up of the new scale of values which the Mariner has learnt through suffering; it is not the gaiety of the wedding-feast which now invites him, but the humble social piety of walking to the church in a goodly company and offering devout and humble prayers to the Creator.

Comprehensiveness of Details. The imaginative power of the poet is combined with an amazing comprehensiveness of details in description. "Every phase of landscape, seascape and cloudscape is touched upon, from the quiet scenery of an English woodland to the lurid scenery of the tropics. The poet touches with equal power and beauty every phase of the life at sea : the ship flying before the freshening gale, the torrid fierceness of the stagnant waters, the freezing cold of the Arctic region, the horror of the becalmed passage, the blessedness of the welcome rain, the clear sky, the storm cloud, the great seafog, the incarnate fury of the storm, the soothing peace of the temperate seas, the loneliness of the great ocean, and the welcome sight of familiar landmarks once again as the Mariner views the peaceful English harbour."

The Technical Beauty. The technical beauties of the poem are remarkable. The form used is ballad and the simplicity of diction is worth noting.

(i) Alone, alone, all all alone,
Alone on a wide, wide sea

(ii) I moved and could not feel my lips,
I was so light-almost
I thought that I had died in sleep
And was a blessed ghost.

Of metre and versification the poet has shown himself to be a master. The medieval rhymes and the alliteration are used with such skill that one can only wonder.

Truth to Nature. The poem provides ample illustration of Coleridge's capacity to excite the sympathy of the reader by a faithful adherence to the truth of nature. Coleridge had undertaken 'to transfer from our inward nature a human interest and semblance of truth sufficient to procure for those shadows of imagination that willing suspension of disbelief for the moment which constitutes poetic faith.' One has only to think of the tortured face of the Ancient Mariner, the frightened and later 'sadder and wiser' Wedding-Guest to realise the extent to which he has achieved success in the undertaking. He has eminently succeeded in giving concrete, sensuous expression to feelings and states of mind. To describe the utter and absolute silence what can be more effective than

And we did speak only to break
The silence of the sea

And note the marvellous expression of the effect on the Mariner of his horrible experiences:

Since then, at an uncertain hour,
That agony returns
And till my ghastly tale is told
This heart within me burns

Coleridge's Insight into Human Psychology. The poet shows great knowledge of human psychology in describing the feelings of the Mariner while in the presence of the supernatural phenomena. Charles Lamb does not like these horrors yet praises the poet's skill in describing these human feelings which makes the poem so convincing—

With throats unslaked, with black lips baked,
We could not laugh nor wail;

Through utter drought all dumb we stood !
I bit my arm, I sucked the blood,
And cried, a sail, a sail, a sail !
We listened and looked sideways up !!
Fear at my heart, as at a cup,
My life blood seemed to sip !

The poem is full of such intense feelings-not merely of fear, but also of remorse, pity and love for all things that live and move.

Theme of the Poem. The theme of *The Ancient Mariner* is not just the story of a sailor who learns through a series of vicissitudes that one shall "be kind to animals." It is rather that experience of guilt, of need for redemption, is shared by all men, which is at the basis of many religious and social customs, and much art. It is no more fantastic, as a modern critic has observed, than *The Pilgrim's Progress*. Far from dealing with a romantic world of unreality the poem reveals an intimate depth of human experience. It is no mere miracle of inventive fantasy, but an inevitable projection into imagery of the poet's own inner discord. It describes the slow and hard path to regeneration. Its symbolism places it in the same category as T.S. Eliot's *The Waste Land*. The real meaning of "He prayeth best who loveth best" is the return of harmony between the Mariner and all living things-not just the assertion of a moral humanitarian law.

Moral of the Poem. The moral of the poem, "He prayeth well who loveth well, both man and bird and beast" grew out of Coleridge's great love of lower animals. In this poem he gives a dramatic expression to the conviction that God is on the side of pity and love, and those who shut themselves against these tender emotions are punished by hardness of heart which does not let them pray or attain to wisdom. Nature and all its beautiful creatures of earth, water, and sky become dead to them. All the physical and moral forces of the world become their enemies till their hearts are softened again by pity and remorse.

Conclusion. During the last decade of the eighteenth century a taste for "supernatural" tales with all their horrible details and blood-curdling incidents has gradually been formed in the public. "Monk" Levis, Mrs. Radcliffe, and other imitators of the German school has freely pandered to it. For a time even Coleridge is tempted, and the first version of *The Ancient Mariner* admits the horrible much more freely than the later and refined version. Happily, he soon recognises his mistake, and employs- his knowledge of psychology, his mastery of colour and detail to create beauty even out of the ghastly incidents of his originals.

(F) SELECTED UNIVERSITY QUESTIONS WITH ANSWERS ON *THE ANCIENT MARINER*

(I) *ANCIENT MARINER* : A GREAT POEM

Q.1. Though some critics have spoken disparagingly of *The Ancient Mariner* yet in all ages and at all times the poem has been appreciated. Elaborate the features which make this poem great.

Ans. Coleridge's bold use of marvellous, without even the decent pretext of allegory or personification, exasperated the critics and did not please the one man who give the poem lofty and adequate praise. "I dislike all the miraculous part in it," wrote Lamb, "but the feeling of a man under the operation of such scenery has dragged me along like Tom Piper's magic whistle." Wordsworth, who seems to have conceived him on the lines of his own human murderer in *Guilt and Sorrow*, has enumerated among the "grave defeats" of the poem that the Mariner has no character. Nor, has he is only a soul that has been "alone on a wide, wide sea," and remains but an embodied memory of what he had undergone. Southey has spoken disparagingly of the poem as "a very Dutch attempt at sublimity."

Except for these discordant notes, critics in all ages and at all times have given the highest praise to the poem. Relying largely on the effect which has been produced by psychological truth, Coleridge can afford to subdue the supernatural, and refine it to the utmost. Scenery, atmosphere, even the colouring of the phrase and rhythm concur in giving to the supernatural the harmonious unity of a possible experience. "He did not need," says Dowden, "as Monk Lewis did, to drag into his verse all the horrors of the churchyard and the nether pit of hell... In *The Ancient Mariner*, where the spectre bark approaches the doomed ship.....a verse full of charnel abomination occurs in the original text which is afterwards judiciously omitted. Coleridge feels that these hideous incidents of the grave only detracted from the finer horror of the voluptuous beauty of his 'White Devil', the "Nightmare Life-in-Death." His tender and keen sense of what is right and delicate makes Coleridge reject from his work, the horrors while producing artistically the terrors of death.

The Ancient Mariner affords ample illustration of the power of exciting the sympathy of the reader by a faithful adherence to the truth of nature. Coleridge always loves nature and has a profound sense of her beauty informs and sounds, for the sudden charm, accidents of light and shade which moonlight or sunset has diffused over a known and familiar landscape. Clearly, connects with this is the extreme simplicity and terseness of expression. Coleridge's words have an unashamed nakedness of scripture, of the Eden of diction ere the voluble serpent has entered.

The terseness and simplicity has never degenerated, with Wordsworth, into baldness and prosaic narration. The magically wonderful, vision is made real which suggests and describes in words that have been chosen with an art that conceals art. Traill has well described these characteristics: "Coleridge had undertaken to transfer from our inward nature a human interest and semblance of truth, sufficient to prose for these shadows of imagination that willing suspension of disbelief, for the moment which constitutes poetic faith. But it is easier to undertake this than to perform it and much easier to perform it in prose than in verse with the assistance of the every day and the commonplace than without it. Coleridge triumphs over his difficulties by sheer vividness of imagery and terse vigour of descriptive phrase, two qualities for which his previous poems did not prove him to possess by any means, so complete a mastery... In *The Ancient Mariner* his eye never seems to wander from his object, and again and again the scene starts out upon the canvas in two or three strokes of the brush. The skeleton ship with the dicing demons on its deck; the setting sun. peering 'through its ribs, as if through a dungeon grate', the water snakes under the moonbeams, with the 'elfish light' falling off them 'in hoary flakes' when they reared: 'the dead crew who work the ship and raise their limbs like lifeless tools', everything seems to have been actually seen, and we believe it all as the story of a truthful eye-witness. The details of the voyage too are chronicled with such order and regularity, there is such a diary-like air about the whole thing, that we accept it almost as it were a series of extracts from the ship's log. Then again the execution-a great thing to be said of such a long poem-is marvellously equal throughout; the story never drags or flags for a moment; its felicities of diction are perpetual; and it is scarcely marred by a single weak line.... Perfect consistency of plan; in short, complete equality of execution, brevity, self-restraint, and an unerring sense of artistic propriety- these are the chief notes of *The Ancient Mariner*, as they are not the chief notes of any other poem of Coleridge." Swinburne went into ecstasies over the poem. This poem is beyond question one of the supreme triumphs of the poetry, he wrote. "For the execution, I presume no human eye is too dull to see how perfect it is, and how high in kind of perfection. There is not the elaborate finish which shows, everywhere the fresh rasp of file or chisel on its smooth and spruce excellence; this is faultless after the fashion of a flower or a tree."

Has the poem any moral ? Mrs. Barbauld has complained that the poem has two defects—it is improbable, and has no moral. Coleridge commenting on this, roundly declared that the poem has too much of the moral element, that it openly obtrudes on the reader as a principle or cause of act on. As Stopford Brooke declares: "The poem illustrates the simple religion of Coleridge.... Its religion is all contained in the phrase-He prayeth well who loveth well, both man and bird and beast. On this the changes are rung throughout; the motiveless slaughter of the bird is a crime; the other mariners who justify the killing of the bird are even worse sinners than *The Ancient Mariner*. They are fatally punished; he lives to feel and expiate his wrong." Mrs. Oliphant remarks in almost the same strain; "And then comes the ineffable, half-childish, half-divine, simplicity of these soft moralisings at the end, so strangely different from the tenor of the tale, so wonderfully perfecting its visionary strain. After all, the poem seems to say after this weird excursion into the very deepest, awful heart of the seas and mysteries, here is your child's moral, a tender little half-trivial sentiment, yet profound as the blue depths of heaven."

(II) SUPERNATURAL WORLD IN *THE ANCIENT MARINER*

Q.2. Discuss the use of the supernatural in *The Ancient Mariner*.

Or

"No other poem in English creates so completely and independently its own atmosphere and order of being, or so merges the world of sense and simplicity with the other world of mystery and profoundity as *The Rime of the Ancient Mariner*." Discuss.

Or

Illustrate and explain the quality of enchantment in Coleridge's *The Ancient Mariner*.

Or

What are Coleridge's distinctive features as a poet of the supernatural ? Discuss with special reference to *The Ancient Mariner*.

Ans. '*The Ancient Mariner* has founded on a dream of Coleridge's friend, Cruickshank, who fancied he has been a skeleton ship, with figures in it. It begun jointly with Wordsworth who contributed a few lines and has suggested the killing of the Albatross, the revenge of the tutelary spirits and the navigation of the ship by the deadman, but he quickly separated from an undertaking upon which he have felt he 'could only have been a clog.' In fact, the poem's theme puts it into the category of the supernatural and romantic which feels to Coleridge in the division of labour on the *Lyrical Ballads*.

What is the supernatural ? Through the ages phenomena which can not be explained by the known laws of nature have been attributed to supernatural powers and influences. If these happenings leads to the happiness of man they are attributed to benevolent powers; if on the contrary they results in suffering and misery, they are ascribed to evil spirits. Literature has continuously been enriched by stories in which the supernatural plays an important part. The desire of hearing about the miraculous adventure is as strong in the civilised man as it is in his primitive ancestors, as it is in the naive child. The folk-lores of all ages and countries abound in tales of magic, fairies, spirits, ghosts and demons.

The interest in the supernatural is an important aspect of the Romantic spirit that has appeared in the eighteenth century. The fashionable cult of the strangeness has turn inevitably to this alluring world of the unknown and exploits it with a reckless carelessness. To Coleridge the supernatural appeals with a special power. The supernatural machinery in *The Ancient Mariner* however, is not merely a series of interesting and often singular details. It works as a controlling imaginative design. The shooting of the Albatross sets the forces of the invisible world in motion. The action of these forces in turn is bound up with the normal evolution, in experience, of cause and consequence.

Supernatural Details in *The Ancient Mariner*. The first supernatural element in the poem is the Polar Spirit who followed the ship from the land of mist and snow in order to avenge the killing of the Albatross. The Polar Spirit has brought the ship into a silent, still sea where the ship gets stuck, unable to move,

> And some in dreams assured were
> Of the spirit that plagued us so
> Nine fathom deep he had followed us
> From the land of mist and snow.

Then comes the appearance from nowhere of the skeleton ship with gossamer-like sails, carrying Death and Life-in-Death being engaged in a gambling contest. This ship sails on the sea without wind or tide and it disappears as suddenly as it has appeared. The stanzas where this incident is described are horrifying in their effect upon us and send a cold shiver down our spine. The manner of the death of all the sailors excepting the Ancient Mariner is supernatural. As each man drops down dead, his soul passes by the old sailor like the whizz of a cross-bow. It is a strange mystery that while all other sailors die, the old sailor lives on. There is something supernatural about the way in which the dead body of the Albatross automatically falls down from the Ancient Mariner's neck into the sea. The moving of the ship upon the sea without a wind is supernatural. The ship is driven by the Polar Spirit, sometimes swiftly. The coming back to life of the dead crew is also a supernatural situation. The dead men gives a groan, they stir and then all gets up. What is more, it is a troop of angelic spirits that enter the bodies. It is to be noted that the bodies of the dead crew do not rot another mysterious element. The two voices talking to each other are also supernatural powers. The two voices relate to each other the long and heavy penance of the old sailor. The angelic spirits' coming out of the dead bodies and appearing in their own forms of light is an other-worldly touch :

> Each corse lay flat, lifeless and flat,
> And, by the holy rood
> A mass all light, a seraph-man,
> On every corse there stood.

These forms of light make signals to the land in order to invite the attention of some boatman. At the end, the sudden sinking of the ship into the sea is a supernatural episode. A loud, roaring noise is heard under the water. This loud and terrible sound reaches the ship and "the ship goes down like lead."

Intermingling of the Natural and the Supernatural. His supernaturalism is refined. He tries to create supernatural effects mostly out of the natural. He arranges the natural in such a clever manner as to achieve something supernatural. Professor Otto and Aldous Huxley call this type of the supernatural as the super-sensible something that is not within our everyday experience but is still within the range of possibility. The art of Coleridge lies in process of accumulation—placing together of some rather extraordinary natural details in such a manner as to achieve a grand super-sensible result. After the strange natural incidents have charmed the reader, Coleridge brings in a few supernatural touches. Even those touches are not decidedly supernatural. They can be considered as super-sensible. Coleridge creates a strange mixture of the sensible, the super-sensible and the supernatural. Therefore, Coleridge's supernatural is more convincing than the crude, horrifying stories of other supernatural writers of the 19th century. As the. Mariner's ship goes from England to the Southern Pacific, from the known to the unknown, from the familiar to the unfamiliar, the change is effected with remarkable subtlety :

> The fair breeze blew, the white foam flew
> The furrow followed free:
> We were the first, that ever burst
> Into that silent sea.

With the same art he shows the scene when dreadful and unnatural things happen. Note the change in the sea when the Albatross first begins to be revenged:

> The very deep did rot: O Christ !
> That ever this should be!
> Yea, slimy things did crawl with legs
> Upon the slimy sea.

His artistic power and imaginative fidelity creates sensuous nature pictures which hold our faith and belief. Those little pictures of sunrise and sunset and the quiet beauty of the moonlight give additional power to the strange and fearful sight.

Realistic Details. In *The Ancient Manner* the poet's eye never seems to wander from his object and again the scene starts out upon the canvas in two or three strokes of the brush. The skeleton ship with the dicing demons on its deck, the setting sun peering through its ribs, as if through a dungeon grate; the water-snakes under the moon beams with the 'elfish light' falling off from them 'in hoary flakes' when they rear : 'the dead crew' who work the ship and raise their limbs like 'lifeless tools'-everything seems to have been actually seen, and we believe it all as the story of a truthful eye witness. The details of the voyage too are chronicled with such order and regularity, there is such a diary-like air about the whole thing, that we accept it almost as it is a series of extracts from the ship's log.

Coleridge's Supernatural is Suggestive : Coleridge do not describe unpleasant details but he simply suggests. Thus he appeals to the imagination and not to the senses. In *The Ancient Mariner* where the ghost ship approaches the sailors, a verse full of details occurs in the original text which is afterwards omitted. Coleridge feel that these terrible incidents of the grave does not add to the suggestiveness of his creation, the Nightmare 'Life-in-Death.' His keen sense of what is rightly delicate makes Coleridge reject all crude and horrible details. He works through suggestion. *The Ancient Mariner* says to have a skinny hand and a glittering eye. The Wedding Guest is hypnotised by The Ancient Mariner. His reactions suggest fear again and again but Coleridge will not describe in detail the cause. Thus he keeps his supernatural to a suggestive level.

Remote Setting to Lend Credibility. In *The Ancient Mariner* the events are natural, but behind them lies a supernatural world. The thoughts which Nature's powers awaken in a sensitive soul are believed by Coleridge to have corresponding existences which derive their being from nature. These bodiless beings may be felt by us as enemies or friends and in circumstances made emotional by loneliness, they may themselves be felt as actual presences by man. But this can only be in primeval solitudes where dwell things to dream of not to tell, or in the midst of untravelled seas, or in the deep forests of romance. In these remote mysterious seas and woods Coleridge lays the scenery of *The Ancient Mariner*, and *Christabel*. It is supernatural, but of the ancient, common, simple kind which belongs to all mankind. We feel the same thrill he desires to convey in *Christabel* if at night we are lost in a forest:

> Like one that on a lonesome road
> Doth walk in fear and dread.

The same expression of the possibility of marvel, and horror, of mysterious sins and their forgiveness, and of the chance of meeting some have forgotten spiritual life which is before man comes on earth, which creeps over us as we read *The Ancient Mariner, belongs* to sea men who have been lost in unvisited spaces of ocean, vexes with everlasting calm.

Human Significance : Psychological Insight. The supernatural is not only made real and natural by its faithful picture of Nature and its psychological insight, but by the simple humanity with which it is saturated. C.M. Bowra says: "The triumph of *The Ancient Mariner* is that it presents a series of incredible events through a method of narration which makes them not only convincing and exciting but in some sense a criticism of life." Coleridge does not confine himself to an outworn dread of spectres and phantoms, he moves over a wide range of emotions and touches equally on guilt and remorse, suffering and relief, hate and forgiveness, grief and joy.

Weird Atmosphere Artistically Unifying the Poem. Among English poets, Coleridge stands out supreme in his uncanny ability to conjure a weird atmosphere whenever necessary in his poem. A cold-blooded analysis of it will perhaps reveal that it is full of improbabilities. In spite of this anyone who reads The Ancient Mariner will inevitably feel its fascination and be gripped by its strangeness and air of mystery.

Coleridge has succeeded in the task that he assigns to himself of imparting to the supernatural an air of naturalness and realism. When we read through the poem, we are not conscious at all that there is a piling up of mysterious and improbable detail. Never for once is any detail clearly defined. *The Ancient Mariner* and the ship are both left unnamed. The seas that they sail, the lands that they must have proposed to visit are also left unnamed. In spite of all this, the surprising thing is that, grips by the atmosphere, no reader feels or is even conscious of the deficiencies. He breathes the air of mystery and romance and is whirled along by the stream of the narrative.

Supreme art and all the gifts of the born story-teller are lavishly employed to conjure up the atmosphere which constitutes the chief fascination of the poem. Terror and beauty, weird mystery and pleasing romance are skilfully alternated in order to produce the necessary effect. The elemental forces of nature are also harnessed in order to conjure up the necessary atmosphere. In fact, it is Nature that is responsible for some of the marvellous and mysterious effects produced in the poem. When the Albatross, the bird of good omen is killed in a wanton fit of cruelty, all Nature protest in horror. The tides do not ebb and flow, the winds cease to blow and everything in nature comes to an absolute standstill.

The ship is becalmed and lies still like a painted ship on a painted ocean.

The introduction of spectre-ship and the game of dice is played by Death and Life-in-Death, is perhaps the most mysterious and terrifying thing in the poem. Though this stands out as something supreme, other mysterious details, superstitious fears and supernatural occurrences are crowded into the poem. The killing of the Albatross by The Ancient Mariner fills the sailors with superstitious dread and they think that all the horrors and privations that follow are a punishment for this crime. The supernatural element is further emphasised when we are told that the bird is the fovourite of the Polar Spirit who now wants to avenge its death. The death of the sailors and their mysterious resurrection for a while, the troop of angels filling the air with sweet sound, the speech .of the two voices, Justice and Mercy, and a hundred other little details help in providing a strange and uncanny atmosphere for the poem.

Coleridge has taken care to introduce what is lovely and pleasant so that the atmosphere may not be over-whelmingly terrifying and oppressive. The bride, red as a rose, the merry band of minstrels, the sweet jargoning of birds and the lovely moonlit harbour-all these relieve the grimness and the gloom, and make the poem beautiful and fascinating.

Conclusion. The too palpable intruders from a spiritual world in almost all ghost literature, in Scott and Shakespeare even, have a kind of crudity or coarseness. Coleridge's power is in the very fineness with which, as by some really ghostly finger, he brings home to our inmost sense his invention, daring as they are : the skeleton ship, the polar spirit, the inspiriting of the dead corpses of the ships' crew. *The Rime of the Ancient Mariner,* says Walter Pater, has the plausibility, the perfect adaptation to reason and the general aspect of life, which belong' to the marvellous, when actually presented as part of a credible experience in our dreams. The modern mind, so minutely self-scrutinizing, if it is to be affected at all by a sense of the supernatural, needs to be more finely touched than is possible in the older, romantic presentment of it. It is this finer, more delicately marvellous supernaturalism, fruit of his own more delicate psychology, that Coleridge infuses into romantic adventure, it also is a new or revive thing in English literature, and with a fineness of weird effect in *The Ancient Mariner* unknown in those older, more simple, romantic legends and ballads.

(III) WILLING SUSPENSION OF DISBELIEF

Q.3. "The first porblem for any poet of the supernatural is to relate it to familiar experience." How does Coleridge solve this problem in *The Ancient Mariner* ?

Or

How far is Coleridge successful in bringing about "a willing suspension of disbelief" in the reader with his *The Ancient Mariner* ?

Or

How are the supernatural elements in *The Ancient Mariner* rendered probable or plausible or realistic ? Has Coleridge succeeded in the attempt ?

Ans. When Coleridge joins Wordsworth in the writing of the *Lyrical Ballads*, it is his aim to select remote, uncommon, or supernatural incidents and so to treat them as to produce an impression of realism. This aim has been achieved in *The Ancient Mariner*. In other words, although this poem contains several impossible incidents, the total effect is that of reality. In Coleridge's own words there is "a willing suspension of disbelief' on the part of the reader. A willing suspension of disbelief obviously implies that the reader suspends the analytical function of the mind and is ready to believe what he is reading. He readily drops his scepticism and believes what he has disbelieved earlier at least for the moment.

Devices Employed by Coleridge. The supernatural is not a part of belief for the readers of Coleridge as it is for the audience of Homer and Shakespeare. In order to win their confidence he has to relate it to something which they know and understand.

1. Characteristics of Dream and Subtlety. Coleridge tackles the problem, in the first place, by exploiting some of the characteristics of dream. A nightmare is a known experience. Through it the people can be led to appreciate the remote mysteries which the poet keeps in reserve. Dreams have the quality, because of their vividness and single, absorbing impression, to stay in the mind. Coleridge is attracted by their strange power. In *Christabel* he speaks of

Such perplexity of mind
As dreams too lively leave behind.

The Ancient Mariner bears the marks of such a liveliness. On the surface, it shows many qualities of dream. It moves in abrupt stages, each of which has its own single, dominating tone. Its visual impressions are remarkably brilliant and absorbing. Its emotional effects change quickly, but they always come with an unusual force. When it is all over, the poem's essence clings to the memory with a strange force. The experiences of the Mariner haunt him and all those who listen to him.

2. Inner Logic. Wordsworth criticises this poem and complains that "the events, having no necessary connection, do not produce each other." This criticism ignores the essential inner logic of the poem. The Mariner kills the Albatross and suffers for it. He violates Natural law. He has to do penance. His companions bless his action and are punished for becoming partners in the crime. Here Coleridge has asserted his belief that spirits watch over human action. It is an old belief and *The Ancient Mariner* may be supposed to have it. Once this is grasped the rest is easy. Both the figures on the skeleton ship and the spirits who guide the Mariner on his northward voyage are sufficiently real for us to feel that their actions are appropriate to their characters and circumstances. Nor is it absurd that, when the ship at last comes home, it sinks. It has passed through adventures too unearthly for it to have a place in the world of common things. The ship and the Mariner bear the marks of their ordeal. It is no wonder that the Pilot's boy goes mad at the sight.

3. Imaginative Realism : Gradual Introduction of the Supernatural. This dream world of strange experience has also been given a life of its own by the exercise of imaginative realism on the part of poet. He has created the unnatural events from natural elements. We feel at home because their constituents are familiar. He uses the atmosphere of dreams to accustom us to his special world. Afterwards at each step he takes pains to see that his unusual subject is real both for the eye and for emotion. The voyage begins in a very cordial human atmosphere:

> The ship was cheer'd, the harbour clear'd
> Merrily did we drop
> Below the kirk, below the hill,
> Below the lighthouse top.

Before our imagination is conjured an image of a little village harbour appears. The supernatural is introduced gradually. The storm-blast is given a living quality-a demoniac life. The sun is not a lifeless thing but bright and red like God's own head. Natural scenes take on a supernatural aura gradually in the poem and prepare us for the appearance of the phantom ship. At the end we are again brought back to the quiet harbour so that the happenings in between becomes an adventure into a nightmarish world.

4. Natural Background. The background of nature that Coleridge paints is very realistic. Anything else may be unreal, but nature is always real. The natural and the supernatural coalesce so that the former makes the latter credible. As Traill has remarked, "Coleridge triumphs over his difficulties by sheer vividness of imagery and terse vigour of descriptive phrase. He writes with his eye on the object and displays a remarkable power of completing his word-picture with a few touches. Everything seems to have been actually seen, and we believe it all as the story of a truthful eye-witness. Commenting upon this quality of the poem Kathleen E. Ryod & remarks: "For vividness of imagery and descriptive power the poem is unsurpassed. We move in a world of unearthly weirdness whose mystery and charm are unbroken by any inconsistency. We see the invisible and almost touch the intangible in this realism, where the things that are too seldom 'dreampt of our philosophy' loom within our ken".

There are quite a number of supernatural incidents. There is the mariner's hypnotic gaze, there is the sudden and mysterious appearance of a skeleton ship, the spectre-woman and her death-mate, the coming back to life of the ship's crew, the spirits talking to one another. The supernatural incidents are cleverly scattered in the poem. With these supernatural incidents the poet has artistically interwoven convincing pictures of Nature like the sun shining brightly at the outset, the mist and snow surrounding the ship, the freezing cold of the Antartic region, slimy creatures creeping upon the sea, the moon going up the sky and a star or two shining beside it, the water snakes moving in the water in tracks of shining white. The blending of these two elements is so skilful that the total effect is realistic. The realistic, the natural and the supernatural, the possible and the impossible, have been so skilfully and artistically blended that the whole strikes us as quite convincing and credible.

5. **Emotional and Psychological Realism.** The poem is made still more realistic by the masterly expression of the thoughts and feelings of the mariners; how at the appearance of the skeleton-ship fear seems to sip the old Mariner's life blood; how while suffering acute mental distress, he tries to pray but can not; how he felt the horror of the curse in the dead men's eyes; and how the sky and the sea lay like a load on his weary eye; and how, finally, he feel relief. This is exactly what any man will suffer under similar circumstances. The poet makes us share the Mariner's experience by truthfully portraying his emotions and mental states. This psychological study, therefore, has its share in contribution to the realistic effect.

Coleridge has given a very realistic treatment of the feelings and emotions of the persons in the poem. We feel that what happens to them might in similar circumstances happen to anyone. We respond readily to their pathos and their misery which is conveyed with a masterly directness. He portrays the helpless agony of thirst in the crew :

> And every tongue, through utter drought
> Was withered at the root !

We could not speak, no more than if
We had been choked with soot.

And, this is how the Mariner expresses himself when his thirst is slaked as he sleeps :

My lips were wet! my throat was cold,
My garments all were dank!
Sure I had drunken in my dreams
And still my body drank.

What is true of physical sensation in *The Ancient Mariner* is no less true of mental states. The mariner passes through an ordeal so weird and fearful that it might seem impossible to make it real for us. Coleridge rises to the occasion and by concentrating on elementary human emotions makes the most of them. The sense of utter helplessness and solitude is fully conveyed :

Alone, alone all all alone
Alone on a wide, wide sea!
And never a saint took pity on
My soul in agony...

This is the true feeling of pain of a guilty man who feels himself abandoned both by God and Man. On the other hand when the ship at last comes to land, the silent presence of the angels fill him with hope and joy:

This seraph band, each waved his hand,
No voice did they impart-
No voice; but oh ! the silence sank
Like music on my heart.

Coleridge distills the extremes of despair and of joy in these brief moments.

6. A Higher Reality. Coleridge's power to convince, so far from being dependent on the back ground of the story, is most fully operative in the story itself, which triumphantly succeeds at the level of a simple tale of adventure. When we read *The Ancient Mariner*, the plain fact is that our disbelief is 'suspended', as it must be with all successful art, whether or not it is 'realistic' in the narrow sense. As Coleridge well knows, imaginative truth is no less real to our experience than is factual truth and it may be more real.

(IV) *THE ANCIENT MARINER* : A ROMANTIC POEM

Q.4. Bring out the Romantic Elements of *The Ancient Mariner*.

Ans. Supernaturalism. *The Ancient Mariner* is a romantic poem, impressing us by bold invention, and appealing to that taste for the supernatural, the longing for a shudder, to which the 'romantic' school in Germany, and its derivations in England and France, directly ministered. Fancies of the strange things which may very well happen, even in broad daylight, to men shut up alone in ships far off on the sea, seem to have occurred to the human mind in all ages with a peculiar readiness, and often have about them, the fascination of a certain dreamy.grace, which distinguishes them from other kinds of marvellous inventions. This sort of fascination *The Ancient Mariner* brings to its highest degree: it is the delicacy, the dreamy grace, in his presentation of the marvellous, which makes Coleridge's work so remarkable.

The sudden and mysterious appearance of the skeleton ship, Death and Life-in-Death who are on board that ship, the coming back to life of the dead crew, the angels of light standing on the corpses, the popular spirits driving the ship are all supernatural elements in the poem. This supernaturalism lends to the poem an atmosphere of wonder, enchantment, and mystery which are romantic qualities.

Medievalism. The poem has a medieval background. Interest in the Middle Ages too, is a romantic characteristic. The Middle Ages are a period of superstition, piety, and love and chivalry. In this poem the first two elements of the Middle Ages have been emphasised. The superstition of the period is seen in the supernatural incidents. Its piety is seen in the religious basis of the poem and in the reference to the hermit. The poem thus carries us back to a remote period of time.

Nature. There are many pictures in the poem showing Coleridge's interest in nature. Love for nature is one of the outstanding qualities of romantic poetry. Every phase of seascape, landscape and cloudscape is touched upon in the poem. The sun shining brightly at the outset, the mist and iceberg surrounding the ship, the moving moon going up the sky, the water burning green, blue and white, the snakes moving in water and leaving tracks of golden fire-these are some of the beautiful and richly-coloured Nature pictures, is giving the poem a romantic interest.

Melodious Movement. The poem is also romantic because of its melody and music. Coleridge here appears as a keen lover of sweet and musical sounds. Alliteration, medieval rhymes, onomatopoeia, etc., are all employed to produce musical effects. As an example of melody the following stanza may be taken:

The fair breeze blew, the white foam flew
The furrow followed free;
We were the first that ever burst
Into that silent sea.

The simplicity and freshness of diction further enhance the romantic effect.

Conclusion. The Romantic Movement of the nineteenth century has been characterised by an upsurge of Imagination. Much of the magic of *The Ancient Mariner* comes from its blend of dark and serious issues with the delighted play of creative energy. The imaginative power of *The Ancient Mariner* gives to it, its complex appeal-there is no final or single approach to it.

(V) MEDIEVAL CHARACTERISTICS

Q.5. "*The Ancient Mariner* seems to throw a door ajar on the vanished life of the Middle Ages". Discuss.

Or

***The Ancient Mariner* shows distinct medieval characteristics in true Romantic tradition. Amplify.**

Ans. The Romantic tradition of the nineteenth century is characterised by a longing and love for the remote and the distant. Except for Wordsworth practically all the Romantic poets incorporates medieval elements in their works. Coleridge has turned to the Middle Ages partly because his temperament is attracted by the remote past and its legends, and partly because of what he set out to accomplish in the *Lyrical Ballads*-to give dramatic truth to incidents and agents of a supernatural kind. The Middle Ages provides Coleridge with themes, setting and atmosphere appropriate to what he wishes to accomplish.

On the face of it *The Ancient Mariner* do not embody the medieval atmosphere as for example, *Christabel* does. But it certainly has many medieval elements. First and foremost, the setting is in the distant past. The key-note is struck in the very opening line- "it is an Ancient Mariner". The word 'ancient' immediately brings up associations with the remote past. The medieval note is enhanced in the mention of the ceremonials painted at the beginning. The 'loud bassoon', the 'merry minstrelsy' are obviously a part of a medieval church setting for a wedding. The ship, the masts, the oars, the sails, the pilot, the light house-these are clear indications of the early days of navigation. The sailors are superstitious as people are in the Middle Ages.

Medieval literature, having been written in a comparatively less advanced age, often dealt with supernatural and superstitious tales. *The Ancient Mariner* has a great degree of the supernatural. It tells the story of a sailor who comes across a ship with Death and Life-in-Death as its crew. The sailor sees his two hundred companions dying of a curse and a group of angels entering the dead bodies of the sailors. On reaching his own country he hears a loud sound and his ship sinks. There is mention of medieval superstition again and again. In the Middle Ages the numbers three, seven, nine etc., has mysterious associations. The Albatross comes and plays with the sailors for nine days. The Mariner suffers for seven days and nights. The death fires and the burning of the sea with various colours are common superstitions mentioned in the stories of the Middle Ages.

References to medieval religious beliefs are not absent. The worship of Virgin Mary, the mother of Christ, is a part of medieval Christianity. In *The Ancient Mariner* Mary (Our Lady) is invoked again and again.

> To Mary Queen the praise he given!
> Heaven's mother send us grace!

References to angelic spirits, to the guardian saint and the hermit are clear testimony to the medievalism of the poem. People of the Middle Ages are comparatively more religious. They has a strong belief in sin, repentance and penance. The moral theme of the poem is distinctly medieval in spirit, dealing as it does with a sin and curse and penance and redemption.

The poem is written in ballad form which is popular in the Middle Ages. All Alliteration which is characteristic of old English poetry is quite often used in this poem. Here is just one of many examples of alliteration:

> The fair breeze blew, the white foam flew,
> The furrow followed free...

Some archaic (old) words have been purposely used by Coleridge to give the poem a medieval atmosphere-for example "eftsoons", "loon", "wist', "ken" and "sheen".

The Ancient Mariner has many medieval features. Without the background of medieval piety and superstition, much of the intensity and agony of the Mariner's experience will be lost on us. However, it is not enough to say that the poem throws a door ajar on the vanished life of the Middle Ages. The substance of the poem is not medievalism; medievalism is merely a suitable setting for the exposition of a universal theme-the idea that the best prayer to God consists in loving all the creatures of God.

(VI) TREATMENT OF NATURE

Q.6. Discuss the treatment of nature in *The Ancient Mariner*.

Ans. Samuel Taylor Coleridge possess a faculty of minute and subtle observation of nature which he has fostered to a degree of delicacy to which neither Wordsworth nor any other worshipper of nature ever quite attained. With this power of minute observation Coleridge has combined a mastery of broad, general effects which is revealed in the description of the ice-fields or the tropical ocean in *The Ancient Mariner*.

In *The Ancient Mariner* we do not come across such sights and sounds of nature we find in the poetry of some other nature-poets like Wordsworth and Keats. There are not many fields, hills, meadows and flowers. There are no lakes and rivers murmuring through the forest groves. Nor do we find here colourful birds for spot white leopards or deer. The poem for most part presents a vast sea-scape where nothing is visible except water and waves and sky. The winds blow, and blow rather fiercely. The sea seems to be heaving in great passion and anger. At other moments it is still as a painting.

The sunrise and the sunset are beautiful on land when from behind the hills the crimson rays seem so deep and flush the whole sky with their light. But the sight of the sun rising out of the waves and then sinking at the eventide beyond the horizon is of wondrous charm.

The Ancient Mariner is famous as a poem depicting supernatural horrors. But in enhancing the impression of horror nature plays a great part. The natural background is carefully drawn and is in subtle harmony with the supernatural incidents introduced. In the natural background we find not the soft and soothing touch of Wordsworth's poetry. There is no bliss of solitude. There is awe and mystery and the very solitude becomes a curse to the mariners when they find themselves

> Alone, alone, all all alone
> Alone on a wide, wide sea.

In the beginning the supernatural horror is introduced against the background of mist and snow, of lonely snowy cliff and growing ice-bergs of the South Pole. Every marvel is preceded or followed by suitable natural imagery.

Unlike Wordsworth, Coleridge has drawn some cruel and unfriendly aspects of nature. When the mariners are proceeding towards the South, a horrible wind pushes them along. The wind is described here as "tyrannous and strong". When again on their return journey the death of the Albatross begins to be avenged, the sky at the Equator has been painted in hot and copper colour:

> All in a hot and copper sky
> The bloody Sun, at noon

When the ship is caught in the snow and mist, the sound of the breaking ice is so pictured that one begins to marvel at the art of Coleridge and his keen observation of the natural phenomena on

> The ice was here, the ice was there
> The ice was all around;

It crack'd and growl'd and roar'd and howl'd
Like noises in a sound.

Prof. Herford says, "All this weird and penetrating supernaturalism is thrown into relief with exquisite instinct by scenes full of innocence of nature."

The play of water-snakes in the water—

Blue, glossy green, and velvet black
They coiled and swam: and every track
Was a flash of golden fire...

is one instance. The simile of the singing birds which express sweetness and purity of the song of the angels is another instance.

Thus we find that the poem is full of beautiful scenes of nature, sometimes showing us the softer and balmy aspects of nature but often picturing the harsher ones. There are striking images of light and luminous colour in sky and sea. But these pictures, beautiful in themselves and finely drawn, are there to serve a purpose. They contribute the unity of effect produced by the poem.

(VII) THE MORAL OF THE POEM

Q.7. It is said that the moral of the *The Ancient Mariner* gives the poem a centrality and added dimension. Do you agree?

Or

How far is it true to say that *The Ancient Mariner* has no moral?

Or

Do you agree with the view that the explicitly stated moral in *The Rime of The Ancient Mariner* lessens the artistic excellence of the poem?

Or

The purpose of *The Ancient Mariner* is "to teach, by his own example, love and reverence to all things that God made and loveth." Discuss.

Or

"The moral of *The Ancient Mariner* is in general conformity with Coleridge's views on 'life in nature' and the essence and function of poetry." Discuss.

Ans. Every story including *The Ancient Mariner* has a moral. No story, written in verse or prose, can be without a moral in its wide and comprehensive meaning. The conclusion or the moral may either be implied or expressly stated. It is not always that an expressly-stated moral lessens the artistic merit of the poem or the story. *The Rime of the Ancient Mariner* is a clear illustration of the truth of these remarks. E.M.W. Tillyard, C.M. Bowra, R.P. Warren and a host of eminent critics agree that the poem has a very serious moral and spiritual bearing on human life and they are certainly right.

The Significance of the Albatross and its Killing. Cheers and sees off at the harbour, the ship with The Ancient Mariner and his two hundred mates steers its course to the region of the icebergs, too easily. There the ship is encircled temporarily by the ice. The crew are much depressed when all of a sudden an Albatross appears through the mist and fog. In itself, the Albatross represents the animal world, another of God's creations. In their lonely gloom, the sailors hail it as though it is a Christian soul. The bird is an auspicious bird, a bird of good omen, which has brought with it a favourable south wind. Thus the Albatross represents the animal, the human and the spiritual worlds. The sailors are right in being hospitable and grateful to it. *The Ancient Mariner*, overlooking all that the bird stands for and the good that it has brought for the sailors, shoots it is dead with his cross-bow. He kills it out of ignorance and wantonness. We are not told why he is killed the bird. It seems to have been an arbitrary and irrational act. On the human level the killing is cruelty and criminal because it is their guest; on the spiritual level it is a sin. The gravity of the Mariner's' misdeed consists in its being at once cruelty, crime and sin. It is a misdeed against animals, human beings and God. The sailors know that it is so. But, when the mist and fog clear, they praise the Mariner and his misdeed. Thus they not only partake of the Mariner's guilt but also become more guilty than the Mariner, because their approval of his misdeed is not due to their ignorance but due to a wilful indifference to their knowledge. The whole crew including the Mariner are now guilty and liable to be punished.

The Consequences of the Killing of the Albatross. Cruelty to living things has its unpleasant consequences. Crime involves punishment, so the sailors are punished with death and The Ancient Mariner is tortured with Life-in-death. The Ancient Mariner has isolated himself and his sailors from the only representative of the living world and symbol of God's love in the region of mist and fog. Consequently, he is in turn cut off from all the living sailors and is left alone on the wide sea. The only living things he can see are the slimy things in the slimy sea. But he recoils from them in horror. As long as he hates them he has no hope of salvation. In hating them he again refuses to acknowledge the worth of God's creation. Naturally, he cannot pray and no saint shows any pity for him.

The Significance and Love of the Slimy Things. The slimy things by themselves represent again the animal world. Since they are living things, they are the only link between The Ancient Mariner and the rest of life or the living world. The Ancient Mariner at last perceives their beauty and admires them. Love gushes forth spontaneously from his heart for life and living things. He blesses the beautiful things unawares just as he kills the Albatross in utter ignorance. He now not only recognises the beauty of the water-snakes but also the fact of the worth of their existence. Now he is able to pray. Thus love dislodges the cruelty, the unconscious blessing replaces the criminality and prayer expiates the sin. Now *The Ancient Mariner* can hope for salvation.

The Way the Moral is Worked Out. Salvation at this stage is only a hope and not a certainty. The Ancient Mariner shows ignorance in killing the bird and liking the slimy things unconsciously. He has not become a self-conscious man. He has not attained realisation. He still has to do penance. The penance consists in his confession to the hermit, to the wedding guest, and to all those he could tell the story of his crime and sinfulness to. It is through this long process of penance that he can achieve self-consciousness and self-realisation which in their turn would make his salvation a certainty.

The Summing up of the Moral. Thus, appreciation of beauty in the living things however ugly they may seem to be and love of all living things whether they are great or small are the best of all prayers. Prayer and penance are but an expression of the appreciation and love of God's creation.

> He prayeth well, who loveth well
> Both man and bird and beast
> ....
> ....
> He prayeth best, who loveth best
> All things both great and small,
> For the dear God who loveth us,
> He made and loveth all:

Is this moral inadequate ? Does the punishment seem in excess of the crime committed? Our view will depend on our entire attitude to life. The Albatross may be a bird, but who is man to judge that he has the right to kill it wantonly? A bird, a water-snake, a man each has a place in the scheme of life as God has created all of them. If we do not take the killing of the bird at face value, we at once realize that the Mariner has violated the inviolable sanctity of life. Thus seen, the moral of the poem is not inadequate. Man must not be arrogant enough to assume the role of judging what deserves to live or die.

The Moral is not a Defect. Some critics argue that Coleridge's statement of the bare moral in the lines quoted above detract from the artistic merit of the poem. They support their view by quoting Coleridge, who says: "... the only or chief fault, if I may say so, is the obtrusion of the moral sentiment so openly on the reader as a principle or cause of action in a work of such pure imagination". This statement is not quite acceptable. It proves nothing more than the fact that Coleridge is being humble in estimating his work. The moral scheme is inherent and central to the very structure of *The Ancient Mariner*. Coleridge believs that all creatures are part of One Life. There is a careful regulated moral atmosphere in the poem which gives it an added dimension. Without it, the poem would merely be a collection of supernatural incidents. But as it is, the poem's structure marks a development in clear stages from crime through punishment to such redemption as is possible in this world. Humphry House is correct about the explicit moral when he says: "But coming in context, after the richness and terror of the poem, it is no more a banal moral apothegm, but a moral which has its meaning because it has been lived."

Q.8. Give an account of the suffering that came upon *The Ancient Mariner* after he had killed Albatross. Do you consider the punishment to be proportionate to his crime?

Ans. *The Ancient Mariner* kills the innocent, loving Albatross. For this he and his companions suffer terribly. The Polar spirit avenges the crime. Their sufferings begin when the ship enters the Pacific Ocean. The wind drops down and the ship stands motionless. The sun burns fiercely and stands directly above the mast. No drinking water is left in the ship. Every tongue is withered at the root. They are unable to speak and are thus condemned to silence. The silent sea is rotting. Slimy creatures of the sea crawl around the ship. Death fires dance around. The water of the sea burns at night with Various colours like witches' oil. Some of the mariners dream that the spirit of the polar region is closely pursuing them in order to punish them. They blame *The Ancient Mariner* for their suffering, curse him with their looks and hang the dead body of the bird around his neck, in place of the Cross. The mariners are almost dead with thirst. Suddenly they see a ship coming from the horizon. Their joy turns to horror as they find that it is a spectre-ship, moving steadily forward without any wind or tide. As it comes near they are paralysed with fear to find that the crew of the ship are Death and Life-in-Death, a woman. The two are playing at dice to decide the fate of *The Ancient Mariner* while the two hundred crew are claimed by Death. Presently the crew drop down dead, one after the other.

The Ancient Mariner is left all alone in that wide sea. He suffers a kind of living death as the curse in the dead men's eyes seems to haunt him. He could not die, though every moment he hankers for death. No saint of heaven takes pity on him. Even God seems to have deserted him. He looks upon the sea and sees only slimy creatures there. He looks at the deck but it is filled with dead bodies. He looks up to heaven and tries to pray but instead of prayer only a wicked whisper comes and leaves his heart as dry as dust. Seven days and seven nights go on in this way. At last a change comes. One moonlit night he sees beautiful water-snakes moving around the ship. Their beauty makes him glad and he blesses them inadvertently. A spring of love seems to come gushing out of his heart. He feels that some kind saint of Heaven has taken pity on him. Thus love purifies his sinful soul and he can pray. As a result the dead body of the bird falls off his neck. Thus part of his penance is done. But his suffering is not yet completely over. The memory of the crime visits his soul from time to time and racks his whole body and mind with a woeful agony. The pain is relieved only when he unburdens his soul by telling his story to somebody who will willingly listen to him.

On a superficial view, the punishment of the Mariner seems to be out of proportion to the crime. It seems that an unduly severe punishment has been given to the Mariner for the mere killing of a bird. But we must remember the true significance of the Mariner's crime. *The Ancient Mariner* shows no respect for the legendary sanctity of life. The bird is innocent, unsuspecting and loving. It comes at the call of the Mariners and takes food from their hands or plays with them. To kill such a bird is a needless act of cruelty and great violation of the law of love and hospitality. He shows hate for one of the creatures of God and thus has committed one of the blackest of sins. That is why his suffering is so terrible. If he is given death, it will be an end of suffering. Hence he is deprived of death and make to perform his penance in full. At last, when love purifies his soul he is able to pray and look forward to salvation. The poet seems to imply that an act of hatred is atoned for by an act of love . In the end his heart is purified as love gushes out for the meanest of God's creatures. Thus views, the punishment of *The Ancient Mariner* does not seem to be out of proportion to his crime.

Q.9. Comment on the attitude of the companions of the Ancient Mariner to the killing of the Albatross. Explain why the Ancient Mariner's life was spared while the companions die apparently for no fault of their own.

Ans. The Ancient Mariner has killed the Albatross with his cross-bow. His companions condemns him for his crime for they believe that it is a bird of good omen that causes the south wind blow and the sun shine brightly. But once the mist clears, the Mariners changes their opinion and says it is right to slay the bird that bring the fog and mist. As the poet says in the marginal commentary of the poem "they justify the same and thus make themselves accomplishers in the crime." It is the first principle of morality and law that is worse than the sinner is the man who approves of the sin. Thus the Mariners of the ship renders themselves guilty by lending their moral support to the crime. Again, when the ships reaches the equator the wind suddenly dropped down. This ship is becalmed. The sailors suffers terribly from heat and loneliness. They saw to their horror a spectre-ship with its supernatural crew. They hung the dead body of the bird around *The Ancient Mariner*'s neck, in place of the cross and cursed him with the terrible look in their eyes.

The variable attitude of the Mariners to the crime of *The Ancient Mariner* is blameworthy. It indicates a want of faith and steadiness on their part. They have no respect for the sanctity of the bird's life. They approves or condemn the killing of the bird, as according to the effect seem to have on their own welfare. This is selfish. Such moral vacillation is highly sinful and implies spiritual deadness. Those who acquiesce in or approve of the sin are doomed to death, without a chance of salvation. But the actual sinner is doomed to Life-in-Death, a state worse than death, in order to suffer-and repent and thereby attain salvation. This explains the apparent paradox that the old sailor, who actually kills the bird, is spared to live while the ship's crew perish apparently for no fault of theirs.

The question may be viewed in another light. It is the old sailor who is the direct sinner while his companions were are accomplices in his crime, because they lean their moral support to it. Hence by the ordinary law of justice the old Mariner who is the actual sinner shall be condemn to death while the accomplices shall be given lesser punishment. But in the higher morality of God, death is a less punishment than Life-in-Death, because the former puts an end to all sufferings. The Mariners end their suffering by death, while the old sailor is doomed to a living death. His life becomes an endless torture and every moment he prays to death to come to him as a welcome relief. But he is denied the blessing of death. Thus his punishment is greater than that of his companions.

Q.10. Draw the significance of Deaths and Life-in-Death.

Ans. Death and Life-in.Death are the two instruments of punishment in the hands of God. There is a Law of Pity prevailing on the earth. The world is on the side of pity and love and the men who violate these laws are punished by hardness of heart. They cannot pray and they cannot bless any creature of the world. All things that God has are beloved to him. God loves those best who love their fellow-men and fellow creatures:

> He prayeth well, who loveth well
> Both man and bird and beast.

Those men who break this law of the universe commit an unpardonable sin. They are either killed or suffer the pangs in life. The ship of The Ancient Mariner has been stuck amidst ice. When an Albatross come through the fog, all hailed the bird with joy and hospitality because with its appearance a good south wind sprang up, the ice split and the helmsman begin to steer the ship through. The Albatross begin to follow the ship. It is perched on the ship for nine days and plays with the sailors. Suddenly the Mariner shot it down. We are not told why. It is obviously a wanton and irresponsible act.

The guardian spirit began to avenge the Albatross. It sends Death and Life-in-Death to punish the sailors. A skeleton ship approaches them carrying two figures. One is a grim-looking, ghastly skeleton or Nightmare, the personification of Death. The other is Life-in Death which has red lips, golden locks, and leprous skin. She represents the life-long torture that a sinful man endures on account of the pin-pricks of his conscience. Life-in-Death curdles one's blood by striking terror into the heart of man. The two ghastly crew are playing at dice to determine who will win the Mariner. Life-in Death wins whereas Death falls upon the sailors.

The sailors fall down dead. But one may argue that death is not always a curse and life is not always a blessing. The Mariners who dies are spared the horrors and pain that the old Mariner has to suffer. He has to do penance for his sin all through his life.

As the souls of the sailors departed from their bodies they passes by the Mariner with the whizzing sound of his cross-bow. It is a perpetual reminder to him of his heinous crime. He is left alone on that wide, wide sea. No saint take pity on him and his soul is in perpetual suffering. The sight of the sea become dreadfully ugly. On the deck the timbers of the ship are rotting and heaps of dead men lay on them. He wishes to pray but his impenitent heart will not allow him to pray. God accepts prayer only of those persons whose hearts are softened by tenderness and pity. The very eyes of the dead seemed to curse him and distracted his attention from the thought of God. For seven days he is thus tortured by the thought of his sin but he can not die, as he himself confess.

It was only after seven days of constant woe that his fate seems to take pity upon his torment soul. In the moonlight, inside the charmed circle of the sea-water reflected by the ship's shadow, he looks with deep interest at the variegated appearance of the water-snakes. Suddenly at the sight of the 'blue, glossy green, and velvet black' snakes a fountain of sympathy and tenderness flows from his heart and he blesses those creatures unawares. This love for the creatures of God is the best of prayers. The ray of pity illumined the darkness of his heart and he became calm and thus able to pray to God who ultimately took pity on him.

But this recovery of human affection does not end the suffering. It, however, opens the door to the future. The Mariner is haunted by the presence of his dead comrades. Thus pursues by memories and fears, the Mariner becomes a symbol of remorse and often he feels the necessity of repeating his confession.

Thus we see that of the two tools of punishment that nature ,utilises to punish, the instrument of Life-in-Death is much more horrible than Death. Execution kills instantly but Life-in-Death like life-imprisonment kills by degrees. Death is a much more humane executioner because it kills a man in few seconds. But Life-in-Death draws the life out of one incessantly, for years.

(VIII) ALLEGORY AND SYMBOLISM

Q.11. What is an allegory? Examine in the light of your definition whether the story of *The Ancient Mariner* is an allegory.

Or

Write a short essay on the allegorical meaning of *The Ancient Mariner.*

Or

The main events in *The Ancient Mariner* have an ethical and-allegorical dimension. Discuss.

Ans. What is an Allegory ? An allegory has been defined as a narrative description of a subject under guise of another suggestively similar subject It is a story within a story. The underlying story always has a moral significance. Allegorical composition serves two absolutely distinct purposes such as to amuse just as any other good piece of literature should, and also to preach as a religious sermon does. A piece of literature which has an apparent instructive purpose is only an inferior kind of literature. Inwardly it may have a moral end in view but outwardly it ought to satisfy the literary urge in the reader. Only a beautiful blending of the two purposes shall make a work of literature really great.

Simple Allegory at the Lowest Level. Reduced to its lowest terms, *The Ancient Mariner* is a simple allegory of guilt and regeneration. It is divided into seven parts. Beginning with the commission of guilt in Part I, each part tells of a new stage in the process towards regeneration , till in Part VII the conclusion comes with whatever redemption is possible in the case.

At the end of Part 1, the Mariner shoots the Albatross, but nowhere does he explain his motives in shooting it. This uncertainty of the motives is quite important. It, in fact, symbolises 'the essential frivolity of many crimes against humanity and the ordered system of the world.' In Part II, the Manner's companions become accomplices in the crime. With Part III the forces of retribution are set into motion. The Mariner's sin being greater, he is condemned to the more dreadful Life-in Death. The Mariner's alienation from both God and His creations is shown at the beginning of Part IV

Alone, alone, all, all, alone
Alone on a wide wide sea!

Then comes the spontaneous blessing for God's creatures, the dead Albatross falls from his neck signifying partial redemption. In Part V the regeneration continues. Sleep comes as the long-awaited rain. But *The Ancient Mariner* has to do more penance before he is reconciled to God. In Part VI there seems to be an obstruction to the healing process the Mariner is haunted by a dreadful fear. But this is remorse which brings repentance and humility; therefore the angelic forms appear to the Mariner's eyes. The last part brings the Mariner to his native land. Life-in-Death continues to work on him as it must for regeneration is a slow process.

Working out of Guilt and Regeneration in the Poem. When the Albatross comes to the ship, the sailors welcome it.

As if it had been a Christian Soul,
We hailed it in God's name.

Here is one of the key-phrases in the poem which explains why the killing of the Albatross assumes a sinister shape in the structure of the poem. 'It is not just killing of an ordinary bird which justifies the spectral persecution of the Mariner; the Albatross is here endowed with a godly personality; it is affiliated to a 'Christian Soul' and therefore demands the respect due to a creature of God. The enormity of the Mariner's crime is felt as much in the status of the life that is taken as in the unprovoked, unexplained nature of the Mariner's action. In the words of Mr. E.M. Bewley, "The transgression of *The Ancient Mariner* in killing the Albatross is a violation of that supernatural charity which shall rule throughout creation... The Albatross becomes, in effect, a person. It is given a kind of inviolability. It has been deliberately placed by the Mariner on the same plane of creation which he himself occupies, and the full play of the will to which this deliberation gives scope brings to the Mariner's act of violence a special guilt". Why the Mariner has killed the bird is a mystery, it is one of those impulsive acts which, by their very irrationality, give a blow to our self-esteem and dump us into the stagnant pool of dejection.

For a moment the enormity of his crime is not brought home to the Mariner: the continuation of fair weather is an external hint that his self-confidence is still unshaken :

> The fair breeze blew, the white foam flew,
> The furrow followed free....

And then there is the shock of

> We were the first that ever burst
> Into that silent sea.

From that point onwards the Mariner's realisation of the nature of his guilt and his expiation for it by suffering supernatural punishment proceed together. The stagnating of the ship, the drought and the parching thirst, the coming of the skeleton-ship with its supernatural passengers, Death and Life-in-Death, throwing dice to settle the fate of the Mariner and the rest of the crew have an inevitability in which the natural and the supernatural become a piece. The mood of depression and self-abasement express in :

> And a thousand thousand slimy things
> Lived on; and so did I !

begins to be charmed away by the magic of nature's vital beauty. The Mariner recovers an interest in the simplest forms of life :

> Beyond the shadow of the ship
> I watched the water-snakes:
> They moved in tracks of shining white,
> And when they reared, the elfish light
> Fell off in hoary flakes....
> O happy living things! no tongue
> Their beauty might declare.

This sympathy with life is the beginning of the man's spiritual regeneration. The sleep which comes to him after many sleepless nights the showers of rain which revive him, the navigation of the ship by 'a blessed troop of angelic spirits' that enter the dead bodies of the crew, the interest taken by other supernatural beings in his spiritual welfare :

> The man bath penance done.
> And penance mote will do-

mark various stages in the process of recovery. The supernatural agents and events perfectly harmonize with the natural motions of the man's spirit. The perfect simplicity and the air of conviction with which they are narrated induce in the reader 'that willing suspension of disbelief for the moment, which constitutes poetic faith'.

The final expiation of the crime is registered in the Mariner's voyage 'coming full circle' –

Oh! dream of joy! is this indeed
The light-house top I see?
Is this the hill ? Is this the Kirk ?
Is this mine own countree ?

The joy in experiencing reunion with the familiar and the intimate is paralleled in the joy and gratitude felt by the Mariner for the seraph-band that stood above the corpses in their own bright forms.

In a mood of humble acceptance the Mariner now rejoins the simple forms and rites of social life from which he has sailed into the romance and the adventures of the uncharted seas:

O sweeter than the marriage-feast
'Tis sweeter far to me
To walk together to the kirk
with a goodly company!

D.W. Harding in his masterly summing up of the theme of the poem conclude: "The buoyancy of the voyager as he first set out....entails a self-reliant thrusting forth into the outer world and repudiates dependence on the comfort of ordinary social ties. But Coleridge's anxieties seem to have shown him this attitude taken beyond all bounds and leading to a self-sufficiency which wants only destroy the ties of affection. The Albatross is killed, and then the penalty must be paid in remorse, dejection, and the sense of being a worthless social outcast. Only a partial recovery is possible. Once the horrifying potentiality has been glimpsed in human nature, Coleridge dare not imagine a return to self-reliant voyaging. Creeping back defeated into the social convoy, the Mariner is obviously not represented as having advanced through his suffering to a fuller life, and he no more achieves a full rebirth than Coleridge ever could. There is nothing but the crushed admission that he will, after all, have done better to have stayed at home in humble companionship. Even the vigour and excitement of the marriage feast are too daring for him, he needs submissive trustful prayer to a great Father."

New Dimension Through Myth of Guilt and Redemption. *The Ancient Mariner* is a myth of guilt and redemption. Coleridge's introduction of this theme into *The Ancient Mariner* gives to it a new dimension. What might otherwise be no more than an irresponsible fairy-tale is brought closer to life and to its fundamental issues. The myth of crime and punishment provides a structure for the supernatural events which rise from it. The shadow cast by the Mariner's crime adds by contrast to the brilliance of the unearthly world in which it is committed, and the degree of his guilt and his remorse serve to stress the power of the angelic beings which watch over human kind. At the same time the Mariner's tale is a story of a voyage into the interior. Not only into the unfathomable depths of the sources of human action to be discerned in the unpremeditated shooting of the Albatross that cause him his suffering and the spontaneous blessing of the water-snakes that begins his restoration but the story also takes us beyond the human world altogether. Again it is a voyage of extreme contrasts, of suffering and of expiation, of the human and social world and an altogether alien cosmos with its own terrible, yet beautiful order. It is exactly right that the listener shall be a wedding-guest and that the Mariner denies him his expectations of the natural enjoyment of the music, the celebration and the happiness of the feast. It is also right that the guest should be afraid of the Mariner and feel that he is a being from another world; he is exactly that.

More than an Allegory. The poem is of course more than an allegory of guilt and regeneration. In any ordinary sense the Mariner is very little guilty. But he has broken the bond between, himself and the life of Nature, and in consequence becomes spiritually dead. What happens to him when he blesses the water-snakes in the tropical calm is a psychic rebirth-a rebirth that must at times happen to all men and all cultures unless they are to dry up in living death, as Graham Hough says.

Conclusion. Thus the story of *The Ancient Mariner* has a multi-faceted richness of meaning. It is a story of spiritual adventure, a story of crime, punishment and reconciliation, a story of sin, expiation and redemption, a story revealing the secret of communal and family harmony and the harmony of the natural order of the universe, all in one. Usually, in an allegory, we find one single current of meaning and moral underlying the superficial facade of the story. But in *The Rime of the Ancient Mariner* several levels of meaning are present pointing always to one single moral :

> He prayeth best, who loveth best
> All things both great and small;
> For the dear God who loveth us,
> He made and loveth all.

This moral is in fact the principle that guides the movement of the universe. Once the principle is broken, the whole order of the universe is broken, with far-reaching consequences. *The Ancient Mariner* has broken the principle by killing the Albatross, and has to suffer the consequences.

Q.12. "*The Ancient Mariner,* like all great poetry, is not confined to make its appeal at one level only ." Amplify.

Or

"*The Ancient Mariner* does not state a result, it symbolises a process". Discuss.

Or

"The description of *The Ancient Mariner* as a story of crime and punishment is grossly inadequate. It does not do justice to the rich symbolism of the poem, especially in the later part". Discuss and illustrate.

Or

"Below its specific surface meaning, there are other more universal meanings." Is that true of *The Ancient Mariner*? Discuss with illustrations.

Ans. *The Ancient Mariner,* like all great poetry, is not confined to making its appeal at one level only. Even the natural description is not straight forwardly 'realistic', though it shows vivid accuracy. The appearances of sun, moon, stars, of storm and calm, of Antarctic and tropic seas are superbly portrayed and enhanced by the sharp contrasts they present. At a purely descriptive level, Coleridge captures the teeming splendour of the tropical sea creatures in memorable lines:

They moved in tracks of shining white, and when they reared, the elfish light Fell off in hoary flakes.

A superficial reading of such a passage is by all means pleasurable; but even the unsophisticated reader is likely to recall that the same creatures are described, forty lines earlier, as 'a thousand thousand slimy things'. How is it that the same water-snakes are at one moment evocative of horror and at another evocative of beauty? We are obliged to refer to the Mariner himself, and are quickly forced to realize that we are not dealing with a poetry of simple natural description only. This is poetry in which natural description has a psychological, a narrative and dramatic function. The descriptive passages, far from being merely decorative, play a part in acting out the spiritual drama which the story, at its deepest level, symbolises.

1. Several Layers of Significance. *The Ancient Mariner* is a symbolic poem, because it has not one, but several layers of significance. Below its specific surface meaning, there are other, more universal meanings. The awareness of a spiritual reality existing behind the surfaces of things is at the heart of all Romantic poetry, and the greatness of *The Ancient*

Mariner lies primarily in the dramatic expression it gives to that awareness. It has been maintained that the story of *The Ancient Mariner* recapitulates the history of mankind, or of every man, or of man's inquiring spirit, or of Coleridge himself. While allowing that such interpretations may be at least partly valid, we shall look at the poem primarily in the light of Coleridge's remark that it has a moral. (He adds that the 'moral sentiment' is obtruded 'too openly on the reader' and of his constant belief that 'the symbolical is always part of that whole of which it is representative'.)

The moral of *The Ancient Mariner* is given explicitly in the lines:

> He prayeth, best, who loveth best
> All things both great and small;
> For the dear God who loveth us,
> He made and loveth all:

2. Moral and Religious Symbols. A moral purpose is central to the whole poem. What it can best be understood by referring to the wedding guest. When he is first seen, he is impatient to enjoy the merriment of the marriage feast and resents being detained. After hearing the Mariner's tale, which concludes on a note of joy and fellowship in Christ, he significantly turns his back on the uproar rude' and we are told he wakes next morning 'a sadder and a wiser man'. Neither strain nor ingenuity is involved in seeing the poem as a story of crime and punishment acted out in a framework of values supplied by medieval Catholicism, with its traditional symbols of saints and spirits, of repentance and absolution. So far, as it draws upon the great Christian 'myth' of sin redeemed by divine grace, it draws strength from that myth and the obscure forces in our life which it is the business of myth to explore and embody. In turning our attention to the action itself, we shall see that the religious and moral symbols used are of crucial importance to an understanding of the poem.

3. Symbolic of a Process. Amid the 'merry din' of the marriage-feast, the Mariner relates a tale that goes back to time when, he carefree and merrily, set out on his voyage a traditional symbol for life itself. The story brings him to an unknown world of danger and ambiguous beauty. Here he kills the Albatross, which is significantly likened to 'a Christian Soul'. For Coleridge, there is only 'one life', which is at the same time 'within us and abroad', and it is just because all life is one that the Mariner cannot commit murder without symbolically destroying all life, including his own. The ship moves into the tropics where the breeze, age-long symbol of life, soon flags, and under an ominous dwarfed and bloody sun the Mariner's punishment begins. The crew by approving it have made themselves 'accomplices in the crime', and are doomed to endure with the Mariner the torments of hell, which are reflected in the entire visible universe. The sterility and corruption of the cardinal sin of lovelessness are conveyed in the vast waste of a rotting and paralysed ocean. At last a 'spectre-bark' appears in this purgatorial world, with its grim crew of Death and Life-in-Death. The figure of Life-in-Death is a harlot figure and, as such, personifies not love, but lovelessness in its disguise; not life, but its diseased semblance only.

For seven days and nights the Mariner endures the hell of his own making. Theologically, hell is the condition of being cut off from God, and to the Mariner in his loneliness God 'scarce seems there to be'. The symbolism of parching heat and drought uses to express life cut off from its source in God is as old as religion itself. It is only through divine grace and the agency of his 'kind saint' that he is resurrected into life and love. The Mariner 'yearneth towards the journeying Moon', which here again is used as a symbol for the imagination which Coleridge believe to be sustained by joy. Significantly, then, there in the light of the moon-of true, imaginative life-the Mariner "beholdeth God's creatures of the great calm' and spontaneously reacts to their beauty and happiness. In his lovelessness the universe about him appears as a corrupt terrifying image of death. As a consequence of divinely-given love, he sees this same universe transfigurs in beauty and alive with God's happy living creatures. Simultaneously, with love comes prayer, and the Albatross, symbol of his guilt, falls from his neck. Sleep, traditionally denies a guilty soul, is sent 'from Heaven', together with life-giving rain.

The Mariner's physical and spiritual paralysis is at an end :

I moved, and could not feel my limbs

The overtones of resurrection are reinforced by the doomsday imagery of the storm, and the 'roaring wind'. This suggests the wind of Pentecost, the breath of God himself. Though restores to *living life* once more, the Mariner must again endure the curse of the dead men's eyes: he has, to face the full significance of his guilt-a Christian condition of finding pardon. Soon the features of his native land re-emerge. There is neither cheering nor merriment, as there has been when the Mariner set out. He is himself a transforms man, and his calm vision is of something far deeper than mere merriment. The Mariner is rewarded by what is specifically called '*a heavenly sight*'. It is with joy once more that he recognizes his rescuers. Through them he is restored to communion with his fellow men, from whom his crime has cut him off. Through the hermit he can make formal confession, accept his penance, and re-enter 'the goodly company' of men, seeking grace through Christ.

Symbol of Imagination. The primary theme, which is the outcome of the fable taken at its face value as 'a story of crime and punishment and reconciliation' is "the theme of sacramental vision , or the theme of 'One

Life' ." The secondary theme is 'concerned with the context of values in 'which the fable is presented' and 'the theme of the imagination'. The two themes are finally fused in the poem. The Albatross, besides being associated with human nature on the level of the primary theme, is also associated with the moon, mist, cloud and fog-smoke, on the level of the secondary theme of the imagination:

> In mist or cloud, on mass or shroud,
> Is perched for vespers nine;

Furthermore the bird is associated with the breeze, which Warren takes to be the 'creative' wind, for which there are countless parallels in other poets. The sun is kept entirely out of the matter. The lighting is always indirect, for even in the day we have only 'mist or cloud' the luminous haze, the symbolic equivalent of moonlight. But not only is the moon associated with the bird, but with the wind also. Upon the bird's advent a 'good south wind sprang up behind'. And so we have the creative wind, the friendly bird, the moonlight of imagination, all together in one symbolic cluster. This 'symbolic cluster' belongs to the imagination and all the imaginative side of man's activity. And in his shooting, the Mariner not only commits a crime against the other, natural and spiritual order of the world, but also a crime against creative imagination; and part of the penalty is, the loss of the wind.

The dual character of the ice near the South Pole-the emerald and the dismal sheen also expresses the dual character of the imagination, that it is partly a blessing and a curse to him who lives by it. It is this cursing side of the imagination which accounts for the particular vengeance of the Polar Spirit on the Mariner as distinct from the punishment is exacted by the sun. And this dual character and special vengeance also explain why the moon is allowed to be the light by which the crew die.

Conclusion. The poem's very richness at once tempts and defeats definiteness of interpretation; as we commit overselves to the development of one strand of meaning, we find that in the very act of doing, we are excluding something else of importance.

(IX) *THE ANCIENT MARINER* : A NARRATIVE POEM

Q.13. Discuss *The Ancient Mariner* as a narrative poem.

Ans. Coleridge is a born story-teller and he knows the art of telling a story in verse. In this respect he presents a striking contrast to Wordsworth who is a poor narrator. *The Ancient Mariner* is a successful literary ballad. It has a direct and sudden opening. The poet does not beat about the bush while starting the story. The poem shows a swift movement. One event follows the other in quick succession. There are no incidents or details which may be described superfluous or unwanted. Every incident carries the story forward.

Coleridge knows the art of arousing suspense. He keeps us guessing throughout the story. We wonder whether *The Ancient Mariner* will be saved or will meet a terrible fate.

The Ancient Mariner like all good stories has a very effective climax. The climax occurs in the fourth part of the poem when *The Ancient Mariner* blesses the water-snakes and when the dead Albatross falls off his neck.

The action has a beginning, a middle and an end. In the first half of the poem, an agency of avenging demon is in the ascendent, in the second, the prevailing power of an angel band. It is an overt act of the Mariner which precipitates the daemonic vengeance, it is an inner impulse counter to the act which brings to pass the angelic intervention, and in the end it is 'the penance of life' which falls upon the rescued wanderer,, a fated wanderer still. Exciting force, rising action, climax, falling action, catastrophe-all are there. And through the transfer to the Mariner of the legendary associations of the Wandering Jew, undying among the dead, Cruikshank's dream-its figures metamorphosed into Death and Life-in-Death-is built into the basic structure of the plot. And under the influence of another ship, sailed by an angelic crew, the suggestion of the navigation of the Mariner's vessel by the bodies of the dead is so transformed as to provide that cardinal antithesis of angelic and daemonic agencies on which the action of the poem turns. And finally, by a stroke of consummate art, ship and poem alike are brought back in the end to the secure, familiar, happy world from which they had set out. The supernatural machinery is a masterpiece of constructive skill.

The poet succeeds in securing the suspension of disbelief on the part of the reader. In other words, the story is narrated by the poet, appears to be convincing and credible. The reader feels that the events described in *The Ancient Mariner* are capable of happening in actual life. Coleridge describes supernatural events against the background of such objects; of Nature as the sea, the sun, the sky, the moon and the stars. He refers to natural phenomena in such a realistic manner as to make us feel that the supernatural events described in the poem also must have happened.

Coleridge also contrasts horror with beauty in order to set in relief the supernatural part of the poem. Thus immediately after describing the spectre-bark (phantom ship) he gives us a beautiful description of the moon going up the sky, attended by a star or two.

(X) FORM OF *THE ANCIENT MARINER*

Q.14 Justify the statement that *The Rime of the Ancient Mariner* is a ballad.

Or

Comment upon Coleridge's use of the ballad form in *The Ancient Mariner.*

Or

What is a literary ballad? Show how *The Rime of the Ancient Mariner* is a literary ballad.

Ans. The traditional ballad form. A 'ballad' is in reality a dance song. In England it was first introduced by the minstrels. It is first applied to the native "sing-song"-a song in short rhymed stanzas. The name is also used for the other folk-songs, lays, gestes and nines. Later on the term come to be applied to short, vivid narratives, consisting of one or more cantos of four-line stanzas in rough rhyme and rhythm. Themes are drawn from the elementary aspects of life, tales of adventure, fighting, of prowess and valour.

The Modern or Literary Ballad. The modern ballad is a literary development of the traditional form. Scott, Cowper, Wordsworth, Longfellow and Tennyson are prominent among those who have written in this style. Unlike the old ballads, these are consciously written poems in that style. As such they do not have that spontaneity, perfect sincerity and has rugged strength of the older ballads.

An important element of romantic poetry is medievalism an interest in medieval subjects and a wilful copying of medieval literary methods. Coleridge, Scott and Keats are mainly responsible for the revival of the ballad form. Ballads written by romantic poets are called literary Ballads. They are a definite re-creation of the atmosphere of times long ago. Their main interest is literary.

***The Ancient Mariner* : A Ballad.** Coleridge combines many of the features of the old form with the modern. All the simple beauty of the old ballad is there with none of its extravagances.

1. Story and Theme. *The Rime of the Ancient Mariner* tells a simple story. The old Mariner kills an Albatross and his sailor-mates applaud his misdeed. Retribution and punishment visit them. The sailors die and the Mariner barely survives a series of harrowing and terrible experiences. When at last he learns to love living things, he becomes free from the spell. In this way, the story is one of crime and punishment. But parallel to this theme, runs the theme of love. Love, in this story is not man-woman love as in most ballads but love of God's creations, big or small, without discrimination.

2. **Adventure.** Most ballads are full of feats of physical strength, fortitude and adventure. *The Rime of the Ancient Mariner* does not lack in them. The high seas are always an apt setting for adventure. From the time the Mariner kills the Albatross to the time he is rescued by the holy Hermit, the Mariner has a series of adventures or encounters with a host of supernatural beings, good and evil, beautiful and ugly, visible and invisible, like the Polar Spirit, the slimy things, the angels that inhabited the bodies of the dead sailors and finally Death and his mate Life-in-Death. In all these encounters, the Mariner's courage and fortitude are put to severe test both physically and morally. He survives them all by his love of living things and his penance. It is a spiritual adventure.

3. **Supernatural Machinery.** Supernatural element is an essential element of ballads of all description. Coleridge in this poem has built a large supernatural machinery to draw an effective and purposeful contrast between artifical and natural things. The supernatural world or life has a logic of its own and once it comes into action it sets into motion a whole series of supernatural characters to impose the due punishment. It even controls, influences and takes advantage of natural elements like the wind, the stars, the rain, the fog and the mist.

4. **Primitivism.** A frequent device in ballads to enlist our belief is to invest the story with a primitive setting and atmosphere. The poem is about an Ancient Mariner. The Albatross is believed to be a bird of good omen and the killing of it to be inauspicious. Together with these superstitions, the whole supernatural machinery, the long drawn marriage feast, the peaceful atmosphere of the church on the top of a hill, the holy hermit are apart of the medieval atmosphere in the poem. The elemental forces, uncontrolled and uncontrollable, like the sea, the wind, the sun and the rain makes the atmosphere more effectively primitive. Against this setting, the elemental passions like the Mariner's whimsical shooting of the bird, his hatred of the grimy, slimy things in the sea, the intense hatred of the sailors for the Mariners and the ardent universal love has preached by the Mariner make the primitiveness of the setting real.

5. **Technical Devices.** Ballads employ certain technical devices to make the narration real, vivid and powerful. One such device is the dramatic touch.

6. **Abrupt Opening ; Events Sudden and Romantic.** In *The Ancient Mariner* for example the story has a very arrestingly dramatic beginning:

It is an ancient Mariner
And he stoppeth one of three

No words are wasted on the description of the Mariner or on giving us information as to who those three are. Similarly, a little later on we are told:

> He holds him with his skinny hand,
> "There was a ship", quoth he.

The Ancient Mariner begins his story abruptly paying no heed to the wedding guest's protest. Similar incidents can be multiplied from the poem. The essence of these is that they are so sudden and so full of surprise that they make the story vivid and dramatic. Further, the story told by the Mariner to the wedding guest with his frequent protests and expressions of fear, and the dialogue between the Two Voices, between the Hermit and the Pilot gives the story a stage-conversational tone. The tense suspense that is created from the time the Albatross is killed to the time the Two Voices appear, makes the poem most dramatic.

7. **Convincing and Economic.** The supreme concern of a ballad is to tell the story fast so as to make the surprise, the suspense and the suddenness of the events most effective. This quickness of narration is achieved by economy in words and simplicity of language. Coleridge is a master in both these arts of economy and simplicity. Besides his famous lines, 'Water, water every where/ Nor any drop to drink". The following lines illustrate his art:

> Alone, alone, all, all alone
> Alone on a wide wide sea.

Only nine letters (a, d, e, i, l, n, o, s, w) have gone in to make these two lines and yet how vivid is the sense of loneliness we experience?

Repetition. Repetition of words, lines and sometimes stanza is a frequent device in ballads, intended for emphasis or for reminding us of the essence of a thing. Coleridge makes use of repetition in a subtle way. Any number of examples can be given of the repetition that occurs in the poem. For instance, the mention of Albatross at the end of each part of the poem brings home to us the seriousness of the Mariner's crime. In the following lines, repetition is clearly meant for emphasis:

> But in a minute she 'gan to stir,
> With a short uneasy motion-
> Backwards and forwards half her length
> With a short uneasy motion.

Archaisms. Finally, archaic expressions are frequently used to enhance the primitiveness of the story. Coleridge makes frequent use of such obsolete expressions and spellings-kirk for church, 'gan for began, skiff boat for light boat; quoth for say, or ever, for never, nor... nor fort neither.., nor; wist, countree, holy rood, eftsoons are all out of date and out of use.

8. The Poetic Form. A ballad is a poem in short stanzas. Usually, there are four lines in a stanza though Coleridge violated this pattern for change and variety occasionally. The lines are in iambic feet, that is, a short or unaccented syllable follows by a long or accented syllable though here Coleridge has took licence to introduce a different syllable or an extra syllable occasionally to relieve the poem of monotony. Of the four lines, the first and the third lines consist of eight syllables or four iambic feet while the second and fourth lines have six syllables or three iambic feet.

Coleridge very frequently employs internal rhymes in the first and third lines as 'blew' and 'flew' or 'first' and 'burst' in the following lines:

> The fair breeze blew, the white foam flew,
> The furrow followed free:
> We were the first that ever burst
> Into that silent sea

Alliteration, in the case of the above stanza, of 'f' and 'b' sounds in sharp contrast to that of 's' sounds in the last two lines, is a fully exploited device in *The Ancient Mariner.*

Modern Touches. *The Ancient Mariner* has a touch of modernity about it as a ballad. The psychological effect in which the poem abounds is something modern and original. In old ballads entire emphasis is laid upon external events. In *The Ancient Mariner,* the poet describes not only the external events but also what happens in the mind of the Ancient Mariner. Thus we are told that *The Ancient Mariner* felt extremely fear-stricken when the ghost-ship disappears all of a sudden on the sea :

> Fear at my heart, as at a cup
> My life blood seemed to sip.

Conclusion. In its form, *The Ancient Mariner* is obviously a ballad, though the traditional ballad stanza is far from being preserved thoughout and is freely extended or modified to serve specific ends and to give greater variety. Its first text is littered with archaisms, which Coleridge wisely pruned; but he uses the direct, sometimes stark, language of the ballads, together with repetition and conventional epithets. The use of dialogue, with a little explicit characterization, the abrupt transitions in narration and, above all, the dramatic pace of a poetry has stripped for action are further characteristics of the ballad form. The marvels, the supernatural eeriness, the atmosphere of terror and superstition in *The Ancient Mariner* links, it in subject matter, too, with great ballad tradition of the late Middle Ages. Omen and weather lore, which play a prominent part in many ballads are used with great effect by Coleridge, whose ominous horned moon with a star 'within the nether tip' is probably suggested by Sir Patrick Spence. After all *The Ancient Mariner* is Coleridge's contribution to a collection of poems called *Lyrical Ballads*.

(XI) IMPORTANCE OF THE WEDDING GUEST

Q.15. Discuss the significance of the part played by the Wedding Guest in the dramatic frame-work of *The Ancient Mariner*.

Or

Why Coleridge introduced the Wedding-Guest in *The Rime of The Ancient Mariner*?

Or

Why did *The Ancient Mariner* pick on a Wedding-Guest to tell his story?

Ans. The Wedding-Guest's Part in the Story. *The Rime of the Ancient Mariner* begins abruptly when *The Ancient Mariner* stops one of the three wedding guests and begins to tell his story. The Wedding-Guest at first is reluctant to hear the story as he is in a hurry to go and attend the wedding. He even recoils in horror from the ghastly Ancient Mariner. But *The Ancient Mariner* holds him by his arresting glittering eye. The helpless Wedding-Guest collapses on a stone nearby and listens to story like a three-year child. On occasions he protests but cannot move away. In the end, he becomes so daze with what he has heard that he does not have the heart or the mind to attend the wedding. He is a 'sadder and a wiser man'. He is sadder for the realisation of the human predicament which *The Ancient Mariner* has so vividly impressed upon him through his story. He is wiser for the profound moral truth that he has learnt, namely the love of all things great or small.

Is the Wedding-Guest Important ? The Wedding-Guest's, part as sketched above is only one of passive listening. On the surface, it looks as though his part are not at all important if only for the reason that the Wedding-Guest is not part of *The Ancient Mariner*'s woeful tale. It is but natural to say, as some people have said, that the Wedding-Guest serves no useful purpose in the story but on the contrary, impedes the even progress of the Mariner's entrancing narrative. This view is superficial, and thoroughly mistaken. The Wedding-Guest has a place and purpose in the story which nobody else could fulfil.

Structurally Important. Structurally, the Wedding-Guest helps to bring out clearly and emphatically the spiritual crisis experienced by the Mariner after he kills the Albatross. He interrupts at important stages of the Mariner's story and draws the reader's attention to significant emotional states. The loud exclamation of the Wedding-Guest draws the much-evaded confession from the Mariner that he has shot the Albatross.

Towards the end of part III, the Wedding Guest suspects the Mariner to be a ghost and then in part V he expresses his fear. Both time the Mariner clarifies the situation for the Wedding-Guest as well as the reader. Thus he marks the stage of development in the story.

A Ballad Characteristic. In popular ballads, it is usual that the story is addressed to some particular individual. It is through this device that the ballad writers make their poems or narratives dramatic and conversational. If the dramatic element is lacking, the story will be dull for lack of surprise and suspense.

***The Ancient Mariner* Must Have a Listener.** The Ancient Mariner suffers fits of agony occasionally and is compelled by a mysterious inner necessity to find a willing listener whom he can discern at once by the power he has now acquired after his long suffering and penance. This time he has found a listener in one of the three wedding guests.

Vividness of Feeling and Emotion. *The Rime of the Ancient Mariner* is a story told not by the poet but by the Mariner himself. While telling the story, the Mariner lives through the past experience and visibly registers all the shades of feeling associated with those experiences and emotions. A description of those feelings and emotions will be bare, bald and unimpressive. Their vividness and dramatic effectiveness will be lost in the description. But the Wedding-Guest's interruptions bring before our mind the appearance and expression of *The Ancient Mariner* in all their vividness and clarity.

> God save thee ancient Mariner,
> From the fiends that plague thee thus;
> Why looks't thou so?

These lines, are spoken by the Wedding-Guest convey the suffering of the Mariner more effectively than a description can ever do.

Link Between Two Worlds. *The Ancient Mariner* has two distinct worlds. One of them is the world of imagination which is the story of the Mariner and his strange experiences. The other world is the world of reality, of which the Wedding-Guest and the church are a part. The Wedding-Guest is the link between the two worlds and consequently is able to live and experience both the worlds.

Target of the Mariner's Moral. It is the Wedding-Guest alone who can give occasion to *The Ancient Mariner* to deliver the moral of his story with telling effect. The Wedding-Guest has protested many times to the Mariner that he wants to attend the wedding. The Mariner has observed the guest's impatience. But in the Mariner's views, it is better to walk to the church and pray in goodly company than to attend the marriage feast. It is spiritual joy that matters and not petty merriment.

Contrast Between two Types of Experience. Finally, in the poem as a whole, a deliberate contrast is certainly presented between the background of the wedding on the one hand and the Mariner's tale on the other. The interruptions of the Wedding-Guest are meant to point out this contrast. The effect of We interruptions of the Wedding-Guest is to show how these two kinds of reality are always co-existent: the total effect of the poem is to show them interpenetrating.

Conclusion. It is clear from the above discussion that the introduction of the Wedding-Guest has a great significance. The Wedding-Guest is neither unimportant nor redundant. The contrast between the spiritual world of the Mariner with its rich moral values with the world of actuality with its mistaken values cannot be effective and perfect without the Wedding-Guest figuring as a link between the two worlds. The Wedding-Guest's suspension of disbelief and the trust with which he accepts the tale assists to create suspension of disbelief in the reader.

(XII) STYLE AND ARTISTRY OF METRICAL COMPOSITION

Q.16. Write a note on Coleridge's stylistic devices in *The Ancient Mariner.*

Or

Discuss the technical beauties of *The Ancient Mariner.*

Ans. *The Ancient Mariner* is a perfect illustration of the influence of imagination upon the natural gift of terse and direct description. With a lucidity which is the outcome of reasoned conviction, Coleridge establishs the true connection between metre and language. Metre is the appropriate garment for a diction essentially different from the ordinary language of prose. In clothing simple, and often baldly simple language with metre, Wordsworth could not escape from the formation of an individual poetic style. But Coleridge, working with a firmer grasp of critical principles, and choosing subjects which might excuse the employment of highly coloured and unfamiliar language, is actually as simple in his diction as Wordsworth. If the connection between the incidents of *The Ancient Mariner* is not always clear, the style in which they are told is as clear and succinct as any prose narrative.

Outcome of Imagination. The poem is a series of pictures drawn with a masterly economy of material. Coleridge describes what he sees with the eye of imagination, suppressing everything which would tend to impair or obscure the reality of vision. The quickness and vividness of Coleridge's imagination, identifying: itself with *The Ancient Mariner* as he tells his tale, conjured up scenes of which every detail was as visible as though it lay before his eyes. Its dramatic power gave life and movement to the objects which it creats and combins: one after another, it touchs them briefly and sufficiently, communicating its magic to each simple word, and clothing them in a metre delicately sensitive to its least demand. It was this influence of imagination over ordinary language and its capacity for evoking the highest music out of the simplest substance that the poetry of the eighteenth century, with its obedience to mechanical laws of fashion, has lost.

Melody and Music. The greatest merit of the poem is that it is delightfully melodious. This poem proves that Coleridge is a lover of musical sound. He has employed here almost all the tricks of musical skill : alliteration, repetition of words, medieval rhymes and onomatopoeia. Here is an example:

> The fair breeze blew, the white foam flew.
> The furrow followed free;
> We were the first that ever burst
> Into that silent sea.

In the above stanza, the second line is a beautiful illustration of alliteration. The repetition of the sounds of 'f', 'b' and 's' is noteworthy'. The first line and third line also show the medial rhyme e.g., 'flew', 'blew' 'First' and 'burst'.

> Alone, alone, all all alone
> Alone, on a wide, wide sea,

The repetition here is employed for the sake of emphasis. Another aim of repetition is to deepen the melody of the verse, e.g.,

> Down dropt the breeze, the sails dropt down;
> 'Twas as sad as sad could be.

Now we take examples of onomatopoeia, i.e., words with sounds conveying sense. For instance, talking of the ice in the Polar region he says :

> It cracked and growled
> And roared and howled,

Or

> With heavy thump, a lifeless lump
> The crew dropped down one by one

Imagery. Now we take the use of figures by Coleridge. He freely uses similes and metaphors. The storm, for instance, is compared to an enemy and the ship, the victim of that enemy. Again,

> Like one that on a lonesome road
> Doth walk in fear and dread,
> And having once turned round walks on

And turns no more his head;
Because he knows a frightful fiend
Doth close behind him tread.

The above lines give us another striking simile to describe the stage of mind of *The Ancient Mariner*. It also reflects the poet's study of human psychology.

Economy of Words and Suggestiveness. Another noteworthy point regarding this poem is that it has not only got a great number of pictures. Both of matter and manner, but also the masterly economy of words with which those pictures have been drawn. Coleridge's suggestiveness is unique indeed. He will never paint horror and mystery to build his supernaturalism as his contemporaries did. Towards the close of *The Ancient Mariner,* the poet wishes to tell us how horrifying the Mariner's face has appeared. He do not describe the face itself; he simply describes the effect of the face upon the pilot's mind

I moved my lips-the pilot shrieked
And fell down in a fit.

We are left to imagine what kind of face it was.

Simplicity and Directness Coleridge utilises some of the stylistic elements of the popular' *ballad* in order to attain the effects of simplicity and directness having 'the eye on the object'. "Coleridge... is deeply interested in the English and Scottish popular ballads. Nothing in the poem is more remarkable than his transmutation of their rude measures, as he knows them, into a music the like of which have never been heard before. The vigorous directness of their plain and home spun phraseology has left its mark upon the poem." Coleridge's distinction lies in the perfection of his handling of metrical language. Whether it is a matter of communicating the awed silence of the crew or a matter of describing the sun as it shone weirdly through the skeleton-ship or a question of expressing the divine music of the angels-Coleridge can tackle it with assured mastery: he knows the secret of attaining the accord of the diction with the unity of impression, which the whole is intended to produce. Sir Arthur Quiller-Couch is fully justified in remarking on the rare perfection of the poem:... "after more than a hundred years, *The Ancient Mariner* is the wild thing of wonder, captured star.. Its music is as effortless as its imagery. Its words do not cumber it: exquisite words come to it, but it uses and straight away forgets them. Not Shakespeare himself, unless by snatches, so sublimated the lyrical tongue, or is obtained effects so magical by the barest necessary means.. throughout, from the picture of the bride entering the hall to that of the home coming in the moon-lit harbour, every scene in the procession belongs to high romance, yet each is conjured up with that economy of touch which we want to call classical."

Q.17. Illustrate Coleridge's descriptive power from the poem *The Rime of The Ancient Mariner,*

Or

Write a short note on the nature pictures drawn by Coleridge in *The Ancient Mariner.*

Or

Write a short essay on the pictorial quality of *The Ancient Mariner*

Or

"Coleridge's scenic descriptions reflect the mood of *The Ancient Mariner.*" Substantiate.

Ans. Descriptions in Coleridge's poetry. As C. M. Bowra aptly remarks, "The Romantics knew how to use their senses, and Coleridge, despite his metaphysical abstractions, was in this respect a true member of their company". *The Rime of the Ancient Mariner* "uses to the full the vividness of visual description which was one of Coleridge's great poetic strengths." What is more, the description, far from arresting the progress of the story or in anyway impeding its progress, always reflects the subtle and delicate stages of the Mariner's mind.

Variety of Scenes Described in the Poem. In *The Rime of the Ancient Mariner,* Coleridge has described every phase of landscape, seascape and cloudscape from the quiet scenery of an English woodland to the vivid scenery of the tropics. There are pictures of the ship moving fast with fresh breeze, cold of the ice-covered polar regions, of the horrors of the becalmed sea, of the torrid fierceness of the stagnant waters, of Death and the Nightmare Life-in-Death, of the sky in various stages of day and night, of the ghastly look on the dead men's laces, of the elfish movements of the water-snakes in the moon light, of the blessedness of the welcome rain and of a host of other things. All these descriptions are not coldly objective and impersonal but highly emotional and suggestive of the Mariner's mental and emotional state.

Description of Objects. Apart from the power of *The Ancient Mariner*'s "glittering eye" and "skinny hand" which we are made to realise through the horror of the Wedding-Guest, the first part of the poem gives a most beautiful and picturesque description of the south sea region:

And ice, mast high, came floating by,
And through the drifts the snowy clifts
Did send a dismal sheen.

It is in the descriptive phrases, "As green as emerald', And "a dismal sheen" that the double mood of admiration and fear is conveyed.

When the ship comes to a standstill, throwing the Mariner into a sea of gloom, Coleridge does not waste many words to describe the state of sailors. Instead, by monotonous repetition of words and by indirectly suggesting the motionless silence around, he conveys to us all the oppressive melancholy of the sailors:

> Down dropt the breeze, the sails dropt down?
> 'Twas as sad as sad could be;
> And we did speak only to break
> The silence of the sea.

Description of Human Scene. Let it not be misunderstood that Coleridge is good only at describing scenes of sadness. In contrast to the above descriptive lines, we can quote the lines describing the merry scene of the wedding:

> The bride hath paced into the hall
> Red as a rose is she;
> Nodding their heads before her goes,
> The merry minstrelsy.

Nature Descriptions. *The Rime of the Ancient Mariner* abounds in picturesque descriptions of the sun and the moon. The sunset in the tropical sea is matchless in its realism and brevity. The same sun is transformed into a horrid object of terror and forebodding, a little later on:

> And straight the sun was flecked with bars,
> (Heaven's mother, send us grace!)
> As if through a dungeon grate he peered
> With broad and burning face.

Similarly, the moon is also described in its two aspects, one of quiet beauty and the other of ghastly horror:

> The moving Moon went up the sky
> And nowhere did abide:
> Softly she was going up
> And a star or two beside

This very moon is charged with an ominous meaning in the following lines, but still is vividly described:

> Till clomb above the eastern bar
> The homed moon with one bright star
> Within the nether tip.

The suddenness of the oncoming of the night and darkness is portrayed with an amazing economy of expression:

> The sun's rim dips, the stars rush out:
> At one stride comes the dark

Descriptions of Supernatural Forces. evil and good. Coleridge does not consider a detail superfluous if it is significant. This attitude to detail is an important feature of all great art. It becomes irrefutably clear in Coleridge's descriptions of the supernatural beings. The water-snakes are ugly and the Mariner has recoiled from them in horror and abomination. That is only one aspect of the water-snakes that he see. But, a little later on,

> Within the shadow of the ship,
> I watched their rich attire:
> Blue, glossy green, and velvet black
> They coiled and swam, and every track
> Was a flash of golden fire.

All these minute details flash into our mind the water-snakes in all their beauty and glory and serve as a transition for the Mariner's admiration and blessing of them.

The description of Life-in Death is in such great detail that we see her terrible figure wanting to thick "man's blood with cold".

In contrast to those horrible shapes, we have the lovely angels who are part of the story. Their description is so rich in delicate detail that we find in them all that we associate with godly beings.

As soon as *The Ancient Mariner* is made aware of his sin by the two voices, the dead sailors are animated once again this time by visible angels. As the ship is neared the harbour, the angels stand on the corpses and

> They stood as signals to the land
> Bach one a lovely light;

Description of States of Feeling. Coleridge is at the highest excellence of his descriptive art when he catches ethereal feelings in concretes pictures. Even when a feeling of acute thirst is described Coleridge remains rigorously simple in expression and yet achieves a great force and power:

> Water, water everywhere
> And all the boards did shrink;
> Water, water everywhere
> Nor any drop to drink.

The state of stagnation is a difficult one to describe or convey to the reader. But Coleridge shows his artistry when he says:

> Day after day, day after day
> We stuck, nor break nor motion;
> As idle as a painted ship
> Upon a painted ocean.

Loneliness is another state which words fail to describe, more so if it is sought to by the very person who experiences it. But Coleridge do not have any difficulty in making *The Ancient Mariner* portray his loneliness convincingly:

For the sky and the sea, and the sea and the sky
Lay like a load on my weary eye.

Or

Alone, alone, all, all alone
Alone on a wide, wide seal

The last two lines are a supreme example of vivid description, reflective of the Mariner's emotional agony, done with unimaginable economy of words.

Conclusion. Examples of Coleridge's descriptive power and his nature pictures can be indefinitely multiplied. No other poem of Coleridge's shows more completely developed in practice the principle of description, which, according to Coleridge is "never to see or describe any interesting appearance in nature without connecting it, by dim analogies, with the moral world."

Q.18. Consider critically the use of metre and versification by Coleridge in *The Ancient Mariner.*

Or

How does Coleridge vary the metre and versification so as to break monotony in *The Ancient Mariner*?

Ans. The unit in the verse which Coleridge uses consists of one unstressed followed by a stressed syllable, to this foot the name iamb is given and the lines contain either four or three iambs. In general, only the former line will be noticed. A perfectly regular line of the type is

and straight/the sun/was flecked/with bars (L. 177)

Variety is introduced by changing the position of the pauses. So we see in most lines at least one case in which the end of a foot is not marked by a natural break in the reading:

It mingl/ed strange/ly with /my fears. (L.458)

At places even the pause at the end of the line is ignored, and the verse overflows into the next-

That to the sleeping woods all night
Singeth a quiet tune. (L.371)

The pauses, whether coming at the end of a foot or in the middle of it, may become more pronounced; they may be so well defined as to be marked by stops:

Strange, by/my faith!/the Her/mit said. (L.527)

The incidence of the stress may be varied. The iamb may be replaced by some other foot, having either the same rhythm a and b or a reversed rhythm, c.

The foot may be an anapaest, i.e. two unstressed syllables followed by a stressed syllable. The two short syllables may either be both distinctly pronounced, as in

For all averred/I had killed/the bird (L. 93)

or one of them may to some degree be slurred over:

From the fiends/that plague thee thus. (L. 80)

The effect of anapaests is to quicken the movement of the verse.

The stress on the second syllable may be so light as practically to disappear, leaving pyrrhic-a foot or two unstressed syllables:

Still treads the shad/ow of This foe (L. 47)

The foot use may comprise a stress followed by an unstressed syllable, changing, that is, to a trochee introducing, in some measure, a falling rhythm;

We were/the first/that ever burst (L. 105)

The bringing together of two short syllables in this way often has an effect of giving lightness and quickness to the verse.

'The stanza used in *The Ancient Mariner*-the ballad stanza-normally consists of two pairs of lines, the first and third each containing four feet and generally not rhyming, the second and fourth each containing three, and always rhyming.

Sometimes the lines of four feet have internal rhyme. The internal rhyme usually occurs in the third line of the stanza, but sometimes, it occurs in the first line as well, when both first and third have internal rhyme:

And through the drifts the snowy cliffs
Did send a dismal sheen:
Nor shapes of men nor beasts we ken-
The ice was all between.

The Stanza of L 203-11 is of exceptional form, which may be denoted by A A B C C B D D B; that is, it consists of nine lines in three sets of three, the first pair of each set being tetrameters rhyming with each other, but not with the tetrameters of any other set, while the last line of each set is a trimeter; these three lines rhyming together. This stanza thus unites all the previous variations.

10

CHRISTABEL

PREFACE

The first part of the following poem is written in the year 1797, at Stowey, in the county of Somerset. The second part after my return from Germany, in the year 1800, at Keswick, Cumberland. It is probable that if the poem has been finished at either of the former periods, or if even the first and second part has been published in the year 1800, the impression of its originality will have been much greater than I dare at present expect. But for this, I have only my own indolence to blame. The dates are mentioned for the exclusive purpose of precluding charges of plagiarism or servile'imitation from myself. For there is amongst us a set of critics, who seem to hold, that every possible thought and image is traditional; who have no notion that there are such things as fountains in the world, small as well as great; and who will therefore charitably derive every rill they behold flowing, from a perforation made in some other man's tank. I am confident, however, that as far as the present poem is concerned, the celebrated poets whose writings I may suspected of having imitated, either in particular passages, or in the tone and the spirit of the whole, would be among the first to vindicate me from the charge, and who, on any striking coincidence, will permit me to address them in this doggerel version of two monkish Latin hexameters.

'Tis mine and it is likewise your;
But an if this will not do;
Let it be mine good friend ! for I
Am the poorer of the two.

I have only to add that the metre of Christabel is not, properly speaking, irregular, though it may seem so from its being founded on a new principle: namely, that of counting in each line the accents, not the syllables. Though the latter may vary from seven to twelve, yet in each line the accents will be found to be only four. Nevertheless; this occasional variation in number of syllables is not introduced wantonly, or for the mere ends of convenience, but in correspondence with some transition in the nature of the imagery or passion.

CHRISTABEL

(A) TEXT, PARAPHRASE AND ANNOTATIONS

PART I

'Tis the middle of night by the castle clock,
And the owls have awakened the crowing cock;
Tu—whit !—Tu—whoo !
And hark, again ! the crowing cock,
How drowsily it crew.

Sir Leoline, the Baron rich,
Hath a toothless mastiff bitch;
From her kennel beneath the rock
She maketh answer to the clock,
Four for the quarters, and twelve for the hour;
Ever and aye, by shine and shower,
Sixteen short howls, not over loud;
Some say, she sees my lady's shroud.

Is the night chilly and dark ?
The night is chilly, but not dark.
The thin grey cloud is spread on high,

It covers but not hides the sky.
The moon is behind, and at the full;
And yet she looks both small and dull.
The night is chill, the cloud is gray :
'Tis a month before the month of May,
And the Spring comes slowly up this way.

(Note how in the very opening lines 1-5 the note of eeriness is struck and a medieval atmosphere of mystery is created by means of minute touches in simple words). L. 1. **the castle clock**—brings the picture of a medieval castle with a clock-tower before our mind's eye. L. 2. **owls**—owls are supposed to be birds of evil omen and its hooting fills our mind with expectant horror. **the crowing cock**—The word crowing is proleptic. The cock crowed after being awakened by the hooting of the owl. The crowing of the cock is generally associated with the approach of the morning and disappearance of ghosts. Here the unusualness of its crowing at midnight is something ominous. L. 3. **Tu-whit**—this is onomatopoeia; the word suggests the sound. L. 4. **hark**—listen. L.5. **drowsily**—sleepily. L. 6. **Sir Leoline, the Baron rich**—The mention of the name of the rich Baron deepens the medieval colouring. The story is now introduced. L. 7. **mastiff**—a breed of powerful watchdog. This is also a medieval touch. toothless-suggestive of decay and death and adds to an ominous

PARAPHRASE OF THE POEM

PART I

L. 1-5. The clock that is put up on the wall of the castle indicates that it is twelve in the night. The screech of the owls has disturbed the cock which is crowing (with a feeble sound), though it is in a sleepy state.

L. 6-13. Sir Leoline, the rich Baron keeps a watch-dog which has lost its teeth (owing to old age). The dog is chained in its house built under the rock, and unfailingly barks when the clock strikes. It may be fair or foul, sunshine or rain, the dog must howl in response to the strokes of the clock. For each quarter, it will howl once and for full hour twelve times, i.e., sixteen short howls, not too loud, for one hour. Some people believe that it does so because the dead body of its mistress has been wrapped up in the shroud is visible to the animal.

L. 14-24. Is the night chilly and dark? It is cold but not dark. The grey cloud which covers the sky is so thin that we can see the sky through it. On this night the moon is full but looks very small and dim behind the cloud. The night is chilly, the cloud is grey and it is the month of April when spring has set in.

---

atmosphere. kennel-a sort of house for dog. **L. 8. rock**—This word suggests that it was a rock-built castle. **L. 9. maketh answer to the clock**—by barking every time the clock struck the quarter of an hour and the hour. **L. 11. by shine and shower**—in sun and rain, in all kind of weather. **L. 13. some say, she sees my lady's shroud**—Here is direct mention of something supernatural and uncanny. People say that the mastiff sees the ghost of Christabel's mother dressed in white shroud. **shroud**—the cloth in which a body is wrapped for burial. **L. 15. The night is chilly, but not dark**—Pitch dark nights are not so suitable for the appearance of supernatural beings as cloudy moonlit nights. **L. 16. thin grey cloud**—almost like a grey veil, through which the moonlight is coming out less bright and almost dim. **L. 17. It covers but not hides the sky**—The cloud is almost transparent. Though it overcasts the sky, it does not hide it. The moon from behind this thin and transparent cloud is easily seen. **L. 18. at the full**—it is a full moon. The full moon, it may be noted, was a benevolent influence for Coleridge; Its being dull and small signifies something wrong. **L. 19. small**—it is a scientific fact. Shining from behind a thin cloud the moon looks smaller than her actual size. **dull**—because the thin cloud partially obstructs her light. **L. 20. the cloud is gray**—Being thin, the cloud cannot obstruct the light of the moon. It cannot, therefore be dark or black cloud. Because of the light of the moon shining through it, it looks grey. **L. 21. 'Tis a month**—It is the month of April, and the Spring sea:on has just begun. (The stanza contributes to an atmosphere of chilly mystery and grips the reader's attention). **L.23. The lovely.....Christabel**—A romantic note is struck here in introducing Christabel. The term 'lovely' had moral implications for Coleridge.

The lovely lady, Christabel,
Whom her father loves so well,
What makes her in the wood so late,
A furlong from the castle gate ?
She had dreams all yesternight
Of her own betrothed knight;
And she in the midnight wood will pray
For the weal of her lover that's far away.

She stole along, she nothing spoke,
The sighs she heaved were soft and low,
And naught was green upon the oak
But moss and rarest misletoe:
She kneels beneath the huge oak tree,

And in silence prayeth she.
The lady sprang up suddenly,
The lovely lady, Christabel !
It moaned as near, as near can be,
But what it is she cannot tell—
On the other side it seems to be,
Of the huge, broad-breasted, old oak tree.

The night is chill; the forest bare;
Is it the wind that moaneth bleak ?
There is not wind enough in the air
To move away the ringlet curl
From the lovely lady's cheek—
There is not wind enough to twirl
The one red leaf, the last of its clan,
That dances as often as dance it can,
Hanging so light, and hanging so high,
On the topmost twig that looks up at the sky.

L. 25. **What makes her**—What makes her to go into the forest? **L. 27. yesternight**—last night. **L. 28. betrothed knight**—the knight to whom she is engaged. **L. 30. weal**—welfare, health and happiness, **that's....away**-either he has gone to the battlefield in some distant land or, otherwise, is living far away. **L. 31. stole along**—walked on quietly. **nothing spoke**—did not speak anything aloud.. **L. 32. heaved**—sighed. **L. 33. naught**—nothing. **L. 34. misletoe**—an evergreen plant. It very rarely grows on the oak. Hence the word rarest has been used here. The Druids worshipped it whenever they found it on an oak tree. (Note the contrast

L. 25-28. What is the lovely Christabel, the darling of her father, doing in the woods at this late hour at a distance from the Castle?

L. 29-32. Last night, she see in a dream the knight to whom she is engaged to be marry. (She is apprehended some calamity to him). That is why she has gone to the woods at night. There she will pray for the well-being of her lover who is far away from her.

L. 31-36. She goes stealthily and silently; she hear low and gentle sighs. With the exception of lichen and mistletoe there is no other sign of greenness on the oak tree. Under it she kneel and pray.

L. 37-42. The lovely lady Christabel spring up suddenly. She hear the sound of sighing coming from very near. But she is not definite about it. It appear that it is coming from the other side of the big oak tree which has its branches spreading in all directions.

L. 43-52. The night is chilly; all the trees in the forest are denuded of their leaves. Is it (the sigh) the dull and cheerless sound of the wind blowing through the trees? But the breeze is too weak to disturb the curls of hair falling on the cheeks of lovely Christabel. There was not sufficient breeze to move even one red leaf that is left hanging loosely on the topmost branch pointing upwards.

---

between the dried tree and the green moss.). L. **37. sprang up suddenly**—was startled. L. **39. as near...can be**—very near. L. **40. she cannot tell**—she did not know. broad-breasted-with a wide trunk. There is a humanising touch given to the oak tree. (Note the noise is introduced in characteristically ballad style.) L. **43. bare**—naked; because the trees had shed their leaves in winter. **L. 44. bleak**—dull and cheerless. L. **47. from...cheek**—a romantic picture. L. **48. twirl**—cause it to turn around quickly. L. **49. clan**—a Scottish word for a tribe. Here it is used for the group of leaves that a tree bears. This leaf is the last left on the trees. L. **51. light**—lightly because it is dead and dry. L. **52. twig**—small branch of a tree. **that.....sky**—the highest branch of the tree: so that the breeze there is not obstructed. Even if the slightest breeze were there, the leaf would have started dancing.

Hush, beating heart of Christabel !
Jesu, Maria, shield her well !
She folded her arms beneath her cloak,
And stole to the other side of the oak.
What sees she there?

There she sees a damsel bright,
Drest in a silken robe of white,
That shadowy in the moonlight shone :
The neck that made that white robe wan,
Her stately neck, and arms were bare;
Her blue-veined feet unsandal'd were,
And wildly glittered here and there
The gems entangled in her hair.
I guess, 'twas frightful there to see
A lady so richly clad as she—
Beautiful exceedingly !

'Mary mother, save me now !
(Said Christabel,) And who art thou?

The lady strange made answer meet,
And her voice was faint and sweet:—
Have pity on my sore distress,
I scarce can speak for weariness :
Stretch forth thy hand, and have no fear !
Said Christabel, How camest thou here ?
And the lady, whose voice was faint and sweet,
Did thus pursue her answer meet—

L. 53. **Hush, beating heart of Christabel**—The heart of Christabel was beating fast on hearing this mysterious moan, so close to her. L. 54. **Jesu, Maria, shield her well**—The whole background, painted so far, is suggestive of trouble and uneasiness. So it evokes a response, this cry. There is a danger, from the influence of which the holy spirits of Christ and Mary are invoked to protect Christabel. It is a characteristic of Middle Age piety. L. 55. **She...cloak**—in prayer most probably to check the effect of anything evil; also partly in fear. L. 56. **stole**—moved quietly and cautiously, out of a lurking fear of the cause of the mysterious moan. L. 57. **What...there**—The poet suggests, that she sees there something unusual. A note of suspense and anxiety is struck. L. 58: Geraldine is introduced, **damsel bright**—a bright maiden. L. 59. **robe**—dress. L. 60. **shadowy**—which shone dimly in the moonlight. L. 61. **that**—refers to the neck of the lady. **wan**—pale. L. 63. **blue-veined**—blue veins, in addition to being considered a sign of beauty, were regarded as a mark of a noble descent. These realistic details make

L. 53-57. May Christabel's heart (which is beating fast on account of fear) calm down. And may Christ and Virgin Mary protect her from harm! She folds her arms beneath her clock and go noiselessly to the other side of the oak. What sight meets her eyes there?

L. 58-70. Christabel see under the oak tree a beautiful maiden dress in white silken robes that shine in the dim moonlight. Her neck is so milky white that her white dress looks pale in comparison with it. Her magnificently beautiful neck and her arms are bare. Her feet are so white that the blue veins in them are easily visible and she is without sandals on. She wear in her hair gems that has glittered here and there. I think that the sight of such a lady, so beautiful and dresses in such brilliant robes, must have been very dreadful. Christabel has prayed in her mind and has asked her who she is.

L. 71-78. In a hollow (ghost-like) and sweet voice the lady Geraldine give the answer which is appropriate to the occasion: "I appeal to you to take pity upon me. I am a distressed lady and am in a sad plight. I am tired and so can hardly talk. Extend your hand and be not afraid of me." Christabel asks her how she has come there, and the lady who has been interrupted in her speech speaks in a faint and sweet voice. Her reply is suitable to the occasion.

---

us accept the supernatural. **unsandal'd**—without sandals. **L. 64. wildly**—with great luster. The term also gives a touch of supernatural. **L. 65. entangled**—interwoven. **L. 66. frightful**—causing fear. **L. 69. Mary mother**-This is the sudden cry for holy protection, which the presence of this strange lady calls forth from Christabel. **L. 71. meet**—proper. **L. 73. sore**—great. **L. 74. Scarce**—hardly, for **weariness**—because of feeling tired. **L. 75. stretch forth**—spread out. **L. 78. did pursue**—feeling tired.

My sire is of a noble line,
And my name is Geraldine :
Five warriors seized me yestermorn,
Me, even me, a maid forlorn :
They choked my cries with force and fright,

And tied me on a palfrey white.
The palfrey was as fleet as wind,
And they rode furiously behind.

They spurred amain, their steeds were white :
And once we crossed the shade of night.
As sure as Heaven shall rescue me,
I have no thought what men they be;
Nor do I know how long it is
(For I have lain entranced I wis)
Since one, the tallest of the five,
Took me from the palfrey's back,
A weary woman, scarce alive.
Some muttered words his comrades spoke :
He placed me underneath this oak;
He swore they would return with haste:
Whither they went I cannot tell—
I thought I heard, some minutes, past,
Sounds of a castle bell.
Stretch forth thy hand (thus ended she),
And help a wretched maid to flee.

Then Christabel stretched forth her hand,
And comforted fair Geraldine:
'O well, bright dame ! may you command
The service of Sir Leoline;
And gladly our stout chivalry
Will he send forth and friends withal
To guide and guard you safe and free
Home to your noble father's hall.

She rose: and forth with steps they passed
That strove to be, and were not, fast.
Her gracious stars the lady blest,
And thus spake on sweet Christabel:

L. 79. sire—father. **L. 81. yestermorn**—last morning. **L. 82. a maid forlorn**—helpless maiden. **even me**—this is intended to emphasise her helpless state. **L. 83. choked**—stopped. **fright**—fear. **L.84. palfrey**—horse. **L.85. fleet**—swift. **L.87. spurred amain**—with power made the horses move with the spurs. **L.88. shade of night**—darkness of the night. **crossed...night**—rode like this the whole night

L. 79-103. "My name is Geraldine and we are descended from a noble stock. Five men has armed with weapons of war laid hands upon me, a weak and helpless woman and is forcibly gagged my mouth at the point of the bayonet, thus preventing me from raising cries for help. They tied me hand and foot, on a white saddle horse. The five warriors rode white horses at full speed in order to keep close to my horse which ran as swift as the wind. I have a faint recollection that we journeyed also for a few hours at night (besides journeying throughout the day). May God never forgive me if I tell a lie! I have not the least idea who those men were nor do I remember how long I have been here, since I was in a state of unconsciousness. One of those five warriors who is the tallest help me get down from the white horse on which I am riding. At that time I was feeling so wearied, both in spirit and in body, that it has appeared I had no life in me. His companions have uttered a few words which has not intelligible to me. The tallest warrior has seated me under this oak tree. He promised on his honour that all of them will come back very soon. I cannot say where they have gone. I fancy that a few minutes ago there fell on my ears the sound of a castle bell ringing. Extends your hand and help me, a miserable lady, run away (from the clutches of the ruffians)."

L. 104-113. When Geraldine has finished speaking, Christabel extends her hand and give comfort to the beautiful lady. She says: "You should have no fear; the services of my dear father are at your disposal. He has a strong cavalry. All the resources of my father—strong horsemen and other friends of his—will be employed to guard you against your enemies and you will be safely escorted back to your noble father's house. Be comforted and have no fear." Saying these words Christabel stands up and both tries to walk fast but (due to tiredness and fear) they can not.

---

long, till day dawned. **L.89. as sure as...**—as I am sure God will help me. **L.90. what men...be**—who they were. **L.92. entranced**—in a fit of unconsciousness. **I wis**—I know. **L. 95. scarce alive**—hardly alive. **L.96. muttered**—whispered. **L.102. stretch...hand**—Geraldine says thus. **L.103. to flee**—to run away. **L.106—107. May.. Leoline**—In the true tradition of hospitality, Christabel assures Geraldine of help that her father can give. **L.108. stout chivalry**—In the Middle Ages, every nobleman had his own band of knights. **stout chivalry**—brave knights. **L.109. withal**—together with that. **forth**—onward. **L. 111. hall**—big house of a nobleman. **L.112. strove to be**—tried to be. **L.114. gracious stars**—good fortune.

All our household are at rest,
The hall as silent as the cell;
Sir Leoline is weak in health,
And may not well awakened be,
But we will move as if in stealth,
And I beseech your courtesy,
This night, to share your couch with me.

They crossed the moat, and Christabel
Took the key that fitted well;
A little door she opened straight,
All in the middle of the gate;
The gate that was ironed within and without,
Where an army in battle array had marched out.
The lady sank, belike through pain,
And Christabel with might and main
Lifted her up, a weary weight,
Over the threshold of the gate:
Then the lady rose again,
And moved, as she were not in pain.

So free from danger, free from fear,
They crossed the court: right glad they were.
And Christabel devoutly cried
To the Lady by her side,
Praise we the Virgin all divine
Who hath rescued thee from thy distress !

Alas, alas! said Geraldine,
I cannot speak for weariness.
So free from danger, free from fear,
They crossed the court: right glad they were.

L.116. at rest—are asleep. **L.117. cell**—a small room in a monastery. **The hall...cell**—the Baron's castle, at this hour, is as silent as a monk's cell in a monastery. **L. 119. may not well awakened be**—It is better that he should not be disturbed in his sleep. **L. 120. as if in stealth**—as if we were thieves. **L. 121. beseech**—request. **L. 123. moat**—a deep ditch round a castle for defence. **L.125. straight**—at once. **L. 127. ironed...without**—bolted with iron bolts on both sides to make it impenetrable by the enemy. **L. 128. where...out**—The big gate was used for army to pass through; on other occasions it would be kept closed. **L.129. belike**—as if. **The lady...pain**—here is the double art of the poet: (i) psychological treatment of the supernatural; and (ii) mystifying the reader. The lady is an evil

L. 114-122. The gracious Christabel thanks her lucky stars, and in this way continues her speech. "All the members of our family are enjoying peaceful sleep. The hall is as silent as the underground rooms there. My father is keeping bad health and it is, therefore, not proper to disturb him. We shall move very noiselessly and stealthily. I beg of you to be so good as to share your bed with me tonight."

L. 123-132. Both crosses the ditch that has been constructed round the Castle Christabel uses the proper key and at once unlocks the door that lay in its middle. In order to make the door stronger, steel has been used on both sides; in the past a regular army drawn up for purposes of war has marched out of this gate. While passing through the threshold of the gate, Geraldine brekes down : possibly through pain; and Christabel uses her full force to lift her who is too heavy a burden (for a delicate girl, like herself).

L. 133-144. Geraldine (who has collapsed) stands up (with the help of Christabel) and begins walking as if her pain has passed away. Being out of the pale of fear and danger, they crosses the compound of the castle, and both of them are exceedingly happy. Christabel speaks these pious words to Geraldine who is walking by her side, "Let us praise the Holy Mother (Virgin Mary) who has saved you from dangers and harms." Geraldine says, "Alas, alas! I am too tired to speak." In this way, being out of the pale of fear and danger, they crosses the court of the castle and they are very happy.

---

spirit. But as she reaches the gate of the castle, the abode of the innocent Christabel, her conscience seems to trouble her, and she loses courage to enter. **L.130. might and main**—with all the strength. **L.131. weary weight**—a dead weight or burden as of a person who has been so thoroughly fatigued as Geraldine told herself to be. **L.132. threshold**—door step. **devoutly**—religiously; piously. **L.136. Virgin**—Mary, Christ's mother. **divine**—because the mother of Lord Christ. **L. 140. rescued**—freed from danger. **L.141. Alas! alas**—instead of saying Amen to Christabel's prayer, she only utters these words. An evil spirit cannot pray. **L.143. So free...were**—The repetition in lines 143—144, increases the suggestion of evil. **L.148. angry moan did make**—The mastiff—bitch seems to have been endowed by the poet with a super—sensitiveness to the presence of supernatural influences. Just as her short howls in answer to the tower—clock were regarded to be due to the fact that she saw the ghost of Lady Leoline, so her angry moan, as Lady Geraldine passed by her, is suggestive of her perception of an evil spirit in that lady.

Outside her kennel, the mastiff old
Lay fast asleep, in moonshine cold.
The mastiff old did not awake,
Yet she an angry moan did make !
And what can ail the mastiff bitch ?
Never till now she uttered yell
Beneath the eye of Christabel.
Perhaps it is the owlet's scritch:
For what can ail the mastiff bitch ?

They passed the hall, that echoes still,
Pass as lightly as you will !
The brands were flat, the brands were dying,
Amid their own white ashes lying;.
But when the lady passed, there came
A tongue of light, a fit of flame;
And Christabel saw the lady's eye,
And nothing else saw she thereby,
Save the boss of the shield of Sir Leoline tall,
Which hung in a murky old niche in the wall.

O softly tread, said Christabel,
My father seldom sleepeth well.

Sweet Christabel her feet doth bare,
And jealous of the listening air
They steal their way from stair to stair,
Now in glimmer, and now in gloom,
And now they pass the Baron's room,
As still as death, with stifled breath !
And now have reached her chamber door;
And now doth Geraldine press down
The rushes of the chamber floor.

L. 149. ail—trouble. **L. 150. yell**—a sharp cry of horror, or agony. **L. 152. scritch**—schreech, howl. **L. 154. echoes**—resounds with the noise of the foot-steps. Another touch of eeriness. **L. 156. brands**—the pieces of wood, burning or partly burned. **L. 158. lady**—Geraldine. **L. 159. a fit of flame**—Here, again, we have a suggestion of the presence of the supernatural. **L. 160. lady's eye**—There are hints in Part II of this poem that there is something serpentine in the constitution of Geraldine.

L. 145-153. In the wintry night, when the moon is shining, the old bitch lay fast asleep outside the kennel. It do not get up, (when the two ladies passes through the court) but in its sleep, it give a growl. The bitch must have some trouble (as it is growling); never before has it given a cry of pain in the presence of its mistress. Perhaps it is the hooting of the young owl; otherwise what else can be responsible for the bitch's trouble?

L. 154-168. They passes through the hall and the hall echoes the footsteps, even though they trod as noiselessly and softly as they can. The burning pieces of wood lay flat; their fire is dying and the faggots lay covered with their own white ashes; yet, when Geraldine passes, the extinguished fire blazes into life and there appears a bright flame of fire. With its help Christabel sees the face of Geraldine and a boss of her father's shield, which is hanging in a dark corner of the wall. Nothing else can she see. Christabel request Geraldine to walk softly and noiselessly lest the sound of their footsteps shall disturb her father who seldom enjoys a sound sleep.

L. 169-174. Christabel put off her sandals and walks very quietly, but still the air nearest her leg can hear the sound of their footsteps. She, therefore, grow jealous of it and tries to walk still more noiselessly. In this way they walk softly from one stair to another, sometimes in faint light and sometimes in darkness. When they are passing near Sir Leoline's room, they suspends their breath and walk as noiselessly as death. Now both of them have reached the door of Christabel's bedroom and Geraldine's feet has pressed down the rushes spread on the floor.

L. 162. **boss**—raised ornament. L. **163 murky**—dark, gloomy, **niche**—shelf built into the wall. **L. 164. tread**—step. **L. 167. jealous**—suspicious. **listening air**—The air that caught up the noise of the footsteps and echoed them. **L. 169. glimmer and gloom**—half light. As they pass through the castle, they are sometimes in partially dark places and some times in total darkness. **L. 171. stifled breath**—almost without breath. **L. 172. chamber**—room. **L. 174. rushes**—mats made of rushes, a marsh plant. Rushes were spread on the floor in medieval castles, for softness and warmth.

The moon shines dim in the open air,
And not a moonbeam enters here.
But they without its light can see
The chamber carved so curiously,
Carved with figures strange and sweet,
All made out of the carver's brain,
For a lady's chamber meet:

The lamp with two fold silver chain
Is fastened to an angel's feet.
The silver lamp burns dead and dim;
But Christabel the lamp will trim.
She trimmed the lamp, and made it bright,
And left it swinging to and fro,
When Geraldine, in wretched plight,
Sank down upon the floor below.

'O weary lady, Geraldine,
I pray you, drink this cordial wine!

It is a wine of virtuous power;
My mother made it of wild flowers.

And will your mother pity me,
Who am a maiden most forlorn?
Christabel answered —Woe is me !
She died the hour that I was born.
I have heard the grey-haired friar tell
How on her death-bed she did say,
That she should hear the castle-bell
Strike twelve upon my wedding-day.
O mother dear ! that thou wert here !
I would, said Geraldine, She were !

L. 176. **here**—in the bed-chamber. L. 178. **curiously**—with artistic designs. L. 179. **strange and sweet**—these two words suggest Geraldine and Christabel respectively. L. 180. **carver's**—artist. L. 181. **meet**—suitable. L. 183. **angel's feet**—the feet of the carved figure of an angel. L. 184. **burns dead and dim**—emits a very dull and dim light. L. 187. **Left...fro**—The poet's pictures are vivid. L. 188—189. **Geraldine...below**—Is it because the brightened lamp shows more clearly the figure of the angel or is it because Geraldine has to make a fierce struggle with good in order to cast her evil spell. L. 191. **cordial**—a tonic; a refreshing wine. L. 192. **virtuous**—wonderful; effective. Note the use of this word also suggests an ethical quality. L. 195. **forlorn**—forsaken. L.196 **Woe is me**—It is an

L. 175-183. The moon is shining dimly outside the bedroom and yet not a single beam is making its way into it, but the two ladies can see the artistic carving-creation of the artist's brain-decorating the walls of the chamber. The carvings of these strange and beautiful figures are perfectly suitable for a lady's bed-chamber. A lamp is hanging by means of double silver chain which is tied to the feet of an angel.

L. 184-189. The silver lamp is burning giving a faint and dim light. But Christabel will trim the candle in order to make it give brighter light, and this is what she do. She allows the lamp to move to and fro, while Geraldine who is feeling miserable and wretched collaps on the floor of the chamber.

L. 190-193. Christabel request Geraldine who is feeling tired and distressed to drink the wine which has been prepared by her mother from wild flowers. It possesses miraculous properties and will revive her spirits.

L. 194--203. Geraldine asks if Christabel's mother will take pity on a miserable woman like her (Geraldine). Christabel answers." Alas! She dies at my birth. I have heard the old priest telling that my mother, while dying, said that she will come on my wedding day, at midnight, to hear the castle bells. I wish my dear mother are here!" Geraldine replied. "I too wish so."

---

exclamation of grief and sorrow. **L. 198, grey-haired friar**—the old friar. A friar is a Roman Catholic priest. **L. 201. that...here**—a childlike pathetic cry. **L. 203. I would...she were**—As in Macbeth (Act III, Sc. iv) the ghost of Banquo appears on Macbeth's hypocritical utterance; : 'would he were here', so Geraldine's words conjure up before her eyes the spirit of the dead mother. Christabel, however, does not see the ghost. Thus, again, the evil in Geraldine has been emphasised, is also her sense of guilt.

But soon with altered voice, said she—
'Off, wandering mother ! Peak and pine !
I have power to bid thee flee.'
Alas ! what ails poor Geraldine ?
Why stares she with unsettled eye ?
Can she the bodiless dead espy ?
And why with hollow voices cries she,
'Off, woman, off! this hour is mine—
Though thou her guardian spirit be,
Off, woman, off ! 'tis given to me.'

Then Christabel knelt by the lady's side,
And raised to heaven her eyes so blue—

'Alas !' said she, this ghastly ride—
Dear lady ! it hath wildered you !
The lady wiped her moist cold brow,
And faintly said, 'tis over now!'

Again the wild-flower wine she drank:
Her fair large eyes 'gan glitter bright,
And from the floor whereon she sank,
The lofty lady stood upright :
She was most beautiful to see,
Like a lady of a far countree.

And thus the lofty lady spake—
'All they who live in the upper sky,
Do love you, holy Christabel !
And you love them, and for their sake
And for the good which me befel,
Even I in my degree will try,
Fair maiden, to requite you well.
But now unrobe yourself; for I
Must pray, ere yet in bed I lie.'

L. 204. **altered voice**—changed voice, because the ghost of Christabel 's mother appears before her. L. 205. **wandering mother**—the ghost of Christable' s mother that has come out of its grave and wanders about. **Peak and pine**—grow weak and die. L. 206. **bid thee flee**—make you disappear. L. 208. **unsettled**—restlessly moving. L. 209. **bodiless dead**—ghost. **espy**—see. L. 211. **This hour is mine**—I am master of this hour. Not the good spirit of her dead mother, but he evil spirit in Geraldine, has control over Christabel at that hour. L. 212. **guardian spirit**—Even Geraldine suggests that the ghost of Christabel 'smother was to act as her guardian. L. 213. **'tis given to me**—Perhaps, it means: "At this hour it is

L. 204-213. Immediately after uttering the words ('I wish she were here') Geraldine changes her voice and said, "Disappear from this place, you spirit (Christabel's mother's spirit). I possess power that will compel you to vanish." What is it that is troubling the mind of Geraldine? Why is she gazing from one side to the other? Is it because she is looking at the dead spirit of Christabel's mother? And why does she utter the following words in a very faint, ghost-like voice, "Get away, O you woman! During this time Christabel is under my influence. I shall rule her destiny for the time being, though you may be her guardian angel, because now the control over Christabel has been given to me.

L. 214-226. There Christabel kneel by the side of Geraldine in a praying attitude with her beautiful blue eyes raises towards heaven. She says, "I feel very sorry because your mind has been bewildered on account of the bad effects of the most frightful ride (you have with the five warriors)." The lady has wiped the cold drops of perspiration that has appeared on her forehead (due to fear, weakness and tiredness), and have answered in a hollow voice, "I am feeling better." She again drink the cordial wine prepares from wild flowers. She stand up erect from the floor where she has collapsed and her large beautiful eyes begins to glitter. She looks most beautiful; she appears a spirit of the next world, and not of this world.

L. 226-234. The tall lady (Geraldine) stand erect in all her majesty and uttered the following words. "You are the soul of goodness and all the angels who live in upper regions love you for your virtues and you love them. I shall try, as much as lies in my power to reward you for your love and for the good lot that has fallen to me through your instrumentality. But now put off your clothes and retire to bed. As for myself, I shall pray before I go to bed."

I who have got full control over Christabel." **L. 216. ghastly**— terrible. **L. 217. wildered**—bewildered, upset. Christabel does not suspect that Geraldine is an evil spirit. **L. 218. moist**—wet; she perspired probably because of her. fierce struggle with the spirit of the mother of Christabel. **L. 219. faintly**—in a faint voice. **'tis...now**—It may mean, either (1) that the fit is over and I am all right now, or (2) now, the struggle with the spirit of the mother is over. **L. 220. wild-flower wine**—wine prepared from wild flowers. **L. 221. 'gan**—began. **glitter bright**—shine brightly. **L. 223. lofty**—tall. **lady**—Geraldine. **upright**—erect. **L. 225. countree**—country. Is it perhaps to suggest that she is from the world of the spirits.supernatural. **L. 227. All they who...sky**—the angels and god **L. 230. good which me befel**—the kindness shown by Christabel. **L. 231. In my degree**—as far lean. **L. 232. requite**—repay. **L. 233. unrobe**—undress. **L. 233—234. I...pray**—This is a lie. The fact is that she is still hesitating to do Christabel harm.

Quoth Christabel, So let it be !
And as the lady bade, did she.
Her gentle limbs did she undress,
And lay down in her, loveliness.

But through her brain of weal and woe
So many thoughts moved to and fro,
That vain it were her lids to close;
So half-way from the bed she rose,

And on her elbow did recline.
To look at the lady Geraldine.

Beneath the lamp the lady bowed,
And slowly rolled her eyes around;
Then drawing in her breath aloud,
Like one that shuddered, she unbound
The cincture from beneath her breast;
Her silken robe, and inner vest,
Dropt to her feet, and full in view.
Behold! her bosom and half her side—
A sight to dream of, not to tell !
O shield her ! shield sweet Christabel !

Yet Geraldine nor speaks nor stirs;
Ah ! what a stricken look was hers !
Deep from within she seems half—way
To lift some weight with sick assay,
And eyes the maid and seeks delay;
Then suddenly, as one defied,
Collects herself in scorn and pride,
And lay down by the Maiden's side !—
And in her arms the maid she took,
Ah wel—a—day !
And with low voice and doleful look

These words did say:
'In the touch of this bosom there worketh a spell
Which is lord of thy utterance, Christabel !
Thou knowest tonight, and wilt know to—morrow

L. 235. Quoth—said. **L. 239. of weal and woe**—of happiness and sorrow. **L. 240. moved to and fro**—passed through her mind. **L. 241. vain**—impossible. **L. 243. recline**—to rest or repose on. **L. 246. slowly rolled her eyes around**—a

L. 235-244. Christabel says, "Be it so" and she undresses herself as ordered by Geraldine. She put off her clothes from her soft body and lay down in the bed. How lovely and beautiful she looks at that time! But so many thoughts of good and evil passes through her brain that she can not get sleep. While she is half-asleep, she gets up from her bed, and supporting herself on her elbow watched what lady Geraldine is about.

L. 245-263. The lady (Geraldine) bends down under the lamp and slowly moves her eyes around. She takes a deep breath like a person who shudders at the sight of danger, and unfastens the girdle from underneath her breasts. Her silken dress and her underwear fell down to the ground, and now her breast and half her side were fully visible. This sight can be better imagined than described. We can see such sights in our dreams; they cannot be put into words. May the heavenly spirits guard Christabel (from the evil influence of Geraldine)! But Geraldine neither speaks nor does she make any movement with her body. Her looks indicate that she is affected with pain and misery. It appears she has half succeeded in her faint and desperate attempt to remove a heavy weight that is oppressing her soul. She looks at Christabel and hesitates going to bed. All of a sudden she realizes that her authority has been challenged. She musters all her courage, summons her pride and contempt and sleeps with Christabel on the same bed and takes her in her arms.

L. 264-278. Woe to the day! Sadly and in a low voice she utters the curse, "this embrace will work such a magic spell upon you that you will lose the power of disclosing the secret of my shame and sorrow. This sign of my disgrace and the mark of my grief will be known to you tomorrow,

---

psychological study of a guilty mind. **L. 247. Then...aloud**— the hint of a snake's hiss. **L. 248. shuddered**—trembled with fear. **L. 249. cincture**—belt. **L. 250. vest**—a knitted or woven undergarment. **L. 252. Behold her**—Coleridge deliberately excites expectant horror, and then increases it by leaving the sight unexplained. **L. 255. nor speaks nor stirs**—She did not speak, nor did she move in the least: it seems as if the conflict in her conscience has paralysed her awhile. **L. 256. stricken**—smitten; she was evil but even she felt the pricks of conscience that made her hesitate to work evil on an innocent and chaste lady, who had been kind to her. **L. 257. Deep from within**—as if some great mental struggle was going on within her. **L. 258. sick assay**—weak attempt. **L. 259. eyes the maid**—looks at Christabel. **seeks delay**—hesitates. **defied**—challenged. **L. 264. Ah wel-a-day**—a similar expression to woe is me. **L. 265. doleful**—mournful, sad. **L. 268. is lord.....utterance**—will control your power of speech.

This mark of my shame, this seal of my sorrow;
But vainly thou warrest,
For this is alone in
Thy power to declare,
That in the dim forest
Thou heard'st a low moaning,
And found'st a bright lady, surpassingly fair;
And didst bring her home with thee in love and in charity,
To shield her and shelter her from the damp air'.

THE CONCLUSION TO PART I

It was a lovely sight to see
The lady Christabel, when she
Was praying at the old oak tree.
Amid the jagged shadows
Of mossy leafless boughs,
Kneeling in the moonlight, To make her gentle vows;
Her slender palms together prest,
Heaving sometimes on her breast;
Her face resigned to bliss or bale—
Her face, oh call it fair not pale,
And both blue eyes more bright than clear,
Each about to have a tear.

With open eyes (ah woe is me!)
Asleep, and dreaming fearfully,
Fearfully dreaming, yet, I wis,

Dreaming that alone, which is –
O sorrow and shame ! Can this be she,
They lady, who knelt at the old oak tree?
And lo ! the worker of these harms
That holds the maiden in her arms,
Seems to slumber still and mild,
As a mother with her child.

L. 269. Thou..........to-morrow—You will never forget. **L. 270. This....shame**—The mark of disgrace. **seal.....sorrow**—suggests that Geraldine was active under some compulsion. **L. 271. warrest**—fight against it. **L. 282. jagged**—uneven. **L. 283. mossy**—covered with moss. **L. 285. To make...vows**—ro pray. **L. 286. slender**—delicate. **prest**—pressed. **L. 287. Heaving sometimes on her breast**—The delicate palms, which were pressed together, lay on her bosom; and, as the bosom of the lady heaved, the palms, too, seemed to be heaving. **L. 288. resigned**—calmly submissive to the will of God; prepared. **bliss or bale**—joy or sorrow. **L. 292.**

but your struggle to regain your power of speech will be quite useless. You can never tell the story of my shame and sorrow to any one. Only one thing is in your power to tell others; how you have heard a low moaning sound in a dark forest, how you find there a bright lady of peerless beauty; how you have brought her home out of love and charity in order to protect her from her enemies and from the cold weather."

L. 279-291. What a lovely sight to see the Lady Christabel kneel, in the moon-lit night, to offer her gentle prayers under the old oak tree where these falling shadows cast by mossy branches of tree that has shed their leaves! She is kneeling with her delicate hands folded. Sometimes she has placed them on her breast. Now as her breast rose and fell (due to her breathing), her hands also rose and fell. Feelings of joy and sorrow are reflected in her face. Her face look fair rather than pale and her blue eyes bright rather than clear, as from each eye a tear seems to fall down.

L. 292-301. It is a matter of grief that, though the eyes of Christabel are open, she is dreaming frightful and horrible dreams. I think the nature of those dreams is so frightful that words cannot describe it. This is a matter of great sorrow and shame. Can this be the same lady who has knelt under the old oak tree? And look! the lady who is the author of all these evils, who embraces Christabel (like a mother embrassing her child) in her arms, appears to be enjoying a quiet and gentle sleep.

With open eyes—so great is the strain on her mind at the sight of Geraldine's bosom etc., that she cannot close her eyes. **L. 294. Fearfully dreaming**—The repetition increases the impression of the misery of Christabel's plight. **I wis**—I think. **L. 295. Dreaming that alone**—Of what was she dreaming? Of nothing else but the hideous sight that she had seen, when Geraldine undressed herself. By suggesting horror Coleridge succeeds in supernatural. **L, 298. the worker of these harms**—Geraldine, who has done all the evil. **L. 300. still and mild**—calmly and sweetly. **L. 301. As a mother with her child**—False Geraldine, the worker of all these harms is usurping the place of Christabel's mother, who was all love for her. Note the contrast between the two situations.

A star hath set, a star hath risen,
O Geraldine ! since arms of thine
Have been the lovely lady's prison.
O Geraldine ! one hour was thine—
Thou'st had they will ! By tairn and rill,
The night—birds all that hour were still.
But now they are jubilant anew,
From cliff and tower, tu—whoo ! tu—whoo !
Tu—whoo! tu—whoo ! from wood and fell !

And see! the lady Christabel
Gathers herself from out her trance;
Her limbs relax, her countenance
Grows sad and soft, the smooth thin lids
Close o'er her eyes; and tears she sheds—
Large tears that leave the lashes bright !

And oft the while she seems to smile
As infants at a sudden light !

Yea, she doth smile, and she doth weep,
Like a youthful hermitess,
Beauteous in a wilderness,
Who, praying always, prays in sleep.
And, if she move unquietly,
Perchance, 'tis but the blood so free
Comes back and tingles in her feet.
No doubt, she hath a vision sweet.
What if her guardian spirit twere.
What if she knew her mother near ?
But this she knows, in joys and woes,
That saints will aid if men will call :
For the blue sky bends over all !

L. 302. A star...hath set etc. It is the next morning. The two stars are the morning star, which sets at dawn, and the sun, which rises, suggesting that a change has come over Christabel. The pure virgin is no more. **L. 304. Lady's prison**—physically as well as spiritually. **L. 306. tairn**—a small mountain lake. **rill**—a small brook. **L. 307. The night-birds still**—even nature stood aghast at the evil done to Christabel holding the breath at this ghastly deed. **L. 308. jubilant**—After that hour, the night—birds begin to call cheerfully again. **L. 310. fell**—a barren hill or rock. **L. 312. Gathers**—recovers. **trance**—a state of semi-unconsciousness. **L. 313. relax**—become less rigid. **countenance**—face. **L. 314. sad and soft**—mellowed with mental suffering. **L. 314—315. Smooth......eyes**—

L. 302-310. O Geraldine! The evening star has set and the morning star has risen since you embracs the lovely Christabel (your embrace is like a prison-house). O Geraldine for one hour you can have Christabel under your complete sway and you could work your will upon her. At that time the birds and streamlets are still. But now they are again feeling jubilant and their cry, 'tu whoo' is heard from the tower of the castle, from the wood and from the rocks and barren mountain sides.

L. 311-318. Look there! the spell cast upon Christabel having broken, she is waking up from the state of deep sleep in which she has lain so far. Her body grows less rigid; her face becomes sad and gentle; the soft eyelids shut; and Christabel sheds big drops of tears that make her eyelashes bright. In the midst of these tears she also smiles very often, just as small children do at the sight of sudden light in the darkness.

L. 319-331. Like a young and beautiful hermitess who lives in a forest and has spend her life in the meditation of God, Christabel at one time weeps and at another time smiles. And if she moves restlessly (if she moves about her legs in a restless manner), it is because part of the blood (that is now free to circulate in her body) comes back to her feet and produces a tightening sensation. Christabel is now surely dreaming a sweet dream. Who knows that it may be the spirit of her mother who is always trying to protect her from evil harm? Christabel knows this moral and spiritual truth that whatever may happen, in joy or sorrow, the saints will come to man's help if they are called upon, because the divine spirit looks after the moral good of till creatures.

---

the tension is now relaxed and she closes her eyes. L. 317. **oft the while**—often. L. 318. **infants**—a child. L. 319. **Yea**—yes. L. 320. **hermitess**—woman living in solitude. L. 321. **Beauteous**—full of beauty. **in a wilderness**—in a place of wild, natural beauty. L. 324. **Perchance**—perhaps. **blood so free**—because she is youthful and her blood is warm and circulates freely. L. 325. **tingles**—causes a sharp thrilling sensation or pain by its sudden rush. L.326. **vision**—dream, **sweet**—pleasant. Geraldine's power is over and Christabel's mother cheers and comforts her now. L.330. **If men will call**—if men will pray for their help. L.331. **blue sky bends over all**—it is love that always triumphs over evil. **The blue sky bends over all**—embracing love of God. Cf. The moral of The Ancient Mariner.

PART II

Each matin bell, the Baron saith,
Knells us back to a world of death.
These words Sir Leoline first said,
When he rose and found his lady dead :
These words Sir Leoline will say
Many a morn to his dying day !

And hence the custom and law began
That still at dawn the sacristan

Who duly pulls the heavy bell,
Five and forty beads must tell
Between each stroke—a warning knell,
Which not a soul can choose but hear
From Bratha Head to Wyndermere.
Saith Bracy the bard, So let it knell !
And let the drowsy sacristan
Still count as slowly as he can !
There is no lack of such, I ween,
As well fill up the space between,
In Langdale Pike and Witch's Lair,
And Dungeon—ghyll so foully rent,
With ropes of rock and bells of air
Three sinful sextons' ghosts are pent
Who all give back, one after t'other,
The death-note to their living brother;
And oft too, by the knell offended,

L.332. **matin**—morning. **matin bell**—The bell that is rung in the morning to intimate people about tie morning prayers in the church. **Baron**—Sir Leoline. **saith**— says. **L.333. Knells**—indicates the sound of the bell that is rung solemnly at death or at a funeral. **Knells us back to**—Reminds us of. **L.335 his lady**—his wife. **L.337. to his dying day**—Upto the time of his death. **L.338. the custom and law**—a custom so well established that it has acquired the force of law. **L.339. still**—always, every day. **sacristan**—A person in a church in charge of the sacred vessels and other movables. It is his duty to ring the bells of a church at the required intervals. **L.340. duly**—at the proper time. **L.341. Five and forty beads must tell**—He must count 45 beads between each stroke. He should repeat "Hail Mary" forty-five times between the strokes of the bell. **L.342. warning knell**—a solemn bell that reminds people about its particular significances, or of death. **L.343. soul**—person. **which not...but hear**—Which every day person must perforce hear. **L.344. Bratha Head**—It is the name of the place where the stream Brathay rises., **Wyndermere**—the largest lake in England and the river flows into it. (As

PART II

L. 332-337. The remark, that the sound of the bell ring each morning to call to prayers takes us back to the world of death, is first made by the Baron, Sir Leoline, when (one morning) he get up and find his wife dead. He will continue to make this remark each morning till his dying day.

L. 338-344. For this reason has started the custom which comes to acquire the force of law. It becomes a part of the duty of the sexton of the parish church always to ring punctually the heavy bell at dawn and to say forty-five short prayers between every two strokes of the bell. It is intended to serve as a reminder to all that they must prepare for death towards which they are heading every moment. The bell is rung so loud that none living in the area from Bratha Head to Wyndermere can help hearing it.

L. 345-349. Bracy the minstrel says: "Let the church bell go on ringing and let the sleepy sexton say prayers slowly and sleepily, because the number of such people is large as will suitably fill up the interval of time between every two strokes of the bell."

L. 350-359. There live imprisoned in Langdale Pike, Witch's Lair and Dungeon-ghyll the ghosts of three wicked sextons. They are bound with the ropes of rocks and the bells of air and they reply, one after the other,

---

we move from Part I to Part II, there is a definite change of scene.) **L.345. Bracy**—Name of the singer in the service of Sir Leoline. **bard**—poet or singer. In the Middle Ages bard were kept in service by kings. These bards sang songs in praise of their masters' brave deeds. **So let it knell**—Let the church bell ring. **L.346. drowsy**—sleepy. **L.347. count**—count the beads of the rosary. **L.348. There is...such**--Such sounds are not wanting. **ween**—think. **L.349. the space between**—the interval between two strokes of the bell. **L.350. Langdale Pike**—The hill of Great Langdale in Grasmere. It is also called Harrison stickle. **Pike**—peak. **Witch's Lair**—Name of a valley nearby. **L.351. ghyll**—valley or ravine with a stream running through it. **foully**—badly. **rent**—torn. **L.352. ropes of....air**—a rosary of rocks and bells of air. Ropes of rock suggest the heavy work of pulling them. The bells of air suggest the echo of sound. **L.353. sinful**—wicked, **sexton**—an officer of the church incharge of its property. **are pent**—are confined in the valley. **L.354. give back**—ring. **L.355. death note**—knell, their living breather—The sexton of Sir Leoline who is alive and rings the morning bell. **L. 356. oft too**—very often. **offended**—displeased. **L. 357. One!two!three**—the strokes of the bell. **L.358. mocks**—makes fun of. **doleful**—sad. **L.359. merry**—happy. This suggests the Devil. **Borodale**—Name of a valley in Cumberland. It is not very far from Langdale. In these lines the superstitious character of the Middle Ages may be seen. As the sexton pulls the heavy bells, the ghosts of the three dead sextons who had led sinful lives echo the sound of the ringing bell. At the end of the stroke, a sound like laughter is heard from the direction of Borodale. It seems to be the Devil mocking at the religious purpose of the bell.

Just as their one ! two ! three ! is ended,
The devil mocks the doleful tale
With a merry peal from Borodale.

The air is still ! through mist and cloud
That merry peal comes ringing loud;
And Geraldine shakes off her dread,
And rises lightly from the bed;
Puts on her silken vestments white,
And tricks her hair in lovely plight,
And nothing doubting of her spell
Awakens the lady Christabel.
'Sleep you, sweet lady Christabel ?
I trust that you have rested well.'

And Christabel awoke and spied
The same who lay down by her side—
O rather say, the same whom she
Raised up beneath the old oak tree !
Nay, fairer yet ! and yet more fair !
For she belike hath drunken deep
Of all the blessedness of sleep
And while she spake, her looks, her air
Such gentle thankfulness declare,
That (so it seemed) her girded vests
Grew tight beneath her heaving breasts.
'Sure I have sinn'd !' said Christabel,
'Now heaven be praised if all be well !'
And in low faltering tones, yet sweet,
Did she the lofty lady greet
With such perplexity of mind
As dreams too lively leave behind.

L. 360. The air is still—The atmosphere is calm. **L.361. That merry peal**—The happy peal of laughter of the Devil, ringing loud—resounding loudly. **L. 362. shakes off her dread**—leaves off her fear; is no more afraid of the spirit of Christabel 's mother. **L. 363. lightly**—quietly, without disturbing Christabel. **L. 364. vestments**—robes; garments **L. 365. tricks**—dresses; arranges. **plight**—pattern; plaits. **L. 366. nothing doubting of her spell**—feeling; quite sure of the effect of her spell on Christabel. **L. 370. spied**—saw. **L. 375. belike**—perhaps. **L. 376. blessedness of sleep**—sleep which brings tranquillity. **L. 377. air**—manner. **L. 379. girded vests**—girdle of the undergarments. **L. 380. heaving**—because of strong emotions. **L. 381. sure I have sinned**—This indicates Christabel's own innocence and generosity.

to the warning knell has sounded by the sexton, thereby reminding the living sextons that their hour of death is fast approaching. And very often when the bells have stopped ringing one, two and three, the devil being offended by the matin-bell, ridicules the sad sound by a joyous peal from the valley of Borodale.

L. 360-369. The air is motionless and we can hear the loud and joyous sound of the peal of bells through fog and cloud. As Geraldine hears the merry peal she sheds her fear and leaves the bed with a light heart. She puts on white silken clothes and arranges her hair in a lovely style. Feeling fully confident that her charm has begun working, she asks Christabel to get up, saying, "Are you still asleep, O gentle lady Christabel ? I am sure you have enjoyed a sound sleep."

L. 370-376. And Christabel gets up and see the same lady who has slept with her, or we shall rather say, who has been rescued by her under the old oak tree. Geraldine now looks lovelier than before because the sound sleep she has enjoyed during the night has refreshed her.

L. 377-386. While Geraldine speak, her looks and her demeanour shows such profound gratitude (to Christabel for the good turn she has done to Geraldine) that is seemed that the tight vests tied round her breasts got tighter on account of (a strong emotion experienced by her) as evidenced by her swelling bosom. Christabel says, "Surely I have sinned (in suspecting Geraldine). Now I offer prayers to God so that everything may turn out well." Then she welcomes the stately lady Geraldine in low, stammering but sweet words, but her mind is so much confused that she can not decide whether Geraldine is as good as she looks to be or whether she is an evil spirit as her vivid dreams has painted her to be.

L. 382. Christabel thinks that what she has seen in her dream is not true. She thanks God that, after all, everything is fine. L. 383. **faltering**—uncertain. L. 385. **perplexity**—uncertainity L. 386. **lively**—distinct.

So quickly she rose, and quickly arrayed
Her maiden limbs, and having prayed
That He, who on the cross did groan,
Might wash away her sins unknown,
She forthwith led fair Geraldine
To meet her sire, Sir Leoline.

The lovely maid and the lady tall
Are pacing both into the hall,
And pacing on through page and groom.
Enter the Baron's presence-room.

The Baron rose, and while he prest
His gentle daughter to his breast,
With cheerful wonder in his eyes
The lady Geradine espies,
And gave such welcome to the same,
As might beseem so bright a dame !

But when he heard the lady's tale,
And when she told her father's name,
Why waxed Sir Leoline so pale,
Murmuring o'er the name again,
Lord Roland de Vaux of Tryermaine?

Alas ! they had been friends in youth;
But whispering tongues can poison truth;
And constancy lives in realms above;
And life is thorny; and and youth is vain;
And to be wroth with one we love
Doth work like madness in the brain.

L.387. arrayed—dressed. **L. 388. Maiden**—virgin. **L. 389. did groan**—suffer. **lie who...groan**—He who suffered very badly on the cross for the sake of mankind. Reference is to Christ, who died on the cross. **Might wash......unknown**— Might excuse her for the sins she had committed. Christabel is still perplexed by the thought whether she has committed a sin. The poet does not clear the mystery. We fail to understand what sin has been committed by Christabel. **L. 391. forthwith**—immediately. **L. 392. sire**—father. **L. 394. pacing**—walking. **L. 395. page**—boy usually in livery, who is employed to attend at the door. **groom**—a servant who looks after the horses. **L. 396. presence-room**—The state room in which Sir Leoline used to receive his guests. **L. 397—98. He preset...his breast**—He embraced his daughter affectionately. **L. 400. espies**—sees. **L. 402. beseem**—be proper; befit. **bright**—beautiful, **dame**—girl. **L. 405. waxed**—grew. **Why waxed...pale?** Why, did Sir Leoline grow so pale on hearing the very name of his father of Geraldine?

L. 387-396. So Christabel leave the bed hastily and quickly dresses herself up and prays to Jesus Christ—He who has suffered a painful death on the cross—to forgive her the sins she has committed unconsciously. Thereafter, she took beautiful Geraldine straightaway to her father, Sir Leoline. The charming Christabel and the tall Geraldine both are now walking into the hall and passing many attendants and household officials, have entered the Baron's drawing room.

L. 397-402. The Baron stand up and while he embraces his gentle daughter, Christabel, his look fell upon Geraldine and his heart is filled with a pleasant surprise. He accords her such a warm reception as befitted the beautiful lady of the status of Geraldine.

L. 403-407. Geraldine relates her story and when she give her father's name, 'Lord Roland de Vaux of Tryermaine' why did Sir Leoline grows pale and why did he repeat over again the name of Roland in a low voice?

L. 408-413. Alas! Sir Roland and Sir Leoline are very intimate friends in their young days. But-evil minded persons who are in the habit of carrying tales and backbiting misrepresent fact and distort truths, thereby creating bad blood and misunderstandings among true and sincere friends. True and steadfast friendship cannot exist on the earth; it is to be found in heaven only. Human life is full of sorrows and disappointments and young men are vain. One who falls out with his dearest friends is driven to madness.

L. 406. Murmuring....again— repeating slowly the name of Geraldine's father. **L. 407. Lord Roland de Vaux of Tryermaine**—Lord Roland was the name of Geraldine's father. Vaux was the name of his family. Tryermaine was the place where he lived. Coleridge has taken the name of Geraldine's father from Walter Scott's Bridal of Triermain. **L. 409. Whispering tongues**—false rumours. **poison truth**—spoil the truth. **L. 410. constancy**—faithfulness; true friendship. **realms**—regions. **constancy.... above**—permanent loyaly is rare on earth. It is found in heaven only. **L. 411. life is thorny**—Life in this world is beset with difficulties and complex problems which cause pain. **youth is vain**—young men are proud. Young men are so confident of themselves that they are apt to be rash and inconsiderate. **L. 412. wroth**—angry. **L. 413. Doth work...brain**—makes the mind unbalanced.

And thus it chanced, as I divine,
With Roland and Sir Leoline.
Each spake words of high disdain
And insult to his heart's best brother:
They parted—ne'er to meet again !
But never either found another
To free the hollow heart from paining—
They stood aloof, the scars remaining,
Like cliffs which had been rent asunder ;
A dreary sea now flows between;
But neither heat, nor frost, nor thunder,
Shall wholly do away, I ween,
The marks of that which one hath been.

Sir Leoline a moment's space,
Stood gazing on the damsel's face:
And the youthful Lord of Tryermaine
Came back upon his heart again.

O then the Baron forgot his age,
His noble heart swelled high with rage;
He swore by the wounds in Jesu's side
He would proclaim it far and wide,
With trump and solemn heraldry,
That they, who thus had wronged the dame,
Were base as spotted infamy
'And if they dare deny the same,
My herald shall appoint a week,
And let the recreant traitors seek
My tourney court—that there and then
I may dislodge their reptile souls

L. 414. **chanced**—happened, **divine**—guess. L. **416. high disdain**—strong anger; scorn. L. **417. To his heart's best brother**—to the friend who was most dear to his heart. L. **418. parted**—separated. **to meet**—to be reconciled. L. **419. another**—another friend. L. **420. To free...paining**—To give relief to the heart which had been pained by the loss of a friend. **hollow heart**—heart made void by the loss of a friend. L. **421. stood aloof**—remained away from each other: **scars**—marks of wounds caused by anger and insult. L. **422. rent asunder**—torn and separated. L. **423. dreary**—cheerless. **sea**—stretch of water. L. **424 heat, frost and thunder**—i.e., no force of nature. L. **425. do away**—bring to an end. **ween**—think. L. **426. of that....had been**—former strong attachment, former feelings of deep love as friends. L. **427. a moment's space**—for an instant. L. **428. damsel**—maiden; i.e. Geraldine. L. **429. The youthful...heart again**—He remembered once again Lord Roland who had been the friend of his youth. L. **431. The Baron forgot his age**—So great was the anger of Sir Leoline at the treatment meted out to Geraldine by the ruffians that he forgot that he was an old man. L. **432. swelled high**—was filled with, **rage**—

L. 414-423. I think a thing like this happens to the two friends, Sir Leoline and Sir Roland. The bosom friends employs contemptuous and insulting language to each other. They fall out and never make up in life. A terrible void is created in their hearts but neither find another true and have devoted friend to fill up that gap, with the result that both feel broken and experiences an acute mental agony. They now lives apart from each other, bearing the marks of sorrow and regret. They are like two rocks which has previously stood united, but which are now separates by the violent action of some natural agent, so that a cheerless and unbridgable gulf of enmity and hate has existed between them.

L. 424-426. But I think that neither heat nor cold nor peals of thunder shall completely wipe off the memory of that which has once existed (i.e., the friendship that has existed between the two Barons).

L. 427-430. For a short time Sir Leoline keeps looking intently at the face of the young and beautiful Geraldine and the remembrance of Sir Roland, the friend of his youthful days, come to his mind.

L. 431-437. Sir Leoline then forgets that he is an aged man. His noble heart is filled with anger and indignation and he swear by the wounds of Jesus Christ who has suffered while he is being crucified. He will announce it throughout the land by the sound of trumpets and according to the established traditions of heraldry that those knights who has disgraced Geraldine are most wicked and dishonourable fellows.

L. 438-443. If they (those knights who has disgraced Geraldine) denies the charge levelled against them let those cowardly rascals enter the lists against him on a day fixed by his herald, when he will expel their foul souls from their human bodies.

---

anger. **L 433. swore**—took an oath. **L. 433. By the....side**—By the wounds on the body of Christ who died on the cross. **L. 435. Trump**—trumpet. **heraldry**—introduction as by a herald's proclamation. **With trump and solemn heraldry**—With a herald blowing a trumpet and making a solemn announcement. In the Middle ages, it was permitted by the Code of Chivalry that a herald could carry a message to an enemy, challenge him to fight or make an offer of peace. **L. 436. They**—the five ruffians or warriors, **wronged**—disgraced. **L. 437. spotted**—blotted. **infamy**— dishonour. **Were as base as spotted infamy**—Were as bad as notorious people stained with dishonour. **L. 438. If they...same**—If they were bold enough to deny the charge levelled against them. **L. 439. appoint a week**—allow a week's time. **L. 440. recreant**—mischievous. **recreant traitors**—Those warriors who had disgraced themselves by breaking the rules of chivalry and wronged Geraldine. **L. 440—441 . seek my tourney court**—come to the tournament court in his castle. In medieval times every castle had an area where tournaments were held where knights and noblemen fought each other to prove their skill. **L. 442. dislodge**—remove. **reptile souls**—people who being wicked resembled snakes. **I may...souls**—I may kill them and thus drive out their poisonous souls from the human bodies which they do not deserve to inhabit.

From the bodies and forms of men !"
He spake : his eye in lighting rolls !

For the lady was ruthlessly seized; and he kenned
In the beautiful lady the child of his friend !

And now the tears were on his face,
And fondly in his arms he took
Fair Geraldine, who met the embrace,
Prolonging it with joyous look.
Which when she viewed, a vision fell
Upon the soul of Christabel,
The vision of fear, the touch and pain !
She shrunk and shuddered, and saw again—
(Ah, woe is me ! Was it for thee,
Thou gentle maid ! such sights to see?)

Again she saw that bosom old.
Again she felt that bosom cold,
And drew in her breath with a hissing sound:
Whereat the Knight turned wildly round,
And nothing saw, but his own sweet maid
With eyes upraised, as one that prayed.

The touch, the sight, had passed away,
And in its stead that vision blest,
Which comforted her after-rest
While in the lady's arms she lay,
Had not a rapture in her breast,
And on her lips and o'er her eyes
Spread smiles like light !

L. 444. his eye in lightning rolls—his eyes flash and roll like lightning in awful anger. **L. 445. ruthlessly**—cruelly. **seized**—caught hold of. **kenned**—saw. **L. 448. fondly**—lovingly. **in his arms he took**—he embraced. **L. 449. who met the embrace**—who embraced the Baron as lovingly as he had embraced her. **L. 450. prolonging it**—keeping the Baron in her embrace for a longer time. **with joyous look**—with eyes full of happiness. **L. 451. she viewed**—Christabel saw. **L. 451—452. a vision....Christabel**—Christabel saw a vision of something fearful. She recollected with a shudder that cold embrace which had given so much pain to her soul the previous night. **L. 454. shrunk**—moved back. **shuddered**—trembled with fear. **L. 455. Ah woe is me**—Alas! what a sad thing to have happened. **L. 457. again she...old**—Once again Christabel was reminded of the touch of Geraldine's bosom when she had laid herself down by her side and taken her in her embrace. **L. 458. that bosom cold**—the cold touch of that bosom. **L. 459. with a hissing sound**—producing a hissing sound like that of a snake. This is a significant sound. **L.460. wildly**—angrily. **L. 462. upraised**—uplifted. **L. 463.**

L. 444-446. He speak these words and his eyes become blood-shot, because the beautiful lady in whom he has recognised the beautiful daughter of his friend (Sir Roland) has been mercilessly abducted.

L. 447-456. Sir Leoline now moves to tears and he embraces Geraldine affectionately. She also allows him to do so willingly and joyously. She remains in his embrace for a little longer time. When Christabel sees this (her father embrace Geraldine who is feeling very happy), a spell is cast upon her. Her soul is seized with fear; she once more feel the horror touch (of Geraldine) and once more passes through the agonising pain (due to her contact with the wicked Geraldine). She shrank back with fear, she has shivered, and sees that vision again. I feel grief-stricken at the thought that a noble and pure-minded lady like Christabel shall be destined to see such horrible sights.

L. 457-462. Christabel once more sees in a vision, the same cold bosom (of Geraldine) as she has previously seen while she has been sleeping in her arms and inhales her breath with a hissing sound. At this, Sir Leoline turns his face like a wild man (to discover the true cause of the sound). But he can see there nothing except his own dear daughter with her eyes uplifted in a prayerful attitude.

L. 463-469. The vision of the (cold) touch (of Geraldine's bosom), and of her father's embrace has vanished. In its place a happy vision fall upon her soul. (This is the vision of her dead mother). This sacred vision is like the first vision that has soothe her feelings as she lay within Geraldine's arms. This fills her heart with ecstasy and brings bright smiles to her lips.

The touch....away—The terrible vision of Geraldine's bosom and its touch vanished. **L. 464. that vision blest**—the happy vision of her guardian-spirit. **L. 465. comforted**—consoled. **after-rest**—After waking up in the morning. **L. 467. rapture**— ecstatic joy **L. 470. with new surprise**—The Baron was surprised on hearing the hissing sound and the uplifted eyes of Christabel.

With new surprise,
'What ails then my beloved child?'
The Baron said—His daughter mild
Made answer, 'All will yet be well !'
I ween, she had no power to tell
Aught else: so mighty was the spell.

Yet he, who saw this Geraldine,
Had deemed her sure a thing divine:
Such sorrow with such grace she blended,
As if she feared she had offended
Sweet Christabel, that gentle maid!
And with such lowly tones she prayed
She might be sent without delay
Home to her father's mansion.
'Nay !
Nay, by my soul' said Leoline.
'Ho ! Bracy, the bard, the charge be thine !
Go thou, with music sweet and loud,
And take two steeds with trappings proud,
And take the youth whom thou lov'st best
To bear thy harp, and learn thy song,
And clothe you both in solemn vest,
And over the mountains haste along,
Lest wandering folk, that are abroad,
Detain you on the valley road.

'And when he has crossed the Irthing flood,
My merry bard ! he hastes, he hastes
Up Knorren Moor, through Halegarth Wood,

And reaches soon that castle good
Which stands and threatens Scotland's wastes.

'Bard Bracy ! bard Bracy ! your horses are fleet,
Ye must ride up the hall, your music so sweet,
More loud than your horses' echoing feet !
And loud and loud to Lord Roland call,
Thy daughter is safe in Langdale hall !
Thy beautiful daughter is safe and free—

L. 471. **What ails**—He asked his daughter the case of her trouble. **L. 472. mild**—gentle. **L. 473. yet**—ultimately. **L. 475. Aught**—anything. **L. 476. deemed**—thought. **L. 478. grace**—beauty. **blended**—combined. **L. 479. offended**—displeased. **L. 481. lowly tones**—soft and gentle voice. **L. 483. mansion**—castle. **L. 485. charge**—special duty. **L. 486. music sweet and loud**—loud but sweet music of harp

L. 469-474. The Baron once again feels surprised and he asks Christabel what troubles her. His gentle daughter replies: "All will yet be well." I guess that she is powerless to give out anything else, because the spell is very powerful.

L. 475-482. Sir Leoline things Geraldine to be a heavenly being (so ravishingly beautiful she is). She wear such sad and charming looks that she creats the impression that she is very sorry having (unintentionally) offended the gentle and sweet Christabel. She entreats the Baron very humbly that she may at once be send home to her father's palace.

L. 483-492. Leoline answers "I say on my honour that you shall not go in this way. O ! Bracy the bard, you are given the duty (of conveying the message to Lord Roland). As you go, take with you your harp which produces sweet and loud music, two horses with grand ornamental harnesses, the harp bearer whom you love most, (and see that you have learnt your songs well). Both of you should be dressed in a dignified manner. Go speedily over the mountains instead of taking the regular road, lest you should be stopped on your way by wandering people (who might compel you to give them your sweet music)."

L. 493-497. When the happy musician (Bracy) has crossed the river Irthing, he hurriedly passes through Knorren Moor and Halegarth wood and reaches Sir Roland's Castle that stands facing the barren moorlands of Scotland.

L. 498-504. Bard Bracy! Your horses are swift and you must ride up to Sir Roland's mansion with the sweet music of your harp sounding louder than the echoing hoofs of your horses. Give loud and repeat calls to Sir Roland saying that beautiful Geraldine is safe and secure in Langdale Hall and that Leoline sends his compliments to him through you.

---

announcing the mission. **L.487. steeds**—horses. **trappings**—beautiful, befittingly dignified. **L. 489. bear**—carry. **L. 490. clothe**—dress. **solemn vest**—ceremonial dress. **L. 491. over the mountains**—go across the mountains instead of the usual road, so that you may not be delayed on the way by people's requests for a song. **L. 492. wandering folk**—people moving about. **abroad**—out of doors. **L. 493. detain**—delay. **L. 494. he**—i.e., the bard. **Irthing flood**—Irthing river. This river rises in the north east of Cumberland and flows into the Eden, which is a few miles in the east of Carlisle. **L. 495. merry**—happy. **L. 496. knorren Moor**—A marsh on the other side of the above river. **Halegarth Wood**—A forest beyond the Moor. **L. 496. that castle good**—The Triermain Castle where Lord Roland lived. **L. 497. Which stands....wastes**—Which overlooks the barren stretches of Scotland in a threatening manner. **L. 498. Fleet**—fast. **L. 499. Ye must...hall**—You must gallop to the Lord Roland's castle. **L. 500. More loud....feet**—Your music should be louder than the sound of the feet of your horses.

Sir Leoline greets thee thus through me !
He bids thee come without delay
With all thy numerous array
And take thy lovely daughter home :
And he will meet thee on the way
With all his numerous array
White with their panting palfreys' foam :
And, by mine honour! I will say,
That I repent me of the day
When I spake words of fierce disdain
To Roland de Vaux of Tryermaine !—
—For since that evil hour hath flown,
Many a summer's sun bath shone;
Yet ne'er found I a friend again
Like Roland de Vaux of Tryermaine.

The lady fell, and clasped his knees,
Her face upraised, her eyes o'erflowing;
And Bracy replied, with faltering voice,
His gracious Hail on all bestowing !

'Thy words, thou sire of Christabel,
Are sweeter than my harp can tell;
Yet might I gain a boon of thee,
This day my journey should not be,
So strange a dream hath come to me,
That I had vowed with music loud
To clear yon wood from thing unblest,
Warned by a vision in my rest !
For in my sleep I saw that dove,
That gentle bird, whom thou dost love,
And call'st by thy own daughter's name—
Sir Leoline ! I saw the same
Fluttering, and uttering fearful moan,
Among the green herbs in the forest alone.
Which when I saw and when I heard,
I wonder'd what might ail the bird;
For nothing near it could I see,
Save the grass and green herbs underneath the old tree.

L. 506. **bids**—asks; requests. **L. 507. numerous**—countless. **array**—retinue. **L. 511. panting**—breathing fast. **palfrey**—horse. **White their...foam**—The retinue appears white due to foam or forth at the mouths of the horses panting from galloping very fast. **L. 512. by mine honour**—I swear by my honour. **L. 513. repent**—regret. **L. 514. fierce disdain**—strong scorn. **L. 516. evil**—inauspicious.

L. 505-518. Leoline asks you (Sir Roland) to come with all despatch with your large retinue to take home your lovely daughter. In order to meet you on the way, he will come, attend his countless servants and soldiers, riding at a galloping speed, his breathless horses foaming at their mouths. I swear by my honour that I shall apologise to him for the contemptuous and haughty language employed by me. Many years have rolls by since that cursed day (when we fell out and parted as enemies), but during these years I have not come across a friend as sincere and has devoted as Sir Roland.

L. 519-530. Geraldine fell down on her knees, grasp Sir Leoline's feet in her arms, raises her face towards heaven and her eyes fills with tears. Bracy replies in broken accents, greeting everybody in the hall in his gracious manner, "Father of Christabel ! The words that you have uttered are sweeter than the notes produced by my harp. Yet I beseech you to grant me one favour. I may kindly be permitted to postpone my journey, as I have dreamt a strange dream. In my sleep I have seen a vision which warns me against an evil spirit and I take a vow not to set out on my journey till I have purged the wood of that is wicked spirit by my loud music."

L. 531-540. For in my vision I have seen that a lovely and gentle creature (in the form of a dove) whom you love dearly and who is called by the name of Christabel. Sir Leoline ! I have seen the dove flapping its wings (in the attempt to fly away) and uttering fearful sounds of pain and distress among the green herbs in the forest. When I have seen her there alone in that state, I wonder what can trouble her as I can see there nothing except the grass and the green herbs that grows under the old oak tree.

---

hath flown—has passed. L. 517. **Many a...shone**—Many years have passed. L. 520. **The lady**—Geraldine. **felt**—knelt. **clasped his knees**—caught hold of the knees of the Baron. L. 521. **upraised**—lifted up as if she were requesting the Baron for something. **overflowing**—full of tears. L. 522. **faltering**—weak, hesitant L. 523. **hail**—welcome. **bestowing**—offering. **His gracious... bestowing**—greeting with kindness all the people present. L. 523. **sire**—father. L. 524. **are sweeter**—because the message given by the Baron is full of kindness and generosity, i.e. the words are sweeter than the harp can make them. L. 525. **gain**—get. **boon**—favour. L. 528. **vowed**—taken an oath; promised. L. 529. **yon**—yonder; there; that. **wood**—forest. **unblest**—evil. L. 530. **vision**—dream. **rest**—sleep. L. 531. **dove**—In Christianity the dove stands for purity and innocence. According to the Bible, the Divine Spirit came down to earth in the form of a dove. L. 535. **fluttering**—flapping its wings, making efforts to fly. **uttering**—speaking out. **moan**—painful sound. L. 536. **herbs**—plants. L. 538. **Ail**—trouble.

'And in my dream methought I went
To search out what might there be found;
And what the sweet birds's trouble meant,
That thus lay fluttering on the ground.
I went and peered, and could descry
No cause for her distressful cry;
But yet for her dear lady's sake
I stooped, methought, the dove to take,
When lo ! I saw a bright green snake
Coiled around its wings and neck.
Green as the herbs on which it couched,

Close by the dove's its head it crouched;
And with the dove it heaves and stirs,
Swelling its neck as she swelled hers !
I woke; it was the midnight hour,
The clock was echoing in the tower;
But though my slumber was gone by,
This dream it would not pass away—
It seems to live upon my eye !
And thence I vowed this self—same day,
With music strong and saintly song
To wander through the forest bare,
Lest aught unholy loiter there.'

Thus Bracy said: the Baron, the while,
Half-listening heard him with a smile;
Then turned to Lady Geraldine,
His eyes made up of wonder and love;
And said in courtly accents fine,
'Sweet maid, Lord Roland's beauteous dove,
With arms more strong than harp or song,
Thy sire and I will crush the snake`!'

L. 541. methought—I thought. **L. 545. peered**—looked carefully. **descry**—see. **L. 546. distressful**—painful. **For her...sake**—For the sake of Christabel. **L. 550. Coiled**—twisted. **snake**—The snake stands for evil and falsehood, as the dove symbolises purity and innocence. L. **551. couched**—rested. **L. 552. crouched**—lay waiting as if for attack. **L. 553. heaves and stirs**—moves. The image clearly looks back on Christabel and Geraldine together. **L. 555. The midnight hour**—The time of Bracy's dream was the same as that of Christabel' s meeting with Geraldine. L. **556. echoing**—striking. **L. 557. slumber**—sleep. **my slumber was gone by**—I was awake. L. **559. It seems...the eye**—The vision is present before my eyes. L. **560. This self-same day**—This very day. **saintly**—holy. **L. 562. bare**—

L. 541-547. It seems to me that in my dream I have seen in search of the wicked spirit that may be lurking there. I have been also anxious to know what troubles the bird that is flapping its wings with fear and lay on the ground in an agitated manner. I have gone and have looked closely but I can find no cause for the cries of anguish that she (Christabel) is uttering. Even then I bend low, for the sake of her dear mother to take the dove in my arms.

L. 548-553. When behold ! I have seen a bright green snake encircling the wings and the neck of the dove. It looks as green as the grass on which it lay ready to attack its victim. It lay with its head bent low near the head of the dove. As the dove struggles for release, the snake also rises and falls with it and as the bird stretches its neck, so does the serpent.

L. 554-563. I have got up. It has been twelve o'clock in the night, as the castle clock is stricking the midnight hour. But though I can not get sleep, the dream I have dreamt will not vanish from my mind's eye. It shall ever haunt me and I can not blot it out of the book of my memory. That is the reason why I take a vow this morning that I will beat this desolate wood singing hymns and playing upon the harp so that it may be purged of any evil spirit lurking there.

L. 564-571. While Bracy is relating his dream, the Baron hears him half-attentively. He (rather feel amused) and smiles. There is an expression of love and wonder in his face and turning to Geraldine he says in the most refined and cultured language. "Sweet Geraldine and beautiful dove (daughter) of Lord Roland (have no fear, because) your father and I will kill the snake with weapons which are stronger than Bracy's harp and his hymns."

---

because during the winter the trees had shed off their leaves and the spring season was just coming **L. 563. aught**—anything. **loiter**—wander, haunt. It may be noted that the bard according to tradition had a sense of sacredness of his vocation and responsibility for interpreting the visions he received. **L. 564. Half listening**—The Baron did not pay full attention to what Bracy said. **smile**—smiled sarcastically because he did not believe in Bracy's dream. **L. 566. made up of**—full of. **L. 567. said in courtly accents fine**—spoke in a gentle and polite language. **L. 568. Lord Roland's beauteous dove**—These words point out the Baron's interpretation of the dream. To him Geraldine was the dove and the warriors who abducted her, the snake.

He kissed her forehead as he spake,
And Geraldine in maiden wise
Casting down her large bright eyes,
With blushing cheek and courtesy fine

She turned her from Sir Leoline;
Softly gathering up her train,
That o'er her right, arm fell again;
And folded her arms across her chest,
And couched her head upon her breast,
And looked askance at Christabel—
Jesu, Maria, shield her well !

And snake's small eye blinks dull and shy;
And the lady's eyes they shrunk in her head,
Each shrunk up to a serpent's eye,
And with somewhat of malice, and more of dread,
At Christabel she looked askance !
One moment—and the sight was fled !
But Christabel in dizzy trance
Stumbling on the unsteady ground
Shuddered aloud, with a hissing sound;
And Geraldine again turned round,
And like a thing, that sought relief,
Full of wonder and full of grief,
She rolled her large bright eyes divine
Wildly on Sir Leoline.

The maid, alas ! her thoughts are gone.
She nothing sees—no sight but one !
The maid, devoid of guile and sin,
I know not how, in fearful wise,
So deeply had she drunken in
That look, those shrunken serpent eyes,
That all her features were resigned.

L. 573 in maiden wise—in the manner proper for a maiden, with the shyness of A Maiden. **casting down**— looking down with. **L. 575. courtesy fine**—with fine show of courtesy. **L. 577. She turned...Leoline**—She turned away from the Baron, at whom she had been looking till then. **L. 577. her train**—the long folds of her dress which trailed behind her. (A medieval dress had this feature) **L. 580. couched**—bent. **L. 581. askance**—obliquely. **L. 584—585. And snake's....eye**—These lines give a graphic description of the look of threat which Geraldine directed towards Christabel. Her large and bright eyes shrank into their slits and became the small blinking eyes of a snake. **L. 584. shy**—because they are not

L. 572-582. As the Baron utters the words (given before), he kisses Geraldine on the forehead and she behave as a maiden shall. She looks downward with her large shining eyes, blushed, makes a charming bow and turns aside from him (Sir Leoline). Then gently collects the folds of her dress, arranging them as before on her right arm, she lays her head low upon her breast and cast an oblique look at Christabel. May Jesus Christ and Virgin Mary protect her against Geraldine's evil influence!

L. 583-596. The eyes of a snake are very small and while casting a dull and unsteady gleam they blink (half shut and half open). Geraldine's eyes withdraws into their socket and become as small as the eyes of a serpent. She casts an oblique look at Christabel more out of fear than out of ill-will.

The charm is wrought in the twinkling of an eye and then the supernatural sight vanishes. But christabel is spell-bound. She feels giddy; her feet totters and she is about to fall down on the ground; she visibly trembles with fear and give out hissing sounds. Geraldine once more turns round to the Baron and eagerly looks at him with her large shining eyes in which there is celestial light. At that time her face is wearing an expression of wonder and grief (because of the hissing sound) and she looks like a person who stand in need of sympathy and comfort.

L. 597-606. How bad! Her brain is confused and upset. She cannot think. She can see nothing except one vision (the dreadful vision of the serpent-woman). I am at a loss to understand as to why Christabel, who is pure and innocent, shall be completely hypnotised by the (hateful and ugly) look of the serpent-woman whose eyes has shrunken into their sockets. Again, I cannot explain as to why Christabel is so deeply influenced by that vision that she can see nothing but that, or why she shall helplessly reproduce Geraldine's look of treacherous hate.

---

fully open. L. 586. **malice**—spite. **dread.**—fear. L. 590. **dizzy**—giddy. **trance**—stupor. L. 591. **stumbling**—staggering. L. 592. **shuddered**—trembled. L. 594. **sought relief**—looked for relief from some affliction. L. 596. **divine**—angelic. L. 597. **wildly**—helplessly. L. 598. **The maid**—Christabel. **her thoughts are gone**—Being in a trance, she has lost the power of thinking. She has lost her will completely. L. 600. **devoid of guile and sin**—knowing no deceit and sin. L.601. **I know not how**—The poet fails to understand how it happened. **wise**—manner. L. 602. **So deeply...look**—so powerful had been the influence of Geraldine's look upon her. L. 603. **shrunken**—become small. L. 604. **features**—looks. **were resigned**—had submitted. L. 604. **this sole image**—i.e., the look of shrunkeneyes. **That all...sole image**—Her face showed the image of Geraldine's look of malice and hatred which was very deeply imprinted on her mind. L. 605. **passively**—without any effort on her part; it seemed as if she was unconsciously prompted. **imitate**—reflect. L. 606. **treacherous**—deceitful.

To this sole image in her mind;
And passively did imitate
That look of dull and treacherous hate !
And thus she stood, in dizzy trance,
Still picturing that look askance
With forced unconscious sympathy
Full before her father's view—
As far as such a look could be,
In eyes so innocent and blue !

And when the trance was o'er the maid
Paused a while, and inly prayed ;
Then falling at the Baron's feet
'By my mother's soul do I entreat
That thou this woman send away !'
She said and more she could not tell,
For what she knew she could not tell,
O'er mastered by the might spell,
Why is thy cheek so wan and wild,
Sir Leoline ? Thy only child
Lies at thy feet, thy joy, thy pride,
So fair, so innocent, so mild;
The same, for whom thy lady died
O by the pangs of her dear mother
Think thou no evil of thy child
For her, and thee and for no other,
She prayed the moment ere she died :
Prayed that the babe for whom she died,
Might prove her dear lord's joy and pride!
That prayer her deadly pangs beguiled,
Sir Leoline !
And wouldst thou wrong thy only child,
Her child and thine ?

L. 608. picturing—reflecting. **L. 609. forced**—unwilling; involuntary. **With forced unconscious sympathy**—With a sympathetic reaction which was forced from her without any effort of will, i.e., unconsciously. **L. 610. Full before..... view**—she presented that look fully to her father. **L. 611—612. As far as...and blue**—So far as that look could be reflected from the blue and innocent eyes of Christabel. L. **614. paused**—stopped. **awhile**—a little. **inly**—inwardly. L. **616. entreat**—request. L. **620. over mastered**—overcome. mighty spell—strong enchantment. L. **621. wan**—pale. **wild**—angry. L. **625. thy lady**—your wife. L. **626. pangs**—

L. 607-612. Christabel stands for some time in this state of utter bewilderment and perplexity. She falls under the hypnotic influence of Geraldine and become almost unconscious, still having the same oblique look of treacherous and malicious hate (as she has seen in the eyes of the witch). She is forced by some mighty and irresistible supernatural power to show sympathy for the witch in the very presence of her father, although she is unconscious of what she is doing. It is some compelling force that bring to her the same malicious and fiendish look of hate so far as the innocent blue eyes of Christabel can have a look full of fierce hate and deceit.

L. 613-620. When the spell is broken, Christabel waits for some time and pray inwardly. When she kneel before the Baron and say, "I appeal to you in the name of my mother to send Geraldine away," she can say nothing more, because being overpowered by the powerful magic, she can not reveal what she know about Geraldine.

L. 621-634. Why is it that the Baron has become pale and haggard? There lies at his feet his only child, who is the joy and pride of his life, who is so beautiful, so pure, so gentle, to give birth to whom the Baroness die. Remember the Throes your wife suffered at the time Christabel has been born, and for their sake do not think evil of the child. When your wife has been lying on deathbed, she has prayed only for you and your daughter. She has prayed that her daughter to bear whom she has given up her own life might grow up to be a source of joy and pride to her father. That prayer lessens the acute pain of child-birth, and will you do injury to your only child by thinking evil of her?

---

pains at the time of child-birth. **L. 627. Think thou...thy child**—Do not think ill of your (laughter. **L. 630. ere**—before. **L. 633. That prayer...beguiled**—That prayer lessened the deadly pain of Lady Leoline.

Within the Baron's heart and brain
If thoughts, like these, had any share,
They only swelled his rage and pain,
And did but work confusion there.
His heart was cleft with pain and rage;
His cheeks they quivered, his eyes were wild.
Dishonoured thus in his old age;
Dishonoured by his only child,
And all his hospitality
To the wrong'd daughter of his friend
By more than woman's jealousy
Brought thus to a disgraceful end–
He rolled his eye with stern regard
Upon the gentle minstrel bard,
And said in tones abrupt, austere–
'Why, Bracy ! dost thou loiter here?
I bade thee hence !' The bard obeyed;
And turning from his own sweet maid,
The aged knight, Sir Leoline,
Led forth the lady Geraldine!

THE CONCLUSION TO PART II

A little child, a limber elf,
Singing, dancing to itself,
A fairy thing with red round cheeks,
That always finds, and never seeks,
Makes such a vision to the the sight
As fills a father's eyes with light;
And pleasures flow in so thick and fast
Upon his heart, that he at last
Must needs express his love's excess

L. 638. **If thoughts like these**–such thoughts as have been described in the above lines, had any share–had any places. L. 639. **swelled**–increased. L. 640. **And did...there**–Such thoughts as these created a confusion in his mind. L. 641. **cleft**–broken into two. L. 642. **quivered**–shook with anger. **wild**–with anger. L. 643. **Dishonoured**– Because he was being asked to send away a girl who was in distress. L. 648. **thus**–By being asked to send away. **with stern regard**–with an angry look. L. 650. **minstrel**–singer; musician. L. 651. **in tones**–in a voice. **abrupt**–sudden. L. 651. **austere**–harsh. L. 652. **loiter**–linger. L. 653 **bade thee hence**–I ordered you to go immediately. L. 654. **aged**–old. L. 655. **Led forth**–went out with. L. 656. **limber**–active, elf–fairy. L. 657. **to itself**– by itself. L. 659. **That always finds**–That finds happiness everywhere. L. 660. **makes**–presents. **such a.....sight**–a very beautiful sight to the eyes. **light**–light of joy and pride. L. 662. **so thick and fast**–such abundance.

With words of unmeant bitterness.
Perhaps 'tis pretty to force together
Thoughts so all unlike each other;
To mutter and mock a broken charm,
To dally with wrong that does no harm.
Perhaps 'tis tender too and pretty
At each wild'word to feel within
A sweet recoil of love and pity.
And what, if in a world of sin
(O sorrow and shame should this be true !)
Such giddiness of heart and brain
Comes seldom save from rage and pain,
So talks as it's most used to do.

L. 665. unmeant—unintende. **bitterness**—harshness. **L. 666—667, 'tis pretty to...each other**—It is strange that such opposite feelings of love and harshness exist side by side in the heart and are complementary to each other. **L. 668. mutter**—speak. **L. 668—669. To mutter no harm**—The meaning of these lines is not clear. Perhaps Coleridge means that Sir Leoline spoke angry words and mocked at Christabel because the charm or attraction of their mutual love had come to an end.He favoured Geraldine because not knowing her real nature he could not see any harm in entertaining her. **daily**—play with. **L. 671. wild'word**—angry word. **L. 670—672. Perhaps 'tis....and pity**—Perhaps it is a part of that very delicate thing which is called human psychology that a person should speak angry words to one whom he loves and while doing so feel a sense of love and pity. recoil—draw back; rebound. **L. 675. giddiness**

(B) INTRODUCTION TO THE POEM

Date of Composition. The first part of *Christabel* has been composed in 1797 when the poet used to live at Nether Stowey. The second part has been composed in 1800, after the poet's return from Germany.

Date of Publication. Coleridge has an elaborate plan about the present poem, but he can not complete it. On Byron's recommendation, Murray published these two parts together with *Kubla Khan* and *The Pains of Sleep* in 1816.

The Plan of the Poem. In 1836, Wordsworth is ben remarked that "he had no idea how *Christabel* was to have been finished and he did not think Coleridge had ever conceived in his own mind, a definite plan for it; that the poem had been composed while they were in habit of definite intercourse, and almost in his presence, and when there was the most unreserved intercourse between them and he had never heard from him any plan for finishing it."

Reasons for Not Completing the Poem. The biographers of Coleridge have assigned several reasons due to which the poem can not be completed. As a matter of fact, a number of unfortunate incidents does not let Coleridge complete this poem. In a note book entry for 3rd November, 1810, Coleridge has written that he suffered a lot due to his quarrel with Lamb and Lloyd and this has prevented him from completing *Christabel*. On 19th December, 1799, he write to Southey, "I am afraid that I have scarce poetic enthusiasm enough to finish *Christabel*."

Despite the two facts mentioned above, Coleridge makes every effort to complete the poem. But he is a very sensitive man. He is almost hyper-sensitive. His quarrel with his two best friends, Lamb and Lloyd, prevents him not only from completing *Christabel*, but also from doing any other thing. His mental peace is further disturbed when he sees Lloyd's novel, *Edmund Oliver*. Lloyd, to humiliate his friend, modelled his hero in the novel on the dark side of Coleridge. So great became his despair and anguish after that "the gulf between his intellect and will, between powers and performance" went on increasing, as Prof. Saintsbury remarks. Consequently, Coleridge could never complete the poem and it remains in its unfinished state as we find it today, though he himself has a strong desire to complete the poem. He writes on one occasion, "The reason for my not finishing *Christabel* is not that I don't know how to do it—for I have, as I always had, the whole plan entire from beginning till the end in my mind, but I fear I can not carry on with equal success of execution of the idea, an extremely subtle and difficult one." But like many unrealised schemes and visions of his, *Christabel* too, remains unfinished.

Joint Plan of Wordsworth and Coleridge. As very close friends, Wordsworth and Coleridge has planned to produce the *Lyrical Ballads* jointly. "It is agreed," says Coleridge, "That my endeavours shall be directed to persons and characters supernatural, or at least romantic. Mr. Wordsworth, on the other hand, is to propose to himself as his object to give the charm of novelty to things of every day, and to excite a feeling analogous to the supernatural. With this view I wrote the *Ancient Mariner*, and is preparing, among other poems, the *Dark Ladie* and *Christabel* in which I shall have more nearly realised my ideal than I have done in my first attempt." Coleridge has already contributed *The Rime of the Ancient Mariner* in the first edition of the *Lyrical Ballads*. *Christabel* is to be included in the second edition of the *Lyrical Ballads*, but Coleridge fails to complete the poem well within time.

(C) THE STORY OF *CHRISTABEL*

Sir Leoline of Langdale has a lovely daughter, named Christabel. Once she goes to the woods at midnight—the hour of witches and ghosts to pray for her absent fiance. In the chilly April night she meet a damsel who is alone and dress in the silken clothes and surpassingly beautiful. She is related her story thus: "My name is Geraldine and I am the daughter of Sir Roland de Vaux of Tryermaine. Yesterday, I am forcibly abducted by five warriors who gagges my mouth and carries me on a white palfrey to this deserted place where they have left me promising to come back soon." The touching story moves Christabel.

As Geraldine enteres the Castle, a few strange things happens. She sank over the threshold of the gate; the old mastiff makes an unwanted angry moan; the smouldering brands give a 'tongue of light or flit of flame.' All these occurrences has an air of mystery about them.

They shares the same bed. At night Geraldine wrought her evil spell upon Christabel. The charm is so powerful that under its effect she could only say that she has succoured a lady of surpassing loveliness in the forest and brings her home and fedd her. She has no power to say anything else concerning Geraldine.

During her sleep Christabel has dreadful and happy dreams one after the other. In the morning, Christabel repents for the evil thoughts that had come to her during her sleep, and she cheerfully led Geraldine to meet her father. When the Baron come to know that the distressed lady is the daughter of his old friend (Alas! the two friends has quarrelled and parted) he make a vow that he would avenge the outrage to Geraldine the noble lady. He has embraced her fondly. At this time Christabel has a vision (this was the second vision). In the vision she see the same cold bosom of Geraldine. She shudders and hiss.

The father can not understand what the real matter is. In the meantime, the witch assumes the pose of injured innocence and wants to be send home. The Baron asks his poet (Bracy) to go to Sir Roland and request him to come with his equipage to take his daughter. Bracy wants permission to postpone his departure. He has seen a vision, he says, and in the vision he has seen a bright green snake (Geraldine) encircling a gentle dove (Christabel) and ready to kill it. The Baron interprets the dream differently and take the snake to mean the ruffians who has abducted her. Geraldine plays the lady and thanks the Baron in the most fashionable manner. She looks at him with her large bright divine eyes, but at Christabel she looks askance. The pure maid has her third vision in which only one image—the dull and treacherous look of Geraldine—seems to be fixed upon her mind.

After the trance is broken, Christabel appeals to her father to send Geraldine away. He carrys the impression that his daughter has grown jealous. He feels insulted and disgraced. He gets enraged and furious and repeates his orders to the Bard. Bracy goes and the Baron turning his back upon his own daughter, lead forth Geraldine.

(D) A CRITICAL SUMMARY OF THE POEM

L. 1-22. According to the clock in Sir Leoline's Castle, it is midnight. The cock has begun to crow. Sir Leoline's mastiff bitch howls sixteen times, and the midnight is chilly; it is a moonlit night, but the cloud obscures the moon light. Being the month of April, spring has only just commenced.

L. 23-36. Christabel, beloved of her father, Sir Leoline, is alone in the forest late at night, praying for the welfare of her lover who is far away; silently, she is kneeling and praying beneath the huge oak tree.

L. 37-78. Christabel is suddenly disturbed in her silent prayers by a nearby moaning sound. It cannot be the wind that makes the moaning sound- for there is very little wind in the air. Christabel walks round to the other side of the oak tree and sees there a beautiful lady lying in some disorder. When asked to explain who she is, the lady says that she is too weary to speak; but, presently, she starts telling her story.

L. 79-103. The lady says that her name is Geraldine; she has been kidnapped by five warriors in the morning; she has been secured on the back of a horse; the whole day they have travelled and when night came, one of the five have taken her from the horse's back and left her at the foot of the oak tree. They have vowed to come back soon. When they left her, she has become unconscious—it is the castle clock that awoke her. Having told her story, the lady requests Christabel once again to stretch forth her hand and help her to escape from her enemies.

L. 104-122. Hearing Geraldine's sad story, Christabel extends her hand to her and promises her that Sir Leoline will send her (Geraldine) safe to her own father's hall. As they walk slowly together, Christabel tells Geraldine that Sir Leoline being too weak in health, shall not be disturbed till the morning. Geraldine can, however, sleep for the night in Christabel's room on the same couch.

L. 123-174. Walking together, Geraldine and Christabel crosses the moat; Christabel opens the door in the middle of the gate, and they cross the court, and then the hall. Seeing them, the mastiff bitch moans angrily: when they pass the dying fire leaps up into a sudden blaze. They find their way from stair to stair, and at last they enter Christabel's room.

L. 175-219. Christabel's room is contrived by clever workmen and sculptors like a real lady's chamber. Christabel trims the silver lamp and makes it bright. Meanwhile Geraldine sinks upon the floor, as though she is very tired. Christabel offers her a cordial wine made Out of wild flowers by her late mother. Geraldine is now suddenly frightened by some mysterious presence-probably the spirit of Christabel's mother-and cries out wildly. She presently recovers her poise and pretends that her fit has subsided and that she is all right once again.

L. 220-244. Geraldine drinks some more wine and regaining her strength, stands erect on the floor; she is alluring and strange, as if she has come from a distant place. She asks Christabel to undress and go to bed. But Christabel cannot sleep now, and hence she reclines on her elbow and observes Geraldine from the bed.

L. 245-278. Slowly and with a shudder as it were, Geraldine too undresses, she neither speaks nor stirs for a time; her face shows sorrow and hesitation; but suddenly she seems to make up her mind and lies down by Christabel's side. She now takes Christabel in her arms and pronounces a charm upon her, which puts her under Geraldine's power.

L. 279-331. Christabel, as she is kneeling and praying at the foot of the old oak tree, looks so innocent so beautiful. Now she is lying by the side of Geraldine, and dreaming the most fearful dreams. Her eyes are open, and yet she is unconscious; such a fearful change has come upon her. But, by her side, Geraldine is slumbering in ease, unmindful of the happiness she has wrecked. An hour passes; the hour of Geraldine's absolute triumph is over. The night-birds are calling lustily and Christabel too comes Out of her night marish trance; she sheds tears of happiness and smiles like a child; for she has now seen a sweet vision, the vision of her guardian spirit, the vision of her dead mother, Lady Leoline.

L. 332-359. It is the custom in Sir Leoline's Castle for the sacristan to count the beads and mutter prayers forty-five times between two consecutive strokes of the morning bell. This is so because, according to Sir Leoline, life is really a living death. When the sacristan rings the bell, the sounds are taken up by the ghosts of three other sacristans in the neighbouring country and each matin bell thus echoes far and wide. When the three echoing sounds cease, the devil himself concludes the series with a merry peal from Borodale.

L. 360-392. When she listens to the devil's jubilant voice, Geraldine rises from her bed and awakens the lady Christabel also. For a little while Christabel is not sure whether the Geraldine she sees is the sinful Geraldine she has met (or had she only dreamt of her) last night or whether it is rather a pure-minded and innocent lady. In spite of her confusion, Christabel greets Geraldine kindly and leads her to meet Sir Leoline.

L. 393-407. Christabel leads Geraldine to Sir Leoline's room. After embracing his own daughter, he gives proper welcome to the lady Geraldine. He learns her story and learns also that her father is Lord Roland de Vaux of Tryermaine. This suddenly and unaccountably upsets the Baron.

L. 408-430. Sir Leoline and Lord Roland de Vaux has been formerly friends; but busybodies and scandalmongers poisons their friendship. Through misunderstanding, each spoke harsh words to the other, and so they parted and never met again. But neither of them is afterwards able to find another equally true friend. Their friendship shatters, they now stood like two cliffs cleft in two with a deep chasm between them. As Sir Leoline now gazes upon Geraldine's face, it appears rather like the face of the youthful Lord Roland, so familiar to him in former times.

L. 431-482. Now the Baron forgets his age and full of anger affirms that he will punish the men who have so infamously wronged Geraldine. He will challenge them to combat and kill them there and then. He also tearfully takes Geraldine in his arms, and she too meets his embrace readily. Meanwhile, *Christabel* sees-as in a flash-the real Geraldine; for a while she is awed and horror-stricken; but presently she sees her guardian spirit, and she is once again calm, and she is even able to smile rapturously. To her father's query, she merely replies, 'All will yet be well!' While *Christabel* knows the truth, but cannot reveal it, Sir Leoline is wholly deceived by appearances and looks upon Geraldine as a thing divine; and Geraldine cunningly begs him to send her away to her father's castle, since she does not want to be a source of annoyance to *Christabel.*

L. 483-518. Sir Leoline calls Bracy the bard and entrusts him with the task of proceedings to Tryermaine and informing Lord Roland of his daughter's safety. Bracy is also to invite Lord Roland, with all his retinue, to Sir Leoline's castle; and the Baron will meet Lord Roland half-way and express regret for the insulting words he has spoken long ago. And so they will be friends again.

L. 519-563. Bracy the bard answers the Baron as follows: "It is always a pleasure to obey you; by your permission let me not go on my journey today. I dream last night that the dove, by name *Christabel,* which you and your daughter alike love, is lying on the ground and screaming in pain. On looking closer at it, I found that a snake has coiled around its wings and neck. Presently, I awoke and found that it is midnight. Today I wish to wander in the forest and drive away with my saintly songs the snake-like unholy creature that, according to my dream, is loitering there."

L. 564-620. When Bracy concludes, the Baron supposing that the dove in the dream signifies Geraldine, tells her, "Your father and I will kill the snake (i.e., your enemies)". Geraldine blushingly turns away from the Baron and archly fixes upon *Christabel* dull, malicious eyes of a snake; immediately

Geraldine's look reverts to its previous brightness as she meets the Baron's gaze. As for *Christabel,* she shudders aloud with a hissing sound, she has no thought but the memory of the serpent glance; her own eyes shrink in irresistible response into the smallness and maliciousness of the serpent eye; and she stares at her own father with this deformed look. After a little while, her features relax, she is again her own sweet self; she prays inwardly and kneeling before her father, earnestly entreats him to send Geraldine away at once. The spell is still so strong that she is unable to say more by way of explanation.

L. 621-655. This request throws Sir Leoline into some confusion. On the one hand, he loves his daughter; his wife has (lied praying for the welfare of his daughter, *Christabel,* his child and his late wife's child, is doubly dear to him. On the other by making this request, *Christabel* has dishonoured him, spoilt his hospitality to his friend's daughter. He suddenly makes up his mind, orders Bracy to go on his errand at once, and leaving *Christabel* alone, leads forth the lady Geraldine.

L. 656-677. As a little child-a nimble fairylike child with beautiful cheeks-*Christabel* is always happy and always gladdenes her father's eyes. On the occasion however, he treats her roughly; but this was due to the very excess of his love. It is strange that contradictory thoughts love and anger should sometimes live together; it is strange that people shall love and at the same time say or do cruel things to the objects of love. But such "Giddiness of heart and brain" is generally caused by anger and pain.

(E) CRITICAL APPRECIATION AND INTERPRETATION

Christabel is written between 1797 and 1800. It is a fragment ,but the reason why it has been left unfinished is not that the poet did not know how to finish it—for he has the whole plan entire from the beginning to end, in his mind—but that he feared he could not carry on with equal success the execution of the idea, an extremely subtle and difficult one.

England has not so far produced a greater writer of supernatural poetry, nor a finer dreamer. Coleridge has been called the master of natural supernaturalism, a wizard who creates an atmosphere of eerie mystery and horror by purely natural means . Christabel, *Ancient Mariner* and Kubla Khan—these three poems stands in a class by themselves. In their own field they are unrivalled in the whole range of English literature.

Christabel is a story of a witch who casts her evil spell upon an innocent soul. It is a supernatural tale of mystery, horror, wizardry and wonders. The dream faculty of the poet has given it a very high rank among works of pure creative art. It is one of the three or four master-pieces of Coleridge on which his reputation as one of the great poets of England rests. About these poems Stoffod Brook remarks, "All that he did excellently well might be bound up in twenty pages, but it should be bound in pure gold."

Supernaturalism. *Christabel* is a tale of enchantment, sorcery and magic. Its place as a work of literary craftsmanship in the realm of supernatural poetry is very high. The pure and innocent Christabel, Sir Leoline's daughter, falls a victim to the wicked influences of Geraldine, a lovely and fascinating sorceress. The charm is so potent that under its effect the poor soul loses her power to disclose the shameful story of the witch even to her father. The language is the language of incantation and the setting and the atmosphere are supernatural.

Mark the masterly skill of the poet in preparing the ground for the meeting between Christabel and Geraldine. It is the middle of night. The owls are screeching 'Tu-whit'! 'Too-Whoo'; they have awakened the drowsy cock. The Baron's toothless mastiff 'from her kennel beneath the rock maketh answer to the clock, four for the quarters, and twelve for the hour, sixteen short howls, not over aloud.' The night is chilly but not dark.' 'The moon is full and yet she looks both small and dull.' The thin grey cloud is spread on high.' 'It covers but not hides the sky. 'It is a month before the month of May.' The forest is bare and bleak. The wind is unusually still and motionless.

Before Coleridge, many writers has trodden the field of supernaturalism and has brought out stories of ghosts and witches. But the only feature of such stories is that they creates sensation and make our flesh creep. They lacks imagination and are divested of human interest. In the hands of writers like Monk Lewis and Anne Radcliffe they have degenerated into a mere orgy of crude sensationalism. But Coleridge changes all this. He gives his supernatural tales a human interest and a semblance of truth. He tells his tales against a psychological background. He creates a willing suspension of disbelief the reader readily believes what he is reading without questioning the possibility of events and incidents recorded in the tales. Doubts never cross his mind. Coleridge's stories are undoubtedly fantastic, unreal and improbable, but by his supreme art he has given them an air of plausibility, has made them look real. In blending the supernatural with the natural lies the greatest achievements of the 'subtle souled psychologist.'

Every word of what has been written in the above paragraph applies to Christabel. It is a 'story from the world of spirits. It is 'witchery by moonlight.' It is, "an imaginative romance pervaded throughout by the supernatural." But, "while we read it, we are all the while in our real and living world." The human and the supernatural elements have been so skilfully blended that it is well-nigh impossible to separate one from the other. Our credulity is never shocked. We do not doubt even for a moment the existence of Geraldine, Christabel or other human characters nor do we ever call in question the raison d'etre of happenings like the visions and dreams recorded in the poem. The supernaturalism of Coleridge is therefore psychological, subtle and refined. It is realistic supernaturalism.

One of the secrets of the success of Coleridge as a great supernatural poet is that his stories are not blood-curdling, nor does he consciously attempt to produce sensationalism in his readers. In *Christabel* the feeling of horror is produced indirectly. Coleridge does not describe or define horror, he only suggests it. He does not actually describe the horrible sight; he merely gives us the effect of that horrible sight:

> Alas! What ails poor Geraldine?
> Why stares she with unsettled eye?
> Can she the bodiless dead espy?
> And why with hollow voice cries she
> "Off woman, off! this hour is mine"

Here what Geraldine sees has not been described; the spirit of the dead body of Christabel's mother has not been dragged into the story. But the poet has succeeded in conveying to us the effect of the dreadful sight Geraldine sees.

Again, Coleridge leaves many things in the poem deliberately vague and indefinite. At several places there is an air of mystery which the poet has not cleared. The poet excites the reader's curiosity but leaves it ungratified till the end. In the lines:-

> Again she saw that bosom old
> Again she felt that bosom cold,
> And drew in her breath with a hissing sound

We are left to conjecture the exact nature of the sight Christabel sees in the cold bosom of Geraldine. It has not been clearly defined.

Medievalism. The scene of the poem is laid in the Middle Ages. The Medieval times are marked by superstition and piety. During that period the people are superstition-ridden; they believe in magic and witchcraft. They are also deeply religious. This period is characterised by feudalism. The feudal lords lives in castles round which moats are built; they take part in tournaments. Now in *Christabel* we find that characters, situations, scenes all belongs to the Middle Ages. The theme of the story is magic. One of the characters is a witch who casts her evil spell upon her innocent victim. There is the chivalry of Middle Ages in Sir Leoline who lives like a feudal lord in a fortified castle, attends by innumerable attendants, pages and heralds, and takes part in tournaments. The piety of the Middle Ages is seen in the prayers to Jesus and Maria and in the reference to the bell. We have a reference to Medieval art in the Chamber of *Christabel*-'Carved so curiously'.

Narrative Skill. Coleridges *Ancient Mariner, Christabel, Love* and *Kubla Khan* all bear eloquent testimony to his narrative skill. He is a storyteller par excellence and a supreme master of this art. His narrative skill in *Christabel* is worthy of a very high praise. The poet has with consummate skill make use of almost all weapons in his armoury to make the story interesting, except at one or two places it never flags; it is a gripping tale. It is full of action and excitement; it is told against a psychological background; there is human interest in it. It arouses curiosity and produces a feeling of suspense; it appeals to us and thrills our souls. Many things in the story have been left intentionally vague and indefinite so that the reader fills up the details according to his imagination. Its language is very simple.

Metre, Imagery, Music, Melody,. etc. In *Christabel,* Coleridge has introduced a new metrical novelty. On this points he himself says: "The metre of *Christabel* is not, properly speaking, irregular, though it may seem so from its being founded on a new principle, namely, that of counting in each line the accent, not the syllables. Though the letter may vary from seven to twelve, yet in each line the accent will be only four. Nevertheless, the occasional variation in number of syllables is not introduced wantonly, or for the mere ends of convenience, but in correspondence with some transition in the nature of imagery and passion."

Art of Picture. Coleridge is deft in the art of picture making with the help of simple words. "Coleridge's success is not a little due to the perfection of his language. From the simplest material of ordinary words he weaves a web of music and imagery. By slight deft touches he creates a picture, the details of which are quickly filled in by a responsive imagination. He is a master of harmony....with that supreme art which ever seems artless, he weaves such a sound, colour and detail as to defy all attempts at analysis".

(F) EXPLANATIONS WITH CRITICAL COMMENTS

L. 1-5. 'Tis middle...... it crew. The poet says that it is midnight. The clock of the tower of the castle of *Christabel*'s father, Sir Leoline, strikes the hour of twelve. The owls, with their hooting sounds, have awakened the cock, which begins to crow in a low and drowsy manner.

The ticking of the clock, the hooting of the owls, and the crowing of the cock have been charged with an unusual significance which is ominous, by manner of the poet's description.

L. 6-13. Sir Leoline......my lady's shroud. *Christabel*'s father, Sir Leoline who is a rich baron, has a bitch with no teeth because she is old. She is in her dog-house beneath the rock. She barks in response to the striking of the hour by the tower clock. In all seasons, whether wet or dry, fair or foul, she barks in response to the striking of the clock.

There are some clocks which strikes the quarters also, i.e., after every fifteen minutes, produce a musical sound. When the hour is complete, first they strike four times to indicate that four quarters have passed, and then they strike the hour. Here the hour is twelve. Hence the clock of the tower strikes four and twelve, i.e., sixteen times. In answer to the sixteen strokes, the old bitch gives out sixteen short growls, which are not very loud. It is her practice to make sixteen short subdued growls exactly at midnight when she hears the clock striking. Some people believe that the bitch thus barks because she sees the ghost of *Christabel*' s mother Lady Leoline.

In this stanza, the poet very faintly suggests the presence of the ghost of *Christabel*'s mother. It can only be conjectured through the instinctive behaviour of the old bitch. This is highly characteristic of Coleridge's treatment of the supernatural, and distinguishes him from the 'School of Horror'. He refrains from the actual description of the horned and the supernatural. He avoids, as far as possible, the repulsive details. But he achieves incomparably stranger effects by such subtle suggestions. In the introduction of the ghost of *Christabel* 's mother, here, we have an example of the fine and delicate presentation of the supernatural. It shall be remembered that, half the poem been finished, as intended by Coleridge, the ghost of the mother will have played a very important part in the development of the story. It is really to be a contest between the two antagonists: Geraldine, the Spirit of Evil, and this ghost, the Guardian-Spirit of *Christabel*. Its mention at the beginning of the poem, is thus, very significant.

L. 14-22. Is the night chilly.......slowly up this way. In these lines the poet gives a description of the night and the weather, which is full of magical beauty. He says that the night is cold, but not dark. The cloud is almost transparent. Though it overcasts the sky, it does not hide it (sky) completely from the view. Behind the semi-transparent thin grey cloud, the moon is easily visible. It is full moon, but shining from behind a thin cloud, it looks smaller than its actual size. At the same time, it looks dull because the thin cloud partially obstructs her light. Being thin, the cloud cannot obstruct the light of the moon. It cannot, therefore, be a dark or black cloud. Because of the light of the moon filtering through it, it looks grey. It is the month of April and the spring season has just began.

According to Prof. Herford, there is an indefiniteness about these lines. It shall be noted that the manner of description is such that little things seem to become very significant. The unexpected tone of the cock's crowing, the cold night, the thin grey cloud, the full moon behind it, all these are made to appear, by the manner of description, as if there are something unusual about them.

L. 23-30. The lovely lady...... that's far away. At this hour of midnight the beautiful Christabel leaves the castle. She goes to the forest which is a furlong away from the gate of the castle. The poet fails to understand the reason why Christabel whom her father loves so dearly shall go to the forest at this hour of the night when it is so cold. He himself gives the answer. He says that last night she has a dream of her dear betrothed knight in the far off lands. That dream is not a happy one. Hence it has made her anxious about the knight to whom she is engaged. So she has come out to the forest to pray for his health and happiness.

Dreams play a large part in supernatural stories. In the times of Coleridge it is considered a superstition to have a belief in dreams. Coleridge himself is greatly attracted by the supernatural power of dreams. After composing the Pains of Sleep, tie wrote: "My dreams become the substance of my life." At another place he writes.

> Such perplexity of mine
> As dreams too lively leav behind.

L. 43-57. The night is chill.........she there? In this stanza, the poet gives a vivid description of the atmosphere in which Christabel finds herself beneath the huge oak tree in the forest. The night is cold. There are no leaves on the trees of the forest. In such a condition there can be nothing on the trees to produce the moaning sound. Then who can make it? Is it made by the wind? *Christabel* rejects this possibility because the wind is not even so strong as to move the light coil of her displaced lock of hair that plays on her cheek. Nor is it strong enough to move the single solitary red leaf that hangs loosely and lightly on the topmost twig of the oak tree and dances rapidly whenever there is a gentle breeze. Hence it becomes clear to Christabel that the moan she hears is not produced by the wind.

The mysterious moaning sound which Christabel has heard makes her heart beat with a lurking fear of evil. She prays to Christ and Man', the mother of Christ, to protect her from all harm. She makes a sign of the cross and crosses her hands under her cloak, in order to ward off evil effect. Then with soft footsteps she goes to the other side of the oak tree. The object that she sees there makes her wonderstruck.

In this stanza, the poet easily and smoothly and in artistic manner gives us an idea of the atmosphere of horror and supernaturalism in which Christabel finds herself under the oak tree at the dead of night. It is a very vivid and graphic picture a minute observation of nature. But this something natural has been given a supernatural and weird significance. The natural is made to look like supernatural. Writing about this stanza, a modern critic has very finely observed: "It is the game of the art of pressing realism into the service of Fantasy, making realistic details of description, not picturesquely telling so much as suggestive of queerness, grotesqueness and extraordinariness of the scene, all gathering into a total impression of something weird and enchanted round us."

L. 58-68. There she sees........beautiful exceedingly. There Christabel see a very beautiful maiden wearing a white silken dress which is shining dimly in the moonlight. Her neck is of such exquisite whiteness that it make her white silken dress appear slightly gloomy and pale in contrast with it. Her majestic neck, her feet in which the blue veins are clearly visible and her white arms are naked. She is bare-footed. She were no sandals on her tender feet whose blue veins are shining clearly through the white delicate skin. The beautiful gems, entangles in her hair are shining with gaiety. The poet thinks that Christabel must have been frightened on seeing a lady, so richly dressed and of such rare beauty, there at that hour of the night.

This stanza is important for three things. First, white colour is associated with noble things, almost divine. Secondly, blue blood flowing through the blue veins implies a noble descent. Finally the use of 'wildly glittered' and 'frightened' suggest horror.

L. 104-111. Then Christabel stretched........father's hall. On hearing the pathetic tale of the strange lady, Christabel move with pity. She gives her hand to Geraldine and consoles her. Then she say to her soothingly, "O beautiful lady! all the things that we have are at your disposal. Sir Leoline and all his brave knights will be at your service. He will send them and his other friends with you to see you back safe in your noble father's house.

Christabel fail to see any evil design behind the proposal of Geraldine to help her. Her miserable plight arouses sympathies of Christabel and as a high-born lady she offeres her courtesy and sympathy. In' this stanza we get a good insight into the delicate inborn kindness of Christabel and the readiness with which she extends her sympathy to someone in misery.

L. 123-134. They crossed the.......were not in pain. The two ladies crosses the ditch that is round the castle. Then they reach the gate of the castle. There *Christabel* take out a key that fits the lock. At once she open a little door in the middle of the gate. The gate is covered with strong iron plates inside and outside. It is so wide that an army in battle order an pass through it. Just as they are to enter. Geraldine, who is so long walking slowly and laboriously, sink down on the ground, as if she is in pain due to extreme exhaustion. The poet here hints at the superstition of the Middle Ages that "evil spirits may not enter a house without help from a mortal." With all her strength, Christabel lift Geraldine, who is like a heavy weight and take her across the threshold of the gate. As soon as Geraldine crosses the gate, she begin to walk on with ease, as if she suffers from no pain.

This stanza reveals three remarkable qualities of Coleridge. First, his knowledge of medieval architecture is very accurate as is shown by the description of the castle. Secondly, he has made a profound study of the psychology of a criminal. Finally, he possesses a good knowledge of people's belief in evil spirits and in the manner how these spirits act when they enter the abodes of innocent persons like Christabel.

L. 135-144. So free from....glad they were. Christabel and Geraldine crosses the courtyard of the castle. They are glad that at last they are free from danger and fear. Then very religiously and sincerely, *Christabel* says to the lady by her side. "Thanks to the holy Virgin Mary, who has freed you from danger." In reply, Geraldine says, "Alas, alas; I cannot speak for I am tired." Thus free from danger and fear, the two ladies are glad to have cross the courtyard of the palace.

Geraldine is an evil spirit. So, like Christabel, she can not pray to Virgin Mary. Hence instead of saying "Amen" to Christabel's prayer, she only said, "I cannot speak as I am tired." Herein lies the poet's art of realistic or psychological treatment of the supernatural.

L. 145-153. Outside her kennel....mastiff bitch ? The two ladies passes by the old bitch, which lay fast asleep outside her kennel, in the cold moonshine. She do not open her eyes, but when Geraldine passes by her with Christabel, she make an angry howling sound. What could be her trouble that she howles like that and she has never done so before in the presence of Christabel! Perhaps, it is in response to the hoot of a small owl. Besides this, there is possibly nothing that can trouble the old bitch.

The bitch seems to have been endowed by the poet with a supersensitiveness to the presence of supernatural things. She has howled in answer to the tower clock because she has seen the ghost of Lady Leoline. She give out an angry growl when Geraldine, an evil spirit passes by her side. But the poet mystifies us. He throws a veil over the yell of the bitch. The suggestion that Geraldine is an evil spirit is very faint and mysterious. The bitch have growled on hearing her pass or on hearing the hoot of the owl. We are left in doubt about Geraldine and the mystery about her is not cleared by the poet.

L. 154-165. They passed.......the sleepeth well. The two ladies passes the hall. Though they walks very softly, yet the hall resounds to their footsteps. There in the fireplace the logs of wood has all but burnt out. Only a few half burnt ends lay on the ashes of the burnt pieces.

But when Geraldine, the evil spirit, passes they suddenly flickeres and give out a sudden flash. In the temporary light thus produced, Christabel sees only the evil glare in Geraldine's eyes and the bright raises knob in Sir Leoline's shield which hung on the wall in a dark corner. Christabel request the lady to walk softly lest they shall awaken Sir Leoline, whose sleep is always light.

In this stanza, we have again a subtle suggestion of the presence of the supernatural. Instead of saying point blank that Geraldine is an evil spirit and a witch, Coleridge simply suggests this idea by the sudden burst of flame of the burnt pieces of wood as Geraldine passes by them. Coleridge here secures the reader in "the suspension of disbelief which is the essence of poetic faith" by placing the normal (the knob of Sir Leoline's shield) side by side with the abnormal (the evil look of Geraldine). As both are seen in the sudden burst of light, belief in the possibility of the abnormal is made possible by the sight of the normal. Christabel sees the eyes as well as the knob and this the poet wishes to sound a timely warning to Christabel against the danger to which she is exposed.

L. 166-174. Sweet Christabel....the chamber floor. In this stanza, the poet gives a graphic description of the stealthy entry of the two ladies in Sir Leoline's castle. Christabel remov the sandals from her feet so that no noise is produced by her footsteps. She feares that even if the air stirres a little, it will transmit the least possible noise to her father's room and he will wake up. Thus with the extreme caution of a thief, the two ladies passes from stair to stair, now in light and now in shade. While passing by the room of Sir Leoline they held their breath as still as death. Sir Leoline is fast asleep and his sleeping room is as silent as death. Finally, they reaches the door of Christabel's bedroom. On reaching there Geraldine presses down with her feet the rushes spread on the floor of the room.

L. 175-183. The moon shines........an angel's feet. In these lines, the poet gives a beautiful description of Christabel's room which Christabel and Geraldine have just entered. Although the moon shines dimly in the sky, its beams does not enter Christabel's room. They can see the beautiful artistic designs of the room in the light of the lamp which hung within, fasten with a double silver chain to the feet of a carved angel in the ceiling. The ornamental designs with which the room is adorned are elaborate and of a fantastic kind. They are the outcome of the artist's own imagination and are quite appropriate for the sleeping room of so young and romantic-looking a lady as Christabel.

L. 184-189. The silver lamp....the floor below. The silver lamp in Christabel's room is giving out a very dull and dim light. So Christabel put its wick in order and it begin to burn brightly. It begin to swing to and fro. Some times it throw light on the face of beautiful Christabel and some times on that of Geraldine. The lamp in the way is brought to light the two opposites-the innocent Christabel and sinister Geraldine. The latter find herself in a very miserable condition and sink down upon the floor below. Her misery is probably due to the fact that she feel afraid at the thought of evil that she has intended to do to Christabel.

L. 190-193. O weary lady....of wildflowers. Like a good hostess, Christabel tries to pull up the spirits of the seemingly weary Geraldine. She offeres her a refreshing wine saying that it will work like a tonic in her present state of exhaustion. She adds that the wine possess wonderful powers of refreshing a tired person and has been distilled by her mother from wild flowers.

The use of the word "virtuous" has a special significance. It has been made by Christabel's mother "who was goodness incarnate." Will such a wine work upon Geraldine, who is an agent of the Supreme Evil? Will she like to take a wine which possesses virtuous and not evil powers?

L. 194-203. And will your ...she were? Geraldine asked Christabel, "Will your mother pity me who is an abandoned and miserable maiden"? Christabel heaving a sigh, replies, "Alas, my mother died at the time of giving me birth. I have heard that she has told the grey haired priest who has attended her on her death-bed that she will hear the castle bell strike twelve on the day of my marriage." The memory of her dead mother made *Christabel* wild with grief. She cries almost like a child in great despair saying, " I wish she was alive and present here," Hearing this, Geraldine says: "I also wish the same thing."

Geraldine being a witch knows that Christabel's mother is dead. Still she asks whether Christabel's mother would pity her. She asks this question only ascertain if Christabel still thinks of her dead mother and invoke her aid in protecting her.

Geraldine's reply, "I wish that she was alive and present here" is perfectly hypocritical. She actually wishes her dead. Her words are ironical. Humphrey House writes that Geraldine must be wishing to say: "To hell with her, she have made all my plans fail. Let her lie in her grave for ever, it's good that she is dead."

Christabel's mother has told the friar on her death-bed that she will hear the castle-bell strike twelve on Christabel's wedding day. This meant that she will be present on the night of her wedding as a spirit. Her spirit can not find rest and will keep hovering about until she see her happily married. It is not altogether improbable, therefore, that here is a suggestion of the wicked design of an evil spirit, who can assume any sex, on Christabel's chastity. But this design is defeat by her guardian-spirit, the ghost of her mother, who keeps a protective watch over her and does not allow any harm to come to her.

L. 204-213. But soon with.... 'tis given to me'. Immediately after that Geraldine see the ghost of Christable's mother appearing before her eyes The ghost which is the guardian spirit of Christabel has been wandering in the air to protect her daughter from the evil designs of Geraldine. As soon as Geraldine see the ghost, the sympathetic tone of her voice changes to one of hateful defiance. Then addressing the spirit of Christabel's mother, she ask it to leave the castle at once. She conjure her to waste away, grow thin and vanish altogether. She further says that midnight is the time appointed to the power of evil to work its ways. As such, she tells the spirit that she possess the power to drive away the good spirit of Christabel's mother.

When Geraldine speaks these words, her eye balls moves wildly. It is because she has seen the disembody spirit of Christabel's mother and looks worried. In a hoarse voice she repeats that though the spirit is the guardian of Christabel, yet at that time Christabel is fully under her influence. She adds that the evil hour of the night is entirely hers and hence the good spirit must move out of sight.

The clue of the theme of the poem seems to be given in these dark words of Geraldine driving the mother's spectre away with her sinister spell. The interest of the poem is centred upon a conflict between the disembodied love of a dead mother and the wicked spell of a witch-like woman, in which, no doubt, love is destined to win, for as the poet assures us, 'the blue sky bends over all.'

L. 226-234. And thus....in bed I lie.' The tall lady Geraldine stands straight and address the following words to Christabel:

"Pure and innocent Christabel. All the angels and good spirits who live in heaven love you. Being holy you also love them. Beautiful maiden, I will do all that is within my' powers to repay you partly for the sake of good spirits and partly for the sake of good that you have done to me. But now, you should undress yourself in order to go to bed. As regards myself I must pray before I go to sleep."

Geraldine's desire to pray before going to bed shows that she is still hesitating to do harm to Christabel. There is a conflict going on in her mind whether she shall harm her or not. Another interpretation is that her prayer is a pretence. By pretending to pray she wants to be silent to work up the charm to harm Christabel.

L. 245-254. Beneath the lamp....sweet Christabel! Geraldine is kneeling beneath the lamp which is burning in the room. It seems as if she is praying. But actually speaking, she is working the charm to harm Christabel. Her eyes are rolling around. The rolling of the eyes has been interpreted in two ways. She looks around because she is still afraid of the presence of the good spirit of Christabel's mother. By rolling her eyes, by looking in this way she is diffusing the spell. Most probably even now there is a conflict in her mind whether she shall harm Christabel or not. Then heaving a long sigh., one like that trembles with fear she unfasten the belt from beneath her breasts. Her upper silken garments and the woven underwear fell to her feet. Thus half her side and bosom became fully exposed to sight. It is too horrible a sight to be described in words. It can only be imagined. The poet prays to the holy spirits to protect the beautiful and innocent Christabel from all harm at the hands of Geraldine.

There have been a number of conjectures about Geraldine's breast. The poet, Shelley thought that she has eyes in her breast. Coleridge wrote to Southey: "It seems that Hazlitt from pure malignity has spread about the report that Geraldine is a man in disguise."

An anonymous pamphlet pronounced Christabel, "The most obscene poem in the English language." Young writes, "Coleridge deliberately excites expectant horror and then enhances it by leaving the sight unexplained." The poet is too great an artist to describe a horrible sight. So he only says that the naked breast of Geraldine presents such a weird sight that it can be better imagined than described. But his prayer to holy spirits suggests that here is something horrible in the breast of Geraldine.

L. 255-264. Yet Geraldine.... wel-a-day ! Neither did Geraldine speak, nor did she move in the least. It seems as if the conflict in her conscience has paralysed her for a while. Though she is an evil spirit, yet she feels the pricks of conscience that makes her hesitate to work evil on a chaste and innocent lady, who has done her so much good. She seems to lift with a weak attempt the heavy load from off her breast. In other words, she appears to overcome her weakness and mental conflict. She fixes her eyes on Christabel for a while, but still she hesitates to do her harm. Then suddenly, the evil in her triumph; she feels the pricks of her conscience as a challenge to her evil nature and pride. She, therefore, shake off her weakness, gathers her strength and lay down by Christabel's side. Then she takes Christabel in her arms. This makes the poet sympathise with Christabel, and he says, "O! What a great sorrow!"

The whole of this scene has unquestionably genuine horror in it and a psychological treatment of the supernatural. It is these qualities which makes Coleridge so great a poet, the greatest poet perhaps, of the supernatural.

Taking Christabel in her arms, Geraldine with a dismal look and in a low voice speeke to her as follows: "There is a charm in the touch of my bosom, Christabel. It will cast a spell on your speech and you will not be able to speak a word of what has happened . This night you will know about this mark of my shame and sorrow which you see on my breast. You will remember it in future, but if you try to talk about it to others, you will not be able to do so. You will only be able to say that in the dark forest you heard a low moaning sound and found there a lady of exceptional beauty, whom you brought home due to love and kindness in order to protect her from the bad weather.

L. 302-310. A star hath.......wood and fell! In this stanza, the poet gives a vivid description of the relief seen in outward Nature as soon as the allotted hour of Geraldine's spell is over. During that period Christabel lay in trance locks in the arms of Geraldine. During that period, She is completely in the power of Geraldine, who does to her what she pleased.

While Christabel thus lay in the close embrace of Geraldine, all the birds of the night hold their breath in horror.

Now it is morning and the star which is so long seen above the western horizon sinks and another stars rises in the eastern horizon. In other words the time of the night passes. With that the evil star set and the propitious star appeares. That is the time of the witch, Geraldine. She cast her spell while that time lasts. The allotted time being over, Christabel is released from the embrace of Geraldine and she recovers from her trance. Geraldine's spell that has cast its influence on nature, too being now over, the owls and the night birds begin to hoot joyfully from rocks, towers, lakes and forests.

L. 311-318. And see ! the ..... sudden light ! During the night, Christabel is in a kind of trance under the influence of Geraldine's charm. In the morning, she slowly recovers from her trance. Her limbs: slackens and her face became sad and soft. Her soft, thin eyelids, which remains open because of the mental tension during the trance, now relaxes. They drop softly on her eyes. So the large tears which stood in her eyes during the trance, rolls down her cheeks. The tears, however, makes the eyelashes bright. Now and then for a moment, she seems to smile like small children when they suddenly see some sweet vision.

L. 319-33 1. Yea, She doth....bends over all ! Some times Christabel smiles and some times she weeps. Thus her tears and smiles alternate. She looks like a beautiful young female ascetic, who always prays whether asleep or awake. If she moves restlessly now and then, it is not on account of some bad dreams, but, perhaps due to the rush of warm blood to her feet, which causes a thrilling sensation.

The poet is confident that during her sleep, Christabel has a happy dream. Perhaps in her dream, she has a vision of the guardian spirit of her mother, who kept constant watch over her well being; or perhaps she feel conscious of the presence of her dead mother near her in order to protect her from all evils. Whatever the case may be, the sense of sorrow and pain that has overtaken her under the spell of Geraldine is gone. Now she feels quite confident that in sorrow as well as in joy, saints help men if they are prayed for. She firmly believes that all men live under the love and protection of God, in the same way as they live under the wide expense of the blue sky.

L. 332-337. Each matin bell...... his dying day ! Sir Leoline says that each stroke of the morning bell takes him a step further back into the world of death. These words are first spoken by him when he rose in the morning and find that his wife is dead.

In the medieval church, the bell is rung early in the morning. It is usually a call to prayer and marks the beginning of the day's activities. But Sir Leoline interprets the ringing of the church bell in a totally different way. To him it is a sad reminder of death and the sorrow that comes in its wake, ever since that morning which find his wife dead. So deep is the sorrow he feel at the death of his wife that the words he speake first about the ringing of the church bell are apt to be spoken by him till the day of his death. To him the morning bell of the church has a special significance. It reminds him of death and not of morning prayer.

L. 338-344. And hence the....to Wyndermere. It is early in the morning when the church bell is ringing that Sir Leoline finds his wife dead. Due to this extraordinary circumstance, he pass the order that the person who ring the church bell must count forty-five beads on his rosary. He must say 'Hail Mary' forty-five times between the strokes of bell. Thus between each stroke of the bell there is to be an interval of about forty-five seconds. The ringing of the church bell in this manner remained a custom for some time, but then it became so well established that it acquires the force of law. The change manner of the ringing of the bell is when some one dies. There are not even one person living from Bratha, where the river Brathay rises to the lake Wyndermere' into which it falls, who do not hear the ringing church-bell in the morning.

L. 345-359. Saith Bracy...from Borodale. Sir Leoline's bard or court-singer, Bracy who uses to hear the ringing of the morning bell, says: "The morning bell is rung solemnly and by a sleepy sexton who counts the beads of his rosary very slowly. As such the interval between the strokes of bell increases. But this matters little because during the time the bell is silent a similar sound comes from the valley of Great Langdale, Witch's Lair and Dungeon Ghyll. The other sound is the knell rung by the ghosts of the three sinful sextons, who for neglecting duties during their lifetime have been punished by being confined within the mountain region of the three valleys. As ghosts, they use rosaries of rocks and bells of air. They ring the knell in response to the morning bell is rung by their living companion, the sexton of Sir Leoline. As soon as they finish ringing their sad notes one after the other, the Devil, very often as if displeased by their death-notes mocks at their sorrow with a peal of joyful laughter from Borodale over the hills and far away.

Langdale Pike, Witch's Lair and Dungeon Ghyll are landmarks in Grasmere. The poet by mentioning these places and Borodale which is a valley in Cumberland, gives a realistic touch to the poem. By doing so, he detracts from it the sense of mystery and delightful vagueness which marks it in the beginning and which is the most enthralling aspect of the poem. Hence many critics of the poem find fault with the localisation of the scene of the poem.

L. 360-369. The air is still !....rested well. In the peaceful atmosphere of the morning, the Devil's peal of happy laughter resounds loudly. Geraldine hears it and being an evil spirit gets rid of all fear. She begins to feel sure that the guardian spirit of Christabel's mother, which has disturbed her the previous night, will not be able to do so again. Then she rises quietly from the bed where she has been sleeping with Christabel. She puts on her white silken dress and arranges her hair in beautiful plaits. She entertains no doubt about the effect of her spell on Christabel. She is definite that Christabel is still under control of the power of the charm which she has cast upon her last night. She then says to Christabel : "Are your still sleeping? I believe you have enjoyed a sound sleep and good rest during the night."

L. 370-386. And Christabel....lively leave behind. *Christabel* awake and she see Geraldine before her. To her Geraldine appears more like the lady she has rescued from distress while she is under the oak-tree in the forest than like the one who has slept by her during the night. Now Geraldine look much more beautiful because like Christabel, she too, has been refreshed by the sound sleep which she has enjoyed at night. While Geraldine talks to Christabel, her looks and her manner seems to express her deep gratitude to Christabel. At the same time her breasts rising and falling with her breath seem to fill her undergarment and make it tight. In such a state Christabel see Geraldine standing before her. When she goes to sleep with her on the previous night she has thought that she has commuted a sin by entertaining such an evil woman and by submitting to her embraces. But now when she see Geraldine standing before her and looking so innocent and beautiful, she feel that she has been unjust in her fears regarding Geraldine. Whatever may have been the case, she still feel confused and fail to decide whether she has done a right or a wrong thing. Her condition is like that of a person whose uncommonly happy dreams leave him in a confused state of mind. Then in a low and weak sweet voice she accosts the beautiful and dignified lady Geraldine.

L. 408-426. Alas! they had been.. ..once hath been. The poet feels sorry when he writes about the relationship of Sir Leoline and Lord Roland. In their young age they are bosom friends and very faithful to each other. But false rumours have the power to rend as under the strongest bonds of love and destroy the fidelity between friends. And this happened in the case of Sir Leoline and Lord Roland. The false rumours set afloat by mischievous persons sows the seeds of discord between the two intimate friends. The poet explains its reasons and tells why it is so. He says that constant faithfulness between two persons is not a thing of this world. Abiding loyalty exists only in heaven and is very rarely find on earth. Life in this world is beset with difficulties and complex problems. Young men are proud. They are so confident of themselves that they are apt to be rash and inconsiderate. When they become angry with the person they love, their minds become unhinged and unbalanced. There is no enmity as strong as the one which comes between those who are very good friends. So it happens in the case of Sir Leoline and Lord Roland. They, who are once very intimate friends, became victims of false rumours and turns into sworn enemies of each other. They bade adieu to their friendly relations and parted, never to meet again.

The poet then describes the manner of their parting, as he thinks it happen. Under the adverse influence of the false rumours, the two friends, who are more dear to each other's heart use very rude and insulting words for each other. Then they are parted and are never reconciled though each feel sorry for the loss of his friend. Neither of them can find another friend who can remove the pain of the heart which has been made void by loss of a true friend. Separated from each other, the two powerful men stand like two mighty peaks which has been torn as under, and between which a gloomy stretch of water flows. Just as a gloomy stretch of water flows between the two peaks, the same way a sea of hatred has surged and swells between the two men. Like the cliffs torn asunder they, too, carry the marks of separation. They always remain conscious of the bitter pain caused to them by parting. The poet thinks that although two bosom friends may part with violent anger, coldness of heart and hot exchange of words, the former strong attachment and feelings of deep love which they have for each other as friends can never come to an end. Off and on they must remind of their mutual affection and grieve at their separation.

These lines contain a reference to Coleridge's temporary estrangement with Charles Lamb, and also to his break with Robert Southey. The personal note introduces here has been criticised as inappropriate to the theme and the manner of the poem. But Coleridge himself regard these lines as the "Sweetest and best lines" that he has ever written. They bring about a reconciliation between Coleridge and Lamb in 1800. Byron like these lines so much that he prefixes them to his Farewell to Lady Byron. But despite their great beauty, they have been criticised for the personal emotion expresses in them, as being not in harmony with the romantic context. "They are like a patch of cloth of gold let into a lace garment and straining the delicate tissue till it tears."

L. 427-446. Sir Leoline, a moment's space...child of his friend! For an instant Sir Leoline stand utterly confouded and looking at Geraldine who has suffered very badly at the hands of five ruffians. He remembers once again Lord Roland who has been the friend of his youth. He recalls happy days when he enjoys the sweet company of Lord Roland. Then, under the influence of indignation, rises by the way his friend's daughter has been treated by the five warriors who abducts her. Sir Leoline forget that he is an old man. His noble heart is filled with a very strong feeling of revenge against the ruffians. He swere by the wounds on the body of Christ who dies on the cross that he will proclaim their guilt in every part of the country. For this purpose he will send a herald blowing a trumpet and making a solemn proclamation in accordance with the code of Chivalry of the Middle Ages. The herald will proclaim that the five warriors who abduct Geraldine are as mean and hateful as dishonour is stained with sin. In case, they are bold enough to deny the charge level against them, the herald will allow them a week's time, at the end of which those guilty men who has wronged Geraldine and who has disgraced themselves by breaking the rules of chivalry will have to come to the tournament court in Sir Leoline's castle. The Baron swere that as soon as they will reach there, he will kill them and thus he will drive out their poisonous souls from the human bodies which they do not deserve to inhabit. When Sir Leoline utters these words, his eyes flashes and rolls in awful anger, he is roused partly because the ruffians has very cruelly seizes Geraldine, but mainly because she is the daughter of his friend.

L. 447-456. And now the tears...sights to see? Sir Leoline is so moved with pity for his friend's daughter, Geraldine, that tears come to his eyes. He, then very lovingly embraces Geraldine. She responce to the affection thus show to her by embracing the Baron as lovingly as he has embraced her. Moreover, she hold Sir Leoline in her arms for a longer time than usual. Her joy at this act of hers can be seen in her eyes because they shine brightly. In fact, her eyes shows the evil gleam of conquest which now she achieve by holding the Baron in her arms. Christabel, who is standing there, see a vision of something fearful in that embrace. She is reminded of that cold embrace which has given her much pain on the previous night. The recollection of that embrace make her move backwards and shiver with fear. The poet sympathises with Christabel and laments at her lot. He thinks that it is really a very sad thing that a pure and gentle maiden like Christabel shall see such shocking and horrible sights. What she see now is a repetition of the ugly vision of Geraldine's bosom and said, "a sight to dream of, not to tell."

L. 457-462. Again she saw....one that prayed. Once again Christabel is reminded of the touch of Geraldine's bosom when she has lain herself down by her side and taken her in her embrace on the previous night. Once again she is reminded of the cold touch of that bosom. This so terrifies and agonises her that she gasps loudly, making a sound like that of a snake. When the Baron hear that queer sound, he frees himself from Geraldine's embrace and turns round angrily to see what the matter is. But he do not find anyone except his own dear daughter with eyes raises towards heaven as if she is praying.

L. 463-469. The touch the....smiles like light ! Christabel's disturbs state of mind and body did not last long. The gruesome vision of Geraldine's bosom which is "a sight to dream of, not to tell," and which she has seen the previous night, when Geraldine has disrob herself, soon vanishs away. The painful memory of the cold touch of Geraldine's bosom which she has experienced while laying beside her in her arms passes away from her mind. Now in the place of that terrible vision, Christabel see the sweet vision of the guardian spirit of her mother which she has witnessed after waking up in the morning. This happy vision fill her heart with a sweet, delicious delight and the sense of rapturous pleasure thrills her to the very core of her heart. Her excessive joy is clearly visible on her face because a sweet smile come to her lips and her eyes begin to shine brightly.

The hissing sound which has escaped from Christabel's lips, and her attitude of prayer, has surprised Sir Leoline. Soon a new feeling of wonder come over him when he sees her smiling in joy on seeing the happy vision of her mother's guardian spirit of which the Baron know nothing. He ask her loving daughter what the cause of her trouble is. In reply, Christabel can only say that everything will be all right ultimately even in spite of what has happened. The poet thinks that so powerful is the spell exercised over her by Geraldine that she can not say anything else beyond that. Though she has a very strong desire to reveal to her father the true nature of Geraldine, yet the spell cast over her by Geraldine is the "Lord of her utterance," making it impossible for her to say anything more.

L. 475-482. Yet he, who..., her father's mansion. Geraldine has observed Christabel very minutely. As a witch, she can divine her feelings. She knows that Christabel dislikes and feel a strong repulsion for her and wants her to go away from the castle. On the other hand, Sir Leoline entertain a very good opinion of her. He regards her as a very gentle and pious lady who combines in her excessive sorrow and uncommon beauty. He take her to be a gentle and bless person in whose manner there is a strange mixture of kindness and sorrow. To him she appears sad and at the same time kind. All these feelings which the Baron has for Geraldine are not foreign to her. The supernatural powers which she possess makes her acquainted even with the inner working of the minds of Christabel and Sir Leoline. With a view to taking advantage of the Barons's soft feelings and posing innocent of Christabel's thoughts, Geraldine begains her afresh. Assuming a look of anxious enquiry on her face as if to know whether she has displeased Christabel in any way, Geraldine in a very soft and gentle voice requests the Baron that she will be immediately send to her father's home. Sir Leoline refuses her request saying that it is not possible. He feel that his first duty is to inform Lord Roland that his daughter is safe.

L. 519-563. The lady fell,........loiter there.' Sir Leoline asks his bard to convey the following message to Lord Roland: "I swear by my honour that when I meet Lord Roland, I will say that I must regret for that day when I speak insulting and contemptuous words to him. Ever since that evil, inauspicious day, when I lost a friend, many years have not found a true friend like Lord Roland."

When Geraldine hear the message to be delivered to her father, she fall at the feet of Sir Leoline and clasps them. Her face is lift up and her eyes are full of tears. This attitude of Geraldine has been interpreted in two ways. It is probably out of gratitude to Sir Leoline for sending the message that she clasps his knees. But probably with her uplifted face and overflowing eyes, she wants to move the Baron's heart so that she may be able to prolong her stay in his castle.

On hearing Sir Leoline's command, Bracy greeting with kindness all the people present, addresse the following words to Sir Leoline in a soft voice, because he fear that what he has to say, will not be liked by the Baron.

"O father of Christabel! Your message by virtue of its magnanimity is sweeter than what it will be even if I sing it to the accompaniment of the sweet music of my harp. Still I beseech you to grant me the favour of postponing my journey to Lord Roland's castle today. The reason why I am requesting you for the posponment of my journey is that I see a very horrible vision in a very strange dream last night and I have taken an oath to clear the nearby forest of the evil influence haunting it."

Bard Bracy has an ominous consciousness of some impending danger. He has sensed some evil influence in the vicinity of the castle. Hence he wants to go on his mission to Lord Roland only after purifying the vicinity with loud singing hymns.

Bracy describes the dream that has filled his mind with grave suspicions and apprehensions. He says to Sir Leoline, "I dreamt of the dove which you love so dearly and which you call Christabel after the name of your own dear daughter. I dreamt that the bird is all alone among the green plants and trees in the forest. It is flapping its wings and giving out a very painful cry. When I see the dove and hear its fearful moaning sound, I fail to understand the cause of its agony because I can see nothing near it except the green grass and green plants under the old tree where it was lying."

In Christian mythology dove is a symbol of purity and innocence. As represents in the Bible, it stands for Divine Spirit which come down to earth in the form of a dove.

The snake is a symbol of evil and falsehood, as the dove is of purity and innocence. The bright green colour of the snake stands for the false and attractive outward appearance which evil things have to tempt men.

After describing the dream, Bracy tells of other details connects with it. He says: "I woke up from my dream. Then it is midnight and the clock in the Tower was striking the hour of twelve. Although I am awake, yet I can not forget the dream. The vision which I see in the dream is still present before my eyes. Hence I swear that this very day I will wander through the forest where the trees have shed their leaves, singing holy songs and producing loud music to remove the influence of an evil thing if it is there". In these words Bracy describe his dream and tell his reason for not going to Lord Roland's castle that day.

Bracy gives a correct interpretation of his dreams. To him the dove stands for Christabel and the green snake for some evil power. He feels that Christabel is going to be harmed by some unholy power, though he does not know what this power is. It is possible that he finds some connection between the evil power and Geraldine who has appeared in the castle in inauspicious circumstances and whose beauty and tale of sorrow fail to produce any effect on him. He is not moved by Sir Leoline's sentimental memories of broken friendship. One thing which deserves special notice is that the time of Bracy's dream is the same as that of *Christabel*'s meeting with Geraldine:

L. 564-582. Thus Bracy said....shield her well ! Sir Leoline has his own interpretation of Bracy's dream. To him Geraldine is the dove and the ruffians who abducts Geraldine are the snake. He, therefore, pay only a little attention to what Bracy says and smile scarcastically. He then looks at Geraldine with eyes full of surprise and love. He tells her in the polished language of courtesy, "O beautiful maid: O lively dove of Lord Roland: Your father and I have more power than that of music and song to kill the snake." When he speak these words, he kisses the forehead of Geraldine. She, in a manner befitting a maiden or with a maidenly show of shyness directed her large and shining eyes towards the ground. She blushes and with a fine show of courtesy turns herself away from Sir Leoline at whom she has been looking till then. Very gently she gathers the long folds of her dress, that traill the floor and places them again on her right arm. She crosses her arms on her breast and loweres her head on it out of modesty and shyness. While standing in that posture, she throw at Christabel a side-glance full of hatred and distrust, which makes her much distressed. The poet prays to Jesus and his mother Virgin Mary to protect her from the threat contain in Geraldine's look.

Bracy's dream has been interpreted differently by different persons. The bard suspects some harm to Christabel from an evil power. The Baron has his own notions and interpretation of the dream. To him the dove is Geraldine and the snake is the symbol of the ruffians who has tried to kidnap her. Only Christabel and Geraldine understand the true meaning of the dream. By introducing the dream and by its vagueness and suggestiveness, Coleridge very skilfully produces the sense of horror and tries to maintain the atmosphere of mystery and supernaturalism with which the poem is commenced.

L. 583-596. And snake's small....on Sir Leoline. Here the poet tells us how Geraldine's eyes looks when she directs them towards Christabel and what effect they produces on her. Geraldine's large and bright eyes sank into their slits and become the small blinking eyes of a snake. They are full of hatred but the fear in them is greater. The hate is for Christabel. The fear is caused by the thoughts that Christabel may confirm Bracy's suspicions. Geraldine's eyes became like those of a snake for a moment only, but during that brief space of time they carry so much hatred and venom in them that they send Christabel into a giddy stupor. Her feet became unsteady. She trembles so violently as if she will fall, and make a hissing sound. Thus having brought Christabel under her control once again, Geraldine turns towards Sir Leoline as if she is anxious for relief from some deep affliction. Then her eyes which has become for a moment small and snake-like eyes on Christabel that she stands in a stupor. She has lost all her power of thinking. She sees nothing but the hateful eyes of Geraldine.

Kathleen Royds says: "Here, as to Part I, the description is not so much of the sight that Christabel beholds as of its effects on her and thus it takes possession of the imagination with a sense of horror all the stronger from its vagueness."

L. 598-612. The maid, alas!. ..innocent and blue ! The very expression of malice and venom which is present on the face of Geraldine can now be seen on the face of Christabel. The poet fails to understand how Christabel who is so free from deceit and sin can assume such a look but it is decidedly there on her face. Giving its reason, the poet says that so powerful has been the influence of Geraldine's look on her that it is now fully reflected on her face. In other words, the look of dull and treacherous hate in Geraldine's eyes has made such a deep impression on Christabel's mind that instinctively without her being aware of it, a similar look is now clearly visible on her face. It seems to have been forced from her by a sympathetic reaction to circumstances in which she is, because she herself by her very nature is incapable of it. Presenting a likeness to Geraldine's treacherous face to the extent to which it can register itself in her blue and innocent eyes, Christabel stand in a giddy stupor in the full view of her father.

L. 636-655. Within the Baron's ...the lady Geraldine ! What Lady Leoline has prayed do not come to be true. The Baron remains silent probably because his mind is filled with this and other thoughts connects with his daughter. But even if such thoughts about his only child has any place in the Baron's heart and mind, they only serve to create a confusion there and increase his anger. He feel enraged because he is requested by his own loving child to send away his friend's daughter. His heart is broken on the one hand, by anger; and on the other, by a feeling of pain caused by his daughter's ingratitude. His suppress anger made his cheek tremble and his eyes red. He feel dishonoured in his old age on being asked by his own daughter to send away a lady who as his friend's daughter has a claim on his hospitality but is thus insulted. He feel that the disgrace done to him is based on nothing else but Christabel's womanly jealousy for Geraldine. Thoughts as these enhances his indignation and looking very angrily at the gentle bard he speake to him in a sudden and harsh voice: "Bracy, why do you linger here? I have commanded you to go from the place quickly." As the bard obeys and left the place, the old Baron turns away in anger from his own dear daughter and in anger and defiance give his arm to Geraldine and go out of the Presence-room.

L. 656-677. A little child,...-it's most used to do. In these lines the poet generalises the reaction of a father's mind to anger and pain on being dishonoured by his own child. The poet says that a little child is an active fairy'. It sings and dances by itself. With its red round cheeks, it is a beautiful thing to look at. The child finds a joy in everything and everywhere. So it never stands in need of the search of happiness. It is so full of unbounded gaiety that it always presents a beautiful sight to the eyes and fills the eyes of its father with the light of pride and joy. The father's love for the child goes on increasing till its abundance brings him to a stage when he becomes severe and harsh to child. Very often this harshness is not intended at all. This is proved by Sir Leoline's conduct towards his daughter. It is only due to his excessive love for her that he severely condemn her request and went out with Geraldine, in utter disregard of her request.

The poet says that it is a very strange thing that such opposite feelings of love and harshness exist side by side in the heart and are complementary to each other. This we find in the case of Sir Leoline. He speak angry wo~ds and mock Christabel because the charm or attraction of their mutual love has come to an end. He favour Geraldine because her real nature being unknown to him, he can not see any harm in entertaining her.

(G) SELECTED UNIVERSITY QUESTION WITH ANSWRES ON *CHRISTABEL*

GOOD AND EVIL; ALLEGORY; THEME

Q.1. *Christable* represents the eternal conflict between the forces of good and evil. Would that be the correct estimate of the theme? Discuss.

Or

How far is *Christable* an allegorical poem in which the struggle of evil and innocence is examined for the purposes of moral realization of the manner in which evil works upon and transforms innocence?

Or

***Christabel*: is an allegory showing the working of evil on an innocent mind. Critically examine this statement.**

Ans. In *Christabel* Coleridge is concerned with a generalised theme-the problem of the inter-action between the forces of good and evil in human life. *Christabel* apparently embodies the invulnerable innocence of unflaw goodness-invulnerable because the innocence possess a spiritual second sight by means of which they can see into the very heart of things and of men. The good lady has perfect confidence in the protecting arms of angels:

But this she knows, in joys and woes,
That saints will aid if men will call
For the blue sky bends over all:

That beautiful and affecting picture of Christabel as she resigns herself to prayer may be regarded as the personification of perfect goodness. The affiliations of that picture with the many representations of Christian saints are probably intentional. The ordeals and agonies through which *Christabel* is obviously intended to pass are also the counterpart of the saints' experiences.

The impression that unseen presences mount guard over the innocence and the meek virtue of Christabel is conveyed by means of natural incidents suggestive of a supernatural purport. The remark that "the thing attempt in *Christabel* is the most difficult in the whole field of romance: witchery by daylight" indicates the peculiar quality of the supernatural element in the poem. In the *Ancient Mariner* daemons and angels and spirits bodily appear on the scene and take a hand in the shaping of the action: the skeleton-ship and its weird shipmates, the navigation of the ship by the dead bodies of the crew, the miraculous movements and final scuttling of the ship are all palpable forms of the supernatural control of human destiny. In *Christabel* nothing so obviously supernatural appears or happens. The poet has cunningly devised a number of incidents, slight, ordinary, natural in themselves, but somehow indicative of a phantom shape. The only thing almost openly weird-'preternatural', as Coleridge refer to it-is the suggested serpent form of Geraldine. The wickedness or evil nature of Geraldine is expressed through psychological suggestions.

Geraldine cannot cross the threshold of the castle. She sink down and it is only with the help of Christabel that she can cross it. The fact is that the threshold of the castle is sprinkled over with holy water and Geraldine, being an evil spirit, dare not cross it. When the two enter the castle, Christabel asks Geraldine to pray to Virgin Mary, but the latter being an evil spirit cannot pronounce the sacred name, she avoids doing so under the pretence that she is too tired to pray. The old mastiff bitch of Sir Leoline gives deep angry moans as soon as Geraldine, the evil spirit, enters the hall. It is the first time that the bitch has behaved in this extraordinary manner. Again the brands in the hall are almost dead (quenched) and instead of flame there are only ashes. But as soon as the evil spirit Geraldine comes the dying brands flash out tongues of flame towards her. This indicates that a supernatural evil creature has entered Christabel' s palace.

When Christabel trims the faintly burning lamps of the hall, Geraldine begins to faint. She being an evil creature cannot bear light. That Geraldine is an evil spirit has been further suggested by the fact that when Christabel tells her that her mother at the time of her death have proclaimed that she will come to hear the wedding bell of Christabel's marriage, Geraldine says in an altered voice :

> Off, wandering mother! peak and pine
> I have power to bid thee flee.

Then the poet dramatically exposes the bosom of Geraldine. The tense scene at the end of the first part of the poem brings to a sharp focus the sinister quality of Christabel's guest. Notice the combined deliberate and shuddering reluctance of Geraldine on the point of undressing herself,

> Beneath the lamp the lady bowed,
> And slowly rolled her eyes around,
> Then drawing in her breath aloud,
> Like one that shuddered, she unbound
> The cincture from beneath her breast...

There is a hush of expectation in the reader as he proceeds to the description of the garments dropping down and then the most subtle suggestion of something shockingly deformed:

> A sight to dream of, not to tell!
> O shield her! shield sweet *Christabel* !

The suggestion is sharpened by the defiant, incantatory words of Geraldine :

> In the touch of this bosom there worketh a spell,
> Which is lord of thy utterance, *Christabel* !

The nature of the mark of her shame, of the seal of her sorrow is left undefined and all the more awe-inspiring. In the words of Professor Vaughan, "It is of the essence of the poem not to feed the mind with facts, still less with gruesome facts, but to spur the imagination by a sense of mystery."

In Part II, the evil Geraldine begins to operate within Christabel herself. When Geraldine is embraced by Christabel's father, Christabel makes a hissing sound. Then Bracy tells his dream about "a bright green snake coiled around" the neck of a dove-

> And with the dove it heaves and Stirs,
> Swelling its neck as she swells hers !

Here it seems as if Christabel and Geraldine-innocence and evil-are held in a precarious kind of balance. It seems Geraldine covets the identity of Christabel and Christabel has unconsciously assumed something of the evil identity of the other. Christable feels herself becoming the image of evil :

> With forced unconscious sympathy....

Evil thus works on an innocent mind-slowly but steadily. In the beginning, Geraldine needs Christabel's' cooperation to work on her but Christabel gradually imbibes a little evil till at the end of the poem, as it exists, she has lost her own free will.

But the poem is incomplete; we cannot just guess how it would have been completed. We can make an evaluation of the theme of good and evil only insofar as it is worked out in the fragment.

Q.2. How far is martyrdom the theme of *Christabel* ?

Ans. It is difficult to interpret *Christabel* on one level because it is too fragmentary.

There are three accounts of how *Christabel* is to have been completed. The Gillman and Derwent Coleridge accounts are almost identical.

The shorter Gillman account says : "The story of *Christabel* is partly founded on the notion, that the virtuous of this world save the wicked. The pious and good Christabel suffers and prays for 'the weal of her lover that is far away' exposed to various temptations in a foreign land; and she thus defeats the power of evil represented in the person of Geraldine. This is the main object of the talc."

The Derwent Coleridge account also says that the sufferings of Christabel are to have been shown as vicarious, endured for her 'lover far away', for 'the holy and the innocent do often suffer for the faults of those they love and are thus made the instruments to bring them back to the ways of peace'. According to this, Christabel goes to the forest because he had dreams all yesternight of her own betrothed knight/And she in the midnight wood will pray/For the weal of her lover that's far away..

Christabel's encounter with Geraldine brings her intense suffering. Her guardian spirit, the spirit of her dead mother is driven away. She is put under a spell so that even in a moment of extreme suffering she cannot speak. At the climactic moment, she makes a hissing sound like a snake and her eyes wear a serpentine look that suggests that she has also absorbed some of the evil. Finally she is discarded by her father, Sir Leoline, who leads forth Lady Geraldine. Thus Christabel is shown to gradually move towards a kind of martyrdom. In Table Talk, Coleridge has written that Crashaw's poem on the martyrdom of St. Teresa directly influenced the writing of the second part of Christabel. Crashaw 's heroine experienced an alienation from her home and family similar to Christabel's except that she is prepared for it, whereas Christabel least expected this form of suffering. Christabel, however, suffers voluntarily with an understanding that the saints above will protect her, 'for the blue sky bends over all'.

Geraldine, according to this interpretation, does not represent the power of evil, she is 'no witch or goblin' or malignant being of any kind, but a spirit who acts as an unwilling instrument of Christabel's martyrdom, obliges to perform her mission in the name of those 'who live in the upper sky'.

There are some objections to such an interpretation. There is nothing in the poem to substantiate the idea that the vicarious suffering of Christabel is for the redemption of her absent lover. It is only from external sources like the two accounts of how the poem is to be finished and Coleridge's Table Talk that such an idea can be entertained. Furthermore, though there is a suggestion in part I that Geraldine is at the mercy of some influence not quite herself, there are also hints to show that she is unequivocally evil. She cannot cross the threshold unaided; she refuses to pray: the mastiff bitch makes an angry moan when she passes by her: the fire embers give a tongue of light and a fit of flame; she drives off the spirit of Christabel's dead mother. These are clear pointers at her evil nature. In Part II, her evil qualities certainly dominate. It is possible that Coleridge may have intended to bring about Geraldine's transformation from an evil to a good thing and to develop a moral theme of goodness suffering for the salvation of the wicked. However, nothing very definite is indicated anywhere.

Thus to consider *Christabel* a story of martyrdom is not warranted by the text.

SUPERNATURAL ELEMENT

Q.3. How is the supernatural element used in *Christabel*?

Or

Discuss Coleridge's mastery over the art of mixing the unreal and the real with reference to *Christabel*.

Ans. *Christabel* is a tale of terror, and it is the skill of Coleridge that makes it rise above other specimen of this genre, even though it is a fragment.

Apt Atmosphere. Knowing that a tale involving the supernatural will no be effective in a contemporary setting, Coleridge places *Christabel* in the distant Middle Ages. We have the medieval castle, the superstitious beliefs of those days, the chivalrous element. Into this medieval setting and atmosphere Coleridge breathes the subtle breath of the supernatural. It is never described at any length. It is but barely suggested, unlike the practice of his contemporaries who revelled in drawing minute details. The object here is plain. The poet gains immensely in power; a hinted horror, which allows full play to the imagination of the reader, is usually far more effective than a described one; just as an unexplained ghost-story terrifies far more than one of which the solution is given.

Gradual Build up of Atmosphere. The atmosphere is gradually built up. Ordinary details are accumulated to weave a mysterious texture. The old toothless mastiff bitch responds in a set manner to the hours struck by the castle clock. We are gently told that "some say, she sees my lady's shroud". Thus the supernatural element is introduced. Then come the lines

> Is the night chilly and dark?
> The night is chilly but not dark.

This has an incantatory effect. The reader is led to accept the slight distortion in the behaviour of various natural objects. The thin grey cloud "covers but not hides the sky". The moon is full but "she looks both small and dull". The cock crows along with the owl's hooting. It is all "as if proportion is thrown out and normal vision perplexed", as Humphry House says. The setting has been built up in which the supernatural will seem real.

Suggestiveness of Evil. Who does not feel the terrible effect of the use of suspense in the story? Christabel goes out into the woods to pray. She kneels beneath the old tree, but springs up suddenly. A moan has disturbed her, 'but what it is, she cannot tell.' The art of the poet in keeping us in suspense is here most evident, for, instead of proceeding to describe the search made by Christabel, he lingers to describe the scenery once more. Then comes the picture of lovely Geraldine with her obviously improbable story of abduction. But we feel no sense of disbelief "Jesus, Maria, shield her well!" says the poet. The supernatural is thus well anticipated and struck by keeping the reader in suspense.

Supernatural dread is again well suggested in the angry moan of the old mastiff and the sudden shooting of 'a tongue of light, a fit of flame, from the brands that burn in the hall. The very air seems to listen to their tread as Christabel and Geraldine mount the stair. Thus step by step we are led on from one anticipation of horror to another till it culminates in two incidents. But again, with his usual reticence, Coleridge, instead of describing them, leaves us to gauge them from their effects on the persons present on the scene. The first is the appearance of the ghost of Christabel's mother to Geraldine alone. Her name has been mentioned, and the witch quietly, but hypocritically wishes she is there; and lo! there she is; but neither we nor Christabel know that she is there, until we listen to the low perturb voice of Geraldine, who bids her be off. With suggestive art the poet speaks of the witch as staring before her with unsettled eye, and poses the questions, "Can she the bodiless dead espy?" "And why with hollow voice cries she, 'off, woman, off! this hour is mine'?" The other, at the mere recitation of which Shelley is said to have shrieked and fled from Byron's room, is the very climax of the poem. Geraldine unrobes herself; Christabel who cannot sleep looks on till she sees

> A sight to dream of, not to tell!
> O shield her! shield sweet *Christabel*

None of us can tell what that sight of shame or anguish reveales to Christabel. But it haunts us as it haunts Christabel all through that night and ever afterwards, although her lips are sealed and she can not unburden herself of the anguish by an open avowal of it. An interesting point here is the omission of the line "hideous, deforms, and pale of hue", which we are told on oral authority, originally stand after the line

"Behold her bosom and half her side." This will have described the horror, which Coleridge did not want to do. An unspoken horror is indeed more terrible than a spoken one.

Sense of Mystery. To add to the effects of the supernatural, Coleridge makes use of mystery also in the poem. He raises a number of questions in the intelligent reader, and leaves them unanswered. What law of the spirit world has *Christabel* transgressed that she shall come under the spell of the witch woman? Was Geraldine really a witch, or did she only seem so to *Christabel*? The angry moan of the mastiff bitch and the tongue of flame that shot up as the lady passes are they omens, or accidents which popular superstition interprets into omens? Is the malignant influence which Geraldine exert over the maiden supernatural possession, or the fascination of terror and repugnance? Did she really utter the words of a charm, or do Christabel dream them? And once more, what is that upon her breast "that bosom old- that bosom cold"? Is it a wound, or the mark of a serpent, or some foul and hideous disfigurement or is it only the shadows cast by the swinging lamp'? We ask ourselves these questions, but we cannot answer them. That is also part of the charm of Coleridge's art in the poem.

Plausible. The poet thus succeeds in rousing supernatural dread. But how does he make it plausible? Surely, by his suggestive art; but that is only one way. Coleridge definitely tells us that the supernatural is to make natural 'by transferring from our inward nature a human interest and a semblance of truth sufficient to procure for these shadows of imagination that willing suspension of disbelief, for the moment, which constitutes poetic faith.' Is the story, which is like a fairy tale, as Coleridge admit it, anything like real life? Has it any elements which make it approximate to reality? Can we suspend our disbelief and say it is quite likely that this thing may have happened. Prof. Dowden supplies the answer: "In *Christabel* the human and the supernatural elements interpenetrate each other more completely and more subtly than in The *Ancient Mariner*. The presence of higher than mortal power for evil and for good is everywhere felt, yet nowhere is thrust forward. We can reconstruct a story almost the same in which the incidents shall proceed in accordance with the acknowledged laws of the world : we can imagine an innocent girl coming under the influence of a woman older than herself of beautiful person and powerful intellect, but of depraved character, who shall disclose to her some bosom-sin under conditions which render indispensable for a time an inviolable secrecy; to shield the maiden from harm she shall possess, besides her own purity of heart, the pious memory of her dead mother. Thus by merely lowering the key all the action of the poem may be transported from the supernatural to the natural. Even the malign influence of Geraldine's look askance can readily be translated into its moral significance the fascinating power of evil over a virginal soul, the mere knowledge of vice seeming to imply a horrible communion with it during, at least, one dreadful moment before the instinctive recoil from sin has had time and force to come into operation" Coleridge's story is much more than this; but we may thus interpret the moral and psychological truth on which Coleridge's story is founded. The poem is not a piece of didactic morality, and yet it is founded in spiritual truth, and, as Christopher North has said, while we read it, we are all the while in our own real and living world, and in the heart of its best and most delightful affections.

MEDIEVALISM

Q.4. Write a critical note on Coleridge's use of medievalism in *Christabel*. How does it enhance the artistic effect of the poem?

Or

How far does the medieval setting in *Christabel* authenticate the supernatural events?

Ans. Medieval Setting: Suitable for Supernatural. Sir Walter Raleigh says that 'romance' throws over us the 'magic of distance.' Ordinary events and experiences, if seen through the glamour of a distance of time or circumstances, assumes a charm which is defined as romantic. This is exactly what Coleridge has done in *Christabel*. Though we cannot exactly place the events of the poem in any, particular century, yet we are not far wrong in associating them with that vaguely defined extent of period known as the middle Ages. It is an age of chivalry, of bold barons and bad knights, of virtuous maidens and glamorous ladies, of courtesy, piety and witchcraft as well. We are required in the poem to look back through several centuries at this remote period. This distance from our own times lends a glamour to the characters and incidents of the tale.

Details of Medieval Setting and Characters. The setting is definitely medieval. We have a Norman castle with its moat, its tourney court and its great gate "ironed within and without, where an army in battle array has marched out", a feudal baron with a retinue, a lady who steals out at midnight into the moonlit wood to pray for her betrothed knight; a sorceress who pretends to have been carried off on a white palfrey by five arm men, and who puts a spell upon the maiden. Pages, grooms, bards and heralds lend a medieval atmosphere to the poem.

Foreboding Dreams. Christabel's dream which leads her to pray in the woods is a medieval touch. Bracy's dream is also very much in the medieval tradition. It is commonly believed in that age that good and wise people get knowledge about the presence of evil spirits beforehand through dreams. Bracy's dream is symbolical. In his dream he has seen Sir Leoline's favourite dove in the grip of a green snake, coils round its body, and the dove fluttering and uttering fearful moans. The dove symbolizes Christabel and the green snake. Geraldine. Regarding his dream to be a real one, he decides

With music strong and saintly song
To wander through the forest bare,
Last aught unholy loiter there.

But Sir Leoline fails to understand the real significance of the dream and identifies the dove with Geraldine, and the green snake with those warriors who has seized her.

Age of Chivalry. In the poem the medieval atmosphere is strengthened by the mention of Sir Leoline's chivalry. It is a tradition in the middle Ages to offer help and chivalry to a woman in distress. Christabel in the same way, offers help and her father's chivalry to Geraldine who is seized by five warriors and left there all alone in the midnight.

In the medieval times women are held in high esteem and it is regarded very mean and cowardly to harm them. Men of honour hates such people. When Sir Leoline listens to the sad story of Geraldine he becomes very angry and even forgets his age. He plans to proclaim it far and wide that those warriors who has thus wronged her are base and wicked men. And if they dare deny this charge he will himself fight with them and kill them. Tournaments are very common in those days where great warriors use to come to show their valour and skill, and fight a duel to prove their truth and honour.

Superstitions and Piety of the Age. We have its faith and its superstition too. The poem is steeped in the simple faith of the Roman Catholics, their entreaties and supplications of Jesu, Maria, their prayers to the saints and their belief in guardian spirits who will listen and aid those who call upon them. There are the superstitions about the gate being guarded by good angels, about animals detecting the presence of evil by instinct. About the ghosts of the dead walking about in the hour of midnight, etc. These again contribute to the old-world atmosphere of the tale.

Medieval Art. Sir Leolione's castle is appropriately decorated in medieval style. It has courts, halls and chambers and flights of stairs. Carved figures of angels adorn Christabel's chamber. The floor is carpeted with rushes. It is the setting of the Middle Ages.

Subdued Light Helps Evoke Distant Past. The absence of strong colours serves to throw a mist over the events of the story. The light is everywhere subdued. As Dr. Bradley has analysed it: "The air, in Shelley's phrase, is woven out of moon-beams' and they are not the beams that lit the bay. A thin grey cloud is spread on high, and, though there is a full moon, it looks small and dull. In its light Geraldine's silken robe, itself colourless, shines shadowy and though the gems entangled in her hair glitter wildly, they flash no tints. The light in the hall, as the flame flickers for a moment from the white ashes, shows no gorgeous hues of tapestries on the wall, it just glimmers on the boss of the shield in a murky niche. The carven work in Christabel's chamber is faintly seen by the light of a silver lamp."

Archaisms. In the poem there is hardly a single word which is not perfectly simple, and yet the whole phrasing is full of the antique. Take such words as "yestermorn," phrases as "right glad they were", "with sick assay," to say nothing of the constant succession of phrases in the style of the old ballads, like "All in the middle of the gate," "Did thus pursue her answer meet". It will be obvious that these constant echoes of old fashion phraseology, never jarring because never too obscure, are basic to the charm which the poem exerts over every reader with some taste.

Conclusion. The medieval setting makes the supernatural events seem probable. Distancing of the atmosphere gives an aura of reality. It is a major method of inducing a willing suspension of disbelief in the reader.

FRAGMENTARY NATURE

Q.5. *Christabel* is all "fragmentary and finally unsatisfying because it leads up to a mystery which is both incomplete and clueless." Do you agree?

Ans. Coleridge intend *Christabel* to be a long poem in five parts, but for some reason or the other he do not complete it. As the poem exists, it has only two parts and is obviously incomplete.

Unmatching Styles. According to Coleridge himself the first part (L.1-331) is written in 1797 and the rest in 1800. The scene of the poem is not defined in the first part but it is fixed in the second in the Lake district with which Coleridge make acquaintance in 1799 with Wordsworth. In Part I there is the castle in the woodland, with oak and moss and mistletoe, a landscape which has its function only in relation to the persons and the atmosphere. There are no proper names but those of the three main persons. In Part II we plunge straight into the detail geography of the region. Wyndermere, Langdale Pike, Dungeon ghyll,

Borodale and the rest organize the reader's attention as if this are matter of history rather than of imagery.

The experience of reading the First part of *Christabel*, says Humphry House, is more an acquaintance with an atmosphere than the apprehension of poetic unity. This atmosphere is achieved partly through description of the setting, partly by the mystery surrounding Geraldine. At point after point in *Christabel* descriptions are used to heighten the mystery by such suggestions of slight distortion in behaviour or of contrast, or surprise. But it is all fragmentary and finally unsatisfying because it leads up to a mystery which is both incomplete and clueless. To a great extent this is true.

Three Possible Developments. Three accounts of how the poem is finished have survived. The two shorter ones are vague, but indicate that Christabel's sufferings 'are represented as vicarious, endured for her "love far away". The third and longest account is much more detailed. In it, Geraldine assumes by supernatural transformation the outward appearance of the absent lover and pays court to Christabel, who not unnaturally senses something amiss. Nonetheless, to oblige her father, she obediently 'consents to approach the altar with this hated suitor'. At this point the real lover returns. The baffled Geraldine then disappears and they all sort themselves out after the joys of rightful marriage. This, however, is so pronounced a piece of Gothic extravagance that critics are divided on whether to take it seriously or not. However, even if in general it elevates its tawdry tradition, the poem undeniably belongs to the literature of a Gothic cult, and characterizes by its flesh-creeping terrors and supernatural happenings in a setting of ruin abbey or castle.

Incomplete but not Unsatisfying. In *Christabel* the struggle of evil and innocence is examined, although within the framework of the typical tale of terror, for the purposes of moral realization of the manner in which evil works upon and transforms innocence. Coleridge's success in achieving this realization by poetic means is due to a dramatic tension building up to a final, irrevocable climax and skilfully regulated by its background of symbols from the natural world, says Charles Tomlinson. The climax of

> And turning from his own sweet maid
> The aged knight. Sir Leoline,
> Led forth the lady Geraldine....

leaves Christabel in that condition of pathological isolation which the Mariner also feels and which Coleridge must himself have known. If one feels a certain incompleteness about the poem it is because we are left with Christabel's pathological isolation which is never, unlike that of the

Ancient Mariner, to be resolved. The 'story', of course, is never completed and the elements concerning the broken friendship between Sir Leoline and the father of Geraldine, relevant as they are to the poem's theme of the division of the inmost being and of the most intimate relationship, are never knit up into a more organic significance. *Christabel* offers, however, despite its abrupt conclusion in psychological stasis, a completeness concerning what do happen, if only we pay attention to the premonitory nature of the symbols at the opening and see the poetic interest as centering on the uncertain balance which is represented here between health anti disease, good and evil, and the end as à tragedy in which neurosis, not death, strikes the final blow. *Christabel,* being bewitched, suffers simultaneously with the disintegration of personality, the disintegration of the will.

In *Christabel* the disease condition of the moon links suggestively with the inability of Christabel's dead mother, her guardian spirit, to operate in her defence. This symbolic use of the moon to reinforce the presentation of a psychological condition is characteristic of Coleridge's natural effects. The disease moon prepares us for her transition from a condition of organic innocence to one of complete division. What is the nature of this division and how has its appearance developed' in the poem? The development, it shall be noticed, takes place through instances of what happens to Christabel rather than what she does; evil works upon her and by the time she feels possessed by it and with force unconscious sympathy, perhaps even becoming evil herself, she has lost her own free will.

To begin with, Christabel finds herself alone. Her lover is absent, her mother dead, her father sick. Here is the position of the typical persecuted woman of the tale of terror, defenceless and vulnerable, her isolation being intensified by its juxtaposition with the fine image of 'the one red leaf, the last of its clan.' In this condition Christabel finds the Lady Geraldine who, according to her own story, has been abducted, then abandoned, and takes her into the castle. Coleridge conveys Geraldine's character of fatal woman in a cumulative series of startling touches. Coleridge gives the situation an adds uncertainty by withholding from us as yet Geraldine's exact intentions. Indeed, whatever they may be the fatal woman, aware of her own fatality seems half to regret what she is about to do. But as she lies down to sleep beside Christabel, she has put by all her scruples. They sleep and the suggestions crystallize into a final irony:

> ....lo, the worker of these harms,
> That holds the maiden in her arms,
> Seems to slumber still and mild
> As a mother with her child.

Christabel has lost her natural father and has found an unnatural mother: the guardian spirit has been worst. The important final image of this passage of the sleeping mother embracing her child comes to mind once more when we hear Bracy's dream of the same night.

In Part One the ground has been prepared: in Part Two the evil of Geraldine begins to operate within Christabel herself. Geraldine, 'nothing doubting of her spell/Awakens the lady Christabel'. Christabel has, on the level of the conscious mind, reassures herself and sees her tormentor as 'fairer yet, and yet more fair!'. But her unconscious fears become conscious once more as her father embraces Geraldine and the latter prolongs the embrace 'with joyous look':

> Again she saw that bosom old
> Again she saw that bosom cold
> And drew in her breath with a hissing sound.

It is the hiss of a horrified intake of breath, but its significance becomes deepen when Bracy the Bard tells his story and with what follows. This moment is one of the most startling and suggestive touches in the poem. We are recalled by the image to that of the two sleeping together; we see in the movement of the snake an attempt to imitate that of the bird as well as to prevent its flight: we remember that the sound Christabel herself may resembled that of a snake. Just as the full moon that is dulled, holds in a frightful balance the image of health with the image of disease, the latter overpowering the former, so now there is a further frightful balance: we are on the brink of the suggestion that the identity of Christabel is coveted by Geraldine and that Christabel has unconsciously assumed something of the evil identity of the other. We come to the most important dramatic climax of the whole, when Geraldine is kissed by Sir Leoline and the significance of Bracy's dream is jestingly ignored by the knight. Our worst suspicion is now confirmed by what follows:

> But Christabel in dizzy trance,
> Stumbling on he unsteady ground
> Shuddered aloud, with a hissing sound.

She shudders with horror still, but she emits the sound a snake will make. Her imagination is so overpowered by 'hose shrunken serpent eyes :

> That all her features were resigned
> To this sole image in her mind...

And not only does she see the image, she feels herself becoming the image.

The idea has rooted itself in her mind. Despite this fact, she still fights against Geraldine's spell by asking her father to send her tormentor away, instead of which he 'leads forth the lady Geraldine' symbolically rejecting his own daughter.' There is an extremely dramatic propriety about this incident as sickness and evil move off together.

One might note finally that Coleridge makes use of the old and familiar material of folk tale: the ageing ruler ignores his wise counsellor, rejects his 'natural' daughter and perfers the unnatural. None of the protagonists in Coleridge's narrative is in him or herself complex; all are stock figures and therefore mere allegory and J.F. Danby, speaking of 'King Lear where Shakespeare uses the same fable, calls 'the unambiguous Morality statement' (Shakespeare's Doctrine of nature). One is compelled to see the characters as symbols relating to every man's condition of inner psychological tension, the evil preying on the good, the sick undermining the health which brings one to the fact-that Coleridge's poem, is limited though it is by its inability to resolve the conflict, presents an extremely individual variant on this basic pattern.

Conclusion. There is no doubt that *Christabel* is of a fragmentary nature. But it is, all the same, a great poem. It is "incomplete and clueless", as Humphry House says, but it is also what Byron called it—'a fine, wild poem".

METRE

Q. 6. Write a note on the metrical art of ***Christabel.***

Ans. When Scott hear Sir' John Stoddart recite, Coleridge's yet unpublished *Christabel,* he is at once struck by the metre and is so haunted by its rhythm that he tries to adopt it for his 'Lay of the Last Minstrel, . The metrical system is in some sense original, and Coleridge took some points to explain it "I have only to add", he writes in his Preface "that the metre of *Christabel* is not, properly speaking, irregular ,though it may seem so from its being founded on a new principle: that of counting in each line the accents, not the syllables. Though the latter may vary from seven to twelve, yet in each line the accent will be found to be only four. Nevertheless this occasional variation in the number of syllables is not introduced wantonly, or for the mere ends of convenience, but in correspondence with some transition in the nature of the imagery of passion."

There are two things to be noted in this metre-first, the number of syllables in each line varies on a very large scale, i.e., from seven to twelve; and secondly, "the light, ample cadence of the anapaest is introduces with delicate felicity among the shorter measures." It has been said that in none of these characteristics can Coleridge claim any originality for the principle of counting the accents and not the syllables is taken to be a revival of the Anglo-Saxon four-stress line with two half lines of two stresses each. But the analogy is more apparent than real, for the essence of the Anglo-Saxon metre is its scansion on alliterative principle quite as much as on accentual.

As regards the anapaestic bias, it is true that eighteenth century poets has used it but always with a jocular or satirical effect. "Only Chatterton and Blake", says Herford, "had at moments elicited the melodies which Coleridge elicited from it, but neither approached his range."

An analysis of Coleridge's lines will reveal the subtleties of his metre which none really has been able to recapture. Take the following lines :

> There is not wind enough to twirl
> The one red leaf, the last of its clan,
> That dances as often as dance is can,
> Hanging so light and hanging so high,
> On the topmost twig that looks up at the sky.

The slow iambics in the first line suggest a quiet night. The second is even more drowsy. The spondee, "red leaf', makes the movement slow and halts the fine. The concluding anapaest-"of its clan"—suddenly accelerates the movement, which is carried on to the liveliness. The fourth line is more rapid still, and in the fifth the iambics and three anapaests correspond to the idea of restless movement.

Coleridge shows poetic power of the first rank in making a trochee take the place of an iambic, e.g., "Mary/mother/save me/now", "Off, woman; off! this hour is mine." It is only poets like Milton or Coleridge who can be trusted to modulate irregular verse and to make such irregularities an aid to emotional expression.

11

KUBLA KHAN

OR

A VISION IN A DREAM A FRAGMENT.

The following fragment is here published at the request of a poet of great and deserved celebrity [Lord Byron], and as far as the Author's own opinions are concerned, rather as a psychological curiosity, than on the ground of any supposed poetic merits.

In the summer of the year 1792[2], the Author, then in ill health, has retired to a lonely farm-house between Porlock and Linton, on the Exmoor confines of somerset and Devonshire. In consequence of a slight indisposition, an anodyne has been prescribed, from the effects of which he fell asleep in his chair at the moment that he is ready the following sentence, or words of the same substance, in 'Purchas's Pilgrimage': "Here the Khan Kubla commands a palace to be built, and a stately garden there unto. And thus ten miles of fertile ground were includes with a wall'. The Author continued for about three hours in a profound sleep, at least of the confidence, that he could not have composed less than from two to three hundred lines; if that indeed can be called composition in which all the images rose up before him as things, with a parallel production of the correspondent expressions, without any sensation or consciousness of effort. On awaking he appears to himself to have a distinct recollection of the whole, and taking his pen, ink, and paper, instantly and eagerly wrote down the lines that are here preserved. At this moment he was unfortunately called out by a person on business from Porlock, and detains by him above an hour, and on his return to his room, found to his no small surprise and mortification. That though he still retains some vague and dim recollection of the general purport of the vision, yet, with the exception of some eight or ten scattered lines and images, all the rest has passed away like the images on the surface of a stream into which a stone has been cast, but, alas! without the after restoration of the latter!

Yes from the still surviving recollection in his mind, the Author has frequently purposed to finish for himself what has been originally, as it is, given to him. Eaμepov aow aew: but the tomorow is yet to come.

As contrast to this vision, I have annexed a fragment of a very different character; describing with equal fidelity the dream of pain and disease.

(A) TEXT, PARAPHRASE AND ANNOTATIONS

In Xanadu did Kubla Khan
A stately pleasure-dome decree:
Where Alph, the sacred river, ran
Through caverns measureless to man
Down to a sunless sea.
So twice five miles of fertile ground
With walls and towers were girdled round :
And there were gardens bright with sinuous rills,
Where blossomed many an incense-bearing tree;
And here were forests ancient as the hills,
Enfolding sunny spots of greenery.
But oh ! that deep romantic chasm which slanted
Down the green hill athwart a cedarn cover !
A savage place ! as holy and enchanted
As e'er beneath a waning moon was haunted
By woman wailing for her demon-lover
And from this chasm, with ceaseless turmoil seething,
As if this earth in fast thick pants were breathing,
A mighty fountain momently was forced :
Amid whose swift half-intermitted burst
Huge fragments vaulted like rebounding hail,

L. 1. Xanadu—the capital city of Kubla Khan. **Kubla Khan**—the famous Mongol Emperor of China in the thirteenth century. Marco Polo—the Venetian traveller, paid a visit to his court and has left a glowing account of the pomp, power and magnificence. Coleridge was reading a well—known book of travel of the 17th century known as Purchas's, pilgrimage' written by Samuel Purchas which contained an account of Kubla Khan and his magnificent court. He dozed off when he came upon the line "Here the Khan Kubla commanded a palace to be built, and a stately garden thereunto : and thus ten miles of fertile ground were enclosed with a wall." **L. 2. Stately**—magnificent; grand. **Pleasure dome**—pleasure—house; a house to which one retires for recreation or pleasure. Dome actually means a structure raised above the roof of large buildings usually hemispherical; a cupola. Here, by a figure of speech it means the building itself. **Decree**—ordered or commanded to be built. **L. 3. Where**—at the point where. **Alph**—the name of this river is a coinage of the poet. He probably had in view two rivers both sacred and flowing underground. The river Alpheus, referred to in Milton's *Lycidas*, is well—known in classical myth and legend. It rises in Arcadia, the ideal region of pastoral poetry. The other river is the Nile venerated by the Egyptians through whose land it flows. **L. 4. Caverns**—deep gorges or hollow places in the earth. **Measureless to man**—of abysmal depth; so very deep that it could be hardly measured. **L. 5. Sunless sea**—deep gloomy waters of the sea. **L. 6. Twice five miles**—i.e. 10 miles. The space enclosed is ten miles square

PARAPHRASE OF THE POEM

L. 1-10. In the capital city of Xanadu, Kubla Khan orders a magnificent pleasure-house to be built for himself. It is erected on the site where the holy river Alph flowed into the dark waters of the sea. The river in its long course, flows through abysmal gorges whose depth could hardly be measured. The chosen site covered a spacious ground, ten miles square. It is enclosed with walls and towers and was rich in vegetation. There are fine gardens inside the walls through which flows sparkling streams in their zig-zag courses. There are a large number of spice plants in full blossom. Part of the ground is covered with forests, old as the hills. Every where, and there inside those forests are beautiful sunlit glades.

L. 11-30. A deep, marvellously beautiful gorge ran down the green slope of the hills shelters by tall cedar trees on either side. It is too beautiful for words. It is a grim and awesome spot. It had an eerie and sanctified look as if under a magic spell. It thus seems to provide the right kind of setting under the waning moon for a woman in love with a demon to come out mourning plaintively for her absent lover. Through the gap in the earth a huge jet of water gushed out every now and then foaming

---

or ten square miles; the phrase by itself however does not make the meaning clear. **Fertile ground**—land rich in vegetation. **L. 7. Girdled round**—fenced around, walled in. **L. 8. Bright...rills**—traversed by streamlets, with their sparkling water. **Sinuous**—zig-zag; winding. **Rills**—streamlets. **L. 9. Blossomed**—flowered. **Incense-bearing tree**—aromatic plants spices bearing tree. **L. 10. Ancient as the hills**—the usual form of simile of old as the hills, i.e. of time immemorial. **L. 11. Enfolding**—enclosing within their confines. **Sunny spots**—places bathed in sun—light. **Greenery**— verdure. Spots of greenery means green grass covered glades in the midst of forests. **L. 12, Oh!**—that was too magnificent and marvellous to be described—this is the significance of the interjection. **Romantic**—Strangely beautiful and magnificent. **Chasm**—a deep hollow, fissure or gorge on the surface of the earth. **Slanted....hill**—sloped down the rock—face covered with verdure. **L. 13. Athwart**—across. **Cedarn cover**—a sheltering forest of cedar trees. The cedar is a large evergreen tree remarkable for the durability and fragrance of its wood (Chambers). **L. 14. Savage**—grim and horrible. **Holy**—sacred, sanctified. **Enchanted**—under a magic spell. **L. 15. Waning**—on the decline (with reference to the phases of the moon. Its opposite is "waxing"). **Haunted**—frequented as if by ghosts and spirits. **L. 16. Wailing**—mourning plaintively. **Demon lover**—demon with whom the woman had fallen in love. **Demon**—an unearthly being. **L. 17. Ceaseless**—perpetual. **Turmoil**—rush and roar of waters. **Seething**—boiling; here foaming and gurgling up from the rocky fissure. **L. 18. Fast thick....breathing**—heaving forth the breath in heavy and quick gasps. **L. 19. Mighty**—of huge dimensions. **Momently**—every moment or second. **Was forced**—was spouted out. **L. 20. Half intermitted**—i.e. half intermitted or having the shortest possible interval between the jets of water spouting from the fountain. **Burst**—fell down suddenly and violently **L. 21, Fragments**— pieces of rocks or

Or chaffy grain beneath the thresher's flail :
And 'mid these dancing rocks at once and ever
It flung up momently the sacred river.
Five miles meandering with a mazy motion
Through wood and dale the sacred river ran,
Then reached the caverns measureless to man,
And sank in tumult to a lifeless ocean :
And 'mid this tumult Kubla heard from far
Ancestral voices prophesying war !
The shadow of the dome of pleasure
Floated midway on the waves;
Where was heard the mingled measure
From the fountain and the caves.
It was a miracle of rare device,
A sunny pleasure-dome with caves of ice !
A damsel with a dulcimer
In a vision once I saw :
It was an Abyssinian maid,
And on her dulcimer she played,
Singing of Mount Abora.
Could I revive within me
Her symphony and song,
To such a deep delight 'twould win me,

---

boulders. **Vaulted**—hitting the rock and leaping from one point to another. **Rebounding**—bouncing. **Hail**—hail stone. **L. 22. Chaffy grain**—grain and husk mixed together. **The boulders hitting the rock**—face bounded up reduced in part to fragments and in part to powder—resembling chaff and grain. **Threshers**—people who beat the heaps of corn on the threshing floor to separate the grain from the chaff. **L. 23. Dancing**—rebounding from one rock to another. **At once and ever**—all together and all the time. The boulders kept bounding up and down simultaneously all the while. **L. 24. Flung up**—threw up; spouted forth. **Momently**—every moment. **L. 25. Meandering**—wandering in a zig-zag course. **With a mazy motion**—having a winding course. **Meandering....motion**—Tautology, both meandering and mazy conveying the idea. Further there is alliteration on "in" the succession of liquids suggesting flow and murmur of the river. **L. 26. Wood**—forest. **Dale**—the valley through which a river flows. **L. 27. Caverns**—a deep hollow place in the earth, crack, fissure, gorge, ravine in the earth's surface. **Measureless to man**—Of limitless depth. **L. 28. Sank**—flowed into. **Tumult**—roar and rush of waters. **Lifeless ocean**—calm stretch of the water of the ocean. **L. 30. Ancestral voices**—the voices of the departed spirits of his fore-fathers. Ancestor-worship had been for long years a venerable custom both in China and Japan. Propehsying—making forecast; foretelling; predicting. **L. 31. Shadow**—reflection. **Dome of pleasure**—house. **L. 32. Floated**—lay suspended and roaring all the while. It seemed as if the whole earth was heaving thick and fast and spouting out this fountain moment by moment. In the midst of these bursts of water, quickly followed each other, huge boulders came toppling down from rock to rock. They seem like hail-stones which bounce off on hitting the ground. Sometimes by impact they break into little fragments and resembles the chaff of grain which came flying up from the threshing-floor when beaten by the short thick sticks of the threshers. In the midst of all these rocks toppling around all the time, jet by jet the fountain fed the waters of the holy river. The river ran along in its zig-zag course of miles through forest and valley. It then tumbles into a gorge of limitless depth and merges in the end with a great uproar into the calm stretch of the waters of the ocean. In the midst of all the rush and roar of waters, Kubla Khan hears the departed spirits of his ancestors warning him about the wars ahead.

L. 31-36. The pleasure-house cast its reflection on the waves of the sea. It stretchs, as it were, sunk half way below the surface of waters. The place lay within the hearing of the blends music of the fountain and the river as it flows through the caves. The building was a work of marvellous art, of such surpassing beauty, the like of which is never seen on earth. It is surmounted by a dome, lit up by the sun. By way of contrast its halls made of dazzling white marbles and alabaster were refreshing too. They resembles in their whiteness and coolness the "caves of ice".

L. 36-54. The poet once has a vision of a young maid playing on her instrument. She is from Abyssinia and is singing about true romantic charms of her native hill of Mount Abora. The poet wishes he can by some chance rouse within himself the memory of that music and song.

---

as it were. **Midway**—half way below the surface. **L. 33. Mangled**—blended. **Measure**—musical rhythm. **L. 35. Miracle**—here an architectural feat of surpassing beauty the like of which was never seen on the earth. **Rare**—marvellous. **Device**—craftsmanship. **L. 36. Sunny pleasure-dome**—cupola was bright and warm with the sunlight. **Caves of ice**—the halls of the building made of marble and alabaster were cool and white like "Caves of ice". **L. 37. Damsel**—young girl. **Dulcimer**—a musical instrument resembling a flat-box, with sounding board and bridge, across which run wires tuned by pegs at the sides, and played on by striking the wires with a small piece of wood in each hand or more usually with two cork—hammers. **L. 39. Abyssinian**—adj. from Abyssinia, the country in the eastern part of Africa having romantic and legendary associations with the Queen of Sheba who visited King Solomon. **L. 41. Mount Abora**—obviously situated in Abyssinia. **L. 42. Revive**—rouse afresh within me. **L. 43. Symphony**—a composition for full orchestra in several movements. Here used in a sense now obsolete : a purely instrumental portion of a work mainly vocal, i.e., musical accompaniment of the song. **L. 44. To such a deep...me**—it would work me up to such a height of ecstasy.

That with music loud and long,
I would build that dome in air,
That sunny dome ! those caves of ice !
And all who heard should see them there,
And all should cry, Beware ! Beware !
His flashing eyes, his floating hair !
Weave a circle round him thrice,
And close your eyes with holy dread,
For he on honey-dew hath fed,
And drunk the milk of Paradise.

L. 46. I would build...in the air—I would create a new pleasure-house in the air by my inspired gifts of song. **L. 47. That sunny....ice**—including those marvellously beautiful features of the building. **L. 48. And all who heard....there**—i.e., every one who listened to that music will have a vision of that magnificent building in the sky. **L. 49. Beware**—take care of him, be on your guard against him. **L. 50. Flashing**—glittering. **Floating hair**—hair streaming in the wind. **L. 51. Weave a circle....thrice**—draw a circle round him three times as a magic spell so that he may not overstep those bounds to do harm to others. **L. 52. Close your dread**—with an unearthly gleam in his eyes and his streaming hair, the poet looks a strange apparition, like one possessed. He strikes awe and wonder into the hearts of all those who look at him. **L. 53. Honey-dew**—a sugary secretion from the leaves of plants in hot weather. **L. 54. Milk of Paradise**—a fancied heavenly food of the same kind as nectar, ambrosia or manna; equivalent to poetic inspiration.

He can work himself up to an ecstasy in that case. He will then create anew that pleasure-house in the air by strains of music, loud and long. People around him will feel awe-struck at his strange looks. There will be a glow in his eyes and his hair will stream in the wind. They will draw magic circles around him to keep him safe from harm. He will look like one possess who has been filled with divine frenzy of the poet and prophet by eating of the heavenly manna.

(B) INTRODUCTION TO THE POEM

This is one of the three most well-known poems of Coleridge. The other two poems are *The Rime of The Ancient Mariner* and *Christabel.* The other, two poems are based on supernatural incidents. The present poem has nothing directly of the supernatural in it. And yet the poet has succeeded in conveying an impression of something strange and mysterious through his description of a river, a landscape and a pleasure dome.

It is said about this poem that it has came to the poet in a dream. The poet himself has said that the whole poem has come to him while he is in a dream under the influence of opium. Actually he said, the poem is much longer. When he woke up, he is able to write down the fifty-four lines of the poem as they exist. Unluckily he is interrupted by some one who has dropped in just then and has kept him busy for over an hour. When the guest has gone, Coleridge can not recapture the words and the images of the dream. Therefore, Coleridge has regarded this poem a fragment or only a part of what he has to write.

According to Coleridge, this dream is the result of his reading a few lines in a famous book, *Purchas's Pilgrimage.*; He is reading that part of the book where it describes how a famous Asian King names Kubla Khan has commanded a palace to be built. This book may thus be describes as the immediate source of the poem.

According to Coleridge, this dream come to him in the summer of the year 1797. The poem has actually publishes however, in 1816.

As the poem stands, it gives an impression of not only being unfinished but also disjointed. The first impression is that there is hardly any connection between the earlier part of the poem and its later part. On closer study, however, one feels that this poem does make a coherent whole and that the various parts of the poem yields a meaning of their own.

In spite of this fact, however, the fact remains that the poem has a quality of jumpiness about it. The transition from one idea to another is not clear. This: is one reason why the poem has been called a dream poem. In a dream, one set of picture follow another and very often two such sets have only a slight connection which can be established by interpretation when we wake up. Again the description itself has something of the quality of a dream about it.

Most critics have regarded this, poem as an example of "Pure Poetry". They feel that the poem has hardly any meaning in the ordinary sense of the work. Its appeal is purely to the imagination and the senses not to our understanding. Other critics, however, feel that the poem is rich in meaning. Only the meaning is not clearly stated it is suggested.

Coleridge's Account of the Composition of *Kubla Khan.* Here is what Coleridge himself wrote as an introduction to this poem when it is published in 1816.

In the summer of the year 1797, the Author, then in ill health has retired to a lonely farm-house, between Porlock and Linton, the confines of Somerset and Devonshire. In consequence of a slight indisposition, Ananodyne has been prescribed, from the effect of which he has fell asleep in his chair at the moment that he is reading the following sentences in *Purchas's Pilgrimage.* "Here Kubla Khan commands a palace to be built, and a stately garden thereunto. And thus ten miles of fertile ground were encloses with a wall." The Author continues for about three hours in a profound sleep, at least of the external senses, during which time he has the most vivid confidence that he could not have composed less than two to three hundred lines; if that indeed can be called composition in which all the images rose up before him as things, with a parallel production of the correspondent expression, without any sensation or consciousness of effort. On awaking, it appears to himself to have a distinct recollection of the whole and taking his pen, ink, and paper, instantly and eagerly wrote down the lines that are here preserved. At this moment, he is unfortunately called out by a person on business from Porlock, and detained by him about an hour, and on his return to his room, found, to his no small surprise and mortification, that though he still retaines some vague and dim recollection of the general purport of the vision, yet, with the exception of some eight or ten scattered lines and images, all the rest has passed away like the images on the surface of a stream into which a stone has been cast, but, also, without the after restoration of the latter.

This account suggests that the poem as it exists is only a part of a much longer poem of two to three hundred lines. Secondly, it is suggested that the poet, in his dream, see all the images, described in the poem along with the actual words that describs them. He saw the things and also the words which describes those things.

As a result of this account given by Coleridge himself, this poem has always been regarded as just a fragment. It has also been regarded as a dream poem because Coleridge himself said so. Without doubting the correctness of this account, however, it may be asserted that a poem need not be judged even according to the poet's own assessment of it. It is possible to regard this poem as a complete whole.

The Source of the Poem. Coleridge himself has pointed out that he is reading a book when he fell asleep, and that certain lines in this book touches off his imagination. These lines are so suggestive that they give rise to the dream in which the poet see all the images and the words.

The book that Coleridge is reading is called *Purchas's Pilgrimage.* The actual lines in the book which describes the pleasure house built by Kubla Khan are as follows :

"In Xanadu did Kubla Can (Khan) build a stately palace encompassing six teen miles of plain ground with a wall wherein are fertile meadows, pleasant springs, delightful streams, all sorts of beasts of chase, game and in the midst therefore of a sumptuous house of pleasure."

These words are of course different from the words ascribed to this book in Coleridge's account of the origin of this poem. Coleridge is obviously quoting from memory. He only presents his summary of the actual lines of the book.

Of course the actual words of the book do not at all matter. The book only serves to start a process of creation in the poet. This poem is an example, therefore, of the poetic process in which the imagination works.

The matter of fact account in Purchas's Pilgrimage is transformed by the poet into a vision. The vision is followed by the description of another. In the end, the process of creation itself is described by the poet in terms of suggestion and poetry.

(C) A CRITICAL SUMMARY

Kubla Khan orders a splendid pleasure dome to be built where the sacred river Alph ran underground down to a dark sea. These encloses ten miles of fertile grounds with walls and towers. Within these walls are gardens full of fragrant flower trees and old forest enclosing green fields. (Lines 1-11)

A romantic chasm leans out against a green hill that lay across a cavern of cedar trees. It is a savage place-here a woman might have bewailed on a dim moonlit night the loss of her demon lover. A mighty fountain throws out jets of water every moment, and scatters fragments of stone like grains under the rod of the thresher. Amidst these dancing rocks the sacred river Alph take its rise and wound its zig-zag course through woods and valleys for five miles until it reaches the caverns measureless to man down to a lifeless ocean. Here Kubla Khan hears his ancestors prophesying war. The shadow of his pleasure dome rested on the middle of the river. It was a palace of wonder-a sunny pleasure dome with caves of ice. (Lines 12-36)

The poet see an Abyssinian maiden playing on a dulcimer and singing of mount Abora. If he can recall the maiden and that song, he will build a similar dome in the air, and whoever hear will call upon men to beware of his flashing eyes and floating hair. They will weave a circle round the poet and close their eyes in fear. For the poet has fed on honey-dew and he has drunk the milk of Paradise. (Lines 36-54)

(D) CRITICAL APPRECIATION, INTERPRETATION AND DEVELOPMENT OF THOUGHT

Development of Thought

***Kubla Khan's* Sunny Pleasure-house.** Kubla Khan orderes a pleasure-house to be built at Xanadu. Alph River ran through underground caves to the dark sea. So ten miles of land are enclosed by walls. There were gardens with zig-zag streams; there are trees with flowers having sweet perfume. There are ancient forests as old as the hills. Also there are sunny spots of greenery.

Noise of River Alph and Ancestral Voices telling of Wars. There is a romantic chasm full of cedar trees. It seems a magical place, where in moonlight, a woman might come weeping over her ghost-lover who has broken her heart.

From this valley, a fountain of water has gushed out of the ground every moment. This burst of water throw up stones, which looks like hail or chaff being scattered around. This fountain is the source of River Alph, which for some miles ran underground and then fell into the silent sea.

In the midst of this noise of water and waves, Kubla heard from far, ancestral voices prophesying war.

Sunny Palace with Caves of Ice. The shadow of the pleasure-house fell mid-way on the waves of the river. It is a strange miracle-a sunny pleasure dome with caves of ice.

The Magic of the Girl's Music. Once the poet saw in a dream, an Abyssinian girl playing on her dulcimer (musical instrument) and signing a song of Mount Abora. If the poet could recall that song, he with the power of music create the sunny pleasure-dome with caves of ice.

People will think him to be a magician, who has eaten honey dew and drunk the milk of Paradise (Heaven).

Critical Appreciation

Contrast With the Other Two Great Poems. Kubla Khan is one of the three great poems of Coleridge. It is the shortest but in some ways the most remarkable of the three. It differs from the other two in that it does not relate a story. It is a piece of description. The first part describes a mighty river and a rare pleasure-dome constructed on it by a mighty conqueror, Kubla Khan. The later part describes the power of poetry and inspiration as well as a poet in the frenzy of creation.

Coleridge's Account of the Origin of the Poem. The poem is described by Coleridge himself as a fragment. According to him it is only a part of the poem of two to three hundred lines which has come to him in a dream. Not only he actually see the picture that he paints in the poem; even the lines and the words came to him, just as they are. But he can not complete the poem as he was interrupted by a visitor and the vision faded.

Is the Poem a Fragment? Ever since then, critics have regarded this poem as a fragment. Not all critics, however, are of this view. For example, George Saintsbury disbelieves Coleridge's statement. He remarks, the prose rigmarole in which Coleridge tells the story of the coming and going of the vision called Kubla Khan is "a characteristic piece of self-description." It is his view that the poem is not a fragment. Says he, "Far from being an opium dream, Kubla Khan is the product of one unexpected lucid interval before the fumes closes up once more the expression of the spirit; moreover, it is complete. It is pure poetry, it is perfect." A modern critic named Humphrey House also holds that the poem is complete. He regards it a poem about the process of poetic creation, about the ecstasy of imaginative fulfilment.

Airy and Unsubstantial. At first reading, the poem gives the impression of being "airy and unsubstantial". It gives us the feeling that it has no coherence and that the two parts of the poem do not hangs together. The first part describes the river Alph. The second part describes a vision and then a poet in frenzy. Even in the first part, the description does not follow an even course. It wanders and wanders like the river Alph. There seems to be no connection between the river Alph and the Abyssinian maiden.

It has Coherence and Substance. A closer study, however, convinces us that the poem is not as innocent as it seems to be. It cannot be explained in rational terms, but when we follow the course of the associations and suggestions that runs through the poem, it does yields a coherent meaning.

An Interpretation Beats His Imagination. The poet's imagination is much aroused by the river Alph and its subterannean course. The measureless caverns, the panting earth, the dancing rocks, sunless and lifeless sea, the tumult of the mighty waves as they rush into the silent ocean, the scene where a woman wails for her demon lover-all these excites his imagination. A feeling of awe and mystery is upon him, and he is lifted into a mood of poetic creation.

The Damsel; Symbol of Creative Power. This suggests him the power of creation in man. It arouses in him the desire to capture the weird beauty of the entire scene, and reminds him that this can be built in colours, strains and words. The symbol of this creative power is the maiden whom he see in a vision.

The poet, therefore, glides into his new theme through suggestion. The two parts are connected by the poet's desire to build a pleasure dome with the help of his imagination. He then describes the poet when the fit of creation is upon him.

Coherence Only of a Dream. Such an interpretation is possible and so the poem can be shown to be complete. But the coherence and the completeness of this poem is the coherence and the completeness of a dream, not of waking life. In fact, the whole poem follows the course of a dream. Even the description of the river Alph has this dream-like quality. The pictures are repeated, and it is not easy to follow the course of the river exactly. It is also difficult to conclude whether the river has an entire course of ten miles or whether this is only a part of the course. Again, it is not at all possible to say with confidence how the wild and the fertile parts of the course of the river are related to each other. Again the transition from the description of the river to the description of the vision is abrupt, and the connection between the first and the second part tenuous. In vividness as well as lack of smooth transitions, the poem is like a dream.

A Series of Pictures. This poem is a master-piece of descriptive art. It has a pictorial quality about it. In fact, the poem is nothing but a series of pictures that follow each other in quick succession. After announcing that Kubla Khan decreed a pleasure-dome, the poet describes the course of river Alph. Then he builds up the picture of a romantic chasm-a scene of vast desolation in the dim light of the moon. Then follows the picture of the mighty fountain. The picture of the course of the river is repeated, and is followed by a picture of the pleasure-dome. Then comes a description of the vision, and finally the description of the poet in frenzy.

Combination of Vagueness and Vividness. These pictures are at once vivid and yet vague. This is exactly what happens in a dream. The impressions of a dream have clear outline, and yet they concentrate only on a few details, the rest being left vague. In other words, the description leaves much to the imagination of the reader they are suggestive, not explicit. For example, what exactly do we know, about the pleasure-dome-that it was situated on the bank of the river Alph, that it had a sunny dome and caves of ice, that its shadow fell on the floating waves and that it was haunts by the tumult of the mighty river.

Equally vague and yet vivid is the picture of the river. We cannot answer a definite question about it. How far, we ask, was the sunless sea from the pleasure-dome? How far is the fountain head of the river? Was the entire course of the river only ten miles? And these questions have no answer because the entire description has the indefiniteness of a dream.

The Mystery of the Scene. This vagueness, however, is the greatest strength of the description. It leaves so much to suggestion that every reader with a little imagination will build a vast scene of his own. The mystery becomes more effective because of this vast vision of vagueness which surrounds the vivid picture of the poem.

The Touch of the Supernatural. Several touches in the poem raises from the region of everyday realities to that of a supernatural world. The details are realistic, and each detail has an actual counterpart somewhere. The total impression, however, is of an unearthly rather than earthly scene.

This is achieved with the help of deft touches scattered in the poem. The very mention of Xanadu', Kubla Khan, Alph, Abora and the Abyssinian maid evokes associations of remoteness, mystery and strangeness. "The woman wailing for her demon-lover," the chasm "seething with ceaseless turmoil," "the earth breathing in thick pants", "the huge fragments" thrown up by the waves "the caverns measureless to man", "the sunless, lifeless ocean", "the ancestral voices prophesying war", "the caves of ice", the poet with "his flashing eyes, his floating hair", fed on honey-dew and milk of Paradise, the circle woven around him thrice-all these are touches which make the poem of a supernatural world.

(E) EXPLANATIONS WITH CRITICAL COMMENTS

L. 17-26. Down the green....seething. While describing the landscape of Kubla Khan's pleasure house, Coleridge introduces a few startling and romantic details. A deep gorges, marvellously beautiful, slope down the green hill side, well hidden by tall cedars on either side. It was too beautiful for words. That particular spot has a grim and horrible look. It seemed at the same time peculiarly sanctifies and lying under a magic sell. On the whole it was rather eerie and grotesque as if the stage is set for the most marvellous happenings. It provides the right kind of setting in which a mortal woman who has loved and lost her 'demon-lover might come out lamenting, passionately. The sickle-moon in the sky would further heighten the grim and grotesque effect of the whole scene.

L. 26-30. Through wood....dome of pleasure. In these lines from Kubla Khan, Coleridge describes the course of the sacred river Alph. The river has its headwaters in a fountain gushing out of gorge on the hill-side in the spacious ground of Kubla Khan's pleasure-house. In its early course, it ran in a zig-zag way through forests and valleys for five miles. It then tumbles into a deep gorge of limitless depth. In the end it emerged from its underground bed and flows into the calm waters of the ocean with a mighty roar. Through this deafening noise, the king hears the voice of his forefathers reaching his ears. They were warning him about the wars ahead. The idea is suggested by the poet's reading. The priests of Kubla Khan and the holy men of Abyssinia (described by Bruce in travels to discover the source of the Nile), both prophesied about wars. Coleridge has lately been writing against the war with France. It may also be noted that ancestor worship is a venerable custom both in China and Japan for long ages. Coleridge is particularly fond of the eerie and supernatural in his poetry. This reference to ghostly spirits warning the king about the wars ahead is a typical touch.

L. 31-36. The shadow......caves of ice. In these lines, Coleridge describes the magnificent pleasure-house of Kubla Khan as it stands on the sea-front and casts its reflection on the waves lapping the shore. The reflection lays suspended, as it is , half-way down below the surface. It stands within hearing of the blended music of the waters of the fountain and river coursing through the caves. The building itself is of surpassing beauty and seems to be hardly the work of human hands. It is nothing short of a miracle. Its dome overhead is bright and warm with sunlight. Down below, however, the halls, built with marble and alabaster, is dazzlingly white and marvellously cool. They seems to be so many "caves of ice".

L. 37-41. A damsel Mount Abora. While describing Kubla Khan's magnificent palace, Coleridge rather abruptly switches off to this image of an Abyssinian maid. One critic observes that he here "runs off the rails". What he actually does is to turn, without preparing the reader sufficiently, from the main theme to dwelling on his own vocation as a poet. He has once a vision of an Abyssinian maid playing on her instrument most ravishingly. She has sang to the accompaniment of her dulcimer about the manifold charms of her native haunt of Mount Abora. The poet heartily wishes, he could capture her art and inspiration. He then makes anew a dream-place in the air with power of his song.

L. 42-48. Could I... see them there. After he has described the magnificent palace of Kubla Khan, Coleridge turns to his own vocation as a poet and the power and vision of poetry. He once has a vision of an Abyssinian maid playing on her own instrument most ravishingly. He wishes he could by some chance get her marvellous gift. He longs to refresh the memory of that music and song. By that means he could work himself up to the fine frenzy of a poet. He can create anew pleasure-house in the sky by the power of his song and music-that splendid building complete with all its marvellous features, the sun-lit cupola and the white and charmingly cool halls of alabaster and marble resembling "caves of ice".

L. 49-54.. And all should.......milk of Paradise. Coleridge switches off râther abruptly from his theme of describing Kubla Khan's pleasure-house to dealing with the poet's mission-his art and vision. He once has a vision of an Abyssinian maid playing on her instrument most ravishingly. He wishes with all his heart that he can capture for himself that maid's marvellous gift of music and song. He will in that case make anew magnificent palace in the air for all to see. It is the poet's art of giving to airy nothings a local habitation and a name. He will indeed look very strange apparition, once inspires, to people around him. They will look with awe and wonder at his gleaming eyes and streaming locks of hair. They would give him a wide berth and draw magic circles around him to keep him at a safe distance. To them he would look like one possessed with those food which is not the food of ordinary men but something exotic like honey-dew or some heavenly stuff of the class of manna or ambrosia or nectar which he fancifully calls "the milk of Paradise".

(F) SELECTED UNIVERSITY QUESTIONS WITH ANSWRES ON *KUBLA KHAN*

ROMANTIC ELEMENTS

Q.1. Consider *Kubla Khan* as an example of Romantic poem.

Or

Bring out the romantic features of *Kubla Khan'*.

Ans. *Kubla Khan* is a concentration of romantic features. Content and style together evoke an atmosphere of wonder and romance and enchantment.

Supernaturalism. A basic feature of Coleridge's poetic art is his ability to render supernatural phenomena with artistry. This is also a characteristic of Romantic poetry. While *Kubla Khan* is not a supernatural poem in the conventional sense, some phrases in the poem collectively give it an atmosphere of other-worldly enchantment. The "caverns measureless to man a "sunless sea", a "woman wailing for her demon lover", 'the mighty fountain forced momently from that romantic chasm"- these are all touches, which create an atmosphere of mystery and arouse awe. But the description is so precise and vivid that no sense of unreality is created.

Sensuous Description. Romantic poetry is also characterized by sensuousness. Like Keats, Coleridge exhibits a keen observation. There are sensuous phrases and pictures in *Kubla Khan*. The bright gardens, the incense-bearing trees with sweet blossoms, the sunny spots of greenery, rocks vaulting like rebounding hail, the sunless caverns these are highly sensuous images. Equally sensuous is the vision of the Abyssinian maid playing on a dulcimer and singing a sweet song.

Distant Setting. References to distant lands and far-off places emphasise the romantic character of Kubla Khan. Xanadu, Alph, Mount Abora belong to the geography of romance and contribute to the romantic atmosphere. There are highly suggestive lines in the poem and they, too, are romantic in character. For instance, the picture of a woman wailing for her demon-lover under a waning moon, is very suggestive- "a savage place......holy and enchanted" Coleridge calls it. Equally suggestive are these lines:

> And mid this tumult Kubla heard from far
> Ancestral voices prophesying war.

Poetic creation. The picture of the divinely has inspired poet in the closing lines is typically romantic. No writer imbued with the classical spirit have written these lines where the poet is presented as a divinely inspired creator. The poet achieves an awesome personality of whom the ordinary persons must "Beware".

Dream-like quality. *Kubla Khan*, is a work of pure fancy, the result of sheer imagination. The dream-like atmosphere of the poem is purely romantic.

SUPERNATURALISM

Q.2. Bring out the supernatural elements in *Kubla Khan.*

Or

"There is a deep psychological realism behind Coleridge's use of the supernatural." Discuss with reference to *Kubla Khan.*

Ans. *Kubla Khan* is a dream vision, a poem of pure magic. It exemplifies Coleridge's mastery over supernatural poetry.

Coleridge creates an atmosphere of mystery in *Kubla Khan* mainly by describing the pleasure-dome and the surroundings in which it stood. It is a beautiful place where the river Alph flows 'through caverns measureless to man down to a sunless sea." The immeasurable caverns and the sunless sea, perhaps some dark, subterranean lake, evokes in our mind a feeling of mystery and awe. There is the deep romantic chasm which lay across forest of cedar trees. From this gorge is momently forced a mighty fountain, the source of river Alph. The manner in which the water is described as intermittently forcing its way out from the spring, throwing up huge pieces of rock, fascinates the reader. The atmosphere of mystery and awe is emphasized when another reference is made to the sunless sea or the lifeless ocean into which the waters of Alph fell with a loud roar.

Suggestiveness is the basic feature of Coleridge's supernaturalism. It is true that a very vivid and graphic description of the surroundings of the pleasure-dome is given in the poem but the supernatural element is suggestive. Coleridge is a superb artist for intermingling the natural and the supernatural so that the probable and the improbable interfuse. Here are lines which for sheer suggestiveness and mystery are perhaps unsurpassed:

> A savage place! as holy and enchanted
> As e'er beneath a waning moon was haunted
> By woman wailing for her demon-lover.

A complete story of love's tragedy is hidden in these three lines; a story comparable to Keat's *La Belle Dame Sans Merci.* And then the following two lines:

> And 'mid this tumult Kubla heard from far
> ancestral voices prophesying war !

The mystery and awe of these lines are striking. What war and why? It is left to our imagination.

Then we come 'to the closing lines which contain a picture of poetic frenzy. Here too we have a superb blending of the natural and supernatural. A poet's inspiration is a well-known and natural fact of human experience, but there is something supernatural about the way in which this poetic inspiration and the creative powers of a poet are shown:

> And all should cry, Beware! Beware!
> His flashing eyes, his floating hair!
> Weave a circle round him thrice,
> And close your eyes with holy dread,
> For he on honey-dew hath fed,
> And drunk the milk of paradise.

But despite the mystery and awe evoked in the poem, the whole description is psychologically accurate because when the poet is in a state of frenzy, he is really like a magician. Out of this creative madness, come the gems of truth and beauty. Touches of realism have been added, even to the description of the chasm and the mighty fountain. Coleridge uses the similes rebounding hail and chaffy grain beneath the thresher's flail which are familiar to our lives and most natural. If Kubla Khan hears prophesies of war in all the tumultuous noise, it is not unrealistic. It is true to human experience. After all he is a brave warrior.

Coleridge never forgets that his real purpose is to make the supernatural natural and to bring about the "willing suspension of disbelief which constitutes poetic faith". Whether Kubla Khan is seen as a poem about poetic creativity or about life, it is a convincing work.

POEM ABOUT LIFE AND POETIC CREATION

Q.3. Critically examine *Kubla Khan* as a poem about life and poetic potentialities.

Ans. G. Wilson Knight analyses the imagery of *Kubla Khan* and shows that it is a poem about life and about poetic potentialities. The pleasure-dome dominates the poem. Its setting is carefully described. There is a sacred river running into caverns measureless to man and to a sunless seas; in other words, the river runs into an infinity of death. The marks out area through which it flows is, however, one of teeming nature, gardens, rills, incense-bearing trees, ancient forests. The river is a symbol of life since the sacred river which runs, through Nature, towards death could easily correspond to life.

Born on a height, the river descends from a deep romantic 'chasm', a place which is savage, holy and enchanted, and which is associated with both a waning moon and a woman wailing for her demon lover. The river's origin blends romantic, sacred and Satanic suggestion. This part of the poem hints at a mystery, blending Satanism with sanctity and romance with savagery.

The lines that follow contain such expressions as the ceaseless turmoil', the earth-mother breathing in fast, 'thick pants', the fountain 'forced' out with 'half-intermitted burst', the fragments rebounding like hail, the 'chaffy grain beneath the flail', the 'dancing rocks'. These expressions create in us a riotous impression of agony, tumult, and power: the dynamic process of birth and creation.

Then the river goes 'meandering in a mazy motion, The maze is, of course, a well-known figure suggesting uncertain and blind progress and is sometimes expressly used for the spiritual complexities of human life. After five miles of mazy progress, the river reaches the 'caverns measureless to man', which represent infinity and nothingness. The river sinks, with great tumult (that is, death-agony), to a 'lifeless ocean', that is, to eternal nothingness, namely death. This tumult is aptly associated with war: the principle of those conflicting and destructive forces that driven man to his end. The ancestral voices suggest that the dark compulsion that binds the race to its habitual conflicts is related by some psychologists to unconscious ancestor-worship, to parental and pre-parental authority.

As far Kubla Khan himself, becomes God, or at least one of those huge and mighty forms, or other similar institutions of gigantic mountainous power, in Wordsworth or we can say that the poet's genius starting to describe an oriental monarch's architectural exploits, finds itself automatically creating a symbolic and universal panorama of existence.

In the second movement of the poem, the dome's shadow falls half way along the river. The river, as indicates above, is the birth-death time-stream. The shadow is cast by a higher, more dimensional reality. It is directly associated with the 'mingled measure' of the sounds coming from the two extremes. The 'mingled measure' suggests the blend and marriage of fundamental oppositions : life and death, or creation and destruction. These mingle under the shadow of the greater harmony, the crowning dome-circle. It is a paradoxical thing, a 'miracle of rare device', 'sunny' but with 'caves of ice' which points to the resolution of opposites in the new dimension, especially those of light and heat, sunny for Eros-fire of mind, and ice for the coldness of inorganic nature, ultimate being, and death, the ice caves being perhaps related to the earlier caverns. Only more optimistically tones, light instead of gloomy, just as 'sunny' suggests to torturing heat. The 'caves of ice' may also hint at cool cavernous depths in the unconscious mind blending with a lighted intelligence; whereby at least coldness becomes kind. These ice and sun fire are the two elemental antitheses, and their mingling may lead us farther. We are at what might be called a marriage-point in life's progress half way between birth and death, and even birth and death are themselves mingled or married. We may imagine a sexual union between life, the masculine, and death, the feminine. Then our 'romantic chasm' and 'cedarn cover' the savage and enchanted, yet holy, place, with its' half-intermitted burst' may be, in spite of the interpretation given earlier, vaguely related to the functioning of a man's creative organs and their physical setting, and also to all principles of manly and adventurous action, while the caverns that engulf the sacred river will be correspondingly feminine with a dark passivity and infinite peace. The pleasure-dome may regard as the pleasure of a sexual union in which birth and death are the great contesting partners, with human existence as the life-stream of a mighty coition.

The third and final movement of the poem starts with the Abyssinian damsel seen in a vision, playing music. The aptness of a girl-image here is obvious. The poet equates the once-experienced mystic and girl-born music with the dome. Could he revive in himself that music which can build the spiritual dome in air, that is, in words, in poetry. Or, may be, he would become himself the domed consciousness of a cold, happy, brilliance, and ice-flashing, sun-smitten, wisdom. The analogy between music and some form of architecture is not unique. After this, the movement of the poem grows ecstatic and swift. There is a hint of a new speed in the drawn-out rhythm of such a deep delight it would win me...? Now the three rhyms lines gather up the poet's message together with his consciousness of its supreme meaning with a breathless expectancy towards the climax. Next follows a fall to a ritualistic solemnity, phrased in long vowels and stately-measures motion, imaged in the 'circle' and the eyes dropps in 'holy dread' before the prophet who has seen and recreated 'Paradise' not the earthly, but the heavenly paradise : the pleasure-dome enclosing and transcending human agony and frustration.

Q.4. *Kubla Khan* is a poem about the act of poetic creation, about the ecstasy in imaginative fulfilment." Justify.

Or

Would it be correct to describe *Kubla Khan* as a finished fragment? Give a reasoned answer.

Ans. *Kubla Khan* is a triumphant positive statement of the potentialities of poetry. How great those potentialities are, is revealed partly in description of its effects at the ending of the second part and partly in the very substance and content of the first.

The precision and clarity of the opening part are noteworthy even in the order of the landscape. In the centre is the pleasure-dome with its gardens on the river bank; to one side is the river's source in the chasm, to the other are the 'caverns measureless to man', and the 'sunless sea' into which the river falls. Kubla in the centre can hear the 'mingled measure' of the fountain of the source from one side, and of the dark caves from the other. The river winds across the whole landscape. Nobody needs to keep this mere geographical consistency of the description prominently in the mind as he reads (though once established it remains clear and constant); but if this factual-visual consistency had been absent, and there have been a mere random sequence or collection of items, such as a dream might well have provided then the absence would be noticeable. The poem will have been quite different, and a new kind of effort, will have been needed to apprehend what unity it might have had. Within this main landscape, too, there is a pervasive order. The fertility of the plain is only made possible by the mysterious energy of the source. The dome has come into being by Kubla's decree. The dome is stately: the gardens are girdled round with walls and towers.

It is so often said that *Kubla Khan* achieves its effect mainly by 'far-reaching suggestiveness', that it is worth emphasising this element of plain clear statement at the outset, a statement which does particularize a series of details inter-related to each other, and deriving their relevance from their interrelation and their order. Furthermore, the use of highly emotive and suggestive proper names is proportionately no large source of the poem's effect, it is only necessary to watch the incidence of them. Xanadu, Kubla Khan and Alph occur once in that form within the poem's opening two-and-a-half lines : and none of them occurs again except for the single repetition of Kubla in line 29. Abyssinian and Mount Abora occur each, in the three lines 39-41. There are no other proper names in the poem at all, unless we shall count the final word Paradise.

Next, the mode of appraisal which relies on suggestiveness is likely to underestimate the strength and firmness of the descriptions. In particular, lines 17-24, describing the source of the river, do not employ 'suggestiveness' at all.

> And from this chasm, with ceaseless turmoil seething
> As if this earth in fast thick pants were breathing,
> A mighty fountain momently was forced:
> A mid whose swift half-intermitted burst
> Huge fragments vaulted with rebounding hail,
> Or chaffy grain beneath the thresher's flail:
> And 'mid these dancing rocks at once and ever
> It flung up momently the sacred river.

The whole passage is full of life because the verse has both the needed energy and the needed control. The combination of energy and control in the rhythm and sound is so great, as in

> at once and ever
> It flung up momently the sacred river

that we are even in danger of missing the force of the imagery, as in 'rebounding hail' and 'dancing rocks'.

A different kind of clarity and precision in the first part leads us nearer to the poem's central meaning the consistency with which the main facts of this landscape are treated, the dome and the river. The dome is an agreed emblem of fulfilment and satisfaction, it is breast like, full to touch and eye, rounds and complete. It is the stately pleasure-dome in line 2, the dome of pleasure in line 31, and 'A sunny pleasure-dome' in line 36. Each time the word 'pleasure' occurs with it. So too, the word river is used three times in the first part, and each time, without fail, it is 'the sacred river'; this is its constant, invariable epithet. The centre of the landscape of this part is, as we have seen, the point at which the dome and the river join:

> The shadow of the dome of pleasure
> Floated midway on the waves.

Here, without possibility of doubt, the poem presents the conjunction of pleasure and sacredness; that is the core of Part One and in part Two the poet who has been able to realise this fusion of pleasure and sacredness is himself regarded as a holy or sacred person, a seer acquainted with the undivided life: and this part is clinched by the emphatic and final word 'Paradise'. The conditional form of Part Two does not annul the presentation of paradise in Part One, though it may hold out the hope of a future fuller vision.

Positively, it causes a distortion of the poem if we try to approximate this Paradise either to the earthly Paradise of Eden before the Fall or to the Heavenly Paradise which is the ultimate abode of the blest. It may take its imagery from Eden, but it is not Eden because Kubla Khan is not Adam. Kubla Khan himself is literally an oriental prince with his name adapted from Purchas. What matters is not supposed fixed and antecedent symbolic character, so much as his activity. Within the landscape treated as literal he must be of princely scope, in order to decree the dome and gardens: and it is this decree that matters, for it images the power of man over his environment and the fact that man makes his paradise for himself. Just as the whole poem is about poetic creation at the imaginative level, so within the work of the imagination, occurs the creativeness of man at the ethical and practical levels. This is what the poet, of all men, is capable of realizing.

> And 'mid this tumult Kubla heard from far
> Ancestral voices prophesying war

This is essential to the full unity of the conception : the Paradise contains knowledge of the threat of its own possible destruction. It is not held as a permanent gift-the ideal life is always open to forces of evil, it must be not only created by man for himself, but also defended by him. It is not of the essence of this Paradise that it must be lost, but there is a risk that it may be lost.

About the river, again, we need not aim to be too precise and make equations. Its function in the poem is clear. The bounding energy of its source makes the fertility of the plain possible : it is the sacred given condition of human life. By using it rightly, by building on its bank, by diverting its water into the sinuous rills, Kubla achieves his perfect state of balanced living. It is an image of these non human, holy given conditions. It is an imaginative statement of the abundant life in the universe, which begins and ends in a mystery touched with dread, but it is a statement of this life as the ground of ideal human activity.

The 'caves of ice' needs a special attention. Some discussions of the poem seems to imply that they belong with the 'cavern measureless to man' but there, surely can be no doubt that in the poem they belong closely and necessarily with the dome-

It was a miracle of rare device,
A sunny pleasure-dome, with caves of ice;

The very line shows the closeness by the antithesis, the convex against the concave, the warm against the cold. It is not necessary to invoke Coleridge's own statement of the theory of the reconciliation of opposites in art to see that it is the holding together of these two different elements in which the miracle consists. They are repeated together, also within the single line, 47, in Part Two. The miracle or rare device consists in the combination of these softer and harder elements. And when this is seen in relation to the act of poetic creation, in the light of which all Part One must be understood, its function is still plainer such creation has this element of austerity in it. For this is a vision of the ideal human life as the poetic imagination can create it. Part One only exists in the light of Part Two. There may be other Paradises, other false Paradises too: but this is the creation of the poet in his frenzy. And it is because he can create it that he deserves the ritual dread.

Thus we may confidently say that *Kubla Khan* is a finished fragment, about the act of poetic creation, about the 'ecstasy in imaginative fulfilment'.

The shadow of the dome of pleasure
Floated! midway on the waves;
Where was heard the mingled measure
From the fountain and the eaves.

When looked at closely, the words 'midway' and 'mingled' prove to be both exact and' consistent with other references made in the poem. Only by its very great height could the dome's reflection extend midway' across the mighty Alph, and the impression of height is confirmed both by the reference to the dome's being 'in air', and by the fact that it must soar clear of the shadow of its surrounding hills and incense-bearing trees' to qualify for the adjective 'sunny', which is twice used. But not only does the dome's shadow reach out across the river, it also falls half way between the tumult of the 'mighty fountain', which is the river's source, and the tumult of the caves in which the river sinks to a 'lifeless ocean', since only at a 'midway' position can the tumults be actually mingled. This kind of precision has been overlooked by those who are content to capitulate before the poem and praise it for its vague stringing-together of dream images.

The poem is in three parts. In part one, Kubla decrees a 'stately pleasure-dome', the central and recurrent image of the poem. We are given the details of the extent of Kubla's pleasure-garden, and of its rich variety of natural beauties, with a clarity and particularity that is astonishing, the profusion being wonderfully conveyed by the swift flow of diverse images. The picture given is an earthly Paradise. Life has frequently been compared to a river flowing into the sea of death, and the epithets 'sacred', use of the river, and 'sunless', use of the sea, are enough to establish the implicit comparison here.

Part two, which is no less rich in its range of images, continues and completes the picture of Kubla's Paradise, but introduces a note of fear and turmoil in its description of the river's source and final annihilation. The raw, elemental imagery which occurs in parts of The Ancient Mariner is fully matched in the lines which describes the chasm:

> A savage place! as holy and enchanted
> As e'er beneath a waning moon was haunted
> By woman wailing for her demon lover!

but, fine though the description of the 'ceaseless turmoil' of the 'mighty fountain' is, it fails to sustain the terrifying power of these lines. The images of 'rebounding hail' and 'chaffy grain beneath the thresher's flail; though exact comparisons, tend to diminish the effect they are meant to convey. What do emerge is a clear picture of the Paradise. The river representing life seethes from the earth itself, flows slowly and with a 'mazy motion', expressive perhaps of life's twists and turns, through a walled garden, and at last enters the 'caverns measureless to man' before sinking to a 'lifeless ocean'. Dominating garden and river alike is the pleasure-dome: as it is the first so it is the last image used. In obvious opposition to the 'sunless sea' of death, the dome is 'sunny'. It is a proud manifestation of life; it is both a work of superb art in itself and a symbol for all artistic achievement.

At the beginning of the third part a sharp literary-geographical change of scene occurs. We move from Kubla's Paradise, taken by Coleridge from *Purchas's Pilgrimage,* to the equally exotic paradise of Mount Abora, takes from Milton. Then a much more fundamental switch occurs this time, a switch of subject. The poet affirms that his touch, could build the whole miraculous dome of Kubla, if he can revive the vision induces in him by the singing of the 'Abyssinian maid'. Her song is in all respects a counterpart to the 'strong music in the soul' spoken of in *Dejection.* From it comes a 'deep delight' - the 'joy' Coleridge persistently insists on as the condition of creative activity. Granted this joy, he will create the fabled splendour of Kubla's dome through a poetry so astonishing that his powers will be thought the result of sorcery and he regarded with 'holy dread'. It will be said by those who hear his poetry that he has fed on honey-dew, and 'drunk the milk of Paradise'. And indeed this will be true: to taste 'the milk of Paradise' is to know the 'deep delight' which expresses itself in poetry.

12

FROST AT MIDNIGHT

(A) TEXT, PARAPHRASE AND ANNOTATIONS

THE Frost performs its secret ministry,
Unhelped by any wind. The owlet's cry
Came loud-and hark, again! loud as before.
The inmates of my cottage, all at rest,
Have left me to that solitude, which suits
Abstruser musings: save that at my side
My cradled infant slumbers peacefully.
'Tis calm indeed ! so calm, that it disturbs
And vexes meditation with its strange
And extreme silentness. Sea, hill, and wood,
This populous village ! Sea, and hill, and wood,
With all the numberless goings-on of life,
Inaudible as dreams ! the thin blue flame
Lies on my low-burnt fire, and quivers not;
Only that film, which fluttered on the grate,
Still flutters there, the sole unquiet thing.
Methinks, its motion in this hush of nature
Gives it dim sympathies with me who live,
Making it a companionable form,
Whose puny flaps and freaks the idling Spirit
By its own moods interprets, every where

L. 1. ministry—office; function. **The Frost performs its secret ministry**—the frost does its work quietly for bringing about a change in the aspect of Nature in the stillness of the night. **L. 2. Unhelped by any wind**—without being helped by the wind. What the poet means to say .is that there was a complete stillness of the night which was not disturbed even by the wind blowing. **owlet**—young owl. **L. 3. and hark again !**—the hooting of the owl is heard again, loud as before—this time also the cry of the owl is as loud as before. The cry of the owlet enhances the impression of the stillness of the night by contrast. **L. 4. inmates**—occupants. **my cottage**—the little cottage at Nether Stowey; Coleridge lived there from December 1796 to September 1798. **all at rest**—all of whom have now gone to sleep. L. 5. solitude—the calm and quiet. **L.5. Have left me to that solitude**—have left me all alone to enjoy the stillness of the night. **L. 6. Abstruser**—deep; profound. **musings**—broodings; meditation. **L.5-6. which suits my abstruser musings**—which is favourable to my profound meditations, L 6. **save**—except, **at my side**—by my side. **L. 7. My cradled infant**—my child lying in the cradle. **slumbers**—sleeps. **L. 8. 'Tis calm indeed**—calm prevails everywhere. **vexes**

A COMPLETE PARAPHRASE OF THE POEM

L. 1-23. There is a silent shower of frost in the cold winter night and there is no wind. In the silence of the night is heard the shrill cry of the owlet. All the members of the house are asleep. I am alone and I could meditate on serious things. Only my child is sleeping peacefully in the cradle by my side. There is silence. But it is so grim and strange that it became oppressive and disturbed my meditative mood. The whole of nature-sea, hill, forest, the populous village with the pulsations of life is silent like pictures in a dream. The thin blue flame on the fire is still. The only thing that is not still and stirred is the film that floats from the flame. I, in my idle contemplation has my thoughts engross in the flapping and fluttering of the film. It seemes to me that it stir in the grim silence in sympathy with me and it is as it is a living companion capable of understanding me. For the idle mind searches for the echoes and resemblances of its own moods in all natural objects and plays with the current of thoughts for this purpose.

---

meditation—our mind is concentrated for working in normal surroundings. The existence of anything unusual—even extreme silence—disturbs the smooth working of the mind. silentness—stillness; quietness. **L. 11. This populous village**—this thickly populated village. **Sea....village**—silence broods over sea, hill, wood, and this thickly populated village. **L. 12. With all the numberless goings-on of life**—innumerable operations of life that go on among the creatures that live in the sea, on the hills, in the wood, and in the thickly populated village. **L. 13. Inaudible as dreams**—silent as the scenes presented in a dream. **L. 14. low-burnt fire**—smouldering fire. **quivers not**—does not tremble at all. **L. 15. film**—a thin, light covering of flame on the fire. **fluttered**—moved in spirals and waves over the glowing fire. **grate**—a frame of iron bars for holdings fire while burning. **L. 16. flutters**—moves. **sole**—only. **unquiet thing**—only thing that disturbs the stillness and quietness of the scene. **L. 17. Methinks**—I think. **its motion**—the flickering of the thin flame. **in this hush of nature**—in the stillness that prevails everywhere. **L. 18. dim sympathies**—"Coleridge believed that the mind of man seeks only an image of itself in the objects of Nature. It colours them bright or gloomy according to the character of its own thoughts. Very few things in Nature have a fixed colour or shape of their own. They change from hour to hour according to the change in the feelings of the observer." **who live**—with a living creature like me. **L. 19. Making it a companionable form**—making it a living companion capable of understanding my thoughts and sympathetically responding to them. **L. 20. puny**—feeble; small. **flaps**— flutterings. **freaks**—little irregular movements. **The idling Spirit**—the poet in an idle contemplative mood. **Whose**—i.e. of the fire. **L. 21. By its own moods**—according to the moods and fancies that visit the 'idling spirit'. **interprets**—explains. **L. 22. Echo or mirror seeking of itself**—the idling spirit seeks everywhere an echo or mirror of itself. In other words, a man in an idle mood searches eagerly for resemblances of his own moods in the whole range of natural objects round him. **L. 23. And makes a joy of thought**—in a mood of relaxation a man's mind drifts into dreams and fancies; plays with thoughts as one plays with.toys.

Echo or mirror seeking of itself,
And makes a toy of Thought.
But O ! how oft
How oft, at school, with most believing mind,
Presageful, have I gazed upon the bars,
To watch that fluttering *stranger* ! and as oft

With unclosed lids, already had I dreamt
Of my sweet birth-place, and the old church-tower,
Whose bells, the poor man's only music, rang
From morn to evening, all the hot Fair-day,
So sweetly, that they stirred and haunted me
With a wild pleasure, falling on mine ear
Most like particulate sounds of things to come!
So gazed I, till the soothing things, I dreamt,
Lulled me to sleep, and sleep prolonged my dreams!
And so I brooded all the following morn,
Awed by the stern preceptor's face, mine eye
Fixed with mock study on my swimming book:
Save if the door half opened, and I snatched
A hasty glance, and still my heart leaped up
For still I hoped to see the stranger's face,
Townsman, or aunt, or sister more beloved,
My play-mate when we both were clothed alike !

Dear Babe, that sleepest cradled by my side,
Whose gentle breathings, heard in this deep calm,
Fill up the interspersed vacancies
And momentary pauses of the thought!

L. 24. school—Christ's Hospital where Coleridge studied. **with most believing mind**—fully convinced that I would see some forms within the fire burning in the fire place. **L. 25. presageful**—full of strange anticipations. **gazed upon**—watched intently. **bars**—bars of the grate. **L. 26. fluttering stranger**—the film of heat over a fire. These films are called strangers' and supposed to portend the arrival of some absent friend. **L. 27. With unclosed lids**—with sleepless eyes. **Already had I dreamt of my sweet birth-place**—every one feels proud of his birth—place. **L. 29. whose bells**—the bells rung in the church tower. **The poor man's only music**—the peal of the church bells was the only music which the humble rustics of that village could afford to enjoy. **all the hot Fair-day**—throughout the summer day when a fair was held in Ottery St. Mary. **L. 31. So sweetly**—the bells rang so sweetly. **stirred**—thrilled me. **haunted me**—the echo of the peals of the church bells lingered on in the mind. **L. 32. a wild pleasure**—a thrill of uncontrollable joy and happiness. **falling on my ear**—the sounds of the church bells heard by me. **L. 33. Most like particulate sounds of things to come**—the music of the bells was not meaningless. It spoke to the poet of things to come. **Particulate**—distinct. **L. 34. So gazed I**—In this way I could continue

L. 24-43. How often, my mind being full of strange anticipations? I look across the bars of my school often awaiting somebody I know but who is a stranger there. And often did I weave dreams, though I am not asleep, about my birth-place and its old church tower. The ringing of the bells of the church was the only music that the poor parishioners could afford to enjoy. In the hot fair-day the music rang all day long. The music is so sweet that it awakens a strange excess of joy in me which remain with me and spoke to me of future happenings. I dream thus looking across the bars, until the calm influence of the sweet thoughts made me fall asleep and dream more of those in my sleep. The next morning I am full of anticipations that something should happen to me to sweeten the dreary atmosphere of the place. The letters of my book swam before me in my excitement. But I fixed my eyes on my book in a show of study in fear of my teacher who is very strict. Only when the door is partially opened, I quickly look through it. I am full of excitement for I still expected that some townsman, or my aunt or my dear sister who has been my playmate when we have like clothes to wear would come to visit me.

L. 44-64. My darling child, you are asleep in a cradle by my side. In the deep silence of the night I can hear your soft breathing which takes up my attention in the short intervals or pauses between the flight of my thoughts. My darling is so beautiful. It fills my heart with joy and tenderness to look at you now and when I remember my hard school days and think that you will learn different things in a different

---

watching the fire in the grate. **the soothing things**—pleasant things I dreamt. **L. 34-35. The soothing things.....sleep**—my mind being refreshed by the pleasant dreams of my native place, I fell asleep. **L. 35. prolonged**—extended in duration. **L. 36. All the following morn**—the whole of the next morning. **L. 37. Awed by**—afraid of. **Preceptor's**—Headmaster's. **L. 38. with mock study**—with a show of study; I pretended as if I was studying the book. **swimming book**—as he was feeling sleepy the letters of the book placed before him seemed to swim before his eyes. **L. 39. Save**—Except. **L. 39—40. I snatched a hasty glance**—I looked hurriedly at the book. **L. 40. And still my heart leaped up**—with the joy of expecting to see something. **L. 41. the stranger's face**—I expected to see there the face of some stranger. **L. 42. Townsman**—local resident. **more beloved**—i.e. than either of the towns man of the aunt. **L. 43. My play-mate when we were clothed alike**—who was my playmate in my childhood when boys and girls wear the same sort of dress. (**Note**—This shows how eagerly the lonely boy at the Boarding School expected to see his relatives from whom he lived far away.) **L. 44. Dear Babe**—his son Hartley, of whom he was very proud. He suffered a great shock when later on Har'ley was expelled from Oxford for intemperance. **L. 45. heard in this deep calm**—heard in the deep stillness of the night. **L. 46. interspersed vacancies**—the gaps or pauses which come now and then in the midst of thinking. **L. 47. momentary pauses of thought**—occasional breaks occurring in the current of thought. **L. 48. thrills**—fills with excitement; stirs deeply.

My babe so beautiful ! it thrills my heart
With tender gladness, thus to look at thee,
And think that thou shalt learn far other lore,
And in far other scenes ! For I was reared
In the great city, pent 'mid cloisters dim,
And saw nought lovely but the sky and stars.
But thou, my babe ! shalt wander like a breeze
By lakes and sandy shores, beneath the crags
Of ancient mountain, and beneath the clouds,
Which image in their bulk both lakes and shores
And mountain crags : so shalt thou see and hear
The lovely shapes and sounds intelligible
Of that eternal language, which thy God

Utters, who from eternity doth teach
Himself in all, and all things in himself.
Great universal Teacher ! he shall mould
Thy spirit, and by giving make it ask.

Therefore all seasons shall be sweet to thee,
Whether the summer clothe the general earth
With greenness, or the redbreast sit and sing
Betwixt the tufts of snow on the bare branch
Of mossy apple-tree, while the nigh thatch
Smokes in the sun-thaw; whether the eave-drops fall
Heard only in the trances of the blast,
Or if the secret ministry of frost
Shall hang them up in silent icicles,
Quietly shining to the quiet Moon.

L. 50. tender gladness—with tender joy. **thus to look at thee**—When I look at you in this manner. **L. 51. lore**—learning; knowledge. **And think you...scenes**—The poet thinks that his son will be educated in a different manner and in different surroundings and scenes from those in which he himself was educated. **L. 52. reared**—brought up. **L. 53. In the great city**—i.e. London. **Pent**—choked up. **Cloisters dim**—the dim, dark walks in a school or college. **L. 54. nought**—nothing. **L. 55. But thou, my babe !**—but you, my child. **Shalt wander like a breeze**—you will move about with untrammelled joy and freedom like a breeze. **L. 56. sandy shores**—shores of river or sea. **crags**—steep or rugged rocks. **L. 57. ancient**—primeval; old **L. 58. image**—reflect. **L. 58-59. Which image....crags**—The poet here refers to the popular belief that clouds take the shape of mountains, lakes, crags, etc. over which they fly. **in their bulk**—in their size. **L. 59. 50 shalt thou see and hear**—what the poet means to say is that the child will learn from and be educated by the various sights and sounds of Nature. **L. 60—61. The lovely shape...eternal language**—The shapes and sounds of Nature constitute a sort of symbolic language which God uses eternally in conveying to mankind the message that he has to convey. **L. 61. eternal language**—an echo of Wordsworth's belief in Nature's great atmosphere. I am a town-bred boy, shut in the midst of dimly lighted convents. The only beautiful things I see were the clear sky and the stars glittering in it. But you will run like the wind by the lakes and on sandy shores of seas under the steep rocks and the clouds which take all the different shapes of lakes, shores and rocks. Living in the midst of natural beauty you will feel God present in all things which in their turn, have their beings in God. God knows all things. He is the great universal teacher. He will shape your mind by his supreme influence which you will find in natural sights and sounds. With every bit of knowledge you will gain by this means, you will be eager to know more.

L. 66-75. You will have a happy time in all seasons-whether it be summer when the earth is covered with green trees or winter when the robin sings sitting between tufts of snow on the bare branch of moss-laden apple-tree when in the rays of the sun snow on the thatched roofs melts away or when the soft sounds of frost falling from the eaves are heard only in the spells of cessation of storm or when small frozen particles of ice hanging from the corners of the eaves shine in the soft and silent moonlight.

---

influence in the formation of our character. God is revealed to us through the beautiful sights and sounds of Nature. **thy God utters**—The sounds produced by natural objects are, as it were, the language in which God speaks. **L. 61. doth teach**—reveals. **L. 62. Himself in all**—an expression of the poet's belief in the presence of God in every objects of Nature, (An illustration of his so—called Pantheism). Wordsworth also gives expression to the same thought in his Tintern Abbey. **All things in Himself**—the Pantheistic theory that everything lives moves, and has its being in God. **L. 63. Great universal Teacher**—the poet here emphasises the fact that God is the great teacher of mankind, because living in close contact with the objects of Nature which are the manifestation of God, one learns as one would if one were placed in God's very presence. **he shall mould thy spirit**—he shall fashion your soul. **L. 64. by giving make it ask**—What the poet means to say is that the more hi's child receives the message from God through the medium of Nature, the greater his curiosity for more knowledge. **L. 65. all seasons shall be sweet to thee**—all seasons will appeal to you; you will learn from all the seasons of the year. **L. 66. clothe—cover, the general earth**—whole earth. **L. 67. with greenness**—with green foliage. **The redbreast**—the robin, a favourite song-bird in winter. **Betwixt**—between. **L. 68. tufts**—clusters; bunches. **bare branch**—branch without leaves. **L. 69. mossy**—covered with moss. **the nigh thatch**—thatch of the cottage nearby. **L. 70. smokes**—emits water vapour. **in the sun-thaw**—in the rays of the sun turning the snow into vapour. **While the nigh thatch...sun thaw**—In the rays of the sun, the snow which has been formed on the thatched roofs begins to evaporate. **eave-drops**—drops of melted snow falling from the eaves. **eaves**—projecting edges of roofs. **L. 71. trances**—intervals. **blast**—storm. **Heard only in the trances of the blast**—heard only when there are lulls in the storm. **L. 72. secret ministry**—silent, quiet working of the frost. **L. 73. icicles**—frozen drops of water. **L. 74. Quietly shilling to the quiet Moon**—The icicles shine in the moonlight. The moonlight has a special charm for Coleridge.

(B) INTRODUCTION TO THE POEM

"This poem was written in February 1798 in honour of the poet's son Hartley Coleridge. It gives us the picture of an evening spent by the poet by his fireside on a frosty night. The mood of the poet is contemplative. Memory floats into the poem and colours with its pensive hue the painting of Nature. The world of reality is far off, the poet is walking in a dreamland in which everything is seen bathed in a low, soft: moonlit night, in a veiled music.' His thoughts wander back to his own past, or are projected forward to the failure of his young child. The stillness of the night is maintained throughout the poem. Nowhere is its harmony disturbed by the vehemence of thought.

The poem shows vividly the deep influence exercised upon Coleridge by Wordsworth. Here Coleridge believes in Wordsworth's theory of the Education of Nature which was embodied by him in his Lucy Poems.

> So shalt though see and hear
> The lovely shapes and sounds intelligible
> Of that eternal language which thy God
> Utters, who from eternity both teach
> Himself in all, and all things in Himself.

(C) A CRITICAL SUMMARY OF THE POEM

It is a frosty night. The frost is falling silently and noiselessly. The shrill cries of the owlet heighten the grim silence of Nature. All the members of the poet's family have gone to bed. The poet alone is left to his solitary musings. His infant is sleeping peacefully in the cradle beside him. It is awfully calm. Indeed, so calm it is that it disturbs the poet's meditation "with its strange and extreme silentness." Sea, hill and wood are as quiet as dreams. The fire in the hearth, too is still. Only the film on the fire flutters which appears to the poet as a welcome companion.

Then the poet is reminded of the monotonous life he live in his school-days as he sits at night dreamily watching the flickering of fire in the grate. Confined within the walls of the school he will dream away his days with the sweet memory of his own village, its church-tower and ringing church-bells which was the only music that the poor men hear. At last the pleasant things he dreamt would lull him to sleep, and his dreams will be prolonged in his sleep. Even in the next morning he is so much overtaken by the pleasant dreams of his native village, that he would be quite indifferent to the class-work, although he will continue fixing his look upon the book, awed by the stern teacher's face. As soon as the door half-opened, he will snatch a hasty glance, for he hopes to see some stranger's face or a townsman or his aunt, or some sister with whom he might have played in his childhood.

Thinking of his dull, monotonous school-life, the poet congratulates his son on the fact that his childhood will be spent in far happier surroundings than his. As for the poet he is brought up in the great city, "pent amid cloisters dim" and see nothing lovely but the sky and stars. He is glad to think that his son "shall wander like a breeze by lakes and sandy shores, beneath the crags of ancient mountain and beneath the clouds". He will hear the language of God in Nature's sound and melody, "who from eternity doth teach Himself in all, and all things in Himself." In this way, God-the great Universal Teacher-will teach his child by exciting in him curiosity for beautiful and lovely objects of Nature.

Therefore, all seasons with their characteristic charms and delights will be dear to his son. Summer with its green foliage will have for him as great an appeal as winter when the red-breast sits and sings between the tufts of snow on the bare branch of the moss-covered apple tree.

(D) CRITICAL APPRECIATION, INTERPRETATION AND DEVELOPMENT OF THOUGHT

Development of Thought

The Deep Quietness and Stillness of a Frosty Night. The frost is falling silently and noiselessly, 'unhelped by any wind.' The shrill cries of the owlet enhance the grim silence of the night. All the members of the poet's family have gone to their rest, leaving him to his solitary musings. Only his infant sleeps peacefully in a cradle near him.

The Awful Stillness of the Scene Disturbs the Calm Meditation of the Poet. It is awfully clam. Indeed, it is so calm that it disturbs the poet's meditation with its strange and extreme stillness. Sea, and hill, and wood, and populous village lie as peacefully as dreams. Even the fire in the hearth is still. The only stirring element is the film on the fire which the poet accepts as a welcome companion. The poet reads in its flappings and flutterings meanings according to the mood of his own mind.

The Poet is Reminded of the Monotonous Life he Lived in his School-Days. The poet is reminded of the dreams and fancies which has inspired him in his school-days by the sight of the flame glimmering in the fire-place. He thought he could discover a form within the flame and gazing at it will be reminded of his native place. He dreams his days away with the sweet memory of his own village, its church tower and ringing church bells whose music has a peculiar appeal and significance to him. The dreams which is visited his mind would linger on to the next day and make him indifferent to the class-work. He will pretend to study the book but it swam before his eyes. At that time, seeing the door half-open, he will snatch a hasty glance, for he hope to see the face of some person from his native village, or of some townsman or of some aunt, or of some sister with whom he may have played in his childhood.

The Poet Thinks that his Son's Childhood will be Spent in a Happier Surroundings Than His. Thinking of his unhappy school-life, the poet congratulates his son on the fact that his childhood will be spent in far healthier and more bracing surroundings. As for the poet he is reared in the great city, 'pent amid cloisters dim' and see 'nought lovely but sky and stars'. He is glad to think that his son shall wander like a breeze by lakes and sandy shores, beneath the crags of ancient mountains and beneath the clouds which 'image in their bulk both lakes and shores and mountain crags'. He will thus allow his child to grow unhampered in the midst of the wholesome atmosphere of Nature, drinking deep of her grand majesty and lyric beauty; hearing the language of God in her sound and melody, seeing Him in all things and all things in Him. So God, the great 'Universal Teacher' shall mould his spirit and excite his curiosity and interest in all 'sweet sounds and harmonies.'

How the Various Seasons will Teach the Poet's Son. In as much as the shapes and sounds of Nature will convey to his son the eternal message of God all seasons will be equally dear to his son. Summer with its green foliage will have for him as great an appeal as winter when the robin sits and sings between the tufts of snow on the bare branches of moss-covered apple tree.

Critical Appreciation and Interpretation

Autobiographical Interest. The poem has autobiographical interest. The poet invites his readers to have a peep into his past life. They are allowed to catch a few glimpses of his school days. This is what all great romantic poets do. They become personal and take the reader into their confidence. From this poem we learn that the poet's school life is wretched and miserable.

> ......For I was reared
> In the great city, pent'mid cloisters dim,
> And saw nought lovely but the sky and stars

Coleridge's Attitude Towards Nature. Like all other romantic poets Coleridge is also a keen lover of Nature. His poems are full of Nature pictures. In his conception of Nature, Coleridge was much influenced, at least in his earlier writings, by his friend, Wordsworth. Frost at Midnight clearly bears the impress of Wordsworth and it is he who has coloured Coleridge's view of Nature. Some of the lines could have been written only by Wordsworth.

Wordsworth's philosophy of Nature was (1) his Pantheistic belief that God pervades all objects of Nature, that the divine power manifests itself in all things of this universe and that all things of this universe have their being in Him: (2) the healing power of Nature; he believes that nature exercised a healing balm on the lacerated heart of humanity; that the companionship of Nature brought real joy and solace to the human mind; (3) moral and educative influence of Nature-Wordsworth looked upon Nature as a great moral teacher as the best philosopher, guide and friend of man. One who receives education in the school of Nature and takes her as one's model, one who establishes a spiritual bond with her and has a mystic union, one who abandons himself completely to be guided and shaped by her, will attain perfection and grow up to be the happiest mortal.

The above view of Nature held by Wordsworth is fully illustrated by the poem *Frost at Midnight*. Coleridge himself has passed his school period in the suffocating and soul-crushing atmosphere of the city of London, but his son (so says the poet) shall have direct association with Nature in all her aspects:

> But thou, my babe I shalt wander like a breeze
> By lakes and sandy shores, beneath the crags
> Of ancient mountains, and beneath the clouds

The above lines refer to the Nature Education Theory of Wordsworth as outlined in his Lucy Poems. Perfection in all spheres of life-moral, spiritual and physical-can be attained only if man suffers Nature to mould his personality.

Coleridge was a pantheist. He strongly believed in the immanence of God. This belief of his is clearly supported by the following lines.

> So shalt thou see and hear
> The lovely shapes and sounds intelligible
> Of that eternal language, which the God
> Utters, who from eternity doth teach
> Himself in all, and all things in Himself
> Great universal Teacher he shall mould
> Thy spirit, and by giving make it ask.

Coleridge's Power of Painting Pictures in Words. This poem also brings out Coleridge's wonderful power of painting pictures in words. With what consummate skill does the poet give us the vivid pictures of his, own school days, the fluttering film, the loveliness of the seasons, the silent icicles quietly shining to the quiet moon. Coleridge is a great master of the art of description and his descriptive powers are marvellous.

Tranquillity in the Poem. Peace and stillness reign supreme in the atmosphere of the poem and the poet is in a meditative mood. In the hush of Nature, the poet establishes a bond of sympathy between his mind and the flickering film. His idling spirit interprets the flickerings of the film according to his own fancies. Memories of his past life crowd upon his mind and the picture of his school days comes before him. The poet has well succeeded in producing in our minds the one impression of quietness and calmness, peace and tranquillity. For this purpose he has made use of all aids-language, meter (blank verse), atmosphere, ideas and feelings.

Conclusion. This poem gives us the picture of an evening spent by the poet by his fireside on a frosty night. The mood of the poet is contemplative, memory floats into the poem and colours it with a pensive hue and painting of nature. The world of reality is far off, the poet is walking in a dreamland in which everything is seen bathed in 'a low, soft moonlit night in a veiled music.' His thoughts wander back to his own past, or are projected forward to the future of his young child. The stillness of the night is maintained throughout the poem. Nowhere is its harmony disturbed by vehemence of thought. The metre, though Miltonic in structure, reflects the sweet subdued mood of the poet.

(E) EXPLANATIONS WITH CRITICAL COMMENTS

L. 15-16. Only that film sole unquiet thing. These lines are taken from Coleridge's poem *Frost At Midnight.* In' these lines he means to say that there is no flicker in the fire except in the part of it that smoulders within the grate, and its flickering is the only sign of animation that can be found. This thin flame in the grating is the only thing that breaks the silence prevailing everywhere.

L. 17-23. Methinks, its motion. ...toy of thought. These lines have been taken from Coleridge's poem *Frost At Midnight..* In these lines the poet tells us that he thinks the flickering of the fire in the grating, when quietness prevails over all objects of Nature, establishes its affinity with him who is a living creature, and makes it a welcome companion. Its tiny flappings and flutterings that the spirit of man in a mood of relaxation interprets according to its own mood fancies, for the idling spirit seeks everywhere echo or mirror of itself, and indulges not in sober thoughts but in idle fancies and dreams.

L. 37-38. A wed by the stern ....swimming book. These lines have been taken from Coleridge's poem *Frost At Midnight.* In these lines, the poets tells us that being afraid of punishment from the stern teacher, the poet continued fixing his eyes in mock attention on his book which appeares to swim before his eyes. The attitude of mock attention is assumed by the poet to deceive his stern teacher whose punishment he dreaded.

L. 58-62. So shalt thou see....in himself. These lines have been taken from the poem *Frost At Midnight* by Coleridge. In these lines, the poet tells us that his child will learn from the various beautiful sights and sounds of Nature which serve as it were, the medium of conveying to human beings the message which God is eternally preaching to mankind. God constantly reveals Himself in everything and there is nothing on this earth which is not a manifestation of God. God exists in everything and everything exists in God; this is the Pantheistic Theory. Here the poet gives expression to the typically Wordsworthian theory of the Nature-education which is so beautifully expounded by Wordsworth in his *Lucy Poems*.

L. 65-74. Therefore all seasons...quiet Moon. These lines have been taken from the poem *Frost At Midnight* by Coleridge. In these lines, the poet, addressing his son, says that all the seasons of the year will be pleasant to him. He will love the summer season which will cover the whole earth with green foliage and green verdue. Nor will he fail to be inspired by the song of the robin which in the winter season will sing, sitting among clusters of snow on the bare branch of the moss covered apple trees, while the snow covering the thatched roof of the cottage nearby begins to emit vapours as it melts in the sun. He will love to hear the spattering sound produced by the falling of the drop of rain, heard only in the lulls of the storm, or he will love to watch the masses of snow hanging from the corners of the eaves congealed by the cold wind of winter when the shower or frost falls silently and quietly, and shining gently in the moonlight. These lines reveal the dream-like quality of Coleridge's poetic genius :

13

DEJECTION : AN ODE

WRITEN APRIL 4, 1802

Late, late yestreen I saw the new Moon,
With the old Moon in her arms;
And I fear, I fear, my Master dear !
We shall have a deadly storm.

BALLAD OF SIR PATRICK SPENCE

(A) TEXT, PARAPHRASE AND ANNOTATIONS

I

Well ! If the Bard was weather-wise, who made
The grand old ballad of Sir Patrick Spence,
This night, so tranquil now, will not go hence
Unroused by winds, that ply a busier trade
Than those which mould yon cloud in lazy flakes,
Or the dull sobbing draft, that moans and rakes
Upon the strings of this Æolian lute,
Which better far were mute.
For lo ! the New-moon winter-bright !
And overspread with phantom light,
(With swimming phantom light o'erspread
But rimmed and circled by a silver thread)

I see the old Moon in her lap, foretelling
The coming-on of rain and squally blast.
And oh ! that even now the gust were swelling,
And the slant night-shower driving loud and fast !
Those sounds which oft have raised me, whilst they awed,
And sent my soul abroad,
Might now perhaps their wonted impulse give,
Might startle this dull pain, and make it move and live !

L. 1. **Bard**—the poet who wrote the old ballad of Patrick Spence. **Weather-wise**—good at foretelling weather. **Who made**—i.e., the ballad etc. **L. 2. The grand**—the splendid. **Ballad of Sir Patrick Spence**—An old Scottish ballad describing how Sir Patrick's ship was wrecked. L. 3. **Tranquil**—Calm: **Go hence**—pass away. **L. 4. Unroused by winds**—without being roused by winds. **That.....trade**—that carry on a more restless activity. The poet means that the winds are more actively engaged than merely driving the clouds about. **Ply a busier trade**—work busily or vigorously. **L. 5. Than those**—than those winds. **Mould**—shape; bring into shape **Yon**—distant. **Flakes**—light fleecy tuft or bunch of snow. **which mould....flakes**—winds that by blowing on that distant cloud work it up into light fleecy tufts of snow. **L. 6. Sobbing**—gasping. **Draft**—draught; current of air. **Moans**—murmurs or complains. **Rakes**—sweeps; moves. **L.7. This Æolian lute**—The Æolian lute is a harp played

PARAPHRASE OF THE POEM

Stanza 1. Well ! if the poet, who wrote the ballad of Sir Patrick Spence, was a reliable prophet of weather (in so far as to be believed, that the sight of old moon in the arms of the new, portends stormy weather), this night which is so calm just now, is bound to be stirred by winds that are blowing more violently here than (winds) that are shaping the distant clouds into large fleecy tufts of snow, or than that gasping current of air which is complaining and sweeping over the strings of the Aeolian lute. It will have been much better if the lute are silent. Look! the new moon shining brightly is covered with an unearthly light, a sort of floating ethereal light, and is encircled by a bright thread of light. I see the old moon in the circular disc of the new. It portends the coming of rain and blowing of violent gusts of wind. Even now the gusts of wind are increasing in violence and intensity. Showers of rain are falling in a slating manner and are both loud and fast. The sound, of the wind and storm which often have elevated my soul in the past and have made my imagination roam abroad, might perhaps give their usual impetus to my soul tonight. They might revive my sense of failure and frustration as a poet and even intensify it.

---

upon by the wind. Coleridge is referring to the sound made by the wind as it plays on the various objects of Nature. **Æolian**—of Æolus, the wind-god. **Lute**—A stringed musical instrument. **L. 8. Which better far**—it would have been much better if. **Mute**—silent. **which better....mute**—He is not in a mood to appreciate the music made by the wind. So he wishes that the wind might be hushed and he might be left to his own melancholy. **L. 9. Lo**—look. **The New-moon winter-bright**—the new moon shining, brightly on a winter evening. **L. 10. Overspread**—covered with. **L. 11. Phantom**—unearthly. **Swimming**—floating. **L. 12. Rimmed**—encircled. **Silver thread**—the crescent moon is slender like a thread. **LI 9—12. For lo !—.....silver thread**—for look, the new moon shining brightly in the winter sky is covered with an unearthly light and is encircled by a thread-like circular line. **L. 13. In her lap**—in her orbit (This is a common phenomenon that during the first quarter, the dark part of the orbit of the new moon is made faintly illuminous by the earth—light and it appears as if the new moon is holding the old moon in its lap) **Foretelling**—predicting; portending. **L. 14 Squally blast**—strong gusts of wind and storm. **Blast**—strong gust of wind. **L. 13—14 I see the old moon....squally blast**—There is a superstition whenever the old moon is seen in the arms of the new, it portends (foretells) the coming of a storm. **L 15. Gust**—sudden violent rush of wind. **Swelling**— increasing in volume and intensity. **L. 16. Slant**—oblique; **Night-shower**—shower of the rain failing at night. **driving**—falling or striking. **L. 17. Those sounds**—sounds of a falling rain and blowing of storm. **Raised**—elevated, lifted up. **Raised me**—have elevated my soul; **L. 17 Awed-terror-struck L. 18 sent my soul abroad**—made my fancy roam. **L. 19. Wonted**—unusual. **Impulse**—impetus; mental incitement. **L. 20. Might startle this dull pain**—may bring about another fit of frustration and self-pity. **It**—pain. **L. 17—20. Those sounds......move and live**—The sounds of the wind and storm which often have elevated my soul in past and have made my imaginative sensibility roam abroad, perhaps now might give their usual impetus to my imagination. They might stir up my sense of frustration and failure and even intensify it.

II

A grief without a pang, void, dark, and drear,
    A stifled, drowsy, unimpassioned grief,
    Which finds no natural outlet, no relief,
    In word, or sigh, or tear—
O Lady ! in this wan and heartless mood,
To other thoughts by yonder throstle woo'd
    All this long eve, so balmy and serene,
Have I been gazing on the western sky,
    And its peculiar tint of yellow green :
And still I gaze—and with how blank an eye !
And those thin clouds above, in flakes and bars,
That give away their motion to the stars;
Those stars, that glide behind them or between,
Now sparkling, now bedimmed, but always seen:
Yon crescent Moon, as fixed as if it grew
In its own cloudless, starless lake of blue;
I see them all so excellently fair,
I see, not feel, how beautiful they are !

L. 21. A grief—pang i.e. a dull leaden sensation, an undefined grief which presses upon him but he cannot define it. **Grief**—sorrow; pain. **Pang**—shooting pain; sudden sharp mental pain. **Void**—a grief which has emptied life of all interest. **Drear**—gloomy; dismal; dull. **Dark**—a feeling of a gloom and depression. **L 22. stifled**—chocked; that which finds no expression. **Drowsy**—sleepy : benumbing. **Unimpassioned**—passionless; that which is too deep for tears; feelingless. **L. 23. Outlet**—expression. **Relief**—lessening of or deliverance from pain. **L 21—24. A grief without a pang...or sigh, or tear**—The poet gives expression to a mood of poignant grief in these lines. He finds himself in a state of mental and spiritual despondency. The sorrow from which he suffers is unattended by pain, is ineffectual, dark and dismal. It is a type of chocked up, sleepy and passionless sorrow which refuses to find an expression or get some relief in the words, sighs or tears. This sorrow has so completely taken possession of his soul, and is so intense and deep—seated that neither heaving of sighs nor shedding of tears brings my relief to the poet. **L. 25. O Lady**—O Sara (Coleridge's wife). **Wan**—pale and apathetic. **Heartless**—Unfeeling. Coleridge describes his mood of mind as one without feeling and utterly apathetic to things that usually interest a man. It shows the depth of his dejection. **L. 26. Other thoughts**—thoughts other than these thoughts of sorrow and suffering. **Throstle**—thrush, an English song bird. **Woo'd**—won. **To other thoughts by yonder throstle woo'd**—having different thoughts from those happy thoughts that are inspiring the distant throstle to sing (Coleridge means that the throstle is in a happy mood of frame as it is singing joyously but he himself is in a very unhappy mood as he is feeling gloomy and depressed.) **L. 27. All this**—throughout this long evening. **Eve**—evening. **Balmy**—fragrant; soothing; healing;

Stanza 2. The sorrow from which I suffer is unattended by pain, is ineffectual, dark and dismal. It is a sort of choked up, sleepy, feelingless sorrow which refuses to find an expression (and get some relief thereby into words, sighs or tears. O my sweetheart! in this vacant and feelingless mood and entertaining different thoughts from those of the distant singing throstle, I have been looking at the sky in the west and at its peculiar yellow-green colour. I am still looking at it (the sky) and I am staring at it with a blank look. I look at those thin clouds worked up into flakes and streaked with bars. These clouds by moving themselves, make the stars move behind or between them. Sometimes these stars look very bright and sometimes very dim but they can be seen always. The distant new moon is fixed to its place and it appears as it grows where it is shining now. I see all these objects of nature which are so exceedingly beautiful but I am not moved or stirred to my depths by their beauty.

Serene—clear and clam, placid. **L.28. Gazing on**—.looking at; **Have...sky**—throughout the long and peaceful serene evening he had been looking at the western sky (just as Wordsworth had looked at Nature in the earlier verses of the Immortality Ode.) **L. 29. Tint**—colour. **Tint.. .green**—colour of the evening sky which is sober yellow. In the description of skyscape Coleridge resembles Shelley and is almost equally felicitous. **L. 30. Blank**—void of interest. **And still...eye**—He looks on at the sky but it strikes no feeling in his mind; it is all blank and negative. **L 31. Flakes**—light fleecy tuft or bunch of snow. **Bars**—streaks. **In flakes and bars**—in various layers and colours. **L. 32. That give away their motion to the stars**—clouds that by floating in the sky, make the stars appear as moving in the sky. **And those. ...stars**—the thin layers of variously coloured clouds that move about the sky and it seems as though the stars peeping through the clouds are really moving and not the clouds. **L. 33. Glide**—move. **Behind them**—behind the clouds. **L. 34. Sparkling**—shining. **Bedimmed**—appearing or growing dim. **L. 33—34. Those stars,....seen**—between the clouds, and some times behind them the stars seem, to be all the time moving, sometimes shining brightly when the cloud moves away and the star is clearly seen, sometimes, dim when the stars arc seen through the thin clouds. But either dim or clear the stars arc always visible. **L. 35. Crescent**—moon of first week; **As fixed**—as rooted to one place. **L. 36. Cloudless**—clear. **Starless lake of blue**—clear sky. **L. 35—36. You crescent......lake of blue**—The new moon that is seen as if it is fixed in the limpid blue sky. In the cloudless sky the moon is, as it were, fixed; when the clouds move about, the stars seem to be moving in and out of the clouds. **L. 37. Excellently fair**—exceedingly beautiful. **L. 38. I see, not feel**—I see these beautiful objects of Nature like the moon and the stars but I do not feel or experience joy on seeing them (I am not stirred to my depths, by their beauty).

III

My genial spirits fail;
And what can these avail
To lift the smothering weight from off my breast ?
It were a vain endeavour,
Though I should gaze for ever
On that green light that lingers in the west :
1 may not hope from outward forms to win
The passion and the life, whose fountains are within.

IV

O Lady ! we receive but what we give,
And in our life alone does Nature live :
Ours is her wedding garment, ours her shroud !
And would we aught behold, of higher worth,
Than that inanimate cold world allowed
To the poor loveless ever-anxious crowd,
Ah ! from the soul itself must issue forth
A light, a glory, a fair luminous cloud
Enveloping the Earth—
And from the soul itself must there be sent

L. 39. **Genial**—jovial: enlivening; warm. **My genial spirits fail**—I feel no longer jovial or cheerful. **L. 40. What can these avail**—How is it possible for the world of external nature to help to raise his spirits ? **L. 41. Lift**—raise, elevate. **Smothering**—stifling; chocking; throttling; suffocating. **And what can these ...breast**—These sight of natural objects cannot relieve me of the stifling burden of sorrow and grief. **L. 42. Vain endeavour**—Useless attempt. **L. 44. Green light**—Green light of clouds and storm. **L. 45. From outward forms**—from external objects of nature. **L. 46. The passion and the life**—Soaring emotions and vital energy. **Whose fountains are within**—Coleridge says that the source of poetic inspiration is the mind or the soul and if the fountains of the inner mind are dry, no external object, however beautiful, can inspire the pod. Inspiration comes from within and not from out. **L. 45—46. 1 may not... within**—I cannot expect to derive from the beautiful objects of the outside world those feelings and that vitality of the springs which lie within the mind. Here, we have the subjectivity of Coleridge. For him everything is coloured by his own mind and he cannot expect to get anything to encourage or enliven him from the outside world. **L. 47. O Lady ! We receive what we give**—We interpret Nature by our own moods or thoughts. **L. 48. And in our life alone does Nature live**—We ourselves attribute emotions and feelings to animate objects of Nature. Thus nature is neither beautiful nor horrible, neither kind or unkind, we make it appear such by attributing feelings and emotions to it. Nature is inanimate. It has no life, no intellect, no spirit. We invest it with all these things. **L. 49. Ours is her wedding garment**—We invest nature with beauty and colour. (wedding garment stands for beauty, splendour and colour). **Shroud**—garment for the dead; coffin. **L. 50. And**

Stanza 3. I feel no longer jovial and mirthful. The sight of the beautiful objects of nature cannot cure the sorrow of my heart by lifting the stifling weight of grief from off my mind. It will be a fruitless attempt even though I shall go on looking at that green light which is still staying out in the west. I cannot expect external objects of nature to' inspire me, because the sources of poetic inspiration lie within the mind or the soul of a person (Thus if the mind is paralysed, no amount of external objects, however beautiful, can inspire the poet.)

Stanza 4. O Sara! we interpret nature by our own moods and whims. We ourselves attribute emotions and feelings to inanimate objects of nature. We invest nature with beauty and colour (sometimes when we are in a happy mood) and we invest it with gloom and sorrow (when we are dejected or depressed). If we read a deeper or inner meaning into nature (Like Wordsworth, for example) the inner meaning is deposited into nature by ourselves, for it is not revealed by the lifeless and cold nature to the feelingless and overanxious common man. The higher or spiritual meaning that we (pretend) to read into nature, only proceeds from our own soul, the light, the splendour, the beautiful brightness with which we invest nature come from within our own soul and are made to wrap up the different objects (of nature). Similarly, the poetic inspiration also proceeds from the soul of the poet. It is nothing but a sweet and

---

would we...behold—If we wish to see anything. **Of higher worth**—having higher value or significance (than that inanimate cold world etc.) **L. 51. Inanimate**—lifeless. **Cold world**—World of nature; nature. **L. 51—52. Allowed to the poor**—revealed to the common. **L. 52. Loveless**—feelingless. **Crowd**—Common man. **To the poor...crowd**—to those poor vulgar multitude who live loveless and laborious days. **L. 50—52. And would we...crowd**—What Coleridge means in this—if we would see in Nature anything that has a higher significance than what the vulgar multitude are permitted to see. Coleridge seems to imply that ordinary men, with their constant anxieties and tragic lack of love, saw Nature without enthusiasm, as though it were something drab and dreary. Anyone who wishes to have a higher conception of Nature for example, as his friend Wordsworth had, he must use his power of imagination. **L. 53. Ah ! from the soul itself must issue forth**—that higher or spiritual significance that we pretend to read into nature, only proceeds from our own soul. We ourselves put these inner meanings into Nature, otherwise nature has no inner significance. **L. 54. Luminous**—bright; shining. **L. 55. Enveloping**—wrapping up. **The earth**—Nature. **L. 53—54. Ah from the soul...cloud**—If he wants to have a higher view of Nature, then there must come from his soul the light and the glory and the radiance that must invest the real world. No doubt Coleridge writes these lines with the memory of Wordsworth's poetry in his mind, perhaps in answer to his friend's attitude in these matters. **L. 54—55. A light, a glory, a fair luminous cloud...earth**—The light, the splendour, the beautiful brightness with which we invest nature, come from within our own soul and are made to wrap up the different objects of Nature; otherwise they have no intrinsic light, splendour or beauty of their own.

A sweet and potent voice, of its own birth,
Of all sweet sounds the life and element !

V

O pure of heart! thou need'st not ask of me
What this strong music in the soul may be !
What, and wherein it doth exist,
This light, this glory, this fair luminous mist,
This beautiful and beauty-making power.
Joy, virtuous Lady ! Joy that ne'er was given,
Save to the pure, and in their purest hour,
Life, and Life's effluence, cloud at once and shower,
Joy, Lady ! is the spirit and the power,
Which wedding Nature to us gives in dower

A new Earth and new Heaven,
Undreamt of by the sensual and the proud—
Joy is the sweet voice, Joy the luminous cloud—
We in ourselves rejoice !
And thence flows all that charms or ear or sight,
All melodies the echoes of that voice,
All colours a suffusion from that light.

L. 57. **Potent**—powerful. **Of its own birth**—born of the soul and an essential Component of all sweet sounds in the world. L. 58. **Element**—component. **Of all....element**.—This voice is the life and essence of all the sweet sounds that are heard. What the poet means is that it is not Nature that really speaks its messages to man, but rather it is man who puts his own voice into nature. The poet's imagination enables him to read in nature a sweet and potent voice which seems to be the essence of all the sweet sounds that he hears. **L. 56—58. And from the soul....element**— Coleridge means that just as the light and glory with which we invest different objects of nature proceed from our soul, similarly poetic inspiration proceeds from or comes from the soul. It is a sweet and powerful echo of the soul and it is the essential component of all the sweet sounds (like music and poetry) in the world. In other words, there cannot be any great poetry or music unless inspiration for it comes from the soul of the, poet. **L. 59. O pure of heart**—O Innocent Sara! **L. 60. Strong music in the soul**—Poetic inspiration, the seat of which is the soul of the poet. **L. 61. It**—music or inspiration. **L. 62. Fair luminous**—beautiful and bright. **This light......this glory**—He explains the radiance that invests this world, and which, in his dejection is shut out from his mind as the reflection of Joy and nothing more. It has no objective reality. **L. 63. This beautiful and beauty-making power**—This inspiration which is beautiful itself and which enables the poet to create beauty or beautiful poetry; creative imagination which endows all objects with beauty. **L. 64. Joy**—poetic inspiration is an exultation or joy. **L. 65. Save**—except. **To the pure**—To the poets with a pure heart. **Purest hour**—In the powerful echo of the soul and it in itself is the very soul and essential component of all sweet sounds (like music and poetry).

Stanza 5. O innocent and spotless Sara! you need not ask me what poetic inspiration is like or where its abode is. It is a light, a splendour, a beautiful mist which is not only beautiful in itself but which enables the poet to create beauty. It is given to poets in their most sublime moments. It is the very soul of life, nay the very stream from which life flows. It is vague as well as beneficial. It is a pure joy. It is spirit and a power which Nature gives to the poets when nature and the poets work in perfect harmony. It is a dowry or gift bestowed by Nature on the poets.

By virtue of possessing it, the poets enjoy the vision of a new earth and a new heaven: a vision which cannot be imagined by those who delight in pleasures of the sense and who are proud. We, the poets, take delight in our poetic faculties or poetic inspiration. From it (the poetic inspiration or exultation) flow all the fine arts that captivate the ear or the eye (like the arts of music, poetry, painting and sculpture). All music is nothing but a reverberation of poetic exultation and all the colours used by the painters in painting are coloured or influenced by it.

---

most sublime moment. **L. 66. Life**—it is the very soul of life. **Life's effluence**—that which issues out of life as showers of rain issue out of clouds. What Coleridge means is that joy is as spontaneous and refreshing as the rain that falls from the clouds. **L. 68. Wedding Nature**—Nature wedding the poet. i.e., when Nature and the poet are in harmony. **To us gives**—gives to the poets. **Dower**—Dowry. **L 69. A new Earth and new Heaven**—By virtue of poetic inspiration a new earth and new heaven arc revealed to the poets. This is the dowry that nature gives to the poets when it weds them i.e., when the poets and nature are in perfect harmony. **L. 67—70. Joy...is the spirit...proud**—It is the influence of joy and its great power that brings about a union between nature and ourselves. And it is as the reward of this union, this close communion that grows up between Nature and us, that we realise a new Earth. Life in other words, is transformed into something enormously beautiful. This beauty is something that the sensual and the proud cannot even imagine. **L. 71. Sweet voice**—voice that expresses this union between man and Nature. This intimate communion overflows into joy. **Luminous**—bright. **L. 72. We in ourselves rejoice**—We reveal or take delight in our joys consequent on our poetic inspiration. **L. 73. Thence**—from the poetic inspiration. All that charms—all those fine arts that captivate the ear or the eye flow from the poetic inspiration. **L. 73. Or ear or sight**—Arts that charm the car are music and poetry, arts that charm the eye are painting and sculpture. **L.74. Melodies**—Music. **Echoes of that voice**—reverberation of the poetic inspiration. **All melodies...voice**— All music seems to be echoes of the voice of that joy. **L. 75. All colours**—All the colours used in painting etc. **Suffusion**—Colouring. **All colours....light**—All colours are nothing but that which spreads from within viz., our joy and over the external world .The idea is that joy issues from the mind and spreads over the external world, making the outside world so exquisitely colourful.

VI

There was a time when, though my path was rough,
This joy within me dallied with distress,
And all misfortunes were but as the stuff
Whence Fancy made me dreams of happiness :
For hope grew round me, like the twining vine,
And fruits, and foliage, not my own, seemed mine.
But now afflictions bow me down to earth :
Nor care I that they rob me of my mirth;
But oh ! each visitation
Suspends what nature gave me at my birth,
My shaping spirit of Imagination.
For not to think of what I needs must feel,
But to be still and patient, all I can;
And haply by abstruse research to steal
From my own nature all the natural man—
This was my sole resource, my only plan :
Till that which suits a part infects the whole,
And now is almost grown the habit of soul.

L. 76. **There was a time**—i.e., in the past. He is referring to the years before his personal life became a burden to him. This would be till 1798. **Though my path was rough**—Though I led an unhappy life; though I had to face many difficulties. L. 77. **This joy**—poetic inspiration. **Dallied**—made sport with; played with. **Distress**—sorrow. **Dallied with distress**—amused itself with my mental troubles: inspite of his sorrow he found relaxation in joy. **L. 78 Stuff**—material. **L. 79. Fancy**—Imagination or imaginative faculty. **L. 78—79. All misfortunes... happiness**—All my sorrows were only materials which my imagination transformed into happiness. Here Coleridge is expressing his favourite conception of the shaping power of imagination. **Whence**—out of which. **L. 80. Twining vine**—a creeper growing round a tree. **For hope grew......vine**—He explains here the reason why he was then able to feel joy. It was because he had taken the capacity for hope; he hoped that life would be happy with the passage of years. But now that hope is gone. Here he refers to the time when hope surrounded his life like the vine. **L. 81. Foliage**—leaves. **And fruits, and foliage.. .mine**—whenever joy and peace of mind seemed to be mine i.e., when he could find pleasure in others' happiness; he could lose his personal identity in that of others. L. 82. **Afflictions**—Misfortunes: sorrow. **Bow me down to earth**—depress me greatly. **L. 83. Rob**—deprive. **Mirth**—jollity; joy **L. 84. Each visitation**—each visit of the fit of mental depression. **L. 85. Suspends**—annuls; cancels **L. 86. My shaping spirit of Imagination**—my imaginative faculty or sensibility which enabled me to compose poetry; i.e., the power of the imagination that makes him give shape to the fancies of his mind, to transform joys into sorrows. It is the creative power of the poet. Coleridge believes that this creative power of

Stanza 6. In the past though I have to face many difficulties yet on account of possessing poetic exultation, I did not mind sorrow. I took misfortunes smilingly. They are, in fact the material, out of which my imagination wove beautiful dreams of happiness for me. I am hopeful and optimistic. I am encircled by thoughts of hope just as a tree is entwined by a creeper, and blessings and joys, which eluded me still seemed to be within my grasp. But now misfortunes crush me completely. I, however, do not mind the loss of my jollity. But what I mind most is that each visit of misfortunes and mental depression annuls or suspends what nature bestowed on me at the time of my birth-my poetic faculty or imaginative sensibility. I realise my helplessness in not being able ~ express what I feel strongly. I am compelled to be silent and resign myself to the loss of my poetic faculty. I fear that the increasing interest I am taking in profound Metaphysics (philosophy) will one day kill the poet in me, though I feel, that by nature I am a poet and not a Metaphysician. My poetic faculty is my only stock or treasure; but Metaphysics which best suits intellect or intellectual faculties, has now infected the whole of my being. The metaphysical way of thinking has become a second nature with me (so that I am now incapable of experiencing a poetic or emotional rapture).

---

imagination can operate only when the mind is free from all worries. **L. 87. For not to think of what I needs must feel**—I am in the helpless condition of not being able to express what I strongly feel. **L. 88. But to be still and patient, all I can**—Having lost my imaginative faculty, all I can is to keep quiet and resign myself to my loss. **L. 89. Haply**—perhaps, by change. **Abstruse research**—profound metaphysical philosophy towards which I am inclining every day; **L. 88—90. And haply...natural man**—Perhaps I may be able by deep research and speculation to find out from within my own nature the natural unsophisticated man that once I was. The poet had lost his natural gifts, 'what nature gave him at his birth'. This was the creative power. Now he thinks that perhaps he might, by philosophical enquiry and research, get back this power that once used to be his quite naturally. This, as he says, was his one determination, his only plan, after this dejection came upon him. He tried to achieve that which Wordsworth actually did—when he spoke of 'the year that brings the philosophic mind'. **L.91. Sole**—only. **Resource**—stock that can be drawn on; means. **This was my sole resource**—Poetic faculty was my only resource or stock. **L. 92. Till that**—till metaphysics. **Suits a part**—which suits intellectual faculties or mind (metaphysics only suits intellectual faculties or intellect) **Infects the whole**—Metaphysics has infected all my faculties. It has superseded the imaginative and poetic faculties. It not only dominates the intellect but also my emotions and feelings. **L. 93. And now is almost grown the habit of my soul**—Metaphysical way of thinking has, become my second nature. My very soul has been infected by Metaphysics so that it is incapable now of emotional rapture or poetic outbursts.

VII

Hence, viper thoughts, that coil around my mind,
Reality's dark dream !
I turn from you, and listen to the wind,
Which long has raved unnoticed. What a scream
Of agony by torture lengthened out
That lute sent forth ! Thou wind, that rav'st without,
Bare crag, or mountain-tairn, or blasted tree,
Or pine-grove whither woodman never clomb,
Or lonely house, long held the witches' home,

Methinks were fitter instruments for thee,
Mad Lutanist! who in this month of showers,
Of dark-brown gardens, and of peeping flowers,
Mak'st Devils' yule, with worse than wintry song,
The blossoms, buds, and timorous leaves among.
Thou Actor, perfect in all tragic sounds !
Thou mighty Poet, e'en to frenzy bold !
What tell'st thou now about?
'Tis of the rushing of an host in rout,
With groans, of trampled men, with smarting wounds—
At once they groan with pain, and shudder with the cold !

L. 94. Viper thoughts—malignant or torturing thoughts pertaining to Coleridge's sense of futility, failure or frustration. **Viper**—a kind of poisonous snake. **Coil**—twist round like a serpent. **L. 95. Reality's dark dream**—consciousness or the dark or unpleasant realities of his failure as a poet. **L. 96. 1 turn from you**—I refuse to think of you or ponder over you. **L. 94—96. Hence, viper thoughts,.... wind**—Leaving aside torturing thoughts which oppress my mind and which force in upon me the consciousness of my failure as a poet, I want to listen to the noise made by the wind in order to escape such unpleasant thoughts. **L. 97. Which**—the wind. **Raved**—howled, roared. **Which long has raved unnoticed**—the wind which has been roaring for a long time, unnoticed by me. **Scream of agony**—cry of pain. **L. 98. Torture**—severe pain. **Lengthened out**—drawn out. **L. 99. sent forth**—produced. **L. 97-99. What a scream of agony...sent forth**—The lute (played upon by the wind) gave expression to a cry of pain that was drawn out on account of the torture felt by the musical instrument (The lute seems to echo the mental torture suffered by the poet. Here we have an instance of pathetic fallacy, i.e., attributing feelings and emotions to inanimate objects) **Rav'st without**—howls outside. **L. 100. Crag**—rock; **Mountain-tairn**—mountainous lake. **Blasted tree**—withered tree. **L. 101. pine-grove**—group of pine trees; a small wood of pine trees. **Clomb**—climbed. **L. 102. Lonely house, long held the witches' home**—a haunted house which has been the abode of evil spirits for a long time.) **L. 103. Methinks**—it appears to me. **Were fitter instruments**— were more suitable instruments than the lute (on which the wind blows) **L. 99—103. Thou wind, that rav'st without......for thee**—Addressing the wind, that is howling outside, the poet reminds it (the wind) that should blow

Stanza 7. Therefore leaving aside tormenting and biting thoughts which oppress my mind and which make me realise the unpleasant reality of my failure as a poet, I turn to listen to the noise made by the wind which has been howling for a long time unnoticed by me. That lute, just now (played upon by the wind) gave expression to a cry of pain that was drawn but because of the torture of the experience. You wind! it would have been far better for you if you blew on bare rocks, mountainous lakes, a withered tree, through a thick group of pine trees never climbed by a woodcutter, or through a haunted house which has been the abode of evil spirits for a long time, rather than on the lute lying in the window. O wind, you are a mad lute player, because in the rainy season you are, by making the weather intensely cold, celebrating an untimely and unholy Christmas festival, with your shrieking songs, by blowing through flowers, buds and timid leaves of trees in the garden. You (the wind) are a perfect actor because you can imitate all the human tragic sounds. You are a powerful poet (because you can express every human sound) and are bold to point of being mad. You seem just now to imitate the sound of a defeated army retreating in a disorderly manner. You seem to imitate perfectly the shrieks of trampled soldiers who are crying on account of

---

on bare rocks, mountainous lakes or a withered tree or through a thick group of pine trees never climbed by a forester or through haunted house which has been the abode of witches for a long time, rather than on the lute lying in the window of the poet's room. These things, he suggests, are more suitable instruments for the wind to blow upon, than the lute. **L. 104. Mad Lutanist**—i.e., the wind. A lutanist means a 'lute player'—one who plays on a lute. **Month of showers**—In the rainy' season. **L. 105. Of dark-brown gardens**—when gardens look dark brown on account of cloudy skies. **Peeping flowers**—when flowers peep around. **L. 106 Devils' yule**—Stormy and tumultuous Christmas. **Yule**—Christmas festival. **With worse......song**—accompanied by something worse than the bleak whistle of wintry winds. **L. 107. Blossoms**—flowers. **Timorous**—timid; easily alarmed. **L. 108. Thou actor**—the wind is addressed as an actor because like an actor it can imitate all human sounds as it blows. **Perfect in all tragic sounds**—It can perfectly imitate all sorrowful sounds. **L. 109. Thou mighty poet**—Wordsworth had addressed the child as the 'mighty poet'. Coleridge applies the address to the wind because like the poet, it plays on human feelings. **E'en.. .bold**—even to the point of being frenzied with poetic passion. **L. 110. What tell'st thou now about**—Which human sounds are you imitating just now. **L. 111. Host**—army. **'Tis of the rushing of an host in rout**—the wind seems to imitate just now the sound of a disorderly retreat of an army which has been defeated. **L. 112. Groans**—cries; **trampled**—trodden. **smarting wounds**—wounds giving acute pain. **L. 113. They**—the defeated soldiers. **Shudder**—tremble. **L. 111—113. 'Tis of the rushing of an host in rout....cold**—The stormy wind as it blows seems to be imitating human sounds. It appears to Coleridge that the wind is producing a noise like the one made by the disorderly retreat of a defeated army. The wind is imitating the shrieks of the trampled and wounded soldiers who groan unanimously on account of pain and who tremble all together on account of cold. L. 114. **Hush**—silence. Deepest silence—most profound silence.

But hush ! there is a pause of deepest silence !
And all that noise, as of a rushing crowd,
With groans, and tremulous shudderings—all is over—
It tells another tale, with sounds less deep and loud
A tale of less affright.
And tempered with delight,
As Otway's self had framed the tender lay,-
'Tis of a little child
Upon a lonesome wild,
Not far from home, but she hath lost her way :
And now moans low in bitter grief and fear,
And now screams loud, and hopes to make her mother hear.

VIII

'Tis midnight, but small thoughts have I of sleep:
Full seldom may my friend such vigils keep !

Visit her, gentle Sleep ! with wings of healing,
And may this storm be but a mountain-birth,
May all the stars hang bright above her dwelling,
Silent as though they watched the sleeping Earth !
With light heart may she rise,
Gay fancy, cheerful eyes,
Joy lift her spirit, joy attune her voice;

L. 115. **Rushing crowd**—running or retreating soldiers of a defeated army. **L. 116. Groans**—cries and shrieks. **Tremulous**—quivering. **Shudderings**—trembling on account of cold. **All is over**—has disappeared; is being heard no longer. **L. 117. It tells another tale**—The wind is now imitating the sound of some other human being. **L. 118. Tale of less affright**—a story of lesser fear (than the fear of the retreating army). **L. 119. Tempered with**—modified or mitigated by delight. **L. 120. Otway's**—Thomas Otway (1652—85). He wrote three great tragedies *viz. Don Carlos,* in rhymed verse, *The Orphan* and *Venice Preserved* (in blank verse) He also wrote a number of tender lyrics and songs. **L. 120—121. As Otway's self...tender lay**—The sound that the wind is producing or imitating is as delightful as a soft song composed by Thomas Otway himself. **L. 121. 'Tis of a little child**—The wind is imitating the cry of a small child. **L. 122. Upon a lonesome wild**—in a lonely forest (the cry of a child who has lost its way in a lonely forest); **L. 123. She**—the child. **L. 124. Moans**—cries. **L. 125. Screams loud**—cries loudly. **Hopes to make her mother hear**—By crying loudly the child hopes to attract the attention of her mother who would come and take her home. **L. 118—125. A tale of less affright....her mother hear**—The wind is now imitating the sound of a less fearful human tragedy. This sound is modified by delight and appears to be as soft as the tender song composed by Thomas Otway. This sound resembles the sound of a little child who has lost her way in a lonely forest situated near her home and who the severe wounds they have received in the battle-field. They seem to be crying with pain all together and shivering with the cold. But silence! there is a pause of profoundest silence. It seems that all the noise of the retreating army accompanied by cries and shivering has vanished. The wind now imitates the sound of some other human being in a softer and less loud manner. It is a story of lesser fear and it is mitigated by a delightful pathos. It is as charming as a charming song composes by Thomas Otway himself. The wind is now imitating the sound of a small child who has lost her way in a lonely forest which is situated near her home. The child seems to cry softly sometimes out of fear and poignant sorrow and sometimes shrieks loudly, in order to attract the attention of her mother.

Stanza 8. It is midnight but I have little inclination to go to bed. I pray, however, that my beloved Sara might never have to keep awake at night like me. O gentle sleep, visit my beloved with your balmy and soothing charm. I wish and pray that this storm be confined to the mountain which has given birth to it and may now blow over the house of my sweetheart. May all the stars shine brightly above her house, and may they shine so serenely and silently as if they are watching the sleeping earth. May my beloved Sara rise from her sleep in the morning in a

---

cries sometimes in low voice and who shrieks at times loudly in order to attract the attention of her mother. L. 126. **Small thoughts have I of sleep**—I have no idea of going to bed. **L. 127. Vigils**—Keeping awake at night. **Full seldom....keep**—I pray that my friend (my beloved Sara) may never keep awake at night like me. She should enjoy sound sleep. **L. 128. Wings of healing**—with your soothing or balmy charm. **L. 129. Mountain-birth**—i.e., be confined to the mountain where it is born. **And may this....mountain-birth**—May this storm be confined to only this mountain. Thus, he prays that this storm should not be blowing over the house of his beloved. **L. 132. Light heart**—in a cheerful frame of mind; In a happy mood; cheerfully. **with light**—the home of his beloved. **Silent as though....Earth**—The stars should shine as serenely and calmly over the house of his beloved as if they are watching in silence the earth which has fallen asleep. **With light heart may she rise**—I pray that my beloved should get up in the morning in a cheerful frame of mind. **L. 133. Gay fancy, cheerful eyes, joy lift her spirit**—May bright thoughts cheerful looks and joy elevate or enliven her soul. **L. 134. Attune**—bring into musical accord. **Joy attune her voice**—her voice should be brought into musical accord. i.e., it should be made musical by joy. **L. 135. From pole to pole**—from one end of the earth to the other. **To her may...to pole**—She may take pleasure in all things that exist in the world. She may feel that all things are full of life and beauty and are to be enjoyed.

To her may all things live, from pole to pole,
Their life the eddying of her living soul !
        O simple spirit, guided from above,
Dear Lady ! friend devoutest of my choice,
Thou mayest thou ever, evermore rejoice.

L. 136. Eddying—whirlpool. **Their life the eddying of her living soul**—The life of all creatures on earth may seem to be only the pulsation of her soul; may her soul be active and operate in all objects of nature, so that they may take from her life and tone and be like her held in balanced harmony i.e., her soul should be surrounded by all living and pleasurable things. **L. 137. O simple spirit**—i.e., Coleridge's beloved, Sara. **Guided from above**—guided by heaven in all thoughts and actions. **L. 138. Friend devoutest**—the most pious friend. **L 139. Thou mayest thou ever, evermore**—Here Coleridge prays that she may feel happy always i.e., his beloved may be never invaded by sorrowful thoughts and that she may enjoy happiness constantly.

cheerful frame of mind. May bright thoughts, cheerful looks and joy elevate her soul and may joy make her voice musical. May all nature always appear to her to be full of joy and beauty and may her living soul be surrounded by all the pleasures of life. O beloved Sara ! you are an innocent spirit who are guided by heaven. You are the most pious friend of mine. I pray that you should enjoy constant and eternal happiness and sorrow may never invade your heart.

(B) A CRITICAL SUMMARY OF THE POEM

Stanza I. Coleridge, on seeing the old moon in the arms of the new, fears that it portends stormy weather. As he is contemplating on the superstition associated with the phenomenon, the storm begins to blow. Coleridge feels that the sounds of the wind and storm which uses to Inspire him in the past, might give their usual impetus to his soul on that night, and might stir up his sense of frustration and even intensify it.

Stanza II. Coleridge gives expression to the grief from which he is suffering. It is such a dark and dismal sorrow that it finds no expression in words, tears or sighs. He feels that nature cannot cure him of his pessimism and melancholy as he is no longer stirred to his depths by nature.

Stanza III. Coleridge believes that the sources of poetic inspiration lie within the human mind or the human soul. Thus when the mind is paralysed nature cannot inspire the poet.

Stanza IV. Coleridge challenges the popular notion of Wordsworthian philosophy. He says that it is we ourselves who invest nature with life, soul beauty or gloominess. It is we who attribute feelings and emotions to inanimate nature. Nature is lifeless—it has neither intellect nor soul. Further, he believes that the poetic inspiration is an echo of the poet's soul.

Stanza V. He defines poetic inspiration as a 'light, a glory, a fair luminous mist' which is not only beautiful in itself but which enables the poets to create beauty. It is joy-exultation. From it flows all fine arts like music, poetry and painting, which captivate the ear or the eye.

Stanza VI. Referring to his past, Coleridge says that he used to feel inspire and hopeful then, inspire of difficulties and hardships. Now, however, misfortunes overpower him. He, however does not lament so much the loss of mirth and joy as the loss of his poetic faculty. He feels that he is drifting more and more towards the study of 'Metaphysics' and fears that by and by this new interest will 'kill' the poet in him, though by nature he is a poet rather than a philosopher.

Stanza VII. He finds escape from torturing and tormenting thoughts of despair by turning to the wind that is raving outside. The wind, so it appears to him, is imitating tragic human sounds. At times it seems to imitate the sound of a defeated army, retreating in a disorderly manner. Like an actor the wind imitates perfectly the sounds of trampled, wounded and shivering soldiers of the defeated army. After a pause, the wind seems to be imitating the cries of a small child who has lost her way in a lonely forest, situated near her home.

Stanza VIII. Though it is midnight, Coleridge has little inclination to go to bed. He, however, prays that his beloved may never have to keep awake at night. Likewise he prays that she may enjoy eternal happiness and that thoughts of sorrow or dejection may never invade her heart.

The poet describes the outburst of a storm after a calm evening and laments his own torpor and inability to be moves by the awful grandeur of the night. His own mood is wan and heartless. The fountains of life fail within him; he lacks that emanation from soul necessary for the appreciation of Nature.

He looks back upon the imaginative days of his youth, when joy and hope has arisen naturally in his heart. But pain and grief have taken all these away; abstruse research has superseded the imaginative faculty. The wind's expression of human cries only re-echoes his afflictions. His one comfort is to pray that those whom he loves may not share such unrest.

(C) INTRODUCTION TO THE POEM

This poem is written in 1802. It gives expression to a poignant mood of pessimism and disillusionment. Coleridge's "sense of failure and sterility" found expression in a number of poems, for instance, *Youth and Age, Work without Hope and Dejection: An Ode*. The last is the greatest of his poems of despair and depression. In it the poet laments the loss of his poetic faculty, "my shaping spirit of imagination." In a letter Coleridge explained his dejection as due to a feeling of the loss of his poetic and imaginative faculties, and complains that sickness and some other worse afflictions has forced him into downright metaphysics while he felt that by nature he has more of the poet in him.

The Ode in its original form is addressed to his friend Wordsworth, but during a personal quarrel, references pertaining to Wordsworth are taken Out and Sara is substituted in place of Wordsworth. It is, however clear, that the poet has Wordsworth in mind when he wrote this poem. The fourth stanza of this *Ode* makes a point reference to Wordsworth's habit of attributing emotions and feelings to inanimate nature. Coleridge contradicts Wordsworth when he says:

O Lady we receive but what we give

In some of his earlier poems, notably *Frost at Midnight* (1798) and *Eolian Harp* (1795), Coleridge like Wordsworth has maintained that Nature is pervaded by the Divine Spirit and that it is possible for human mind to commune with in. In *Dejection: An Ode* Coleridge accuses Wordsworth as well as himself of what Ruskin term as the Pathetic fallacy (*i.e.,* attributing feelings and emotions to inanimate objects of Nature).

The poem is in some respect similar to and in others different from Immortality Ode by Wordsworth. Like Wordsworth, Coleridge laments in Dejection the loss of his ability to experience the enthusiasm and power which he uses to when he uses to rejoice in nature, when hope grew round him like the twining vine and laments that Nature cannot move and inspire him now. But in many respects this poem presents a sharp contrast to the immortality Ode. As in the Eolian Harp, Coleridge blends philosophical opinions with tender lyricism in this poem.

(D) CRITICAL APPRECIATION, INTERPRETATION AND DEVELOPMENT OF THOUGHT

Background. The subject of Coleridge's poem is depressing. Yet this ode is one of his triumphs. It is one of Coleridge's chief glories that he found expression of some unheard of pains and agonies of the mind. When he write this poem he is already estranged from his friend Wordsworth who use to exercise a very healthy influence on him. The genial spirits of the poet are failing. Life has nothing to offer him and Nature has no joy for him. But the poet has not yet lost his gift of expression. He fitted that gift to his depressed and bleak state of mind and produced a great poem.

Development of Thought. In a letter Coleridge explained his dejection as due to a feeling of the loss of his poetic and imaginative faculties, and complained that sickness and some other adverse afflictions has forced him into 'downright metaphysics', while he felt that by nature he has more of the poet in him. The original poem is addressed to Wordsworth, but, during an estrangement, the personal references were taken out by Coleridge.

The poet describes the outburst of a storm after a calm evening, and laments his own torpor and inability to be moved by the awful grandeur of the night. His own mood is wan and heartless. The fountains of life fail within him; he lacks that emanation from the soul necessary for the appreciation of Nature. He looks back upon the imaginative days of his youth, when joy and hope has arisen naturally in his heart. But pain and grief have taken all these away; abstruse research has superseded the imaginative faculty. The wind's expression of human cries only re-echoes his afflictions. His one comfort is to pray that those whom he loves may not share such unrest.

***Dejection* : Throws a Flood of Light on Coleridge's Inner Character.** He is given to self-dissection and introspection. Having lost the simple joy of living, he take to the fatal pleasure of abstruse and futile thinking. He regrets this habit of his in verse that rings with moving pathos. He looks back upon his past and see it as only a poet can see it, when-

> Hope grew round me, like the twining vine
> And fruits and foliage, not my own, seemed mine

The Poem States a Crisis in the Poet's Life : But now his shaping spirit of imagination has gone. Now, he is only wrestling with his 'viper thoughts' reality's dark dream. The poem is 'thus a clear-eyed statement by a poet of a crisis in his life when he felt that he is about to part for ever with his poetic faculties. Indeed, after this poem is composed, Coleridge, the poet is practically dead but Coleridge the subtle logician survived.

Coleridge's Attitude to Nature. The poem has another point of interest- it presents a view of Nature which challenges Wordsworth's view, Wordsworth believes in a joyous life of Nature independent of man, a life man could take part in by giving up his artificial existence. Coleridge however says-

> O lady I We receive but what we give
> And in our life alone does Nature live,
> Ours is her wedding-garment, ours her shroud I -

In the first edition, these lines are addressed to Wordsworth. Coleridge is no longer a follower of Wordsworth. He believe that one can win from outward forms the passion and the life, whose fountains are within man.

Pictorial Artist. But whatever be the biographical interest of the poem, the art of the poet does not show any sign of decay here. Coleridge, the colourist and the poet of atmosphere appears at his best in the first stanza where he describes the swimming phantom light spread over the moon which is rimmed and circled with a silver thread and notices the peculiar tint of yellow green on the western sky, and gazes upon the thin clouds above in flakes and bars giving their motion away to the stars. The stormy atmosphere describe in the last stanza shows the same artistry of touch. The moaning of the wind render in various keys is wonderful.

Music. Coleridge the musician is no less evident in this ode. His skill is best seen in the weaving together of long lines with short lines.

A Comparison with the *Immortality Ode* of Wordsworth. "*Dejection* ....should be read in conjunction with Wordsworth's Intimation Ode. Both poems mourn the passing of a glory from life: for Wordsworth this passing is one of time's casualties: Coleridge, more modestly, finds the cause in personal failure. Wordsworth ends on a note that is strong but forced; Nature that takes away delight will bring wisdom Coleridge, downcast still, invokes a blessing as he makes his farewell, but the storm which has arisen during the course of the poem is still raging'

It is indeed impossible to avoid the idea that there is an intimate connection between the two poems. Originally the poem is addressed to Wordsworth, perhaps in answer to the opening stanzas of the great Ode or vice versa. The first four stanzas of the '*Immortality Ode* are written in March 27, 1802; Coleridge write his on April 4. It is known from Dorothy Wordsworth's Journal that during this fateful week, the two poets met very frequently, and if we read the two poems side by side, we must note the similarity, not only in the metre, but in the problem posed. For both the poets are disturbed that something has passed away from their vision which they can not recapture. The reader shall read carefully lines 1-18 of the Immortality Ode and lines 21-37 of Coleridge's poem. In both the passages, the poets speak of the change that had come over them so far as their feeling for Nature was concerned. But where is the difference ? In the first place, Wordsworth has not yet lost the capacity for feeling. Listening to the sound of the cataract and the song of the birds and the shout of the shepherd boy, he can yet say " No more shall grief of mine the season wrong". Coleridge, on the other hand is suffering from a more oppressive burden which nothing can lift. He also wishes-

> Those sounds which oft have raised me, whilst they awed,
> And sent my soul abroad,
> Might now perhaps their wonted impulse give
> Might startle this dull pain, and make it move and live....

But he finds with feelings of the utmost bitterness that it is not to be. To him the winds do not come from the friends of sleep, but they speak to him of :

> The rushing of an host in rout,
> With groans of trampled men and smarting wounds

The reason for this difference is that Wordsworth's domestic circumstances helps him to retain his serenity which is quite beyond

Coleridge's reach. Further Coleridge found his own mind reflect in Nature with all its fears and agonies and wild despair, whereas Wordsworth hark back to the past, to memory instead of to the imagination or which Coleridge depend so entirely. For imagination creates out of material supplied by personal experience, but memory handles with things remote and seen through a haze of idealisation.

One other fact has to be noted-the fact that Wordsworth who usually kept hammering at a poem until he complete it to his satisfaction (as we know from Dorothy) gave up this poem at lines 56-57. He resume it again some two years later and completed it in 1806. It seems clear that Wordsworth did wish to be able to solve Coleridge's spiritual doubles on the high poetic level, but he found himself incapable of doing so after listening to the Dejection Ode. Hence, he held over his answer to Coleridge's problems, and later, taking a hint from Coleridge's Neo-platonic doctrines, modifies it in terms of his own theory of memory and the part it play in his life. It is thus that the poem is completed for his own satisfaction. Hence, the two poems must be read together to get the full human significance behind it.

Conclusion. *Dejection* is one of the most exquisite lyrics by Coleridge. The poem gives expression to a poignant mood of pessimism and disillusionment and is of a piece with his *Youth and Age* and *Work without Hope*. It successfully challenges comparison with Shelley's stanzas written in Dejection, Near Naples. In both we hear that piercing note of sadness which is known as lyric-cry.

(E) EXPLANATIONS WITH CRITICAL COMMENTS

1. L 3-8. This night, so tranquil now....were mute: These lines suggest the background against which the poet sat to write his most famous ode. Nature is in a violent state. It is night. The poet see the old moon in the lap of the new moon and this is a natural foreboding of something inauspicious. When the night has set in, it is not so terrible. It was tranquil. But he apprehends the weather to grow violent. The wind is blowing gently then. The gentle puff of the wind waft lazy patches of cloud here and there, and sometimes the soft and moaning wind harped a sad and melancholy tune on the strings of the Aeolian lute. But the poet thinks that this dull wind will soon be replaced by a terrible storm blowing with a violence. The poet thus creates a suitable background against which he expresses his own feelings. The poet has been roused to a mood of intense pathos and self-pity. He is fill with an infinite longing to revive the creative imagination in him which is nearly dead. But he is utterly helpless and the natural setting suggests this intense pathos born of the poet's sense of helplessness. The Aeolian lute has a symbolic value in the poem. The poet himself is the Aeolian lute charges with a deep-seated melancholy. His feelings are like the strings of the lute. The terrible storm that is raging furiously has also disturbed him. He too has been upset and so powerfully is he overwhelmed with a sense of grief that the tempest that is about to blow does not let him rest in peace. But the poet wants the lute to be silent.

2. **L. 15-20. And oh....move and live:** In these lines, the poet speaks of the changes of weather. He says that the wind is growing in violence. It is gradually increasing in its tempo and the storm is nearly to come. It is raining in thick showers. These showers and storm have often filled him with a rare inspiration. The fury of the storm and the downpour of heavy rain have often synchronised with a similar gust of passion in the poet. The poet expects that the storm that blows now and the slanting showers of rain will as usual fill him with a driving inspiration, and give him the same impulse as of old. The poet is seething with a deep sense of grief. He has been greatly moved and agitated. A powerful feeling of grief has overwhelmed him and it is struggling for expression. The poet urges the fury of the storm and drift of the showers to impel him to still greater fierceness of pain. He wants the dull and benumbing pain, which has almost frozen in his body to be roused and become vocal. He wants his intense feeling of pathos to find suitable utterance.

3. **L. 21-24. A grief without a pang...or tear:** In these lines the poet gives expression to his sense of grief. He says that he has been seized by an unutterable grief. So deep is the feeling of pain in him that he has been rendered speechless. His is a grief without a pang-a grief which has been so deeply seated in his heart that the poet's sensitiveness to the pain has been dulled completely. In the rest of the lines he tries-even struggles hard-to give a feeling and expression to his sense of pain. But he cannot say precisely what his pain is like. Therefore he tries to explain the nature of his pain. It is blank, dark and desolate. He feels stifled and breathless for the pain. It is a benumbing grief which has deadened his sensitiveness and the grief has completely frozen in him. His is a feeling of grief which finds no outlet-either in word or sigh or tear. The four lines referred to are suffused with an intense note of pathos. They speak of the mute tragedy of the poet.

4. **L. 31-38. And those thin clouds above...they are :** The poet in these lines regrets the loss of his creative imagination. The fountain of the joy of life has dried up in him. He is dead and insensitive to the beauties of Nature. He has no feelings and he never waxes to a cheerful mood-that Nature is beautiful. He sees the majestic cloud floating in the sky-in

patches and in long lines. These majestic clouds lend their dignified grace and movement to the stars which sometimes glide in between the flakes of cloud and sometimes he concealed behind them. In other words, the stars sometimes twinkle brightly in the sky and sometimes grow dim. But they are always present and visible. He sees also the crescent moon. This moon seems fixed and immobile. It shines eternally in the blue sky and the poet says that the moon remains fixed to the place where it arose-among the cloudless, starless lake of blue. All these objects of Nature are extremely beautiful. The poet sees them all. But they do not stir his emotion or arouse a response in him. In fact, the poet has grown insensitive to the appeal of natural beauties. He has no feelings for them. His feelings have died. He stares at them with blank eyes.

5. **L. 39-46. My genial spirits fail...fountains are within:** The poet, in these lines laments the loss of his inspiration. He says that the spirit of joy has died and the objects of nature, however beautiful, will do little to allay his pain. He is seized by a deep seated melancholy. He is dulled with too heavy a weight of depression. These scenes of beauty will be all meaningless and will fail to lift the heavy weight of depression that burdens his soul. He gazes at the beauty of Nature even now. Even now he looks hard on the green light that lingers in the west. But what if the objects of Nature are beautiful ? It is not outer objects that arouse the passion and feelings of the poet. His own feelings of joy and warmth of passion add a natural lustre to the objects of natural beauty. They do not have any intrinsic beauty in them. But they assume a beauty invested by the poet's rich fancy. But the poet regrets to say that his feelings have died. He has grown insensitive to the appeals of natural beauty.

The fountain of life has dried up in him because of the heavy drain of his poetic potentialities in the family distractions. The lines express the poetic creed of Coleridge and a lamentation for the flickering away of his poetic genius.

6. **L. 59-66. O pure of heart' and shower:** The poet addressing his beloved Sara Hutchinson as a pure hearted lady tells her in touching language the significance of joy in life. He says that she need not ask him what this strong music in the soul is. Explaining the nature of this joy the poet says that it is a beautifying force—it is the spirit of beauty; it is beauty itself. It is the light and glory of life. It is the fair luminous mist. The poet says that there is something divine about the nature of joy. Joy is given only to the pure and in their purest hour. When this blessing is beauty, it accumulates like cloud and rains down in thick showers. Joy, therefore, is an enviable gift. It is given to the pure in the purest hour and whoever receives it, receives all that is good and graceful in life.

7. **L. 71-75. Joy is the sweet voice.......from that light:** The poet is trying to explain the nature of joy. He says that joy is everything. Joy is life. Joy is the charm of life. It is the sweet voice in us and the luminous cloud above. It is joy that is sweet. So whoever speaks sweetly is inspired by joy. Similarly the lovely luminous cloud is another expression of joy. Thus, all that is sweet in sound—is the audible manifestation of joy. Again, joy is the luminous cloud. The poet means to say that the luminous cloud which shines with a mellowing lustre in the sky is the visual manifestation of the spirit of joy. So whatever is sweet and beautiful, is the external manifestation of the spirit of joy. It is from this spirit of joy that all that is charming to the eyes and sweet to the ears flow out. All the sweet music of the world is the echo of this spirit of joy and all the charming colours of the world are the suffusion of the light of joy.

8. **L. 76-81. There was a time....seemed mine:** The lines are suffused with a rich memory of the past. The poet says that there is a time when he has plenty of joy in him. He is so full of the stirring spirit of joy that his sorrow and distress can hardly be a match for the joy. The times are rough indeed. He is beset with distress but even in his misfortune, he see dreams of future happiness. His creative imagination is a glow with a radiance which turns sorrows and sufferings into dreams of happiness and joy. In these days he is full of hope. Hope grow round him as vine twists round a tree. He is full of rich blossoms and rich fruits. Probably Coleridge refers to the six years of his early married life which are full of rosy dreams and cheerfulness. These lines of Coleridge remind us of almost similar lines in Wordsworth's ode:

> There was a time when, meadow, grove, and stream,
> The earth, and every common sight
> To me did seem
> Apparelled in celestial light
> The glory and freshness of a dream

9. **L. 82-86. But now afflications bow me...Imagination:** The poet refers to his miseries in very touching language. He says that now the fountain of joy has dried up in him. His life is full of untold miseries. The afflictions of life have bent him down. He stoops and staggers under the heavy weight of troubles and sufferings. These troubles and sufferings have not only a negative value. They do not simply rob him of all his joys; more than that they darken the very glow of life in the poet. He does not regret so much the loss of joy, but what he feels very deeply is that each blow of pain kills his creative imagination and leaves him all ashes and cold. They extinguish the very flame of genius-the fire of passion, which he inherit from his birth.

10. L. 97-107. What a scream of agony...leaves among: The poet hears the rattling of the storm. He becomes aware of a painful and bitter tune plays on the strings of the Aeolian lute. He explains with anguish that a sad and tragic note has been played by the furious storm on the strings of the lute. The tune has vibrated the chord of his feeling and he is deeply touched by the sad and pathetic note on the lute. The poet says that the terrible storm shall not have struck a sad note on the Aeolian lute. This lute is meant for a sweet note. The storm shall have rather blown away its fury in its usual places-such as naked steep rocks, mountain lakes, blasts trees, unfrequented pine groves, lonely houses haunts by witches-which are more suited for its terrible note of wilderness and melancholy. The poet addresses the storm as a mad lutanist, because in this month of sunshine and showers i.e., in the month of April with its beauty of buds and blossoms, the storm shall have played a lovelier tune. But instead of playing a sweet and harmonious note, the storm howls like the Devil's cry. The tune that the storm has played is cold and bitter, painful and biting. Instead of playing some soft tune in this month, it has played a cold and chilly note.

11. L. 118-125. A tale of less affright...mother hear : The poet in these lines suggests the change in the tempo of the storm. The storm has become less fierce. In the preceding stanza, the storm rustled through the wilderness. From rattling to rustling and from rustling to moaning is the order of the decrease of the tempo of the blowing storm. The poet says that now the tone of the storm has changed to a faint but painful moaning. The roar is now less terrible than what it is. The storm has lost much of its fierceness. It is now tempered with delight. Its moan is low and poignant, full of rare softness and delicacy. The storm now reminds one of the tragic plays of Otway, the Resoration tragedian. Otway has a reputation for soft and delicate tragic feelings. The storm too has changed its violent tone into a soft and gentle moaning suffuses with a pathetic touch. The tenderness of this moan is like that of Otway's plays. The poet tries to explain the softness of the moon and its tender pathos by comparing it with a girl wailing in the wilderness in the midst of a storm. She has lost her way and is shouting in a tender and pitiable voice in the storm to make her mother hear her cry. The poet means to point to the tragic tale of Lucy Gray. A sense of intense pathos is born Out of the tragic end of the girl. She goes out in the storm, with a lantern in her-hand to guide her mother in the storm. She lost her way and as indications are there, she fell down from a bridge in a pool of water and died. The storm that blows is suffused with the same tenderness and pathos which characterises Wordsworth's tragic tale of Lucy Gray.

12. L. 126-139. 'Tis midnight, but small thoughts have...... evermore rejoice : Coleridge prays in this stanza that his beloved may never share his dejection or unrest. He says: Though it is midnight, yet I have little inclination to go to bed. I at night pray, however, that my beloved may not have to keep awake like me. O gentle sleep, visit my beloved with your balmy and soothing charm. I wish and pray that this storm should be confined to the mountain and not blow over the house of my sweetheart. May all the stars shine brightly above her house, and may those stars shine so serenely and silently as if they are watching the sleeping earth. May my beloved rise from her bed in the morning in a cheerful frame of mind. May bright thoughts, cheerful looks and joy elevate her soul and may joy make her voice musical. May all nature appear to her to be full of life and beauty; may her living soul be surrounded by all the pleasures of life. O dear Sara, you are like a heavenly spirit who are guided by heaven, you are the most pious friend of mine. I pray that you should enjoy constant and eternal happiness.

(F) SELECTED UNIVERSITY QUESTIONS WITH ANSWERS ON *DEJECTION : ON ODE* AND *FROST AT MIDNIGHT*

Q.1. What are conversation poems? Why did Coleridge use this form? What success did he achieve in these poems? Critically consider some of the conversation poems to develop your answer.

Ans. "Conversation poems" are also called "poems of friendship" because it is impossible for us to understand them unless we know of the persons Coleridge is thinking about when he write these poems. Even though in form these poems are soliloquies or monologues, a listener may be supposed to be present at least in the writer's imagination; and it is for this reason that they may be regarded as "conversation poems". The best among these poems by Coleridge are : *The Eolian Harp, Reflections on Having Left a Place of Retirement, This Lime Tree Bower My Prison, Frost at Midnight, Fears in Solitude, The Nightingale, Dejection : An Ode* and *To William Wordsworth.*

As a form, the *Conversation Poem* has an attraction for Coleridge. He is temperamentally incapable of making the sustained effort essential to produce a great philosophic poem, but he knew the necessity of keeping his craft alive for the time when he tell himself he will be fit to undertake a great work. By writing Conversation poems he is saved from self-accusations of total indolence, and equally saves from facing the bitter truth of his inability to cope with a major project. The form offered still further advantages. In a Conversation poem themes can be taken up, developed, dropped and resumed, and shifts of tone can be made, much more acceptably than in most other poetic forms. Critics are agreed that what Coleridge himself called 'the divine chitchat of Cowper' furnished him with a model, but in fact he wholly transformes his model, and there is little in these poems that can be appropriately called 'chitchat'. They do, however, share the intimacy of tone, freely-ranging development of theme which characterizes Coleridge's own conversation, and they closely resemble the note-books, alike in their sensitive recording of nature, their tentative exploration of ideas and concern for self-analysis.

The range and flexibility which Coleridge achieves in the *Conversation poems* is already apparent in *The Eolian Harp,* which he calls 'the most perfect' of his early poems. With *The Nightingale* it celebrates his first happiness in love and he begins and ends with a reference to Sarah Fricker; but in theme it moves from the tranquil beauty of the cottage at Clevedon to 'all of animated nature', from the simple lute clasps in the casement to a Paradisal Fairy-Land, from an intuition of life's oneness to a personal confession of weakness and a need for orthodox religion. The sudden transitions and varied themes come from the association formed in the mind of the poet as he contemplates his surroundings.

The greater part of the poem makes an immediate impact on the reader by its individual, emotionally direct use of language:

> And what if all of animated nature
> Be but organic Harps diversely fram'd,
> That tremble into thought, as o'er them sweeps
> Plastic and vast, one intellectual breeze
> At once the soul of each, and God of all?

Here, for the first time, Coleridge's poetry takes on a full organic life of its own. The language, sustains by the free rhythmic development, moves surely and with increasing intensity to a climax which is only formally a question, and is in effect a positive and joyful statement of faith in God's presence at the heart of all His creation. This intuition, wholeness and oneness, which is of absolute importance to our understanding of all Coleridge's poetry, is reaffirmed in the four magnificent lines that were later added to the poem:

> O! the one life within us and abroad,
> Which meets all motion and becomes its soul,
> A light in sound, a sound-like power in light,
> Rhythm in all thought, and joyance everywhere.

Coleridge demonstrates in practice the sort of imagination he is later to analyse and define in theory. It is the expression of a new age : a poetry of vision. Coleridge, like every genuine Romantic, admits no limitations: the oppositions between thing and thing, between God and man, are apparent only to our reason, and are reconciled at the deeper level of our spiritual experience. In the conclusion to the poem, Coleridge denies this experience and the poetry is cramped into artifical conformity to Sarah's views. It suffers accordingly, becoming stilted and Miltonic in manner.

Representative as *The Eolian Harp* is Coleridge's handling of form in the Conversation poems, it will be misleading to suggest that the last two passages quoted are typical of the poetry of the group, taken as a whole. In general, the poems are written at a much more modest level: they are meditative-descriptive poems of great charm and ease of manner, and are better represented by such a passage as this:

> Pale beneath the blaze
> Hung the transparent foliage; and I watch'd
> Some broad and sunny leaf, and lov'd to see
> The shadow of the leaf and stem above
> Dappling its sunshine!
>
> This Lime-Tree Bower

Subdued though this is, the poetry achieves its vividness and clarity by a technique so unobtrusive that we are no more conscious of it than we are conscious, while watching a film, of the cinematographic equipment that gives us a brilliant close-up.

Instances of vividly realized detail, an extraordinarily sensitive recording of visual impressions and colour, abound in the Conversation poems, whether in the well-known particularization of the 'Western sky' in Dejection, with its peculiar tint of yellow green, or in such lines as:

> the dell
> Bathed by the mist, is fresh and delicate
> As vernel cornfield, or the unripe flax,
> When, through its half-transparent stalks, at eve
> The level sunshine glimmers with green (Fears in Solitude)

But for all the delicate exactness of his description, Coleridge hardly ever writes purely descriptive poetry. Without distorting the eternal scene, he constantly invests it with his own mood.

With the exception of Dejection, which is really a later poem, the *Conversation poems* are to a remarkable extent a poetry of withdrawal. This is so not only in an obvious 'physical sense -in the celebration of pretty cot', 'lime-tree bower' or 'silent dell' but also in the way in which nature is presented in its tenderest aspects under 'late twilight' or 'dimness of the stars'. Not least, we are aware of withdrawal in the way in which the poet, even in the act of perception of outgoing to the external scene, still almost comfortingly gathers it back to himself at the inmost centre of his own mind. It is as if the 'wilder'd and dark' Coleridge, as he calls himself in '*The Eolian Harp,* were fabricating in these poems a world of intimate security which he felt orphaned from in real life.

In *Frost at Midnight,* one of his finest poems, Coleridge harmonizes the physical world about with his own mood. The inmates of the cottage have retired for the night and only his 'cradled infant'. Hartley, sleeps at his side. He is curtained in the 'hush of nature', which mutes 'the goings on of life' and makes them 'inaudible as dreams'. From the very first lines of the poem the silent operation of the frost in indistinguishable from the stealth of his own mind working in contemplation.

As his eyes come to rest on the fragile life of a soot-flake on the grate, he recognizes, even explicitly, that it is intimately associated with his mind's activity:

> Methinks, its motion in this hush of nature
> Gives it dim sympathies with me who live,
> Making it a companionable form,
> Whose puny flaps and freaks the idling spirit
> By its own moods interprets, everywhere
> Echo or mirror seeking of itself...

As the flame plays with a furtive life of its own, so the poem develops in an interplay of memory and thought emerging from and shifting back into a physically external environment, until the mind comes full circle to rest in the almost tranced contemplation of:

> Silent icicles,
> Quietly shining to the quiet moon

Though predominantly a poetry of withdrawal, the Conversation poems are very occasionally disturbed by Coleridge's attempts to face the harsh realities of politics and the world of affairs. Since his deepest psychological needs were for serenity and security, it is not surprising that these attempts usually fail. In *Reflections on Having Left a Place of Retirement* the recommendation of active life is less convincing than the nostalgia felt for the 'Valley of Seclusion ,and it is hardly unfair to suggest that in Fears in Solitude the poem's success is all in the solitude and its failure all in the fears. Insecurity and violence are too closely related to the terrors haunting Coleridge as a man to be a fit subject for his poetry.

Though Coleridge's poetic efforts in the supernatural sphere are praised highly, and justly so, the Conversation poems have their own special appeal to the modern reader.

Q.2. Consider *Frost at Midnight* as. artistically unified in design.

Ans. What makes Frost at Midnight an achieved artistic whole is the design and the organisation in the movement of the thought.

The centre is the Ego, the "I", the seeing, remembering, projecting mind the man sitting in a cottage-room at night. From the room the mind moves out, by stages, first to the physical context of weather and sound, then to the village, then to the world "all the numberless goings-on of life". Next with a swift contracting transition, unexplained, in the middle of a line (L. 13) it comes again to the fire. The movement of the film on the grate suggests the very kind of movement which the mind itself is here making-"the idling spirit by its own moods interprets".

But the film, the "fluttering stranger" sets the mind off again outside, now backwards in time, through memory. And in the school boy reminiscence the same process happens again that has already happened in the cottage. From Christ's Hospital the boy's mind goes back and outwards to Ottery : then forwards outwards to the possible visitor who might come to him out from school. Just as the poem as a whole is anchored to the original cottage rooms with the "low-burnt" fire a phrase which comes centrally in the first paragraph, so the Christ's Hospital paragraph is anchored in the central phrase which produces the image of the school boy:

> Awed by the stern preceptor's face, mine eye
> Fixed with mock study on my swimming book.

From the memory of school the mind next comes back to the cottage room, by comparison between the two childhoods : the London school boy (Coleridge) seeing" nought lovely but the sky and stars" and Hartley (the poet's son) to see everything that Nature has to give.

This leads into the short passage of six lines on the Theistic Metaphysics (Pantheism) of Nature. More is not necessary, for this includes and justifies the whole poem. God is

> Himself in all, and all things in himself.

The quiet transition to the last passage is one of the most beautifully effective things in the whole poem. It returns to the opening context of seasons, weather and sound through the imagining of Hartley's future, and comes round fully at the end to "the secret ministry of frost", and the quietness of the winter night with which it began.

Not only do the movements of the mind give the poem its design and unity, but the poem as a whole leaves, us with a quite extraordinary sense of the mind's very being in suspense, above time and space: the mind with all its powers of affection and memory and its power of reading "Nature as the language of God". The predominant emotion is the deep, tender affection for the child. Not only is the ending one of the finest pieces of short descriptive writing in the language, intricate and yet at the same time sparsely clear, compressing so much of the moods of various weathers, but it also perfectly rounds the movement of the mind which has been the poem's theme.

Q.3. "*Dejection* is a poem of despair". Critically examine this statement.

Or

"*Dejection: An Ode* is a dirge over the grave of creative imagination". Discuss.

Ans. Though originally a verse-letter addresses out of despairing love to Sarah Hutchinson, *Dejection* is at the same time an answer in kind to the first part of Wordsworth's *Immortality Ode* and is written at a time of crisis. Coleridge's health is failing, as is his marriage, and he believed the poet is dying inside him. While the poems have a good deal in common, even in vocabulary and imagery, it is important to remember that Dejection is a poem of despair, primarily despair over the failure of the imagination, while Wordsworth's Ode, though it shares Coleridge's theme of anguish in its first four stanzas, goes on to assert a new confidence in its author's poetic powers.

The quiet opening of *Dejection*, in which the poet soliloquizes on the tranquil evening sky, creates an atmosphere superficially like that of the earlier Coversation pieces. There are, however, differences, minute at first, but significant. Such wind as stirs is a:

> sobbing draft, that moans and rakes
> Upon the strings of this Aeolian lute.

In Romantic poetry the Eolian lute is a standard symbol of the poet's mind works upon by natures inspiration (the wind), and the lute, moaning to the 'sobbing draft', conveys to the reader a mood of despair. The moon, which Coleridge always uses as a symbol of the imagination, is overspread with phantom light, and therefore suggests the death of the imagination, which is the central theme of the poem. Then comes an invocation violently at odds with the serene withdrawal characteristic of the earlier poems:

> And oh! that even now the gust were swelling,
> And the slant night-shower driving loud and fast....

The reasons for this invocation are supplied by the reflective passage which follows. In it, Coleridge tells us that joy, which is linked with love, is denied him. The external glory of nature, which originates in the joy of the beholder and is known through the 'Shaping spirit of imagination', can be seen by him to exist, but can no longer be emotionally experienced by him; he therefore inhabits a world of life in death. Metaphysics offers no way out, it induces in him what Blake called 'Newton's sleep', a sleep in which the full reality of imaginative living shrinks into a merely mechanical knowing. The storm is invoked, therefore, as the only means of unfreezing the dull pain' of a life that is emotionally numbed. Coleridge is so tragically different now from the poet who at Nether Stowey, in a briefly grasped joy, can be moved to fine poetry by a flame flickering in the grate, that he must invoke the eruption of all nature in a desperate attempt to bring the dead poet in him back to life.

As the storm explodes the poet is conscious of a released emotion exploding within himself. The violence he invoked to stimulate feeling is now both externally present in the storm and inwardly present in his own paroxysm. The lute sends out:

> a scream
> Of agony by torture lengthened out;

and the storm makes 'Devil's yule'. Coleridge has unleashed his emotion through a violence that is by no means accidentally linked with demonic forces. He is confronted by the nightmare of his private hell:

> With groans, of trampled men, with smarting wounds-
> At once they groan with pain, and shudder with the cold!

Still in parallel movement with the storm, which subsides in 'soundless deep and loud', the terror subsides in exhaustion and pathos, and his vision is now of:

> A little child
> Upon a lonesome wild,
> Not far from home, hut she has lost her way.....

That Coleridge is lamenting his own condition in that of the lost child is clear enough.

With the passing of the storm, Coleridge recreates a serene world, not unlike that of *Frost at Midnight,* of stars hanging bright over the 'sleeping Earth'. This world is briefly glimpsed, but it is no longer a possible world for him. It can only exist for those in whom joy has not died for Sarah Hutchinson:

> Visit her, gentle sleep! with wings of healing....
> Joy lift her spirit, joy attune her voice.

The pathos of this is enriched by the implied contrast of the living death awaiting Coleridge himself. Only for her can the storm be a 'mountain-birth' and wholly external, only for her can 'gentle Sleep' – the sleep denied Macbeth in a meaningless world of nightmare, the sleep denied the Ancient Mariner before he finds grace restore the living principle of joy. Coleridge himself must keep vigil: 'small thoughts have I of sleep". He has momentarily recaptured the vision of what life can be for others, but it is a life from which his own spiritual failure now excludes him.

Dejection has all the vividness of the earlier Conversation poems and in the self-analysis that Coleridge gives of his failure-a - post-mortem by a merely medically alive Coleridge on the poet that has died inside him thought and feeling are integrated more surely and powerfully than in any other of his poems. On miniature scale, the poem resembles a tragedy. From a calm but menacing beginning it works to a tragic climax and subsides into something not unlike 'calm of mind, all passion spent'. True, he does not transcend his neurotic state but he does indeed give it an adequate verbal shape. The poetical faculties of Coleridge have by no means declined as far as his style is concerned. There is a beauty in the images, an intensity of feeling in the language that makes this "dirge over the grave of creative imagination:" a great artistic achievement.

Q.4. How does Coleridge's attitude to nature and poetic inspiration differ from Wordsworth's? Compare *Dejection and Immortality* Ode in this regard.

Ans. The problem which concerns both Coleridge and Wordsworth is that of poetical inspiration. Each feels that his hold on it was precarious and asks why this is so. Wordsworth faces the problem in the first three stanzas of the *Ode to Immortality* and then abandons it for at least two years Coleridge, slower perhaps to start but quicker once he has started, told of his crisis in the poem which he afterwards calls Dejection.

Dejection is a cry from Coleridge's heart to his most intimate friends, and though he abridged and altered it, keeps its essential substance.

Long before Wordsworth completed his Ode, Coleridge has given full and powerful voice to his own crisis, and Wordsworth could not but take heed of it. Wordsworth's Ode, at least in its eight last stanzas, is a kind of answer to Coleridge's *Dejection*. From one angle it may be regarded as a poem of comfort and encouragement, but it is much more than that. It is a declaration of belief, intended to counteract the searching doubts and melancholy fears which Wordsworth saw in Coleridge and has felt to a lesser degree in himself. The two poems are concerns with central problems in the Romantic outlook and show to what different conclusions two men could come who shares their innermost thoughts, and followed, as they believed, very similar aims.

At the outset we notice a great contrast of temperament between the poets. Both find themselves in somewhat similar situations, and it is no accident that in the first text which he sent to Sarah Hutchinson Coleridge more than once has a conscious echo of Wordsworth. When Wordsworth says.

> The things which I have seen I now can see no more,

and Coleridge says

> But oft I seem to feel and evermore I fear
> they arc not to me now the things which once they were,

We see that both poets share a common crisis. But each interprets it characteristically in his own way. When Coleridge examines himself and speaks with fearful candour of his inner being, he sees nothing but an empty, lifeless depression

> A grief without a pang, void, dark, and drear...

Perhaps at some moment which the Ode has left behind Wordsworth felt something like this, but he has conquered and suppressed it. In the Ode, almost as if in answer to Coleridge, he stresses his own confidence and the delight which he still takes in nature, despite his loss of something most valuable. There is in Wordsworth something tough and bellicose which Coleridge lacks. Coleridge's sensitiveness is part of a gentle, in some ways passive, nature. When things goes wrong with him, he did not know what to do and is prone to lament defeat. Wordsworth is made of sterner stuff and sought for a new scheme of life to replace the old.

The difference between the two men is well illustrated by the different scenes which they describe. While Wordsworth speaks of a fine morning in spring, Coleridge speaks of a stormy night with the moon shining between clouds. If there is one thing which more than another touchs Coleridge to poetry, it is the moon. He, whose metaphysics Carlyle rudely describs as "bottled moonshine", knew all the enchantment of the moon and see in it almost a symbol of the poet's power to transform the material world into a world of the imagination. It is appropriate that he shall use it to illustrate his dejected state. It is no less appropriate that Wordsworth shall speak of a spring morning. His poetry is inspired not by vague forms and indefinite contours, but by the stirring of light and life, the budding of flowers, and the sunshine on the meadows. While Coleridge is at his best among the dimly described shapes. Wordsworth moves happily and confidently among solid forms. The contrast shows the more delicate nature of Coleridge's genius and illustrates why, when his crisis came, it is more fearful and more final than Wordsworth's.

The differences of personality which are illustrated by the Ode and by *Dejection* are enhanced by differences of outlook on the task of poetry and the place of the imagination in life. In the first place, the double crisis shows how differently Coleridge and Wordsworth reacted to the external world. Whatever relics of Locke's universe Coleridge may have kept in his philosophical opinions, as a poet he is an idealist who believes that the mind fashions the universe for all purposes that really matter. His present grief has come because he feels that he has lost his power to create through the imagination, that he can no longer shape experience into beauty and impose his will on nature:

> O Lady we receive but what we give,
> And in our life alone does nature live:
> Ours is her wedding garment, ours her shroud!

Because he has lost his inner joy, he has lost his gift of imaginative creation, and he cannot but lament the circumstances which are responsible for this:

> But now afflictions bow me down to earth:
> Nor care I that they rob me of my mirth:
>   But Oh! each visitation
> Suspends that nature gave me at my birth,
>   My shaping spirit of Imagination.

For Coleridge, who believes that the imagination is the primary instrument of all spiritual and creative activities, this is indeed a bitter confession. He has lost not only his poetical gift but what makes life worth living.

With Wordsworth it is quite different. For him nature exists independently and needs only to be used and interpreted. Even in the first three stanzas of the Ode, when the memory of his crisis is still fresh,

Wordsworth sees nature as not merely living its own life but full of beauty and joy:

> The Rainbow comes and goes,
> And lovely is the Rose,
> The Moon doth with delight
> Look round her when the heavens arc bare;
> Waters in a starry night
> Are beautiful and fair.

As he develops his poem, Wordsworth stresses this independence and this essential joyfulness of nature. Whereas Coleridge puts all his trust in his own imagination and is in despair when it fails him, Wordsworth continues to believe that nature stands outside him and has still much to give him, if he will only be ready to receive it.

A second point of contrast reveals by the two poems is between the different ways in which Coleridge and Wordsworth are inspired to write poetry. On his own experience Coleridge is emphatic. For creation he needs joy. It may not be all that he needs, but, so far as it goes, it is indispensable:

> Joy, Lady! is the spirit and the power....

This pure joy is the "strong music in the soul" which enables Coleridge to create, and this is what he has lost. Without it he feels helpless and miserable. When stirred, Wordsworth's creative energy is not joy, as Coleridge describes it, but something more complex. Nature might delight him, but it also did something else. It woke hidden powers in him by a process which was not always enjoyable. Though such experiences may at the time be frightening, in retrospect they became a matter for gratitude. For Wordsworth, beauty and awe were closely mingled in any keen appreciation of natural things, and each contributs to his conception of this task. In comparison with the strange workings of Wordsworth's creative faculty, those of Coleridge are indeed frail, since they are founded in a joy which be lost early and never regained.

A third point of comparison between Coleridge and Wordsworth turns on their conception of the world which the imagination finds beyond the senses. On this point Coleridge does not say much in Dejection, but what he says is to the point. He insists that from the soul must issue

> A light, a glory, a fair luminous cloud
> Enveloping the Earth.

Through the exercise of the imagination the "inanimate cold world" is transformed into something real and living. The imagination creates reality by absorbing the given into the world of spirit. This is the only reality for

Coleridge, but it is not what Wordsworth sought or found. There are moments when by some mysterious and magnificent process he passed beyond the visible world into some other order of being, vaster and more wonderful. In The Prelude he speaks of times when

> The light of sense
> Goes out in flashes that have shewn to us
> The invisible world. (VI,600-602)

To this experience Wordsworth's poems bear eloquent witness. Instead of examining nature with a close, observant eye and extracting all that he could from it, he found himself unaccountably transported into another sphere of being, shapeless and frightening and beyond the reach of exact words. While Coleridge seeks to transform the given world through the imagination, Wordsworth knows moments when he passes beyond it to something else, and he believes that this task is essentially one of the imagination.

14

LOVE

(A) TEXT, PARAPHRASE AND ANNOTATIONS

ALL thoughts, all passions, all delights,
Whatever stirs this mortal frame,
All are but ministers of Love,
And feed his sacred flame.
Oft in my waking dreams do I
Live o'er again that happy hour,
When midway on the mount I lay,
Beside the ruined tower.
The moonshine, stealing o'er the scene
Had blended with the lights of eve;
And she was there, my hope, my joy,
My own dear Genevieve!
She leant against the armed man,
The statue of the armed knight;
She stood and listened to my lay,
Amid the lingering light.
Few sorrows hath she of her own,
My hope! my joy ! my Genevieve !
She loves me best, whene'er I sing
The songs that make her grieve.
I played a soft and doleful air,
I sang an old and moving story—
An old rude song, that suited well
That ruin wild and hoary.
She listened with a flitting blush,
With downcast eyes and modest grace;
For well she knew, I could not choose
But gaze upon her face.

L. Passions—sentiments, feelings; emotions. **delights**—joys, pleasures. **Stirs**—moves, effects, influences. **L. 2. Mortal**—subject to death. **Mortal frame**—the human body which is mortal i.e., which dies sooner or later. **L. 3. But**—only. **Ministers**—servants, attendants. **L. 4. Feed**—strengthen. **Sacred**—holy, divine. **Flame**—fire. **L.5. Oft....waking dreams**—a waking dream or reverie is a dream one gets not

PARAPHRASE OF THE POEM

L. 1-4. Love turns to his own purpose all thoughts and impulses that touch the human heart. And they serve but to keep the holy fire of love burning in the human heart.

L. 5-8. Often in my reveries I recall before my mind's eye the happy time when half way up the mountain I lay beside the ruins of the tower.

L. 9-12. It is when the moonlight mingles with twilight. My love Genevieve is then with me.

L. 13-16. She rested herself against the statue of an armed knight, in the soft twilight which still lingers in the moonlight as she listens to my song.

L. 17-20. My darling is pure and guileless. She loves me best when I sang songs of distress which makes her sad in sympathy.

L. 21-24. I play a tender and sad note and sang an old, touching ballad that is in harmony with the atmosphere of the ruined tower, grey with time.

L. 25-28. Her colour comes and goes when she listens to my song with her eyes down cast and with graceful modesty. For she know I cannot help gazing at her with yearning.

---

during sleep but during waking hours. It sometimes happens that one's mind wanders from one's immediate surroundings. This experience is called a waking dream. L. 6. **Live o'er**—relive—remember, as though he were having the same experience again. Hour—time. L. 7. **Mount**—mountain. **L. 8. Ruined**—old and broken. L. 9. **Stealing o'er**—spreading slowly. **O'er**—over. **Scene**—place. L. 10. **Blended**—mixed, intermingled. **Eve**—evening. **L. 11. My hope my joy**—beloved, my sweet heart. **L. 13. The armed man**—the statue of an armed knight. **L. 15. Lay**—telling a story. L. 16. **Lingering light**—the light of the day which was gradually fading. The word 'lingering' means reluctant to go. The idea is that the light of the day wished to continue but as it had to make way for the night, it was trying to prolong its stay as much as possible. **L. 17. Hath**—has. **L. 21. Soft**—gentle. **Doleful**—sad, melancholy, pathetic. **Air**—tune. **L. 22. Old**— ancient. **L. 23. Rude**—rough. **Suited well**—Properly suited. **L 24. Wild**—desolate and dreary. **Hoary**—old (literally it means white with age) **L. 25. A flitting blush**—a blush that came and went again and again. 'Blush' means the reddening of the face which is caused by a sense of shame or modesty. **L. 26. Downcast**—bent down. **Modest**—shy, bashful. **Grace**—beauty, charm. **L. 27. Well she knew**—She knew quite well. **Could not choose**—could not help. **L. 28. Gaze**—stare, to look continuously at some object. **L.**

I told her of the Knight that wore
Upon his shield a burning brand;
And that for ten long years he wooed
    The Lady of the Land.
I told her how he pined: and ah !
The deep, the low, the pleading tone
With which I sang another's love,
    Interpreted my own.
She listened with a flitting blush,
With downcast eyes, and modest grace;
And she forgave me, that I gazed
    Too fondly on her face!
But when I told the cruel scorn
That crazed that bold and lovely Knight,
And that he crossed the mountain-woods,
    Nor rested day nor night;
That sometimes from the savage den,
And sometimes from the darksome shade,
And sometimes starting up at once
    In green and sunny glade, –
There came and looked him in the face
An angel beautiful and bright;
And that he knew it was a Fiend,
    This miserable Knight !
And that unknowing what he did,
He leaped amid a murderous band,
And saved from outrage worse than death
    The Lady of the Land !
And how she wept, and clasped his knees;
And how she tended him in vain–
And ever strove to expiate
    The scorn that crazed his brain;–
And that she nursed him in a cave;
And how his madness went away,
'When on the yellow forest-leaves
    A dying man he lay;–

---

29. Wore–carried. **L 30. Shield**–A weapon of defence. **Burning Brand**–a burning piece of wood. **L. 31. Wooed**–courted, made love to. **L. 32. The lady of the Land**–The knight's beloved was a princess, the daughter of the king of the country. **L. 33. Pined**–suffered. **L. 34. Low**–whispering. **Pleading**–appealing, touching, moving. **Tone**–the matter of speaking or singing. **L. 35. Sang**–described in a song. **L. 36. Interpreted**–revealed. **L. 40. Too Fondly**–too lovingly, too ardently. **L. 41. Told**–described. **Scorn**–contempt, hatred. **L. 42. Crazed**–drove him mad, made him

L. 29-32. I have sung of the knight whose sign of heraldry is a flaming torch carved on his shield (symbolical of his consuming love) and who courts the lady of the land on which he lives for a long time.

L. 33-36. I sing how he languishes for his lady's love. The appealing tone in which I sing of the knight's love, sometimes in deep and sometimes in sad voice. Thus, I tell her of my own love for her.

L. 37-40. Her colour changes as she listens to me with graceful modesty and with her eyes cast down. She is not crossed with me when I look at her with longing.

L. 41-44. I have related the scornful rejection of the knight's suit by the cruel lady. It makes the brave and fair knight mad and he wanders day and night through the forest without stopping.

L. 45-52. Sometimes when he is in the den of wild beasts, or in dark cover of the wood or in the clear bright and green spaces in the wood a beautiful spirit come and tempts him. But the unfortunate knight, though he is crazy, has sense enough to understand that it is the devil in the angel's disguise.

L. 53-56. Then not knowing what he is doing he suddenly intervenes with a band of desperate robbers and saves the lady from a dishonour to which death is preferable.

L. 57-60. Then the lady weeps with repentance and embraces his knees. She nurses him and tries to atone for her cruelty which drives him mad. But all is in vain (for the knight was to die soon.)

L. 61-64. She nurses him in a cave. He regains his sanity just before the death when he lays on the dry leaves of the tree.

---

crazy, unhinged his mind. **L. 43. crossed**— wandered, roamed. **L. 44. Nor rested day nor night**—in his madness the knight wandered aimlessly and without rest over the mountain forests. **L. 45. Den**—cave. **Savage den**—the cave of a savage animal. **L. 46. Darksome**—dark. **Shade**—shadow. **L. 47. Starting up**—appearing suddenly as if from nowhere. **L. 48. Sunny**—full of sunshine. **Glade**—valley. **L. 49. Looked him in the face**—stared in his face. **L. 51. A fiend**—a devil or demon, an evil spirit. **L. 52. Miserable**—unhappy, wretched. **L. 54. Murderous**—a group of murderers or dacoits. **L. 55. Outrage**—disgrace, dishonour, a horrible crime. **L. 57. Clasped**—held between her arms. **Clasped his knees**—begging his pardon. **L. 58. Tended**—nursed, looked after. **L. 59. Ever**—always. **Strove**—struggled hard, strained every nerve. **Expiate**—to atone for one's sins. **L. 60. Scorn**—hatred, contempt. **Crazed**—turned him mad. **L. 61. Nursed**—tended. **L. 63. Yellow forest-leaves**—The yellow leaves indicate autumn and death.

His dying words-but when I reached
That tenderest strain of all the ditty,
My faultering voice and pausing harp
    Disturbed her soul with pity
All impulses of soul and sense
Had thrilled my guileless Genevieve;
The music and the doleful tale,
    The rich and balmy eve;
And hopes, and fears that kindle hope,
An undistinguishable throng,
And gentle wishes long subdued,
    Subdued and cherished long !
She wept with pity and delight,
She blushed with love, and virgin-shame;
And like the murmur of a dream,
    I heard her breathe my name.
Her bosom heaved—she stepped aside,
As conscious of my look she stepped—
Then suddenly, with timorous eye
    She fled to me and wept.
She half enclosed me with her arms,
She pressed me with a meek embrace;
And bending back her head, looked up,
    And gazed upon my face.
'Twas partly love, and partly fear,
And partly 'twas a bashful art,
That I might rather feel, than see,
    The swelling of her heart,
I calmed her fears, and she was calm,
And told her love with virgin pride;
And so I won my Genevieve,
    My bright and beauteous Bride.

L. 66. Tenderest—The most touching. **strain**—note, point in the story. **Ditty**—song. **L. 67. Faultering**—Unsteady. **L. 68. Disturbed her soul with pity**—her soul was filled with pity. **L. 69. impulses**—desires, wishes. **Impulses of soul and sense**—Spiritual and physical desires. **L. 70. Thrilled**—excited, agitated. **Guileless**—simple and innocent. **L. 71. Doleful**—sad, melancholy. **L. 72. Rich**—beautiful. **Balmy**—quiet, soothing like balm. **L. 73. kindle**—arouse, inflame, set afire. **L. 74. Undistinguishable throng**—a jumbled crowd. (The phrase refers to the medley of emotions aroused in Genevieve by her lover's song). **L. 75. Subdued**—repressed, kept under strict control. **L. 76. Cherished**—entertained, treasured. **L. 77. Delight**—

L. 65-68. When I come to his last words-and that is the most touching part of the song-my voice trembles and the music of the harp falters as I shook with emotion. This strongly moves her.

L. 69-72. The faltering music, the beautiful fragrant evening, the sad mournful song rouses her emotions and overwhelmes her.

L. 73-76. There are such a mixture of feelings in her heart that one cannot be distinguished from another. There are hopes in her mind. There are also fears, and out of fears again rose hopes. (In the tumult of her feelings, the succession of hopes to fears is quick and constant that the one may be described as caused by the other). And there are soft feelings of love for the poet hidden in her heart. The feelings are long concealed by her but they are always present.

L. 77-80. She weeps with pity for the dead knight and with delight at having her lover by her side. She blushe in her maiden modesty at the thought of her love which is like the faint murmuring sound which is heard in a dream.

L. 81-85. Her bosom swells with strong emotions. She turned aside to hide her blush, conscious of my gaze. Then with fear in her eyes she run into my arms impulsively and wept in joy and fear.

L. 86-88. In her modesty she huges me gently and bending her head a little she looks at my face. (In her modesty, she did not abandon herself passionately).

L. 89-92. Her action is the result of a strange mood where love and fear mingles together. Also there is perhaps a modest woman's artifice that I shall rather feel than see her bosom swelling with emotions.

L. 93-96. I calm her fears by comforting her. With maiden dignity she relates her love. Thus I have my beautiful and cheerful bride-my Genevieve.

---

happiness. L.78. **Blushed**—her face glowed with colour. **Virgin-shame**—the modesty of a maiden. L . 79. **Murmur**—soft and low sound. L. 80. **Breathe**—Utter, whisper. L. 81. **Bosom**—Breast. **Heaved**—rose and fell. L. 82. **Conscious**—aware. L. 83. **Timorous**—timid, shy. L. 84. **Fled**—ran. **Wept**—with joy, of course, L. 86. **Meek**—timid, modest. L. 90. **A bashful art**—a shy and yet skillful device. L. 92. **Swelling**—throbbing. L. 93. **Calmed**—soothed, set at rest. L. 94. **Told**—declared, confessed.

(B) INTRODUCTION TO THE POEM

This poem is composes in 1799 and is jointly published by Wordsworth and Coleridge in 1800 in the second edition of their *Lyrical Ballads.* Coleridge attaches a great importance to this poem and actually say to one of his friends that the poem can be excelled but not imitated like his *Ancient Mariner.* Herford says, "The poem *Love* stands in somewhat the same relation to all previous ballads of love and chivalry as the "*Ancient Mariner*" does to all previous tales of wonder. In both cases Coleridge's originality lies in the delicate and subtle psychology. As the sea-horrors are portrayed through the mind of the Mariner, so here we follow the romantic story of the knight and the Lady of the Land through the medium of the changing emotions which it excites in the guileless Genevieve."

The poet says that all the impulses that move the human heart help to feed the holy flame of love. He relates how once under the mystic moonlight, lying by the side of a ruined tower on an ancient mountain he was singing an ancient ballad. Genevieve, his lady love is standing by a statue and listening to his song. The song deal with the love of another but it reflects the poet's own love for his beloved. It is the story of a knight who goes mad due to the scorn of his beloved and who goes on wandering in the woods and the caves of the wild beasts, where he is tempted by the devil but did not yield. The knight has an occassion to save his lady love from the hands of the robbers who are bend upon outraging her as brutally as ever. There came a change in the lady who give up her scorn and cruelty to the knight and begin to nurse him with great tenderness. The knight get back his senses for a while but died very soon afterwards. When the poet is singing the last words of the dying knight, Genevieve is so deeply moved at heart that she at once confesses her love for the poet who win in the long run his bright and beauteous bride.

(C) CRITICAL SUMMARY OF THE POEM

All thoughts and feelings help in arousing love in the heart of a lover or beloved. All thoughts and feelings help in arousing love in the heart of a lover or beloved.

The Lover Remembers An Evening. The lover still remembers an evening when he lay near a broken tower half-way up a hill. He met his beloved Genevieve there.

Genevieve Leaned against the Statue of a Knight. Genevieve leaned against the statue of a knight and listened to his sad and touching song.

The Song Dealt with the Story of a Disappointed Knight. The song sung by the lover dealt with the story of a disappointed knight. This knight courted a beautiful maiden for ten long years. She did not respond to his love. This knight felt disappointed and wandered aimlessly in forests and caves.

The Disappointed Knight went Mad. The disappointed knight went mad. One day, he came across a party of murderers who wanted to insult his beloved. He saved her from them. She was impressed by his courage and self-sacrifice. She nursed him in a cave but in vain. When the knight lay dying on forest leaves, he wants to say a few words by way of farewell to her.

Genevieve was Moved by this Story. When the lover goes to tell Genevieve what the dying knight said, he feels greatly agitated. Her heart melts with pity. The music, the sad story, the pleasant evening, all produces on Genevieve the effect which the lover desires.

Genevieve Surrendered Herself to Her Lover. She weeps with pity and delight. She blushes on account of love and shyness. She calls her lover by his name and embraces him. She confesses her love in an indirect manner.

The Lover Won the Heart of Genevieve. In this way the lover won the heart of Genevieve-the bright and beautiful bride.

(D) CRITICAL APPRECIATION, INTERPRETATION AND DEVELOPMENT OF THOUGHT

Development of Thought

The poet says that all the impulses that move the human heart help to feed the holy flame of love. He relates how once under the mystic moonlight lying by the side of a ruined tower on an ancient mountain he is singing an ancient ballad. Genevieve, his lady love is standing by a statue and listening to his song. The song dealt with the love of another but it reflects the poet's own love for his beloved. It is the story of a knight who goes mad due to the scorn of his beloved and who goes on wandering in the woods and the caves of the wild beasts, where he is tempted by the devil but did not yield. The knight has an occasion to save his lady love from the hands of the robbers who is bend upon outraging her as brutally as ever. There came a change in the lady who give up her scorn and cruelty to the knight and began to nurse him with geat tenderness. The knight get back his senses for a while but died very soon afterwards. When the poet is singing the last words of the dying knight, Genevieve is so deeply moved at heart that she at once confesses her love for the poet who win in the long run his bright and beauteous bride.

Critical Appreciation and Interpretation

***Love* is a Lyrical Ballad.** It was published in *The Lyrical Ballads* jointly issued by Wordsworth and Coleridge in 1800. It has almost all the important features of old ballads. It is replete with simplicity of language and naivete of tone. It contains a story and it can be sung. In fact, it is a story as well as a song. It gives us a peep into the heart of the lover. This subjectivity of the poem makes it lyrical whereas the story of the Knight and the Lady of the Land makes it a ballad. Old ballads usually have tales of adventure for their theme. In this one, we find the handsome knight rescuing his sweetheart from a band of murderous ruffians. Old ballads are full of the feeling of love, hatred and pity. All the three feelings are present in this poem. The lover and the knight represent love. The Lady of the Land represents hatred, whereas Genevieve-pity. Again, like traditional ballads, *Love* is characterised by 'rapidity of narration and a certain childlike naivete.'

***Love* not only Possesses the Qualities of Traditional Ballads but of Modern Ones as Well.** Modern ballad is only a literary development of the traditional form. Though it maintains the qualities of the traditional ballads, yet it makes its modernism evident 'in its tendency to greater elaboration, the enlargement of description and psychological interest, and a more finished style of art' (Hudson). *Love* similarly has an abundance of psychological interest and possesses a finer style of art than the traditional ballads. Though *Love*' has all the sterling qualities of old ballads, yet it is essentially modern and has nothing imitative about it.

Medievalism of the Poem. Love has a medieval atmosphere. The ruined tower, and the statue of the armed knight dominates the whole scene and make it look medieval. The hopeless love between the Lady of the Land and the Knight who is driven mad may be narrated by any poet of the Middle Ages. It reminds us of the poems of Wyatt and Surrey who always shows the beloved to be a disdainful mistress and the lover an entreating fool. The sight of a love-loin knight is very in the middle ages. In the poem we find the knight saving his sweetheart from a band of ruffians who are about to inflict 'shame worse than death upon her'. This action of the knight too reminds us of the good old days of chivalry. Thus the atmosphere of the poem is medieval.

Supernaturalism in the Poem. Usually Coleridge's ballads have an atmosphere of mystery and supernaturalism. But curiously enough Love has this element in a very small quantity. In stanza thirteen he mentions an evil spirit coming in the garb of an angel to tempt the knight:

> There came and looked him in the face
> An angel beautiful and bright:

And that he knew it was a Fiend
This miserable Knight....

Except this solitary hint, there is nothing supernatural about the poem.

***Love* is a Psychological Poem.** Shelley called Coleridge a 'subtle souled psychologist'. Coleridge shows this quality of his in this poem. Here we find the lover making a psychological approach to his sweetheart Genevieve. The lover rightly understands the mind of his beloved. He says:

Few sorrows hath she of her own,
My hope My joy, my Genevieve.
She loves me best, whenever I sing,
The songs that make her grieve.

Therefore, he 'played a soft and doleful air', and sings 'an old moving story'. The lover know that his beloved can be persuaded only by sorrowful tales of love. He, therefore, sing the story of a knight who is turned insane by the scorn which his sweetheart showed him. In his song, he from time to time, hints at the parallelism between the love of the knight and his own. Genevieve is moved to pity for the knight and she is persuaded not to follow the example of the cruel Lady of the Land.

She wept with pity and delight
She blushed with love and virgin shame
And like the murmur of a dream
I heard her breathe my name.

Thus it is through psychological approach, that the lover wins the heart of his bright and beauteous Genevieve.

Theme of the Poem. It has the usual theme of the love between a young man and a beautiful maiden. The poet wants to show that all ideas, all feelings and all joys which have the strength of moving a man's or woman's soul are the source of love. He rightly says :

All thoughts, all passions, all delight
Whatever stirs this moral frame,
All are but ministers of love,
And feed his sacred flame.

In the story too, we find the feelings of pity for the knight which moves the soul of Genevieve and inspires love in her.

Technique of *Love*. The rhyme scheme of the poem is *a b c b*. The diction of the poem is seldom archaic. 'Doleful', and 'brand' in the sense of 'the sword' are two archaic words used by Coleridge in this poem. The poet initiates the old ballad technique by repeating some lines and expressions. The words :

She listened with a flitting blush,
With downcast eyes and modest grace,

appear twice. Again in stanza 4, we have

She leant against the armed man,
The statue of the armed knight.

Mr. J.H.F. Fowler, remarks: "The qualities that give *The Ancient Mariner* its high place in English Literature are largely present here also. There is the same revival of the simplicity of the ancient ballad; there is the same subtlety of psychological analysis, so foreign to the ancient ballad which stamps the poem as the work of a reflective philosopher. There is the same power of vividly representing a scene by a few strokes of the pen. There is the same fascination of melody, increasing the power of the poem upon us each time we read it."

Opinion of Lamborn and Wheeler about the Poem. They say: "The poem, though like everything of Coleridge's it contains gold, is not gold all through. Its first stanza is a statement, as imperishable as it is complete, concise and assured, of love's supreme and all-pervading power. But the narrative told in illustration is out of place here. The mere narration of events employs too many words, which is worse, poor words, that is words which have no value but the immediate one of conveying a meaning, without any secondary or more poetic suggestion. The music too of such verse must necessarily have the simple, freely moving rhythm which carries on the story easily and pleasantly but does not entrance our ear with its own subtleties and holds us back to listen to it. Much of it in this poem is mere jogtrot, which conveys meaning without reinforcing it or helping it to produce an emotional reaction to it". In all this, *Love* differs entirely from the *Ancient Mariner* which is not a narrative but a vision like Dante's. It is not told in verse but conjures up before us by the spell of music; scenes-if those can be called scenes which have no more to do with this world than the *Book of Revelation*. This story can be read with interest by anyone in his senses. But the story of *Ancient Mariner* is mere delirium to anyone who has not surrendered his mind to the intoxication of musical magic.

(**Note**. It is upto the students to weigh the contradictory statements made by J.H.F. Fowler on one hand and Messrs. Lamborn and Wheeler on the other. They shall adopt any view which appears congenial to their own appreciation of the poem).

Conclusion. This poem is matchless in its beauty and simplicity. The poet seems to abandon himself completely to the charms of love and romance. He is completely led by his heart with the melodies of his verse. The atmosphere is medieval and it reminds one of the legends of

Mallory or the romances of, Spenser. The only thing which interferes with our perfect enjoyment of the poem is the excess of art on the part of the poet.

This poem like the "*Ancient Mariner*" or "*Kubla Khan*" may be regarded as a dream poem. Every one of these poems bears a peculiar charm of atmosphere and music which are woven by the magic words, the strong emotions and romantic surroundings. It also reflects Coleridge's power of psychological analysis, which is a mark of the growth of his mind and the consummation of his art. The poem reflects Coleridge's love which is at once warm and tender and also platonic or spiritual.

The metre of the poem is an imitation of the English ballad measure. The simplicity of its diction, the cadence of its rhymes are remarkable. The poem is an illustration how even from the simplest elements a romantic poet can build a lyrical ballad, which is not only a thing of beauty and music but also a thing of joy for ever..

(E) EXPLANATIONS WITH CRITICAL COMMENTS

L. 1-4. All thoughts... .sacred flame. These lines rosin the open stanza of Coleridge's Love. The central idea of the poem is summed up in these lines. The poet regards love as the supreme fundamental human sentiment. In his opinion, all other thoughts, feelings, passions or delights are subordinate to it. He compares Love to a deity and says that all other sentiments are the priests or worshippers who keep the sacred fire burning in its temple i.e., human heart. All feelings sad or happy lead to and strengthen love. The poem is an illustration of this truth. The lover is able to kindle the flame of love in the heart of his shy beloved by arousing her pity for the plight of the ancient knight. Thus, the feeling of pity intensifies the sentiment of love which is present in the heart of Genevieve.

L. 17-20. Few sorrows...her grieve. These lines occur in Coleridge's poem *Love*. The poem describes how a young man wins the love of his sweet heart by relating to her the story of the disappointed love of a knight.

This is a pathetic story, but the young man says that his beloved loved such stories. She is quite happily placed and had never known any sorrow of her own. But she is fond of hearing sad stories which bring tears to her eyes and melts her heart with pity. That is why the young man selects this pathetic tale to relate to her.

This poem is based on practical psychology. Here the poet is making reference to a well-known psychological fact: that though we hate tears in actual life, we love them on the stage and in literature. The girl is a soft hearted, gentle and tender maiden, and she finds delight in the feeling of pity which such stories arouse in her.

L. 25-28. She listened...open her face. These lines occur in Coleridge's poem *Love.* This poem is the story of how a young man wins his beloved by relating the story of a knight's disappointes love. The story moves the girl deeply, and she cannot help expressing her own love.

The present lines describe the effect of the story on the girl and also describe her attitude as she listens. She is a soft hearted, modest young girl. As she listens to her lover, there is a little redness on her cheeks. This is the blush aroused in her by the story of love. She is so modest that she cannot look her lover in the face. Her eyes are cast down. She looks more beautiful because of her shyness and bashfulness. She does not look up because she knows that her lover is all the time staring at her lovely face with eyes full of tenderness and love.

This stanza paints a beautiful picture of the maiden and arouses tender feeling for her in us. It brings out the grace and the gentleness of her character.

L. 29-36. I told her...Interpreted my own. These lines have been taken from *Love* written by S.T. Coleridge. The theme of the poem is that all human feelings and passions kindle and feed the flame of love. This truth is illustrated by the manner in which a man wins the heart of his beloved by arousing her pity for the poor lover who has gone mad on account of unsuccessful love.

In these lines, the lover tells us that he tells his beloved how a knight suffered deep anguish and languished because his proud beloved did not respond to his love. The story of the lover is so much like that of the knight's own that it may be said to interpret his experiences to his beloved, Genevieve. In other words the lover actually narrates his own woes when he describes the sufferings of the unhappy knight. Through this story the young man is suggesting to his beloved, the consequences if she treats him as the Lady of the Land treats the knight.

L. 45-52. That sometimes from... This miserable Knight. These lines occur in Coleridge's poem, *Love.* The poem is the story of how a young man wins his lady love by relating the story of a knight's love to her. The present lines form a part of this story of the knight.

The knight is scorned by his lady love and went crazy. He wanders in the forests. He is haunted by many apparitions. Again and again, he see a beautiful and bright angel. He see this angel in all sorts of places in-dens, shady groves and bright glades. This delusion pestered him at all places and at all times. The knight know that the angel is in reality a demon. The knight is miserable because of this haunting vision.

Coleridge's imagination reveals in the supernatural. The present poem is a realistic poem, and yet he introduces a touch of the supernatural even here.

L. 65-68. His dying words...her souls with pity. These lines occur in Coleridge's poem *Love*. The poem is the story of how a young man wins his lady love by-relating the story of a knight's love to her. This is a pathetic story, and his beloved is deeply moved by it. Her heart melts.

The present lines occur towards the end of this story within the story related by the lover. They describe the tone and voice in which the lover narrates the story, and the effect of this narration.

The lover says that he reaches the end of the story and is just about to narrate the dying words of the miserable knight. This is the most pathetic part of the song. His voice begin to tremble with emotion as he related the story. He pauses, in his play upon the heart. This make the story even more moving than it would have been otherwise. Her very soul is disturbed with a feeling of pity for the poor knight who has died so miserably.

L. 69-76. All impulses of soul....and cherished long. These lines occur ill Coleridge's poem, *Love*. The poem narrates how a young lover melts the heart of his sweet-heart by relating the story of a knight's disappoints love. The poem describes the effect of this story on the girl.

The present lines bring out the reasons why the girl is so deeply moved as to forget herself and rush into his arms. The lover explains that the story has aroused the deepest feelings in his beloved, Genevieve. She is an innocent and unsophisticated girl, and therefore her very soul is stirred by the story. Again the setting is also helpful in melting her to pity. The evening is beautiful and soothing. The story is sorrowful and melting. It is told in the form of a song, and this also adds to its power.

Again, the girl identifies herself completely with the lady in the story. Their love seem to be like her own love, and their story. Her heart is filled with the hopes of a bright future with her lover, but this hope give rise to the fear that this future may become as dark as that of the lady in the story. Therefore, the story arise a crowd of hopes and fears in her heart. All these are so mixed together that they could not be distinguishes from each other.

The result is that the desires and the feelings of love which she has subdued for a long time out of modesty now break forth. These feelings she has felt and at the same time suppresses. But these are now released so that she can no longer restrain herself.

L. 81-84. Her bosom heaved ...fled to me and wept. These lines occur in Coleridge's poem *Love*. The poem shows how the tragic story of a knight's love affects a simple girl when it is told to her by her lover. The story melts her heart. So powerful is her feeling of pity and so great are her fears about her own future that her shyness and sense of modesty can no longer keep her back from rushing into the arms of her lover.

The present stanza describes how this happens. As the story reaches its most pathetic moment, she begin to breathe hard. Her breast rose and fell with emotion. She know that her lover's eyes are upon her. She wants to hide her emotion from him and so she steps to one side. Suddenly, however, she run to him and starts crying. In her eyes there is a sense of fear. Her self-restraint breaks down and she seeks protection in the arms of her lover.

L. 85-88. She half enclosed...and gazed upon my face. These lines occur in Coleridge's poem, *Love*. The poem narrates how a lover relates the story of the tragic love of a knight to his beloved, and how this moves her, so that she comes running to his arms. So powerful is the effect of the story on her that her self-restraint breaks down.

The present stanza describes the girl's coyness even when she is arise. Even at this moment of deep feeling, she is hesitant out of her modesty. She rushes to her lover, but only half-embraced him. She presses him to her breast, but gently. She bends her head backward and looks up into his face.

The stanza presents a lovely picture of the girl and brings out her shyness and sweetness. This is the first time that she has looked her lover in the face. We have been told twice earlier that her eyes were down-cast because she will not meet the gaze of her lover. Now, however, she abandons her modesty and looks up.

L. 89-92. 'Twas partly love...the swelling of her heart. These lines occur in Coleridge's poem *Love*. The poem narrates how a young lover wins his lady-love by singing to her the story of the tragic love of a knight. The story moves his beloved so much that she rushes into his arms.

The present stanza points out why the girl rushes to her lover. The lover explains that to some extent this is the result of her love for him.

It was also the result, however, of the fear which the story has aroused in her. She is afraid that their love may meet the fate of the knight's love. Finally, this is the result of a combination of her shyness and a little lover's trick. She does not want that her lover shall see her in this emotional state when she is so deeply moved. She does not want him to see her heaving breast. She draws near him so that he shall not be able to watch her. Perhaps she also has a conscious desire of using this opportunity of showing her love.

15

THE EOLIAN HARP

(A) TEXT, PARAPHRASE AND ANNOTATIONS

My pensive Sara ! thy soft cheek reclined
Thus on mine arm, most soothing sweet it is
To sit beside our Cot, our Cot o'ergrown
With white-flower'd Jasmin, and the broad-leav'd Myrtle,
(Meet emblems they of Innocence and Love !)
And watch the clouds, that late were rich with light,
Slow saddening round, and mark the star of eve
Serenely brilliant (such should Wisdom be)
Shine opposite How exquisite the scents
Snatch'd from yon bean-field ! and the world so hush'd!

The stilly murmur of the distant Sea
Tells us of silence.
    And that simplest Lute,
Placed length-ways in the clasping casement, hark!
How by the desultory breeze caress'd,
Like some coy maid half yielding to her lover,
It pours such sweet upbraiding, as must needs
Tempt to repeat the wrong ! And now, its strings
Boldlier swept, the long sequacious notes

L. **Pensive**—Plunged in thought; melancholy. **Sara**—Coleridge's wife. **reclined**—supported by; lying or leaning against. L. **2. Soothing**—pleasant; comfortable. L. **3. Cot**—cottage. **O'ergrown**—covered by. L. **4. Jasmin**—jasmine shrub or plant; **With white-flower'd Jasmin**—with Jasmine plant having white flowers. **Myrtle**—Myrtle plant having flowers sacred to Venus. **Broad-leav'd**—having broad leaves. **L. 5. Meet**—proper. **Emblems**—symbols. **They**—the Jasmine and Myrtle flowers. **Innocence**—the white Jamsine flower is symbolical of innocence; **Myrtle**—is symbol of love because flowers of myrtle are sacred to Venus. **L. 1—5. My pensive...Love**—My melancholy Sara with your soft cheek resting or leaning on my arm, it is very pleasant to sit by the side of our cottage which is covered with Jasmine and Myrtle plants which have white flowers and are proper symbols of innocence and love (because the Jasmine flower is of a white colour and the myrtle is sacred to Venus, the Roman Goddess of Love. **L. 6. That late were rich with light**—which were of bright colour early in the day.

PARAPHRASE OF THE POEM

L. 1-12. My melancholy Sara, how pleasant it is, with your soft cheek resting or leaning on my arm, to sit by the side of our cottage which is overgrown with jasmine and myrtle plants having white flowers befitting symbols of innocence (which is white or spotless like jasmine flower) and love (because the flower of Myrtle is sacred to Venus, the Roman Goddess of Love). It is very pleasant to look at the clouds which were very bright early in the day but which are growing darker and dimmer now owing to the descending shades of the evening. It is very soothing to mark the rise of the evening star which is shining opposite these clouds. The evening star is calmly brilliant. (This reminds me) that true wisdom also should be serenely brilliant. The scent of the distant bean-field which comes to us wafted by the wings of the wind is extremely pleasant. There is profound silence and the quiet murmur of the ripples of the distant sea reveals that the sea is calm tonight.

L. 13-23. The simple musical instrument the lute placed lengthwise in the folding window is being played upon by the random breeze and is producing music. The lute is like a shy maiden who partly surrenders herself to her lover and who, when she is teased by her lover, rebukes

---

L. 7. **Slow saddening round**—The clouds are growing dimmer and less bright as the sun is about to set. **Star of eve**—the evening star. **L. 8. Serenely**—calmly; **Such should wisdom be**—true wisdom should be calmly brilliant. **L. 9. Shine opposite**—the evening star is shining opposite the clouds. **L. 6—9. And watch....Shine opposite**—It is very pleasant to look at the clouds which are very bright early in the day but which are growing darker and dimmer now on account of the shades of the evening. It is also very pleasant to mark the rise of the evening star which is calm as well as brilliant. True wisdom should be calmly brilliant like the evening star which is shining opposite the clouds. **L. 9. Exquisite**—excellent; beautiful. **L. 10. Snatch'd from**—snatched by the wind from. **Yon**—distant. **Bean-field**—field of beans (bean is a plant bearing seeds in long pods). **Hush'd**—silent. **L. 11. Stilly**—Quiet. **L. 12. Tells us of silence**—shows the sea is calm. **L. 9—12 How exquisite the scents...silence**—the scent of the distant bean-field which comes to us flying on the wings of the wind is extremely pleasant. There is perfect silence and the quite murmur made by the ripples of the distant sea tells us that the sea is calm tonight. **L. 13. Lute**—Guitar-like instrument; **Length-ways**—length wise. **Clasping**—folding; **Casement**—window; **Hark**—listen. **L. 14. Desultory**—casual; unmethodical; **Caress'd**—kissed; touched; fondled. **L. 15. Coy**—shy. **L. 15. Half yielding**—partly surrendering herself; **L. 16. Pours**—gives out; **Upbraiding**—reproach; rebuke; chiding. **Must needs**—must necessarily. **L. 17. Tempt**—persuade the lover. **To repeat the wrong**—To make love again to her (the shy maiden). **Its strings**—the strings of the lute placed in the window. **L. 18. Boldlier swept**—moved more violently than before in the wind. **Sequacious**—inclined to follow; servile. **Notes**—Notes of music.

Over delicious surges sink and rise,
Such a soft floating witchery of sound
As twilight Elfins make, when they at eve
Voyage on gentle gales from Fairy-Land,
Where Melodies round honey-dropping flowers,
Footless and wild, like birds of Paradise,
Nor pause, nor perch, hovering on untam'd wing !

O ! the one Life within us and abroad,
Which meets all motion and becomes its soul,
A light in sound, a sound like-power in light,
Rhythm in all thought, and joyance every where—
Methinks, it should have been impossible
Not to love all things in a world so fill'd;
Where the breeze warbles, and the mute still air
Is Music slumbering on her instrument.

And thus, my Love ! as on the midway slope
Of yonder hill I stretch my limbs at noon,
Whilst through my half-clos'd eye-lids I behold
The sunbeams dance, like diamonds, on the main,
And tranquil muse upon tranquillity;
Full many a thought uncall'd and undetain'd,
And many idle flitting phantasies,
Traverse my indolent and passive brain,
As wild and various as the random gales
That swell and flutter on this subject Lute !
And what if all of animated nature

Be but organic Harps diversely fram'd,
That tremble into thought, as o'er them sweeps

L. 19. **Surges**—surging waves of music; moving waves of music. **L. 17. 19. And now, its strings Boldlier swept.....rise**—Suddenly the strings of the lute are more boldly struck by the wind and the long notes of music which follow the striking of the strings sink and rise on the surging waves of music. **L. 20. Witchery**—fascinating charm. **Such a soft floating witchery of sound**—the strains of music (of the lute) as they float in the atmosphere have a fascinating charm. **L. 21. Elfins**—elves, supernatural, **fairy**—like dwarfish creatures. **Twilight Elfins**—supernatural creatures that sing in the evening. **At eve**—in the evening. **L. 22. Voyage on**—fly on the wings of. **Gentle gales**—soft breeze. **L. 23. Melodies**—sweet music. **Honey**—dropping flowers-flowers of the fairy-land which drop honey. **L. 24. Footless**—softly. **Wild**—swiftly. **Birds of Paradise**—birds of heaven. **L. 25. Pause**—Stop. **Perch**—sit. **Hovering**—hanging or flying in the air. **Untam'd**—wild. **L. 26. The one life**—The Divine spirit; God pervading all things. **Within us**—within human mind. **And abroad**—and pervading all him sweetly and thereby persuades her lover to tease her again. Suddenly the strings of the lute are struck more boldly by the wind, and the strains of music, which follow the striking of strings, rise and sink on sweet waves of music. These strains of music of the lute floating in the air have a fascinating charm as the music produces by elves (supernatural creature) who, in the evening ride the gentle winds from the fairy land where sweet music whispers to flowers dropping honey, and who fly as softly and swiftly as birds of heaven, on their wild wings without stopping or sitting anywhere. Well, I think that the Divine Spirit pervades both the mind of human beings and external nature. It is the soul of every object. It is at the heart of light as well as at the heart of sound. It is the soul of harmony in all thought and a source of joy everywhere. It appears to me that it will be impossible not to love all things which are so pervaded by the Divine Spirit in this world. In this world even the breeze makes a continuous and thrilling sound and the so-called silent and quiet air is nothing, but music which has fallen asleep on its instrument.

L. 24-48. Similarly my sweetheart, when 'I am reclining on mid-way on the slope of that distant hilt at noon and while through my half-closed eyes I watch the rays of the sun dancing like diamonds on the water of the ocean and while I ponder over calmness in a calm frame of mind, many thoughts and idle passing fancies, not deliberately entertained by me, flash across my slothful and inert mind. These whims and fancies are as formless and as numerous as the haphazard winds that grow louder in volume as they play on this lute. And it is just possible that all living

---

objects of nature. **L. 27. Which meets all motion**—which pervades all moving objects. **L. 28. light in sound**—which is at the heart of sound, the Divine spirit is at the heart of music. **A sound-like power light**—the Divine Spirit pervades light and is at its heart. **L. 39. Rhythm**—harmony. **Joyance**—Joy. **L. 30. Methinks**—it appears to me. **Ll 30—31. It should have been impossible. ..so fill'd**—it would be impossible not to love everything which is so pervaded by the Divine Spirit in this world. **L. 32. Warbles**—sings in gentle, continuous, thrilling manner. **Mute**—silent; **still**—quiet. **L. 33. Slumbering**—sleeping on. **L. 34. And thus, my love**—and similarly, my sweet heart. **L. 35. yonder**—distant. **I stretch my limbs**—I lie. **L. 37. Sunbeams**—rays of the sun. **Diamonds**—bright precious stones. **Main**—sea, ocean. **L. 38. Tranquillity**—in a calm manner. **Muse upon**—ponder over. **Tranquillity**—calmness **L. 39. Full many a thought**—numerous fancies. **Uncall'd**—not deliberately entertained by me. **Undetain'd**—Not retained by me. **L. 40. Flitting**—passing. **Phantasies**—whims and images. **L. 41. Traverse**—cross; flash across. **Indolent**—lazy. **Passive brain**—inert mind. **L. 42. As wild and various**—These whims, fancies and images are as shapeless and as numerous. **Random gales**—haphazard winds. **L. 43. Swell and flutter**—grow inflated and flit over. **On this subject Lute**—on this lute over which they blow. **L. 44. And what if**—and it is just possible. **Animated nature**—All objects possessing life. **L.**

Plastic and vast, one intellectual breeze,
At once the Soul of each, and God of all ?
But thy more serious eye a mild reproof
Darts, O beloved Woman! nor such thoughts
Dim and unhallow'd dost thou not reject,
And biddest me walk humbly with my God.
Meek Daughter in the family of Christ !
Well hast thou said and holily disprais'd
These shapings of the unregenerate mind;
Bubbles that glitter as they rise and break
On vain Philosophy's aye-babbling spring.

For never guiltless may I speak of him,
The Incomprehensible ! save when with awe
I praise him, and with Faith that inly *feels;*
Who with his saving mercies healed me,
A sinful and most miserable man,
Wilder'd and dark, and gave me to possess
Peace and this Cot, and thee, heart-honour'd Maid !

---

45. **Organic**—having organised physical structure. **Diversely**—differing in nature or qualities. **L. 46. That tremble into thought**—that awaken into thought; that are startled into thinking, that are led to think. **L. 47. Plastic**— supple; flexible; easily bend. **L47. Vast**—huge. **Intellectual breeze**—divine spirit. **L. 48. Soul of each**—soul of every animated object. **L. 49. But thy more serious eye**—but your (Sara's more serious look). **Mild reproof**—a gentle rebuke. **L. 50. Darts**—emits suddenly. **Ll 49—50—But thy...Darts**—But you, Sara, being more serious seem to rebuke me gently with your eye or look, because you do not approve of what I say. **L. 50. beloved woman**—Sara, Coleridge's wife. **L. 51. Dim**—vague; undefined. **Unhallow'd**—unholy. **L. 50—51 Nor such thoughts....thou not reject**—you reject these vague and unholy thoughts about the creator and the universe. (Coleridge means that his wife does not approve of his thoughts because they are not in strict conformity with Christian doctrines and because Coleridge appears to be presumptuous in giving expression to these thoughts concerning the creator and the universe) **L. 52. And biddest me walk humbly with my God**—You ask me to be humble (and not presumptuous) in discussing matters divine, You want me to' worship God humbly without taking upon myself the duty of explaining the ways of God or expounding the 'mysteries. **L.45. Sweeps**—moves. **L. 53. Meek**—gentle, **In the family of Christ**—A devout member of the worshippers of Christ, a faithful follower of Christ. **Meek daughter in the family of Christ**—Sara is addressed as 'meek daughter in the family of Christ' that is as a devout faithful follower of Christ. **L. 54. Holily**—solemnly. **Disprais'd**—disapproved of. **L. 55. Shapings of**—vague fancies or thoughts of. **unregenerate**—unreformed; unimproved. **L. 56. Bubbles**—The fancies and the whims of the

nature is but a series of well-constructed harps with different nature and that they all become vocal when the soul of God like an intellectual breeze blows over them. This soul of God is both flexible and vast and is at the same time the soul and master of every object in nature.

L. 49-64. But O my beloved Sara; I find that you seem to be gently rebuking me with your look for my presuming to explain the mystery of the universe and the ways of God. You also do not seem to be approving of my vague and unholy thoughts. On the other hand, you want me to be a humble worshipper of God. O gentle follower of Christ, you do well disapproving solemnly of the vague fancies of my unreformed mind which are just like bubbles that shine as they rise and dissolve in the ever murmuring spring of arrogant or fruitless philosophy. I feel that I may never discuss the way of God without committing a sin, unless when I praise him in a mood of reverential awe and with a sincere and heart-felt faith. God is to be thanked and praises for His showing great mercy to a sinful and miserable person like me. Without his mercy I felt utterly strands and is in the dark. He give me such priceless gifts as peace of mind, this cottage and Sara who is the object of my sincere adoration.

---

poet which are like bubbles. **Glitter**—shine. **L. 57. Vain**—arrogant, **aye-babbling**—ever murmuring. **L. 55—57. These shapings. ...babbling spring**—These vague and undefined fancies of my unreformed mind are like bubbles that shine as they rise and break on the surface of ever murmuring spring of arrogant philosophy (which presumes to explain the mystery of the universe). **L. 58. For never guiltless**—for never without guilt. **Of him**—of God. **L. 59. The Incomprehensible**—God whose ways cannot be comprehended or understood by human beings. **Save**—except. **Awe**—reverential fear. **L. 60.1 praise him**— I praise God. **Faith that inly feels**—Faith that instinctively realises. **L. 58—60. For never...inly feels**—because I can never speak of God without feeling guilty except when I praise him in reverential fear and believe in him with sincere faith. **L. 61. Saving mercies**—great mercy. **healed me**—cured me. **L. 62. A sinful and most miserable man**—I who am a sinful and miserable person. **L. 63. Wilder'd**—bewildered. **Dark**—ignorant. **Gave me to possess peace**—Gave me peace of mind. **L. 64. Cot**—cottage. **Heart'd honour**—sincerely respected. **Maid**—Sara, Coleridge's wife.

(B) INTRODUCTION TO THE POEM

The Eolian Harp is written in August 1795. It occupies an important position in the poetry of Coleridge. It is in a sense the first important and characteristic poem by Coleridge "The poem is written in blank verse, beautiful in cadence and easily as fluent as Milton's." It anticipates by three years Wordsworth's great poem *Tintern Abbey*. Coleridge regards it as his most perfect poem. As a matter of fact, this poem is one of the six "poems of Friendship or Conversation" written by Coleridge-the others beings, *Frost at Midnight, On Having Left a Place of Retirement, Fears in Solitude, This Lime-Tree Bower, My Prison and The Nightingale.* All these six poems have common characteristics." "These six 'poems are in blank-verse of apparently artless simplicity, very delicate however, and unsurpassed for flexible grace. Its music is of a kind rarely hear before, except now and then in brief passages in Elizabethan dramas and in Cowper's Task. The process of his thought too, is quiet and natural. The poems all begin serenely, with some notice of the time and place, then generally pass into a mood of self-examination, and with a return or transposes repetition of the original cheerful tune and mood."

Coleridge gives expression to the belief that both the mind of man and external nature are pervaded by the Divine Spirit:

> O the one life within us and abroad,
> which meets all motion and becomes its soul,
> A light in sound, a sound-like power in light
> Rhythm in all thought, and joyance everywhere

It is probable that Wordsworth is influenced by these lines when wrote in *Tintern Abbey:*

> A motion and a spirit that impels
> All thinking, all objects of all thought
> And rolls through all things

Coleridge "pictures Nature as a series of harps playes upon by one-the soul of God, which is the same in all things. God is imagines as a great musician who calls forth the harmony latent in all creation."

(C) CRITICAL SUMMARY OF THE POEM

Addressing his wife Sara, the poet points out that it is very pleasant to look at their cottage, the clouds and the evening star. He next tells her that the lute placed in the window is giving forth music as it is being played upon by the wind. This music is elfish (ethereal) and sweet. He thinks that the Divine spirit pervades both the mind of man and the external nature. This Divine Spirit is the soul of every animate or inanimate object. He recalls how when he reclines on a slope of the hill, vague whims and fancies flash across his mind. He conjectures that all living nature is just a series of harps which give forth music when the soul of God, like an intellectual breeze, blows over them. Suddenly he remembers that his beloved Sara seems to be disapproving of his thoughts and philosophy and is reminding him not to be presumptuous but to worship God like a humble Christian. He agrees with her, praises and thanks God for His great blessings, like their cottage, his peace of mind and Sara.

(D) CRITICAL APPRECIATION, INTERPRETATION AND DEVELOPMENT OF THOUGHT

Development of Thought: There are two ideas expresses by the poet in the poem. First, that the Divine Spirit pervades both the mind of man and external nature:

> O the one life within us and abroad,
> Which meets all motion and becomes its soul
> A light in sound, a sound-like power in light
> Rhythm in all thoughts, and joyance everywhere.

The second idea in the poem is that God is a great musician who brings forth the latent music in every animate object by making the Divine Spirit blow over it:

> And what if all the animated nature
> Be but organic harps diversely framed
> That tremble into thought, as o'er them sweeps
> Plastic and vast, one intellectual breeze....

Critical Appreciation and Interpretation. *The Eolian Harp* is written in 1795. In both substance and form it is the fist important poem written by Coleridge. It marks an era in the development of Coleridge's power of expression, both as regards melody and individuality. "Coleridge for the first time for himself, discoveres the countryside, and this new influence give him a lyrical intensity, enriched his imagery, stimulated his thought, make his verse fluent and easy". The poem does not, as has been wrongly supposes by some critics, owe its inspiration to Wordsworth because the two poets first meet in September while the date of the composition of *The Eolian Harp* is August 20, 1795. On the other hand, this poem anticipates by three years, in two of its passages, Wordsworth's famous poem *Tintern Abbey*. Some of the lines bear a remarkably close resemblance. For instance, we have in Coleridge's *Eolian Harp* the following lines:-

> O ! the one life within us and abroad,
> Which meets all motion and becomes its soul,
> A light in sound, a sound-like power in light
> Rhythm in all thought and joyance everywhere...

whereas we have in Wordsworth's Tintern Abbey:

> A motion and a spirit that impels
> All thinking things, all objects of all thoughts,
> And rolls through all things.

It is reasonable to believe that Wordsworth make use of the philosophy of *The Eolian Harp* in his *Tintern Abbey*. Coleridge's poem anticipates his friend's not only in its single emotional curve· but also, if the essential form of the poem is borne in mind, in every stage through which that curve passes.

In the *Eolian Harp* Coleridge thinks as he feels and feels as he thinks. His philosophical opinions are blended with his tender lyricism.

The theme of the poem is that nature is a-series of harps and God is the great musician. The soul of God like an intellectual breeze blows over every living object and brings forth the latent music.

The Eolian Harp, like *Frost at Midnight* and *The Nightingale* has been classed as a 'Poem of Friendship' or Conversation. Coleridge's poems of friendships have certain common characteristics which are shared by '*The Eolian Harp*. "They are written in blank verse of apparently artless simplicity, very delicate however and unsurpassed for flexible grace. Its music is of a kind rarely heard before except now and then in brief passages in Elizabethan drama. The process of his thought, too, is quiet and natural. The poems all begin serenely, with some notice of the time and place, then generally pass into a mood of self-examination, and end with a return or transposes repetition of the original cheerful tone and mood".

The Eolian Harp is written in blank verse, beautiful in cadence and easily as fluent as Milton's.

(E) EXPLANATIONS WITH CRITICAL COMMENTS

L. 14-17. How by the desultory breeze...repeat the wrong. The poet compares the wind blowing on the lute to the wooing of a shy maid by a lover. Just as the shy maid who is caressed by her lover, rebukes him playfully, affecting to be unwilling, and persuades the lover (with her rebuke) to make love to her again; similarly when the wind blows on the lute it gives forth sweet music and tempts the wind to blow over it again.

L. 20-25. Such a soft floating......on untamed wing. Coleridge compares the sweet strains of the music of the lute floating in the air to the music made by elves (supernatural fairy-like creatures) who in the evening fly on the wings of breeze blowing from the fairy-land where sweet music whispers to the flowers dropping honey. The elves fly softly but swiftly, like birds of heaven on their wild wings and neither stop at any place nor sit on any branch of tree.

L. 26-31. O the one Life... World so fill'd. These lines are taken from Coleridge's poem *The Eolian Harp*. The poet listens to the music that the breeze produces by passing through the musical instrument called the Eolian Harp which is placed in the open window. Listening to this music, the poet begins to speculate in his usual way about the existence and function of one pervading spirit throughout the world. But for the operation of such a spirit, how can a breeze produce such music out of a harp ?

The poet believes that this spirit pervades the mind of man and the material world outside man. It is the guiding impulse behind till forms of movement. It is on account of the operation of such a spirit that light and sound are so closely associated and that human thought has in it such order and harmony. This spirit creates a sense of joy everywhere. Once a man becomes a pantheist, once he feels the pervading spirit of joy everywhere, he begins to love everything for to him every thing appears to be a part of God.

L. 26-29. O the one Life...everywhere. Coleridge here anticipates Wordsworth who in *Tintern Abbey* gave expression to the belief that both the mind of the man amid nature are pervaded by the Divine Spirit. Compare Wordsworth's famous lines:

> Whose dwelling is the light of the setting sun,
> Arid the round ocean and the living air..
> And the blue sky, and in the mind of man
> A motion amid a spirit that impels
> All thinking things, all objects of all thoughts,
> And rolls through all things.

Coleridge means that the Divine Spirit pervades both man and nature. It is the soul of every object in the world. It is at the heart of light as well as at the heart of sound. It makes thought harmonious with its presence and is the cause of joy everywhere in the universe.

L. 32-33. Where the breeze warbles.. ..her instrument: Coleridge thinks that every object of nature is instinct with music. Only it needs being played on. Thus the breeze is full of music and the so-called silent and quiet air is nothing but quiet and dormant or latent music which has gone to sleep on its instrument. Thus every object contains latent music which is brought out when the Divine Spirit blows over it.

L. 44-48. And what....and God of all: These lines are taken from Coleridge's poem The Eolian Harp. Seeing how a breeze blowing through the harp is producing wonderful music, the poet begins to speculate about the nature of the relationship between God and the universe. It seems to him that a Divine harmony or music pervades everywhere in Nature. In this Divine scheme, each life or living being is like an Eolian harp, each having its own peculiar power. Now, the thoughts which come to all living beings are like music produced by a breeze of the all-pervading spirit that creates and sustains the universe. All thoughts come from God, because God is the source and motive force of all spiritual activity. Hence, man's thoughts have a preordained order of harmony.

16

REFLECTIONS ON HAVING LEFT A PLACE OF RETIREMENT

(A) TEXT, PARAPHRASE AND ANNOTATIONS

Low was our pretty Cot: our tallest Rose
Peep'd at the chamber-window. We could hear
At silent noon, and eve, and early morn,
The Sea's faint murmur. In the open air
Our Myrtles blossom'd; and across the porch
Thick Jasmines twined: the little landscape round
Was green and woody, and refresh'd the eye.
It was a spot which you might aptly call
The Valley of Seclusion ! Once I saw
(Hallowing his Sabbath-day by quietness)
A wealthy son of Commerce saunter by,
Bristowa's citizen: methought, it calm'd
His thirst of idle gold, and made him muse
With wiser feelings; for he paus'd, and look'd
With a pleas'd sadness, and gaz'd all around,

Then eyed our Cottage, and gaz'd round again,
And sigh'd, and said, it was a Bleassed Place.
And we were bless'd. Oft with patient ear
Long-listening to the viewless sky-lark's note
(Viewless or haply for a moment seen

(The first few lines betray Coleridge's weakness for minute details of natural objects, without producing any unity of impression—a defect which is to be found in the early Nature-poems of Coleridge).

L. 1 .**Low**—situated low. **Cot**—cottage. L. 2. **Peep'd at the chamber window**—peeped in at the window of our pretty cottage. **L. 3. at silent noon**— at noon when everything is quiet. **eve**—in the evening also calm and silence pervade the whole Nature. **L. 4. The Sea's faint murmur**—the faint murmuring noise produced by the breaking of the waves against the shore of the sea. **L. 5. Myrtles**—shrubs with shiny evergreen leaves and white scented flower. **blossom'd**—were laden with flowers. **porch**—covered approach to entrance of building. **L. 6. twined**—interwoven or twisted together. **L. 7. woody**—was covered with trees. **refresh'd the eye**—pleased or charmed the eye. **L. 9. Seclusion**—Retirement ; a place away

A COMPLETE PARAPHRASE OF THE POEM

L. 1-9. Our cottage is beautiful but not very high. The rose is visible at the chamber window. We can hear the gentle sound of the seawater in the morning at noon and in the evening. The ever-green myrtle plants are smiling with their flowers outside the cottage, and across the cottage door the jasmine flowers grew in abundance. The surrounding lands looks green and overgrown with trees, and the view soothed the eye. It is a place which you might rightly regard as the valley of loneliness.

L. 10-17. Once I see a rich merchant of Bristol loitering in the place and enjoying his Sunday. It seems to me that his hankering for vain riches are subdued at that moment and he knew better. For he stood there and looks witn a mixed feeling of sadness and pleasure. He looks all around and see our cottage. Then he looks round again with yearning and said with a sigh that it is a happy place. He is right. We are really fortunate to live there.

L. 18-26. Often we have long listened patiently to the song of the skylark unseen or seen perhaps only for a moment when it soared on its wings shining in bright sunlight. And I have said to my darling softly, "My Love, the divine music of happiness is like this song of soaring

---

from the human resort. L. 10. **Hallowing**—honouring as holy with absolute suspension of all work. **Sabbath-day**—Sunday. **quietness**—by absolute rest from work. **L. 11. A wealthy son of Commerce**—a wealthy merchant. **saunter by**—walking in a leisurely way; strolling about. **L. 12. Bristowa's**—in the Middle Ages, Bristol, known as Bristowa, was a very important town. **methought**—I thought. **calm'd**—satisfied, appeased. **L 13. idle**—vain; useless. **muse**—comtemplate; reflect. **L. 12—14. Methought, it calm'd...feelings**—It seemed as if he dismissed from his mind all thoughts of money, and indulged in holier and more pious thoughts. **L. 14. paus'd**—stopped for some time. **L. 15. pleas'd sadness**—with a mixed feeling of pleasure and sadness. He was pleased because he found himself in the lovely surroundings; he was sad because he could not live in the midst of this bloom and wealth of Nature, for his business required him to remain in the city. **L. 16. eyed**—looked at; saw. **gaz'd round again**—looked at the lovely scenes once again. **L. 17. And sigh'd**—that he could not live in that blessed place. **L. 18. Oft with patient ear**—listening with patience. **L. 19. Long-listening**—listening for a long time. **to the viewless sky-lark's note**—to the song of the skylark which sings as it flies high in the sky and so unseen to the human eye. Also it is a small bird which is not easy to see among the leaves of the trees. **view-less**—unseen to the human eye. **L. 20. haply**—perhaps.

Gleaming on sunny wings) in whisper'd tones
I've said to my Beloved, "Such, sweet Girl !
The inobtrusive song of Happiness,
Unearthly minstrelsy ! then only heard
When the Soul seeks to hear; when all is hush'd,
And the heart listens!'
          But the time, when first
From that low Dell, steep up the stony Mount
I climb'd with perilous toil and reach'd the top,
Oh ! what a goodly scene ! Here the bleak mount,
The bare bleak mountain speckled thin with sheep;
Grey clouds, that shadowing spot the sunny fields;
And river, now with bushy rocks o'er—brow'd,
Now winding bright and full, with naked banks;
And seats, and lawns, the Abbey and the wood,
And cots, and hamlets, and faint city-spire;
The Channel there, the Islands and white sails,
Dim coasts, and cloud-like hills, and shoreless Ocean—
It seem'd like Omnipresence ! God, methought,
Had built him there a Temple: the whole World
Seem'd imag'd in its vast circumference:
No wish profan'd my overwhelmed heart.
Blest hour! It was a luxury,—to be !

Ah! quiet Dell ! dear Cot, and Mount sublime !
I was constrain'd to quit you. Was it right,
While my unnumber'd brethren toil'd and bled,

L. 21. Gleaming—shining faintly. **sunny**—bright; as its wings flash in the sunlight for a moment. **L. 21. in whisper'd tones**—in suppressed or subdued voice. **L. 23. inobtrusive**—spontaneously flowing. **L. 24. Unearthly minstrelsy**—divine music. **then only heard**—is heard only when. **L. 25. the Soul seeks to hear**—one is spiritually and mentally keen to listen to the divine music. **all is hush'd**—when everything is silent We can listen to the immoral music of the soul only when our bodies are asleep and our souls are alert to hear. **L.27. low Dell**—low-lying valley. **Mount**—hill. **L. 28. with perilous toil**—with strenuous labour, running the risk of falling down every moment. **L. 29. Here**—Mark this dramatic visualising of the scene (as if the poet is actually on a mountain top and directly looking at the whole prospect). **L. 31. bare**—without trees. **bleak**—barren; dreary. **speckled thin**—thinly scattered over. **L. 32. that shadowing**—that casting the shadows. **spot**—dot; mark. **sunny**—bright; sunlit. **L.32. Grey clouds,...fields**—Grey clouds mark the sunlit fields with their shadows. **L. 33. bushy rocks**—rocks over-grown by bushes and shrubs. **over brow'd**—hanging over. **And river,...over brow'd**—At one place the river was over hung by rocks over grown with prickly shrubs and bushes. **L. 33. winding**—running in a circuitous or zig-zag course. **Now winding...banks**—In another place one could see the bright clean waters skylark. It can be heard when the soul longs to hear it, when all discords sleep and we are in a mood to listen to it."

L. 26-42. I see the most marvellous scene when I first go up the high mountain and reached the top with hard labour. I saw the bare dreary mountain where a few sheep roamed, the grey clouds the shadow of which fell on the sunny fields, the winding rivers, with bushy rocks hanging over them at some places and bare at other places, the lawns, forest, abbey, cottages, church spires of a distant city dimly seen. On the other side of the mountain are the channel, islands, ships sailing with white sails in coasts far away and finely seen, cloud-like hills and oceans the shores of which can not be seen. It seems all things with all aspects are represented there.

Nature is so magnificent there that it seems that the very temple of God has been built there. The whole scene is so full of rich details that it seems to be the reflection of the whole world. No vain craving rose in his heart which is overflowing with joy and adoration for God. It is a happy hour and to be alive then is all that a man could wish for.

L. 43-62. But I have to leave that calm valley, dear cottage and beautiful mountain. For when millions of men are working hard for their living it is not proper for me to waste my time, which God has given me to do some useful work, in idle dreams, ease and luxury, fighting shy of active life and

---

of the river flowing in a zig-zag course between the banks over grown by neither bushes nor trees. **L. 34. seats**—places meant for sitting. **Abbey**—church. **L. 35. hamlets**—villages. **faint city-spire**—the dimly visible spire of some cathedral in a distant city. **L. 36. The Channel there**—there lies the channel etc. **white sails**—of the ships. **L. 37. dim coasts**—dimly seen coasts. **cloud-like hills**—hills white and hazy like clouds. **shoreless Ocean**—vast ocean seemingly without any shore. **L. 38. It seem'd like Omnipresence**—It appeared as if this lovely and beautiful scene stretched everywhere, throughout the universe. **L. 38—39. God... Temple**—it appeared as if God had built for Himself a splendid temple—so beautiful and' lovely appeared the landscape on all sides. **L. 40. imag'd**—reflected. **L. 39—40. the whole World... circumference**—The whole landscape was so full of rich scenery that it appeared to be an exact image of the whole world. It appeared as if the whole world was brought within the boundaries of the lovely scene. **L. 41. profan'd**—polluted. **overwhelmed**—with adoration for God at the majestic beauty and loveliness of Nature. **L. 42. Blest hour**—it was a blessed time. **It was a luxury**—it was the highest and the richest joy. **To be**—to be alive. **L. 43. quiet Dell**—how quiet the valley was ! **sublime**—great. **L. 44. constrain'd**—compelled. **quit**—leave. **you**—*i.e.*, the valley, cottage, and the mountain. **right**—on my part. **L. 45. unnumber'd**—numberless; innumerable, **brethren**—fellow-beings. **toil'd**—laboured for their livelihood. **bleds**—worked hard and strenuously for a living; painfully struggled for a livelihood. **L. 46, dream away**—pass in merely dreaming. **entrusted hours**—The idea is that this life is given as a sort of trust to man on the strict condition that he should make the best use of it by spending it in the service of his fellow-men.

That I should dream away the entrusted hours
On rose-leaf beds, pampering the coward heart
With feelings all too delicate for use?
Sweet is the tear that from some Howard's eye
Drops on the cheek of one he lifts from earth:
And he that works me good with unmov'd face,
Does it but half: he chills me while he aids,
My benefactor, not my brother man!
Yet even this, this cold beneficence
Praise, praise it, O my Soul ! oft as thou scann'st
The sluggard Pity's vision-weaving tribe!
Who sigh for Wretchedness, yet shun the Wretched,
Nursing in some delicious solitude
Their slothful loves and dainty sympathies!
I therefore go, and join head, heart, and hand,
Active and firm, to fight the bloodless fight
Of Science, Freedom, and the Truth in Christ.

Yet oft when after honourable toil
Rests the tir'd mind, and waking loves to dream,
My spirit shall revisit thee, dear Cot !
Thy Jasmin and thy window-peeping Rose,
And Myrtles fearless of the mild sea-air.
And I shall sigh fond wishes—sweet Abode !
Ah !—had none greater! And that all had such !
It might be so—but the time is not yet.
Speed it, O Father ! Let they Kingdom come !

L. 47. On rose—leaf beds-lying in a soft and luxurious bed made of rose-leaves, i.e in the great possible luxury and ease. **pampering**—over-indulging. **coward heart**—a heart that fights shy of active habits. **L. 48. too delicate for use**—the poet believes such a life of imagination and poetic joy to be of little practical use to humanity. **L. 49. tear**—sympathy. **Howard's**—a reference to John Howard (1726—1790). An English philanthropist well known for his exertions on behalf of prison reform. In 1777 he published The State of Prison in England and Wales. He travelled all over Europe to study the conditions in jails, and died while travelling through Russia on one of his charitable missions. **L. 50. Of one he lifts from earth**—of one whose sufferings he relieves. **L. 51. works me good**—does good to me. **with unmov'd face**—without exhibiting any feeling of sympathy by his face. **L. 52. Does it but half**—helps me only partially. **chills**—leaves me cold; depresses me. **aids**—helps me. **L. 53. My benefactor. ...man**—such a man is my benefactor; he is not my brother sympathising with me in my sufferings. **beneficence**—one who does good. **L. 54. this cold beneficence**—this cold and passionless charity shown towards the miserable. **L. 55. scann'st**—critically examine. **L. 56. sluggard**—slow moving. Pity—(Pity is personified here.) Pity that takes time to be stined up to action. **tribe**—of the same kind. **vision-weaving tribe**—It must be remembered that Coleridge's love and sympathy for the poor and distressed ended only in visionary schemes of various kinds for their permanent good. This line is reminiscent of the 18th century delighting in too fine sentiments to be of any use of humanity. The tears of sympathy which fall from the eyes of a lover of humanity like Howard on the cheeks of one whom he relieves are sweet. A man who relieves me from a cold virtuous reasoning without being moves to pity does not help me fully. He does not sympathise with me like a brother and therefore cannot inspire strong feelings in me. Yet thanks are due to his cold virtuous reasoning when we consider the inactive visionary schemes of people who grieve for the unfortunate condition of men but who without giving any practical help to them meditate in luxurious solitude on their love and sympathy which are too fine and idle to be of any benefit to them. So I must leave this to fight whole-heartedly and actively the spiritual war for the cause of science, liberty and truth.

L. 63-71. But after my share of work, when I shall rest and dream while I am still awake, I shall recall the dear cottage to my mind and go there in spirit. I shall vividly see the jasmine and the rose that touch my window, and the myrtles unmolested by the mild breeze coming from the sea. And I shall wish for the golden age when all may have such a cottage. It can be so, but the time has not yet come. O God, let it come soon. Make this world an ideal world.

---

habit of personification. **L. 57 Wretchedness**—misery and despair. **yet shun the Wretched**—yet avoid the wretched sufferers. **L. 58. Nursing**—nourishing. **in some delicious solitude**—in some pleasant and lovely place of retirement. **L. 59. Their slothful loves**—love which is not activated into doing something. **dainty**—fine but somewhat useless. **L. 60. join head, heart and hand**—help the cause of the miserable and the poor with all my head and heart. The poet wants to do something practical for the good of suffering humanity. **L. 61. Active and firm**—actively and steadfastly, **bloodless fight**—spiritual war. **L. 61. Of Science, Freedom,....in Christ**—to banish ignorance and superstition from people's mind by making them acquainted with the laws of Science, to work for the freedom of the people, and to establish the kingdom of Christ on earth by making people have absolute faith in Christ. **L. 63. When after honourable toil**—after having worked hard for honourable schemes devised for the permanent good of mankind. **L. 64. Rests the tir'd mind**—When the tired mind of man seeks rest. And waking loves to dream—and when refreshed the mind once again loves to indulge the pleasures of imagination. **L. 65. My spirit...Cot**—I shall remember you, 0 lovely cottage. **L. 66. Thy Jasmin.......sea—air**—the poet says that he will relive his experience by recollecting in his tranquil moments the jasmine plants, the roses peeping in at the window of that cottage, and the myrtles boldly blossoming in the open air. **L. 68. fond wishes**—refers to his dream of Pantisocracy (a community in which all are equal and all rule). **L. 69. Ah!-had none greater**—Nothing is more desirable to me than the realisation of these dreams. According to him this is the best service to humanity. **And that all had such**—that all people had means to enjoy the pleasing sights of Nature. **L. 70. It might be so....yet**—such a state might come in future, but it is not so as yet. **L. 71. speed it, O Father!**—O God, bring it soon. **Let they kingdom come**—the ideal condition of the world, according to Christians is the establishment of "the kingdom of Heaven on earth," when falsehood, tyranny, injustice, violence and war will cease, and Love, Justice, Freedom, Truth and Humanity shall reign. The poet wants God to bring about this blissful state in the world soon.

(B) INTRODUCTION TO THE POEM

This poem is first published in the Monthly Magazine October 1796, under the title "Reflections on entering into Active Life. A poem, which affects to be not poetry." Towards the end of 1795 the Coleridges were living in the Clevedon Cottage; and the poem was composed immediately after they left the place in December 1795. It shows Coleridge's interest in and enjoyment of Nature even before he had come under the influence of Wordsworth.

Coming, as this poem does, within the second period of Coleridge's poetic life, it is not marked by that fine outburst of poetic imagination which characterised the later poems of Coleridge. It is reminiscent of the style of the eighteenth century. Here and there it echoes with eighteenth century sonorities and stock phrases found generally in the style of the early precursors of the Romantic Movement-Gray and Collins.

The poem is a beautiful record of a passive mood of voluptuous ease enjoyed by the poet in the midst of a 'soft floating witchery of sound and scent' of nature. But this mood remains with the poet for a very short time only. The sight of toiling humanity in a neighbouring city breaks up the spell. The poet condemns the life of ease, sloth and indolence and contemplation lived in the midst of beautiful surroundings of Nature. He is filled with an angelic ardour for the service of humanity. He, therefore, resolves to,

> Go, and join head, heart, and hand
> Active and inn, to light the bloodless fight
> Of Science Freedom, and the 'Froth in Christ.

(C) A CRITICAL SUMMARY OF THE POEM

In the first stanza the poet gives us a minute description of the lovely surroundings in the midst of which is situated their cottage. It is such a lovely and beautiful place that it might aptly be called "The Valley of Seclusion". On a certain day the poet see a commercial magnate of Bristol enjoying a listless stroll before his cottage. This wealthy merchant seemed to be pleased with the lovely scenery that stretched before him. He has dismissed from his mind all thoughts of gold-piling and is now drinking deep of the beauty of the landscape. He is right in thinking that the poet is really bless in living in that lovely spot. Often as the poet listen to the faint musical songs of the sky lark soaring high in the heavens, he said to his beloved, "Such is the divine music which we hear only when we are laid asleep in body and become a living soul." (Stanza 1.)

The poet, then, gives a vivid and dramatic description of the marvellous landscape and seascape stretched out before him. In the foreground he sees the dreary mountain scattered over with sheep, grey clouds, rocks, sunny fields, naked banks, and winding rivers. In the background he sees the channel, the islands, white sails, dim, coasts, cloud-like hills and shoreless ocean. In the majesty and magnificence of this charming aspect of nature, the poet thinks, lies the very temple of God. At this time when the overpowering beauty of Nature pervades the whole frame, his heart is filled with an adoration for the Omnipresent, and the only desire that crosses his mind is to be merely alive. (Stanza 2)

But the poet must leave his cottage. It is not right on his part to lead a life of ease and indolence and contemplation in the midst of the rich beauties of Nature and to indulge in the idle day-dreams of a poet while thousands of his fellow-men are toiling hard and bleeding for their livelihood. He envies the great philanthropists like Howard who have devoted their lives to the mission of relieving the pain and trouble of suffering humanity. The poet thinks that even those people who show cold and passionless charity towards the sufferers without really sympathising with them in their troubles are much better than he who simply 'nurses in some delicious solitude his slothful loves and dainty sympathies.' What is the use of his wasting time in visionary schemes for the good of the people? He must act at once and devote himself heart and soul to the service of mankind. (Stanza 3.)

The poet says that he will recollect the cottage and the lovely surrounding scenery in moments of peaceful rest enjoyed after the honourable toil. He concludes with a pious wish that soon the Kingdom of Heaven will be established on this earth when all have enough of leisure to enjoy the beauties of Nature. (Stanza 4.)

(D) CRITICAL APPRECIATION, INTERPRETATION AND DEVELOPMENT OF THOUGHT

Development of Thought

The whole poem can be conveniently and is easily divided into four parts. The first part of the poem (Lines 1 to 26) shows the poet's delight in pure Nature, but essentially as a dwelling-place for man. The poet gives here a minute and detailed description of the various objects of nature he sees before him, without producing any unity of impression at the same time. This loose and disjoints manner of the delineation of Nature in all the aspects of her beauty of colour, fragrance and melody is a besetting weakness to be found in Coleridge's early Nature-poems. Lack of imaginative intensity, unity of impression and emotional rush and sweep characterize the whole body of Coleridge's early Nature poetry.

In the second part, (Lines 26-42) the poet gives us a vivid and dramatic description of the marvellous landscapes lying idly about as seen from a mountain-top. In the foreground is a magic blend of light and shade and colour on bleak mountains, sunny fields and naked banks, grey clouds and winding rivers. In the background lie the islands and white sails, dim coast, and cloud like hills and shoreless ocean. In the majesty and magnificence of this charming and lovely scenery of Nature, the poet thinks, lies the very Temple of God, the Omnipresent. In such an atmosphere of heavenly beauty the poet has no other desire than to be merely alive.

In the third part, the poet pleads for a life of activity of devotion to the cause of humanity in preference to the mere selfish joys of a contemplative life led in the midst of beautiful surroundings of nature. The poet feels that a life of active sympathies for the poor and the distresses is much better than a life full of pious intentions and dainty sympathies, but devoid of all practical measures for the relief of suffering humanity. The poet promises, therefore, to-

> Go, and join head, heart, and hand
> Active and firm, to fight the bloodless fight
> Of Science, Freedom, and the Truth in Christ.

In the fourth part, the poet says that at certain moments, in his imagination, after "honourable" toil, he will visit the lovely cottage with its beautiful surroundings. He concludes with a pious wish for the speedy establishment of the kingdom of Heaven on earth, when all will have sweet leisure for the enjoyment of the rich beauties of Nature.

Critical Appreciation and Interpretation

The Poem Reflects Coleridge's Interest in and Enjoyment of Nature even Before he had Come Under the Spell of Wordsworth. The first part of the poem reflects Coleridge's delight in the various sights and sounds of Nature which he considers as the fittest and sublimest abode for the human soul. The second part of the poem is a more dramatic and less imaginative description of Nature. Here the poet discovers the temple of the Omniscient God in the bleak mountain, in the bushy rocks, in the winding rivers, in the grey clouds and in the bright lawns. The third part of the poem reflects the poet's abrupt change of mood, his philanthropic desire to serve his fellow beings, his reflections upon the so-called philanthropists of the world who serves humanity with 'an unmoved face' and above all, his personal consideration that the highest bliss of life lies in retirement in old age, into the very arms of Nature, which he regards as the kingdom of God. Incidentally, he expresses his dislike for the selfish joys of a contemplative life in beautiful surroundings of nature.

The Poem is Written in Blank Verse in a Somewhat Miltonic Style of Verse-paragraphs. There are touches of feeling as well as of expression like those of Wordsworth and Keats, which form a striking contrast with some of his 18th century conceits, which are distinctly traceable particularly in the third part of the poem. We note in it, on the one hand, lack of imaginative intensity, unity of impression, emotional rush and sweep and on the other occasional subtle touches of relief produces by the poets's keen desire for the enjoyment of Nature as well as for the service of humanity.

Coleridge as a Man Highly Sensitive to Nature. Coleridge appears here as a poet highly sensitive to the beauties of Nature and to the keen delights of love. He is fond of seclusion and meditation. He cannot forget the quiet cottage at Clevedon with its jasmine and myrtle even when he has left them behind.

He is a man full of noble moments of earnest thinking. He is not satisfied with the life of ease and pleasure that he is leading at Clevedon, and wants to do something real for his fellow-men. He is inspired by the examples of other philanthropists. He hates his life of dreams.

But in all this, he shows his truly romantic character. His dissatisfaction is romantic rather than practical. Keats and Shelley too, occasionally felt dissatisfies with their dreams. Coleridge leaves his happiness and quiet to follow a course of action that does not suit him.

Lastly, we note the idealistic strain in him. He wants to fight the battle of science against ignorance and superstition, the battle of Christ against the Devil. He wishes for a time when all men will be virtuous and happy. His constant prayer to God is that he shall send His millennium soon to the earth.

A Loose Blend of Descriptive and Meditative Verse Paragraphs. In the first few lines of the poem we notice the looseness of minute description and the want of unity of impression. As a matter of fact, this looseness and disjointed manner of delineation of Nature in all her forms, colours and sounds is a typical defect of Coleridge's early nature-poems. Of course, in the second part of the poem the description of Nature rises to a climax in passionate intensity and emotional unity. After a loose survey of the lowlands Coleridge rises to the very summit of a hill where from he views all the splendour of landscape and seascape. There is a dramatic touch in the very manner of description because the reader feels with the poet as if he is actually standing on the top of a sublime mount and visualising the whole prospect.

There are meditative touches in the poem. Note the lines 22-26 "such, sweet girl! The inobstrusive song...and the heart listens". The touches are all at once Wordsworthian, Shelleyan and Miltonic because Coleridge talks of the viewless skylark's note, of the unearthly minstrelsy and of the heart listening when all is hushed. Mark also the lines 39-44 which are deeply contemplative as well as most poetic in conception and imagery.

The third part of the poem reflects the influence of Gray and Collins upon Coleridge. It shows how Coleridge fails to strike a fully romantic note and how the present poem like all his early poetry is full of commonplace metaphors, far-fetched images and eighteenth century conceits.

(E) EXPLANATIONS WITH CRITICAL COMMENTS

L. 22-26. 'Such sweet Girl !....Heart listens ! These lines have been taken from the poem Reflections on Having Left A Place Of Retirement. At Clevedon, the poet and his beloved willl often listen to the song of the skylark. At times they would see the glittering wings of the bird, and at times the bird will be invisible, but only his melody would be heard. The poet would explain to his beloved that the song of true happiness is like the song of that bird, that it is always quiet and peaceful. This song could be heard only when a man would listen to it with his heart in quietness. In other words, true happiness is to be found only in seclusion and in the heart not in the accumulation of wealth or fame or success.

L. 38-40. It seem's like Omnipresence ! ..... vast circumference. These lines have been taken from the poem Reflections on Having Left a Place of Retirement. When Coleridge surveyed the vast scenes all around him from the top of the mountain, he is very much impressed. The scene reminded him irresistibly of God. He felt as if the vast scene is a Temple built by God for himself, for it appears to reflect the whole universe in its circumference. In other words, the landscape stretching up to the horizon on one side, and the seascape on the other, reminds the poet of the vastness of the universe, and of the Omnipresence of God. Only a scene like that could do it.

L. 44-48. Was it right....delicate for use? Coleridge is dissatisfied with the happy lice of ease and pleasure that he is living at Clevedon in the company of his newly-wedded wife. He is thus neglecting his duties. Man is given his life not because he should fritter it away in idle enjoyments, but because God expects him to do some good to the world. So the poet is dissatisfied with his quiet and easeful life. His heart dared not face the stern realities, and the poet is over-indulging his heart with fine feelings excited by the beauties of Nature of love or quiet contemplation. What did these feelings matter to the rest of the world ? They are utterly useless. So the poet can not any longer justify his idyllic existence at Clevedon.

L. 49-53. Sweet is the tear....brother man! The poet is here pleading for whole-hearted kindness and charity. If a man simply does some mechanical act of charity without showing his compassion: that he himself is deeply moved by it, then he is a mere benefactor. He cannot evoke a warm gratefulness from the man who is receiving his help. The latter is not thrilled or ennobled by the help he receives. This is only charity half done. A true philanthropist appears not as a benefactor but as a brother to the poor and the distressed. He relieves their pain and want with emotions of love and pity. He is like John Howard who used to shed tears on the criminals whom he will help and try to reform.

L. 54-59. Yet even this....dainty sympathies ! The poet is here speaking of his own inaction and sloth. He is full of pity for the sufferers, but his pity leads to no action. It only calls up certain dreaming faculties of his mind which go on weaving visions of reform and help. But these visions do not make the poet actually go to the sufferers and relieve them. These visions are only poetic in nature. The poet's faculties like only to indulge in wishful thinking, and in delicate feelings of love and sympathy in solitude. So the poet, comparing himself with those who help the sufferers without any warmth of feeling, concludes that the action of the latter, though not full-hearted, is much better than his inaction.

L. 63-70. Yet oft Kingdom come ! This has a Wordsworthian touch. Wordsworth used to move revisiting scenes and objects of Nature after his stay in the city and participation in the worldly activities. Coleridge opines here that he has no better wish in his heart than revisiting his old dear cottage and enjoying the loveliness of us natural surroundings. He wishes here that all people wish in their heart to revisit Nature after their "honourable toil". He emphasises that the entire mankind shall revisit Nature after the fulfilment of their worldly duties. But, he himself feels that his time has not come to do so because as yet he has not done anything to serve his fellowmen. In the end, he wishes that day is not far away when he will have finished his duties of life and returned to Nature for contemplation which in his opinion is the happiest life.

17

FRANCE : AN ODE

(A) TEXT AND ANNOTATIONS

I

Ye Clouds ! that far above me float and pause,
Whose pathless march no mortal may controul !
Ye Ocean-Waves ! that, wheresoe'er ye roll,
Yield homage only to eternal laws !
Ye Woods ! that listen to the night-birds singing,
Midway the smooth and perilous slope reclined,
Save when your own imperious branches swinging,
Have made a solemn music of the wind !
Where, like a man beloved of God,
Through glooms, which never woodman trod,
How oft, pursuing fancies holy,
My moonlight way o'er flowering weeds I wound,
Inspired, beyond the guess of folly,
By each rude shape and wild unconquerable sound !

L. 1—4. Float and pause—now moving, now pausing. **whose....controul**—no man can control the movement of the clouds in the pathless sky. **yield...laws**—are bound only to the eternal laws of the nature that control the ebb and flow of the waves; they are not subject to human tyranny.

L. 5—8. Night-birds—birds of night. **Midway...reclined**—while the trees on the hills rest upon the slope dangerously. **Save**—except; you listen to the night—bird's song except when etc. **Imperious**—commanding. **Save when... wind**—Except when your branches, from the commanding heights of the hill swing and sway in the wind and have made a solemn music of your own. The trees listen to the night bird's song except when its branches swing in the wind and make a murmuring music.

L. 9—14. Where—through the woods. **Like...God**—as though the poet is under the special care of God.. **Glooms**—dark forests. **which...trod**—which have never been visited by the wood-cutter. **Pursuing...holy**—following my sacred thought, my 'religious musings'. Moonlight **way**—pathway lighted up by the moon. **O'er... wound**—I wandered over wild flowering woodland. **Wound**—wandered. **Inspired...sound**—I felt inspired by the wild sounds and shapes of nature in a manner that fools cannot imagine. The poet addresses the woods and says that he has often wandered through them all alone and also over the wild flowering woodland, rapt in the thoughts inspired by the shapes and sounds of nature.

O ye loud Waves ! and O ye Forests high !
And O ye Clouds that far above me soared !
Thou rising Sun ! thou blue rejoicing Sky !
Yea, every thing that is and will be free !
Bear witness for me, wheresoe'er ye be,
With what deep worship I have still adored
The spirit of divinest Liberty.

II

When France in wrath her giant-limbs upreared,
And with that oath, which smote air, earth, and sea,
Stamped her strong foot and said she would be free,
Bear witness for me, how I hoped and feared !
With what a joy my lofty gratulation
Unawed I sang, amid a slavish band:
And when to whelm the disenchanted nation,
Like fiends embattled by a wizard's wand,
The Monarchs marched in evil day,
And Britain joined the dire array;
Though dear her shores and circling ocean,
Though many friendships, many youthful loves
Had swoln the patriot emotion
And flung a magic light o'er all her hills and groves;

L. 15—20. Blue rejoicing Sky—blue sky that seemed to rejoice in its blueness. **Every thing....be free**—Coleridge summons as his witness everything in Nature that is free. This line suggests the idea that concludes the poem that Nature alone is free,—and thus gives to the poem that organic unity which Pater praised. **Bear witness for me**—be a witness on my behalf. **Still**—always. **Adored**—worshipped.

L. 22—27. In wrath—full of fiery anger against the tyrants. **Her giant-limbs upreared**—lifted up the terrible arms of her people with the might of a giant. **With that oath**—i.e., took that vow of freedom. **And with...sea**—i.e., which struck all Nature with fear and wonder. **Stamped...foot**—made a gesture of passionate defiance. **Said...free**—Proclaimed that she would make herself free. **Bear witness...feared**—Let all Nature bear witness how he hoped for the success of the revolution and feared lest it should fail . **Gratulation**—feeling of gratification, joy or exultation. **Unawed**—without the least fear. **Amid a slavish band**—amid a people whose feelings were slavish, who did not respond to this cry for liberty.

L. 28—35. Whelm—overwhelm crush. **The disenchanted nation**—i.e., France, who had freed herself from the enchantment of slavery. So long France was under the spell of servitude; now she has thrown off this spell. **Like fiends...wand**—like so many evil spirits brought into the field by the magical power of wizards. **The Monarchs....day**—The kings of Europe marched against the republic on a most inauspicious day.

Yet still my voice, unaltered, sang defeat
To all that braved the tyrant-quelling lance,
And shame too long delayed and vain retreat !
For ne'er, O Liberty ! with partial aim
I dimmed thy light or damped thy holy flame;
But blessed the paeans of delivered France,
And hung my head and wept at Britain's name.

III

'And what', I said, 'though Blasphemy's loud scream
With that sweet music of deliverance strove !
Though all the fierce and drunken passions wove
A dance more wild than e'er was maniac's dream !
Ye storms, that round the dawning East assembled,
The Sun was rising, though ye hid his light !"

Dire array—terrible army. The reference is to England's declaration of war against France in 1794. Though...ocean—Though England's shores and the seas that surround her are dear to me. Swoln—inspired. And flung....groves—And had thrown over her hills and groves the light of an enchantment that kept me spell—bound. The poet means to say that although he had many friends and beloved ones in England to inspire in him a patriotic feeling, and his love for them had thrown a magical enchantment 'on her hills and groves he remained faithful to his revolutionary principles and to his support for France.

L. 36—42. Yet still—in spite of all my feelings of patriotism. **Unaltered**—unchanged in revolutionary zeal. **Sang defeat**—wrote poetry wishing for the defeat of his own country and those others who had joined the war against France. **To all....lance**—wished defeat for all those nations who faced and opposed the army of the republic that had overthrown the tyrant kings of France. **Braved**—opposed. **Tyrant-quelling lance**—power of the new republic that overthrew tyrants. **And shame. ..retreat**—and I wished them the shame of humiliation that had been delayed so long, and utter defeat at the hands of France.

L. 43—48. Blasphemy's—impiety. **Blasphemy's loud scream**—the harsh language of impiety. The French Revolution preached atheism and denounced all religion. **Sweet....deliverance**—the sweet appeal of freedom. **Strove**—struggled. **And what....strove**—what does it matter that the impious language of atheism tried to drown the sweet voice of liberty, though atheism counteracted the blessings of freedom. **The fierce...passions**—the savage and cruel passions that made them so bloodthirsty. **Wove**—formed, arranged. **Maniac's**—madman. **Though...dream**—All wild and cruel passions led the people to commit crimes of violence more savage than even a mad man would have dreamt. **Ye storms**—Oh you stormy passions. The poet addresses the wild stormy passions that swept France during the Revolution. **That round...assembled**—that gathered round the East where the sun of liberty was rising. These evil passions like

And when, to soothe my soul, that hoped and trembled,
The dissonance ceased, and all seemed calm and bright;
When France her front deep-scarr'd and gory
Concealed with clustering wreaths of glory;
When, insupportably advancing,
Her arm made mockery of the warrior's ramp;
While timid looks of fury glancing,
Domestic treason, crushed beneath her fatal stamp,
Writhed like a wounded dragon in his gore;
Then I reproached my fears that would not flee;
'And soon', I said, 'shall Wisdom teach her lore
In the low huts of them that toil and groan !
And, conquering by her happiness alone,
Shall France compel the nations to be free,

---

storm clouds had almost hidden the dawning light of freedom in France. It is significant that neither Wordsworth nor Coleridge was frightened by the violence of the Revolution. **The sun....light**—The dawn of liberty was appearing although its light was hidden by these evil passions.

L. 49—52. **Dissonance**—wild discord and disorder. He is referring to the time when the Revolutionary Government after the Reign of Terror, had established order in the Republic. **Her front...gory**—when France suffered wounds and blood—shed. **Deep—scarr'd**—marked by the deep wounds. **Gory**—blood stained. The poet is referring to the sufferings of France from foreign attacks. **Concealed......glory**—covered all her suffering with the joys of glorious victory. The poet means that France had suffered deeply from foreign invasions which wanted to restore the King and abolish the republic, but all her suffering were concealed by this glory of the victories. She defeated her invaders.

L. 53—57. **Insupportably advancing**—marching forward without any help or support. **Ramp**—threats of violence. **Her arm...ramp**—the armies of the new republic treated the threats of the enemies with utter disdain; made the threatening invaders look contemptible. **Timid....glancing**—casting furtively timid looks of anger; casting looks of fear and anger. **Domestic treason**—treachery at home; the attempt on the part of the royalists to overthrow the republic. **Crushed...stamp**—utterly destroyed by the deadly power of the republic; crushed underfoot by the deadly power of the republic. **Writhed**—twisted and turned painfully. **Dragon**—monstrous reptile; the term is applied to 'domestic treason'. *Gore*—blood. **While timid......gore**—while casting fearful looks of anger, the enemies of the state at home were utterly destroyed by the republic and felt the pain and agony of being crushed underfoot.

L. 58—63. **1 reproached my fears**—I blamed myself for being afraid. **That...flee**—fears that kept pursuing my mind. Lore—lessons. **In the low ...groan**—in the humble cottage of those who yet groan under tyranny. Conquering....alone—and France conquering other nations by the example of the

Till love and Joy look round, and call the Earth their own'.

IV

Forgive me, Freedom ! O forgive those dreams !
I hear thy voice, I hear thy loud lament,
From bleak Helvetia's icy caverns sent !
I hear thy groans upon her blood-stained streams !
Heroes, that for your peaceful country perished,
And ye that, fleeing spot your mountain-snows
With bleeding wounds; forgive me, that I cherished
One thought that ever blessed your cruel foes !
To scatter rage, and traitorous guilt,
Where Peace her jealous home had built;
A patriot-race to disinherit

---

happiness that the revolution had brought. **Shall....free**—France will help nations to be free from the tyranny of kings. **Till love....own**—until the spirit of love and joy will become powerful in this earth. Coleridge says that the toilers in the cottages will soon learn wisdom, and France will conquer other people by the example of her happiness, and the whole earth will be filled with joy and love.

L. 64—71. Freedom—He asks forgiveness of freedom because, to have expected France to help the cause of freedom was an insult to the spirit of freedom. **Those dreams**—that France by her example, shall compel other nations to be free. **I hear......lament**—The poet imagines that he can hear the lament of Freedom when France attacked Switzerland. **Helvetia**—the Roman name for Switzerland, the country of the Helvetia. **I hear......streams**—I seem to hear the lament of freedom that issues out of the icy caves of Switzerland. **Heroes**—Heroes of Switzerland who shed their blood for the freedom of your country. **That for...perished**—who died in defence of your peace-loving country. **Ye that**—your soldiers of freedom who. **Fleeing**—running away before the attacks of your cruel enemy. **Spot**—stain. **With bleeding wounds**—with the blood that issues Out of your wounds. **Cherished**—entertained in my mind. **One thought...foes**—even once I wished happiness and success to your enemies. The poet is now repenting that he should ever have wished even once blessings and happiness for France. **Cruel foes**—the French. Coleridge recants his previous homage to France hence the ode was originally called 'Recantation.'

L. 71—77. To scatter rage, etc.—i.e., how ignoble it was for France to scatter rage, etc. **Scatter...guilt**—spread evil passions and the crime of being false to her faith. **Traitorous guilt**—the crime of being a traitor to one's own faith (France had turned against the religion of freedom which she had professed when she attacked Switzerland). **Where**—in that country. viz., Switzerland. **Where peace...built**—which had been the zealously-guarded home of peace. This refers to Switzerland's peaceful history. **A patriot....race to disinherit**—to deprive a patriotic people of their fatherland. The Swiss had inherited their country from

Of all that made their stormy wilds so dear;
And with inexpiable spirit
To taint the bloodless freedom of the mountaineer—
O France, that mockest Heaven, adulterous, blind,
And patriot only in pernicious toils!
Are these thy boasts, Champion of human kind ?
To mix with Kings in the low lust of sway.
Yell in the hunt, and share the murderous prey;
To insult the shrine of Liberty with spoils
From freemen torn; to tempt and to betray ?

---

their ancestors, and now France had 'disinherited' them. **Of all....dear**—disinherited them of everything that made the wild tempestuous regions of their country so dear to them. **Inexpiable**—that for which there is no pardon. **With inexpiable...mountaineer**—to destroy the freedom of the mountain-people who are free from the guilt of bloodshed, in a manner which cannot be pardoned.

L. 78—84. That mockest Heaven—you mock at the very gods by the way in which you have broken your vows. **Adulterous**—having been wedded to the republic, you are now proving faithless to the republican ideal (like a wife unfaithful to her husband). **Blind**—You have shut your eyes to your duties. **Patriot...toils**—you show your patriotism only in your hateful and evil deeds. **Are these thy boasts**—viz., that you must scatter anger and crime against freedom in a place which has been the home of liberty; that you must deprive a patriotic people of everything that made their wild country so dear to the Swiss; and that you must destroy in an unpardonable manner the unsullied. **freedom of the mountaineer**—do you boast of these, you who call yourselves champions of the human race? **Champion**—you who pose as the champion of mankind. **To mix....sway**—that you should act like kings and be moved by the desire to rule other countries. A republic should not envy other countries and hence should not desire to conquer them. But France now began to act not as a free republic but as kings do. **Yell in the hunt**—You shout and run like a pack of hunters running after their prey. **Share....prey**—claim your share in the country which had fallen a victim to your conquest. Coleridge is referring to France's efforts to conquer a part of Italy and share that country with Austria. **To insult....torn**—You offer on the temple of freedom what you have snatched and plundered from free man—an offering that is an insult to liberty. The poet means that France is now worshipping liberty with what she has acquired from other countries by plunder. **To tempt...betray**—You tempt nations with hopes of freedom and then you betray them into slavery. France has given up her republican ideals and taken to conquest and the desire to build up an empire.

V

The Sensual and the Dark rebel in vain,
Slaves by their own compulsion ! In mad game
They burst their manacles and wear the name
Of Freedom, graven on a heavier chain !
O Liberty ! with profitless endeavour
Have I pursued thee, many a weary hour;
But thou nor swell'st the victor's strain, nor ever
Didst breathe thy soul in forms of human power.
Alike from all, howe'er they praise thee,
(Nor prayer, nor boastful name delays thee)
Alike from Priestcraft's harpy minions,
And factious Blasphemy's obscener slaves,

L. 85–88. **The Sensual**–(as opposed to the spiritual); those who pursue pleasures of the senses or material pleasures. **The Dark**–the ignorant. Rebel in vain–revolt against bondage but they do so in vain. **Slaves. ...compulsion**–they are compelled to be slaves by their very nature; they remain slaves to their own passions. **In mad game**–In a spirit of senseless light–heartedness; not with any serious purpose. **Burst**–break through. **Manacles**–chains. **Wear...freedom**–claim to be called free people. **Graven....chain**–But that claim to freedom is described as chains more heavy. In other words, while they claim to be free, they are really more than ever enslaved–they are enslaved by their own passions.

L. 89–98. **With profitless endeavour**–I have followed you without any gain to myself (because I have not been able to find Liberty in France where I expected to find her). **Many.....hour**–many hours full of weary efforts. But thou....strain–You do not add to the songs of triumph sung in honour of the victorious. **Nor swell'st....power**–nor has liberty given life to power of victorious nations (The French had started on a career of conquests. Coleridge says that liberty does not flatter the conqueror in any way. It is not to be found among victorious people. It does not influence in any way the vainglorious power–seekers). **Alike from all**–The construction is–Thou speedest on thy pinions alike from all those who praise you; i.e., liberty avoids the company or association of all who praise her. **Howe'er.. ..thee**–however much they may praise you; i.e., the flattery of men cannot win the favour of the spirit of Liberty; you may praise liberty but that does not mean that thereby you become free. **Nor prayer....delays thee**–Liberty cannot be arrested by prayer or praise. **Boastful name**–i.e., stops liberty in her flight. **Alike from...minions**–i.e., liberty flies in the same way from the avaricious slaves or priests i.e., those who submit to priesthood are really full of cruel avarice. Liberty avoids all association with such people. **Priestcraft's**–arts used by priests to extend their influence. **Harpy**–grasping;

Thou speedest on thy subtle pinions,
The guide of homeless winds, and playmate of the waves !
And there I felt thee ! – on that sea-cliff's verge,
Whose pines, scarce travelled by the breeze above,
Had made one murmur with the distant surge !
Yes, while I stood and gazed, my temples bare.
And shot my being through earth, sea, and air,
Possessing all things with intensest love,
O Liberty ! my spirit felt thee there.

---

full of cruel avarice (The harpy is a monster with a woman's face who always feeds upon human beings). Minion—favourites; dependants. **Factious...slaves**—liberty also flies from the indecent slaves of impious men. **Factious**—full of unscrupulous party spirit. **Blasphemy's**—(personification) men full of impiety; irreligious men. Obscener—more indecent. Speedest—flies away quickly. **Subtle**—delicate. **Pinions**—wings. **The guide...winds**— liberty guides the restless wandering winds, playmate of the waves—liberty is the happy companion of waves.

L. 99—105. There I felt thee—I felt the presence of liberty in the elemental forces of nature. **Sea cliff's verge**—the limits of the rocks that overhang the sea. **Whose pines**—the pine trees on that cliff. **Whose pines...above**—The high winds hardly ever travel over those pine trees. **Had made....surge**—i.e., make one continuous murmur in harmony with the faraway waves of the sea. The poet means that he had felt the presence of liberty on the mountain cliffs over which stand the tall pines that are hardly ever touched by the wind that travels over them. **My temples bare**—i.e., my forehead being exposed to the wind. **Shot my being....air**—I projected myself into the world of nature; my personality penetrated earth, air and sky. **Possessing....love**—and while I possessed all things with a deep passionate love. **My spirit....there**—I could feel your spirit there.

(B) INTRODUCTION TO THE POEM

The poem are published in the *Morning Post* in 1798, and is originally named *Recantation* because it is a public confession of what he has conceived to be his error. With Wordsworth and Southey, he has fully shared the revolutionary enthusiasm that swept a section of Englishmen when the French Revolution break out. But he is the first to confess that his sympathy with the revolution is wrong. The immediate occasion of the poem is the war declared by the French Revolutionary government against the sister republic of Switzerland in the winter of 1797-98. This is a betrayal of fundamental principles, and in this ode he has withdrawn all support from the Revolution. A Note on the French Revolution: The French Revolution plays a considerable part in influencing the course of the English Romantic movement. It is possible to distinguish three phases of the French Revolution, each of which affect English Romanticism: (1) the Doctrinaire phase—the age of Rousseau; (2) the Political phase—the age of Robespierre and Danton: and (3) the Military phase-the age of Napoleon. Rousseau's sentimental influence touched Blake, Wordsworth and Coleridge; his intellectual influence affected Godwin, and through Godwin, Shelley. A love of external Nature and simple ways of life found expression in the earlier poets. The compelling power of love is what Shelley reiterated with such ecstatic eloquence. The doctrinaire side of the French Revolution, the revolution as an intellectual theory, give substance not merely to Godwin's philosophy but to Blake's spiritual creed. Freedom to him is a kind of mystical rapture, so exalted and impassioned, so free from dross that it sounds the same note as Shelley's lyrical poems.

In 1789, the second phase of the Revolutionary movement opens, and in the first flush of the struggle it stirred to the depths the imagination of the English Romantic writers, and Wordsworth, Coleridge and Southey caught the enthusiasm. Truly, as Wordsworth exclaimed :

> Bliss was it in that dawn to be alive,
> But to be young was very heaven.

The spiritual asceticism and stoical vigour of Wordsworth's genius are soon horrified by the blood and fire across the sea. But Wordsworth's recantation and the lapse of Coleridge must not blind us to the fact that the best works of both poets has been done in the days of their revolutionary enthusiasm.

Yet the most whole-hearted singer of the revolution is Shelley, and this is not because he looks more leniently on the horrors of the revolution, or looks beyond the immediate disaster to a future reconstruction, but because his imagination was far less concrete than that of his great contemporaries. Ideas inspired him; not episodes; so he drank in the doctrines of Godwin, and ignored the tragic perplexities of the actual situation.

(C) CRITICAL SUMMARY

The poet invokes and calls upon the clouds and the waves, and the woods and the sun to bear witness to the deep feeling of worship with which he has adored the spirit of divinest liberty (St 1.) and how he has hope and fear when France rose in all her mighty strength determined to be free. He calls upon them to testify how when even England joins the kings of other nations to crush France, inspite of his deep patriotism he wishs that his country may will be defeated. For he would never do anything that dimmed the light of liberty. He, therefore, blessed France and hung his head and wept in Britain's name.. (St. 2).

Though the sweet music of liberty is disturbed in France by impiety and fierce and drunken passion, yet he has no idea that the sun is rising in the east. Therefore when at last disorder ceased and she emerg victorious over her enemies and destroys all traitors, she is happy to feel that soon her leaders will learn wisdom, and France will compel the nations to be free, and the earth will be filled with love and joy. (St. 3).

But these hopes are all doomed to bitter disappointment. They seem an insult to freedom. He asks pardon of the freedom-loving people of Switzerland to forgive him for honouring France in the name of freedom. For France destroys the peace and freedom of the people of Switzerland. The poet is filled with bitter indignation that France under Napoleon has joined the hated Kings and insulted the temple of liberty with offerings plundered from the free men of Switzerland whom they tempted and betrayed. (St. 4).

Those who are plunged in the darkness of the passions strive vainly for freedom. They are compelled by their nature to remain slaves. They take the name of freedom but remain bound by their slavery. The poor had vainly pursued liberty all these years. He has now realised that Liberty avoids the avarice of the priest and the wickedness of the impious. True liberty is to be found only in Nature, and he feels the spirit of liberty in the sweep of the wind and the surge of the wave. (St. 5).

(D) CRITICAL APPRECIATION, INTERPRETATION AND DEVELOPMENT OF THOUGHT

This is one of the great Odes of English Literature, although it is not among the greatest. The style is rhetorical; it has the passion that rises into a noble eloquence, but not one which stamps itself upon the mind with an indelible impression. It begins splendidly with an invocation that is matchless for its pomp and splendour. But this high tone is not consistently maintained, and the poem remains unequal. Its essential motive is a strong patriotic sentiment which expresses itself in an indignant reaction against Coleridge's earlier sympathy for the revolution. As Walter Pater said, however, in spite of some turgid lines, the composition justifies itself as poetry and "has that true unity of effect which the Ode requires."

The conclusion, moreover, is typical of the general note of frustration that pervades romantic poetry. After all its passionate ardour the poem loses itself in a tame negation that true liberty can not be found among men. While he proclaims the abandonment of his youthful social ideals with a fiery passion and freedom of expression not always to be found in his work, under the influence of Wordsworth all that he can think of as a substitute is a glorification of Nature. Wordsworth's meditative spirit can withdraw from the revolution and take shelter in Nature, but Coleridge's subtle evasive temperament clutches at it eagerly, but hardly with a note of confidence. Hence the inspiring exordium exhausts itself in something like an anti-climax.

(E) EXPLANATIONS WITH CRITICAL COMMENTS

L. 80-84. Are these...to betray. These lines are taken from Coleridge's Ode France. Here Coleridge is expressing his indignation at the fall of France from her great ideals of liberty. She has posed as the liberator of humanity. But now she is following the path of kings. She is trying to conquer other countries. She is like a cruel hunter running after her prey with deadly intent. She wants to worship liberty by enslaving other peoples. This is not worship but insult. She tempts other peoples with hopes of freedom and then enslaves them, and thus betrays them.

L. 85-89. The sensual...heavier chain. These lines are taken from France by Coleridge. Coleridge has once rejoiced in the revolution of France; he has welcomed even the excesses of the revolution. But when France starts on a war of conquest, he was disillusioned. He regrets that he has ever praised France. Here he concludes his Ode to France by asserting that though France claims to have won freedom, she is really not free. Because she is really enslaved by her own passions, her lust for conquest. The poet asserts that those ignorant people who seek a life of material gain, of sensual pleasures, cannot really rebel against their bondage. Their rebellion is all in vain. They are compelled to be slaves to their own blind passions; while they claim to be free they are really not free. They break the chains of their political subjection, but they wear other chains-the chains of their own passion. They call themselves free, but really they are slaves to their own passions.

L. 93-98. **Alike from all... Waves.** These lines are taken from

Coleridge's Ode to France. Coleridge has once welcomed the French revolution and sung its praises. But when republican France attacks freedom-loving Switzerland and tries to conquer other lands, he is disillusioned. Here he says that he no longer expects to find liberty among men. Liberty flies away from all classes of men. Man may pray to liberty or praise her in lofty language, but that will not prevent liberty from running away from man. One will not find liberty among these slaves who are under the artful influences of priests, or of impious men who are worse than priests, for liberty avoids all association with such people. Liberty flies from the human world and 'one finds her a guide and companion of winds and waves. (The fact that with all his love of liberty Coleridge finds liberty not in the human world but with Nature, shows Coleridge's neutral and negative attitude).

L. 99-105. On that sea-cliffs...felt thee there. These are the concluding lines of Coleridge's poem France. Coleridge has welcomed the French Revolution, and believes that France would be the standard-bearer of freedom. But he is disappointed, for the French begin to seek ways and means to conquer other peoples. Thereafter he despaires of finding liberty among human beings. He finds liberty in nature. He imagines himself standing on the verge of a sea-cliff. The wind there hardly travels over the pine trees which murmur in harmony with the sound of the waves. Standing there, he imagines his personality mingle and become one with nature. His forehead is open to the wind and he felt that he now loves all things in nature as though they are his own. It is then that he felt that liberty existed not in the world of man, but in the world of nature.

18

THIS LIME-TREE BOWER MY PRISON

(Addressed to Charles Lame, of The India House, London)

In the June of 1797 some long-expected friends paid a visit to the author's cottage; and on the morning of their arrival, he met with an accident, which disabled him from walking during the whole time of their stay. One evening, when they had left him for a few hours, he composed the following lines in the garden-bower.

(A) TEXT AND ANNOTATIONS

Well, they are gone, and here must I remain,
This lime-tree bower my prison, I have lost
Beauties and feelings, such as would have been
Most sweet to my remembrance even when age
Had dimm'd mine eyes to blindness ! They, meanwhile,
Friends, whom I never more may meet again,
On spring y heath, along the hill-top edge,
Wander in gladness, and wind down, perchance,
To that still roaring dell, of which I told;
The roaring dell, o'erwooded, narrow, deep,
And only speckled by the mid-day sun;
Where its slim trunk the ash from rock to rock
Filings arching like a bridge;—that branchless ash,
Unsunn'd and damp, whose few poor yellow leaves
Ne'er tremble in the gale, yet tremble still,
Fann'd by the water-fall ! and there my friends
Behold the dark green file of long lank weeds,
That all at once (a most fantastic sight !)
Still nod and drip beneath the dripping edge
Of the blue clay-stone.
Now, my friends emerge
Beneath the wide wide Heaven—and view again
The many-steepled tract magnificient
Of hilly fields and meadows, and the sea,
With some fair bark, perhaps, whose sails light up
The slip of smooth clear blue betwixt two Isles

L. 2. **bower**—Arbor or a sheltered place in a garden or a park with overhanging creepers and branches of trees. L. 5. **dimm'd mine eyes to blindness**—as one becomes older the eyesight becomes poorer. L. 8. **Perchance**—perhaps. L. 11. **speckled**—having specks or spots all over. L. 12. **slim**—slender. L. 13. **filings**—throws. L. 15. **gale**—violent wind. L. 17. **file**—row. **lank**—hanging straight and limp. L. 19. **Still....edge**—The weeds make a quick forward motion and they let drops of water flow down from the edge of the clay stone. L. 22. **many-steepled**—having many steeples.

Of purple shadow ! Yes ! they wander on
In gladness all; but thou, methinks, most glad,
My gentle-hearted Charles ! for thou hast pined
And hunger'd after Nature, many a year,
In the great City pent, winning thy way
With sad yet patient soul, through evil and pain
And strange calamity ! Ah ! slowly sink
Behind the western ridge, thou glorious Sun !
Shine in the slant beams of the sinking orb,
Ye purple heath-flowers ! richlier burn, ye clouds !
Live in the yellow light, ye distant groves !
And kindle, thou blue Ocean ! So my friend
Struck with deep joy may stand, as I have stood,
Silent with swimming sense; yea, gazing round
On the wide landscape, gaze till all doth seem
Less gross than bodily; and of such hues
As veil the Almighty Spirit, when yet he makes
Spirits perceive his presence.
A delight
Comes sudden on my heart, and I am glad
As I myself were there ! Nor in this bower,
This little lime-tree bower, have I not mark'd
Much that has sooth'd me. Pale beneath the blaze
Hung the transparent foliage; and I watch'd
Some broad and sunny leaf, and lov'd to see
The shadow of the leaf and stem above
Dappling its sunshine ! And that walnut-tree
Was richly ting'd, and a deep radiance lay

L. 27. **methinks**—it seems to me. L. 28. **pined**—longed intensely; L. 28—30. **Thou hast....city pent**—Lamb was in the city of London where he could not be in communion with nature for a long time. All along he had been yearning to be in the midst of natural beauty. L. 34. **slant**—oblique. L. 41. **gross**—not subtle. L. 41—43. **Less gross....his presence**—Nature has the pervading spiritual power of the Almighty. Here the pantheistic belief of the poet is clearly portrayed. L. 45—47. **Nor in this....sooth'd me**—The two negatives make the sentence affirmative in effect; i.e., I also have not failed to observe quite a few beautiful things that have comforted me. L. 52 —55. **and a deep....lighter hue**—To usurp means to take the place of. Ivy is an evergreen plant that can grow on other three or on walls. The ivy has hidden the elm tree beneath its own leaves. It is not to be forgotten that in this poem the poet does not indulge in self—pity as in the poem Pains of Sleep although the poem pains some pictures of loneliness, imprisonment etc. The poet is not unhappy when nature denies him certain benefits. He tries to rejoice in the joy of others. Also he makes a careful scrutiny of things around and finds many things that do give him real joy. "Nature never

Full on the ancient ivy, which usurps
Those fronting elms, and now, with blackest mass
Makes their dark branches gleam a lighter hue
Through the late twilight : and though now the bat
Wheels silent by, and not a swallow twitters,
Yet still the solitary humble-bee
Sings in the bean-flower! Henceforth I shall know
That Nature ne'er deserts the wise and pure ;
No plot so narrow, be but Nature there,
No waste so vacant, but may well employ
Each faculty of sense, and keep the heart
Awake to Love and Beauty ! and sometimes'
'Tis well to be bereft of promis'd good,
That we may lift the soul, and contemplate
With lively joy the joys we cannot share.
My gentle-hearted Charles ! when the last rook
Beat its straight path along the dusky air
Homewards, I blest it ! deeming its black wing
(Now a dim speck, now vanishing in light)
Had cross'd the mighty Orb's dilated glory,
While thou stood'st gazing; or, when all was still,
Flew creeking o'er thy head, and had a charm
For thee, my gentle-hearted Charles, to whom
No sound is dissonant which tells of Life.

---

deserts the wise and pure" is the conviction of the poet. L. 53. **ancient**—very old. L. 54. **fronting**—appearing in front. L. 65. **to be bereft of**—to be denied. L. 72. **dilated**—enlarged. L. 76. **dissonant**—discordant.

(B) INTRODUCTION TO THE POEM

The period June, 1797 to September 1798 may be called the *annus mirabilis* (wonderfully miraculous year) in the life of Coleridge who rose to the zenith of his poetical career in that short period, thanks to the close companionship of Wordsworth and his sister Dorothy. Almost all his good poems are written then because Coleridge is free from domestic anxiety. In the case of Coleridge there is no gradual development of the poetic gifts as evolved by the actual circumstances of his personal life, with some retardation when they were unfavourable and some enrichment when they are favourable. There has been a sudden blossoming through one short season, to the perfect point and unfortunately we find deterioration thereafter something akin to a young man's growing prematurely old. After this short period Coleridge turns into a literary critic and a philosopher without much of the poetic gift.

Wordsworth, Charles Lamb and others pays a visit to Coleridge and stayed with him for a couple of days. One day Sara, the wife of Coleridge accidentally spills boiling milk on his foot rendering him incapable of walking. The friends later went for a walk in the woods while Coleridge are compelled to stay behind in the Lime Tree Bower in his garden. These lines are written at that time. The poem is copied and sent to Southey with a covering letter on 9th July, 1797 explaining the circumstances of the composition of the poem. When written there has been some references to Wordsworth and his sister but this part is deleted later due to the estrangement of the two poets.

(C) CRITICAL SUMMARY

The poet is unhappy he is compelled to stay behind under the lime tree bower while his friends are on a walking tour in the dell i.e., a small secluded valley. He mentally pictures the excursion of his friends along the heath or the tract of wasteland and then to the dell which is thickly wooded. The poet is sorry that he is deprived of many beautiful natural scenes, the sweet memory of which would have comforted him in his old age when his eyes would become dim and practically blind. The friends are then imagined to be looking at the dark green weeds growing in a long line dripping and nodding beneath the edge of a clay-stone.

Then the poet fancies his friends emerging into the open land viewing the fields and meadows with many small hillocks rising like the steeples of a church. They can see the sea also with perhaps a small ship whose sails make the sea look brighter. Of all the friends Charles (Lamb) will have been the happiest because he had been living in the congested city of London for a long time with a great longing to be in the company of nature. Here the poet refers to the domestic misfortunes of Charles Lamb whose sister has become insane and killed their mother. In order to look after her properly, Charles Lamb remained a bachelor throughout his life. Although he is sad, he has been patient throughout that period of evil, pain and strange calamity. The poet then wants the glorious sun to sink slowly behind the Western ridge; the purple-coloured heath-flowers to shine in the slanting rays of the setting sun, the clouds to burn more richly, the distant groves to be brightened by the yellow light and the blue ocean to be kindled up. The poet is sure that this splendid scene would delight Charles Lamb so much as to make him stand spell bound in the same manner as the poet himself has stood before, gazing round the wide landscape and feeling the pervading presence of the Almighty over the entire area.

Then the poet feels delighted as though he himself are present there. Not that he has not observed certain things in the bower itself which has soothed him much. The transparent foliage appeares pale in the blazing sun. Broad leaves shone brightly. The lovely shadows produces by the leaves and the branches above dappled the sunshine. They mark it with different spots. The walnut tree has a richer colour. The ivy overgrowing the elm tree has a brighter radiance. In the twilight the dark branches of the elm tree has a brighter radiance. In the twilight the dark branches of the elm trees gleames brightly. Sometimes a bat passes by whirling. The twittering of the swallow was no longer heard. The solitary bee humms amongst the bean flowers. The poet is convinced that Nature never leaves the pure hearted people. The beauty of Nature is manifest even in narrow plots of land and vacant waste tracts too. The beauty of Nature keeps the heart awake to Love and Beauty. The poet feels that even though we may be denied certain benefits despite our eager expectations, it is eventually conducive to our own good, because it has the power to elevate the soul when men can joyously contemplate the lovely joys he may not personally feel.

In the concluding lines the poet admirably sums up everything by referring to certain remarkable features. The poet apostrophises Charles Lamb and tells him that the last rook flying towards his nest is blessed by him. Probably Lamb himself might have stood gazing at it as it flew above. It must have made a croaking sound as it flow overhead. No sound which tells of life can be dissonant to him and so it must have a charm for him.

(D) CRITICAL APPRECIATION, INTERPRETATION AND DEVELOPMENT OF THOUGHT

Development of Thought

Coleridge's friend has left on a trip to the hills and the roaring dell.

He is denied the pleasure of accompanying them because of his inability to walk. This makes him sorry because the beautiful sights of nature he might have seen, could have been treasured within his mind for a long time even in his old age when his eyes will become dimmed to view them clearly.

This personal loss does not prevent the poet from indulging in fanciful thoughts about the various things that will be seen and enjoyed by his friends. He feels as though he is bodily transported to that region. Nature cannot but accord joy to its votaries, the wise and the pure-hearted. Man may be denied certain benefits but that does not mean that through the help of Nature man cannot elevate his soul to appreciate love and beauty. Wordsworth's influence over Coleridge is clear in the lines 40-43. But to Coleridge nature is not a moral teacher. Still, a pantheistic belief is the necessary corollary of the appreciation of Nature and its extensive bounties.

Critical Appreciation

Description of Nature: Several scenes from Nature are realistically describes in this poem. His description is such that all those objects appear to come before our mind's eye. The description of the ash tree with its few yellow leaves fluttering due to the waterfall, although the gale itself is unable to shake them is a wonderful example:

> ....that branchless ash
> Unsunned and damp, whose few poor yellow leaves
> Ne'er tremble in the gale, yet tremble still
> Fanned by the waterfall

The poet observes his surroundings so very minutely as to appreciate all the beauties of the nature in and around the lime-tree bower where, he has complained before, he has been kept a prisoner.

Friendship with Lamb. Another noteworthy feature of the poem is the full description of the poet's friendship and respect for Charles Lamb who stoically braved many domestic calamities. The friendship dated from their school days. Appropriately, Coleridge uses the term "gentle-hearted" for Lamb. It is deep affection for his friend that makes Coleridge call upon the objects of Nature to look more beautiful so that Lamb would be able to feast his eyes upon them. The closing lines of the poem emphasises Lamb's love of Nature and picturise him standing and gazing at the flight of a rook.

The Poet's Variation of Moods. The poem presents a variation of moods. It begins on a note of regret, but goes on to express joy-the poet's joy at the idea of his friends feeling happy amidst natural beauty. The poet's joy also has a source in his appreciation of his immediate surroundings. Towards the end, the exuberant joy is sobered down to a meditative mood as the poet thinks of those occasions in life when a man finds himself "bereft of promised good". Thus the poem ends on a contemplative note:

> No sound is dissonant which tells of Life.

A Conversation Poem. This poem belongs to the category of Coleridge's conversation poems'. Coleridge handles blank verse successfully. There are vivid word pictures of natural sights, showing Coleridge's observation powers.

Coleridge's Love of Nature. Coleridge's love of nature comes through in this poem. He cherishes the charms of Nature and the power of Nature to cheer and soothe our mind. In a pantheistic vein he speaks of the hues of Nature "veiling the almighty Spirit". Here Coleridge seems to be Wordsworthian in his belief of the Universal spirit pervading the objects of Nature.

(E) EXPLANATIONS WITH CRITICAL COMMENTS

L. 26-32. Yes they wander on...catamily: Coleridge imagines his friends wandering amidst natural sights, enjoying their close contact with Nature. Gentle-hearted Lamb, he feels, must be the happiest of them all, because after his long stay in crowded London he will have been longing for the sights of Nature. He must be delighted to see them now. The poet makes a reference to the unhappy life that Lamb has been leading on account of domestic misfortunes. These misfortunes were, of course, the insanity of his sister and the death of their mother at his sister's hands. The poet admires Lamb's patience in facing his misfortunes.

The lines bring out Coleridge's affection for his friend. They also snow his love of Nature. He feels that Nature has a fascination for all, offering a welcome sojourn from the fever and fret of a congested city life'.

L. 59-64. Henceforth......and Beauty: These lines have an echo of Wordsworthian sentiment. "Nature never did betray a heart that loved her", said Wordsworth in his Tintern Abbey. Coleridge feels similarly that the sights of Nature have a great significance for those who are wise and pure of heart. To the discerning mind, even the narrowest piece of ground and the emptiest tract of land have features which stimulate the faculties of human beings.

19

THE PAINS OF SLEEP

(A) TEXT AND ANNOTATIONS

Ere on my bed my limbs I lay,
It hath not been my use to pray
With moving lips or bended knees;
But silently, by slow degrees,
My spirit I to Love compose,
In humble trust mine eye-lids close,
With reverential resignation,
No wish conceived, no thought exprest,
Only a sense of supplication;
A sense o'er all my soul imprest
That I am weak, yet not unblest,
Since in me, round me, every where
Eternal Strength and Wisdom are.

But yester-night I prayed aloud
In anguish and in agony,
Up-starting from the fiendish crowd
Of shapes and thoughts that tortured me:
A lurid light, a trampling throng,
Sense of intolerable wrong,
And whom I scored, those only strong !
Thirst of revenge, the powerless will
Still baffled, and yet burning still !
Desire with loathing strangely mixed
On wild or hateful objects fixed.
Fantastic passions ! maddening brawl !

L. 1. **Ere**—before. L. 7. **reverential**—expressing honour and respect; with love and awe. **resignation**—the quality of being submissive to God's will. This indicates that the poet was devout but did not belive in making a show of it by praying loudly in front of others or kneeling down to make others see it. L. 8. **Conceived**—think L. 9. **Supplication**—imploring humbly, entreaties with earnest request. L. 13. **Eternal**—everlasting. L. 15. **Anguish**—extreme distress of mind. **agony**—excessive pain in body or mind. L. 16. **fiendish**—devilish. L. 18. **lurid**—ghastly and gruesome. **Throng**—crowd. **trampling**—crushing under the feet. L. 19. **intolerable**—excessively unbearable. L. 20. **Scorned**—treat with contempt. L. 23. **Loathing**—dislike. L. 25. **fantastic**—unbelievably great, imagined and fanciful. **brawl**—noisy quarrel.

And shame and terror over all !
Deeds to be hid which were not hid,
Which all confused I could not know
Whether I suffered, or I did:
For all seemed guilt, remorse or woe,
My own or others still the same
Life-stifling fear, soul-stifling shame.

So two nights passed: the night's dismay
Saddened and stunned the coming day.
Sleep, the wide blessing, seemed to me
Distemper's worst calamity.
The third night, when my own loud scream
Had waked me from the fiendish dream,
O'ercome with suffering strange and wild,
I wept as I had been a child;
And having thus by tears subdued
My anguish to a milder mood,
Such punishments, I said, were due
To natures deepliest stained with sin,—
For aye entempesting anew
The unfathomable hell within,
The horror of their deeds to view,
To know and loathe, yet wish and do!
Such griefs with such men well agree,
But wherefore, wherefore fall on me?
To be beloved is all I need,
And whom I love, I love indeed.

L. 30. **remorse**—distress on account of guilty feeling. **L. 32. Life-stifling**—suffocating and smothering. **L. 33. dismay**—loss of courage due to excessive alarm. **L. 36. distemper**—bodily disorder. **Calamity**—great misfortune. **L. 41. subdued**—suppressed. **L. 45. entempesting**—moving as if by means of a violent gust of wind. **L. 46. unfathomable**—difficult to gauge.

(B) INTRODUCTION TO THE POEM

Though written as early as 1803, *The Pains of Sleep* has been published only in 1816 along with *Christabel*. Brilliance of intellect is sometimes denies robust health. Coleridge had never been as healthy as he deserves to be. Rheumatism, spasmodic attacks of dysentery, etc. has plagued him always. He becomes an addict to laudanum, a tincture of opium, in order to relieve himself from pain. The habit cannot leave him. He has taken the stuff in increasing quantities which results in further deterioration in his health. He uses to spend sleepless nights and if at all he has some sleep now and then it is vitiated by horrid dreams. This miserable plight is due to the strong doses of opium that he has indulged himself in but he is helpless. Coleridge is very unhappy over his ill-health. He wrote to a friend; "God forbid that my worst enemy shall ever have the nights and sleeps that I have had night after night surprised by sleep, while I struggle to remain awake, starting up to bless my own loud screams that has awaken me-yea, dear friend, till my repeated night-yells has made me a nuisance in my own house."

(C) CRITICAL SUMMARY

L. 1-13. In the beginning we are given a sort of background to the poem. While going to bed it is the practice among devout Christians of those days to kneel down and pray to God in more or less audible words. But Coleridge says that he do not do so habitually. His practice was to pray silently with his eyes closes. He do not openly pray for any fulfilment of his wishes. There used to be a sense of supplication with reverential submission to the Almighty whose strength and wisdom he can perceive everywhere around him. He is fully conscious of his weakness but at the same time he is convinced that God will not keep him unblessed.

L. 14-32. The poet goes on to give us a vivid picture of the sufferings he has to undergo on a particular night. He has painful hallucinations of a crowd of shapes and thoughts torturing him. He has a sense of intolerable wrong and unbearable injustice. Persons meriting his scornful contempt are seen in dreams as too powerful for him to contend with. In spite of his eagerness to punish them, he is baffled and powerless to do anything. Loathing for certain things become strangely mixed with keen desire for them. He is overwhelmed by fantastic passions and maddening brawl. He is unable to decide whether he perpetrates certain blameworthy actions or suffers on account of the same when performed by others. Guilt, remorse and woe instilled fear and shame in him. After these dreams and horrible experiences the poet got up and prayed to God aloud.

L. 33-52. The last section of this lyrical piece is devoted to the recurrence of the horrid dreams for two nights and its effect on him. The day following the fearful dreams also is sorrowful. Sleep is a blessing experienced by people all over the world but unfortunately the poet who has a bodily disorder found it calamitous. After experiencing the horrible dreams on the third night the poet is so overwhelmed that he begin to cry like a child. He is somewhat relieved after the anguished cry. Then the poet with excessive self-pity wonders why he should be tormented with such griefs and worries when he had been sinless and devoid of criminal tendencies. The poet concludes the piece with the avowal of his serious aim in life.

(D) CRITICAL APPRECIATION, INTERPRETATION AND DEVELOPMENT OF THOUGHT

Development of Thought

In this personal and autobiographical poem, Coleridge confides in the reader about the misery he experiences on certain nights. The poem begins with the poet expressing his feeling of faith in God, even though he do not follow the ostentatious practice of kneeling and praying aloud at bed-time. His practice is to pray silently. Then the poet goes on to describe what he underwent on a particular night so as to be forced to pray about. He see a crowd of horrible shapes in his sleep and is tortured by terrible thoughts. He feel overpowered by hostile people, and also experiences a dreadful desire for hateful things. All this is accompanied by a feeling of guilt and remorse. Walking up in a state of misery, he prays aloud to God. In the last section of the poem, the poet tells us of the effect of such dreams. He feel depressed throughout the day after such miserable nights. Sleep, which is a universal blessing for mankind, has become a calamity for the poet. When on the third night of such horrid dreams, he awake with loud screams, and overwhelms by suffering he weep like a child, he reflects that he did not deserve such hideous punishment. All that he askes is to be loved by those whom he loved sincerely.

Critical Appreciation

This autobiographical poem emphasises on personal experience. True to the characteristic style of a romantic poet this work gives a lot of illuminating glimpses of Coleridge's temperament and personal idiosyncrasies.

The distress and sorrow that dominates the mood of the author when he pensed these few lines can be clearly understood from the series of grief stricken words uses in the poem such as "agony", "anguish", "woe" "torture" "dismay", "calamity", "horror" "scream", "lurid light" "baffled", "maddening" etc. The hallucinations of the poet are clearly portrayed.

His experience of fantastic passions and maddening dreams, the strange confusion of the mingling of desire with loathing, the feeling of guilt, remorse and woe-all these indicate the sick mind of the poet. We are able to understand that all these psychological upheavals are the result of excessive addiction to the opiatic drug.

The agonising experiences of the poet are the experiences of many other people also who unfortunately fall a prey to the habit of the use of laudanum. The poet begin the odious habit to get some relief from rheumatic pain but ultimately landed himself in more trouble. The remedy happened to be more disastrous than the original malady. The poet's outbursts of self-pity and the protests that he has been guileless and free from sin may awaken the feelings of compassion in our hearts. Those who are habitually prone to deadliest of sins and offences against God and His creations may well deserve such punishments but simple folk desirous of loving and being loved by others should be spared. Moreover, the poet is a believer in God and his mercy and this religious devotion in him also merits kindness from the Almighty. The last section of the poem can be called a specimen of the poet's vigour of expression.

As a literary piece the poem merits our praise. The feelings of terror and shame and guilt are effectively conveyed through intensity of language.

(E) EXPLANATIONS WITH CRITICAL COMMENTS

L. 14-32. But yester night....stifling shame. Unlike his usual practice of praying silently the poet has to pray aloud on a certain night because of the horrifying experience of terrible dreams. He gets up in a state of excessive agony and remorse and prays to God aloud. The diabolical shapes and fantastic images so terrifies the poet that he finds relief only in the supplication for mercy. The vision of intolerable injustice and the prevalence of the power of strong but detestable persons is too much for him. He wants to take revenge on them but finds himself powerless. Many things come before him for which he has a keen desire and an excessive distaste simultaneously. Everything is confusing and contradictory. He has feelings of fear as well as shame.

The lines are a vivid expression of the experience of drug taking.

L. 35-52. Sleep the wide blessing...love indeed. Sleep is universally acknowledged as something necessary for us to recoup our energy and give relief to our mental tensions. But the author says that he finds it to be a curse because he has some bodily disorder. He never wants to go to sleep because he is terribly afraid of the horrid dreams and hallucinations. There is some meaning, if sinful persons are punished by God or man and society, but the poet feels that a sinless and guileless man like him should not have been tormented by these life-stifling fears and soul-stifling, shames. If guilty persons are punished they will realise their mistakes. Punishment to them will be a deterrent and hence necessary. On the contrary if an innocent person is punished he may become callous and is likely to commit some crime just to spite those people who tortured him. So, it is necessary that society should mete out punishment to those who deserve it. Further, the poet wants to love others and be loved by them. All the more reason that he should be pitied and not punished. The lines show a strain of self-pity in the poet. However, the pathetic lines evoke our sympathy for the poet.

20

TO DISAPPOINTMENT

A. TEXT AND ANNOTATIONS

Hence ! thou fiend of gloomy sway,
That lov'st on withering blast to ride
O'er fond Illusion's air-built pride.
Sullen Spirit ! Hence ! Away !

Where Avarice lurks in sordid cell,
Or mad Ambition builds the dream,
Or Pleasure plots th' unholy scheme
There with Guilt and Folly dwell !

But oh ! when Hope on Wisdom's wing
Prophetic whispers pure delight,
Be distant far thy cank'rous blight,
Demon of envenom'd sting.

Then haste thee, Nymph of balmy gales !
Thy poet's prayer, sweet May ! attend !
Oh! place my parent and my friend
'Mid her lovely native vales.

L. 1. **Hence**—This is an adverb used in different meanings such as, from this time, consequently. Here it is used in the sense 'go away'. The poet wants Disappointment to go away, never to return. **Fiend**—evil spirit' or demon. **Of gloomy sway**—capable of spreading gloom or lowness of spirits and dejection. L. 2. **Withering**—Causing loss of force and vitality. **Blast**—plight or frustrating influence. Disappointment is a devil that loves to ride on the withering blast. L. 3. **Illusion's**—mistaken idea, fancy, hallucination. Air—built pride—elation without any foundation. Disappointment removes all our elation due to mistaken fancies. L. 4. **Sullen**—morose. L. 5. **Avarice**—excessive greed. **Lurks**—lies hidden. **Sordid**—grossly base, filthy and dirty. L. 6. **Ambition**—desire for honour and success. L. 7. **Pleasure**—desire for enjoyment. **Plots**—plans secretly. L. 8. **Guilt**—feeling of responsibility for some serious offence. **Folly**—foolishness. Disappointment should not trouble a person free from mean qualities. L. 9. **Hope**—eager expectation of some bright result. **Wisdom's**— sensible insight. L. 10. **Prophetic**—characteristic of an inspired utterance. L. 11. **Cank'rous**—full of spreading sore that destroys tissues. L. 12. **Envenom'd**— poisonous. L. 13. **Nymph**—semi-divine female angel. **Gales**—strong winds. **Balmy**—gently soothing. The poet invokes the month of May as a beautiful spirit having the

Peace that lists the woodlarks' strains,
Health, that breathes divinest treasures,
Laughing Hours, and Social Pleasures
Wait my friend in Cambria's plains.

Affection there with mingled ray
Shall pour at once the raptures high
Of filial and maternal Joy,
Haste thee then, delightful May !

And oh ! may Spring's fair flowerets fade,
May Summer cease her limbs to lave
In cooling stream, may Autumn grave
Yellow o'er the corn-cloath'd glade;

Ere, from sweet retirement torn,
She seek again the crowded mart:
Nor thou, my selfish, selfish heart
Dare her slow return to mourn !

---

power to bring joy and delight to everyone by means of enjoyable breezes. He requests May to delight his 'parent' and 'friend' (the reference is to Mrs. Evans whom he loves much) who is in her native land of Wales. **L. 17. Peace**—freedom from disturbance of every sort. **Lists**—listens to, hears attentively. **Woodlarks'**—a small song-bird living among the woods. Strains—sweet and agreeable sound of melody. L. **20. Cambria's**—Old name for Wales. In this stanza the poet eagerly wishes for mental peace, health, ample occasion for laughter and social pleasure for his friend Mrs. Evans who was enjoying retired life in the rural atmosphere of Wales. **L. 21. Affection**—tender attachment. **mingled**—mixed. **Ray**—beam of light. **L. 27. raptures**—emotional ecstasies. **L. 23. filial**—befitting a son or a daughter. The poet wants May to hasten its visit to the land of Wales in order to make her happy and joyous. The affection has two types of ray mingled together. One, the filial one that flows from him to her as from a son to his mother. The other, the maternal one that flows from her to him like that of mother to her son. L. **25. Flowerets**— small flowers. L. **26. Cease**—stop. **Lave**—wash, cleanse with water. **L. 28. Corn-cloath'd**—covered with ripening corn. **Glade**—grassy open space in a forest. **L. 29. retirement**—withdrawal from actual participation. L. 30. Mart—market.

(B) INTRODUCTION TO THE POEM

To Disappointment is included in the *Letters of Samuel Taylor Coleridge* in 1895. This short poem has been composed in 1792 when Coleridge is just twenty years of age. His acquaintance with the family of a widow, Mrs. Evans, began as early as 1788 when he is still a student in the charity school of Christ's Hospital in London. One of the sons of Mrs. Evans is his schoolmate. The poet has fallen in love with Mrs. Evans' daughter Mary, about whom he use to compose romantic poems, apostrophising her by the name Lewti. Although his sentiments are not taken seriously by Mary, the poet's respect and affection for the kindly and considerate Mrs. Evans continues unabated. In this poem he eulogises her as "parent" and "friend". At the time when the acquaintance begin, that family is staying in London but at the time of the composition of the poem the mother and the daughter are staying in Wales. The fact that Mary did not encourage his romantic attentions, did not prevent Coleridge from respecting the mother and praying for her peace and happiness at her rural resort far away from the "crowded mart" of the metropolitan city.

(C) CRITICAL SUMMARY

The poet orders Disappointment to go away. He calls it the 'find of gloomy sway which destroys all one's hopes and illusions. He condemns Disappointment to the company of Avarice, Ambition, Pleasure, Guilt and Folly. Disappointment is not to come near Hope because it will always try to poison and kill hope.

Addressing the sweet month of May, the poet then goes on to ask it to provide every kind of happiness to Mrs. Evans, whom he considers his 'parent' and 'friend'. He requests the sweet month of May to go quickly and shower her with peace, good health, laughing hours and social pleasures.

Finally the poet expresses his desire that Mrs. Evans shall continue to enjoy the peace and leisure of retirement in the Wales countryside. She shall not disturb herself and come back to the crowded city. The poet do not want his selfish heart to be disappointed at her delayed return to the city. Heather wishes her peaceful stay in Wales.

(D) CRITICAL APPRECIATION, INTERPRETATION AND DEVELOPMENT OF THOUGHT

Development of Thought. In the poem. *To Disappointment*, Coleridge actually dismisses Disappointment to the company of mean qualities such as Avarice, Ambition, Guilt and Folly. He tells Disappointment not to come near Hope because its effort is always to kill hope. The poet addresses the sweet month of May to shower happiness of every kind on Mrs. Evans in her peaceful sojourn in the Wales countryside. He says that Mrs. Evans should enjoy herself and not disturb herself by coming back to the crowded city. He is determined not to feel disappointed at her delayed return. Indeed, he will be selfish if he is to mourn her delayed return to the city.

Critical Appreciation. Many of Coleridge's poems reveal intense morbidity and pitiable unhappiness that has been his lot throughout his life. Yet poems like this piece can be seen to express his moods of joy too. The poet wants disappointment to be dismissed and done away with. He celebrates the month of May which, he hopes will confer all kind of happiness on Mrs. Evans.

Theme. Though the poem is named after Disappointment, the real theme is the expression of the poet's love and respect for Mrs. Evans whom he considers as his parent and friend. He would like her to enjoy peace, health, laughter, social pleasures and hours of rest and retirement amidst the calm loveliness of the Wales countryside. The poet's sincere feelings of love and respect are expressed.

Synthesis of Romanticism and Neo-classicism. Another noteworthy feature in this poem is its happy synthesis of romanticism and neoclassicism. The expression of personal feelings and the induction of autobiographical elements are all features of romanticism. At the same time, the poet has also personified the different qualities of head and heart such as Hope, Wisdom, Avarice, Ambition, Folly, Guilt, besides Disappointment. This is peculiar to the Neoclassical School of poetic art.

Simple Poem. The poem is simple and devoid of complex philosophical thoughts or religious mustings. No portion of it can be called obscure. The poet's desire to associate with nature is also manifest. He craves for favours of Nature to enjoy them. There is no hint here of Nature as a moral teacher. He refers to Spring's flowerets, cooling streams of summer and corn-clothed glade of the Autumn without any craving for edification. He expresses sincere and simple love for an elderly lady who has shown a mother's affection for him.

The melody of the lines heightens the aesthetic pleasure we derive from this poem.

(E) EXPLANATION WITH CRITICAL COMMENTS

L. 1-3. Hence...air built pride. Coleridge bids Disappointments go away. Disappointment is regarded as a fiend having the power to spread gloom. Disappointment loves to shatter the pride that one feels on the basis of some illusory hope. Disappointment destroys one's hopes and the pride arising from these hopes.

In picturesque language, Coleridge conveys the idea of the pleasantness of nursing an illusion.

L. 25-32. And Oh...to mourn. In his To Disappointment Coleridge hopes that Mrs. Evans will enjoy all happiness possible in her retirement in the Wales countryside. Coleridge says that she may continue her sojourn in Wales till all the beauties of the various season come to an end. Only then is she to come to the crowded city. The poet may miss her company but he is determined not to feel disappointed at her absence when she is amidst the joy, beauty and tranquillity of the countryside.

Coleridge's sincere feelings of affection to Mrs. Evans are expresses in the characteristic Romantic manner.

FEARS IN SOLITUDE

Written in April 1798 , during the alarm of an Invasion

(A) TEXT AND ANNOTATIONS

A GREEN and silent spot, amid the hills,
A small and silent dell ! O'er stiller place
No singing sky-lark ever poised himself.
The hills are heathy, save that swelling slope,
Which hath a gay and gorgeous covering on,
All golden with the never-bloomless furze,
Which now blooms most profusely : but the dell,
Bathed by the mist, is fresh and delicate
As vernal corn-field, or the unripe flax,
When, through its half-transparent stalks, at eve,
The level sunshine glimmers with green light.
Oh ! 'tis a quiet spirit-healing nook !
Which all, methinks, would love; but chiefly he,
The humble man, who, in his youthful years,
Knew just so much of folly, as had made
His early manhood more securely wise !
Here he might lie on fern or withered heath,
While from singing lark (that sings unseen
The minstrelsy that solitude loves best),
And from the sun, and from the breezy air,
Sweet influences trembled o'er his frame;
And he, with many feelings, many thoughts,
Made up a meditative joy, and found
Religious meanings in the forms of Nature !
And so, his senses gradually wrapt
In a half sleep, he dreams of better worlds,
And dreaming hears thee still, O singing lark,
That singest like an angel in the clouds !
My God ! it is a melancholy thing
For such a man, who would full fain preserve
His soul in calmness, yet perforce must feel
For all his human brethren – O my God !
It weighs upon the heart, that he must think

L. 1. **amid**—in the middle of. L. 2. **dell**—valley. ***stiller***—quieter. L. 3. **poised**—balanced; stayed. **L.4. save**—except. **swelling**—bulging. L. 6. ***furze***— gorse bushes. L. 7. **profusely**—abundantly. L. 9. **vernal**—*fresh;* happening in spring. L. 12. **nook**—corner. L.19. **minstrelsy**—music. L. 23. **meditative**— thoughtful. L. 29. **melancholy**—*sad.* L. 30. **full fain**—very gladly. L. 31. **perforce**—*of* necessity. L. 33. **weighs upon the heart**—*it* makes one sad or depressed.

What uproar and what strife may now be stirring
This way or that way o'er these silent hills—
Invasion, and thunder and the shout,
And all the crash of onset; fear and rage,
And undetermined conflict — even now,
Even now, perchance, and in his native isle:
Carnage and groans beneath this blessed sun!
We have offended, Oh ! my countrymen !
We have offended very grievously,
And been most tyrannous. From east to west
A groan of accusation pierces Heaven !
The wretched plead against us; multitudes
Countless and vehement, the sons of God,
Our bethren ! Like a cloud that travels on,
Steamed up from Cairo's swamps of pestilence,
Even so, my countrymen ! have we gone forth
And borne to distant tribes slavery and pangs,
And, deadlier far, our vices, whose deep taint
With slow perdition murders the whole man,
His body and his soul ! Meanwhile, at home,
All individual dignity and power
Engulfed in Courts, Committees, Institutions,
Associations and Societies,
A vain, speech-mouthing, speech-reporting Guild,
One Benefit-Club for mutual flattery,
We have drunk up, demure as at a grace,
Pollutions from the brimming cup of wealth;
Contemptuous of all honourable rule,
Yet bartering freedom and the poor man's life
For gold, as at a market ! The sweet words
Of Christian promise, words that even yet
Might stem destruction, were they wisely preached,
Are muttered o'er by men, whose tones proclaim
How flat and wearisome they feel their trade:
Rank scoffers some, but most too indolent
To deem them falsehoods or to know their truth.
Oh ! blasphemous ! the Book of Life is made
A superstitious instrument, on which

L. 37. **onset**—attack. **rage**—anger. L. 39. **perchance**—perhaps. L. 40. **carnage**—great destruction of life; slaughter. L. 48, **pestilence**—**deadly** epidemic disease. L. 52. **perdition**—damnation. L. 59. **demure**—affectedly modest; putting up a show of gravity. L. 68. **Rank**—utter; out-and-out. *Scoffers – mockers;* insincere people. *indolent*—lazy; L. 69. **deem**—consider. L. 70. **blasphemous**—impious. *Book of Life*—the Bible.

We gabble o'er the oaths we mean to break;
For all must swear — all and in every place,
College and wharf, council and justice-court;
All, all must swear, the briber and the bribed,
Merchant and lawyer, senator and priest,
The rich, the poor, the old man and the young;
All, all make up one scheme of perjury,
That faith doth reel; the very name of God
Sounds like a juggler's charm; and, bold with joy,
Forth from his dark and lonely hiding-place,
(Portentous sight !) the owlet Atheism,
Sailing on obscene wings athwart the noon,
Drops his blue-fringed lids, and holds them close,
And hooting at the glorious sun in Heaven,
Cries out, 'Where is it ?'
Thankless too for peace,
(Peace long preserved by fleets and perilous seas)
Secure from actual warfare, we have loved
To swell the war-whoop, passionate for war !
Alas! for ages ignorant of all
Its ghastlier workings, (famine or blue plague,
Battle, or siege, or, flight through wintry snows.)
We, this whole people, have been clamorous
For war and bloodshed; animating sports,
The which we pay for as a thing to talk of,
Spectators and not combatants ! No guess
Anticipative of a wrong unfelt,
No speculation or contingency,
However dim and vague, too vague and dim
To yield a justifying cause ; and forth,
(Stuffed out with big preamble, holy names,
And adjurations of the God in Heaven,
We send our mandates for the certain death
Of thousands and ten thousands ! Boys and girls,
And women, that would groan to see a child
Pull off an insect's leg, all read of war,
The best amusement for our morning meal !
The poor wretch, who has learnt his only prayers
From curses, who knows scarcely words enough
To ask a blessing from his Heavenly Father,
Becomes a fluent phraseman, absolute
And technical in victories and defeats,
And all our dainty terms for fratricide;

L. 72. **gabble**—speak unintelligibly. L. 78. **perjury**—*false* swearing. L. 89. **war-whoop**—war-cry. L. 93. **clamorous**—demanding loudly. L. 98. **contingency**—liability. L. 101. **preamble**—introductory words of explanation. L. 102. **adjurations**-causing to swear. L. 103. **mandates**—*orders;* sanctions. L. 113. **fratricide**—*the* act of brother killing brother.

Terms which we trundle smoothly o'er our tongues
Like mere abstractions, empty sounds to which
We join no feeling and attach no form !
As if the soldier died without a wound;
As if the fibres of this godlike frame
Were gored without a pang; as if the wretch,
Who fell in battle, doing bloody deeds,
Passed off to Heaven, translated and not killed;
As though he had no wife to pine for him,
No God to judge him ! Therefore, evil days
Are coming on us, O my countrymen !
And what if all-avenging Providence,
Strong and retributive, should make us know
The meaning of our words, force us to feel
The desolation and the agony
Of our fierce doings ?
Spare us yet awhile
Father and God ! O ! spare us yet awhile !
Oh ! let not English women drag their flight
Fainting beneath the burthen of their babes,
Of the sweet infants, that but yesterday
Laughed at the breast ! Sons, brothers, husbands, all
Who ever gazed with fondness on the forms
Which grew up with you round the same fire-side,
And all who ever heard the sabbath-bells
Without the infidel's scorn, make yourselves pure !
Stand forth ! be men ! repel an impious foe,
Impious and false, a light yet cruel race,
Who laugh away all virtue, mingling mirth
With deeds of murder; and still promising
Freedom, themselves too sensual to be free,
Poison life's amities, and cheat the heart
Of faith and quiet hope, and all that soothes,
And all that lifts the spirit ! Stand we forth;
Render them back upon the insulted ocean,
And let them toss as idly on its waves
As the vile sea-weed, which some mountain-blast

L. 114. trundle—roll. **L. 119. gored**-covered with blood. **L. 121. translated**-i.e., transferred. **L. 122. pine**—grieve. **L. 126.** *retributive*—rewarding or punishing suitably. **L. 132. burthen** – burden. **L. 137. Sabbath-bells** – *church* bells on Sunday. **L. 138. infidel's**—disbeliever in one's religion. **L. 143. sensual**—given to the pleasures of the senses. **L. 144. amities**—friendship. **L. 149. vile**—worthless.

Swept from our shores ! And oh ! may we return
Not with a drunken triumph, but with fear,
Repenting of the wrongs with which we stung
So fierce a foe to frenzy !
I have told,
O Britons ! O my brethren ! I have told
Most bitter truth, but without bitterness.
Nor deem my zeal or factious or mistimed;
For never can true courage dwell with them,
Who, playing tricks with conscience, dare not look
At their own vices. We have been too long
Dupes of a deep delusion ! Some, belike,
Groaning with restless enmity, expect
All change from change of constituted power;
As if a Government had been a robe,
On which our vice and wretchedness were tagged
Like fancy-points and fringes, with the robe
Pulled off at pleasure. Fondly these attach
A radical causation to a few
Poor drudges of chastising Providence,
Who borrow all their hues and qualities
From our own folly and rank wickedness,
Which gave them birth and nursed them. Others, meanwhile,
Dote with a mad idolatry: and all
Who will not fall before their images,
And yield them worship, they are enemies
Even of their country !
Such have I been deemed.—
But, O dear Britain ! O my Mother Isle !
Needs must thou prove a name most dear and holy
To me, a son, a brother, and a friend,
A husband, a father! who revere
All bonds of natural love, and find them all
Within the limits of thy rocky shores.
O native Britain ! O my Mother Isle !
How shoudst thou prove aught else but dear and holy
To me, who from thy lakes and mountain-hills,
Thy clouds, thy quiet dales, thy rocks and seas,
Have drunk in all my intellectual life,
All sweet sensations, all ennobling thoughts,
All adoration of the God in nature,
All lovely and all honourable things,
Whatever makes this mortal spirit feel
The joy and greatness of its future being ?
There lives nor from nor feeling in my soul

L. 153. **frenzy**-madness. L. 156. **factious**—seditious. L. 160. **Dupes**—those who are cheated or deceived. **belike**—probably; perhaps. L. 172. **Dote**—to be weakly affectionate; to be stupid. **idolatry**-worship of an image held to be the abode of a superhuman personality.

Unborrowed from my country ! O divine
And beauteous island ! thou hast been my sole
And most magnificent temple, in the which
I walk with awe, and sing my stately songs,
Loving the God that made me !
                                        May my fears,
My filial fears, be vain ! and may the vaunts
And menace of the vengeful enemy
Pass like the gust, that roared and died away
In the distant tree: which heard, and only heard
In this low dell, bowed not the delicate grass.
But now the gentle dew-fall sends abroad
The fruit-like perfume of the golden furze:
The light has left the summit of the hill,
Though still a sunny gleam lies beautiful,
Aslant the ivied beacon. Now farewell,
Farewell, awhile, O soft and silent spot !
On the green sheep-track, up the heathy hill,
Homeward I wind my way ; and lo ! recalled
From bodings that have well-nigh wearied me,
I find myself upon the brow, and pause
Startled ! And after lonely sojourning
In such a quiet and surrounded nook,
This burst of prospect, here the shadowy main,
Dim-tinted, there the mighty majesty
Of that huge amphitheatre of rich
And elmy fields, seems like society–
Conversing with the mind, and giving it
A livelier impulse and a dance of thought !
And now, beloved Stowey ! I behold
Thy church-tower, and, methinks, the four huge elms
Clustering, which mark the mansion of my friend;
And close behind them, hidden from my view,
Is my own lowly cottage, where my babe
And my babe's mother dwell in peace ! With light
And quickened footsteps thitherward I tend,
Remembering thee, O green and silent dell !
And grateful, that by nature's quietness
And solitary musings, all my heart
Is softened, and made worthy to indulge
Love, and the thoughts that yearn for human kind.

L. 198. **filial**–proper for a son or daughter. **vaunts**–boasts. L. 200. **gust**–wind. L. 202. **bowed**....grass–i.e., did not reach or affect the place. L. 207. **Aslant**–slantingly. ivied–covered with ivy. **beacon**–light-house placed for guiding ships, etc. L 210. **wind** my way, make one's way along a winding path. L. 211. **bodings**–omens. L. 212. **brow**–top of the hill. L. 213. **sojourning**–stay. L..215. **burst of prospect**–suddenly visible scene. main-expanse of sea. L. 223. **mansion of my friend**-probably the house of Coleridge's friend and benefactor, Thomas Poole, in Stowey. L. 225. **lowly**-humble. L. 227. **tend**-move. L. 230. **musings**–thinking.

(B) INTRODUCTION TO THE POEM

Fears in Solitude is a long poem of 232 lines. It is composed and published in 1798 at a time when England is facing the grave danger of being invaded by France. The fears expresses in the title of the poem, of course, turned out to be baseless later as the poet himself expresses (in lines 197-199). The poet has been an admirer of the French Revolution but unhappily within a few years after the revolution, the condition in France has deteriorated much. Throughout the poem we find ruthless criticism of the misdeeds of the poet's countrymen and the expression of his love for the land with its natural beauty. The fact that he loves the land does not blind him to the misdeeds of his countrymen. The poet, under the influence of Wordsworth, has begun to see in Nature a profoundly religious aspect, as is evident in this poem.

(C) CRITICAL SUMMARY

Fears in Solitude, Coleridge's longest 'conversation poem', begins with a quiet description of the poet's surroundings. It is a still and silent spot where the singing skylark poises himself because there cannot be a stiller place elsewhere. The hills are mostly covered with tracts of wastelands except a swelling slope where the furze grows in plenty. The poet thinks that this is a corner that can quietly exert its spirit-healing power. All people must necessarily love this beautiful spot and referring to himself, the poet says that a man like him must love it all the more. He is a humble man. It is possible that during his early youthful years he might have been guilty of many foolish acts. Possibly this has made his early manhood 'securely wise. The poet then says that he can conveniently lie down on the fern or the faded heath from where he can listen to the songs of the lark and feel the soothing influence of the sun and the gentle breeze. Under the influence of this exquisite pleasurable atmosphere the poet begins to experience meditative joy and finds religious meaning in the forms of Nature. He dreams of better worlds.

The poet now comes to the crux of the matter. While dreaming of better worlds, the poet is compelled to think of realities also in the form of an imminent attack of the foreign soldiers on his beloved motherland. The poet feels that the external danger might have been the result of a series of wrongs and sins has committed by his own countrymen. War means a great deal of angry shouts, fearful crashes and reckless conflicts. Carnage is inevitable. People will be groaning due to pain even beneath the blessed sunshine. The poet then addresses his countrymen and reminds them that all these troubles shall be attributed to their own faults and offensive behaviour in the past. From east to west all over the world the people belonging to various nationalities have begun to accuse Englishmen in loud tones for making them wretched and miserable. People of other lands too are the Sons of God and our own brethren. The British people utilised their military might in extending the pernicious system of slavery and forced labour all over the world. The damage done is not confined to the body alone. Even the soul is contaminated and make prone to perdition. The individual dignity and power became confined to "Courts, Committees, Institutions, Associations and Societies", i.e., different organisations that the British people, evolves in different places for the purpose of perpetuating their overlordship at different places. All the rulers *i.e.,* the British people are avaricious, with money-making as their sole aim. These associations, the poet says, were mere "Speech-reporting Guilds" and "Benefit-Clubs for mutual flattery". One member praises another and is praised by him in return. The poor man's life and freedom is bartered for gold. The poet then points an accusing finger at the Christian missionaries of those days. The Bible and the words of God are intended for stemming destruction by preaching them wisely. But the priests who goes overseas considered their own professional job wearisome. They are lazy and they did not study scriptures thoroughly to understand the truth and spiritual revelation contained in them. The Book of life *(i.e.,* the Bible) is considered to be an instrument to take oaths on. People mutter something unintelligibly, touching the book. They swear by the Bible but break the oaths with impunity. The briber and the bribed equally swear. The Merchant, the lawyer, senator, priest, the rich, the poor, the old and the young—all are guilty of perjury (false swearing). God's name descends to the level of a juggler's charm. The owl does not like the bright sunshine. Similarly Atheism does not want devout feelings and Godfearing habits to flourish. How absurd it will be when the owl hoots at the glorious sun in the sky and loudly proclaims "where is the Sun"? The Atheists behave like that with regard to God and His benign overlordship over the destinies of men and matters.

After narrating the misdeeds of those Britons who goes overseas accompanying the trading companies and wrought havoc in those distant colonies, the poet turns to the Britons in England itself who has been abetting the crimes of those who went out. England has been free from external attacks for a long time. The peace within the country can be preserved because the land is surrounded by perilous seas and the fleet possessed by the British is formidable. Hence the local people has never been victims of naval attacks and bombardment. This immunity has not, however, ennobled them but make them indulge in war cries and passionate advocacy of war elsewhere. For a long time the British people has been unaware of the ghastly inhuman results of war, namely famine, plague, blockades and flight of refugees from place to place. But instead of continuing to be peace-loving people they have begun to clamour for war and bloodshed. They consider war on a par with animating sports for which they pay to remain mere spectators and not actual participants. If there has been a wrong done to them, they may have adjust cause for fighting. But they do not take the trouble of ascertaining whether war is just. Everything is dim and vague. Still the orders are to fight. Small boys and girls and women who are too sensitive to bear an insect's leg being pulled off, seem to revel in reading about war. All those who fluently speak about war do not bother to think about the wounds and sufferings of the fighting soldier. They seem to believe that a soldier dying in the battle is immediately taken to Heaven. They do not care for his wife and children who suffer on account of his death. After listing all the wrongs of his countrymen the poet concludes this section by warning them that Providence may take retributive steps to force them realise their mistakes and the disastrous consequences.

The poet goes on to fervently pray to God to spare his countrymen the fierce disaster foretold by himself. He also calls upon his countrymen to resist the attack of the impious foe. The poet eagerly implores that they shall be saved from the evil consequences of a deadly war. He appeals to all the people—sons, brothers, husbands, sisters, daughters, mothers, etc. who grow up around the same fireside to resist the attack of the infidel. The foe must be repelled and driven away. They are so ruthless as to laugh away all virtue. They mix mirth and indecent joy with their own deeds of murder. They speak highly of freedom. Still they do not want others to enjoy freedom. Amity, faith and hope elevate the spirit of man. But the enemy's activities poison the atmosphere. The Britons shall stand together and see that the enemy is swept back from the shores of their country like sea-weed by a mountain blast. Of course, they must not be proud of their victory; they must feel sorry for all the wrongs,— their own as well as their enemies."

The poet goes on to request his countrymen not to misinterpret his ideas. He does not want them to consider his advocacy of sanity and peace for all to be wayward comments of a factious Spirit and dub him as a traitor to the country of his birth. The poet frankly admits that what he says is the bitter truth but avers that he does not express them with bitterness of spirit. If people do not pay heed to their own conscience, if they do not realise their own mistakes and admit their vices they cannot be considered truly courageous. Delusion has been cheating them for a long time. Perhaps there may be some people in England who wish to change the form of the government in power in order to bring about better results in this context. 'They are mistaken if they believe that a mere change of government will sweep off all the ills rampant in the land. People can, at will, change their clothes but a government is not akin to robes wherein the ills and sufferings are tagged on like fancy points and fringes. By the mere pulling off of this robe no serious changes in the land can be brought about. The enemies that are likely to attack them are mere tools and menials who work under the behest of Providence that wishes to punish them for their wrongs. Radical causation shall not be attributed to their activities. If at all they have any inherent strength, it is drawn from the folly and wickedness of the British people. Truth such as the poet speaks may be deemed traitorous by those who want everyone to worship them. People who do not fall down before their images are soon branded as enemies of their own country.

The poet affirms his loyalty to the land of his birth. He respects all the bonds of natural love such as that of son and father, of brother and sister, of husband and wife, and also that of a friend to another friend. He apostrophises his motherland within whose boundary he finds love flourishing. He takes inspiration from her lakes, mountains, hills, clouds, valleys etc. His sweet sensations, ennobling thoughts, worship of God in the form of Nature, indeed, everything that makes the human spirit feel the joy and greatness of the bright future that his country is destined to have—all these things he has acquired from his motherland. He has treated the beautiful Island as his shrine of worship.

The poet expresses the hope that his fears regarding his country will prove false and the enemy will not be able to do anything that he boasts of In the concluding lines, the poet bids farewell to the green silent spot where he has been thinking and dreaming. He says that he is going back to his own cottage. He wants to give practical form and shape to his all-embracing love and sympathetic consideration for the entire mankind. The sunlight has disappeared from the top of the hill. Oblique rays can be seen in the ivied beacon *i.e.,* the light-house covered with ivy shrub. The poet walks homeward along the sheep-track. The thoughts and musings that he has indulged in this quiet heathy spot has given him joy. The distant village where his friend and he live appears like a great amphitheatre with the elm-trees and fields. The poet's heart has become softened and light through the influence of nature. He feels full of love and universal brotherhood.

(D) CRITICAL APPRECIATION, INTERPRETATION AND DEVELOPMENT OF THOUGHT

Development of Thought

The poem begins on a quiet note with a description of the natural surroundings of the poet as he sits and muses upon the danger of war threatening his country. He reposes in a green dell, above which sings a sky lark in the clouds. Such natural beauty and the religious spirit it invokes must appeal to all. Sadly, however, the poet is forced to think of the peace being shattered by war. Coleridge rises above narrow partisan views. He do not hesitate to condemn his countrymen for their various acts of omission and commission such as greed of wealth, overlordship of colonial regions, indulgence in slave trade etc. The local society is hard-hearted, frivolous and prone to flattery and corruption. They speak enthusiastically about wár and show no sensitivity to the suffering of the soldiers actually fighting and dying and their wives and children. The pacifist outburst is soon followed by a sincere hope that his countrymen will be able to resist the impious foe. The poet is not behind anyone in his patriotism for his own country but it does not make him narrow-minded. He wants no war. He wants people to be large-hearted and work for universal brotherhood. The poem ends on a hopeful note. The poet is grateful that his quiet meditative sojourn amidst nature's beauty has softened his heart which is full of love for mankind.

Critical Appreciation.

Love of Nature and Minute Observation. The poem reflects Coleridge's love of Nature and his minute observation. At the very beginning we have a beautiful scene of nature brought to us through a few vivid details of description. We are struck by the sense of light gleaming through the half transparent stalks of crops—

> The level sunshine glimmers with green light.

Similarly the concluding passage also shows a vivid picturisation of natural scenes:

> ....the gentle dew-fall sends abroad
> The fruit-like perfume of the golden furze...

The feeling for natural beauty is heightened because of the poet's perception of Nature's religious aspect. The natural beauty is imbued by God's spirit—a spirit that soothes and comforts and teaches man the true value of life. The poet finds "religious meaning in the form of Nature".

Patriotism through Love of Nature. It is the natural beauty of the land that makes Coleridge apostrophise his country. He loves his motherland—his native isle with all its lakes, mountains, rocks and seas—for these have inspired his intellectual life and stimulated in him beautiful feelings and adoration of God. The poet is grateful to his land for having provided him with the spirit of joy and hope in the future. He is thus truly patriotic and loves his country and wants no harm to befall it. It is because he is patriotic that he does not want the effects of bloody war to touch it. His patriotism is not of a narrow and partisan kind. He does not think it patriotic to glorify war. Nor does he think that to be patriotic one must worship those who claim loudly to be the leaders of the nation and who condemn anyone who disagrees with them as unpatriotic.

Severe Condemnation of the British Society. Coleridge delivers a scathing attack on the contemporary British society. He pinpoints their faults and folly. He condemns their commercial greed, their imperialistic designs, their hypocrisy even in religion. He is disgusted at their perjury—their abusing God's name in trying to achieve personal material success and power over other human beings. He clearly avers that it is not just the political system that needs change, it is the people's heart that must change and become sensitive to human suffering everywhere. A change of government cannot improve matters, for the government is not a robe by the removal of which the country's "vice and wretchedness" will disappear.

Hatred of War Part of Humanism. Coleridge advocates pacifism because he loves humanity. The idea of war excites people and makes them eloquent on the subject. His sensitivity to the reality comes out in the lines where he tells his countrymen to think of the impact of war on the soldiers who actually fight it. No soldier dies without a wound; every one who dies on the battle field suffers the pangs of death and is not simply transferred to heaven, and each dead soldier's widow and child feel the sorrow of his death. The poet realizes that war in defence of one's country is a necessity but he asks his countrymen not to gloat over the bloodshed and not to give in to a feeling of "drunken triumph".

Sincerity of Feeling Expressed in the Style. The style of the poem matches the theme and effectively expresses the sincerity of the poet's feelings. Vigorous and forceful vocabulary emphasises the poet's severely critical attitude towards contemporary society. There is no artificiality in the lines in which he speaks of the horrors of war. The tone is appropriately subdued and mellow in the passages where he praise & his motherland. It is a poem marked by quiet sincerity.

(E) EXPLANATIONS WITH CRITICAL COMMENTS

L. 49-63 Even so, my countrymen.......as at a market : In Fears in Solitude, Coleridge criticises his countrymen severely. As a Romantic and a humanist Coleridge finds it disgusting that the English have enslaved people in distant lands and caused them much suffering. The English have done worse in inflicting the people of those lands with their own vices and thus crushing them physically and spiritually. Cruel and unjust to people oı other lands, the English in their own land are leading a meaningless existence. Committees, associations, and societies have been formed and the members of these have been spouting words unaccompanied by any useful action. They merely compliment one another and indulge in mutual flattery for mutual gain. They have all been guilty of commercial greed. They have ignored the principles of honourable living and are polluting their life with their desire of making money. These people have bartered freedom and the poor people's life for money and commercial gain. Coleridge is obviously referring to the English policy in the colonies at the time. He delivers an unbiased criticism of the mercenary and evil behaviour of his countrymen.

L. 108-121. The poor wretch...not killed : The poet delivers a diatribe against war in *Fears in Solitude.* He rightly points out that his countrymen read with amusement accounts of war and bloodshed taking place at other places in the world. The vocabulary of war is freely used. The speakers do not seem to realize the dreadful nature of war. They seem insensitive to the suffering and tragedy. The dead in the battlefield are spoken of as so many casualties as if they did not die of painful wounds. They talk of those dead in battles as if they were transferred without pain to heaven.

The language used by Coleridge is strong and vigorous in this passage where he condemns the insensitivity of his countrymen. In the process his own humanitarian impulses come out clearly.

L. 160-166. Some belike...at pleasure : In Fears of Solitude, Coleridge points out that some people think that by changing the government, the ills besetting the country will be removed. This is a wrong idea. The government is not a robe on which the ills are like fancy work, that with the removal of the government the ills will also go. Coleridge rightly feels that the folly and wrongs of a nation springs from the attitude of the people.

L. 198-202. May my fears...grass : Coleridge wrote *Fears in Solitude* at a time when war seemed imminent. However, the fear of war is unfounded. Coleridge here prays that his fears about the well-being and security of his country should prove false. In a striking manner, he conveys the idea that the danger from the enemy shall pass over his country without harming it, just as the wind which may be heard but does not actually blow near enough to bend even a blade of grass in the valley where the poet stands.

22

ODE TO TRANQUILLITY

(A) TEXT AND ANNOTATIONS

Tranquillity ! thou better name
Than all the family of Fame!
Thou ne'er wilt leave my riper age
To low intrigue, or factious rage;
For oh ! dear child of thoughtful Truth,
To thee I gave my early youth,
And left the bark, and blest the steadfast shore,
Ere yet the tempest rose and scared me with its roar.
Who late and lingering seeks thy shrine,
On him but seldom, Power divine,
Thy spirit rests ! Satiety
And Sloth, poor counterfeits of thee,
Mock the tired worldling. Idle Hope
And dire Remembrance interlope,
To vex the feverish slumbers of the mind :
The bubble floats before, the spectre stalks behind.
But me thy gentle hand will lead
At morning through the accustomed mead;
And in the sultry summer's heat
Will build me up a mossy seat;
And when the gust of Autumn crowds,
And breaks the busy moonlight clouds,
Thou best the thought canst raise, the heart attune,
Light as the busy clouds, calm as the gliding moon.

L. 3. **riper age**—maturity and manhood. L. 4 **intrigue**—mean plots and secret stratagems to injure others. **Factious rage**—anger causing dissension, partisanship. L. 7. **Bark**—a kind of ship with three masts. Here it refers to the launching of an ambitious campaign. **steadfast**—stable. This alludes to a peaceful sober life of quiescence. L. 9. **late and lingering**—being beyond the stipulated time in an inopportune moment and then halt and be inactive intermittently, **shrine** – temple; sacred place of worship. L. 10. **seldom**—not often. L. 11. **Satiety** – sense of over-satisfaction. L. 12. **Sloth** – laziness. **counterfeits** – things imitated in order to defraud people. L. 13. **worlding**-worldly minded foolish persons. L.14. **dire**—dreadful. **Remembrance**—memory. **Interlope**—intrude and interfere. L. 15. **vex**—irritate and annoy by means of petty pinpricks. L. 16. **spectre**—demon. **stalks**—follows closely to overpower and destroy. L. 18. **mead**—meadow, low-lying grassland. L. 24. **Light...moon**—Tranquillity will enable us to think deeply but

The feeling heart, the searching soul,
To thee I dedicate the whole !
And while within myself I trace
The greatness of some future race,
Aloof with hermit-eye I scan
The present 'works of present man—
A wild and dream-like trade of blood and guile,
Too foolish for a tear, too wicked for a smile!

---

those thoughts will not be a burden to us. Like the floating clouds they are very light, like the moon that softly sails across the sky they generate calmness in the mind. **L. 25. The feeling heart**—The heart that is capable of feeling sympathetic with those who suffer. The searching soul—The soul capable of analysing things and seeing everything in the proper perspective. **L. 27-28. within...trace**—The poet feels within himself that at some future date some nobler species of people will inhabit the earth. **L. 29. scan**—scrutinise carefully. **with......hermit eye**—a hermit does not get himself involved in worldly problems. He can view everything disinterestedly. **L. 31. Trade of blood and guile**—people shed blood of one another in wars and scuffles. People cheat others in various ways.

(B) INTRODUCTION TO THE POEM

An ode is a lyric poem with the special characteristics of nobility of feeling and solemnity of style. It takes its origin from the Greek literary practice. When this poem is originally published in a periodical in 1801, it has two more stanzas thus making the minimum of fifty lines. The two stanzas are later deleted because the political allusions were no longer topical or relevant. Earnest craving for quietude is manifest throughout the poem. Coleridge's life is marred by unhappiness. Hence his deep search for peace of mind.

(C) CRITICAL SUMMARY

Tranquillity gives pleasanter experience than what Fame and allied glory can be expected to give us. The poet hopes that through it 'low intrigue and factious rage', can be avoided in the mature years of his life because he has, worked for it during the early years of his youthful life. A life of ambition will lead to uncertainty and instability just like a voyage in a boat. Hence it has been the poet's earnest endeavour to live a sober life of adhering to the stead fast shore to avoid the roaring tempest. The poet addresses Tranquillity as the "dear child of thoughtful truth". One must be truthful and constantly ponder over the problems of life in order to arrive at the proper solution and hence a peaceful and calm life.

Those who are 'late and lingering' in seeking the temple of tranquillity cannot be blest by the Divine power with the serenity of mind. Worldly-minded people mistake sloth and satiety for real tranquillity. The man of vexed mind cannot expect peaceful sleep. Idle hope is akin to a bubble that gets dissolved even as we pursue it. "Dire Remembrance" is the series of painful memories resembling a spectre that stalks us in order to overpower us.

The poet is certain that Tranquillity will come to him and that it will lead him in the morning through accustomed fields and will provide him with a moss-covered seat. There he can spend the hot hours of the summer days. When the winds of Autumn blow, Tranquillity will comfort the poet, ennoble his thought and appease his heart.

The poet dedicates his heart and soul to the service of Tranquillity. In his mind's eye, he can see a vision of a future time when a nobler race of human beings will inhabit this planet. As for the present, the poet finds mankind's actions disappointing. He only sees bloodshed and treachery all around. These deeds of human beings are so foolish that it is futile to shed tears over them. They are so wicked that they cannot be seen in an amusing light.

(D) CRITICAL APPRECIATION AND INTERPRETATION AND DEVELOPMENT OF THOUGHT

Development of Thought

The poet feels that he has not blundered like other people. Very early in his life he had been dedicating all his endeavour for the realisation of tranquillity that eludes the worldly-minded people. The poet has no truck with the unsteady bark, so he has been clinging to the steadfast shore of a contented and stable life. Ambition and thankless tasks have been avoided by hint Hoping for vain and useless things of the mundane life will cause only restlessness. Painful memories of the past cannot but perturb the mind.

Disappointment and depression do not make Coleridge pessimistic. He is confident that Serenity will be attending him in his morning walk through the fields familiar to him. The sultry summer's heat will be alleviated by a moss-covered seat provided to him by Tranquillity. The gusts of the Autumnal winds may blow but they will only raise noble thoughts in him and attune his heart to peace.

Since the poet's heart is of the feeling type and his soul is searchingly analytical he can remain aloof from the turmoils of everyday life like a hermit. Scenes of bloodshed and treacherous cruelty all over the world are depressing undoubtedly; To him this "trade of blood and guile is too foolish for a tear, too wicked for a smile". People are ignorant and they do not know what they are doing. Shedding tears on this account is futile; nor is it amusing. Still the poet does not lose heart. He thinks that at some future date a nobler race of people will inhabit the Earth when the situation will improve.

Critical Appreciation

Reflective Tone. The *Ode to Tranquillity* is written in a reflective tone. The writer's meditative mood gives rise to a number of thoughts. He is critical of the world of' his time. Philosophically, he reflects on the worthlessness of satiety and sloth in the quest of tranquillity. A worldly type of man sleeps restlessly. Painful memories from the past perturb him. The world is a scene of bloodshed and guile.

Too foolish for a tear, too wicked for a smile! The world do not seem to have changed much even today, nearly two centuries after Coleridge wrote these lines.

Optimistic Note. Coleridge however is not depressed. He is hopeful of finding tranquillity and peace of mind. He is even hopeful of a nobler race of human beings inhabiting Earth at a future date. Tranquillity will soothe the poet amid the storms of life. Peace of mind or Tranquillity is idealised by Coleridge in the poem.

Eighteenth Century Style. The poem is written more in the eighteenth century style than in the Romantic tradition. Qualities are personified – Tranquillity, Fame, Sloth, Satiety, Hope, Remembrance. There is also a moralistic or didactic note in the poem. There is more of philosophical reflection in it than Romantic emotion and feeling. Of course, we cannot deny that there are appropriate metaphors and felicity of word and phrase. But, on the whole, the poem is in the tradition of the neo-classical school of the eighteenth century.

(E) EXPLANATIONS WITH CRITICAL COMMENTS

L. 9-16. Who late...stalks behind. In his *Ode to Tranquillity* Coleridge personifies Tranquillity ; He calls it a divine power which does not favour a man who constantly makes a conscious and deliberate effort to woo it. Only through contentments in life can Tranquillity be achieved. A worldly person is soon overwhelmed by indolence and over-indulgence. He can get no peace of mind. Indolence and satiety are poor substitutes for Tranquillity. Mad pursuit of ambition again cannot lead to Tranquillity. It can only result in futile hope or memories of past failures and sorrows. The poet compares the hope of such men to a bubble that quickly dissolves. The painful memories are like a demon which pursues people to devour them.

Coleridge writes in a didactic manner here, condemning worldly ambitions. He puts forth the value of peace of mind which cannot come to those with ambitious hearts.

L. 25-33. The feeling heart..for a smile: At the end of the *Ode to Tranquillity,* Coleridge dedicates himself entirely to tranquillity. He has a heart which feels and a soul which is searching and analytical. His heart and soul will help him worship Tranquillity. He visualises a future when a nobler race of human beings, will inhabit the earth, though what he sees of the present is disappointing. The poet, like a hermit, does not involve himself in the world's affairs, he merely surveys the scene. He can only see bloodshed and treachery, the consequence of avarice and commercial greed. The deeds he witnesses are too foolish to provoke sadness; but they are also too wicked to deserve an amused response.

The lines show a mixture of criticism of the present and an optimism for the future.

23

YOUTH AND AGE

(A) TEXT AND ANNOTATIONS

Verse, a breeze mid blossoms straying,
Where Hope clung feeding, like a bee–
Both were mine ! Life went a-maying
With Nature, Hope, and Poesy,
When I was young!
When I was young ? – Ah, woful When !
Ah ! for the change 'twixt Now and Then !
This breathing house not built with hands,
This body that does me grievous wrong,
O'er aery cliffs and glittering sands,
How lightly then it flashed along :–
Like those trim skiffs, unknown of yore,
On winding lakes and rivers wide,
That ask no aid of sail or oar,
That fear no spite of wind or tide !
Nought cared this body for wind or weather.
When Youth and I lived in't together.
Flowers are lovely ; Love is flower-like;
Friendship is a sheltering tree;
O ! the joys, that came down shower-like,
Of Friendship, Love, and Liberty,
Ere I was old.
Ere I was old ! Ah woeful Ere,
Which tells me, Youth's no longer here!
O Youth ! for years so many and sweet,

Ll 1-2. Verse...bee–In his young days, Coleridge hoped to attain fame by means of his poetry. **L. 3. both:** hope and verse, a-maying–indulging in the pleasures of summer in the month of May. Poesy–poetry. **L.7. Now and then**–in and old age and in youth. **L. 8. breathing house**–body. **L. 9. This body....wrong**–i.e., Coleridge suffered from an ailing body. **L. 10. aery**– high. **L. 11. it flashed along**–i.e., my body then could move swiftly. **L. 12. trim skiffs**–light boats, here Coleridge means the steam boats unknown of yore–the first steam, boat in Europe was built in 1812. **ask no aid–i.e.,** move without the help of. **L. 17. When......together**–When I was young and was not afraid of rough weather (dangers). **L. 18. Flowers....Flower-like**–Both Love and flowers are beautiful but short lived. **L. 23. Ah ! woeful Ere**–The bitter memory of a happy past.

'Tis known, that Thou and I were one,
I'll think it but a fond conceit–
It cannot be, that Thou art gone !
Thy vesper-bell hath not yet toll'd :–
And thou wert aye a masker bold!
What strange disguise hast now put on,
To make believe, that thou art gone ?
I see these locks in silvery slips,
This drooping gait, this altered size :
But Spring-tide blossoms on thy lips,
And tears take sunshine from thine eyes
Life is but thought : so think I will
That Youth and I are house-mates still.

Dew-drops are the gems of morning,
But the tears of mournful eve!
Where no hope is, life's a warning
That only serves to make us grieve,
When we are old :
That only serves to make us grieve
With oft and tedious taking-leave,
Like some poor nigh-related guest,
That may not rudely be dismist :
Yet hath outstay'd his welcome while,
And tells the jest without the smile.

L. 26. Thou and I were one–Youth and the poet lived together as intimate Friend. **L. 27. fond conceit**–foolish thoughts. **L. 29. vesper-bell**–the evening bell which announces the departure of the day and calls people for prayer. **L. 30. masker**–The man who wears a mask or disguises his face. gait–manner of walking. **L 34. Altered size**–i.e., he has grown fatter or heavier. **L. 36. tears sunshine**–get their brilliance. **L1. 35-36. But....eyes–But** the bloom of youth is still on your lips and the brilliance of your eyes still shines through your tear. L. 37. **Life is but thought–man** is happy or sorrowful according to his thoughts. **L1 39-40. Dew drops....eve**–In youth the world appears to be romantic and life pleasant, but old age brings sorrow. **L. 46. Nigh-related guest**–*a* near relative as a guest. **L1 45-47. With oft.....dismist**–Life becomes dull and unwelcome like a poor relative who comes as a guest and delays his departure outstaying his welcome.

(B) INTRODUCTION TO THE POEM

The first 38 lines of *Youth and Age,* has appeared in *The Bijou* and *The Literary Souvenir* in 1828. The remaining eleven lines (L. 39–49) has first appeared in 1832 in *The old Man's Sigh* in Blackwood's Magazine. The present version of the poem has appeared in 1834. As indicated by the title, the poem offers a contrast between old age and youth.

(C) CRITICAL SUMMARY

Youth and Age expresses the poet's deep regret at the loss of youth. Coleridge recalls his young days when he freely enjoyed the pleasures of Nature, Hope and Poetry. Life in those days is like the month of May, full of joyful festivities. Now, in old age, a great change has come over him. His body is no longer as it was in his youth—light and frolicsome as a light steam boat moving about confidently without fear of danger. He is now fat and afflicted with illness.

In his youth, the joys of friendship, love and liberty are showered upon him copiously, friendship is like a sheltering tree and love is like a lovely flower. It is hard for the poet to believe that his youth is gone; he has been long in the habit of identifying himself with youth. He thinks that youth is playing a trick upon him; perhaps it has not really gone from him, but only putting on a disguise of grey hair, drooping gait, and alters size to induce him to believe that it has really gone. But Life is what one thinks it to be. Liveliness still shines on his lips; and youthful lustre in the eyes; and since a man is what he thinks himself to be, the poet will think that youth has not yet gone from him.

Life is the same in youth as it is in old age, with this difference that it is full of hope in youth, while in old age all hope is gone. The dew drops for instance are the same in the morning and evening, but in the evening they are the signs of the approaching night. This loss of hope warns us of approaching death and makes us grieve. The old man feels like a long-staying poor relation; and like jokes of a poor relation who has outstayed his welcome, the old man feels he is no longer required on earth.

(D) CRITICAL APPRECIATION, INTERPRETATION AND DEVELOPMENT OF THOUGHT

Development of Thought

In his youth the poet's life seems to be a constant festivity and had been associated with nature, hope and poesy. He is then not fat, and could lightly skip over hill and sandy tract. He then enjoys the delights of friendship, love and liberty. But now it seems that youth has forsaken him, However, he persuades himself into the belief that he is still young, because the bloom on his lips has not yet quite faded and the brilliance of the eyes has not altogether disappeared. The truth is that the essential element of life is the same in youth and in old age. What makes the great. difference between youth and old age is the disappearance of hope and the creeping in of the shadow of death. The old man, in the absence of hope, feels that his presence is no longer necessary on this earth.

Critical Appreciation and Interpretation.

Autobiographical Reference. The sincerity of the lyrical utterance in the poem can be tested by referring them to some of the incidents in the life of the poet himself. First, there is the reference to his hope that in his youth he thought of :building his fame upon poetry. As he grew older, he thought he has failed in building a poetic fame owing partly to his love of metaphysical speculations and partly to his habitual idleness and addiction to opium. Then, he pathetically refers to the loss of friendship, particularly of Wordsworth's, who treates him rather coldly. He also thinks of the estrangement from his wife in his later years. He also refers to his youthful scheme of establishing liberty in the country. Other minor details such as his excessive fatness, the glow of his lips and eyes, also find a place in the poem.

Mood of Sentimental Regret. There is a wistful nostalgia for the lost pleasures of the youth in the poem. Coleridge's appeal to the reader in this poem is a sentimental one, though it is an appeal difficult to resist because of its plaintive charm. The grief of the lines

> When I was young ? Ah, woeful When
> Ah I for the change 'twixt Now and Then

is touching. We find it touching also that he tries to delude himself that youth has not really left him but is just putting on the disguise of an old man.

Style. The nostalgaic note of the poem is expressed beautifully, especially in lines such as

> Dew-drops are the gems of morning
> But the tears of mournful eve

Beauty clothing pathos is also evident in :

> O, the joys, that came down shower-like
> Of Friendship, Love, and' Liberty,
> Ere I was old I

Coleridge has used appropriate similes in the poem. He compares the lightness of a young man's body with a lightness of the sleek steam-boats that rode the waters without the help of sails or oars, not bothered by wind or tide. Then there is the comparison between the old man and a poor relation who has outstayed his welcome. The poor relation do not want to go, but go he must sometime. Similarly the old man knows he is near death though he does not want to die.

The sad burden of Coleridge's later poems from *Dejection* onwards, contrast with the earlier days when

> hope grew round me, like the twining vine,
> And fruits, and foliage, not my own, seemed mine.

Youth and Age of Byron and Coleridge. The poem *Youth and Age* is written by Coleridge when he is actually approaching old age, and has reason to regret the loss of the joys and powers of youth, while Byron's poem is written when he is still a young man but was fast losing the capacity for enjoyment through mental disgust and physical lassitude, arising out of a life of dissipation. Coleridge's regret is only for the loss of buoyancy of youth:

> This body does me grievous wrong...

But Byron complains more bitterly of the loss of some power—the loss of the 'tender bloom of heart ere youth itself be past'. The thought launches Byron into despair, and the loss of youth brings to him 'mortal coldness of the soul', but to Coleridge, the loss of youth does not involve the loss of the feelings and emotions; he can think that youth and age are not different in the matter of thought and emotion; since life is but thought, he will think that youth and he are friends still. Another point of contrast is the melody of the two poems. The long iambic lines rhyming in pairs, as in Byron's poem, have a melodramatic ring; but Coleridge's lines are all music, a kind of elfin melody running through the lines and sustaining his thoughts; these thoughts are those of a metaphysical thinker in verse.

(E) EXPLANATIONS WITH CRITICAL COMMENTS

L. 1-5. Verse, a breeze...was young. In Youth and Age Coleridge recalls his youth when the pleasures of poetry and hope come easily to him. Poetry is like a breeze blowing gently over flowers, and hope, like a bee feed on the nectar of flowers, is fed by his poetic dreams. Life is like the festivities of May. Nature, Hope and Poetry are the blessings of his life in his youth.

The lines ring with a beautiful nostalgia and their plaintive charm appeals to the reader.

L. 39-43. Dew-drops.. .are old. In this touching passage from *Youth and Age* Coleridge compares youth and old age to dew-drops. In the morning dewdrops look like gems; they give us pleasure. In the evening the dew-drops look like tears of mourning because day is about to end. Similarly in youth, which is the morning of life, a man has hope to look forward to the future happily.

In old age, which is the evening of life, there is no hope. The old man has nothing to look forward to; he can only feel sad at life

L. 46-49. Like some poor....smile. A striking simile is used by Coleridge to illustrate the feeling of futility in old age. An old man is compared to a poor relation who has outstayed his welcome at his host's place. The poor relation is treated hospitably at the beginning of his stay, but soon enough the host tires of him. He can be openly rude to his guest and asks him to go away but his behaviour towards the poor relation gets colder and colder. Even the jokes of the guest evoke no smile. Similarly, an old man feels sad at the nearness of death. He will not like to die, though die he must. He is aware that he is of little use and life has no welcoming pleasure for him. He has outstayed his welcome in this world.

24

ODE TO THE DEPARTING YEAR

(A) ARGUMENT

The Ode commences with an address to the Divine Providence that regulates into one vast harmony all the events of time, however calamitous some of them may appear to mortals . The second Strophe calls on men to suspend their private joys and sorrows, and devote them for a while to the cause of human nature in general. The first Epode speaks of the Empress of Russia, who died of an apoplexy on the 17th of November 1796; having just concluded a subsidiary treaty with the Kings combined against France. The first and second Antistrophe describe the Image of the Departing Year, etc., as in a vision. The second Epode prophesises, in anguish of spirit, the downfall of this country.

I

SPIRIT who sweepest the wild Harp of Time!
    It is most hard, with an untroubled ear
    Thy dark inwoven harmonies to hear !
Yet, mine eye fix'd on Heaven's unchanging clime
Long had I listen'd, free from mortal fear,
    With inward stillness, and a bowed mind !
    When lo ! its folds far waving on the wind,
I saw the train of the Departing Year !
    Starting from my silent sadness
    Then with no unholy madness,
Ere yet the enter'd cloud foreclos'd my sight,
I rais'd the impetuous song, and solemnis'd his flight.

II

    Hither, from the recent tomb,
    From the prison's direr gloom,
From Distemper's midnight anguish;
And thence, where Poverty doth waste and languish;
    Or where, his two bright torches blending,

L. 1. Wild Harp of Time—Time is compared to a harp, a stringed musical instrument. It is God who regulates all the events in the world. L. 4. Clime—climate: it may mean region also. **L. 5. mortal**—that which is associated with death. L. 8. **train**—the flowing garments. Note that the year is personified. **L. 12. impetuous**—forcibly violent. solemnis'd—*celebrated* with great honour. **L.15. Distemper'**—bodily disorder. **L. 17. blending**—mixing properly.

Love illumines Manhood's maze;
Or where, o'er cradled infants bending,
Hope has fix'd her wishful gaze;
Hither, in perplexed dance,
Ye Woes ! ye young-eyed Joys ! advance!
By Time's wild harp, and by the hand
Whose indefatigable sweep
Raises its fateful strings from sleep,
I bid you haste, a mix'd tumultuous band !
From every private bower,
And each domestic hearth,
Haste for one solemn hour;
And with a loud and yet a louder voice,
O'er Nature struggling in portentous birth,
Weep and rejoice !
Still echoes the dread Name that o'er the earth
Let slip the storm, and woke the brood of Hell:
And now advance in saintly Jubilee
Justice and Truth ! They too have heard thy spell,
They too obey thy name, divinest Liberty !

III

I mark'd Ambition in his war-array !
I heard the mailed Monarch's troublous cry—
'Ah ! wherefore does the Northern Conqueress stay !
Groans not her chariot on its onward way ?'
Fly, mailed Monarch, fly
Stunn'd by Death's twice mortal mace,
No more on Murder's lurid face
The insatiate Hag shall gloat with drunken eye !
Manes of the unnumber'd slain !
Ye that gasp'd on Warsaw's plain !
Ye that erst at Ismail's tower,
When human ruin choked the streams,

L. 24. indefatigable – untiring. **L. 26. tumultuous** – noisy. **L. 34. brood of Hell**– In the name of freedom , hellish deeds were done. **L. 35. Jubilee** – great celebration. **L. 40. Northern Conqueress** – *reference* to the Russian empress. **L. 42. mailed**– protected with good armour. **L. 46. Manes of the unnumber'd slain** – The ghosts and spirits of the numerous people who were murdered. **L. 48. erst**—erstwhile, here-tofore. **Ismail's tower**—reference to the massacre of Ismail.

Fell in Conquest's glutted hour,
Mid women's shrieks and infants' screams !
Spirits of the uncoffin'd slain,
Sudden blasts of triumph swelling,
Oft, at night, in misty train,
Rush around her narrow dwelling !
The exterminating Fiend is fled—
(Foul her life, and dark her doom)
Mighty armies of the dead
Dance, like death-fires, round her tomb !
Then with prophetic song relate,
Each some Tyrant-Murderer's fate !

IV

Departing Year! 'twas on no earthly shore
My soul beheld thy Vision ! Where alone,
Voiceless and stern, before the cloudy throne,
Aye Memory sits: thy robe inscrib'd with gore,
With many an unimaginable groan
Thou storied'st thy sad hours ! Silence ensued,
Deep silence o'er the ethereal multitude,
Whose locks with wreaths, whose wreaths with glories shone.
Then, his eye wild ardours glancing,
From the choired gods advancing,
The Spirit of the Earth made reverence meet,
And stood up, beautiful, before the cloudy seat.

V

Throughout the blissful throng,
Hush'd were harp and song:
Till wheeling round the throne the Lampads seven,
(The mystic Words of Heaven)
Permissive signal make:
The fervent Spirit bow'd, then spread his wings and spake!
'Thou in stormy blackness throning
Love and uncreated Light,

L. 50. **glutted**—having a supply more than required. L. 52. **uncoffin'd**—*not* interred properly in a coffin during burial. L. 56. **exterminating**—destroying. L. 60. **relate**—narrate. L. 68. **ethereal**—airy. L. 69. **wreaths**—garlands. L. 72. **reverence meet**—proper respect.

By the Earth's unsolaced groaning,
Seize thy terrors, Arm of might !
By Peace with proffer'd insult scared,
Masked Hate and envying Scorn !
By years of Havoc yet unborn !
And Hunger's bosom to the frost-winds bared !
But chief by Afric's wrongs,
Strange, horrible, and foul !
By what deep guilt belongs
To the deaf Synod, 'full of gifts and lies !'
By Wealth's insensate laugh ! by Torture's howl!
Avenger, rise !
For ever shall the thankless Island scowl,
Her quiver full, and with unbroken bow ?
Speak ! from thy storm-black Heaven O speak aloud !
And on the darkling foe
Open thine eye of fire from some uncertain cloud !
O dart the flash ! O rise and deal the blow !
The Past to thee, to thee the Future cries !
Hark ! how wide Nature joins her groans below !
Rise, God of nature ! rise.'

VI

The voice had ceas'd, the Vision fled;
Yet still I gasp'd and reel'd with dread.
And ever, when the dream of night
Renews the phantom to my sight,
Cold sweat-drops gather on my limbs;
My ears throb hot; my eye-balls start;
My brain with horrid tumult swims;
Wild is the tempest of my heart;
And my thick and struggling breath
Imitates the toil of death !
No stranger agony confounds
The Soldier on the war-field spread,
When all foredone with toil and wounds,
Death-like he dozes among heaps of dead !
(The strife is o'er, the day-light fled,
And the night-wind clamours hoarse !
See ! the starting wretch's head
Lies pillow'd on a brother's corse!)

L. 76. **Lampads** – torch-bearers in front of holy persons. L. 82. **unsolaced** – not comforted. L. 91. **Synod** – religious council. L. 92. **insensate** – lacking in sense and understanding. L. 95. **quiver** – pouch where arrows are kept. L. 103. **ceas'd** – stopped L. 104..**dread** – great fear.

VII

Not yet enslaved, not wholly vile,
O Albion ! O my mother Isle!
Thy valleys, fair as Eden's bowers
Glitter green with sunny showers;
Thy grassy uplands' gentle swells
Echo to the bleat of flocks;
(Those grassy hills, those glittering dells
Proudly ramparted with rocks)
And Ocean mid his uproar wild
Speaks safety to his Island-child !
Hence for many a fearless age
Has social Quiet lov'd thy shore;
Nor ever proud Invader's rage
Or sack'd thy towers, or stain'd thy fields with gore.

VIII

Abandon'd of Heaven ! mad Avarice thy guide,
At cowardly distance, yet kindling with pride—
Mid thy herds and thy corn-fields secure thou hast stood,
And join'd the wild yelling of Famine and Blood !
The nations curse thee ! They with eager wondering
Shall hear Destruction, like a vulture, scream !
Strange-eyed Destruction ! Who with many a dream
Of central fires through nether seas up-thundering
Soothes her fierce solitude; yet as she lies
By livid fount, or red volcanic stream,
If ever to her lidless dragon-eyes,
O Albion ! thy predestin'd ruins rise,
The fiend-hag on her perilous couch doth leap,
Muttering distemper'd triumph in her charmed sleep.

IX

Away, my soul, away !
In vain, in vain the Birds of warning sing—
And hark ! I hear the famish'd brood of prey
Flap their lank pennons on the groaning wind !

L. 122. **Albion**—old name for England. L. 126. **bleat**—the cry of lamb. **L. 128. ramparted**—protected like a fort. **L. 130. Island-child**—i.e. England. The ocean protects the island as a father protects a child. **L. 134. sack'd**—plundered; destroyed, **gore**—blood **L. 135. Abandon'd of Heaven**—England is regarded as deserted by God. **Avarice**—commercial greed. L. 142. **nether**— underground. L. 143. **she**—i.e. Destruction, **livid**—angry. **L. 147. fiend-hag**—devilish old woman. L. 148. **distemper'd-** mad; insane. **L. 152. lank**-limp. **pennons**-wings.

Away, my soul, away !
I unpartaking of the evil thing,
With daily prayer and daily toil
Soliciting for food my scanty soil,
Have wail'd my country with a loud Lament.
Now I recentre my immortal mind
In the deep Sabbath of meek self-content;
Cleans'd from the vaporous passions that bedim
God's Image, sister of the Seraphim.

L. 161. Seraphim-six-winged heavenly beings.

(B) INTRODUCTION TO THE POEM

This poem is composed during the Christmas festivities in the year 1796 and published on the last day of the year. At that time Coleridge has prefixed an "Argument" to the piece in which he has explained the theme. Three distinct items have been stressed in this ode of nine stanzas of uneven length; first, the avowal of the Divine Spirit that regulates all the events of time into one vast harmony; secondly the listing of various iniquities and acts of cruelties perpetrated by various persons including the Empress of Russia; and thirdly, the greatness as well as weakness of his own country and countrymen.

(C) CRITICAL SUMMARY

The poet begins by invoking the Divine Spirit that blows upon the wild Harp of Time. Time is like the stringed musical instrument on which the Spirit produces sweet harmonious melodies. In the argument Coleridge himself explains it, stating that Divine Providence regulates all the events of time. The poet then acknowledges that he patiently listened to the harmony though it is difficult to hear it an: understand it. The poet is free from fear; he has inward stillness i.e., tranquillity; he is humble. Then he saw a vision of the eventful year 1796 making its ceremonious exit. The poet has glimpses of the main events of the year 1796. The poet feels that the silent sadness of the year is the reason that prompted him to describe the exit. Fortunately before the vision fades the poet composes the ode to bid a ceremonial farewell to the departing year.

In Stanza II the poet summons all types of woes and all types of joys on the earth to come together in the form of a mixed group so that they can either weep over their misfortunes or rejoice over their glorious achievements over the period of time. He calls the grief of persons due to recent death, the sufferings of prisoners, the sleeplessness or broken sleep vitiated by nightmarish dreams of persons suffering from bodily disorder. The poet then refers to the sorrows of poor people. Then the poet refers to various types of joy-the joyous tryst of lovers, the joy of parents over their children in the cradles, hoping for a bright future for their children and wishing for their prosperity. The Divine Spirit which is indefatigable plays on the harp of time. Woes and joy of the world must give vent to their respective feelings in loud tones for at least one solemn hour because Nature is struggling to give birth to marvellous events and momentous miracles. The last five lines of this stanza (i.e., 33-37) refer to the French Revolution 1789-1791. The stormy period of the actual revolution might have been criminally horrible due to the excessively hellish deeds of the leaders but by the year 1796, beneficent results of the revolution were also being enjoyed by the people, viz., justice, truth and liberty.

In Stanza III the poet refers to the misdeeds of the Czarina, the Empress of Russia who died of apoplexy in the month of November, 1796. She has been very ambitious. She proudly called herself "Northern Conqueress". She has allied herself with certain other countries against the French Republic. She has attacked Poland, leading to the suffering of thousands of people in the capital city of Warsaw. She has attacked Persia. At Ismail's tower in that country thousands of people are massacred. The poet calls the Empress an "insatiate hag" and "exterminating fiend". She has poisoned even her own husband to realise her ambition to become a powerful monarch. Although the Empress is dead and gone, the poet says that her soul cannot rest in peace; the ghosts of those for whose death she is responsible, would dance around her tomb and give her no peace.

In Stanza IV the poet continues the description of the vision of the Departing Year. Memory sits before the cloudy throne of the Almighty. The departing year has a robe inscribed with blood. This indicates that numerous persons has met with unnatural death in the year under review. The year stands amidst an assembly of angels in heaven. The spirit of Earth respectfully bows in front of God and waits for the permission to speak.

In Stanza V, the poet briefly mentions how the spirit of Earth describes the atrocities on Earth and how it prays for the vengeance of God on all the exploiters of the weak nations. Many critics are of the view that this section contains a lot of unintelligible allusions. The style is also somewhat affected.

Earth's groans are not comforted. People mask their hate, and show scorn to hide their envy. Wealthy people have wrought havoc over many years all over the Earth, especially in Africa from where people are exported as slaves. Those slaves are ill-treated. They are exposed to hunger and starvation. The Council of Religious leaders too has become deaf to the lamentations of these unfortunate human beings. Wealthy people lack sense and understanding. They are brutally foolish and arrogant. This being the case the Spirit of Earth prays to God to open His eyes of fire, and take action to stop the cruelty. The poet's humanitarianism is deep and genuine.

In Stanza VI the poet says that though the vision has ended it has has a powerful effect on him. He gasps for breath and reels with great fear when he recalls it. Sometimes in the night the vision reappears to him in the form of a terrible nightmarish dream. On such occasions he sheds cold drops of sweat, his ears become hot, his eye-balls smart with pain, his brain begins to whirl, and his heart becomes agitated due to excessive excitement. The poet begins to gasp for breath like a dying man. He feels that even a dying soldier sprawling on the battlefield does not have to face an agony more acute than what the poet feels at the remembrance of the vision.

In Stanza VII we find the loving patriotism of the poet exquisitely reflected in every line. Albion is the old Celtic name of the British Isles. The poet apostrophises his native land who has never been enslaved. England's valleys are as beautiful as the gardens of Paradise. The greenery with plenty of sunshine and rain is splendid. Flocks of sheep and cattle graze over the pasture lands. The rocks act like walls of a great fort around his island country. The ocean accords good protection to the land from external invaders. Over a long period England has remained free from the fear of invasion. There has been stability and peace.

In Stanza VIII the poet's mood changes from patriotism because he is again aware of the misdeeds of the people living here. A splendid land can be ruined by the misdeeds of its inhabitants. Mad avarice has become the guide of the inhabitants of England. Hence even Heaven will not hesitate to disown this land. The greed for empire and flourishing overseas trade has kindled the pride of the Britons. People of England are free from hunger and ravages of war but they have spread famine and bloodshed over vast territories all over the world in their eagerness to establish their overlordship. The other nations which suffer on account of the misdeeds of British curse their land. Wickedness will not go unpunished. Destruction waits like a vulture, to work havoc through fires, volcanoes etc. Personifying Destruction, Coleridge says that it has the eyes of a dragon which have no lids and so are ever wide open. The devilish female spirit of Destruction may appear to be sleeping but it is likely to triumph. It is possible that England may be ruined. The poet's warning is that his countrymen should not enjoy plenty and security at the cost of other nations' suffering.

In Stanza IX, the poet composes himself after lamenting the misdeeds of his countrymen. Though other people indulge in misdeeds the poet avers that he is aloof from all of them. He does not partake of their evil actions. He is devout and prays daily. He seeks refuge in his contentment.

(D) CRITICAL APPRECIATION, INTERPRETATION AND DEVELOPMENT OF THOUGHT

Development of Thought

Ode to the Departing Year begins with the poet's address to the Divine Spirit who regulates the events of time into one vast harmonious whole. The poet then calls on human beings to ignore for a while their personal sorrows and joys and instead devote some thought to the general happenings of the year that is about to pass. After paying tribute to Liberty, the poet speaks in a condemnatory note of the Empress of Russia who has concluded a subsidiary treaty with some other rulers against France. He then describes the vision of the departing year. In this vision he hears the Spirit of the Earth narrating to God the atrocities and barbarities committed on the backward peoples of the world. The poet expresses his patriotic love for his country. However, he is not blind to the fact that his countrymen are much to blame for their commercial greed and insensitivity to others' sufferings; smug in their social security, his countrymen do not bother about their tyrannical cruelty over other people in far off lands. He prophesies that such a wickedness will not go unpunished by God. Having lamented the wicked behaviour of his countrymen, the poet composes his mind and seeks shelter behind his contentment that he himself is devout and full of love for all humanity. He is optimistic that simple people like him will prevail in the end.

Critical Appreciation

Topical Interest. The poem is in a way topical. It pertains to the international political situation in 1796, and particularly refers-to the misdeeds of the Empress of Russia who dies in November 1796. Coleridge considers her as the personification of "the evil spirit". He is clearly critical of her ambitious political actions which results in much suffering and bloodshed in places like Poland and Persia. The poem is not just condemnatory of the Empress of Russia. The poet is deeply critical of all those who have perpetrated cruelty and injustice on people and exploits and people in different lands. The Africans get Coleridge's special sympathy for being victimis and exploits by the English. Coleridge is deeply disgusted with the avarice and insensitivity of his own countrymen. He warns his countrymen that such wickedness will not go unpunished. His country will be destroyed for enjoying smug security while perpetrating atrocities on other people.

Patriotic Element. In this poem too, as in *Fears in Solitude,* Coleridge praises his native land. He loves his 'Albion...(his) mother Isle" whose

...valleys, fair as Eden's bowers
Glitter green with sunny showers,
...Grassy uplands, gentle swells
Echo to the bleat of flocks.

In other words his land is beautiful and he loves the island country which has been so well endowed naturally by God. He is only disgusted with the people of his country who have been overcome by commercial greed and political ambition and become blind to the suffering of those over whom they tyrannise.

Humanitarian Impulse and True Religious Faith. Every line of the poem show Coleridge's deep humanitarian impulses. He loves all mankind. That is why he is disgusted with his countrymen for their cruelty over other people, especially the Africans. He speaks vehemently against the exploitation of the African slaves by the avaricious and insensitive. His moral indignation and courage of conviction find sincere expression in the poem.

Coleridge expresses a true religious faith in the poem. He is a believer in the brotherhood of man. He shows an unshakable faith in God and is sure that wickedness will be punished by the Almighty. He is also convinced that simple folk like him who believe in the brotherhood of man and pray sincerely to God will prevail in the end.

Style. Parts of the poem ring with sincere anger at the inhuman behaviour of people. However, the style is uneven. The rhetorical manner of writing with the eighteenth century style of personification somewhat detracts from the overall effect. The affected phrases such as 'bowed mind', 'foeman', 'recentre', 'bedim', 'frost-winds', 'strange-eyed Destruction,' etc. have no place in lyric poetry. However, "this ode, not withstanding it is affected in some parts, and unintelligible in others, breathes the genuine spirit of poesy."

(E) EXPLANATIONS WITH CRITICAL COMMENTS

L. 122-134. O Albion...gore. In these lines from his *Ode to the Departing Year,* Coleridge addresses his native land. He admires England's natural endowments—the valleys as beautiful as those of paradise, the 'grassy uplands' and 'glittering dells' that make it a beautiful island. He is glad that the island has been endowed with a natural protection of rocks which fortify it and the surrounding ocean, that makes it secure. It has always enjoyed social stability and peace, and has not been enslaved or conquered

Coleridge apparently wants to convey the fact that as God has been so kind to their country, the people should not forget to be thankful. They have no right to be smug in their security and inflict cruel wrongs on the people of other lands.

L. 135-148. Abandon'd of Heaven...charmed sleep. Coleridge is unsparing in his criticism of his countrymen. After expressing patriotic admiration for his lovely land in the *Ode to the Departing Year,* he goes on to say that the beautiful land is doomed to destruction because its people have succumbed to avarice and indulge in exploitation of people in far off lands. Secure from invasion and free from hunger, its people have wrought destruction and famine on other lands. Obviously Coleridge is referring to the colonial exploitation by the British especially in Africa. These exploits nations are cursing England and Destruction is waiting like a vulture to swoop and annihilate the land.

Coleridge has personified Destruction in the eighteenth century style. He has given a striking picture of Destruction as a vulture waiting to sweep upon the dead with a scream.

L. 158-161. Now I recentre.....seraphim. After lamenting the misdeeds of his countrymen in the *Ode to the Departing Year,* Coleridge calms himself. In the typical manner of odes, Coleridge ends the poem on a calm note. He himself is a simple man who loves mankind. He will return to a calm state of mind. He will free his mind from passions that make God's image dull. He will take refuge in the mind's contentment.

SELECT BIBLIOGRAPHY

1. M.F. Schulz : *The Poetic Voices of Coleridge (1963)*
2. I.A. Richards : *Coleridge on Imagination (1934)*
3 Stephen Potter : *Coleridge and S.T.C. (1936)*
4. J.L. Lowes : *The Road to Xanadu (1927)*
5. Humphry House : *Coleridge (1953)*
6. E.K. Chambers : *Samuel Taylor Coleridge (1938)*
7. J.D. Campbell : *Life of S.T. Coleridge (1894)*
8. E. Blunden : *Coleridge, Study by Several Hand (1934)*
9. J. Beer : *Coleridge the Visionary (1959)*
10. Kathleen Rain : *Samuel Taylor Coleridge (1957)*
11. R.P. Warren : *A Poem of Imagination : The Ancient Mariner (1946)*
12. Herbert Read : *The True Voice of Feeling (1953)*
13. Walter Pater : *Appreciations (1889)*
14. D.G. James : *The Romantic Comedy (1948)*
15. S. Dutt : *The Supernatural in English Poetry (1938)*
16. E Dowden : *New Studies in Literature (1902)*
17. C.M. Bowra : *The Romantic Imagination (1950)*
18. G. Watson : *Coleridge : The Poet (1966)*
19. H.D. Traill : *Coleridge (1884)*
20. M.Suther : *The Dark Night of Samule Taylor Coleridge (1960)*
21. M.H. Ahbrams : *The Mirror and the Lamp (1963)*
22. E.M. Bewley : *The Poetry of Coleridge, Security VIII, (1940).*
23. E. Blunden and E.L. Griggs, Ed. : *Coleridge, Study by Several Hands (1934)*
24. J.D. Boulger : *Twentieth Century Interpretations of 'The Rime of the Ancient Mariner' (1969)*

25. Kathleen Coburn : *Coleridge, A Collection of Critical Essays (Twentieth Century Views) 1967.*

26. Allan Grant : *A Preface to Coleridge (1972)*

27. D.W. Harding : *The Theme of 'The Ancient Mariner' Scrutiny, IX, 1941*

28. Graham, Hough : *The Romantic Poets (1953)*

29. Alan R. Jones; and William Tydeman, ed. : *Coleridge: The Ancient Mariner and Other Poems (Casebook Series) (1973)*

30. G. Wilson Knight : *The Starlit Dome (1941)*

31. Elder Olson : *A Symbolic Reading of The Ancient Mariner: reprinted from Modern Philogy, XLV (1984) in Critic and Criticism, ed. R.S. Crane 1952.*

32. P.S. Sastri : *The Vision of Coleridge (1966)*

33. Elizabeth Schneider : *Coleridge, Opium and Kubla Khan (1953)*

34. M.F. Schulz : *The Poetic Voices of Coleridge (1963)*

35. N.P. Stalknecht : *The Moral of The Ancinet Mariner PMLA, XLVII, (1932)*

36. M. Suther : *The Dark Night of Samuel Taylor Coleridge (1960)*

37. Robert Penn Warren : *A Poem of Pure Imagination, The Ancient Mariner, reprinted, from The Kenyan Review, VIII, 1946 in Selected Essays, (1958)*

38. William Walsh : *Coleridge : The Work and the Relevance (1966)*

39. G. Watson : *Coleridge : The Poet (1966)*

40. Geoffrey Yarlott : *Coleridge and the Abyssinian Maid (1967)*

LIST OF OUR PUBLICATION

1 ENGLISH POETS

1.1 Geoffrey Chaucer
The Prologue to the Canterbury Tales
1.2 Geoffrey Chaucer
The Pardoner's Tale
1.3 Tennyson
Selected Poems
1.4 John Milton
Paradise Lost Book I
1.5 John Milton
Paradise Lost Book II
1.6 John Milton
Paradise Lost Book IV
1.7 John Milton
Paradise Lost Book IX
1.8 Alexander Pope
The Rape of the Lock
1.9 John Donne
Selected Poems
1.10 John Donne
Selected Poems (Enlarged Edition)
1.11 John Keats
The Odes
1.12 John Keats
Odes and Other Poems
1.13 John Keats
Selected Poems : Odes, Other Poems, Hyperiona nd Fall of Hyperion
1.14 John Dryden
Mac Flecknoe and Other Poems
1.15 John Dryden
Absalom and Achitophel
1.16 John Dryden
Mac Flecknoe Other Poems, and Absalom and Achitophel
1.17 Robert Browning
Selected Poems
1.18 Robert Browning
Selected Poems (Enlared Edition)
1.19 William Wordsworth
The Prelude Book I & II
1.20 William Wordsworth
Selected Poems
1.21 William Wordsworth
Selected Poems and The Prelude Book I & II
1.22 William Blake
Songs of Innocence and of Experience
1.23 P.B. Shelley
Selected Poems
1.24 P.B. Shelley
Selected Poems (Enlarged Edition)
1.25 S.T. Coleridge
The Ancient Mariner
1.26 S.T. Coleridge
Selected Poems and The Ancient Mariner
1.27 W.B. Yeats
Selected Poems
1.28 T.S. Eliot
The Wasteland and other Poems
1.29 Mathew Arnold
Selected Poems
1.30 W.H. Auden
Selected Poems
1.31 Hopkins
Selected Poems

2. ESSAYISTS AND PROSE WRITERS

2.1 Francis Bacon
Selected Essays
2.2 Addison & Steele
Selected Essays from the Spectator
2.3 Charles Lamb
Essays of Elia
2.4 Bertrand Russel
Unpopular Essays
2.5 Jonathan Swift
The Battle of the Books
2.6 John Ruskin
The Crown of Wild Olive

3. NOVELS AND NOVELISTS

3.1 Henry Fielding
Tom Jones
3.2 Henry Fielding.
Joseph Andrews
3.3 Charles Dickens
David Copperfield
3.4 Charles Dickens
Great Expectations
3.5 Charles Dickens
Oliver Twist
3.6 Charles Dickens
Hard Times
3.7 George Eliot
The Mill on the Floss
3.8 George Eliot
Adam Bede
3.9 John Glasworthy
The Man of Property
3.10 E.M. Forster
A Passage to India
3.11 Virginia Woolf
To the Lighthouse
3.12 Virginia Woolf
Mrs. Dalloway
3.13 D.H. Lawrence
Sons & Lovers
3.14 D.H. Lawrence
Women in Love
3.15 D.H. Lawrence
Rainbow
3.16 Thomas Hardy
Jude the Obscure
3.17 Thomas Hardy
Tess
3.18 Thomas Hardy
Far from the Madding Crowd
3.19 Thomas Hardy
Mayor of Casterbridge
3.20 Thomas Hardy
The Woodlanders

3.21 Thomas Hardy
The Return of the Native
3.22 Jane Austen
Emma
3.23 Jane Austen
Persuasion
3.24 Jane Austen
Pride & Prejudice
3.25 Charlotte Bronte
Wuthering Heights
3.26 Thackeray
Vanity Fair
3.27 Joseph Conard
Heart of Darkness
3.28 Joseph Conrad
Lord Jim
3.29 James Joyce
A Portrait of the Artist as a Young Man

4. CRITICS AND CRITICISM

4.1 Aristotle
Poetics
4.2 William Wordsworth
Preface to the Lyrical Ballads
4.3 Mathew Arnold
Essays in Criticism
4.4 T.S. Eliot
The Critic
4.5 John Dryden
An Essay on Dramatic Poesy
4.6 Dr. Johnson
Preface to Shakespeare
4.7 Dr. Samuel Johnson
Life of Milton
4.8 Dr. Samuel Johnson
Life of Pope

5. ENGLISH DRAMATISTS

5.1 Christopher Marlowe
Dr. Faustus
5.2 Christopher Marlowe
Edward the Second
5.3 Bernard Shaw
Saint Joan
5.4 T.S. Eliot
Murder in the Catherdral
5.5 William Shakespeare
King Lear
5.6 William Shakespeare
As You Like It
5.7 William Shakespeare
Macbeth
5.8 William Shakespeare
Hamlet
5.9 William Shakespeare
Richard II
5.10 William Shakespeare
Henry IV Part I
5.11 William Shakespeare
Twelfth Night
5.12 William Shakespeare
The Tempest
5.13 William Shakespeare
Much Ado About Nothing
5.14 William Shakespeare
The Merchant of Venice
5.15 William Shakespeare
Othello
5.16 William Shakespeare
Julius Caesar
5.17 Bernard Shaw
Major Barbara
5.18 Bernard Shaw
Arms and The Man
5.19 Bernard Shaw
Candida
5.20 Bernard Shaw
Man and Superman
5.21 Bernard Shaw
The Apple Cart
5.22 Ben Jonson
Volpone
5.23 John Dryden
All for Love
5.24 Webster
The Duchess of Malfi
5.25 Webster
The White Devil
5.26 William Congreve
The Way of the World
5.27 R.B. Sheridan
The Rivals
5.28 R.B. Sheridan
The School for Scandal
5.29 John Osborne
Look Back in Anger
5.30 J.M. Synge
Riders to the Sea
5.31 J.M. Synge
The Playboy of the Western World

6. AMERICAN LITERATURE

6.1 Walt Whitman
Selected Poems
6.2 Robert Frost
Selected Poem
6.3 Arthur Miller
Death of a Salesman
6.4 Henry James
The Portrait of a Lady
6.5 Ernest Hemingway
A Farewell to Arms
6.6 Ernest Hemingway
The Old Man and the Sea

7. ANGLO INDIAN LITERATURE

7.1 Mulk Raj Anand
Untouchable
7.2 R.K.Narayan
The Guide
7.3 Rabindranath Tagore
Gitanjali
7.4 Sarojini Naidu
Selected Poems
7.5 Raja Rao
Kanthapura
7.6 R.K. Narayan
The Man-Eater of Malgudi Days
7.7 Mulk Raj Anand
Coolie